Norton Rose on

Cross-Border Security

Norton Rose on

Cross-Border Security

Edited by Norton Rose

With contributions by:

Allen Allen & Hemsley
Stikeman Elliott
Norton Rose
Rossbach & Fischer
Mulla & Mulla & Craigie Blunt & Caroe
Nishimura & Partners
Trenité Van Doorne
Prol & Asociados
Hammarskiöld & Co
Milbank, Tweed, Hadley & McCloy LLP

Butterworths

London, *Charlottesville*, Dublin, *Durban*, Edinburgh, *Hong Kong*, Kuala Lumpur, *New Delhi*, Singapore, *Sydney*, Toronto, *Wellington*

2000

United Kingdom	Butterworths, a Division of Reed Elsevier (UK) Ltd, Halsbury House, 35 Chancery Lane, LONDON WC2A 1EL and 4 Hill Street, EDINBURGH EH2 3JZ
Australia	Butterworths, a Division of Reed International Books Australia Pty Ltd, CHATSWOOD, New South Wales
Canada	Butterworths Canada Ltd, MARKHAM, Ontario
Hong Kong	Butterworths Asia (Hong Kong), HONG KONG
India	Butterworths India, NEW DELHI
Ireland	Butterworth (Ireland) Ltd, DUBLIN
Malaysia	Malayan Law Journal Sdn Bhd, KUALA LUMPUR
New Zealand	Butterworths of New Zealand Ltd, WELLINGTON
Singapore	Butterworths Asia, SINGAPORE
South Africa	Butterworths Publishers (Pty) Ltd, DURBAN
USA	Lexis Law Publishing, CHARLOTTESVILLE, Virginia

A CIP Catalogue record for this book is available from the British Library.

ISBN 0 406 05463 0

ISBN 0-406-05463-0

9 780406 054630

Printed by Redwood Books, Trowbridge, Wiltshire

Visit us at our website: http://www.butterworths.co.uk

Preface

The phenomenon of globalisation requires neither introduction nor explanation. National barriers to trade and cross-border economic activity are being eroded at great speed. But national boundaries remain important to those who finance or advise upon international transactions. In particular the validity and sufficiency of any security arrangements will generally depend on the law of the country where the charged assets are to be found – regardless of the international or cross-border nature of the transaction as a whole. The business world may become global; but at least for the present laws dealing with property and security retain their essentially national characteristics.

For the reasons just given, a book dealing with security for international transactions must nevertheless concentrate on the individual legal systems of separate jurisdictions. This book considers the legal framework applicable to guarantees and security in 12 different jurisdictions (or, in appropriate cases, federal subdivisions), namely Australia, Canada, France, Germany, India, Italy, Japan, The Netherlands, Spain, Sweden, England and Wales and the United States of America. Its main purpose is to set out the steps necessary to ensure that the creditor obtains a satisfactory security interest in the assets concerned and (where necessary) considers the steps which must be taken in order to realise the security. The various chapters examine the nature of the forms of the security available in each jurisdiction and the formalities required to ensure that such security is valid and binding. It also examines the priority of competing security interests.

The main topics covered are:

(a) the types of security available in each different jurisdiction;
(b) the formalities required in order validly to constitute the security (including board resolutions, methods of execution, registration requirements and the payment of any stamp duties or other fees);
(c) priorities as between competing security interests and as against unsecured creditors;
(d) remedies and enforcement;
(e) vitiating factors; and
(f) enforcement of foreign guarantees and security.

It is hoped that this Book will provide a useful introductory guide for those contemplating security arrangements in the jurisdictions concerned. It is not, of course, a substitute for proper advice in individual cases.

In conclusion we would like to thank all of the contributors and Butterworths for their hard work and patience in bringing this project to fruition. Mention should also be made of the work of the assistants at Norton Rose, including Georgia Cocks who performed the overall editorial role, and Edward Sunderland who assisted in the preparation of the England and Wales contributions. Thanks are also due to Sara Whitaker who typed the manuscript for the English chapter and monitored the progress of the text as a whole.

Norton Rose
October 2000

The contributors

AUSTRALIA

Andrew Jinks

Allen Allen & Hemsley

CANADA

Jean Farley

Stikeman Elliott, London

FRANCE

Martin Gdanski

Norton Rose, Paris

GERMANY

Florian Wolff

Rossbach & Fischer, Frankfurt

INDIA

Shardul Thacker

Mulla & Mulla & Craigie Blunt & Caroe

Italy

Roberto Cornetta

Norton Rose, Milan

Japan

Masaru Ono and Daniel C Hounslow (senior foreign counsel)

Nishimura & Partners, Tokyo

The Netherlands

Roel Botter and Bas Boris Visser

Trenité Van Doorne, London

Spain

Francisco G Prol

Prol & Asociados

Sweden

Bengt Kärde

Hammarskiöld & Co

England

Charles Proctor

Norton Rose, London

United States of America

Warren F Cooke

Milbank, Tweed, Hadley & McCloy LLP

Contents

2 Canada 23

3 France 67

Table of cases

Canada

India

The Netherlands

Spain

Sweden

1 Australia

Andrew Jinks

Allen Allen & Hemsley

INTRODUCTION

Background

For those familiar with English law, much of the Australian law relating to the creation and enforcement of securities will not be a surprise. English common law was brought to Australia with the settlers and, even though different political and cultural imperatives have meant a steady divergence between the approaches of courts in the two jurisdictions, English authorities (particularly those of the higher courts) are still often considered, even if not always applied, by Australian courts.

Formative English legislation – such as the Companies Act 1862 and the Statute of Frauds 1677 – was the model for most early Australian legislation. Although with time the statutes have varied, much has been retained of the basic concepts. The Australian legislatures are also willing to look at international legal developments, including those in the UK, when reviewing and updating domestic law.

Nevertheless, there are sufficient substantive differences, both practical and theoretical, between Australian and English law in this area, to warrant close attention – it is dangerous to assume that because much is the same, *all* is the same.

This introduction discusses some of the major sources of differences between English and Australian law, and the basis for many of the requirements for taking effective security either over assets in Australia, or from an Australian resident, which are also discussed in more detail later.

Federal structure

Australia is a federation. It is comprised of the Commonwealth (the federal jurisdiction) and six States (New South Wales, Victoria, Queensland, Western Australia, South Australia and Tasmania). There are two mainland federal Territories (Northern Territory and Australian Capital Territory), and several small offshore federal Territories which are not included in this discussion.

The Commonwealth and each State has its own Constitution. The Federal Constitution vests specific exclusive legislative powers in the federal parliament as well as numerous non-exclusive powers which may be exercised by the States to the extent that such exercise is not overridden by valid federal legislation. The State Constitutions empower the State parliaments to legislate for the well being of the State – that is, to exercise either those powers which are shared with the Commonwealth or those powers on which the Federal Constitution is silent (which are exclusive to the States).

Some examples of relevant federal powers are taxation, foreign investment, customs and excise, copyright, patents, trade marks, trading and financial corporations and banking. Some examples of relevant State powers are real property law, stamp duties, corporations, consumer credit and certain special types of taxation. Importantly, although corporations fall within State powers a national corporations law is in place to allow uniformity of the provisions dealing with the incorporation, management and regulation of companies. Similarly, a uniform Consumer Credit Code has been implemented by the States (other than Western Australia, which has in place a regime similar to the other States).

This multiplicity of jurisdictions means that when taking security over Australian property or from an Australian resident the laws of more than one jurisdiction will almost invariably be involved. Commonwealth legislation will usually apply, while the laws of the situs of the relevant property and the place of incorporation and/or residence of the security provider may also be relevant.

Corporations Law

The Corporations Law covers all aspects of corporate existence in Australia, from incorporation and management, through the raising of finance by corporations and treatment of their insolvency to dealings in company shares. Many aspects of the Corporations Law are readily recognisable to an English practitioner; others are either novel or involve a different treatment of familiar concepts.

For the purposes of taking security from an Australian company, the following provisions of the Corporations Law may be relevant.

1 Part 2B.1, which deals with company powers and how they are exercised.
2 Chapter 2E, which deals with financial benefits to related parties of public companies.
3 Chapter 2J (especially ss 260B and 260D), which deals with the transactions affecting share capital.
4 Chapter 2K, which deals with company charges (in particular the registration of charges and their ensuing priority).
5 Chapter 5, which deals with the administration of an insolvent company.
6 Division 2 of Part 5B.2, which deals with foreign companies.
7 Certain provisions of Chapter 6, which deal with the acquisition of shares (relevant in the case of enforcement of securities over shares).

Various aspects of these provisions are dealt with in more detail below.

Taxation

The majority of Australian taxation legislation will be irrelevant to foreign lenders and security takers. The following issues may, however, be of concern:

1 the Income Tax Assessment Act 1936 ('ITAA') s 25(2), which provides that interest on money secured by a mortgage over any property in Australia is deemed to be derived from a source in Australia; and
2 of the ITAA s 128B, which imposes (by way of a withholding) income tax on interest received by foreign persons from an Australian resident.

These issues are discussed in more detail below.

Real property

There are a number of different forms of title to land in Australia. Some are rarely encountered by financiers: for example, Crown Land held on leasehold and 'old system title' (where title must be proved by a history of possession through title deeds). However, the form of title most commonly encountered in Australia is 'Torrens title'.

Torrens title land (named after Sir Samuel Torrens, who is credited with developing the system of title) is freehold title, interests in which are created by registration in a central land registry of the relevant State or Territory. Each parcel of land is represented by a specific certificate of title. The original certificate is retained by the registry and in most States a duplicate certificate is issued to the owner. Dealings with the land is carried out by pro forma instruments which become effective on registration. Ordinarily the relevant certificate of title (or any registered plan referred to in it) will reveal the position and dimensions of the land, the present owner and any leases, mortgages and registered easements to which it is subject. The certificate is conclusive evidence (except in limited circumstances, such as fraud) of the matters stated in it.

Torrens title land may take the form of 'strata title'. Strata title was developed to facilitate the creation of, and dealings with, apartment units. Under this system, each proprietor of a unit has title to, and may freely dispose of, their unit. All proprietors are members of a 'body corporate', which monitors compliance with rules governing the apartment block. Certain parts of the property, such as stair wells, entrance lobbies and the like are known as 'common property' and are owned by the body corporate as a whole rather than by individual proprietors.

As is discussed below, different considerations apply when taking security over Torrens and strata title property. In addition, each State or Territory has different legislation governing these forms of title.

Stamp duty

Stamp duty is a tax levied by the States and Territories which is imposed on specified classes of documents, and in certain circumstances, on transactions. Documents on which duty is levied include transfers of marketable securities in Australian companies, conveyances of land and other property, declarations of trust, loan security documents and leases. In some cases the duty is merely nominal; in others, duty is levied at an ad valorem rate which will vary depending on the nature of the transactions: 0.3% generally on listed share transfers; up to 5.5% on the conveyance of real property; and between 0.35% and 0.4% on loan securities in the States.

Failure to stamp a document which is subject to duty renders the person required to stamp the document liable to a penalty, and may also constitute a criminal offence. In certain circumstances, an unstamped document will also not be admissible as evidence in a court in the relevant jurisdiction until such time as it is duly stamped.

TYPES OF SECURITY

Background

The types of security available to lenders and devised to allow recourse to property of a borrower in priority to third parties are far too numerous to examine all of them in detail.

The general law in Australia governing charges, mortgages, pledges and possessory liens is based heavily on English law and the differences in application are usually small.

The same can be said of areas such as reservation of title, subordination and flawed asset arrangements.

Floating securities

As in the UK, Australia recognises the ability of companies to create floating charges. In addition, individuals may arguably give floating charges under Australian law. Unlike fixed securities, floating charges do not attach to specific assets but instead 'float' over a class of assets which may change from time to time, allowing the chargor to deal with those assets and to give third parties title to those assets free from any encumbrance. It is usual for the chargor's right to deal with the assets to be limited by a requirement that such a dealing is in the 'ordinary course of business'.

This should be compared to assets which are subject to a fixed charge, where the chargor requires the consent of the chargee each time an asset subject to the fixed charge is to be disposed of.

A floating charge may 'crystallise' and become a fixed charge over the relevant class of assets owned by the chargor at the time of crystallisation. Crystallisation may occur by implication – liquidation, cessation of business – or following the occurrence of a specific event stipulated in the charge documents. Australian authority has followed the view that crystallisation may occur upon any event agreed by the parties, and therefore 'automatic' crystallisation (without the need for action by the chargee) is allowable. However, it is still unresolved whether a floating charge, once crystallised, can decrystallise without creating a new charge (giving rise to issues relating to stamp duty liability and voidable transactions in insolvency, among other things).

The instrument which creates a floating charge will usually grant the chargee a number of powers on default by the chargor, including a right to appoint a receiver to the charged property and to sell the charged property.

Merely labelling a security 'fixed' or 'floating' will not necessarily be conclusive as to its legal effect. A purportedly fixed security under which the chargor is in fact entitled to deal with the charged assets in its business will be treated by the courts as a floating security. Conversely, a floating charge which is too restrictive will operate as a fixed charge.

Securities over land

The law relating to the granting of securities over real property is made complex both by the fact that each State and Territory has separate governing legislation, and because, although most land in Australia is Torrens title, there is also legislation dealing with other forms of title.

In relation to old system title, the position in Australia is broadly the same as in England until the passage of the Law of Property Act 1925. That is, a legal mortgage arises by the conveyance of the real property, subject to reconveyance by the mortgagee on due payment of the outstanding debt by the mortgagor. All jurisdictions require a conveyance of real property to be in writing, in most cases by deed. The relevant Acts in Tasmania and Victoria set out a short form of deed of mortgage which is sufficient to create a security over old system land in those States. Some jurisdictions also provide various protections for mortgagors: for example, a right of early redemption.

Under Torrens title, registration of a mortgage using the prescribed form executed by the mortgagor is required in order for the mortgagee to obtain both the remedies granted by statute and the statutory priorities against other secured creditors. To this extent the mortgagee is said to have a legal (ie registered) title. However, registration does not transfer title in the property: the mortgagor remains legal owner of the property. Instead, the Torrens mortgage operates as a statutory charge. The mortgagee does not obtain an estate in the property but does have an interest in the land which is marked on the register and the 'certificate of title' for the property. A search of the register by any subsequent lender will reveal the existence of the prior mortgage. A registered mortgage also gives the mortgagee the benefits of 'indefeasibility of title' under the Torrens system: that is, title cannot (subject to various exceptions, such as fraud) be set aside on the grounds of a pre-existing defect in title.

A mortgagee will retain the relevant certificate of title until the mortgage is discharged. Although the certificate is not a document of title as such, the procedure for replacement is sufficiently onerous to act as a deterrent against most mortgagor fraud.

Once the mortgagor has repaid the debt, a discharge is lodged with the registrar and the mortgage is noted as having been released.

An unregistered mortgage over Torrens title land is treated as an equitable mortgage, over which registered mortgages will generally have priority.

Securities over shares

Nature of shares

The Corporations Law s 1085(1) provides that company shares are personal property, transferable as provided by the company's articles of association. Section 1085(2) then states that the laws applicable to ownership of and dealing with personal property apply to company shares. Thus, both legal and equitable securities may be created over shares.

Legal mortgage over shares

A person does not have legal title to shares until such time as that person is registered as a holder of the shares by the company. Therefore, in order to grant a legal mortgage of shares a mortgagor must transfer the shares to the mortgagee, who is then registered as a shareholder and receives and holds the certificates of title to those shares in its name. The mortgagor has an equity of redemption to pay out the secured moneys and have the shares re-transferred; the mortgagee on the other hand can foreclose or exercise its powers under the mortgage documents. A mortgagee also seems to have an implied power of sale independent of any agreed powers.

However, the legal transmission of shares raises certain issues, including the following.

1. The constitution of most companies provide that shares are to be transferred by an instrument in writing in any usual or common form or in any other form which the directors approve. The Corporations Law s 1091 provides that a company is not to register a transfer of shares unless a proper instrument of transfer has been delivered to the company, which instrument must show the jurisdiction of incorporation of the company (s 1091(1A)). Any legal mortgage of shares must therefore be accompanied by a duly executed transfer in the form prescribed by the relevant company's constituent documents.
2. The Corporations Law s 113 provides that the constituent documents of a proprietary company must restrict the number of shareholders of the company to no more than 50 non-employee shareholders.
3. Each Australian jurisdiction requires that a transfer of shares is duly stamped before it is registered by the company.
4. As a member of the company, the mortgagee may be liable for unpaid calls on the mortgaged shares. The mortgagee would also be responsible for voting on shares, which may not only present administrative problems for the mortgagee but may leave it exposed to an action for negligence or for some other liability by a disgruntled mortgagor or shareholder in relation to any voting the mortgagee may undertake. On the other hand, the mortgagee will be entitled to receive bonus and rights issues and dividends as a shareholder of the company.
5. The constitution of a proprietary company may require director consent to a transfer of its shares. Where a security (legal or otherwise) is being obtained over shares in such a company the mortgagee should obtain an undertaking from the directors of the company or an amendment to the company's articles that the transfer will be registered. Alternatively, in the case of a legal mortgage, funding should not be provided to the mortgagor until the relevant transfer is approved and registered.

Legal mortgages of shares are not particularly common in Australia.

Equitable mortgage

Under an equitable mortgage, the mortgagor remains the registered holder of the shares but the mortgagee has a right in equity to require the shares to be transferred to it or a third party upon the occurrence of certain specified events.

As the mortgagor remains owner of the shares, it is usual for the mortgagee to receive a transfer 'in blank' signed by the mortgagor together with the share certificates for the charged shares. The transfer should contain the minimum amount of information (details of shares and name of company in which the shares are held) and should not be dated nor signed by the transferee. In this way no stamp duty should arise on the transfer as a conveyance of shares. The transfer in blank does not need to be notarised or otherwise certified.

In order to ensure that a subsequent exercise of the security can be made without any restrictions, the points raised in paras 1 and 2 above under 'Legal mortgage over shares' should be observed. That is, the transfer should be in appropriate form, while an amendment should be made to the company's articles or an undertaking obtained from the company's directors.

Another problem with an equitable mortgage is that it may lose priority to other securities in certain circumstances. It is therefore possible in some jurisdictions to serve on the company in which shares have been charged (with a copy to the Supreme Court of the jurisdiction) a stop notice restraining the company from permitting dealings with the shares for a period of eight or ten days (depending on the jurisdiction) unless proper notice has been given to the chargee. The procedure has the same effect as a writ of *distringas*. The notice does not give the chargee any priority in respect of its interest, but prevents the registration of a transfer of shares or payment of dividends without giving the chargee an opportunity to stop the transaction (for example, by injunction). If no action is taken by the chargee within the requisite period the transaction may proceed.

In those jurisdictions where no stop notice, or 'notice in lieu of *distringas*', is available it seems that a chargee can only seek an injunction if the chargee becomes aware of the transaction before it occurs.

CHESS

As of December 1995, all shares in Australian listed companies are eligible to be traded on CHESS (which stands for Clearing House Electronic Subregister System). CHESS is a settlement system for share transfers run by the Settlement Clearing House (SCH), which can be used for settlement of both on-market and off-market transactions. Under CHESS, a listed company's register of members consists of up to three subregisters, namely:

1 an electronic CHESS subregister held by the SCH;
2 a certificated subregister containing the names of all shareholders who have share certificates; and
3 an uncertificated issuer-sponsored subregister.

An equitable mortgage over CHESS-approved shares may be vulnerable, even if the relevant mortgagee holds the share certificates, because in some circumstances certificated shares can be converted to uncertificated shares without the need for share certificates to be surrendered, and without notice being provided to the mortgagee unless the mortgagee is a registered holder of shares.

Various techniques are available to improve an equitable mortgagee's position in relation to CHESS-approved securities. However, it must be said that the system as it currently exists does not, and cannot, give equitable mortgagees the amount of protection that legal mortgagees enjoy.

Stamp duty

Generally, a charge over shares will have a nexus with an Australian jurisdiction (and therefore potentially attract a stamp duty liability):

1 if the charge is executed in that jurisdiction although a number of jurisdictions, such as New South Wales, no longer levy duty on the basis solely of place of execution;
2 if the shares are kept on a register maintained in that jurisdiction;
3 in the case of certain jurisdictions, if the company is incorporated in that jurisdiction; or
4 if the charge secures property in that jurisdiction or relates to any matter or thing done or to be done in that jurisdiction.

Securities over goods

Each State and Territory, other than Victoria, has bills of sale legislation, although in some cases that legislation now has limited application. The purpose of the legislation is to protect, by registration, third parties where an assignor of property capable of transfer by delivery is left in possession of the property. It is an attempt to deal, in relation to individuals, with the 'false wealth' doctrine encountered in and dealt with by many jurisdictions throughout the world.

In essence the legislation provides that:

1 a bill of sale (being a document that effects a legal or equitable assignment or which gives no proprietary interest but rather grants a right to seize or, in some cases, which creates a charge, subject to certain exceptions);
2 of personal chattels;
3 where the grantee has power to seize and take possession of any property subject to the bill of sale;
4 which is not filed or recorded within a specified period after its making (except in Queensland and the Northern Territory, where no time limit is specified);
5 is null and void;
6 against certain specified individuals (generally the official receiver, the trustee in bankruptcy, the sheriff seizing goods in the course of execution and the judgment creditor on whose behalf such execution was issued, but in Queensland against any person other than the grantor and grantee); and
7 to the extent of the property in or right to possession of the personal chattels comprised in the bill of sale which are in possession or the apparent possession of the person making the bill of sale.

In Western Australia the definition of 'chattels' has been limited to 'stock and wood or growing crops when separately charged or bailed'. The Northern Territory has provision for removing a range of goods from the reach of the legislation, although as yet only motor vehicles have been so removed.

In the other jurisdictions, a chattel comprises goods, furniture and other articles capable of complete transfer by delivery.

FORMALITIES

Power

Corporate power

One of the most important aspects of corporate authorisation in Australia is that, at least in relation to companies incorporated under the Corporations Law, the doctrine of ultra vires has been abolished.

The Corporations Law s 124 states that a company has 'the legal capacity of a natural person', together with certain additional powers, such as issuing shares and debentures and granting floating charges. This capacity exists regardless of any objects stated in the memorandum of association of the company. Section 125 provides that a company's constitution may include express prohibitions on the exercise of a power, but a breach of the prohibition does not by itself render the act invalid (and thus a third party acting in good faith will be able to rely on that act: for example, the granting of security).

Where a non-incorporated entity (such as a governmental authority, building society or statutory corporation) is giving security a lender should carefully review the constitution and powers of that entity to ensure it has the ability to grant the security.

Officer's powers

Even though the act of granting a security will be within the powers of a company by reason of the Corporations Law, there is the additional question as to whether the directors or other agents of the company have properly exercised their powers when entering the relevant transaction.

In order to ensure that an individual executing the relevant documentation has actual authority from the company, it used to be that an extract from the minutes of the meeting of the board of directors resolving to enter into the transactions was obtained. This is because, for most companies, the board has general management power for the company and thus a resolution of the board was sufficient to empower an individual to act on behalf of the company.

To a large extent these issues have been resolved by statutory implementation of the so-called 'indoor management rule', the common law rule that persons dealing with a company in good faith may assume that acts within the company's constitution have been properly performed. The Corporations Law ss 128 and 129 contain the current legislative expression of this notion.

Under s 128(1):

1. a person having dealings with a company is entitled to make certain assumptions in relation to these dealings; and
2. the company may not assert in any proceedings relating to the dealings that the assumptions were incorrect.

Section 129 sets out the assumptions that can be made, which include:

1. that the company's constitution have been complied with (s 129(1));
2. that a person who appears from returns lodged with the Australian Securities and Investments Commission (the 'ASIC') to be a director or secretary has been duly appointed and has authority to exercise usual powers (s 129(2));
3. that a document has been duly executed if it appears to have been signed by two directors or a director and secretary of the company, or if the company has only one director who is also the only secretary, that person (s129(5));
4. that a document has been duly sealed if the company's common seal appears to have been fixed to the document and the seal has been attested by two persons who may be assumed to be a director and a secretary of the company by reason of s 129(2) (s 129(6)); and
5. that the directors, secretaries, employees and agents of the company properly perform their duties to the company (s 129(4)).

The effect of those provisions is that the preferred approach for confirming due execution of documents is often *not* to obtain any board minutes. Instead, relevant searches are made at the ASIC (which will show the names of all directors and secretaries of the company) and a review of the constitution is undertaken. This will generally be sufficient to allow reliance on ss 128 and 129.

A further benefit of reviewing searches at the ASIC is that it will reveal any registered charges and any notices of winding-up applications or receiverships that may have been lodged. It should be borne in mind, however, that such searches are not always up to date and are not always totally accurate.

Notwithstanding ss 128 and 129, a board resolution should be obtained where:

1. the relevant security provider is not subject to the Corporations Law;
2. the transaction documents, or any power of attorney pursuant to which the transaction documents are signed, are not under seal; or
3. the Corporations Law s 128(4) applies (see below).

It is preferable that an extract, rather than full minutes, be provided as full minutes will require the mortgagee to examine whether that the relevant meeting was held in accordance with the company's constitution (quorum, identity of directors etc). It will be significantly more difficult in the latter case to rely on the common law indoor management rule.

Section 128(4) states that the assumptions in s 129 cannot be made if a person dealing with the company knew or suspected, at the time of the dealings, that the assumption was incorrect. The requirement of knowledge or suspicion can cause problems, particularly if the mortgagee is a large corporation where knowledge held by certain employees is not communicated to other employees involved in the transaction.

Corporate benefit

Even though the mortgagor may have corporate power to grant a security, and the transaction has been properly authorised by the company (whether by an application of ss 128 and 129 or otherwise), there is a further concern when obtaining security from an Australian company particularly if the security is a third party security or involves a guarantee. This concern arises under the so-called 'doctrine of corporate benefit'.

Directors of a company which enters into a guarantee or provides security where no advantage is conferred on the company will be in breach of their fiduciary duties and will have abused their powers as directors. If the person in whose favour the guarantee or security was given was actually aware of the facts giving rise to the abuse (ie was aware that the guarantee or security was not in the interests of the company) then the relevant guarantee or security is voidable at the option of the company and, it would seem from Australian authority, at the option of creditors of the company.

When giving a guarantee or security, a company must obtain a benefit in substance and not just in form. Moreover, the benefit should be to the company as a single entity and not merely to the general group of companies of which the company may form a part.

Therefore, guarantees or securities given in exchange for payment of real consideration are in the interests of a company. Generally, it can also be said to be in the interests of a parent company to guarantee or secure the borrowings of its subsidiaries, as such borrowings will almost invariably enhance the parent's position as shareholder of the borrowing company.

However, a sister company giving a guarantee or security in support of another sister company in the same group of companies without any other consideration arguably would not be receiving sufficient corporate benefit for the guarantee or security unless it receives (for example) a reasonable fee, or some other actual benefit.

Notwithstanding that a guarantee or security is not in the interests of a company, because the issue of commercial benefit involves abuse of power by directors the company can, as with most issues of directors powers, ratify the giving of the guarantee or security (and thus ratify the directors' abuse of power).

The most important consideration with respect to such ratification is whether the company giving the guarantee or security was solvent at the time that its shareholders ratified the giving of the guarantee or security. This is because, although it is not correct to say that the directors owe a duty to creditors of a mortgagor, recent cases have indicated that the interests of creditors are to be taken into account by the directors where the mortgagor is insolvent or the transaction in question may jeopardise the solvency of the mortgagor. The granting of a mortgage or guarantee may thus be set aside if it results in the mortgagor or guarantor being unable to pay its creditors. Shareholders are unable to consent to the giving of the guarantee or security if it would be to the detriment of the creditors' interests.

Therefore, despite the assumption in the Corporations Law s 129(4), it is usual for banks which are granted securities or guarantees which may not be in the interests of the grantor to require shareholder ratification, accompanied by a declaration of solvency. Such ratification must be made following full disclosure of all relevant matters to the shareholders, including the fact that the transaction might not be in the best interests of the company and the directors might be in breach of their duties to the company.

Execution/sealing

Natural persons

Few formalities are required in relation to the granting of a security by a natural person. Apart from general restrictions such as those relating to contracts executed by minors and the mentally disordered, and the rules governing third party guarantees and securities, a natural person may execute a security quite simply.

For example, in relation to a deed no seal is required if the deed is expressed to be a deed or an indenture. The relevant attestation clause will merely express that the document is 'signed, sealed and delivered' by the mortgagor. The signature must be witnessed. If the deed is executed under power of attorney, the power of attorney must itself take the form of a deed (usually in the form of a deed poll).

An agreement may be executed by the relevant natural person without any need for a witness, although it is common practice for the execution of agreements also to be witnessed.

Companies

Under the Corporations Law s 127, a company may execute documents, including deeds, whether under seal or not, provided that such documents are executed in the prescribed manner, namely, the document must be witnessed, if under seal (s 127(2)), or signed, if not under seal (s 127(1)), by:

1 two directors of the company; or
2 a director and the company secretary; or
3 for a proprietary company that has a sole director who is also the company secretary, that director.

Hence, a company may now bind itself without affixing its common seal. Moreover, by virtue of ss 128 and 129, any person dealing with the company will be entitled to rely on the assumptions therein, as explained above.

Further, a company may delegate its power to execute deeds or other documents on its behalf. Section 126 states that a company's power to deal with contracts may be exercised by an individual acting with the company's express or implied authority. This power may be exercised without the use of a common seal: s 126(1). Such an agent binds the company by 'signing' the company's name, just as a person may bind a natural person where authorised to 'sign' that person's name.

However, if the legal act is one for which an individual is required under common law to execute by deed, this obligation would also apply to a company. For example, conveyancing legislation derived from the Statute of Frauds requires certain dispositions of land to be by deed.

Again, if a deed is executed under a power of attorney the power of attorney itself must take the form of a deed. In addition, s 127(3) provides that a company may execute a document as a deed if the document is expressed to be executed as such and in accordance with s 127(1) or s 127(2). Therefore, it appears that s 127(3) may not be satisfied by mere use of the word 'deed' in the document or its name. In case of uncertainty companies should execute documents using a common seal or, where it is not possible to do so (for example, stamp duty reasons or because execution is taking place offshore), a power of attorney itself executed under common seal can be used.

It is often the case that agreements and offer letters are signed by a director on behalf of the relevant company, without any further consideration. However, it is arguable that a director (even a managing director) has limited powers to bind a company when acting alone, so some further evidence of the director's power (including in appropriate circumstances a board resolution) should be obtained.

Each company incorporated in Australia, and each foreign or other company registered under the Corporations Law, is allotted a unique nine digit registration number allotted to it on incorporation or registration (as the case may be) and which remains unchanged and unchangeable until the company is dissolved or deregistered. In the case of an Australian incorporated company this is called the Australia Company Number or ACN; in the case of a registered company it is an Australian Registered Body Number or ARBN. The ACN or ARBN is required to be set out on each public document of the company that is signed, issued or published, and every negotiable instrument of the company that is signed or issued, after the company's name 'where it first appears' (s 219(3) and s 362(4)). In most contracts this 'first appearance' is taken to be on the first page, where the parties' names are set out. However, if Australian companies are referred to in schedules or are defined in the body of the documents it is also usual practice to include the ACN of that company for identification purposes (even if that company is not a party to the contract).

Registration of securities

General

There are a number of specific circumstances where registration of a security will be required or prudent: for example, a ship mortgage will need to be registered under the relevant legislation, while securities over motor vehicles can be registered under State legislation. However, registration will be of general concern in the following instances:

1 powers of attorney;
2 registerable securities granted by companies;
3 registerable bills of sale; and
4 mortgages over real property.

Registration of real property mortgages and bills of sale are discussed above.

Powers of attorney

All States and Territories in Australia have legislation which deals with the registration of powers of attorney. South Australia and Western Australia require registration only when the dealing which was executed under the power concerns land. Victoria provides for the power to be produced when the relevant dealing in land is itself lodged. New South Wales and the Australian Capital Territory require registration of any power of attorney used to execute conveyances and deeds (arguably whether involving land or not). Tasmania requires registration of powers of attorney under which any act, deed or instrument is done, registered or signed. Finally, Queensland requires registration of powers of attorney authorising dealings with land, and according to some commentators, for *all* powers of attorney. In most cases, failure to register will (depending on the jurisdiction) either render the dealing invalid or prevent registration of the relevant dealing.

When registering a power of attorney with the appropriate registry (usually the land title registry of the relevant State or Territory), it is necessary to comply with requirements as to form, size and sometimes specific wording. A registration fee will be charged in all jurisdictions other than Victoria. This can be quite expensive where a number of powers of attorney have been granted with respect to property in a few jurisdictions.

Importantly, although in most jurisdictions it is possible to register the powers after execution of the dealing, in both Tasmania and Western Australia the power should be registered *before* any document is executed pursuant to it.

Company charges

Under the Corporations Law, companies are required to register with the ASIC certain charges over their property. If a registerable charge is not registered within the required 45-day period, it will be void against a liquidator or administrator if they are appointed within six months of the registration of the charge (but not against other creditors or receivers).

A registerable but unregistered charge will also lose priority to a registered charge (even if created after the unregistered charge) unless the registered charge was created after the unregistered or later registered charge and the chargee had notice of the previous security at the time of creation of their charge.

A registerable charge for the purposes of the Corporations Law includes a floating charge, a charge on books, debts and a charge (legal or equitable) on a marketable security (including a share) except to the extent that the charge was created in whole or in part by the deposit of a document of title for the marketable security.

A charge must be stamped before it can be finally registered, although provisional registration is available for charges which are in the process of being stamped.

Consents and notifications

The most important consents and notifications which may be relevant to a secured lender are:

1 government consent under the Foreign Acquisitions and Takeovers Act 1975 ('FTA');
2 shareholder consent under the Corporations Law s 260B if by granting the security a corporate mortgagor is giving financial assistance for the acquisition of its own shares;
3 shareholder consent under Chapter 2E of the Corporations Law if the mortgagor is a public company providing a financial benefit to a related party in specified circumstances;
4 in some circumstances, notice to a listed company where the lender becomes a 'substantial shareholder' of that company; and
5 securities taken over companies in special areas (eg broadcasting).

Foreign Acquisitions and Takeovers Act

The FTA governs investment in Australian assets by foreign companies. The FTA applies where:

1 a 'foreign person' proposes to acquire shares in an Australian corporation ('foreign person' includes a foreign corporation or an Australian corporation in which a foreign corporation holds a 'substantial interest' – that is, in which the foreign corporation or one of its subsidiaries holds 15% of the shares);
2 the purchaser acquires more than 15% of the capital of the corporation; and
3 the corporation has assets which exceed A$5,000,000 in value (or A$3,000,000 if more than 50% of its assets are attributable to Australian rural land).

Acquisitions of business valued over A$5,000,000 (or A$3,000,000 if 50% or more of the business comprises rural land), or of urban land regardless of value, or assets in certain other sensitive areas (such as media or broadcasting), also require notification under the FTA.

The FTA applies even where the vendor of the assets is itself a foreign person.

If the FTA applies to a transaction, the purchaser is required to give notice of the proposed acquisition in the prescribed form. The Australian government (through the Foreign Investment Review Board or 'FIRB') may then approve or reject the proposed purchase, based on an assessment of whether the acquisition is contrary to the national interest. It is rare for proposals to be rejected, but a failure to give notice and obtain consent can lead to monetary penalties and imprisonment for offending corporate officers and may also lead to the divestment of the purchased shares.

Where a target company is valued at less than A$50 million, the Australian government's policy guidelines state that the proposed acquisition will generally be approved without review (except where the target is involved in certain sensitive industry sectors).

Generally, FIRB is required to respond to a notice within 30 days. If it does not respond within that period, the transaction may proceed. Where the target company owns urban land the procedure is slightly different, and the requirements are more onerous.

The FTA will have relevance to secured lenders in three respects:

1 where the relevant secured funding is for the purchase of assets, the purchase by the purchaser of the target assets; and
2 any sale of the secured assets to a foreign person by the Lender on enforcement of its securities. It should be noted that, under the FTA s 5(1), 'acquisition' does not include an acquisition by way of enforcement of a security held solely for the purposes of a moneylending agreement (defined as 'an agreement entered into in good faith in the ordinary course of carrying on a business of lending money, not being an agreement dealing with any matter unrelated to the carrying on of that business'); and
3 the creation of the security. Again, an interest in assets will not be subject to the FTA if the interest is held solely as security for the purpose of a moneylending agreement.

Corporations Law s 260B

The Corporations Law s 260A provides that a company may financially assist a person to acquire shares in the company only in limited circumstances. Such financial assistance can only be given if it:

1 does not materially prejudice the interests of the company or its shareholders or the company's ability to pay its creditors; or
2 has been approved by shareholders by special resolution at a general meeting pursuant to s 260B; or
3 falls within one of the exemptions specified in s 260C.

No definition of 'financial assistance' is given, except that it may take the form of paying a dividend (s 260A(2)(b)).

Therefore, if the security from a target company to any lender is designed to facilitate the acquisition of the target company by a purchaser, the proposed transaction would not contravene the Corporations Law provided it falls into one of the above categories.

If a company provides financial assistance in circumstances that breach s 260A, that assistance and any related contract or transaction would not be rendered invalid. Nevertheless, the relevant company officers involved in the contravention, but not the company itself, may be subject to civil penalties under the Corporations Law.

The procedure for shareholder approval under s 260B referred to above is as follows:

1 the notice of the meeting of members must be accompanied by a statement setting out all relevant information material to the decision on how to vote on the resolution (s 260B(4));
2 before the notice of the meeting is sent to members, the company must lodge a copy of the notice, as well as any document relating to the financial assistance to be given, with ASIC (s 260B(5));
3 at least 14 days before giving the financial assistance, the company must lodge with ASIC a notice in the prescribed form stating that the assistance has been approved (s 260B(6));
4 any special resolution giving shareholder approval consent to the transaction must also be lodged with ASIC within 14 days after it is passed (s 260B(7)).

It should also be noted that holding company approval may be required in certain circumstances (s 260B(2) and (3)).

As 21 days' notice of a meeting to cast a special resolution is required (unless consent to short notice has been given by not less than 95% of voting members), the procedure under s 260B takes some time to implement (ie a minimum of approximately 45 days).

Corporation Law Chapter 2E

The basic prohibition in Chapter 2E of the Corporations Law arises under s 243H, which states that:

> 'A public company must not give a financial benefit to a related party except as permitted by Part 2E.4 or 2E.5.'

The prohibition does not apply if the financial benefit is provided on arm's length terms no more favourable than would be the case if dealing with an unrelated party (s 243N).

A 'financial benefit' is stated in s 243G(1) as to be intended to operate broadly and to include indirect financial benefits. Some examples given in s 243G(4) are lending money, guaranteeing a loan, providing security for a loan, issuing securities and giving money or property.

A 'related party' of a company is defined in s 243F(1) and includes:

1 a director of the company;
2 a director of a parent entity of the company;
3 a spouse or de facto of such a director;
4 a parent, son or daughter of such a director or spouse;
5 an entity (other than a child entity of the company) over which such a person (or two or more of them together) have control; or
6 a parent entity or sibling entity of the company.

A 'related party' includes an entity that was a related party within six months prior to the relevant time, and an entity which believes (or has reasonable grounds to believe) that it will become a related party. A 'parent entity' is an entity which is a holding company or has control of the relevant company, a 'child entity' is an entity of which the relevant company is a parent entity, and a 'sibling entity' of the company is an entity which has the same parent entity.

A financial benefit which breaches s 243H is not invalid by reason only of the contravention (s 103). However, parties to contraventions may be required to account for profits or compensate for loss suffered by the company (ss 1317HB or 1317HD), or pay a civil penalty of up to A$200,000 (s 1317EA).

All this would not seem at first to be of much relevance to a lender. Unfortunately, the penalties also apply to a person who is:

1 'involved' in the contravention; or
2 'by an act or omission, directly or indirectly, recklessly concerned in, or party to' the contravention (s 243ZE(3)).

Section 79 states that a person is 'involved' in a contravention if, and only if, they have (a) aided, abetted or procured the contravention; (b) induced the contravention; (c) been in any way directly or indirectly involved in the contravention; or (d) conspired with others to effect the contravention.

'Reckless' is not defined, but would indicate a total disregard for the possibility that there may be a contravention.

Therefore a financier who obtains a guarantee or security from a public company to support the obligations of a related party of the company in contravention of Part 3.2A, and who is 'involved' in the contravention or recklessly concerned in or party to it, may be required to account to the company for money received under the guarantee or security.

Consequently, a financier receiving such a security should decide whether an exception applies (eg the transaction is arm's length, or the related party is a member of the same corporate group as the public company sharing 100% ownership) Otherwise, approval by the public company shareholders is required. The procedure for a shareholder's approval is strict (ss 243U to ZD), requiring advance notice to the ASIC and explanatory statements to shareholders. Interested shareholders cannot vote.

Substantial shareholding

Under the Corporations Law s 709 , a person who becomes entitled to not less than 5% of the voting shares in any class of shares issued by a listed company (a 'substantial shareholder') is required to give a written notice to the company (with a copy to the Australian Stock Exchange) of that entitlement, in the prescribed form, within two business days of becoming aware of the relevant interests which caused the person to become a substantial shareholder.

Similarly, s 710 requires a substantial shareholder to notify a 'notifiable change' in its entitlement (being a change of entitlement, whether an increase or decrease, of 1% of the shares in the relevant class).

The tests of whether a person is 'entitled' to, or has a 'relevant interest' in, shares is very broad but basically turns on the ability to vote in relation to, or dispose of, the shares. The interests of associates of the relevant shareholder must be included when calculating a substantial shareholding.

A failure to comply with ss 709 or 710 will give rise to a liability to pay damages to any person who suffers loss or damage as a result of the contravention, unless the contravention was due to inadvertence, mistake or a lack of knowledge about a relevant fact or occurrence (s 716).

These provisions will not be relevant to a mortgagee if the Corporations Law s 38 applies. That section states that a relevant interest in a share is disregarded if the person's 'ordinary business includes lending money' and the relevant interest arises 'only because of a security given for the purposes of a transaction entered into in the ordinary course of business in connection with lending money'.

As few lenders who fall outside s 38 would be in a position to finance the acquisition of 5% or more of a listed company, s 38 is of somewhat more practical use for lenders than its limited scope may at first indicate.

OTHER CONSIDERATIONS

Stamp duty

All Australian jurisdictions other than the Australian Capital Territory and the Northern Territory impose stamp duty on charges, mortgages and other loan securities. The rate of duty is generally 0.4% of the amount secured by the loan security. In addition, all jurisdictions impose stamp duty on transfers of property (with various exemptions from jurisdiction to jurisdiction). Therefore, the enforcement of a security and transfer of assets on enforcement may be subject to stamp duty.

However, before stamp duty is imposed by a jurisdiction in relation to a loan security there must be a nexus with that jurisdiction. Further, a mortgage or charge will generally only be stampable to the extent that it secures moneys 'advanced or lent'. Therefore, to determine whether stamp duty is payable in relation to the charge it is necessary to determine whether:

1 the security has a nexus with an Australian jurisdiction;
2 the security falls within the definition of 'mortgage' or 'security' in that jurisdiction; and

3 the security covers money to be secured or lent (in most cases a security which secures debts such as a defined purchase price or an indemnity will not be dutiable as a loan security).

Failure to pay stamp duty on the security will generally render it inadmissible in the courts until such time as the duty is paid, together with any relevant penalties.

Stamp duty can be basically defined as a tax on instruments. In certain cases, legislation requires parties to create an instrument and then imposes tax on that instrument. There are also a few cases where duty is imposed on transactions.

The problem of stamp duty is made more difficult by the fact that each State or Territory has its own legislation, which differs (often markedly) from others.

It is hoped that the stamp duty rewrite referred to above will alleviate some of these problems (although it is not yet clear whether all Australian jurisdictions will introduce conforming legislation). The rewrite is also intended to simplify some of the complexities of existing stamp duty legislation, and to abolish some inconvenient nominal duties. The practical effect of much of the rewritten legislation will be similar to the existing legislation.

Revocable transactions

There are a number of circumstances under which securities can be avoided and the lender, previously secured, required to rank as an unsecured creditor. A detailed examination of these circumstances is beyond the scope of this chapter, but set out below is a list of provisions of the Corporations Law to which a prospective lender may have regard.

1 Under the Corporations Law s 266, a registerable charge which is either not registered within the 45-day period referred to in 'Company Charges' above or at least six months before the winding up of the chargor will void against the liquidator of the chargor.
2 Under the Corporations Law s 267, certain charges in favour of officers and associates of the chargor are void.
3 A transaction entered into by a company is voidable and may be set aside under Part 5.7B of the Corporations Law if, among other things:
   (a) it is either an unfair preference under s 588FA (being a transaction which results in a creditor of the company receiving more than it would have in a winding up of the company) or an uncommercial transaction under s 588FB (being a transaction which a reasonable person in the company's position would not have entered into having regard to certain specified matters); and
   (b) the transaction occurs or is effected when the company is insolvent or causes the company to become insolvent (an 'insolvent transaction': s 588FC) and was entered into within a specified period prior to the company's winding up (being six months for an unfair preference, two years for an uncommercial transaction, four years if a related party benefited from the transaction and ten years if the transaction was entered into to defeat creditors).

   Despite the above, a transaction will not be void against a creditor who can prove certain matters set out in s 588FG (including good faith and no reasonable grounds for suspecting insolvency of the company)

4 An unfair (ie extortionate) loan made at any time on or before the day when a company's winding up begins is voidable.
5 If an administrator is appointed in respect of a company under Part 5.3A of the Corporations Law, a moratorium on disposal of the company's assets and enforcement of securities over the company's assets will apply except in relation to:
   (a) creditors holding security over all or nearly all of the assets of the company who enforces the security within 10 days of notice of the administrator's appointment;
   (b) secured creditors who have enforced prior to the appointment; or
   (c) holders of security over perishable property.
6 Section 566 of the Corporations Law provides that a floating charge on the property of the company created within six months before the commencement of the company's winding up is (unless the company was solvent immediately after the creation of the charge) invalid except to the amount of any moneys paid to the company at the time of or subsequently to the creation of and in consideration for the charge together with interest on that amount at a prescribed rate.

Tax

Although not strictly a 'vitiating factor', certain taxes will be relevant to offshore lenders who take security over Australian assets in that they may operate to reduce the ultimate return under the relevant loan.

Two areas of particular concern are:

1 the ITAA s 25(2); and
2 interest withholding tax.

Income Tax Assessment Act 1936 s25(2)

Section 25(2) provides that interest on money secured by a mortgage of any property in Australia is deemed to be derived from a source in Australia (except to the extent that any double tax treaties apply). Section 25(2) does not apply to payments outside Australia to a non-resident in relation to debentures issues by a company outside Australia.

Section 25(2) can have the effect that interest on a secured lending between non-Australian residents can be subject to Australian income tax where even a small amount of the overall security property is situated in Australia.

In some cases it may be possible to structure the security as an issue of debentures and thus fall within the exception expressed in the section. Alternatively, the property might be moved outside Australia (for example, if shares are secured they can be moved to a branch register outside Australia). Another possibility, where the value of the Australian assets is small when compared to the overall assets and the amount of interest payable, is to create a separate loan facility (for an amount less than the value of the Australian assets) secured by the Australian assets. In that way, only the interest on that loan (if any) will be subject to Australian income tax under s 25(2).

Interest withholding tax

Under the ITAA s 128B(5), a person who is not a resident of Australia and who receives interest income in the course of its foreign business from an Australian entity as an outgoing of that Australian entity's Australia business is liable to pay income tax on the gross amount of that interest. The rate of that income tax is currently 10%. Although the liability falls on the non-resident, the entity paying the interest is required to deduct the tax from the interest payment and to remit to the Commissioner of Taxation the amount deducted within 21 days of the end of the month in which the deduction was made (ss 128(C)(1), 221YL(2A) and 255).

Consumer credit

The States and Territories of Australia have adopted a uniform code, known as the Uniform Consumer Credit Code, to govern the provision of consumer credit. Basically, any credit provided to a natural person wholly or predominantly for personal, domestic or household purposes in the course of the lender's business and for which a charge is made will be subject to the Code. No monetary threshold applies.

The Code does not apply to credit provided to corporations. It also does not apply to certain specified transactions (for example, credit for less than 62 days and bill or promissory note facilities).

Where the Code applies, the relevant credit (including related securities) is subject to various disclosure and documentation requirements, and enforcement of the credit contract and any related securities will be subject to certain restrictions (such as a 30-day grace period). The courts also have wide powers to re-open and vary credit transactions under the Code.

Environmental legislation

Each Australian jurisdiction has enacted legislation regulating the environment and health. Among other things, a proprietor of contaminated land (which can include a mortgagee in possession) may be required to rectify the contamination. Therefore, when funding the acquisition of, or taking security over, property which may be subject to such legislation a lender should consider whether any environmental due diligence or insurance is required in respect of the property.

Special sectors

There are a number of business and financial sectors which present special problems for lenders who propose to take security, given the legislative and regulatory environment in which they operate. Although beyond the scope of this chapter, they include banking, aviation, shipping, media, broadcasting, telecommunications and mining. Secured financing over assets in any of these areas requires detailed consideration by a prospective financier.

2 Canada

Jean Farley[1]

Stikeman Elliott, London

INTRODUCTION

This chapter reviews generally the taking of security over personal and real property in Canada. Under the Canadian federal system, the legislature of each of the ten provinces has responsibility for 'property and civil rights' within the province.[2] Each province of Canada has enacted legislation governing the taking of security. Consequently the first step in any analysis of taking security in Canada is to determine the relevant province or provinces (generally speaking the province where the debtor is located or the location of the assets upon which the security is to be taken) and analyse their conflict of laws rules in order to determine the applicable legal regime. The federal law of Canada also has application as the Bank Act (Canada)[3] contains provisions dealing with the taking of security by banks in Canada. Restrictions contained in federal and provincial corporations legislation on the ability of corporate debtors to grant financial assistance must also be considered when structuring transactions.

There are differences in the legal regimes from province to province, some of which are significant. Other than the Province of Quebec, which has a civil code based upon the Napoleonic model, each of the provinces has a common law regime. All of the common law provinces have, however, enacted comprehensive personal property security legislation in the personal property security Acts ('PPSAs') and other legislation in the context of real property. The provincial PPSAs generally follow the model set by the Province of Ontario, which first enacted PPSA (itself based largely upon art 9 of the United States Uniform Commercial Code) in 1976. PPSAs are in force in British Columbia, Alberta, Saskatchewan, Manitoba, Ontario, New Brunswick, Nova

1 Jean Farley is a lawyer in the London office of Stikeman Elliott. The author would like to acknowledge gratefully the assistance of his colleagues at Stikeman Elliott in the preparation and review of this chapter: Sterling Dietze, Peter Hamilton, Josée Gravel, C. Mario Paura and Justin McKellar.

2 Constitution Act 1867 (UK) s 92(13).

3 Bank Act (Canada), SC 1991 as amended (hereinafter referred to as the 'Bank Act').

Scotia, Prince Edward Island, Newfoundland and the Yukon Territory.[4] Draft PPSA legislation has been enacted but has not yet received royal assent in the Northwest Territories.

In the PPSA jurisdictions the rules governing the creation, attachment and perfection of a 'security interest' in personal property are relatively uniform. The concepts of attachment and perfection are terms of art and will be discussed in greater detail below. Briefly, a security interest must attach before it may be perfected. 'Attachment' occurs when a debtor has signed an agreement in respect of collateral, value is given and the debtor has rights in the collateral. Perfection is the process whereby the secured party establishes the greatest measure of rights in the collateral as against third parties, either by possession or registration. In a PPSA jurisdiction, perfection may always be established by registration and the form of security document is largely irrelevant.

Beyond the scope of this chapter are Canadian legal issues relating to secured party remedies and enforcement (other than in connection with specific documentation issues) and the bankruptcy and insolvency regimes in Canada.[5]

In order to give a practical demonstration of the issues arising for non-Canadian lenders and their counsel in taking security in Canada as well as to outline the manner of documenting and completing such a transaction, at the end of this chapter a model transaction involving cross-border security is set out. This part of the chapter will discuss structural issues such as financial assistance as well as searches, documentation and opinions.

SECURITY OVER PERSONAL PROPERTY

PPSA jurisdictions

Currently, nine of Canada's ten provinces are PPSA jurisdictions: British Columbia, Alberta, Saskatchewan, Manitoba, Ontario, New Brunswick, Nova Scotia, Prince Edward Island and Newfoundland as well as the Yukon Territory. The provisions of the various provincial PPSAs are quite similar as each is modelled upon the Ontario PPSA and as such the relevant provisions of the Ontario PPSA will be discussed in this chapter, with provisions of other provincial PPSAs noted only to the extent of significant variations.

4 PPSA (British Columbia), RSBC 1996; PPSA (Alberta) SA 1988; PPSA (Saskatchewan), ss 1993; PPSA (Manitoba), RSM 1987 (Note: the Manitoba PPSA has been repealed by SM 1993 (which is not yet in force); PPSA (Ontario), RSO 1990; PPSA (New Brunswick), SNB 1993; PPSA (Nova Scotia), SNS 1995-96; PPSA (Prince Edward Island), SPEI 1997; PPSA (Newfoundland), S.N. 1998; PPSA (Northwest Territories), SNWT 1994 (not yet proclaimed in force) and PPSA (Yukon), RSY 1986. Nunavut was created and became the third territory of Canada on 1 April 1999. Pursuant to the *Nunavut Act* (Canada) 1999, Nunavut has generally adopted the legislation of the Northwest Territories. Therefore, whenever reference is made to the legislation of the Northwest Territories, such reference applies equally to Nunavut.

5 For a discussion of bankruptcy and insolvency in Canada see Houlden and Morawetz *Bankruptcy and Insolvency Law of Canada* (3rd edn, 1993).

Application

The PPSA provides that it applies to any transaction that in substance creates a security interest in personal property regardless of the form of document creating the security interest.[6] The effect of this 'substance' driven scheme is broad. The PPSA defines a 'security interest', in part, as an interest in personal property that secures payment or performance of an obligation. The definition extends to conditional sales, chattel mortgages, leases that in substance are financing arrangements and not true leases,[7] debentures, trust deeds, accounts (or assignments of book debts), general security agreements and purchase-money security agreements.[8] The definition also extends to one specific case of a transaction not intended to create security which is an outright assignment of accounts or chattel paper.[9]

The term 'personal property' is broadly defined in the PPSA. It includes chattel paper, documents of title, goods, instruments, intangibles, money, securities and fixtures except for building materials that have been affixed to real property. Virtually all personal property of any kind is encompassed.[10] The applicability of the PPSA to a transaction does not generally turn on how the parties characterise the transaction.[11]

From a documentation perspective, therefore, the form of security document used is largely irrelevant so long as it effectively creates a security interest in the assets to be covered as collateral. Absent non-PPSA considerations, a single general security agreement can change all present and future assets of a debtor. Registration requirements of other regimes may, however, dictate one or more specific documents where a transaction involves real property or property located in a non-PPSA jurisdiction. For example, a debenture may be drafted so as to create a security interest over all present and future real and personal property of a debtor. The security interest in all present and future personal property may be perfected by the registration of a

6 PPSA s 2.

7 The definition of leases intended as security is increasingly interpreted as being so broad that the distinction is of little value.

8 PPSA s 1(1).

9 In *Canadian Western Bank v Gescan Ltd* (1991) 2 PPSAC (2d) 142 (Alta Master) the assignment of a single receivable was found to be within the scope of the Alberta Personal Property Security Act. The policy reasons for including absolute assignments focus upon the intangible nature of accounts receivable and their inability to be transferred by a visible change in possession thereby rendering registration necessary.

10 PPSA s 1(1). Dispute exists as to whether it is possible to create a security interest which is capable of perfection under the PPSA in some forms of intangible personal property, such as quotas, licences and dental patient records and charts. Recent case law suggests that the courts are ready to acknowledge the commercial reality that, for certain types of business, a licence is the debtor's most significant asset and inability to grant security over it will make it difficult for certain businesses to obtain conventional financing. For example, in *Sugar v Duca Community Credit Union Ltd* (1998) 38 OR (3d) 429 (Ont GD) a creditor obtained a valid secured interest in a nursing homes licence issued under the Nursing Homes Act. Security interests in some forms of intellectual property require registration under the PPSA as well as applicable federal statutes (for example, the Copyright Act, RSC 1985, as amended; the Trade Marks Act, RSC 1985, as amended; the Patent Act, RSC 1985), although registration under specific federal statutes may be duplicative without ensuring any further benefit to the secured party.

11 PPSA s 2 provides that, subject to certain exceptions, the PPSA applies to every transaction without regard to form and without regard to the person who has title to the collateral that in substance creates a security interest.

financing statement in PPSA jurisdictions at the same time the debenture itself (with appropriate descriptions of real property) is registered in a real property registry to charge real property. Thus a single document can in appropriate circumstances be effective for more than one purpose. This is illustrated in the discussion of the model transaction at the end of this chapter.

Certain types of property must be registered pursuant to other types of legislation or must be registered in multiple jurisdictions. A ship within the meaning of the Shipping Act (Canada) is required to have its mortgages registered in the vessel's port of registry.[12] Pursuant to the Canada Transportation Act, documents evidencing a sale, lease, mortgage or bailment of rolling stock located on railway lines in Canada may be filed with the Registrar General of Canada.[13] Security interests in aircraft on the other hand must be perfected under the applicable laws of all jurisdictions in which the aircraft travels. Additionally, although the issue is not free from debate, general practice when taking security over intellectual property including copyrights, trade marks, industrial designs and patents is to register a full copy of the security agreement with the relevant federal office.

Conflict of laws

In general, conflicts analysis in a secured transaction is not wholly dependent on the choice of law of the security document. Subject to addressing any issues relating to the proper law of the contract, it is open to parties to choose the laws of another province or country to govern the security agreement. Location of a debtor or its assets in a province will, however, force consideration of the conflicts and, potentially, other laws of that province. The PPSA has a non-exclusive internal conflicts regime which sets out conflict of laws rules for three classes of collateral: goods; intangibles such as accounts; and a third class of collateral consisting of securities, instruments, negotiable documents of title, money and chattel paper. Where a specific PPSA conflict rule does not apply to a given circumstance, the common law rules will apply.

In the case of goods, a possessory security interest in a security, an instrument, a negotiable document of title, money or chattel paper, the PPSA rule provides that the validity, perfection and effect of perfection or non-perfection of a security interest shall be governed by the law of the jurisdiction where the collateral is situated at the time the security interest attaches (the so-called *lex situs* rule).[14] The PPSA varies the *lex situs* rule with respect to goods that are of a type normally used in more than one jurisdiction if the goods are equipment or inventory leased or held for lease by a debtor to third parties, in which case the validity, perfection and effect of perfection or non-perfection of a security interest in such goods is governed by the law of the jurisdiction where the debtor is located at the time the security interest attaches.[15]

The PPSA conflicts rule for intangibles and a non-possessory security interest in a security, an instrument, a negotiable document of title, money or chattel paper provides that the validity, perfection and effect of perfection or non-perfection of a security

12 RSC 1985.
13 SC 1996.
14 PPSA s 5(1).
15 PPSA s 6(1).

interest in these types of collateral is also governed by the law of the jurisdiction where the debtor is located at the time the security interest attaches. For the purposes of these latter two conflict rules, the PPSA deems a debtor to be located at the debtor's place of business if there is one, at the debtor's chief executive office if there is more than one place of business and otherwise at the debtor's principal place of residence.

The PPSA also provides a specific rule where parties to a security agreement creating a security interest in goods in one jurisdiction understand at the time the security interest attaches that the goods are to be kept in another jurisdiction. If the goods are moved to that other jurisdiction within a specified time period (30 days in Ontario), the PPSA provides that the validity, perfection and effect of perfection or non-perfection of the security interest shall be governed by the law of that other jurisdiction.

Where goods are moved into Ontario, whether subject to a security interest created and perfected under the laws of another jurisdiction or not, the PPSA provides rules for perfection or continued perfection, as the case may be, of the security interest in respect of such goods in Ontario. Where the security interest was previously perfected (or the functional equivalent of perfection in non-PPSA jurisdictions) in another jurisdiction, the PPSA rules ensure the continuity of perfection of such a security interest provided that it is re-perfected in Ontario within the time allowed (in Ontario, 60 days from the date the goods are brought into the province or 15 days from the time the secured party receives notice of the relocation). This period can also be abridged by reference to the date the security interest in respect of the transferred goods would have lapsed in the original jurisdiction. The rationale for this latter rule is that a secured party should have no greater rights by virtue of the transfer. During the interim period the PPSA deems the security interest perfected. If it is not re-perfected within the applicable time period, the deeming provisions do not apply. In each case, however, the PPSA provides that such a security interest will be subordinate to the interest of a buyer or lessor of the goods who acquires the goods from the debtor as consumer goods in good faith without notice of the security interest and before the security interest is perfected in Ontario. A security interest in respect of goods bought in Ontario that was not previously perfected pursuant to the laws of another jurisdiction may be perfected in Ontario.[16] The perfected status only takes effect from the time of perfection in Ontario.

In the case of a security interest in intangibles, goods normally used in more than one jurisdiction or a non-possessory security interest in a security, an instrument, a negotiable document of title, money or chattel paper, if the location of the debtor changes to Ontario, the PPSA provides rules for perfection or re-perfection in Ontario of such a security interest on the same terms as for transfer of goods, as discussed above.[17]

The PPSA specifically exempts from the application of its conflicts rules certain procedural and substantive matters. Procedural matters affecting the enforcement of the rights of a secured party in respect of collateral other than intangibles are governed by the law of the jurisdiction in which the collateral is located at the time of exercise of those enforcement rights. Procedural matters affecting the enforcement of the rights of a secured party against intangibles are governed by the law of the forum. Substantive matters affecting the enforcement of the rights of a secured party against collateral are

16 PPSA s 5(4).
17 PPSA s 7(2).

governed by the proper law of the contract between the secured party and debtor.[18] This last conflicts rule is important if security documentation is governed by the laws of a jurisdiction other than Ontario. In that situation, the common law conflicts rules under the proper law of the contract will govern.

Exclusions

Liens

Liens created by statute or rule of law are not governed by the PPSA.[19] Excluded liens include liens of innkeepers,[20] stockbrokers,[1] landlords,[2] solicitors,[3] warehouseman's and repair and storage liens. These latter transactions must be registered in accordance with the applicable provincial legislation.[4]

Deemed trusts

Common legislative devices for creating a priority for amounts owing to a government are the statutory deemed trusts or liens. The PPSA expressly recognises the priority of deemed trusts created under provincial statutes relating to employee entitlements such as holiday pay and pensions.[5] As the term suggests, certain legislation deems assets of the debtor to be segregated and held in trust for the satisfaction of government claims. Deemed trusts are typically created under taxation statutes which contain provisions deeming certain monies owed to the government by the debtor, such as employee source deductions, to be held in trust on behalf of the government. The case law to date has tended to find that for deemed trusts to be effective on a bankruptcy the trust must satisfy the common law requirements for a true trust. At common law the subject matter of the trust must be identifiable and traceable.[6] Deemed trusts rarely meet these tests because it is unusual in a business context to find that assets have actually been segregated to meet these liabilities. The federal Bankruptcy and Insolvency Act[7] (which applies to individuals and most business corporations in every province), however, specifically recognises certain deemed trusts created under the

18 PPSA s 8.

19 PPSA s 4(1)(a); note, however, s 31, 'where a person in the ordinary course of business furnishes materials or services with respect to goods that are subject to a security interest, any lien that the person has in respect of the materials or services has priority over a perfected security interest unless the lien is given by an Act that provides that the lien does not have such priority'.

20 *Bank of Montreal v 414031 Ontario Ltd (Red Dog Inn)* (1983) 45 CBR (NS) 77 (Ont Dt Ct).

1 *Jones v Davidson Partners Ltd* (1981) 121 DLR (3d) 127 (Ont HCJ).

2 *Commercial Credit Corpn v Harry D Shields Ltd* (1980) 112 DLR (3d) 153 (Ont HCJ) affd 122 DLR (3d) 736 (Ont CA).

3 *Budinsky v Breakers East Inc* (1993) 7 PPSAC (2d) 166 (Ont Gen Div).

4 Repair and Storage Liens Act, RSO 1990 ('RSLA'). Registrations are effected in the same manner and with the same registry as under the PPSA. The RSLA effected the repeal of the *Ontario Mechanics' Lien Act*, RSO 1980, the Unclaimed Articles Act, RSO 1980 and the Warehouseman's Lien Act, RSO 1980. While only Ontario has consolidated its liens legislation in this matter, other PPSA provinces also utilise their PPSA registries for registrations relating to such liens.

5 PPSA s 30(7).

6 *Principal Savings & Trust Co (Liquidator of) v British Columbia* (1994) 26 CBR (3d) 104 (Alta QB).

7 Bankruptcy and Insolvency Act, SC 1992, as amended.

Income Tax Act, the Canada Pension Plan and the Unemployment Insurance Act and certain comparable provincial statutes.[8] Other deemed trusts and liens created by provincial law would not, as a result of recent case law, be effective in bankruptcy.[9]

Assignment of interests in real property

PPSA regimes do not apply to the creation or assignment of an interest in real property such as a mortgage, charge or lease of real property. Where security is taken over real property which also contains personal property, the relevant PPSA legislation will apply to the personal property. An interest in a fixture and an assignment of a right to payment under a mortgage, charge or lease where the assignment does not convey or transfer the assignor's interest in the real property are subject to the PPSA.[10]

8 Income Tax Act, RSC 1985, 5th Supp as amended (hereafter referred to as the Income Tax Act); Canada Pension Plan, RSC 1985, as amended; Unemployment Insurance Act, RSC 1985, as amended.

9 The Supreme Court of Canada has on several occasions held that a provincial legislature cannot, by purporting to constitute itself a secured creditor of the debtor, successfully subvert the order of priorities set out in the Bankruptcy and Insolvency Act. Of course, in the case of provincial trusts and statutory liens, a constitutional issue exists because of the federal power prevailing over bankruptcy and insolvency.

In one of the leading cases in the area, a statutory lien created by Quebec legislation for taxes owing to the provincial Crown was held to be ineffective once the debtor became bankrupt: *Re Bourgault: Deputy Minister of Revenue of Quebec v Rainville* [1980] 1 SCR 35, (1979) 33 CBR (NS) 301.

More recently, it was authoritatively settled by the Supreme Court that a bankrupt's assets will be distributed in accordance with the provisions of the Bankruptcy and Insolvency Act and to the exclusion of any contradictory provincial legislation, even where assets are realised by a secured creditor outside the bankruptcy proceedings and without the involvement of the trustee in bankruptcy: *Federal Business, Development Bank v Commission de la Santé et de la Securité du Travail* (1988), 68 CBR (NS) 209.

Therefore, it appears to be settled that any statutory lien created by a provincial legislature will be rendered ineffective as a 'secured claim' in bankruptcy proceedings. (See, further, *Canadian Acceptance Corpn Ltd v Gillespie, Metro Construction (1978) Ltd and R in Right of New Brunswick* (1985) 56 CBR (NS) 197 (NBCA); *Bank of Montreal v Titan Landco Inc* (1989) 41 BLR 14 (BCSC); and *Husky Oil Operations Ltd v Minister of National Revenue*, [1995] SCR 453 (SCC) as other examples of decisions applying *Bourgault and Deloitte* to strike down, after bankruptcy, a provincial statute creating a lien or claim on the debtor's property that operated in violation of the priorities set out in the Bankruptcy and Insolvency Act.)

The Supreme Court of Canada has also dealt with the question of the effectiveness of deemed trusts after bankruptcy: *R in Right of British Columbia v Henfrey Samson Belair Ltd* (1989) 75 CBR (NS). It held that the exclusion of trust property from property of the bankrupt that is stipulated in the Bankruptcy and Insolvency Act should be confined to trusts arising under general principles of law (namely where the trust property is identifiable or traceable). As long as the property in question is identifiable or traceable and meets the requirements for trusts under the general principles of trust law, the provincial statutory trust can be valid and effective even after bankruptcy. However, where the monies in question are no longer identifiable or traceable—as is almost invariably the case in insolvency situations—the 'trust' which is deemed by the provincial statute to exist will not be effective.

10 PPSA s 4(1)(e). A notice of a security interest may also be registered in the proper land registry office where (a) the collateral is or includes fixtures or goods that may become fixtures or crops or minerals or hydrocarbons to be extracted or timber to be cut; or (b) a security interest in a right to payment under a lease, mortgage or charge of real property to which the PPSA applies PPSA s 54(1).

The term 'fixture' is not defined by the PPSA. Generally, fixtures are items which attach to the realty but which may nevertheless be removed without causing major damage to the premises.[11] Personal property such as building materials, which becomes permanently affixed to or incorporated into real property, is not subject to the PPSA. As a result, suppliers of building materials may only take a security interest in such goods before they are affixed to the realty. To the extent that a security interest is granted in something that goes beyond a fixture and extends to the real property, appropriate registrations of the interest may be made in the applicable land registry office as discussed below.

Other exclusions

The PPSA does not apply to:

1 an assignment for the general benefit of creditors to which the Assignments and Preferences Act applies;[12]
2 a sale of accounts or chattel paper as part of a transaction to which the Bulk Sales Act applies;[13]
3 an assignment of accounts pursuant to a factoring arrangement;[14]
4 an assignment of an unearned right to payment to an assignee who is to perform the assignor's obligations under the contract;[15] and
5 transactions governed by a Pawnbrokers Act.[16]

The PPSA does not affect the rights of buyers and sellers under provisions of the Sale of Goods Act which grant to unpaid sellers the right to repossess undelivered purchased goods in transit.[17] Where the PPSA expressly states that it does not apply, the requirements of any other applicable statute or common law principle must be satisfied.

Transfers of interests or claims under or in insurance policies or annuity contracts are likewise not governed by the PPSA. Entitlements to these types of interests can be ascertained by reference to records maintained by the insurers themselves.

11 *Deloitte & Touche Inc v 1035839 Ontario Inc* (1998) 14 PPSAC (2d) 44 (Ont CA), which adopted the following general rules with respect to fixtures which were originally set out by the court in *Stack v T Eaton Co* (1902) 4 OLR 335 (Div Ct): (a) articles not attached to land other than by their own weight are not considered part of the land unless it can be demonstrated that they were intended to be part of the land; (b) articles that are affixed to the land even slightly are considered part of the land unless it can be shown that they were intended to continue as chattels; (c) the degree of annexation and the object of annexation are of relevance in determining the characterisation of objects; (d) the intention of the person affixing the article is material only to the extent that it can be presumed from the degree of annexation of the article; and (e) tenant's trade fixtures form part of the land, subject to the right of the tenant as against the landlord to remove them. In the recent case of *Sawridge Manor Ltd v Selkirk Springs International Corpn* (1994) 7 PPSAC (2d) 139 (BCSC), water bottling equipment which was affixed to a warehouse yet was removable without great difficulty was prima facie considered to be fixtures.

12 PPSA s 4(1)(f); Assignments and Preferences Act, RSO 1990.

13 PPSA s 4(1)(g); Bulk Sales Act, RSO 1990.

14 PPSA s 4(1)(h).

15 PPSA s 4(1)(i).

16 For example, Pawnbrokers Act, RSO 1990; PPSA s 4(1)(d).

17 PPSA s 4(2), Sale of Goods Act, RSO 1990.

True leases versus leases intended as security

Generally speaking under the PPSA system, financing leases must be perfected in accordance with the PPSA in order to protect the interest of the lessor in the leased goods. The critical issue is the distinction between a non-financing (or a true lease) as opposed to a lease intended as security (or a financing lease). As the PPSA expressly states that, form notwithstanding, it will apply to transactions which in substance create a security interest, the PPSA may be found to apply to a lease transaction even in the face of an explicit statement by the parties to the contrary.[18]

In considering this issue, courts traditionally focus on the relative position and intention of the parties and the effect of the transaction[19] as evidenced by the following specific criteria:

1 whether the lessee is obliged to purchase the leased goods at the end of the lease term;[20]

2 whether the option price is nominal in contrast to the actual fair market value of the leased goods at the time when the option is to be exercised;[1]

3 where the lessee is required to make an additional payment at the end of the lease in respect of any deficiency under the lease should the lessee fail to exercise the option to purchase or, where end of term purchase is mandatory, the risk of ownership is deemed transferred to the lessee[2]; and

18 *HOJ Franchise Systems Inc v Municipal Savings & Loan Corpn* (1994) 6 PPSAC (2d) 302 (Ont Gen Div).

19 *Re Speedtrack Ltd* (1980) 33 CBR 209 (Ont SC), where a lease was found to be in essence a financing transaction requiring perfection under the PPSA.

20 *Federal Business Development Bank v Bramalea Ltd* (1983) 144 DLR (3d) 410 at 413–414 (Ont HCJ); aff'd 150 DLR (3d) 768 (Ont CA) where the court found that a lease whereby the lessee was obliged to purchase the leased vehicles was a transaction creating a security interest to which the PPSA applied. In *Zuccarini Importing & Distribution Co v Royal Bank* (1986) 6 PPSAC 46 (Ont Dist Ct), the court likened the terms of the lease to a conditional sales contract intended as security to which the PPSA applied. In *Price Waterhouse Ltd v Leggat Leasing (Halton) Ltd* (1985) 6 PPSAC 300 (Ont SC (in Bankrupty)), a lease was found to be a true lease and therefore outside the scope of the predecessor PPSA as the lessee had the option to exchange the leased vehicle for another of similar condition during the term of the lease, a term found to be inconsistent with a purchase and moreover the purchase option was not so nominal and favourable that a reasonable lessee would automatically exercise it. In *Dunwoody Ltd v Wood-Land Tractor Inc* (1994) 7 PPSAC (2d) 133 (Ont Bankrupty), a lease which could be converted into a purchase agreement but where the conversion to purchase was not exercised was found to be a true lease, the court noting that in the circumstances the lessor was aware that the chances of the lessee raising sufficient funds to buy out the lease were remote.

1 *First City Capital v Hall* (1989) 60 R (2d) 12 (Ont HCJ) where the option price was substantially less (less than one-tenth of the original purchase price) than fair market value of the goods resulting in the leases being considered to be conditional sales; *Unilease Inc v Graphic Centre (Ontario) Inc* (1982) 43 CBR (NS) 234 (Ont Co Ct) where the option price of one dollar was found to be nominal. In *Re King* (1993) 4 PPSAC (2d) 283 (Ont Ct J (in Bankruptcy)) where a security agreement stipulated that the lessee would be required upon the lessor's request to purchase the leased goods at the expiry of the lease term for a sum which was found to be a realistic estimate of the fair market value of the leased goods, the lease was found to be a true lease. In *Mitsui & Co Canada v Royal Bank* (1993) 22 CBR (3d) 95 (NSCA) and *MTC Leasing v National Bank Leasing Inc* (1997), 12 PPSAC (2d) 319 (Man. QB), a lease with an option to purchase at fair market value was found to be a true lease.

2 *Re Cronin Fire Equipment Ltd* (1993) 5 PPSAC (2d) 219 (Ont Bankruptcy).

4 whether the term of the lease coincides with the useful economic life span of the leased asset and no meaningful residual value remains at the end of the lease term.

Recently, courts have demonstrated an increasing tendency to regard any lease transaction which is in substance a financing as caught by the requirements of the PPSA, even without a careful analysis of any purchase option.[3] As a result, compliance with the provisions of the PPSA is advisable where any doubt exists as to whether a lease is a true lease or a financing lease. A lessor registering under the PPSA in connection with a lease will not generally suffer a disadvantage since the PPSA provides that registration does not create a presumption that the PPSA applies to the related transaction.[4]

Consignments

A true consignment is exempt from the scope of the PPSA. Again, where the consignment is viewed as in substance securing payment or performance of an obligation, it will be deemed to create a security interest. In a true consignment relationship the consignor is a principal and the consignee an agent with no obligation to pay for consigned goods. Title to the consigned goods does not pass through the consignee to the purchaser but rather flows directly from the consignor to the purchaser.[5] In such cases, no security interest is created because the consignor retains title to the goods until title is passed to the purchaser.[6] Again, it may be wise to register under the PPSA to protect against the eventuality that a consignment is found to be a secured as opposed to a true consignment.[7] Registration and transaction under the Ontario PPSA will not generally compromise a true consignment. In Alberta, British Columbia and Saskatchewan, the interest of a consignor who delivers goods to a consignee under a commercial consignment must be perfected in accordance with the applicable rules.[8]

3 *Adelaide Capital Corpn v Integrated Transportation Finance Inc* (1994) 6 PPSAC (2d) 267 (Ont Ct (Gen Div)).

4 PPSA s 46(5)(b).

5 *Newcourt Credit Group Inc v GA Finance Inc* (1998) 13 PPSAC (2d) 372 (Ont Gen Div); *Seven Limers Coal & Fertilizer Co v Hewitt* (1985) 52 OR (2d) (Ont Div Ct); *Re Toyerama Ltd* (1980) 34 CBR (NS) 153 (Ont SC (in Bankrupty)). In *Re Stephanian's Persian Carpets Ltd* (1980) 1 PPSAC 119 (Ont SC), the consignee had no obligation to purchase the goods and, as such, the arrangement was found to be a true consignment. In *Northshore Firearms In.* (1995) 39 CBR (3d) 309 (Ont GD (in bankruptcy)) the court held that, as every conditional sales agreement reserves title, this in itself is not determinative of a consignment; the applicant must show that the relationship was in the nature of a bailment.

6 *Re Revere Electric Inc* (1993) 13 OR (3d) 637 (Ont Gen Div).

7 In *D & A MacLeod Co Ltd (Trustee) v Manhattan Electric Cable Corpn (indexed as Glengarry AET Inc (Trustee of) v Manhattan Electric Cable Corpn* (1986) 6 PPSAC 112 (Ont SC), the court found that the parties had created a true consignment despite the fact that the agreement between the parties stated that the consignment was one of security. See also *Canadian Imperial Bank of Commerce v Otto Timm Enterprises Ltd* (1991) 2 PPSAC (2d) 58 (Ont (Gen Div)) where the agreements and conduct of the parties were held to be inconsistent with a true consignment.

8 PPSA (Alberta) ss 1(1)(g) and 3(2)(c); PPSA (British Columbia) ss 1(1) and 3(b); and PPSA (Saskatchewan) ss 2(1)(h) and 3(2).

Attachment and perfection of security interest

As noted in the introduction, perfection of a security interest is the process by which a secured party establishes the most effective rights in personal property of a debtor as against third parties. The PPSA provides that a security interest is perfected when it has attached and all steps prescribed in the PPSA for perfection have been completed.[9] Perfection may be effected, depending on the nature of the collateral, either by registration[10] or possession[11] (or both).

A perfected security interest in collateral will extend to the identifiable or traceable proceeds of such collateral. Proceeds are in effect born perfected so long as the original collateral is perfected at the time the proceeds arise. If perfection was achieved by way of registration, perfection in the collateral remains effective so long as the registration remains effective. A security interest in proceeds of collateral in which the security interest was perfected by possession becomes unperfected ten days after the debtor acquires an interest in the proceeds unless the security interest in the proceeds is itself perfected by registration or possession of the proceeds.[12]

The PPSA also provides that a perfected security interest in collateral will extend to secure future advances made under an agreement which explicitly contemplates such advances.[13] In almost all circumstances, priority is independent of the timing of the advance.

Attachment

Attachment is the PPSAs term to describe the satisfaction of all preconditions for the creation of a security interest and is required in order for a security interest to be enforceable against third parties.[14] It occurs when the secured party (itself or through an agent other than the debtor) obtains possession of the collateral or the debtor signs a security agreement containing a description of the collateral sufficient to enable it to be identified,[15] value is given[16] and the debtor has rights in the collateral, unless the parties have agreed to postpone the time for attachment in which case the security

9 PPSA s 19.

10 PPSA s 23.

11 PPSA s 22.

12 PPSA s 25.

13 PPSA s 30(3) and (4) and s 13.

14 PPSA s 11(1). In provinces other than Ontario attachment is not a precondition to enforceability generally (Manitoba) or as between the debtor and the secured party, as opposed to as against third parties (Alberta, British Columbia and Saskatchewan).

15 The requirement that the collateral be sufficiently described in a security agreement so as to enable it to be identified is, of course, subject to interpretation. There is jurisprudence to the effect that where a schedule listing equipment was completed but not stapled to the security document or where an invoice containing a retention of title provision was not signed by a debtor who only executed a purchase order which did not feature this provision but contained a description of the collateral, the description requirement was not satisfied and attachment did not occur. See *Royal Bank of Canada v Concorde Investments Corp* (1991) 2 PPSAC (2d) 314 (Sask QB) and *Universal Handling Equipment Co Ltd v Redipac Recycling Inc* (1992) 4 PPSAC (2d) 15 (Ont Ct Gen Div).

16 'Value' is defined by the PPSA as any consideration sufficient to support a simple contract and includes an antecedent debt or liability: PPSA s 1(1).

interest attaches at the agreed time.[17] The failure of a security interest to attach will result in the security interest being unenforceable as against third parties, although the security interest will still be effective as against the debtor.[18]

The requirement that the debtor have rights in the collateral assists in establishing the time from which attachment (and consequently perfection) exists in, among other things, after-acquired property. Although there had previously been debate as to the validity of after-acquired property clauses in security agreements, the PPSA has settled this issue as it expressly provides that a security agreement may cover after-acquired property.[19] Subject to certain exceptions relating to consumer goods and crops, property acquired by a debtor after execution of a security agreement granting a security interest over after-acquired property will automatically and without any specific appropriation be subject to be a perfected security interest with priority as against third parties dating from the date of original perfection.

Perfection by possession

Perfection by way of possession of the collateral is available where a security interest is given in chattel paper, goods, instruments, securities, negotiable documents of title, and money during the time in which these goods are actually held as collateral.[20] The party perfecting by possession may be the secured party or a person acting on behalf of the secured party, other than the debtor or the debtor's agent.

Perfection by possession is usually not a practical approach[1] except where the collateral consists of securities. Possession does, however, make realisation much easier and prevents the debtor from fraudulently disposing of the security. There is the risk, however, that if possession is lost for any reason the state of perfection will also lapse and registration may also be done as an added precaution. Where possession has been lost, repossession of the collateral will suffice to perfect a security interest in the collateral[2] although, in some western Canadian provinces, repossession in the course of realisation will not operate to perfect a security interest.[3]

17 PPSA s 11(2). Additional timing rules apply in the case of specific types of collateral such as crops, fish, the young of animals, minerals and hydrocarbons and timber: s 11(2).

18 PPSA s 11(1).

19 PPSA s 12.

20 PPSA s 22.

1 Although heavy equipment remaining on the debtor's premises can be rendered unusable in order to demonstrate the act of possession of such collateral: see *Re Darzinskas* (1981) 340R (2d) 782 (Ont SC (in Bankruptcy)).

2 *Re Charron* (1985) 54 CBR (NS) 301 (Ont SC (in Bankruptcy)); *Royal Trust Corpn of Canada v No 7 Honda Sales Ltd* (1987) 35 BLR (Ont Dist Ct); rev'd (1988) 40 BLR 109 (Ont Div Ct).

3 In *Bank of Nova Scotia v Trans Canada Credit Corpn* (1993) 4 PPSAC (2d) 56 (Sask QB), the court observed that the possession of collateral by a secured party perfects a security interest only while it is actually held as collateral. In this case, the unsecured creditor who repossessed the collateral did not do so to hold it as collateral but rather to sell it and realise payment of a debt owed to the secured party. See also *Re Glencoe Express Inc* (1992) 3 PPSAC (2d) 239 (BCSC) where seizure made prior to the bankruptcy of a lessee was found to have been made with an intent to satisfy a debt and not to perfect a security interest.

Perfection by registration

Under the PPSA regimes security documents are not themselves registered. Instead, a financing statement in the prescribed form is registered.[4] Registration does not, however, constitute constructive notice or knowledge to or by third parties of the existence of the financing statement (or indeed of the underlying security document) nor does it create a presumption that the PPSA applies to the transaction.[5]

Financing statements are registered in person or in some cases electronically with the government office designated in the relevant PPSA. Except where the collateral is consumer goods, a financing statement can be registered at any time before or after the execution of the security agreement.[6] In the case of consumer goods, the financing statement can be filed at any time after the execution of the security agreement.[7] Since priority may depend upon the timing of registration, early registration is recommended whenever possible.

A secured party can select the period for which a registration is effective and may register for an indefinite period, except where consumer goods are involved, in which case a registration may only be made for a maximum of five years.[8] The choice of the registration period is usually governed by the anticipated term of the financing plus an appropriate additional period to ensure that perfection continues and priority is maintained if the debtor defaults. The costs of registration tend to increase as the selected registration period increases. The registration period can be reduced or increased by registering a financing change statement before the expiry of the registration.

The requirements for proper completion of a financing statement are extremely technical and minor errors, including spelling mistakes, can lead to disastrous results. The appearance of the debtor's name has been an ongoing source of litigation.[9] If the

4 PPSA ss 23, 45(1) and 46(2). A financing statement can be registered to perfect a security interest in more than one security agreement between the same parties (except with respect to consumer goods) even if the agreements were entered into at different times (PPSA s 45(4) following pre-existing case law: see *West Bay Sales Ltd v Hitachi Sales Corpn* (1978) 1 PPSAC 20 (Ont SC).) There is unfortunate jurisprudence to the effect that any subsequent agreements which seek to rely on a prior registration must be capable of being linked to the overall transaction to which the prior registration related. The case of *Adelaide Capital v Integrated Transportation Finance Inc* (1994) 6 PPSAC (2d) 267 (Ont Ct (Gen Div)) suggests that subsequent transactions should be related to prior transactions to which the PPSA registration relates, but the case of *Royal Bank v Agricultural Credit Corpn of Saskatchewan* (1994) 7 PPSAC (2d) 1 (Sask CA) found that a single financing statement was able to perfect multiple security interests even though the other subsequent loans constituted separate and distinct transactions. The better view is that subsequent security interests may be perfected by a prior registration even when they derive from transactions which are separate and distinct from the original transaction to which the registration relates.

5 PPSA s 46(5).

6 PPSA s 45(3).

7 PPSA s 45(2).

8 PPSA s 51(1) and (5).

9 The case law makes clear the importance of being very precise about the debtor's name. A failure to refer to the correct debtor name in a registration may invalidate the registration and result in an unexpected windfall for unsecured creditors. For example, in *Re Weber* (1990) 1 PPSAC (2d) 36 (Ont Bankruptcy) a financing statement which omitted the debtor's middle initial was found to be invalid. Although the PPSA contains curative provisions with respect to immaterial errors, this provision will often not assist the secured party. The standard in applying the curative provisions of the PPSA is an objective one – whether a reasonably competent user of the system would be misled: see *Re Best* (1997) 33 OR 416 (Ont GD).

debtor is a corporation and has both an English and a French form of name (which is quite common especially where a corporation does business in Quebec), both versions must be entered on the financing statement.[10] The accurate corporate name can be verified by conducting a corporate name search and if the debtor conducts business under a trade name then this name may also be set out along with the correct corporate name. Registration against a trade name in lieu of the proper corporate name is ineffective and will result in the loss of perfection and priority. In the case of a partnership, a search should be conducted to ensure that the name referenced in the security agreement and on the financing statement is the name registered under the relevant legislation governing partnerships. In the case of an individual, reference should be made to a birth certificate, passport, driver's licence or other official document to confirm the correct legal name.[11]

Other information which must be included on the financing statement is the address of the debtor,[12] the name and address of the secured party,[13] a classification of the collateral[14] and where consumer goods are involved, the principal amount secured and the date of maturity or an indication that there is no maturity date.[15] A copy of the registered financing statement or financing change statement must be delivered to the debtor within 30 days of registration.[16]

10 These specific provisions regarding the content of financing statements are found in the Regulation to the PPSA (hereafter referred to as the 'PPSA Regulation') ss 16 and 17.

11 *Canadian Imperial Bank of Commerce v Melnitzer (Trustee of)* (1994) 23 CBR (3d) 161 (Ont Bankrupty) where a debtor is foreign born, the name shown on the debtor's citizenship certificate should be used in preparing financing statements.

12 PPSA Regulation s 3(1)(d).

13 PPSA Regulation s 3(1)(e).

14 A financing statement includes collateral classification boxes for 'consumer goods', 'inventory', 'equipment', 'accounts', 'other' and 'motor vehicle included'. A secured creditor must indicate in which type of collateral it claims a security interest. Collateral classification boxes must be correctly completed or a security interest may not be perfected in respect of such collateral: *Re Laverty* (1982) 47 CBR (NS) 109 (Ont SC (in Bankrupty)) where the 'other' box was checked instead of the 'equipment' box it was held to exclude the named class of collateral which should have been indicated in the 'equipment' box and as a result, the secured party could not claim priority with respect to certain equipment; *Adelaide Capital Corpn v Integrated Transportation Finance Inc* (1994) 23 CBR (3d) 289 (Ont Ct (Gen Div), where collateral which was inventory in the hands of the debtor was not indicated as such and the curative provisions of the PPSA were not applied to save the registration. Certain financing statements which contained a general collateral description, however, were found to be effective as the collateral description provided sufficient information to put other parties on notice of the security interest and, as such, a reasonable person would not be materially misled. In *Hong Kong Bank of Canada v National Bank of Canada* (1990) 73 OR (3d) 28 (HCJ) the 'book debts' box was not checked but there was a description in the collateral description box (the completion of which is optional) and, as a result, the court reasoned that no one would be materially misled by the error. In *Central Guarantee Trust Co v Red Coach Rentals Corpn* (1995) 9 PPSAC (2d) 146 (OntGD) the court held that, if a financing statement is to be valid despite a misclassification of collateral, there must be an unequivocally clear description of the collateral elsewhere on the financing statement. As a rule, however, the general collateral description portion of the financing statement form is not completed as it is not mandatory to complete this section and may in fact place the secured party at risk of limiting the scope of the collateral by employing language which indicates something less than intended. In the two preceding cases, however, the completion of a general collateral description prevented the security interest from being unperfected in certain collateral.

15 PPSA Regulation s 3(1)(i), (j).

16 PPSA s 46(6).

Under the PPSA, the secured party or the agent of the secured party completes, executes and registers the financing statement. A failure to correctly complete the signature portion of the financing statement may also affect the validity of the registration.

As discussed above, certain errors made in the preparation of financing statements and financing change statements are fatal to the validity of the registration, whereas others can be remedied by resort to the curative provisions set out in the PPSA. The test is that a financing statement or a financing change statement will not be invalidated or its effect impaired by reason only of an error or omission in its execution or registration unless a reasonable person is likely to be misled materially by the error or omission.[17] What is materially misleading has been a fertile ground for disagreement. Where an error has been made on a financing statement (or financing change statement) which is curable, the registration can be remedied by the filing of a financing change statement.

Maintaining perfection

Generally speaking, if a security interest is originally perfected and subsequently re-perfected (in each case in any manner permitted under the PPSA) it will be deemed to be continuously perfected. This has the important effect for priorities purposes of dating the perfection of the security interest at the date of original perfection. However, the occurrence of certain events relating to the debtor or the collateral may require action by the secured party in order to maintain the perfection of the security interest. Examples of such transactions include transfer of collateral by the debtor[18] and the change of the debtor's name (which frequently occurs upon corporate amalgamations).[19]

A security interest perfected by registration whose registration has lapsed can be subsequently reperfected. However, the security interest may be subject to the rights of a person in the collateral in the intervening time.[20] Lapse of a security interest does not impair the validity of the security agreement.[1]

Priorities

The two broad categories of priority rules under the PPSA are for unperfected and perfected security interests. Additionally a special regime operates for purchase-money security interests which, if properly perfected under the PPSA, will take priority with respect to the purchased asset over a perfected security interest in after-acquired property which covers the same asset.

17 PPSA s 46(4).

18 PPSA s 48 (1) and (2). Where the secured party has given its prior consent to the transfer it has 15 days to register a financing statement before its security interest in the transferred collateral becomes unperfected and where the secured party has not given its prior consent, it has 30 days from the date of the transfer (if the secured party had prior knowledge of the transfer and the information required to file a financing change statement) or from the date it becomes aware of the information required to file a financing change statement.

19 PPSA s 48(3). The secured party has 30 days from the time it learns of the name change and the new name to register a financing change statement or take possession of the collateral before the security interest becomes unperfected.

20 PPSA s 30(6).

1 See *Canadian Imperial Bank of Commerce v Klunkovski* (1983) 3 PPSAC 216 (Ont HC).

These rules, however, do not constitute a complete priorities analysis. As a general rule, the priorities rules in the PPSA only apply to priorities issues arising in respect of competing PPSA security interests. Priorities as between PPSA and non-PPSA interests (such as security under the Bank Act) must be resolved outside the PPSA. The analysis as to priority as between PPSA and non-PPSA security is complex and many issues remain uncertain. For example, notwithstanding that under the PPSA the concept of title to assets is not relevant, title may be relevant in priority disputes between PPSA and non-PPSA security.

Unperfected security interests

Although an unperfected security interest is valid in accordance with its terms and will be enforceable against third parties to the extent it has attached, a security interest which has not been perfected does not provide a secured party with the level of protection that perfection affords. In particular, an unperfected security interest is subordinate to the interest of:

1 a person who has a perfected security interest in the same collateral or who has a lien given under any other legislation or rule of law or who has priority under any other legislation;
2 a person who assumes control of the collateral through execution, attachment, garnishment, charging order, equitable execution or other legal process; or
3 persons entitled by the Creditors' Relief Act or otherwise to participate in the distribution of the property over which a creditor in 2 above has assumed control, or the proceeds of that property.[2]

In addition, an unperfected security interest is not effective in the following circumstances:

1 against a person who represents the creditors of a debtor, including an assignee for the benefit of creditors and a trustee in bankruptcy;
2 where the security interest is in chattel paper, documents of title, securities, instruments or goods, against a transferee who takes under a transfer that does not secure payment or performance of an obligation and who gives value and receives delivery without knowledge of the security interest; and
3 where the security interest is in intangibles other than accounts, against a transferee who takes under a transfer that does not secure payment or performance of an obligation and who gives value without knowledge of the security interest.[3]

In a competition between two unperfected security interests, the PPSA provides that priority is determined by the order of attachment of the security interests.[4]

Perfected security interests

In addition to the rules set out above with respect to disputes involving unperfected security interests, the PPSA contains rules of priority which apply to disputes involving perfected security interests. Subject to the special priority rules discussed below, these rules are as follows:

2 PPSA s 20(1)(a).
3 PPSA s 20(1)(b), (c) and (d).
4 PPSA s 30(1), (4).

1 in situations where the competing interests were both perfected by registration, the first to register has priority regardless of the order of perfection;
2 in situations where one of the competing interests was perfected by registration and one of the interests perfected otherwise than by registration:
   (a) the registered interest takes priority if it was perfected and registered before the perfection of the other security interest; and
   (b) the interest perfected otherwise than by registration takes priority if it was perfected before the registration of the registered interest;[5] and
3 in situations where both interests were perfected otherwise than by registration, the first to perfect has priority.[6]

These rules will apply irrespective of where legal title to the collateral lies and irrespective of the state of knowledge of the parties. In a race to perfect, the common law concepts of good faith and notice generally have no application.[7]

Purchase-money security interests

The special priority provisions relating to purchase-money security interests are the most common exception to the general priority rules relating to perfected security interests and were designed to facilitate purchase-money financing in the face of pre-existing general security extending to after-acquired property. The policy behind this special priority is that a person holding general security is not harmed by such a priority in that the debtor's net asset position has not changed.

The PPSA defines a purchase-money security interest as being a security interest taken (a) in collateral to secure payment of all or part of the purchase price of such collateral, or (b) by a person who gives value for the purpose of enabling the debtor to acquire rights in collateral to the extent that the value is actually applied for the purpose of acquiring such rights.[8] The definition goes on expressly to exclude a sale and lease back transaction from being a purchase-money security interest. A purchase-money security interest can achieve the special priority afforded by the PPSA if the requirements set out in the PPSA are satisfied.[9] These requirements are dependent upon the nature of the collateral but essentially involve the giving of notice by the purchase-money

5 PPSA, s 30(1), (2). The PPSAs in British Columbia, Alberta and Saskatchewan do not contain this rule but are subject to the general rule that the first to register, possess or perfect takes priority. It is thus conceivable that, in a limited number of cases, the result of a priorities analysis might be different in these provinces. The Manitoba PPSA has yet to be amended to bring it into line with the other provinces and there the rule is that the first to perfect has priority. However, when Manitoba's *Personal Property Security and Consequential Amendments Act*, SM 1993 is proclaimed in force, its provisions will on this point mirror those of British Columbia, Alberta and Saskatchewan.

6 PPSA s 30(1).

7 See *National Trailer Convoy of Canada v Bank of Montreal* (1980) 1 PPSAC 87 (Ont SC). However, with respect to good faith, in the case of *Bank of Nova Scotia v Royal Bank* (1998) 14 PPSAC (2d) 10 (BCSC) the court held that one of the creditors acted in a way so misleading that it qualified as being in bad faith; in such cases, the 'integrity' of the system may be subjugated to prevent an unjust result. There is also a good faith requirement in certain PPSA legislation: eg British Columbia, s 68(2) requires that the parties act in good faith and in a commercially reasonable manner.

8 PPSA s 1(1).

9 PPSA s 33.

security holder of its interest to other secured creditors who appear on the PPSA register.

Where the purchase-money security interest is in inventory, the interest must be perfected by the earlier of the time the debtor obtains possession of the inventory or a third party obtains the inventory at the request of the debtor.[10] The security holder must then, before the debtor obtains possession of the inventory, give notice to other registered secured parties who have indicated in their registration (by checking the appropriate collateral classification box) that inventory is part of their collateral, stating that such person has or expects to acquire a purchase-money security interest in the inventory specified in the notice. Once properly constituted a purchase-money security interest's special priority extends to the proceeds of the inventory. The PPSAs in British Columbia, Alberta and Saskatchewan address the inherent priority competition between the holder of a purchase-money security interest in the proceeds of inventory and the holder of a security interest in accounts receivable. In Ontario the holder of the purchase-money security interest over inventory has priority but in the Western provinces the holder of the purchase-money security interest over accounts receivable has priority so long as new value is given and the interest is registered.[11]

For collateral other than inventory, the purchase-money security rules[12] are similar to those described above except that the holder of such security is not required to give notice to existing secured creditors and perfection of the interest can occur before or within ten days of the debtor (or a third party as described above) obtaining possession of the collateral. Where the collateral is an intangible, perfection must occur before or within ten days of attachment of the interest in the intangible.[13]

Finally, in situations of competition for the same collateral between more than one holder of a purchase-money security interest (presumably the seller of collateral and one or more financiers of the same collateral), the PPSA provides that the interest of the seller of the collateral has priority.[14]

Other priority rules and results

While a perfected security interest provides a secured party with the greatest protection possible under the PPSA it is subject to certain limitations. A perfected security interest will be defeated (a) where the collateral is goods, by a sale or lease in the ordinary course[15] even though the buyer or lessee knows of the security interest, unless the buyer or lessee also knew that the sale or lease constituted a breach of the security agreement, (b) where the collateral is chattel paper, an instrument or a negotiable document of title, by a transfer of the collateral to a purchaser for value who purchased the collateral without knowledge that the collateral was subject to a security interest,[16]

10 PPSA s 33(1).

11 BC PPSA s 34(5), Alta PPSA s 34(6) and Sask PPSA s 34(6). In each of these provinces, the purchase-money security interest must be registered before it is perfected or its financing statement is registered.

12 PPSA s 33(2)(a).

13 PPSA s 33(2)(b).

14 PPSA s 33(3).

15 PPSA s 28(1) and (2).

16 PPSA s 28(3) and (4). Section 29 of the PPSA provides that 'the rights of a person who is (a) a holder in due course of a bill, note or cheque within the meaning of the Bills of Exchange Act (Canada) or (b) a transferee from the debtor of money are to be determined without regard to the Act'.

and (c) where the collateral is a security, whether certificated or not, a sale to a purchaser in the ordinary course even though the purchaser knows of the security interest, unless the purchaser knew that the sale constituted a breach of the security agreement[17]. Additionally, the security granted over crops,[18] goods that become accessions[19] or are co-mingled[20] and fixtures[1] enjoy priority over certain other security interests. The common law rights of distress of a landlord in respect of unpaid rent have also been judicially recognised as conferring on the landlord a lien and are thus viewed as being outside the scope of the PPSA priorities scheme.[2]

The PPSA also expressly recognises the effectiveness of contractual subordination.[3] The provision goes beyond an agreement between secured parties and has been interpreted to permit a third party to enforce a contractual provision made for its benefit absent privity of contract.[4]

Bank Act security

The final type of security to note in connection with a priorities analysis is the security that can be granted over certain types of assets by certain classes of borrowers to a Canadian chartered bank pursuant to the terms of the Bank Act (Canada) ss 426 and 427. The security provisions of the Bank Act are based upon the common law provisions respecting title to property and are thus at odds with the PPSA regimes. This has led to extremely difficult problems between competing security interests created under the different regimes.[5]

The possibility of the existence of Bank Act security is important to a foreign lender because it may have priority over such lender's security notwithstanding that such security is properly perfected under a PPSA or other provincial legislation. The existence of Bank Act security can be determined by conducting searches with the register maintained by the Bank of Canada.

17 PPSA s 28(7).
18 PPSA s 32(1).
19 PPSA s 35.
20 PPSA s 37.
1 PPSA s 34.
2 See *Commercial Credit Corpn v Harry d Shields Ltd; Braukmann Holdings Ltd v Commercial Credit Corpn* (1981) 1 PPSAC 310 (Ont CA).
3 PPSA s 38.
4 See *Euroclean Canada Inc v Forest Glade Investments Ltd* (1985) 4 PPSAC 271. Note, though, that a subordination agreement must be in 'clear and unequivocal terms': *Sunlife Assurance Co. of Canada v Royal Bank* (1995) 10 PPSAC (2d) 246 (Ont Gen Div).
5 See Crawford and Falconbridge Banking and Bills of Exchange (8th edn), p 435 in the following terms:

> 'When [competing interests] may arise under wholly separate systems that are not founded upon common principles, those problems are compounded perhaps beyond the point of completely logical resolution. But that is precisely the situation which now exists in Canada.'

For more detailed analysis see Jacob S Ziegel 'Interaction of Personal Property Security Legislation and Security Interests Under the Bank Act' (1986) 12 Can Bus LJ 73 at p 80; Cuming and Wood 'Compatibility of Federal and Provincial Personal Property Security Law' (1986) Can Bar Rev 267; Cuming 'The Relationship between Personal Property Security Acts and Section 178 of the Bank Act: Federal Paramountcy and Provincial Legislative Policy' (1988) 14 Can Bus LJ 315; Jacob S Zeigel 'Personal Property Security Interests and the Conflicts of Laws' (1996) 11 BFLR 323.

Bank Act security was originally intended to assist wholesale manufacturers and producers of primary products to obtain bank financing. However, it is now available to virtually any type of borrower. Section 426 security can be taken by a Canadian chartered bank from any borrower, guarantor of a borrower or other person in assets comprised of hydrocarbons and minerals. Section 427 security can be taken from farmers, foresters, fishermen and aquaculturists and other natural resource producers, manufacturers, wholesalers, retailers, shippers and dealers in the products of such persons over assets comprised of the produce or goods, wares and merchandise of such persons. In both cases, the terms of the Bank Act detail the method of taking such security and registration as well as the rights and priority of the bank in connection with the collateral.

The priority scheme set out in the Bank Act[6] provides that the bank shall, if the security has been properly taken and registered in respect of property owned by the debtor at the time of the grant of security or of which the debtor becomes the owner thereafter, have priority over all rights subsequently acquired in respect of that property and also over the claim of an unpaid vendor. Thus unless a prior claim impacts on the issue of whether a debtor 'owns' property, Bank Act security will generally have priority.[7]

Where Bank Act security competes with security properly taken and perfected or registered under another regime, the first principle to be considered is the constitutional authority of the legislature enacting the competing regimes to legislate in that area. As the federal parliament has constitutional authority over the area of banking, the priority rules set out in the Bank Act should prevail over conflicting rules of provincial law.[8] Because the Bank Act provides in effect that the bank will obtain all the right and title that the borrower has as 'owner', it is left to the law of property to determine whether the borrower is 'owner' for these purposes and, if so, the consequences of the bank holding such an interest. The common law rule that a debtor can only give to a secured party rights as good as he possesses (the *nemo dat* principle) has the effect of giving priority to interests created first in time but again does not provide a complete answer

6 Bank Act s 428(1).

7 The Bank Act does, however, recognise the existence of certain liens such as that of an unpaid vendor of property where the bank has knowledge of the lien (s 428(2)) as well as certain claims of employees for wages and other remuneration against a company in bankruptcy proceedings and of growers and producers of products of agriculture (s 427(7)).

8 The decision of the Supreme Court of Canada in the case of *Bank of Montreal v Hall* (1990) 9 PPSAC 177 (SCC) held that the federal parliament has occupied the field in connection with legislation that impacts in any manner on a security interest taken by a Canadian chartered bank (here with respect to enforcement procedure) and, notwithstanding that the legislation in question was intra vires the provincial legislature, the provisions of the federal Bank Act were paramount. The provincial PPSAs in British Columbia (s. 4(b)), Alberta (s. 4(b)), Saskatchewan (s. 4(k)), Manitoba (s 3(f)), New Brunswick (s 4(l)), Nova Scotia (s 5(j) and (k)), Prince Edward Island (s 4(j) and (k)) and Yukon (s 3(k)) expressly recognise that the security interests created under federal statutes such as the Bank Act prevail. In other PPSA jurisdictions, application of the decision in *Bank of Montreal v Hall* should lead to the same result.

It should also be noted that federal security interests can be created under other statutes such as the Farm Credit Act, Corporation Act, SC 1993, the Canada Shipping Act, RSC 1985, as amended, and the Canada Transportation Act, SC 1996 although these interests are less common. Somewhat more common are security interests created under federal statutes governing intellectual property, which are discussed below.

given the variety of different types of interests that can be created at common law.

Perhaps the most difficult analysis is where the priority question involves a PPSA security interest as title to collateral is not generally relevant notwithstanding that a dispute between a PPSA security interest and a Bank Act security interest will likely utilise traditional property law concepts.[9] Thus, where a bank takes Bank Act security over collateral owned by a debtor free of any third party interest, the case law indicates that Bank Act security will take priority over subsequently created PPSA security interests and, as well, subsequently created interests arising under federal chattel security legislation or under the Bank Act itself.[10]

The most debated area is the case of a prior perfected PPSA security interest. Here the case law seems to support the view that such an interest will take priority over subsequent Bank Act security.[11] However, even this cautious conclusion must unfortunately be qualified. One caveat is that such a PPSA security interest may not prevail if it is unperfected and if the bank is able to enhance its position by invoking the priority rules of the PPSA by means of registering a financing statement under the PPSA with respect to its s 427 security.

Civil jurisdiction: Quebec

The security regime in the civil law jurisdiction of Quebec often appears a complex morass for those trained in the common law. The civilian system includes concepts

9 The leading case dealing with such a dispute is the decision of the Ontario Court of Appeal in *Rogerson Lumber Co Ltd v Four Seasons Chalet Ltd* which involved a competition between a bank with pre-existing s 427 security and a conditional seller with a title reservation and security under the PPSA. The seller's security agreement was signed before the date the bank appointed an agent to realise its security; the seller's financing statement was filed under the PPSA shortly thereafter. The majority of the Court of Appeal considered the seller's security interest to be valid and concluded that there was no provision in either the PPSA or the Bank Act which would take away the seller's priority or preclude the enforcement of his security agreement. The court concluded that the buyer, having paid nothing on account of the purchase price, did not have an *interest of any value* in the collateral. Hence, the bank could acquire no greater right or title than the buyer himself possessed.

10 See *Bank of Montreal v Pulsar Ventures Inc* [1988] 1 WWR 250 (Sask CA); *Royal Bank of Canada v Queen Charlotte Fisheries Ltd* (1981) 13 BLR 306 (BCSC), affd (1983) 50 BCLR 128 (BCCA); *Royal Bank of Canada v Bank of Montreal* (1976) 67 DLR (3d) 755 (Sask CA); *Union Bank of Halifax v The Indian & General Investment Trust* (1908) 40 SCR 510. Also, if a bank fails to file a notice of intention to take security, as required by the Bank Act s 178(4), the bank's interest will be void ab initio as against creditors: *Discovery Enterprises Ime v Hongkong Bank of Canada* (1995) 9 PPSAC (2d) 183 (BCCA).

11 *JI Case Credit Corpn v Canadian Imperial Bank of Commerce* (1985) 60 CBR 235 (Sask QB). In that case, the security agreement was signed and the secured party filed a financing statement under the Saskatchewan PPSA. Subsequently, a bank obtained s 178 (the predecessor to section 427) security and made the required filing of its notice of intention. The court noted that, unlike the situation in *Rogerson Lumber*, the security interest of the seller was created *before* the creation of the s 178 security. The court observed that s 179(1) (currently s 428(2)) of the Bank Act does not purport to grant to a bank priority over pre-existing encumbrances but only priority over rights subsequently acquired. Moreover, the Court further observed that, insofar as the bank knew of the seller's security interest at the time the bank acquired its s 178 security, the bank could not claim priority under the provision in of the Bank Act s 179(1) dealing with the bank's priority over certain 'unpaid vendors'.

unknown in the common law and, even where concepts are the same or similar to those found in the common law, the names attaching to them are different. As such, this section is prefaced with a rough (and in no way definitive or completely accurate) translation of some of the concepts found in the Civil Code of Quebec[12] and discussed in greater detail below.

Quebec concept	*PPSA/common law equivalent*
movable property	personal property whether tangible or intangible
immovable property	real property
publication	perfection (by possession or registration)
title	document evidencing title
hypothec (either movable or immovable)	charge/security interest (on personal or real property)
conventional hypothec	charge/security interest created by an act of a debtor
legal hypothec	lien arising at law
universality of property	all assets of debtor in a particular category
movable hypothec with delivery	pledge
conventional movable hypothec without delivery	non-possessory security interest

The most significant security device in Quebec is the hypothec (a term which encompasses the concept of a security interest) which can be used to create security over real and personal property. Hypothecs will be discussed in detail below.

Conflicts of law

The Civil Code of Quebec (CCQ) contains the vast majority of the relevant provincial rules relating to the granting of security on real (immovable) and personal (movable) property in Quebec. The Civil Code makes a distinction between the rules governing the validity of a security, which are contained in Book Six, and the rules governing the publication of a security, which are contained in Book Nine. The general rule concerning the validity of security over movable property (whether tangible or intangible) is that it is governed by the law of the jurisdiction in which the property is situate at the time of creation of the security. Publication of such security and its effects are governed by the law of the jurisdiction where the property charged is situate at the time of determination.[13] If the movable property is not intended to remain in the jurisdiction in which it is situate, it may be charged in accordance with the law of the jurisdiction for which it is destined. Conversely, a security published according to the law of another jurisdiction where the property was situated at the time of creation of the security will be deemed to be published in Quebec from the date and time of the first publication if it is published in Quebec within the required time period.

12 S.Q. 1991 ('CCQ').
13 CCQ Art 3102.

This general rule has one exception: despite its publication in Quebec, security published in another jurisdiction at the time of its creation may not be asserted against a buyer who has acquired the property in the ordinary course of the activities of the grantor.[14]

If the security either charges tangible movable property ordinarily used in more than one jurisdiction or an intangible, the validity of the security is governed by the law of the jurisdiction where the debtor is domiciled at the time of creation of the security. Publication of such security and its effects are governed by the law of the jurisdiction in which the debtor is currently domiciled.[15] If the debtor changes domicile and establishes domicile in Quebec, rules analogous to those outlined above and applicable to property moved to Quebec after the security has been published in another jurisdiction apply.[16]

An important exception to the rule in respect of intangible movable property is that security relating to bearer instruments or securities will be governed by the jurisdiction in which such property is situated.[17]

As examined above, the legal test in order to determine the appropriate law applicable to a security charging either tangible movable property ordinarily used in more than one jurisdiction or intangible movable property is that of the domicile of the debtor. The domicile of a corporation is at the place and address of its head office, which is generally interpreted as the same as its registered office.[18] In contrast, the test under the PPSAs is the 'principal place of business' of the debtor. The Civil Code does not give any guidance as to the domicile of a general partnership or a limited partnership, even though these entities may grant certain types of security. Neither is the domicile of a trust made clear.

Unlike non-possessory security interests which need to be published at the Register of Personal and Movable Real Rights (the 'Register'), possessory security interests are deemed to be published by virtue of the creditor holding the property or title and remain so only as long as the creditor continues to hold it.

In respect of 'security published by the holding of a property or title exercised by the creditor' (in most cases a pledge), the rule is that the validity of the security and publication and its effect are governed by the law of the jurisdiction in which the property is situate. For negotiable instruments and, in particular, negotiable instruments in bearer form, this poses no apparent difficulty since it may be argued that the title is situated where the instrument is held. Shares of private corporations with transfer restrictions noted on the share certificates are likely not, under certain corporate statutes, to be negotiable instruments. Case law concerning successions and the jurisdiction of Quebec courts is to the effect that shares are situated at the head office of the issuer corporation or at the place where such shares are transferable on the registers of the corporation.[19] If this case law is followed in interpreting the Civil Code as it relates to the validity of a pledge of the shares of a private corporation, the validity of such security

14 CCQ Art 3104.
15 CCQ Art 3105.
16 CCQ Art 3106.
17 CCQ Art 3105.
18 CCQ Art 307.
19 *Brassard v Smith* [1925] AC 371 (PC), *Black-Clawson Co v Montreal Locomotive Works Ltd* [1960] BR 514, *Farr Co v Curtiss-Wright Corpn* [1980] CS 159, *Bern v Bern* (1995) [1995] RDJ 510 (C.A.).

will be governed by the law of the jurisdiction of the registered office of such corporation or of the place where the shares are transferable on the registers of the corporation.

Hypothecs

One of the major objectives of the reform of the civil law in Quebec, which culminated in the enactment of a revised Civil Code effective from 1 January 1994, was the creation of a single security device for both consensual and non-consensual security interests. This device has replaced the vast majority of former consensual and non-consensual security devices over movable property including, in the case of a conventional movable hypothec, pledges (a hypothec involving delivery of movable property is still referred to as a pledge), commercial pledges, pledges over agricultural and forest products, transfers of property in stock, specific assignments of claims, general assignments of book debts and trust deeds.[20]

A hypothec is defined in the Civil Code as a real right on a movable or immovable property made liable for the performance of an obligation.[1] The hypothec confers on the creditor the right to follow the property into whosoever hands it may be (the '*droit de suite*'), to take possession of it or to take it in payment or to sell it or cause it to be sold and, in this latter case, to have a preference upon the proceeds of sale. As collateral security, a hypothec is (subject to certain exceptions) merely an accessory right and subsists only as long as the obligation whose performance it secures continues to exist.[2] A hypothec is indivisible and subsists in its entirety over all and every part of the charged property even when the property or the obligation is divisible.[3] It secures not only the principal of the obligation secured, but also accrued interest and legitimate costs incurred for recovering or conserving the charged property.[4] Registration of a hypothec preserves the creditor's security for interest due during the current year and the three preceding years.[5]

A hypothec can charge any type of movable or immovable property but only to the extent of the debtor's interest in such property. A hypothec will also extend to the proceeds of property originally charged.

Who may grant a hypothec

In principle, in order to have the capacity to grant a conventional hypothec, a person need only have the capacity to alienate (transfer) the hypothecated property and may be the principal debtor or guarantor.[6] A natural person who operates an enterprise may grant a movable hypothec without delivery on the property of that enterprise. Since 1999, a material person may also grant a moveable hypothec without delivery on certain specified property, including certain motor vehicles, boats and aircraft.

20 Civil Code Commentary, note 305, Vol II, pp 1653, 1679.
1 CCQ Art 2660.
2 CCQ Art 2661.
3 CCQ Art 2662.
4 CCQ Art 2667.
5 CCQ Art 2959.
6 CCQ Art 2681.

Only a person or a trustee carrying on an enterprise may grant a hypothec on a universality of property (all of its assets)[7] or a floating hypothec on the property of the enterprise.[8] Corporations or, as the Civil Code terms such entities, legal persons, are persons for the purposes of these provisions. Insofar as corporations are concerned, a corporation which does not carry on an enterprise may, if its law of incorporation or its constating documents provide for borrowing powers and powers to hypothecate, grant a hypothec on a universality of property or grant a floating hypothec.[9] It is, therefore, necessary when determining the capacity of a corporation to grant certain hypothecs, to ensure that it has the appropriate borrowing and hypothecating powers.

In respect of partnerships, the Civil Code does not specifically recognise most partnerships as 'persons'[10] but acknowledges that a limited partnership will be able to grant a hypothec.[11] Although the issue is not free from doubt, the general view based upon interpretation of the limited partnership references as well as the registration provisions of the Regulation respecting the Register of Personal and Movable Real Rights (Quebec)[12] (the 'Regulation') is that partnerships that carry on an enterprise may grant hypothecs on a universality of movable property and floating hypothecs.[13]

Holder of a hypothec

In principle any creditor may be the holder of a hypothec. Since a hypothec may be a unilateral deed it is not necessary that the creditor sign the deed of hypothec provided that the creditor manifest its intention to benefit from the hypothec.[14] This may be done at the time the parties contract the principal obligation or at some later time.

If the hypothec secures payment of bonds or other titles of indebtedness issued by a trustee, a limited partnership or a legal person authorised to do so by law, such a hypothec must be granted by notarial deed executed before a Quebec notary in favour of the person holding what the Civil Code calls a 'power of attorney' of the creditors (the *'fondé de pouvoir')* or else the hypothec will be void.[15] The actual nature of the relationship between the creditor and the holder of the power of attorney is unclear. The Civil Code in other circumstances equates a power of attorney to a mandate which is:

> 'a contract by which a person, the mandator, empowers another person, the mandatory, to represent him in the performance of a juridical act with a third person, and the mandatory, by his acceptance, bends himself to exercise the power'.[16]

This provision is likely to give rise to some difficulties since in certain public financing structures the grantor of the security executes the security instruments in favour of

7 CCQ Art 2684.
8 CCQ Art 2686.
9 See Special Corporate Powers Act, RSQ ss 27, 34.
10 CCQ Art 2188.
11 CCQ Art 2692.
12 QOG 1 Dec 1993 (Vol 125 No 50).
13 As a further argument, a partner may, on certain conditions, hypothecate his 'share' in the partnership assets or profits (CCQ Art 2211). Since this is the case, it should be possible for a universality of the assets of the partnership to be hypothecated by the partnership.
14 *Lemay v Cliche et associés Ltée* [1977] RP 279 (CA).
15 CCQ Art 2692.
16 CCQ Art 2130.

the 'holder of a power of attorney' prior to the issuance of bonds or other titles of indebtedness to public investors and, therefore, prior to the identification of any creditor. To suggest that the holder of the power of attorney is equivalent to a trustee is not completely satisfactory since this implies that a trust relationship has been established and a hypothec is not a trust.

There is no specific definition in the Civil Code as to what constitutes a bond or other title of indebtedness. In a financing where one or more notes are issued pursuant to a credit agreement, it will be necessary to review the structure of the financing in order to ascertain if it will be subject to the Civil Code requirements for a hypothec in notarial form.

A question also arises as to whether the practice of constituting a security agent for purposes of holding security for a number of lenders is acceptable for security over movable property in Quebec. Other than specific cases involving a title of indebtedness issued by a person and a creditor who, with the consent of the grantor, holds the property through a third person,[17] the Civil Code does not specifically permit security to be granted to a security agent for the benefit of others and it has been argued that the specific language in certain articles of the Civil Code would mean that the creditors must directly hold the security.[18] While it may be argued that the rules concerning agency or mandate in the Civil Code are sufficient in order that a security agent may hold a conventional movable security for the benefit of a syndicate of existing but not future lenders, in such event and for registration purposes, the prudent view is that the principal creditors and not the security agent are the true holders of such security and they should all be registered in the Register. This approach will, however, entail further registrations upon the occurrence of subsequent events such as the assignment by a lender of its interest in the loan secured by the hypothec or the amendment, cancellation or reduction of the hypothec.[19]

Obligations secured

A consensual hypothec may secure any obligation whatsoever.[20] A hypothec granted to secure payment of a sum of money is valid even if when it is granted the debtor has not yet received such sums. Furthermore in some instances the hypothec will subsist even if the secured obligation is extinguished. This will apply in particular to hypothecs securing lines of credit and issues of bonds or other titles of indebtedness. In fact, if the deed of hypothec contains a provision pursuant to which the debtor obliges itself again for future obligations, even if at any particular subsequent time there is no obligation between debtor and creditor, the hypothec will continue to exist.[1]

A line of cases decided under the former Civil Code put into doubt the possibility of securing all present and future obligations of a grantor under a hypothec over immovable property unless there was at least a reference to an existing obligation of the debtor to

17 CCQ Art 2692.

18 See Arts 2660 and 2748.

19 Relying upon the Supreme Court of Canada decision in *Montana v Les Développements du Saguenay Ltée* [1977] 1 SCR 32, some suggest that a trust may be used as a vehicle for holding the security.

20 CCQ Art 2687.

1 CCQ Art 2797.

the creditor in the deed of hypothec.[2] Although there may have been some doubt as to the correctness of this line of cases[3] it is now clear that a hypothec may secure all present and future obligations of a debtor, even if such obligations were non-existent at the time of the granting of the hypothec and even if the deed of hypothec does not specifically refer to an existing obligation.[4] The possibility of securing any obligation is a major improvement over the pre-1994 regime since a mainstream security device may now be granted for any type of obligation and may be relied upon for subsequent financing, thus reducing transaction costs and the cost of borrowing.

Types of hypothec

Non-consensual or legal hypothecs

The first of the two categories of non-consensual hypothecs on movable and immovable property provided in the Civil Code is government claims for sums due under fiscal (tax) laws and claims of legal persons established in the public interest.[5] In all cases, such security only takes effect from registration in the appropriate register.[6] Application for registration of a legal hypothec is made by filing a notice indicating the legislation pursuant to which the hypothec is granted, the property of the debtor on which the creditor intends to exercise its security, the cause of the claim of the creditor and the amount of the claim. The registration by the government of a legal movable hypothec for sums due under fiscal laws does not prevent it from exercising any prior claim attributed by the Civil Code to the government such as the creation of a deemed trust or lien.[7]

Claims arising from judgments constitute the second category of legal hypothecs on movable property. Judgment creditors may acquire a legal hypothec on movable or immovable property of the debtor by registration.[8]

In all cases, a creditor who registers a legal hypothec preserves its rights to follow movable property not alienated in the ordinary course of business of an enterprise in accordance with the same conditions as the holder of a consensual hypothec.[9]

Pledge

A pledge is also called a movable hypothec with delivery. It is granted by delivery of the property or title in the property to the creditor or, if the property is already in the creditor's hands, by the creditor continuing to hold it with the debtor's consent to secure the creditor's claim.[10] A pledge is considered to be published under the Civil

2 See for example, *La Banque Mercantile du Canada v Yves Germain Inc* [1984] CS 856; *Hamon v La Banque Toronto-Dominion* [1992] RDI 620 (CS).

3 *St-Jacques v Carbonneau* (1999) JE99, CA.

4 CCQ Arts 2687, 2688 and 2797.

5 CCQ Art 2724. Legal persons established in the public interest would include, for example, entities such as the *Commission de la santé et de la sécurité au travail* (the workers' compensation authority in Quebec) and Hydro-Quebec.

6 CCQ Art 2725.

7 For discussion of prior claim, the state and what constitutes fiscal laws, see discussion under the heading 'Prior Claims' below.

8 CCQ Art 2730.

9 CCQ Arts 2700, 2732.

10 CCQ Art 2702.

Code by the creditor holding the property or title and remains published only as long as the creditor continues to hold the property or title. Holding is continuous even if it is prevented by the act of a third person taken without the consent of the creditor or is temporarily interrupted by the handing over of the property or title to the grantor or to a third person for evaluation, repair, transformation or improvement.[11] A third party may hold the property for the creditor with the consent of the debtor and possession by the third party is equivalent to publication only from the time the third party receives evidence in writing of the hypothec.[12]

Although it is not necessary to register rights under most pledges in the Register in order for the pledge to be valid against third parties, it is possible to publish it by registration at a later date provided the creditor continues to hold the property or title.[13] If the pledge is over a universality of claims, that is, including property of a type other than that which can be charged by a pledge, the pledge must be registered in the appropriate register.[14]

The Civil Code does not define what constitutes a title capable of being held under a pledge. However, it would appear to include negotiable instruments and at least the shares of a private corporation. In respect of pledges of securities entered into the book entry system of a clearing house approved by the Quebec Securities Commission (which includes only the Canadian Depository for Securities), the Securities Act (Quebec)[15] states that hypothecation of such securities may be made by book entries in the accounts maintained by such clearing house.

Conventional movable hypothec without delivery

The conventional movable hypothec without delivery constitutes the main non-possessory security device employed in Quebec. A movable hypothec without delivery may cover intangible movable property such as accounts receivable, patents, trade marks and other intellectual and industrial property, existing tangible property such as equipment or machinery or future tangible property such as inventory or charge a universality or specific category of property, such as certain receivables, inventory or equipment.

A conventional movable hypothec without delivery is void if not in writing. A sufficient description of the property or, in the case of a universality of property, an indication of the nature of that universality, must be contained in the deed constituting the hypothec.[16] The deed constituting a hypothec must also indicate the specific sum

11 CCQ Art 2704. In respect of shares of the capital stock of a corporation, CCQ Art 2677 requires registration of a renewal in the event of transformation of the share originally pledged such as redemption, conversion or cancellation. One may make the argument that transformation as used in CCQ Art 2704 has a similar meaning, when applied to shares of a corporation that are held by the creditor.

12 CCQ Art 2705.

13 CCQ Art 2707.

14 CCQ Art 2711.

15 RSQ s 10.2 as amended.

16 CCQ Arts 2696, 2697.

for which it is granted.[17] This rule applies even when the hypothec secures the performance of an obligation the value of which may not be determined or is uncertain.[18] The sum is not considered to be indeterminate if the deed, rather than stipulating a fixed rate of interest, contains the necessary particulars for determining the actual rate of interest on the obligation.[19] It should be noted that the specific sum for which the hypothec is granted is not necessarily equivalent to the amount of the obligation secured by such hypothec.[20] In fact, the hypothec constitutes security in property up to the limit of the specific sum indicated in the deed of hypothec. The intention of the Civil Code is that the specific sum is used to inform third parties of the extent of the security granted.[1]

Floating hypothec

A floating hypothec is defined in the Civil Code as a hypothec where some of the effects are expressly provided in the deed to be suspended until the creditor crystallises the hypothec following default by serving a notice of default and crystallisation on the debtor or the grantor.[2] A floating hypothec has effect only if it has itself been published, but is not valid against third parties except by registration of the notice of crystallisation,[3] which determines the rank of the floating hypothec (other than in respect of other floating hypothecs) and not initial registration.[4]

If a universality of property is charged, a floating hypothec will also charge properties acquired by the grantor after crystallisation. A creditor holding a floating hypothec on a universality of property may, from the date of registration of the notice of crystallisation, take possession of the property to administer it in priority to any other creditor who has published a hypothec after the date of registration of the floating hypothec.[5] A floating hypothec would, therefore, not have preference over a hypothec charging a universality of property registered prior to the initial registration of such floating hypothec. If there are several floating hypothecs on the same property, crystallisation of one enables the creditors holding the others to register their own notice of crystallisation and, amongst such creditors, priority is determined by the date of initial registration.[6]

17 There is no prohibition in the Civil Code for denominating a loan in currency other than the lawful money of Canada. If the debtor grants a conventional movable hypothec without delivery, however, the sum must be determinate or specific. Although nothing in the Civil Code requires that such be in Canadian currency, the current practice is to state the charging provision in lawful money of Canada. The Currency Act, RSC 1986 permits contracts in foreign currency but judgment only in Canadian currency. CCQ Art 3161 also provides a manner for conversion to Canadian funds of a sum payable in foreign currency pursuant to a foreign decision.

18 CCQ Art 2689.

19 CCQ Art 2690.

20 Commentary, above note 305, Vol II, p 1684.

1 Ibid.

2 CCQ Art 2715.

3 CCQ Art 2716.

4 CCQ Art 2955.

5 CCQ Art 2721.

6 CCQ Arts 2722, 2955.

In light of the inferior priority afforded by the floating hypothec, the floating hypothec is not frequently used as a mainstream security device over movable property.[7]

Movable hypothec on claims

The Civil Code treats conventional movable hypothecs on claims (ie book debts) differently to other hypothecs. Whether such a hypothec is with or without delivery, the creditor may not set up the hypothec against the debtors of hypothecated claims unless such debtors have acquiesced to the hypothec or received a copy or a pertinent extract of the deed of hypothec or any other evidence of the hypothec which may be set up against the grantor.[8] From the date of execution of the deed of hypothec over claims, a creditor is entitled to collect revenues produced by such claims and any principal falling due while the hypothec is in effect. The creditor gives acquittance for the sums it collects[9] and unless otherwise stipulated, must apply the amounts collected to payment of the secured obligations even if they are not yet exigible.[10]

Most deeds of hypothec, however, contain a revocable authorisation from the creditor permitting the debtor to collect the hypothecated claims as they fall due. The Civil Code requires that such authorisation be in the deed constituting the hypothec. In order for the creditor to withdraw such authorisation, the creditor must register and serve notice on the grantor and on the account debtors that the creditor will henceforth collect sums falling due.[11]

Documentation and registration

A movable hypothec without delivery is void if not in writing. It is only in the event that the hypothec secures the payment of bonds or other titles of indebtedness issued by a trustee, a limited partnership or a legal person authorised to do so by law that a movable hypothec must be in notarial form in favour of the person holding the power of attorney of the creditors.[12] It is not necessary that the hypothec be witnessed or that the creditor intervene to it since a hypothec may be unilateral.

For registration purposes, however, it is desirable that the hypothec contain the proper designation of the parties including, for a natural person, such person's name, date of birth and residential address. In the case of a legal person, its name, the address of the head office or name and address of the establishment directly concerned, together with any business styles used in Quebec including the French version of its name, should be included. In the case of a partnership, its name, juridical form (such as general or limited partnership) and address should be included. The hypothec should include

7 In spite of this inferior priority, the floating hypothec on claims is notifiable to account debtors upon registration of the notice of crystallisation and publication thereof in certain newspapers (CCQ Art 2718) and not by notification of each individual account debtor as required for conventional movable hypothec on claims (CCQ Art 2710). This possibility has led some to suggest obtaining both a conventional movable hypothec on claims and a floating hypothec.

8 CCQ Arts 1641, 2710.

9 CCQ Art 2743.

10 CCQ Arts 1570, 2743.

11 CCQ Art 2745.

12 CCQ Art 2692.

the date on which the document was signed and its place or places of signature, where applicable.

Under the Civil Code, rights and not documents are required to be registered in connection with movable property by presenting an application containing the prescribed information for registration at the Register.

It is currently not possible to register in advance rights under a conventional movable hypothec and the Registrar will not accept an application for registration if the date the application is signed is prior to the date of the constituting deed of movable hypothec.

The Civil Code does not require that notice be filed of a change of name of debtor in order for security granted by such debtor to continue to be valid against third parties but does permit registration of a change of name of a holder or a grantor and, if an application is tendered for registration, it must be accompanied by a certified copy of the document evidencing the change.[13]

The Civil Code states that rights conferred by a hypothec are valid against third parties only when the hypothec is published. Publication makes rights valid against third parties, establishes rank and, in certain circumstances where the law so provides, gives them effect. Between the parties, rights are effective even before publication unless the law expressly provides otherwise.[14] A right that has been registered in the Register is presumed known by a person acquiring or publishing a right in the same property and also carries, in respect of all persons, a simple presumption of the existence of that right.[15]

Other security devices

The Civil Code does not take the functional approach adopted in UCC and PPSA jurisdictions to the creation of a security interest and therefore there are a number of security or quasi-security devices available to creditors contemplating financing arrangements in Quebec. Such devices include instalment sale (similar but not identical to a conditional sale), sale with right of redemption, sale with resolutory clause, trust, consignment agreement, leasing (*crédit-bail*) and leases. It is also possible, in general, to use title retention and title manipulation to meet the particular needs of a financing transaction. As many of these devices are established in the Civil Code notwithstanding the use of terminology which may sound familiar to common law trained lawyers care must be taken to ensure that the specific requirements relating to the particular device are satisfied. Amendments to the Civil Code which came into force in 1999 require registration of rights associated with certain instalment sales contracts, sales with right of redemption, trust, leasing and leases in order for such rights to be valid against third parties. Assignment of these rights must in certain circumstances be registered.

13 CCQ Art 3015.
14 CCQ Art 2941.
15 CCQ Arts 2943, 2944.

Priorities

Prior claims

The Civil Code recognises a limited number of prior claims which constitute non-consensual security for specified creditors. A prior claim entitles its beneficiary to the right to be preferred over other creditors, including hypothecary creditors.[16] Notwithstanding any agreement to the contrary, prior claims are in all cases ranked in the following order:

1 legal costs and expenses incurred in the common interest (by a creditor exercising rights on behalf of all creditors) (against movable and immovable property);
2 claims of a vendor who has not been paid the price of a movable sold to a natural person who does not operate an enterprise;
3 claims of persons having the right to retain movable property, provided that the right subsists;
4 government claims for amounts due under fiscal laws (only against movable property); and
5 claims of municipalities and school boards for property taxes on taxable immovables (probably, although this is not clear, only against immovable property).

Prior claims are opposable to other creditors without requiring registration. Prior claims rank among themselves according to the order attributed by law, without regard to their date and rank prior to movable or immovable hypothecs.

General principles

Unless otherwise stipulated by law, the priority of rights is determined in accordance with the date, hour and minute entered on the memorial of presentation, provided that the entries have been made in the proper register.[17]

The first exception to the general principle noted above relates to pledges. The Civil Code specifically states that when publication by delivery is authorised by law, rights rank according to the time at which the property or title is delivered to the creditor.[18]

Another exception relates to a movable hypothec on property represented by a bill of lading, another negotiable instrument or on claims, whether established by pledge or by conventional movable hypothec without delivery, which is opposable to other creditors of the grantor from the time the creditor holding such security gives value provided that, in the case of the pledge, the title is remitted to the creditor within ten days from that time and, in the case of a conventional movable hypothec without delivery, such hypothec is registered within ten days.[19]

Although it appears that the intent of the Civil Code is to facilitate receivables financing by adopting this rule, in fact, prudent secured creditors may wait ten days from registration of their security before advancing money in order to undertake searches and ensure that there is no prior ranking hypothecary creditor.

16 CCQ Art 2650.
17 CCQ Art 2945.
18 CCQ Art 2945.
19 CCQ Arts 2699, 2708.

The Civil Code does not have a concept similar to a purchase-money security interest available under a PPSA. The Civil Code does, however, provide that a vendor's hypothec created in the deed of acquisition and published within 15 days of the sale will outrank a prior registered conventional movable hypothec granted by the purchaser on movables of a third party or future movables.[20] This means, for instance, that the vendor would outrank a general charge taken by a financial institution on all present and future movable property of a nature similar to the movable property sold by the vendor to the grantor.

It may also be argued that this priority would extend, subject to a further registration in the case of a specific movable, to property that replaces such movable if sold by the grantor in the ordinary course of its enterprise, and to proceeds of alienation if no property replaces the sold movable.[1]

Registration of the notice of crystallisation, not the initial registration of the floating hypothec, determines the rank of a floating hypothec.[2] However, among floating hypothecs, rank is determined by their respective initial registration regardless of the registration of the notices of crystallisation. A creditor holding a floating hypothec on a universality of property does, however, have priority in taking possession of the property for purposes of administration in preference to any other creditor having published a hypothec after the date of the initial registration of the floating hypothec.[3]

Secured creditors may enter into agreements[4] amongst themselves in order to determine the priority that will be afforded to their security. Creditors may also determine that, in spite of the apparent priority of registration, priority will be otherwise. Between the parties, this is an enforceable obligation; however, the Civil Code states that such a cession of rank must be published in order to be valid against third parties.[5] Where a cession of rank occurs, the rank of the creditors is inverted to the extent of their respective claims but in such a manner as not to prejudice any intermediate creditors.

SECURITY OVER REAL PROPERTY

In Canada parcels of land are generally identified and dealt with under either the older land registry system or the more modern land titles system in the common law provinces and by a civil law regime for the registration of real property rights in the Province of Quebec. Considerations relevant to establishing an effective charge are very similar to those involved in conveying property and may be different depending upon the applicable legal regime as well as from province to province. As a result, this portion of the chapter provides only a brief overview of the real property legal regimes in Canada and the issues associated in taking real property security.

20 CCQ Art 2954.
1 CCQ Art 2674.
2 CCQ Arts 2716, 2955.
3 CCQ Art 2721.
4 CCQ Art 1691.
5 CCQ Arts 2941(2), 2956.

Common law jurisdictions

The land registry system

The registry system applies to part of the Province of Ontario, the Maritime provinces (Nova Scotia, New Brunswick, Newfoundland and Prince Edward Island) and a very small part of the Province of Manitoba. The registry system seeks to provide a method for orderly registration of different and potentially competing interests (thereby creating a public record) and to establish the priority of such interests by their registration.

The land titles system

The land titles system is in place in the Western provinces of British Columbia, Alberta and Saskatchewan as well as most of Manitoba and a large and increasing portion of Ontario. The model for such legislation in the Western provinces is the so-called 'Torrens' system developed in Australia in the mid-nineteenth century while in Ontario the model is the early land titles legislation of England. Most land titles legislation requires registration of an appropriate instrument within the system in order to create any interest in the land. The land titles statutes[6] provide that no person dealing with a property is in any way affected by any actual or implied notice of any unregistered interest in the land, notwithstanding any rule or law of equity to the contrary. However, this principle has been infringed upon by case law.

The most significant difference between the two systems is that under the registry system an inventory of instruments affecting title is provided, whereas under the land titles system a statement of title is provided. In other words, both the registry and land titles system are regimes that allow the public to register instruments creating or disposing of interests in land or affecting the use of land. However, the registry system does not produce any statement as to the status of title. The statement of title produced under the land titles system constitutes a qualitative assessment of title which, with certain qualifications, is guaranteed by the state.

Documentation and registration

In every case documents must satisfy the form requirements of the legislation in order to be registrable.

The process of protecting an interest in land under either system is essentially the same, that is, through registration in prescribed form in a public land registry office. Under the registry system, once an instrument has been presented to the land registrar and accepted for registration, it is deemed registered. Under the land titles system, the land registrar must first certify the instrument and its entry before it is deemed registered. Once this routine certification is completed, the effective date of registration is retroactive to the time when the instrument was received for registration. In Ontario, for example, the regulations to the Land Registration Reform Act[7] provide for the prescribed form in which each instrument must be presented to the Registrar for registration. If a document is not presented in this form it will be refused by the Registrar.

6 The Land Titles Act (Ontario) RSO 1990 s 78(5); the Land Title Act (British Columbia) RSBC 1996, s 29; the Land Titles Act (Saskatchewan) RSS 1978, as amended SS 1994.

7 RSO 1990, as amended.

Each jurisdiction has its own specific requirements and therefore care should be taken to ensure such requirements are met when preparing and executing registration documents (for example, certain jurisdictions require documents to be made under seal (Nova Scotia) while others prefer that documents not be sealed (British Columbia)). There are certain other quirks to be wary of (ie all registration documents in British Columbia must be signed in black ink to permit better microfiching). To ensure compliance with the applicable requirements, it would be wise to contact local counsel to ensure documents are prepared in proper form.

Priorities

The land registry system

Fundamentally the priorities scheme in the land registry systems operates on the basis of notice, whether actual or constructive, to establish priorities. The general rule is that the first to register has the first interest. The registration of an instrument constitutes, for most purposes, notice to third parties of the interest. Persons with subsequent registrations are thus aware of others with prior interests and are subordinate to such interests. There is an exception to this rule where the person who is first to register had, prior to registration, actual knowledge of an existing, but unregistered, interest.[8]

The land registry legislation also addresses the priority of a mortgage lender who makes funds available by way of multiple advances.[9] Technically, such a lender is entitled to rely upon the priority of a registration for advances over subsequently registered instruments, unless before making the advance the lender had actual notice of the registration of the subsequent instrument. Future advances will, however, be subject to construction and other liens and, as such, it is essential to search title prior to making any mortgage advance.

The land titles system

In land titles the register itself reflects title to land and all other interests created in land. The legislation provides that, absent fraud, priority is determined on the basis of the first to register, without regard to the time at which instruments were executed or to any knowledge of prior unregistered instruments by the holder of a registered interest.[10] Despite the explicitness of these provisions however, courts have continued to breathe life into the equitable doctrine of notice, sometimes treating the registration of an interest in property with actual knowledge of an unregistered interest as tantamount to fraud.[11]

8 The Registry Act (Ontario) RSO 1990, s 71; Registry Act (Nova Scotia) RSNS 1989s 18; Registry Act (New Brunswick) RSNB 1973; Registry Act (Prince Edward Island) RSPEI 1988.

9 Registry Act (Ontario) RSO 1990.

10 Land Titles Act (Ontario) RSO 1990 s 78(5); Land Titles Act (British Columbia) RSBC 1996 s 29; Land Titles Act (Saskatchewan) RSS 1978 as amended SS 1994; Land Titles Act (Alberta) RSA 1980 as amended SA 1988.

11 See *United Trust Co v Dominion Stores Ltd* [1977] 2 SCR 915.

Civil law jurisdiction: Quebec

The land registration system in Quebec is based on the basic division of property into units called 'cadastres'. Most of the province has been divided into cadastres except for a few remote northern areas. Upon creation of a cadastre, which in many cases dates back 120 years, the property within the cadastre was further divided into a number of original lots bearing the numbers set forth on the official cadastral plan deposited in the appropriate registry office. Over time, the original lots have often been subdivided, replaced or renovated, particularly in urban areas such as Montreal and Quebec City where there is a relatively high degree of economic development. Each lot or subdivided lot has a corresponding register where immovable hypothecs and other pertinent entries are recorded.

Documentation and registration

Security on real property in the Province of Quebec can be taken by having a debtor grant to its creditor a hypothec on a specifically designated immovable property or, in the case of a person or a trustee carrying on an enterprise, as part of a grant over a universality of the debtor's property. Unlike the hypothec taken on personal or movable property, the immovable hypothec must be created in a notarial deed '*en minute*' which may be prepared by an attorney but must be signed before a notary who is a member of the Chamber of Notaries in the Province of Quebec. The hypothec must be for a determined sum of money, regardless of whether the underlying debt is fixed or fluctuating.

An immovable hypothec would normally affect a parcel of land and any buildings, structures, or permanent constructions erected on the property. Moreover, real rights on immovables, such as emphyteusis (a long-term lease pursuant to which the lessee agrees to make improvements to the property), superficies (a transfer of surface rights for the purpose of construction), usufruct or co-ownership may also be hypothecated. In addition, a hypothec on present or future rents or on insurance proceeds which are produced or paid under insurance contracts covering such rents is artificially classified as an 'immovable' hypothec and is therefore also subject to the formalities mentioned in this section.

The hypothec is itself registered at the appropriate registration office in the cadastre in which the property is situated. For registration purposes, the description of the charged immovable property in the deed must be complete and precise in that it must identify or describe all lots or parts of lots which compose the said property on the cadastral plan. If the property is composed of parts of lots, it may be necessary to have a qualified surveyor certify the boundaries and measurements of the property with a certificate of location.

Since cadastral reform, replacement or renovation as well as subdivision operations occur frequently in the Province of Quebec, it is ill-advised to extract a property description from a prior deed or document no matter how recent and to insert it in the deed constituting the hypothec. For each transaction, in order to ensure the validity of a hypothec, the description of the target immovable property must be verified and updated, if necessary. Furthermore, a major cadastral reform is currently under way in the Province of Quebec which will have a significant impact on the lot numbering system.

Priorities

A hypothec on real property can only be fully effective against third parties if it is entered on the land registry at the appropriate registry office. The hypothecary creditor's priority of rank is then established on the basis of the date, time and minute of registration of its hypothec. The priority of immovable hypothecs may, however, be outranked by certain priorities and legal hypothecs, such as those guaranteeing legal fees, municipal property taxes or amounts payable to a contractor or other persons having taken part in the construction or renovation of an immovable to the extent such work has created added value to the property.

The regime of the Civil Code of Quebec governing the exercise of hypothecary rights is essentially the same for immovable and movable hypothecs and confers on the creditor in most cases the basic right to follow the charged property into the hands of whoever its owner may be. Consequently, where the debtor is in default and its claim is due and payable, the creditor may exercise any one or more of the following four rights:

1 to take possession of the charged property for purposes of administration;
2 to take it in payment of its claim;
3 to cause it to be sold by judicial sale; or
4 to sell it.

Depending on which recourse is chosen, different formalities and conditions (such as prior notice, court authorisations) apply and must be strictly followed to achieve the desired outcome.

MODEL TRANSACTION

The scenario outlined in this part of the chapter is very typical of cross-border transactions where security is to be taken over assets located in Canada and will illustrate the operation of the legal regimes outlined above as well as provide a practical guide to some of the other issues that arise under Canadian law in such a transaction.

Facts

An international syndicate of banks (the 'Banks') led by a financial institution acting as agent bank and security trustee ('Agent') is to make available a credit facility to a UK multinational corporation ('Parent') with a wholly-owned Canadian subsidiary ('Canco'). To secure the obligations of Parent to the Banks, all of Parent's subsidiaries are to provide guarantees of the obligations of Parent and all other group companies backed up by security over all their assets. Canco is incorporated under the federal companies legislation, the Canada Business Corporations Act ('CBCA')[12] and carries on business and has assets including both real and personal property in the provinces of Ontario and Quebec. Canco's registered and head office is located in Toronto, Ontario.

12 RSC 1985 as amended.

Canco's guarantee is to be governed by English law[13] with security documents governed by Ontario law (except in the case of the Quebec security documents which will be governed by Quebec law) and the Banks expect to receive the customary Canadian legal opinions in connection with the transaction.

Determining relevant jurisdictions

The first step in determining the relevant jurisdictions is to determine the provinces in which Canco has assets and carries on business. As noted above, the facts indicate that the relevant provinces are Ontario and Quebec. This information should be obtained from Canco and will be included as part of the officer's certificate that will be required in connection with the transaction opinion (as discussed below) as the question as to whether a person is carrying on business in a particular jurisdiction is complex and is not easily ascertainable by a third party.

The analysis does not end here, however, as the nature of the assets to be secured may entail further inquiry. If the assets include intangibles, goods that are normally used in more than one jurisdiction, accounts payable by debtors in other jurisdictions or securities, the laws of other jurisdictions may be involved. For purposes of the model transaction it will be assumed that no other jurisdictions are involved.

As soon as the relevant jurisdictions are determined and a list of assets to be secured prepared, the searches against Canco and those assets described below should be commenced as the time frame for obtaining results varies. Such searches may uncover secured creditors with prior interests in the assets whose existence may be required to be dealt with in the structuring of the transaction. Corporate searches against Canco itself will also provide confirmation as to its corporate status and provide copies of its constating documents (although not its by-laws) which must be reviewed to establish that Canco has the corporate capacity to enter into the transaction. In the case of real property, searches will also assist to confirm the exact legal description of the property to be charged.

Structuring issues

The most significant structuring issue which arises on these facts relates to the potential application of the financial assistance provisions contained in the CBCA[14] (and the

13 It is very common in transactions such as the model that lead counsel for the Banks tends to want the guarantee to be governed by the law of their own jurisdiction. There is an attraction to this because the law is familiar and it may facilitate opinion-giving. However, careful consideration should be given to splitting the governing law as between the guarantee and security documents. When the assets comprising the security supporting guarantee are in Canada there are advantages from an enforcement perspective in having all documents governed by a single law. There should be no disadvantage to having the guarantee governed by the laws of one of the Canadian provinces as they are, from the perspective of legal issues, quite 'clean' jurisdictions.

14 CBCA s 41.

other provincial corporate statutes).[15] The restrictions operate to prohibit, otherwise than as excepted, a corporation from granting financial assistance by means of a loan, guarantee or otherwise[16] unless it can meet the prescribed solvency tests.[17] The exceptions to the prohibition allow a corporation to provide 'downstream' financial assistance (ie to a subsidiary) and 'upstream' financial assistance (ie to a parent, but in this latter case the company providing the assistance must be wholly-owned by the parent).

There is, however, no exception to the prohibition for guarantees of the obligations of a sister company. Where a lender requires a sister guarantee from the CBCA company common practice is to put a structure in place whereby the parent company guarantees the obligations of the sister and the CBCA company guarantees all obligations of the parent which will of course include its own guarantee obligations. In the model transaction this issue arises as the Banks require each subsidiary in the group to guarantee the obligations of Parent and all other subsidiaries. Canco's guarantee of Parent will, however, achieve the same result without directly guaranteeing its sisters' obligations so long as Parent has guaranteed the obligations of each of its subsidiaries.

Another significant point that arises when a foreign lender is actually lending to a Canadian company is the exigibility of Canadian non-resident withholding tax on interest payments. In general, non-resident withholding tax is payable at a rate of 25% (unless, as is often the case, reduced by a treaty between Canada and the lender's home jurisdiction) on interest payments made by a resident of Canada to a non-resident of Canada where the debt instrument provides for the possibility of repayment of more than 25% of the principal within five years.[18] Should a Canadian guarantor such as Canco assume interest payment obligations of another party such as Parent, withholding tax will be exigible. This point is generally addressed by including a withholding tax indemnity and gross-up in the guarantee.

Finally, it is also important to be aware of the provisions of the Bank Act which prohibit a foreign bank (defined to be a foreign entity which is a bank under the laws of a jurisdiction other than Canada) or any entity affiliated with a foreign bank from undertaking any banking business in Canada.[19] The Bank Act does not define what constitutes banking business, but, case law indicates that the classic elements of banking business are lending and accepting deposits.[20] As a result, Canadian counsel typically advise that a loan transaction be undertaken by a foreign bank to a Canadian borrower from outside Canada. All activity by the bank in connection with the loan, including execution of the loan documentation, should be undertaken from offices

15 The financial assistance provisions of the provincial corporate statutes are largely the same as those in the CBCA. The notable exceptions are Quebec, whose statute has restrictions on upstream guarantees and New Brunswick and Nova Scotia whose statutes permit a corporation to opt out of the restrictions by placing appropriate provisions in its constating documents.

16 The term financial assistance is not defined but is generally viewed as being very expansive.

17 CBCA s 44(1)(c) and (d). Solvency is tested on both a net asset as well as an operating basis (ie ability to pay liabilities as they become due).

18 Income Tax Act, RSC 1985 (5th Supp), as amended 1994; 1995 s 212(1)(b).

19 Bank Act (Canada), Part XII.

20 See, for example: *R v Milelli* 45 BR 209, leave to appeal to Supreme Court of Canada refused (1990) 107 NR 160n.

outside Canada. If this is done, the bank should not be viewed as undertaking banking business in Canada simply by virtue of taking security from a Canadian guarantor.[1]

As a result, opinions rendered that a transaction such as the model transaction is not in breach of any applicable law will usually be made on the express assumption that activity related to the financing, such as analysis and credit decisions, negotiations, execution of documents and funding, have occurred or will occur outside of Canada.

Searches

As noted above, in a transaction such as the model it is customary to undertake a number of searches, the results of which may impact on the structuring of the transaction and will provide the basis for certain parts of the legal opinions.

The first category of searches relate to the debtor. Basic corporate searches confirm the complete name of Canco (and any predecessor names or business names) and provide copies of all of Canco's articles of incorporation (and all amendments) thereby confirming the legal regime pursuant to which it is established and enabling a review of its powers. It is also customary to obtain a certificate of compliance or status (the name of the certificate is dependent upon the corporate statute under which the corporation is created) confirming that as of the date of the certificate the corporation exists and has not been dissolved. This certificate, along with confirmation from an officer of Canco that, as of the date of the officer's certificate (which will match the date of the opinion), Canco carries on business and is up to date in all required filings in the relevant jurisdictions, will form the basis of the opinion as to required corporate registrations and authority to carry on business in a particular province.

In addition to corporate searches, bankruptcy and insolvency searches also provide information as to the status of the debtor. Searches are undertaken with the federal bankruptcy office to ensure there have been no receiving orders, petitions in bankruptcy or bankruptcy orders made against the debtor. A search will also be done with the relevant court office in the particular province in which bankruptcy or receiving orders are made to ensure there have been no filings with such office. Finally, a search of the court register in each judicial district in which Canco is known to have assets may be made for execution orders which would permit a judgment creditor to seize its assets. Here, however, given the large number of potential searches that could be undertaken, most common practice would be to search for execution orders only in the most significant centre in the province unless the debtor had a substantial presence elsewhere.

The second type of search provides information on existing security over assets of the debtor. In the case of real property, land titles and registry searches not only reveal existing encumbrances but also (together with appropriate surveys) confirm the accuracy of the legal description of the property. In the case of personal property, searching in the PPSA jurisdictions is very straightforward with the most difficult point being to ensure that all of the correct names are searched, including predecessor and business names and, as applicable, the French, English and combined version of the name. The

1 See the decision of the Privy Council in *Koh Kim Chai v Asia Commercial Banking Corp Ltd*, [1984] WLR 850 (PC) which held that the taking of security from a resident of Malaysia did not constitute banking business within that jurisdiction.

result of a PPSA search is a computer printout of all PPSA registrations against Canco certified as to a particular date. As mentioned earlier, a PPSA search will not provide a copy of any underlying security document but only a classification of the collateral covered and the description of such collateral that the secured party chose to include.

It will also be necessary to search in the Bank of Canada office in Toronto, where Canco's principal place of business is located, to determine if Canco has granted security to a Canadian chartered bank under the Bank Act. Finally, if any of Canco's assets include patents or trade marks, searches should also be done with the federal patents and trade marks registries.

Where it is a condition of a transaction that the lender receive a first or other specific ranking security interest in collateral, arrangements must be made to discharge any existing security and searches will be done immediately prior to completion of the transaction to confirm the discharges and that there have been no registrations in the intervening time since the original searches.

Documentation

The documentation objective is generally to ensure that lenders receive the best security using the fewest possible different documents. A single guarantee can be obtained from Canco, but, different security documents will be required to secure all of Canco's assets. In the model transaction the assets to be charged are located in the provinces of Ontario (PPSA jurisdiction) and Quebec (civil law jurisdiction). Notwithstanding that there is more than one security regime in operation in Canada it is possible to a certain degree to use documentation that is capable of effectively creating a security interest or charge over personal property and real property that is appropriate for registration purposes in more than one of the provinces.

The most useful security document for the model transaction will be a debenture which can charge all Canco's present and future property, real and personal, in Ontario and, potentially, Quebec (see discussion below). In Ontario, the PPSA does not mandate any particular form of document and the security interest created in a typical debenture can be perfected by registering a financing statement indicating each type of collateral covered by the debenture under the PPSA. This debenture can also be drafted in such a manner that it is appropriate for registration in either the land titles or registry system to charge Canco's real property located in Ontario. In such circumstances a detailed legal description of the property is appended to the debenture. It must be remembered, however, that under the real property registration systems the entire security document is placed on the public register thus potentially exposing information about the financing to anyone who cares to search the register.

In Quebec it is generally not the practice to use the form of debenture executed for use in Ontario. However, a single deed of hypothec can be used to create an interest in both movable and immovable property. The deed of hypothec itself will be filed at the land register to evidence the interest created in the immovable property and a description of the hypothec created in movable property will be filed at the Register of Personal and Movable Real Rights to evidence the interest created in the movable property.

A registration issue arises on the facts of the model transaction given that there is more than one lender. As mentioned above, although there is debate on the issue, prudent practice appears to be that each of the Banks as a member of the banking syndicate should be named as a beneficiary or holder of a hypothec and not simply the Agent. This can create practical difficulties should the composition of the syndicate change in future, since amendments to the various registrations will be required and may be difficult to accomplish, especially with respect to registrations relating to immovable property. Although a full discussion of this issue and the manner in which it may be addressed is beyond the scope of this chapter, it should be mentioned that a practice has developed in Quebec whereby a debenture executed for use in the common law provinces may be used. In this situation the debenture (which contains a covenant to pay) is itself viewed as the primary obligation which is then secured by a hypothec in favour of the Agent acting on behalf of the Banks. In this case the registration relating to the hypothec need only note the Agent as the *fondé de pouvoir* (a Quebec civilian concept which is more than an agent) of the Banks.

Along with the guarantee and security documents a certificate as to certain factual matters relating to Canco will also be obtained to provide a factual basis for certain opinions as well as to provide comfort on certain matters which are not covered by opinions. The certificate ordinarily is made by a senior corporate officer such as the chief executive officer, chief operating officer, chief financial officer or corporate secretary. In transactions where it has not been possible to structure around financial assistance prohibitions an officer's certificate will include statements that the relevant solvency tests are satisfied so as to permit the financial assistance to be given. Matters typically covered in an officer's certificate include statements of the corporate history (with copies of relevant documents certified as accurate and complete attached); that the company is not insolvent and no 'insolvency' steps or actions have been taken or have occurred, corporate power and capacity and the absence of contractual restrictions on corporate action; the holding of relevant licences, consents etc; shareholders of the corporation; the corporation's places of business, location of assets and chief executive and registered office. Additionally, such a certificate often attaches a copy certified to be true, accurate and complete of the resolutions of the directors authorising the transaction and all related activity including execution, delivery and performance of the various documents.

Opinions

Lawyers in Canada qualify to practise law on a province by province basis and therefore, where a transaction such as the model involves the laws of a number of different provinces, opinions will be required from lawyers qualified in each relevant province. Trans-Canada law firms may be in a position to provide omnibus opinions drawing on the qualifications of lawyers from different provinces or, where a province in which a firm does not have offices is involved, by relying upon the opinion of local counsel. Practice as to who gives opinions varies in different provinces. In most circumstances (the notable exceptions being Quebec and British Columbia) in a domestic transaction opinions are rendered to the lender by borrower's counsel. In cross-border transactions practice is mixed and largely depends on the wishes of the lender.

In the model transaction opinions will be required from Ontario counsel as to:

1 the corporate status of Canco (which, although not strictly an opinion, will generally also include a report of the results of the various corporate searches)

and its power and authority to enter into and perform the obligations under the transaction documents and that such documents do not breach Canco's constating documents or any applicable law;
2 the enforceability of the choice of law clause in the guarantee and the ability to enforce a judgment obtained in England on the guarantee against Canco in Ontario;
3 the enforceability of the Ontario security documents;
4 title to the subject real property; and
5 the details regarding registrations made in connection with the security in Ontario (and, if relevant, any federal patent and trade mark registration) and the sufficiency and completeness of such registrations.

The opinions required from Quebec counsel are as to:

1 the enforceability of the Quebec security documents and the ranking of the hypothec over immovable property;
2 the ownership of the subject real property; and
3 the details regarding registrations made in connection with the security in Quebec and the sufficiency and completeness of such registrations.

Certain other opinions may also be requested in cross-border transactions such as that there are no stamp, registration or other documentary duties or similar taxes payable in connection with the transaction (which is not a difficult opinion to give as there are generally no such taxes or duties payable in any jurisdiction in Canada). More difficult issues arise where opinions are requested regarding enforcement and remedies which are not traditionally the subject of domestic opinions. Given that in Canada there are statutory[2] and common law[3] restrictions on the ability of secured parties to exercise their remedies strictly in accordance with the terms of the relevant contract, a number of qualifications will be required if these types of opinions are sought.

Additionally, depending on the facts of any particular transaction, certain regulatory statutes may be applicable to the exercise of remedies and thus may require opinion qualifications. The Investment Canada Act, which regulates the acquisition of Canadian businesses by non-residents of Canada, specifically addresses the situation of a foreign lender who acquires a Canadian business through the exercise of enforcement remedies by providing an exemption from the provisions of the Act in these circumstances so a qualification here will generally not be required.[4] A similar exemption is not, however, available under the Bank Act for a foreign bank (which is defined very broadly for the purposes of the Bank Act and will probably include any entity in a corporate group that also includes a bank) which acquires substantially all of the assets of a Canadian entity,[5] a transaction which requires federal cabinet approval. It should be noted that a foreign lender that acquires property through the exercise of enforcement remedies may become subject to Canadian income tax as it relates to such property.

2 See, for example, Part V of the Ontario PPSA which prescribes certain mandatory time periods and procedures relating to the exercise of remedies by a secured creditor.
3 For example, the doctrine of reasonable notice between the making of a demand for payment and the exercise of remedies, as articulated in the leading case of *Lister (Ronald Elwyn) v Dunlop Canada Ltd* [1982] 1 SCR 766.
4 Investment Canada Act, RSC 1985 (1st Supp) par 10(1)(c).
5 Bank Act (Canada) s 521.

Finally, mention should also be made of a few additional opinion qualifications or assumptions which are unique to Canada but standard in connection with a transaction such as the model. The first relates to the fact that under the terms of the Currency Act (Canada)[6] a court in Canada is only permitted to render a monetary judgment in Canadian dollars. If the payment obligations under a contract are expressed in another currency a court will convert sums due into Canadian dollars at a prescribed rate. As discussed above, an assumption will also generally be appropriate as to the extent of the foreign lender's activities in Canada in connection with the Bank Act (Canada) prohibition on a foreign bank conducting banking business in Canada. A qualification will also be required if a document contains an *exclusive* submission to the jurisdiction of the courts of a particular jurisdiction as the exclusive nature of the submission is unlikely to be recognised by a court in Canada as usurping their own jurisdiction.[7]

Finally, it should be noted briefly that difficult issues may arise where Canadian lawyers are asked to opine on the enforceability of agreements governed by the laws of a foreign jurisdiction rather than (or in addition to) opining on the enforceability of a choice of law clause nominating a foreign jurisdiction as the governing law of the contract. It is beyond the scope of this chapter to review these issues[8] beyond noting that Canadian lawyers generally feel more comfortable opining on the enforceability of a choice of law clause as the case law articulates the relevant legal tests.[9] Opining on the enforceability of a contract governed by foreign law on the basis of an assumption that the governing law was that of the relevant Canadian province is problematic as there may be a number of concepts or terms in or implied in the contract which have a meaning of which a Canadian lawyer would be unaware. If there is particular concern in a transaction regarding any given obligation should the choice of law provision fail, enforceability of such obligations can be specifically addressed.

6 Currency Act (Canada), RSC 1985 s 12.

7 See *Pirrana Small Car Centres Inc v Rumm* [1981] 5 WWR 79 (BCSC).

8 For a full discussion of the issues involved see Peter Hamilton 'Multi-Jurisdictional Opinions', *Opinions in Commercial Lending Transactions* (Toronto, The Law Society of Upper Canada, 1996).

9 The leading case is the decision of the Privy Council in *Vita Food Products Inc v Unus Shipping Co* [1939] AC 277 (PC). See also *Amchem Products Inc v British Columbia (Workers' Compensation Board)* [1993] 1SCR 897 (SCC).

3 France

Martin Gdanski

Norton Rose

GUARANTEES

English-law guarantee agreements are frequently structured along the lines of an on-demand guarantee, requiring the guarantor to pay on first demand of the beneficiary without being entitled to raise any defences to payment possessed by the underlying obligor. In addition, and as an independent obligation, the guarantor indemnifies the beneficiary against non-payment by the underlying obligor.

Under French law, the basis and therefore the scope of contractual guarantees is different. Although French court decisions have specifically recognised the principle of first-demand guarantees (*garanties à première demande*), and such guarantees, originally adapted from international practice, are in fact now in frequent use in France, they are not the statutory form of guarantee provided for under the French Civil Code (the 'Civil Code'). The Civil Code guarantee, which goes under the name of *cautionnement*, is a somewhat weaker instrument, since the guarantor may require the beneficiary of the guarantee to avail itself of certain remedies with respect to the assets of the underlying obligor before the beneficiary can exercise the guarantee. Some of the shortcomings of the *cautionnement* may be cured by obtaining a *cautionnement solidaire*, pursuant to which the guarantor waives such requirement. However, even in such case, the guarantor is entitled to refuse payment under the guarantee by raising certain defences of the underlying obligor inherent to the underlying obligation.

Only in the case of the first-demand guarantee is the guarantor obliged to pay independently of the terms of the underlying obligation. The drawback of the first demand guarantee in France, however, is that both the case law (*jurisprudence*)[1] and

1 The use of the term 'case law' in the French context should not be taken to mean exactly the same as its counterpart in Anglo-American legal systems, because the French court system does not recognise the principle of *stare decisis*. However, when a line of decisional authority becomes sufficiently long, or a principled decision is made by the French *Cour de Cassation* (the highest court in civil and commercial matters), there is said to be a '*jurisprudence*' and the lower courts will generally follow the principle.

the learned commentary (*doctrine*)[2] have concluded that, since the obligations under a first-demand guarantee are autonomous from the underlying obligation, it is necessary for the guarantee to refer to a specific amount or maximum amount payable thereunder, and the scope of such a guarantee may not be determined by reference to an underlying obligation. In a *cautionnement*, on the other hand, there are no such constraints, since a *cautionnement* is considered as being accessory to the underlying obligation.

Statutory guarantees (*Cautionnnement*)

The rules regarding *cautionnement* are set forth in Art 2011 to 2041 of the Civil Code. The basic rule is that the *cautionnement* is an agreement whereby the guarantor (known as the *caution*) undertakes to perform the obligation of the underlying obligor in the event that the obligor does not perform such obligation. For this reason, the *cautionnement*, unlike the first-demand guarantee, is considered to be 'accessory' to the underlying obligation. This has several practical consequences. First, a person cannot purport to be both a principal debtor and a guarantor of the same obligation. Second, a *caution* will not be valid where the underlying debt is itself invalid as a matter of law. Third, although a *cautionnement* is typically given for a sum of money, this is not a statutory requirement, and the *cautionnement* agreement can require the *caution* to perform in kind the obligation of the underlying party.[3]

The courts have construed liberally the kinds of obligations which may be the subject of a *cautionnement*. Thus, for example, it is possible to grant a *caution* of obligations which will arise only in the future, such as drawings under a line of credit, as long as the obligation guaranteed is sufficiently identified (although a *cautionnement* of obligations which are purely potential (*éventuelle*) is not deemed to be valid). It is also possible, subject to the rules described under 'Board Resolutions' (p 106 below), for a *caution* to be granted for an obligation which is undetermined or unlimited in amount. On the other hand, *cautionnement* of obligations which are or which are declared to be null and void (*nulles*) or illicit (such as *cautionnement* of gambling debts) will not, unlike the first demand guarantee, be enforceable. Moreover, the Civil Code Art 2013 specifies that the *cautionnement* may not exceed what is due by the underlying debtor or be contracted under conditions more onerous than those contained in the underlying contract. Hence, a *caution* cannot be called upon to pay prior to the time that the underlying debt is due. On the other hand, the parties may agree contractually that only a fixed fraction of the underlying debt or a fixed amount thereof will be the subject of the *cautionnement*.

The actual language of the *caution* is important in determining the amount of the underlying debt covered by the guarantee. The courts have determined that, in the

2 In France, considerable weight is given in the context of statutory construction to the writings of learned commentary, including law journal articles and commentary on court decisions (*notes sous arrêts*) by respected law professors and practitioners. Such writings, known as *doctrine*, are often accorded status equivalent to that of *jurisprudence* (as described in the previous footnote) if there is no *jurisprudence* on the point, or if the court decisions are in conflict.

3 However, the remedy of specific performance is generally unavailable under French law, so that in the event of the failure of the guarantor to perform in kind the underlying obligation, the remedy of the beneficiary will generally be a suit for damages.

absence of express language to the contrary, where a specific sum is set forth in the text of the *cautionnement*, only such amount of principal is covered by the guarantee, to the exclusion of interest, costs, expenses and other ancillary amounts. On the other hand, where the *cautionnement* does not refer to a fixed amount and merely states that it guarantees the underlying debt, the courts have ruled that the *cautionnement* covers all amounts incidental to the principal amount covered, including interest (although some courts have required that this fact be mentioned in the text of the guarantee), costs of calling on the guarantee (including court fees) and damages resulting from non-performance of the underlying obligation by the obligor (including any amounts specified in the underlying agreement as liquidated damages).[4]

Where the guarantor is not a merchant (see 'Execution' p 108 below), the Civil Code requires (with certain exceptions), in order for the guarantee to be enforceable, that the amount guaranteed be acknowledged, both in letters and in numbers, by the guarantor in his own hand (where there is no determinable amount guaranteed, then mention of this fact must be acknowledged in handwriting by the guarantor). However, where the guarantor is a merchant (which is very frequently the case in situations where cross-border guarantees are obtained), no such manuscript acknowledgment is required; indeed, as described under 'Execution' (p 108 below), in such cases it is not even necessary for the *cautionnement* to be evidenced in writing.

The beneficiary of a *cautionnement* may call upon the guarantor for payment at any time once the underlying debt is due. In the event of an extension of time being granted by the beneficiary to the underlying debtor, the *cautionnement* remains in force; however, the guarantor is entitled to bring an action against the underlying obligor to cause it to pay. The *cautionnement* may also provide expressly that the underlying obligation may not be extended beyond its initial due date without the agreement of the guarantor, or that the guarantee is given for a limited period only. On the other hand, the guarantor does not automatically benefit from any grace period or moratorium granted by law or by a court to the underlying debtor[5], unless the law or court decision in question specifically applies to *cautions* as well. Unless there is specific contractual language to the contrary in the terms of the *cautionnement*, the guarantor is obliged to pay only at the original maturity date of the underlying debt and not upon acceleration of maturity due to an event of default.

The Civil Code makes an important distinction between a simple guarantee (*cautionnement simple*) and a surety (*cautionnement solidaire*). In the case of a *cautionnement simple*, the guarantor is only obliged to pay if the underlying obligor does not pay at the due date. Moreover, the guarantor is entitled in this case (unless

4 The French Civil Code Art 1156 provides that liquidated damage clauses (*clauses pénales*) are enforceable but that the court may increase or decrease the payment to be made if such payment is found to be clearly insufficient or excessive in relation to the true loss suffered by the party not in breach.

5 In respect of payment obligations, a French court has power under the French Civil Code Art 1244-1 to postpone or spread over time the payment of the sums due for a period not in excess of two years, taking into account the situation of the debtor and the needs of the creditor. In such case, the judge may also provide separately that any payments which are postponed will bear interest at a reduced rate (but not less than the legal minimum), or that payments will initially be allocated to principal rather than interest. The judge may also subject such measures to the effecting by the debtor of acts which facilitate or secure the payment of the debt.

the right has been expressly or tacitly waived[6] or if the underlying debtor in insolvent or has granted security over all of its assets) to require the beneficiary first to attempt to satisfy the debt out of the assets of the underlying debtor (*bénéfice de discussion dans les biens du débiteur*). In addition, if there is more than one *cautionnement simple*, then, although each guarantor is theoretically required to pay the full amount of the debt, each guarantor may (again, unless the right has been waived), require the beneficiary to divide its action pro rata to the amount of each guarantee (*bénéfice de division*).

In the case of a *cautionnement solidaire*, the guarantor must pay at the due date upon demand of the beneficiary, whether or not demand has been made on the underlying debtor and whether or not the underlying debtor has in fact paid. Moreover, the *caution solidaire* may not raise the *bénéfice de discussion* or (in the case of several guarantors) the *bénéfice de division*. However, unlike the case of the first demand guarantee, a *caution* (including a *caution solidaire*) is entitled, under the Civil Code Art 2036, to raise against the beneficiary any defences to payment possessed by the underlying obligor and which are inherent to the debt (but not those defences which are personal to the underlying obligor).[7]

For this reason, the *cautionnement* can be extinguished for any of a variety of reasons, many of which are related to the underlying debt. Obviously, payment by the underlying obligor of the debt will extinguish the guarantee; however, payment by a third party will not extinguish the guarantee, since such third party will be subrogated to the rights of the creditor. Acceptance by the beneficiary of property in payment of the underlying debt (a procedure known as *dation en paiement*) will also extinguish the *caution* up to the value of the property so transferred. Extinction of the underlying debt by settlement (*transaction*) between the creditor and the underlying obligor also extinguishes the *caution*, as does the forgiveness of the underlying debt (*remise de dettes*)[8]. Prescription of the underlying debt due to expiration of a limitations period will also liberate the *caution*.

In the event of novation of the underlying debt, the *caution* is normally liberated from its obligations under the *cautionnement*. In the event that the creditor desires the preservation of the *cautionnement* and the *caution* refuses, then the prior debt subsists. In the event that the *caution* agrees to guarantee the novated debt, then it can no longer raise any defences inherent to the prior debt. The *caution* may also be freed from its obligations in the event of set-off (*compensation*) between the creditor and the underlying obligor.[9]

Other defences to payment which may be raised by the *caution* include the following:

6 Under legislation dating from 1994, any such waiver by a physical person of a guarantee of professional debt in favour of an individual entrepreneur is invalid unless the amount of the guarantee is limited to a stated figure inclusive of interest, principal, costs and expenses.

7 Nevertheless, any judgment rendered in favour of the beneficiary against the underlying debtor is binding as against the guarantor, and any judgment rendered against any guarantor is binding against any co-guarantors and against the underlying debtor.

8 The converse is not true: forgiveness of the *caution* does not free the underlying obligor of its obligations.

9 Under the Civil Code Arts 1289ff, when two parties each owe the other a liquid and certain debt in cash or in fungible commodities, an automatic set-off (*compensation*) occurs up to the amount of the debt.

1 non-performance by the creditor of its own obligations under the underlying contract;
2 nullity of the primary obligation as a matter of law (eg due to lack of proper corporate authorisation of the underlying obligor);
3 failure of the beneficiary to declare the underlying debt in a timely manner in bankruptcy proceedings affecting the underlying obligor;
4 expiration of the underlying obligation pursuant to the terms of the instrument creating the underlying obligation.[10]

However, the *caution* is not entitled to raise defences to performance which are purely personal to the underlying obligor, such as lack of personal capacity, declaration of moratorium or supervening illegality (including exchange controls prohibiting transfer of funds by the underlying obligor to the creditor).

It is important to specify with precision the duration of the guarantee in the text of the *cautionnement*. The case law is to the effect that an 'indefinite' *cautionnement*, ie one which specifies no duration whatsoever, can be terminated on a unilateral basis by the *caution*. However, the courts appear to be wary of applying this rule, and have refused to do so where the guarantee is of a loan which has a specific term, even though the guarantee had no fixed term, or where the *cautionnement* was stated to apply 'until full reimbursement of the underlying debt'.

First-demand guarantees

Unlike the case of the *cautionnement*, there is no statutory basis for the first-demand guarantee in the Civil Code. Historically, the French first-demand guarantee was adapted from international practice by French banks in order to compete with foreign banks in the market for bid bonds, performance bonds, prepayment bonds and maintenance bonds for projects in developing countries in which their clients (frequently large French construction companies) participated. In such cases, the French banks often used forms of first-demand guarantee originally developed for use in other legal systems, modified to provide for French law and jurisdiction. Since the text of these guarantees differed considerably from the statutory *cautionnement* by their insistence that the guarantor was required to pay on demand without being able to raise defences intrinsic to the underlying obligation, it was left to the French courts to determine whether such an instrument was valid under French law or whether it amounted to an impermissible attempt by the parties to contract out of the mandatory parameters of the *cautionnement*.

10 Under Law no 84-148 of 1 March 1984 (recently codifed as Arts. L. 621-1 ff of the Commercial Code), when a *cautionnement* has been given to a credit institution to guarantee the debt of a business enterprise, the credit institution must notify the guarantor, no later than 31 March of each year, of the amount of principal, interest, costs and other amounts remaining due at the previous 31 December in respect of the underlying obligation, as well as the remaining term of such obligation. Failure by the bank to provide such information results in loss of coverage over interest due from the time of the last such notification made and the time when the information is in fact reported to the *caution*. Although the law uses the word '*caution*', many practitioners provide the same information in the event of a first-demand guarantee as well.

Beginning in 1982, the *Cour de Cassation*, the highest French court in civil and commercial matters,[11] determined in a number of cases that the first-demand guarantee (*garantie à première demande*, or *garantie autonome*), was valid as a matter of French law and that it was distinguishable from the statutory *cautionnement*. Since that time, a complex body of *jurisprudence* and *doctrine* has developed regarding the circumstances under which a guarantee is to be properly construed as a first-demand guarantee rather than as a *cautionnement*, and the limited scope of defences to payment under such a guarantee, but there remains no statutory basis for such a guarantee under French law.[12]

In construing a guarantee as a first-demand guarantee, both the courts and the authors of the learned commentary have laid particular emphasis on the 'autonomous' nature of the first-demand guarantee. Unlike the *cautionnement*, the first-demand guarantee must, under French law, be separate and independent from the underlying obligation. Therefore, where a French-law instrument refers simply to an obligation to guarantee payment of 'all amounts which may fall due, whether in principal, interest, costs or expenses, under the [loan agreement or other underlying obligation]' or, a fortiori where the guarantee is an 'all moneys' guarantee covering all amounts which may be due by the underlying obligor to the creditor for any reason whatsoever, there is a significant risk that the instrument will be construed by the French courts as a *cautionnement* rather than as a first-demand guarantee. The courts and the commentary have insisted, in order for an instrument to qualify as a first-demand guarantee, that the instrument refer to a specific amount (or a specified maximum amount) to be paid by the guarantor to the beneficiary upon simple demand rather than a mere reference to amounts due under the underlying debt instrument. The courts have also emphasised that the guarantee instrument must contain an unequivocal statement of its unconditional nature, distinct from that of the underlying obligation. The courts have not hesitated to look beyond the qualification given to the guarantee by the parties to the actual text of the agreement, requalifying instruments entitled 'first-demand guarantee' as *cautionnements* and vice versa, depending on whether the parties have indicated that the guarantee obligation is intended to be unconditional and autonomous, or not.

In the event that a guarantee is construed to be an autonomous guarantee, then the French courts will require performance in accordance with the terms of the guarantee, but only in accordance with such terms. Performance may be made subject, by the terms of the guarantee itself, to submission of documents (eg customs certificates). The guarantee may be called only within the time limit specified therein; calls made after the

11 France does not have a single Supreme Court. The *Cour de Cassation*, which sits in five different civil chambers, is the highest court for civil and commercial matters, as well as for matters determined by the specialised labour courts (*prud'hommes*). A separate chamber of the *Cour de Cassation* is the highest court for criminal matters. It is possible (and not infrequent) that the same point of law is decided differently by the different chambers of the *Cour de Cassation*. In such case, the court will occasionally meet in a plenary session in order to adopt a unified position. The highest court for matters of administrative law (which can also include issues of tax law) is the *Conseil d'Etat*, a body which also promulgates certain regulations. Issues of constitutionality of legislation are determined by a special body, the *Conseil Constitutionnel*, a body which includes, inter alia, all prior Presidents of the French Republic.

12 The parties are free to adopt by contract the rules of the International Chamber of Commerce on first-demand guarantees if they wish to provide for a more formalised set of rules.

deadline will not be honoured by the French courts; however, 'extend or pay' clauses have been accepted by the courts. The guarantee will be honoured only up to the amount set forth in the guarantee instrument.

The principal advantage of the first-demand guarantee over the *cautionnement* is, of course, that the guarantor is obliged to pay notwithstanding any defences which would exonerate the underlying obligor from performance. The guarantor may not raise any exception to payment drawn from the underlying obligation, or invoke a claimed nullity thereof as a defence to performance of the guarantee. Nor may the guarantor refuse payment on the grounds that it will not be able to exercise an action for reimbursement against the underlying obligor due to the bankruptcy of the obligor or because political difficulties in the country of the underlying obligor render such recourse impossible, or require the prior approval of the underlying obligor as a condition to payment. The courts have even gone so far as to say that it is not a defence to payment under the guarantee that the underlying agreement constitutes a violation of French public policy.

The French courts have accepted a number of limited defences to payment under a first-demand guarantee, and such defences have been held to be the exclusive defences available to such payment. These defences are as follows :

1 where a call on the guarantee constitutes an outright fraud. The courts have found such fraud to exist in a variety of cases where it was manifestly clear from the facts that the underlying obligation had in fact already been performed and the beneficiary was attempting to obtain double payment, or where the beneficiary, in collusion with other parties, had rendered impossible the performance of the agreement by the underlying obligor;

2 where a call on the guarantee constitutes a manifest abuse of the terms of the guarantee. The courts have found such a manifest abuse to exist in the following fact situations:
   - (a) where the underlying agreement had been previously terminated by the beneficiary of the guarantee;
   - (b) where the guarantee had been given for a company which was entirely foreign to the transaction in question;
   - (c) where the beneficiary expressly refused to perform its own obligations under the underlying contract;
   - (d) where the purpose of the call on the guarantee was to reopen a dispute which had already been the subject of a settlement agreement;

3 where the beneficiary of the guarantee had succeeded by law to the rights and obligations of the underlying obligor (since, in this case, the beneficiary would be in a position to refuse to perform the underlying obligation and then to call on the guarantor to perform under the guarantee); and

4 where the guarantee has expired due to a cause imputable to the beneficiary.

Frequently, it is the underlying obligor (*donneur d'ordre*) rather than the guarantor who seeks to raise such limited defences to payment under the guarantee. In such cases, the obligor will typically petition the court for a temporary seizure of the funds of the guarantor necessary to make the payment (*saisie conservatoire*). Where the guarantor itself seeks to avoid payment it will raise the defence when an action is brought by the beneficiary.

Joint and several obligations

The statutory rules regarding joint and several obligations (*obligations solidaires*) are set forth in the Civil Code Art 1200–1216. Joint and several obligations are stated to exist where each of the obligors may be called upon to pay the entire amount of the debt, and where payment of the debt made by any single obligor liberates all of the other obligors vis-à-vis the creditor. Under Article 1202, joint and several liability must be expressly contracted and will not be implied. However, the French courts have held on numerous occasions that this restriction is inapplicable to commercial debts, and indeed are inclined to consider that where two or more persons have contracted for payment of the same commercial debt, or where two or more merchants (*commerçants*) have contracted for the same debt, joint and several liability is to be presumed. Article 1202 also states that the requirement of an express statement of joint and several liability is not required where such liability exists automatically by virtue of the provisions of a law: such liability, referred to as *solidarité légale*, arises out of several disparate provisions of French law, the most typical example being the liability of partners in a French partnership (*société en nom collectif*).[13]

Joint and several liability may exist even where one of the obligors has contracted on a basis different that the others with respect to the payment of the debt, eg on a conditional basis, whereas the other debtors have contracted to pay unconditionally, or subject to a limited duration not granted to the other debtors.

The creditor of an obligation contacted by several obligors on a joint and several basis may require full payment from any of such obligors, and such obligor is not entitled to the *bénéfice de division* described under 'Statutory guarantees' (p 70 above). In the event that any obligor refuses to pay, the creditor may require payment from another co-debtor, even if it has instituted proceedings against the initial debtor. Indeed, the courts have extended this rule to hold that the creditor may waive its rights as against one of the debtors, or assign such rights to a third party, without losing its right to require full payment from any of the other debtors.

An obligor called upon to pay a joint and several obligation may raise any defences resulting from the nature of the obligation (eg nullity, force majeure, novation, or expiration of a limitations period), any defences which are personal to the obligor (eg the condition under which the obligor contracted the obligation or the limited duration granted to such obligor), as well as any defences which are common to all of the obligors, but not any defences which are personal only to some of the other obligors. Payment by any obligor of the full amount due liberates all of the other co-obligors of their obligations vis-à-vis the creditor.

Under French law, each obligor with joint and several liability for a debt is considered to represent all of the other debtors, even in the absence of an express stipulation to this effect, except where to do so would increase the liability of the other debtors or where the creditor has brought an action against all of the debtors. From this concept of 'joint representation' there results a number of consequences set forth in the relevant Articles of the Civil Code:

13 Joint and several liability of tortfeasors (*obligations in solidum*) are subject to somewhat different rules and will not be discussed further in this chapter.

1 a formal notice to perform (*mise en demeure*) sent to a single co-obligor is deemed binding on all joint obligors;
2 an action commenced against a single co-obligor interrupts any relevant limitation period with respect to all co-obligors;
3 a claim made against a single co-obligor for the payment of default interest (*intérêts moratoires*) commences the running of default interest against all co-obligors;
4 a novation of the debt agreed with one co-obligor liberates the other co-obligors; provided, however, that in the event that the creditor requests the other co-obligors to accede to the novated debt and they refuse, then the co-obligor remain liable for the prior debt;
5 any co-obligor may appeal from a judgment rendered against a single co-obligor, and in the event that such appeal is not lodged in time by any co-obligor, he may join in any timely appeal filed by any other co-obligor.

Subrogation and contribution

Cautionnement

A *caution* who has paid the creditor is entitled to seek reimbursement from the underlying obligor, either directly pursuant to the Civil Code Art 2028, or by availing itself of subrogation to the right of the creditor to payment under the Civil Code Art 2029. In certain cases, the Civil Code Art 2032 entitles the *caution* to obtain advance reimbursement of the amount of the guarantee, even before paying such amounts to the beneficiary of the guarantee. However, the *caution* loses its rights to such reimbursement if the underlying obligor pays the beneficiary a second time due to failure of the *caution* to inform the underlying obligor that it has already paid the debt (although in this case the underlying obligor may seek reimbursement of its payment from the beneficiary), or if the *caution* has paid, without any action having been brought against it to pay and without notifying the underlying obligor that it is contemplating payment, where it can be shown that the underlying obligor possessed the means to have the obligation cancelled (eg due to the expiration of a limitations period or some other defence to payment).

Article 2028 provides that a *caution* who has paid under the guarantee has a direct right to reimbursement from the underlying obligor, whether the guarantee was given with or without the knowledge of the underlying obligor. This right may be exercised in the event of full or partial payment; however, the courts have held that language in the *cautionnement* which prohibits the guarantor from exercising its rights to reimbursement until it has paid the full amount of the underlying debt is enforceable. The guarantor is entitled to obtain reimbursement of all sums paid to the beneficiary, plus interest from the date of payment at the legal rate (and not the contractual rate set forth in the underlying obligation), plus damages where the *caution* has suffered damage in addition to being required to pay.

Alternatively, Art 2029 provides that the *caution* who has paid the debt is subrogated to all of the rights which the creditor had against the underlying obligor. The French courts have interpreted this provision to permit recourse by the *caution* against not only the underlying obligor but also any other person against whom the creditor would have been able to take action to recover the debt in question, including co-debtors and owners of property pledged for the underlying debt. In the event of partial payment, the *caution*'s rights as subrogee rank below those of the creditor for the remaining sum due.

The rights of subrogation under Art 2029 can in certain circumstances be more advantageous than the direct rights to reimbursement under Article 2028, because the *caution* is subrogated to all rights of the creditor against the underlying obligor, including any rights under pledges, mortgages or other forms of security interests granted by the underlying obligor to the creditor.

Pursuant to the Civil Code Art 2032, a *caution* may bring an action for reimbursement by the underlying obligor even prior to effecting payment to the beneficiary in the following cases:

1 where an action has been brought against the *caution* by the creditor;
2 where the debtor is in bankruptcy;
3 where the underlying obligor undertook to discharge the guarantor within a certain time period and has not done so;
4 where the underlying debt has become payable due to the passage of the contractual due date;
5 at any time after 10 years, where the underlying obligation does not have a fixed term; and
6 as described earlier, where the underlying obligor has obtained an extension of the time to pay by the beneficiary.

Although the Civil Code is silent on the point, the French courts have determined that an action under Article 2032 is available only in the event that the beneficiary of the guarantee has not already brought an action for payment of the underlying obligation against the underlying obligor.

Where several *cautions* have guaranteed a debt and one *caution* has performed its payment obligations, it has a right of contribution against each of the other co-guarantors for their proportionate share of the debt, but only where the *caution* has paid under one of the cases normally entitling it to reimbursement prior to payment under Art 2032.

The *caution*'s right to subrogation to the rights and security enjoyed by the creditor is considered to be crucial, and for this reason the Civil Code Art 2037 provides that in the event the *caution* is no longer able to enjoy the right to subrogation due to an act of the creditor, the *caution* is relieved of its guarantee obligations. This right is available both to *cautions simples* and to *cautions solidaires*, and cannot be waived (any such waiver is by law given no effect). The courts have found that Art 2037 applies both when the actual security itself (eg mortgage, pledge of going business, share pledges, pledge of stock (inventory), liens, or even another *cautionnement*) is terminated due to an act or the negligence of the creditor, and when the value of the security is reduced (eg by reduction of the value of the collateral, loss of ranking, lack of perfection) due to the creditor. The security must have been in existence at the time of the granting of the *cautionnement*.

First demand guarantees

Since the first demand guarantee is not based on the terms of the Civil Code, none of the statutory provisions of the Code relating to reimbursement of the guarantor by the underlying obligor or subrogation to the rights of the beneficiary against the obligor are directly applicable to such guarantees. The French courts have ruled that a guarantor who has performed its obligations under a guarantee may bring an action against the underlying obligor for reimbursement of the amount so paid, even where, following payment by the guarantor, it develops that the call on the guarantee was not justified. However, it remains unclear at the present time whether a guarantor under a first demand guarantee is subrogated to all of the rights of the beneficiary against the underlying obligor, including any security of the beneficiary. In practice, the terms of the guarantee agreement will typically deal both with reimbursement and subrogation rights.

The French courts have also found that the underlying obligor is entitled to claim directly from the beneficiary any payments made by the guarantor upon proof that such amounts were unjustly paid, eg where the obligor had already performed under the underlying obligation, where the non-performance of the obligor was due to the fault of the beneficiary or where the underlying obligation was null and void; in such cases, the courts have held that the underlying obligor is not required to prove that the call on the guarantee constituted fraud or manifest abuse.

Joint and several obligations

As a matter of law (Civil Code, Art. 1213), once the creditor has received full payment from one co-obligor, the debt in question is divided between all of the co-obligors (theoretically on an equal basis, although the court is entitled to allocate liability on an unequal basis if it determines that the responsibility of each co-obligor does not present the same degree of gravity).[14] The co-obligor who has paid the debt in its entirety to the creditor then has an action against each of the other co-obligors for reimbursement of its proportion of the debt. The Civil Code provides that in the event that any such co-obligor should be insolvent, the loss occasioned by such insolvency is divided between the other co-obligors and the co-obligor who paid the debt to the creditor.[15]

A co-obligor of an *obligation solidaire* who pays the debt is automatically subrogated to the rights of the creditor (including any security enjoyed by the creditor) against the other co-obligors (Civil Code Art 1251-3). However, unlike the case of a *caution*, the co-obligor is not entitled to refuse performance of its obligations on the grounds that it is no longer able to enjoy the right to subrogation due to an act of the creditor.

14 However, if the matter for which the debt was contracted on a joint and several basis concerned only a single co-obligor, then such co-obligor is liable for the full amount of the debt to the other co-obligors.

15 The Civil Code also provides that where the creditor has waived its rights against one of the co-obligors and thereafter one or several other co-obligors become insolvent, the portion of the debt attributable to such insolvent co-debtors is, in the event of an action in contribution by an obligor against the other co-obligors, divided between all the co-obligors, including the obligor against whom the debtor waived its rights.

TYPES OF SECURITY

Introduction: lack of a comprehensive security structure and other differences with Anglo-American practice

As explained elsewhere in this book, the general framework for the taking of security in the US and the UK and other jurisdictions, inspired by the 'common law' systems of such countries, permits, with certain exceptions, the obtention of a more or less full security package by means of a single comprehensive document, which is styled in England and Wales a 'guarantee and debenture', including a floating charge with (probably but not necessarily) separate assignments of book debts, insurance policies and intellectual property. There may be other specific security documents, depending on the nature of the assets concerned. Typically (again with certain exceptions), the registerable forms of security will be registered at a single location, either the relevant UCC filing office (in the case of the US) or at Companies House (in the case of the UK).

France does not possess such a unified regime for the taking of security over assets. Rather, each category of assets is subject to a different set of statutory provisions which provides the framework pursuant to which security over such assets are created and perfected. Hence, in order to obtain the equivalent in France of a general guarantee and debenture, it is necessary to execute a number of different instruments and to obtain perfection of the security created under each such instrument in a different manner. This often comes as a surprise to lawyers and bankers practising in legal systems modelled on the Anglo-American model, and can require the expenditure of greater time and expense in France in order to obtain security analogous to that which they would expect to receive in their home jurisdictions.

It should also be noted that there is no exact equivalent under French law of a floating charge. While it is possible, as will be explained below, in the case of certain categories of assets (for example, book debts and, in certain limited respects, the going concern value of a business) to obtain the functional equivalent of a floating charge, this is not generally the case, and in certain instances it will be necessary to content oneself with an undertaking or promise by the chargor to create additional security upon the acquisition of further assets at the time of such acquisition.

Another central principle of French law on the taking of security which often comes as a surprise to foreign bankers and lawyers is that, as a general rule, security over tangible movable assets is created and perfected only by the physical delivery of the pledged asset either to the pledgee or to a third party (*tiers convenu*) mutually agreed upon by the pledgor and the pledgee. Failure to accomplish this formality will render the pledge of the asset unenforceable as against both the pledgor and third parties. Fortunately, there are several exceptions to this general rule, as will be detailed below, permitting pledge without dispossession (*gage sans dépossession*) of certain categories of assets in certain circumstances.[16] However, the existence of the general rule can

16 In addition to the various categories of security described in this section, special legislation exists for the granting of pledges over automobiles (Decree no 53-968 of 30 September 1953), films (*Code de l'industrie cinématographique* Arts 33ff), bills of exchange (Commercial Code Art 122) life insurance policies (Law of 13 July 1930 Art. 65), and computer software (Law of 10 May 1994).

create significant difficulties in certain cases, for example that of stock in trade (inventory).

Finally, another important principle of French law which stands in contradiction to the practice in certain other jurisdictions is that the remedies of the secured party are limited in many cases to the sale of the pledged asset at public auction, pursuant to specified procedures for such auctions and the satisfaction of the secured debt out of the proceeds of such sale, or petition to a court for judicial self-attribution, but only after an evaluation of the value of the pledged asset by a court-appointed expert (see under 'Power of sale or attribution of the secured asset', p 117 below). Contractual clauses in the pledge instrument which permit the pledgee to sell the asset by private sale (*clause de voie parée*) or to appropriate the asset for the pledgee's own use (*pacte commissoire*) are null and void, and, where considered by a court to be central to the pledge instrument, may even void the pledge altogether. This general principle has, as will be detailed below, many applications which can be surprising to the foreign practitioner.

Charges over land: real estate mortgages (*hypothèques immobilières*)

French real estate mortgages (*hypothèques immobilières*) are governed by the provisions of the Civil Code s 2114ff.[17] Under such provisions, a mortgage is defined as a right over real property granted to a creditor (known as a *créancier hypothécaire*) by a debtor, relating to real property which the debtor owns and has the right to dispose of, in order to secure payment of a debt by the mortgagor to the mortgagee.[18] The mortgage will automatically cover any personal property which is a fixture (*immeuble par destination*) of the real property, and any improvements (*améliorations*) made to the property during the term of the mortgage. Assignment of a mortgaged debt by the creditor to a third party automatically transfers the benefit of the mortgage, and such transfer is noted on the mortgage register.

The creation of a mortgage gives the creditor the right to obtain attachment (*saisie*) of the mortgaged property despite subsequent transfer of title to the property (*droit de suite*) and to be paid out of the proceeds of the sale of the attached property (*droit de préférence*). The real estate mortgage is generally considered to be among the most effective of the forms of security interest available under French law, because very few liens created by operation of law have priority over the mortgage. However, enforcement of the mortgage may be very slow (often extending into several years) and creation of the mortgage is expensive. For these reasons, it is relatively rare for the creation of a mortgage to be requested in the context of a cross-border transaction.

17 Separate Provisions of the Civil Code (Arts 2085ff) also permit the taking of a pledge (*antichrèse*) over real estate; for such security to be valid the owner of the real estate must be dispossessed of the real estate.

18 Certain mortgages may be created by operation of law (*hypothèque légale*) or by petition to a court in order to secure amounts due under a judgment (*hypothèque judiciaire*), but this is very infrequent in the context of cross-border secured transactions. The remainder of the discussion in this section will therefore concentrate on mortgages created by contract (*hypothèque conventionnelle*).

The granting of mortgages (*hypothèques*) over real estate located in France is subject to a statutory monopoly in favour of French notaries (*notaires*);[19] in order to be valid, the mortgage deed must be signed as an *acte authentique*, which in practice means before such a notary. In practice, the mortgage deed is a highly stylised document which should be prepared directly by the notary rather than simply witnessed by him; however, in international financing transactions it is often preferable for the banks' French counsel to prepare a French-language summary of the credit facility which is attached to the mortgage deed, thereby enabling the *notaire* to concentrate on the preparation of the deed itself and avoiding the cost of translating the credit facility into French (which could otherwise be required by the *notaire* or the land registry). The deed must contain certain specific information required by law, including a detailed description of the property and the amount of the debt. It should also be noted that it is necessary to provide a fixed amount in the mortgage deed for the amount secured; it is not acceptable to provide in such a deed that the amount secured is equal to 'all amounts falling due under the credit facility'. There is no statutory rule which would prohibit the debt from being denominated in a currency other than the French franc or the Euro; however, in the event of enforcement of the mortgage, the proceeds will be paid in French francs or Euros and calculated on the basis of the then-current exchange rate.

The granting and registration of mortgages requires a lengthy time-period. The first step is for the *notaire* to obtain proof of title from the local land registry; as these institutions are frequently slow, even this step may take from one to two months, and actual registration may take as long as six months or more. However, the creditor has an actionable document once execution of the mortgage deed has occurred. Perfection of the mortgage and enforceability as against third parties requires registration of the mortgage (*inscription*) with the local land registry (*conservation des hypothèques*). The priority of mortgages is normally determined by the order of filing. However, in the event that two mortgages are filed on the same day over the same property, the mortgage granted pursuant to the deed bearing the earliest date will have priority; if both deeds bear the same date, then they have equal priority regardless of the time of day at which the mortgages were actually filed.

Once properly recorded, the mortgage is effective as against any subsequent purchaser of the property (subject to the 'purging' rights described below), any subsequently-filed (and therefore lesser-ranking) mortgage, and all unsecured creditors. The mortgage will secure the amount of principal of the debt secured and three years of interest. The registration is effective until the date specified in the registration, provided that where (as will usually be the case), the mortgage is recorded prior to the due date of the amount secured thereby, the date so specified cannot exceed the second anniversary of the due date (or, where the amount secured is to be paid in instalments, two years from the due date of the final instalment) or 35 years in all from the date of registration. In the event that the mortgage is registered on or following the due date (or where the mortgage instrument does not specify a due date), then the total duration

19 In general, *notaires* in France occupy a position quite different from their counterparts in Anglo-American jurisdictions. Several categories of transactions, such as real estate conveyancing and establishment of wills, may be effected only if subscribed to before a *notaire* while other instruments, which may be signed without the benefit of notary (*actes sous seing privé*) have additional evidentiary effect if signed before a notaire (*actes authentiques*).

of the mortgage cannot exceed ten years from the date of registration. The inscription is renewable.

The costs of obtaining a mortgage are relatively high and virtually impossible to summarise. Taxes and registration fees will in and of themselves can account for up to 0.6% of the amount being secured under the guarantee, and notarial fees will generally account for approximately an additional 0.55% of the amount being secured. It should be noted that it is the amount secured, and not the value of the real estate, upon which such taxes and fees are calculated. Hence, it may be attractive to the creditor to agree to limit the amount secured by the mortgage to a sum lower than the value of the real property in order to reduce registration fees.

In the event of default by the debtor, the mortgagee may cause the mortgaged property to be attached (*saisie immobilière*) and sold at public auction (*vente aux enchères*), with the proceeds of the sale being used to satisfy the amount due. The sale must occur publicly pursuant to the strict rules on *saisie immobilière* provided in the French Civil Procedure Code. Any clause in the mortgage deed which permits the mortgagee to sell the property itself (*clause de voie parée*) or to dispose of the property directly (*clause de pacte commissoire*) is null and void.

In the event that the mortgaged property is transferred by the mortgagor to a third party, the mortgagee continues to benefit from the mortgage (*droit de suite*), so long as certain notices are served on both the mortgagor and the transferee. However, the transferee may choose to 'purge' the mortgage by offering to pay to registered mortgagees the purchase price (or the value of the real estate if acquired without payment of a purchase price). If the creditors accept the offer, they are paid out of the purchase price (even if the total amount of the purchase price is not sufficient to satisfy the full amount of the debt secured by the mortgage). If the creditors do not accept the offer, then they must request that the mortgaged property be put up for auction, and undertake to submit or cause to be submitted at such auction a bid for 10% higher than the purchase price.

The right to a mortgage can be transferred independently from the underlying debt obligation; such a transfer is referred to as '*subrogation à l'hypothèque*' and is noted on both the mortgage deed and the mortgage register. The holders of two different-ranking mortgages can agree to exchange priorities under an agreement known as a '*cession d'antériorité*'. Such exchange can occur even prior to the actual constitution of the lesser-ranking mortgage. The exchange is noted on the mortgage register. If there is an intermediate-ranking mortgage between the two mortgages, the transferee ranks ahead of the intermediary mortgagee only up to the amount of the lesser of the two debts secured.

A registered mortgage can be removed from the register (*radiation*) either pursuant to agreement between the mortgagor and the mortgagee (*mainlevée*) or upon petition to the court by the mortgagor or any other creditor upon proof that the mortgage is no longer justified (eg the maximum permitted duration described above has been exceeded). Removal from the register requires execution of a notarised deed and payment of a recording fee equal to 0.1% of the amount secured. For this reason, and since a mortgage is in any event deemed to be extinguished if the underlying debt is extinguished, mortgagors frequently fail to require removal from the register, and prefer to obtain a simple declaration from the mortgagee to the effect that the debt has been repaid.

Charges over share accounts and fractional ownership interests in French companies

In certain jurisdictions, the pledge of shares or other securities simply require execution of a pledge agreement and delivery of the physical share certificates representing the shares to the pledgee or to an agent bank or depository acting on behalf of the pledgee. The pledge agreement will in such case frequently provide that immediately upon the occurrence of an event of default, the dividend and voting rights in the shares may be exercised by the pledgee, and the shares may be sold to satisfy the debt. Due to various statutory restrictions in France, the practice is different.

Dematerialisation of securities; creation and perfection of share accounts or fractional ownership interests

Since 1981, shares in French companies have not been materialised by physical share certificates. In companies in which ownership interests are represented by negotiable securities (*valeurs mobilières*), such as the *société anonyme*,[20] ownership is evidenced solely by entries on a master share movement register (*registre de mouvement de titres*) and on individual share accounts (*comptes d'actionnaires*) opened in the name of each shareholder; transfers of ownership interests are recorded by changes to the register and debit and credit entries on the share accounts, with new accounts being opened as necessary.[1]

The legal structure of certain forms of closely-held companies, such as the private limited liability company (*société à responsabilité limitée*) is such that ownership interests are not represented by negotiable securities, but rather by fractional ownership interests with limited transferability (*parts sociales*). In these cases, ownership is recorded by statements in the Articles of Association (*statuts*) of the company, with transfers being recorded by amendment to the Articles.

Obviously, it is impossible in either case to deliver physical share certificates in order to create and perfect a pledge of shares. For this reason, legislation was adopted in 1983 which created, in the case of companies issuing shares (or other negotiable securities), a streamlined procedure for the pledge of such securities. Pursuant to those provisions as originally adopted in 1983, such a pledge was created by the simple delivery, by the pledgor to the entity acting as the share registrar of the shares (usually the issuer company itself), of a statement of pledge (*déclaration de gage*). The registrar

20 French commercial companies may be constituted using several different structures. The most popular of these structures are the following :

1. *société en nom collectif* ('SNC'), roughly equivalent to a general partnership;
2. *société en commandite simple* ('SCS'), roughly equivalent to a limited partnership;
3. *société à responsabilité limitée* ('SARL'), a private limited liability company equivalent to a Dutch BV or a German GmbH;
4. *société anonyme* ('SA'), equivalent to a corporation;
5. *société en commandite par actions* ('SCA'), equivalent to a corporation in which certain shareholders have limited liability.;
6. *société par actions simplifiée* ("SAS") a recently-created form of company akin to a 'close corporation'.

Of these kinds of companies, only SA, SCA and SAS may issue negotiable securities (*valeurs mobilières*).

was then obligated to record the pledge on the books of the company by transferring the entry in the register relating to the pledged shares to a special account in the name of the pledgor but which states the existence of the pledge in favour of the pledgee. The registrar then issued a certification of pledge (*certification de gage*) to the pledgee.

The 1983 law was modified substantially by Law n° 96-597 of 2 July 1996 on modernisation of financial activities (which also transposed the EU Investment Services Directive into French law) and supplemented by Decree n° 97-509 of 21 May 1997. These modifications have the effect of broadening the scope of the streamlined procedure originally applicable only to dematerialised negotiable securities to any account in which there are deposited one or several 'financial instruments' (a term which includes not only shares or other securities which can give rise to share capital or voting rights but also other negotiable instruments, shares in collective investment units and all other financial instruments payable at term).

As it is henceforth the account, rather than the financial instruments deposited therein, which is pledged, the composition of the portfolio of financial instruments contained in the account may change from time to time, permitting considerable flexibility. The revised version of the law provides that the pledgee must agree with the account holder as to the conditions under which the holder may dispose of the financial instruments and the sums recorded as pledged. The parties have full discretion to agree as they wish; they may decide to grant the pledgor the right to dispose freely of the financial instruments and sums or for greater or lesser supervision and control by the pledgee.

The account itself may be administered by an authorised intermediary, a central depository (eg Sicovam, the French securities clearing organisation, or any of the international clearing centres) or by the issuer of the financial instruments (eg the issuer of company shares).

Under the text of the 1983 law, as modified, the pledge is perfected as soon as the pledgor has delivered the declaration of pledge to the account administrator (*teneur de compte*). The delivery by the account administrator to the pledgee of a certification of pledge is now optional at the request of the pledgee; however it is still good practice to request such a certification in the case of pledge of share accounts (and, for that matter, to request photocopies of the relevant pages of the register of movements and the individual share accounts) as a condition to closing of any financing transaction.

Although it is sufficient, in order to have a pledge over the shares of a *société anonyme*, for the shareholder/pledgors[2] each to deliver a declaration of pledge to the share registrar of the issuing company, it is preferable to have a short-form French-law share pledge agreement which contains, as annexes, the forms of the statement of pledge and the certification of pledge and contains certain clauses relating to French legal issues.

1 For purposes of this chapter it is assumed that the company in which the shares are to be pledged are held by less than 100 persons. In companies with 100 shareholders or more, share ownership is recorded by a double-entry accounting system. In listed companies, share ownership is recorded by a system maintained in accordance with the rules and regulations of SICOVAM, the French domestic securities clearance system. Publicly -traded companies may also issue bearer shares, which are registered on securities registers maintained by banks or other financial intermediaries.

2 A *société anonyme* is required under French law to have at least seven shareholders, and each member of its Board of Directors is required to hold at least one share.

In the case of a *société à responsabilité limitée* and certain other French companies, the rules are different. Since fractional ownership interests in such companies are not represented by recording on a share movement register or on individual share accounts, pledges of such interests cannot be created by simple declaration nor perfected by recording on a register. For this reason, the pledge of such equity interests is accomplished in the same manner as any other pledge of intangible rights under French law (see 'Charge of intangible property and contractual rights', p 92 below), ie either by service of a written pledge instrument on the company by authorised bailiff (*huissier*) or acceptance of such an instrument by the company by notarised deed (*acte authentique*), in both cases following registration (*enregistrement*) of such written instrument with the tax authorities (Civil Code Art 2075). Of the two alternatives, service by *huissier* is far less costly, since French *notaires* usually work on a scale fee basis. It should be noted that whichever alternative is chosen, the pledge instrument should first be registered with the local tax authorities, as described under 'Registration and Stamp duty' (p 110 below).[3]

Shareholder pre-emptive rights

Once a pledge of share account or equity interests is created and perfected in the manner described above, there may be an additional formality to accomplish if the pledge is to be fully enforceable. The transfer of shares in companies with *parts sociales* (such as *sociétés à responsabilité limitée*) is permitted only following approval of such transfer by a meeting of shareholders; in the event that such approval is not obtained, the shareholders must find another purchaser for the shares. In companies with negotiable securities (such as *sociétés anonymes*), transfer is normally free, but the articles of such companies may contain pre-emption clauses (*clauses d'agrément*) having a similar result by requiring board approval for transfer.[4] In either case, this means that the enforcement of a pledge granted over the shares of such companies upon the occurrence of an event of a default, which would perforce result in the transfer of the shares, would require shareholder approval at the time of realisation. Obviously, as a practical matter it is too risky for lenders to wait until enforcement of a pledge and then seek appropriate approval. For this reason, the French company law (Law no 66-537 of 24 July 1966 (the 'French Company Law') (recently codifed as Arts L. 210-1 ff of the Commercial Code) provides that approval of a pledge agreement by the relevant corporate body is deemed to constitute approval of the transfer of shares in the event of enforcement of the pledge. It is highly preferable to obtain such approval as a condition precedent to the taking of any pledge over the shares or equity interests in such a company.[5]

3 In order to meet the requirement of dispossession, some practitioners recommend also delivering a copy of the SARL's Articles of Association to the pledgee.

4 The Articles of Association of a French company are publicly available through the Registry of Commerce and Companies with jurisdiction over the place in which the *siège social* (corporate seat) is located.

5 In certain cases, the Articles of Association of the company may also grant individual shareholders first refusal rights on the transfer of shares (*clause de préemption*) or even prohibit the transfer of shares altogether. In such circumstances, a resolution by the Board of Directors will not be sufficient to protect the rights of a pledgee to enforce a pledge of shares : it is necessary to modify the Articles of Association to exempt from application of such provisions the enforcement of the pledge.

Dividend and voting rights relating to the pledged shares

During the term of existence of the pledge, the pledgor retains all voting rights with respect to the pledged shares. The practice prevalent in certain jurisdictions of providing by contract that, upon the occurrence of an event of default in the underlying financing documentation, the pledgee may exercise voting rights, has traditionally been considered as not being enforceable under French law, since the effect of such provisions would be assimilated to a *pacte commissoire* (see 'Power of sale or attribution of the secured asset' p 117 below); the sole rights of a pledgee of share accounts or fractional ownership interests to enforcement of the pledge being, as detailed below, deemed to be to sell the pledged asset at public auction and to be satisfied out of the proceeds of such sale, or to petition to a court for judicial self-attribution, but only after an evaluation of the value of the pledged shares by a court-appointed expert.

However, by way of exception to the foregoing rule, the 1983 law as modified and supplemented in 1996 and pursuant to the 1997 decree, specifies that the pledgee may, with respect to negotiable securities in the pledged account, whether issued by French or foreign entities, which are traded on a regulated market (eg a stock exchange), as well as any shares in collective investment undertakings (UCITS) and cash in the pledged account, enforce the pledge eight days (or such other period previously agreed between the parties) following formal notice to the debtor[6] (*mise en demeure*), by any of the following means:

1 full title transfer to the pledgee for amounts in cash;
2 sale on a regulated market; or
3 self-attribution up to the value of the debt (with no requirement to obtain a court order permitting such attribution), on the basis of the most recent quotations[7].

The law as modified and supplemented provides that all 'fruits and proceeds in any currency' are subject to the pledge. When read with other text in the revised version of the provision, the statute now appears to permit the parties to determine whether dividends on negotiable securities deposited in the account will be paid to the pledgor or the pledgee. The effect has been to legitimise contractual provisions by which the parties agree that, upon an event of default in the underlying financial documentation, the pledgee will be entitled to receive dividends directly, even prior to enforcement of the pledge. In practice, however, pledgors generally negotiate the right to retain dividends unless and until the pledge is enforced upon the occurrence of an event of default.

Exchange controls

In the event that the sale or judicial self-attribution of the shares pursuant to enforcement of the pledge gives rise to their transfer to a foreign entity, then French exchange control regulations may be applicable. Under current exchange control regulations, the

6 The *mise en demeure* must also be sent to the pledgor if the pledgor is not the debtor, and to the account administrator (*teneur de compte*) if it is not also the pledgee.

7 Similarly, shares in UCITS may be presented for repurchase to the UCITS or be self-attributed on the basis of the most recent valuation.

acquisition of shares in an existing French company (as opposed to the creation of a new company) may require prior government approval; however, these provisions have been steadily relaxed and under current regulations such approval will be required only where the acquisition would violate public policy, public health or public security. Acquisition by entities controlled by EU nationals are, in theory, exempt from such requirement (in practice, the authorities will require proof of EU ownership, which amounts to a pre-clearing process).[8]

Judicial pledge

Under Law no 91-650 of 9 July 1991, it is also possible for a creditor able to prove the existence of a debt founded in principle against a debtor whose situation is compromised, to petition the courts for a judicial pledge (*nantissement judiciaire*) of shares owned by the debtor.

Charges over goods – pledge of stock-in-trade (inventory)

Unless covered by one of the exceptions described in the following sections, charges over goods are difficult propositions under French law, because the relevant provisions of the Civil Code and the Commercial Code[9] provide that in order to create and perfect an effective charge over tangible personal property, it is necessary for the pledgor to be physically dispossessed of the assets in question and for control over such assets to be exercised either by the beneficiary of the pledge or by a third party (*tiers convenu*) named by mutual agreement of the pledgor and pledgee (a process known as *entiercement*). Failure to comply with this formality renders the pledge ineffective both as between the parties and vis-à-vis third parties; indeed, even if the pledgor is properly dispossessed of the asset at the commencement of the pledge, a return of the asset to the pledgor prior to the reimbursement of the underlying debt will result in cancellation of the pledge. Moreover, unlike the situation in several other jurisdictions, there is no public register at which pledges over tangible personal property (other than those assets which are pledged pursuant to one of the exceptions described in the following sections) are recorded; the physical delivery of the pledged asset is both necessary and sufficient for the perfection of the pledge. Indeed, where the pledge of tangible assets secures a 'commercial' debt as opposed to a 'civil' debt (which will be the case in most cross-border financing transactions), it is not even necessary for the agreement to create the pledge to be in writing.

Due to the exceptions to the foregoing rule existing for pledges of going concerns and certain purchase money security interests (see below), the practical consequences in the context of cross-border secured financial transactions are felt most particularly in the case of pledges of stock-in-trade (inventory), due to the manufacturer's

8 Regulations applicable to particular industries (eg telecommunications) in which administrative authorisation is required to conduct regulated activities may also result in a requirement of government authorisation for transfer of shares, including upon enforcement of a pledge over the shares.

9 See Civil Code Art 2076; Commercial Code, Art L. 521-2.

understandable desire to retain control over the flow of its finished products.[10] However, there do exist companies specialised in acting as *tiers convenu* and in the construction and supervision of 'on-site' third-party controlled inventory pledge warehouses in such capacity. A portion of the pledgor's plant is closed off by fencing erected by the specialised institution, and all inventory is moved into this closed-off area by the pledgor as completed. Access to the area is supervised by the specialised company, which permits inventory to be moved out of the closed area only either upon instructions signed by both the pledgor and the pledgee or upon satisfying itself that the inventory remaining in the closed area has an aggregate value in excess of the amount secured by the pledge.

During the existence of the pledge, the pledgee enjoys the right to retain the pledged asset as long as the debtor has not paid the interest, principal and costs relating to the secured debt (*droit de rétention*). In the event that the pledged asset is stolen or the pledgee otherwise involuntarily loses the possession thereof, the pledgee has a cause of action for recovery of the asset (*droit de revendication*), provided that such action must be brought within three years of the theft or loss and that the current possessor of the asset who has purchased such asset at a fair or in a market, at public sale or from a merchant, is entitled to reimbursement of the price paid for the purchase of the asset.

The rights of enforcement of a pledgee of tangible goods are limited to sale of the pledged goods at public auction and satisfaction out of the proceeds of such sale, or to petition to a court for judicial self-attribution, but only after an evaluation of the value of the pledged goods by a court-appointed expert; contractual clauses which permit the pledgee to dispose of the asset at private sale or to appropriate the asset for the pledgee's own use are null and void. In the event that there exist several pledges on the same asset (which, as a practical matter, could occur in the event that the asset is delivered physically to a *tiers convenu* rather than to the pledgee), then the order of the creation of the pledges determines the order of priority. This is why, even though a written pledge instrument is not required to create a pledge over tangible goods where the pledge is 'commercial' rather than 'civil', it is good practice to execute a pledge agreement and to submit it for voluntary date stamping in accordance with the procedures described in under 'Registration and stamp duty' (p 110 below).

Charge over going business

The French Law of 17 March 1909 (the 'FDC Law' (recently codifed as Arts L. 141-5 ff of the Commercial Code)) provides a statutory framework under French law for the pledge of the 'going business' (*fonds de commerce*) of a French company without the pledgor being required to be physically dispossessed of the pledged assets and in a manner which results in public registration of the pledge.

A *fonds de commerce* is the bundle of assets, other than real estate, which constitute the means by which a company exercises its business to satisfy its clientele, including material and equipment, inventory, lessee's rights under a lease, patents, trademarks

10 Specific legislation relating to warrants permits a debtor having deposited goods in a warehouse to undertake to pay a specific sum and to pledge the warehoused goods as security for payment of the debt. Such warrants can be endorsed to third parties. Certain categories of goods may also be pledged by warrant when the goods are retained by the owner, but in practice this system is very rarely used except in the case of pledge of agricultural products.

and other intellectual property rights, licences, and other tangible and intangible rights including goodwill. It is important to note that the core concept of a *fonds de commerce* is the existence of clientele and the operation of a business to serve such clientele; for this reason it is sometimes difficult to evidence the existence of a *fonds de commerce* within a newly incorporated company, which means that a pledge would not then be available. This has practical consequences where an ad hoc company is created for the purposes of structuring a transaction: in such case, unless such newly-created company is the transferee of an existing business, it will not be possible to obtain a pledge of a *fonds de commerce* at the outset of the transaction.

A *fonds de commerce* has a legal existence under French law, and can be sold, leased and pledged as a unit. A pledge of a *fonds de commerce* may cover all or some of the following elements thereof: the commercial name and any logos, the right to be a lessee under a lease (but not the leased asset itself), goodwill and client lists, commercial furniture and equipment used in the exploitation of the business, licences, trademarks, patents, industrial designs and other intellectual property, and any rights to occupy land (but not the land or other real estate itself).

Stock-in-trade or inventory (*marchandises*), although encompassed in the concept of a *fonds de commerce*, cannot be pledged within the framework of a *fonds de commerce* and therefore can be pledged only pursuant to the procedures described under 'Charges of goods – pledge of stock-in-trade' (p 86 above). Other assets which do not form part of a *fonds de commerce* and which are therefore not included in a pledge of a going business include real estate (which can be mortgaged as described under 'Charges over land: real estate mortgages' p 79 above), book debt or accounts receivable (which can be assigned or pledged as described under 'Security assignment or pledge of book debt' p 93 below), and most contractual rights (which can be pledged as described under 'Charge over intangible property and contractual rights' p 92 below). In the event that the written pledge instrument does not contain an enumeration of the components of the *fonds de commerce* to be pledged, then the following elements are deemed to be covered: commercial name and logos, leasehold rights, goodwill and client lists.

Unlike a pledge of inventory, a pledge of a *fonds de commerce* does not require the pledgor to be physically dispossessed of the pledged assets, perfection being accomplished by public filing of a written pledge agreement. In order to obtain a pledge of the going business of a French company, it is necessary first to execute a written agreement to such effect. That agreement must then be registered and date stamped by the local tax authorities as described under 'Registration and stamp duty' p 110 below and thereafter recorded with the commercial court having jurisdiction over the place in which the business is carried out (also at nominal cost), and the commercial courts of any branches in which the business is also carried out if the intention is to cover such branches in the pledge and this is made clear in the pledge agreement.[11] Such recording must occur no later than 15 days following execution of the pledge agreement.

11 Unlike the UK, France does not have a nationwide Companies House. Filings are made with the local Registry of Commerce and Companies for the district in which the *fonds de commerce* is exploited. Hence, if a company has several branches in different administrative districts and the intention is that the pledge cover such branches, it is necessary to make a filing in each such district.

In addition, where intellectual property such as trade marks and trade names are included in the going business, an additional filing must be effected with the French National Institute of Industrial Property (*Institut national de la propriété industrielle*) no later than 15 days following the filing with the Registry of Commerce and Companies. Notifications to the company's insurers are also recommended if (as is usually the practice) the pledgee is to have priority over proceeds of any insurance payments made in the event that the *fonds de commerce* is damaged. The registration of a pledge of a *fonds de commerce* is valid for ten years and then expires if not renewed prior to the end of such term.

It should be noted that it is necessary to set forth the elements being pledged with some precision and therefore it is particularly important to put one's French counsel in direct contact with the management of the pledgor company or its own counsel well in advance of the date by which the pledge must be taken.

While the pledge agreement can provide, in respect of certain components of the *fonds de commerce*, that the pledge created thereunder extends to such elements as they are replaced, modified or improved over time, this is not generally the case, and additions to the going business (eg new equipment, new leases and new patents or trademarks) are not covered. Thus, despite a certain surface resemblance, the pledge of a *fonds de commerce* should not be considered as a functional equivalent of a floating charge. As mentioned above, French law does not generally recognise the concept of a floating charge, and a pledge instrument which purports to create one will not be enforced by a French court. On a practical level, the agreement can provide that the pledgor promises to create additional pledges following the acquisition of additional components of its *fonds de commerce*, as well as upon creating or acquiring new *fonds de commerce* (eg upon commencing a new line of business or opening branch offices or factories). However, a new pledge agreement (or supplement to the original pledge agreement) would be required at the time of creation of each subsequent pledge. It should also be noted that a pledge of a *fonds de commerce* is valid for ten years and must be renewed prior to the expiration of such period in order to retain its effect. If the loan facility being secured by the pledge has a maturity greater than that time it will be necessary to include covenants in the pledge agreement to the effect that renewals are the responsibility of the pledgor.

Pledges of a *fonds de commerce* are a matter of public record and lists of all existing pledges over a specific *fonds de commerce* can be ordered from the relevant Registry of Commerce and Companies by mail or can be viewed (and 'hard' copies ordered) via any of a number of computer network databases accessible via the French national 'Minitel' network or on the Internet. Rank of pledges is determined by order of filing: two pledges filed the same day will have equal priority. However, the existence of publicly-filed pledges having priority over later pledges does not automatically mean that such prior-ranking pledges actually continue to exist. Due to a quirk in the FDC law, although the filing of a pledge over a *fonds de commerce* requires only the submission of a private agreement, the extinguishing (*radiation*) of such a pledge on the public register is a costly matter, requiring submission to the Registry of Commerce and Companies of a notarised deed (*acte authentique*). On the other hand, if the underlying debt secured by a pledge is discharged, then the pledge is also automatically discharged as a matter of law, even if the debtor does not proceed to the formality of *radiation*.

For this reason, debtors often deliberately omit to seek *radiation* of prior pledges, even if the debt secured thereby has been discharged for some time, due to the costs of *radiation* (since in any event the filing will, as explained above, expire ten years from the date of filing). An initial examination of the public record may therefore indicate the existence of several pledges of the *fonds de commerce* having priority over the pledge to be created, some or all of which represent debt reimbursed by the pledgor. In such a case, written confirmation should be sought from the beneficiaries of the previous pledges stating that the debt secured thereby has in fact been repaid.

In the event of default by the debtor, the pledgee of a *fonds de commerce* may cause the going business to be attached and sold at public auction (*vente forcée*), with the proceeds of the sale being used to satisfy the amount due; unlike the case of the pledgee of tangible assets (or of the beneficiary of a purchase money security interest, as described in the following section), the pledgee may not apply to the court for an order of judicial self-attribution. As usual, any clause in the pledge agreement which permits the pledgee to sell the property itself or to dispose of the property directly is null and void.

As in the case of a real estate mortgage, a registered pledgee of a *fonds de commerce* enjoys a '*droit de suite*' which preserves the benefit of the pledge if the going business is sold to a third party; however, also as in the case of a mortgage, the purchaser may 'purge' the pledge by notifying the pledgee of the purchase and offering to pay the pledgee out of the proceeds of sale. If the pledgee does not accept the offer of 'purge', it has 15 days in which to request that the going business be sold at auction, by undertaking to offer to submit a bid of at least one-tenth higher than the planned purchase price (excluding equipment and merchandise).

Sale of a *fonds de commerce* generally is subject to a strict procedure pursuant to which the fact of the sale must be rendered public and all creditors of the seller (including both pledgees of the same *fonds de commerce* and unsecured creditors) are entitled to challenge the sale and to require the *fonds de commerce* to be sold at public auction by offering to bid at a price equal to at least one-sixth higher than the original purchase price; however, failure of a pledgee to challenge the sale does not deprive it of its *droit de suite*. In addition, the owner of the *fonds de commerce* is required to inform the pledgee of any proposed move of the business or of any pledged branch at least fifteen days prior to the proposed move. Failure so to notify results in the immediate acceleration of the debt secured by the pledge. Within 15 days of the notification or the date on which it became aware of the move, the pledgee must cause the change of location of the *fonds de commerce* to be noted on the filing with the Registry of Commerce and Companies (or, if the business has been moved to a location within the jurisdiction of another Registry of Commerce and Companies, to cause a new filing to occur with such other Registry). Failing such filing, the pledge may be cancelled by court order at the request of a third party who can show that he has been misled due to such failure. The pledgee may not challenge the move itself, but can petition the court for an order declaring the immediate acceleration of the debt secured by the pledge if the effect of the move is to depreciate the value of the business.

Purchase money security interest over material and equipment

Under a separate Law of 18 January 1951 (the '1951 Law' (recently codifed as Arts L. 525-1 ff of the Commercial Code)), a specific security interest can be granted over material and equipment (*outillage et matériel d'équipement*) (including material and equipment which are part of the *fonds de commerce* of a business) to secure the purchase price of such equipment or loans made or guarantees given to secure loans made to finance such purchase price.[12] Such purchase money security interest (hereinafter a 'PMSI') has the advantage of giving the pledgee a preferred ranking if there are two secured creditors having equal rank, including ranking over pledges of the *fonds de commerce* which includes such material and equipment.[13]

The general rules applicable to a PMSI under the 1951 Law are very similar to those prevailing under the FDC law for the pledge of a going business, the 1951 law even referring specifically in several instances to thc FDC law. However, certain procedures and consequences of a PMSI are different from those relating to a pledge of a *fonds de commerce*. The pledge must be contained in the sale or loan instrument itself rather than in a separate document, and the instrument in question must contain a detailed description of the material or equipment in order to distinguish it from similar assets belonging to the pledgor. The pledge must be concluded no later than two months following the delivery of the material or equipment on the site where it is to be used, and must be registered and date-stamped with the local tax authorities[14] and then registered with the Registry of Commerce and Companies no later than 15 days following such execution. In addition, the pledgee is entitled to require the pledged assets to bear a plaque stating the date, place and registration number of the pledge. In the event of sale of the pledged asset, the pledgee will enjoy a *droit de suite* only if such plaque has been affixed to the asset.

Unlike the complicated procedure for challenging the sale of a going business provided for in the FDC Law, the 1951 Law provides simply that for so long as all of the sums secured under the PMSI have not been paid or reimbursed, the pledgee wishing to sell all or part of the pledged assets must request the prior approval of the pledgee and, if such approval is not forthcoming, a special petition must be filed by the pledgor with the emergency motions judge (*juge des référés*). If the pledged asset is sold prior to the end of the term of the pledge, the rights of the pledgee will be automatically transferred so long as the pledged assets bear the plaque described in the previous paragraph.

A PMSI over material and equipment remains in force in the event that the pledged asset becomes a fixture. In the event of enforcement of the pledge, the PMSI will have priority over all other secured creditors, including over a pledgee of a pledge of the *fonds de commerce* of which the material and equipment is a part or a mortgagee of the real estate in which the pledged asset is located, even if such pledges or mortgages have been concluded prior to the PMSI, provided that in such case the pledgee has notified the existence thereof to the other secured creditors and furnished them with a copy of the instrument pursuant to which the PMSI was created, within two months from the date of such creation. Even if such notice has not been served, the PMSI will have preference over any other security interest normally having equal rank (eg a pledge

12 Under a separate Law of 30 September 1953, a purchase money security interest can be created to secure the purchase price of an automobile. Security over aircraft and ships are subject to specific rules described below.

13 In order for the beneficiary of a PMSI to enjoy priority over a pledgee of the *fonds de commerce* recorded prior to the date of recording of the PMSI, the PMSI beneficiary must notify the existence of the PMSI to the pledgee of the *fonds de commerce* within two months of the conclusion of the PMSI.

14 Registration with the tax authorities is not required if the instrument is signed before a French notary.

of *fonds de commerce* filed the same day), and over most liens created by law. A PMSI is valid for a period of five years from the date of registration, and guarantees principal and two years' interest. The PMSI can be renewed twice.

Unlike the case of the pledge of a going business, in the event of default by the debtor, the pledgee under a PMSI may both cause the going business to be attached and sold at public auction, with the proceeds of the sale being used to satisfy the amount due, or apply to the court for an order of judicial self-attribution. Interestingly, the latter possibility is not contemplated expressly in the text of the 1951 Law but has been determined by a plenary decision of the *Cour de Cassation*.

Charge over intangible property (*meubles incorporels*) and contractual rights (*créances mobilières*)

Under French law, the pledge of intangible property (*meubles incorporels*), including rights under contract (*créances mobilières*) is considered to be akin to the pledge of tangible goods, and therefore is subject generally to the rules described under 'Charges of goods – pledge of stock-in-trade (p 86 above) with certain exceptions as described below.

As in the case of tangible goods, a pledge over intangible rights theoretically requires that the pledgor be physically 'dispossessed' of the pledged asset. Under the Civil Code Art 2075, this is accomplished by registration of the pledge instrument with the local tax authorities at nominal cost, followed either by the official serving of such instrument on the underlying contractual debtor by authorised bailiff (*huissier de justice*) or the acceptance of the pledge by the underlying debtor in a notarised deed (*acte authentique*). As the fees of *huissiers* are generally lower than those of notaries, service by *huissier* is the more frequently-chosen approach.[15] Due to language found in a number of early court decisions, some practitioners also require an original signed copy of the contract containing the rights to be pledged to be physically delivered to the pledgee, but this practice is not universally followed.

In the view of the French courts, if the pledge is not served on the underlying debtor, then the pledge is not valid, even as between the pledgor and the pledgee. However, there appears to be no rule requiring such service to occur within a specified time period following the signature of the pledge instrument. For this reason, a pledge instrument which has not been properly served has been construed to constitute a promise to pledge, which can be perfected subsequently by proper service. Naturally, in practice it is prudent to effect service as soon as possible in order to avoid problems of priority.

Enforcement rights of a pledgee of intangible property are theoretically identical to those of a pledgee of tangible goods. In practice, where the property pledged consists solely of a debt to pay a sum of money, it is generally felt that it is permitted to provide that the pledgee may receive directly the payment of such sum and use such amounts to reduce the amount of the debt owed to it (or, if the sum is due and paid prior to the time that the secured debt is due, to retain the proceeds as a *gage-espèces* (see under

15 Due to the specific wording of the Commercial Code, Art L. 521-1, there is an argument that, where the pledge of intangible rights is commercial rather than civil, the pledge instrument is not required to be registered with the tax authorities prior to being served. In practice, the parties typically have the document registered prior to service.

'Cash collateral charge' p 96 below) for the debt). However, it should be noted that the debtor of the underlying obligation is entitled to raise against the pledgee any defences to payment which is had against the pledgor.

Article 2075 provides a simple means for creating and perfecting a pledge over contractual rights. However, the requirement of service of the pledge instrument on the underlying debtor renders the technique inefficient where the pledgor does not for commercial reasons wish the underlying debtor to be aware of the pledge, or where there are a great number of underlying contracts all of which are to be pledged. For this reason, Art 2075 is not well-suited to the creation of charges over book debt (accounts receivable). Such charges are generally created pursuant to the specific legislation described in the following section.

It should be noted that, except pursuant to the specific procedures described in the following section, the concept of a 'security assignment' of contractual rights is not well understood in France. The Civil Code Art 1690 provides a mechanism for the creation and perfection of outright assignment of intangible rights similar to that provided under Art 2075 for pledges (ie service of the underlying contract by *huissier* or acceptation in an *acte authentique*, no prior registration with the tax authorities being required), but, despite several early decisions of the French courts which appear to uphold the use of such a procedure for a security assignment (*cession à titre de garantie*), more recent events have cast doubt on the effectiveness of this technique. There is a view held by some parties that the effect of a genuine security assignment is similar to that of a *pacte commissoire*, since it leaves the secured party/assignee with full rights over the pledged asset. In practice, it has been difficult to convince French bankruptcy administrators that there is a genuine difference between a security assignment and an outright assignment. For the foregoing reasons, it is generally advisable to avoid preparing a French-law document which purports to create a security assignment of contractual rights or other intangible rights outside of the specific statutory framework described in the following section.[16]

Security assignment or pledge of book debt (accounts receivable)

French Law no 81-1 of 2 January, 1981, as modified (usually known as the '*Loi Dailly*' from the name of the senator who proposed its adoption) provides a statutory framework for either the assignment by way of security or the pledge of book debt/accounts receivable in favour of a credit institution in order to secure credit granted by such credit institution to the assignee/pledgee. Until passage of the *Loi Dailly*, assignments or pledges of book debt was a cumbersome process, since, as described in the previous section, each individual assignment or pledge required service of notice thereof on the underlying debtor by authorised process server (*huissier*) or acceptation in a notarised deed. Under the *Loi Dailly*, perfection of the assignment or the pledge is accomplished by the simple delivery to the credit institution of a list of the accounts being assigned or pledged (*bordereau*).

16 It is even clearer that no attempt should be made to structure a security assignment of tangible moveable assets under French law. The French courts have expressly refused to recognise a security assignment created under foreign law over an asset physically located in France.

Liquid and current accounts may be so assigned or pledged, as may accounts resulting from an agreement already executed or to be executed, but the amount and the term of which are not yet determined, provided in all such cases that the debt is owed to the assignor or pledgor by legal entities or by individuals in the exercise of a professional activity.

The *bordereau* itself must, by law, contain, in addition to the name and address of the credit institution and a specific reference to the *Loi Dailly*, an enumeration or individualisation of the receivables being assigned or pledged or information susceptible of effecting such designation or individualisation, for example by indication of the underlying account debtor, the place of payment, the amount of the account and their term. Thus, a simple statement to the effect that the security assignment or pledge covered 'all accounts now and future owing to the assignor (or pledgor) by any customer during the term of this credit agreement' would not be permitted. In practice, in order to avoid this problem, the parties generally execute a 'master agreement' (*convention cadre*) requiring the French assignor or pledgor to provide *bordereaux* to the credit institution with an agreed-upon frequency (for example, on a monthly basis) so as to cover all future accounts receivable which are booked during the life of the credit to be secured thereby. As receivables mature and are paid by the underlying debtor, they are replaced with new receivables which are booked and recorded on the next *bordereau* delivered. Note that the use of *bordereaux* which are superseded on a frequent basis by new *bordereaux* provides the financing bank with a quasi-floating charge, one of the rare instances where this is feasible under French law.

The *Loi Dailly* is one of the few circumstances under French law where an assignment of rights by way of security (*cession à titre de garantie*) has received statutory recognition. An amendment made to the basic text of the law in 1984 specifies that even 'when made by way of security', an assignment of book debt made pursuant to the law passes actual title to the account of the assignee. For this reason, most security granted pursuant to the *Loi Dailly* has taken the form of security assignments rather than pledges. This provides the credit institution with a significant advantage in the event of the bankruptcy of the assignor, since the receivables listed in any *bordereau* executed prior to the date of the bankruptcy filing will be the property of the credit institution.[17]

Assignments or pledges effected pursuant to the *Loi Dailly* are effective as against third parties (including the underlying account debtor) once the *bordereau* is dated by the recipient credit institution[18], even if the fact of assignment or pledge is not notified to the underlying debtor (the master agreement usually provides that during this time, the assignor/pledgor will continue to collect the receivables, but as the agent for the credit institution). The assignor/pledgor is thereafter estopped from modifying the nature or the scope of the underlying account without the permission of the credit institution.

However, the credit institution may also, at any time (eg if and when it begins to feel uncomfortable about its own customer), notify the underlying account debtor that all future payments in respect of the account must be made directly to the credit institution.

17 Transfer of book debt under the *Loi Dailly* also automatically transfers any security granted in respect of such debt, unless the agreement specifies to the contrary. Also unless the agreement specifies otherwise, the transferor guarantees the payment of the book debt transferred.

18 Although the *bordereau* is signed by the assignor, it is dated by the assignee.

Thereafter, any payments made by the account debtor to the bank customer are made at the customer's risk. Moreover, the credit institution may obtain from the account debtor a written undertaking to pay only the credit institution. If the underlying debtor executes such an undertaking, it may not oppose to the credit institution any defences to payment which it had against the bank's customer unless the credit institution, in acquiring the book debt, knowingly acts to the detriment of the debtor. Frequently, the master agreement will provide that notification by the credit institution to the underlying debtor and/or the solicitation of such an undertaking from the underlying account debtor may occur only upon the occurrence of an event of default relating to the assignor/pledgor under the credit secured by the *Dailly* assignment/pledge; however, where it is felt that the credit of the borrower is weak, banks have required that these steps be available to the bank at any time.

Assignments or pledges under the *Loi Dailly* are a very powerful security tool. Because they do not have to be notified to the underlying account debtor by *huissier* or accepted in a notarised deed in order to be created and perfected, they are less expensive than the forms of assignment and pledge of contractual rights provided for in the Civil Code, and are also more acceptable to the assignor/pledgor who is wary of its own customers becoming aware that their accounts are being assigned or pledged to a bank. However, in the context of international lending, there are two unresolved questions of law with respect to use of the *Loi Dailly*.

First, there is some doubt as to whether a *Loi Dailly* assignment or pledge would be valid in favour of a bank other than one which is registered in France as a licenced credit institution or enjoying 'passport rights' under the EU Second Banking Directive. The literal text of the *Loi Dailly* states that such assignments or pledges can be granted in favour of a 'credit institution' (*établissement de crédit*) which has extended credit to the assignor/pledgor. The term 'credit institution' is identical to the term used under the French banking law (Law no 84-46 of 24 January 1984) to refer to a bank or financial institution licensed by the French banking authorities to effect credit operations in France. There is therefore an argument that an assignment under the *Loi Dailly* is effective only when the accounts receivable are assigned to a French bank (or the subsidiary or branch of a foreign bank licensed by the French banking authorities to operate in France or an EU bank enjoying 'passport rights' to lend into France) which has granted the credit. There is some doctrinal authority in France to the effect that such an assignment should be valid in favour of any banking institution that is licensed under the laws of its home country, but the question has not yet been formally raised in any court decision, and there is some intimation that the Bank of France does not share this view.

A second issue arises from the fact that the literal text of the *Loi Dailly* refers to the assignment or pledge being possible in order to secure amounts due under 'credit which the credit establishment *grants to*...[the assignor/pledgor]'. The most restrictive reading of this provision would permit a *Loi Dailly* assignment or pledge to secure only amounts actually lent to the assignor or pledgor, and not amounts which are lent to a different entity and only guaranteed by the assignor/pledgor. In other words, there is some doubt as to whether a *Loi Dailly* assignment or pledge is the proper vehicle for providing security for a guarantee of third-party debt as opposed to an outright loan. For this reason, French lawyers are far more comfortable with the use of a *Loi Dailly* assignment or pledge when the assignor/pledgor is also a permitted borrower under the main credit facility. The Dailly master agreement can then provide that the amounts secured are both those directly drawn down by the assignor/pledgor and those due by it under the guarantee. A severability clause then provides that the assignment or pledge remains valid for amounts due directly by the assignor/pledgor in the event that it should be found to be invalid with respect to the guaranteed amounts.

Charges over cash and bank accounts

French law recognises two forms of charges over cash, the cash collateral charge and the charge over account balance.

Cash collateral charge (gage espèces)

In the cash collateral charge (*gage espèces*), a specific sum of cash is remitted by the pledgor to the pledgee, or more frequently, placed on account with a bank which is either itself the pledgee or acting as the agent of the pledgee, as security for the debt. Such a pledge is assimilated under French law to a pledge of tangible personal property (see under 'Charges of goods – pledge of stock-in-trade' p 86 above). By analogy to such pledges, a written instrument is required solely if the pledge is civil rather than commercial (although it is good practice to execute such an instrument in any event to specify the rights and responsibilities of the parties). The physical dispossession of the pledged asset required for perfection of a pledge of tangible goods is deemed accomplished by the remittance of the cash or the payment of the pledged sums into the account maintained by the pledgee or the bank acting as its agent; service of the pledge instrument by *huissier* is not required. In order to maintain such dispossession, the pledgor must have no rights to withdraw sums from the account or otherwise control the flow of funds into or out of the account. Some practitioners extend this to a prohibition on the payment of interest to the pledgor on the pledged sums, but this is not universally recognised[19].

The French *Cour de Cassation* has ruled that, since by definition there can be no dispute as to the value of cash and since money is perfectly fungible, there is no requirement upon enforcement of a *gage espèces* for the pledgee to sell the pledged asset at auction or seek judicial attribution of the asset; the pledgee is therefore entitled to retain the cash pledged and satisfy the secured debt out of such cash; the prohibition against *pactes commissoires* (ie the self-appropriation of the pledged asset rather than sale at auction) apparently therefore does not apply to *gages-espèces*. The leading French learned commentary has discerned in this ruling the commencement of a recognition in France of the concept of a fiduciary assignment (*cession fiduciaire*), since the effect is identical to that of an assignment of the cash to the pledgee coupled with an obligation to return the cash to the pledgor if the secured debt is entirely repaid.

19 In practice any amounts paid to the pledgor are typically stated to constitute an indemnity for immobilisation (*indemnité d'immobilisation*) of the pledged funds rather than interest.

*Charge over bank account (*nantissement de solde de compte*)*

In the charge over account balance (*nantissement de solde de compte*), a charge is created over the balance of a bank account rather than over a specific sum of cash deposited in the account and, in the event of enforcement, only such funds as are actually standing to the credit of the account at the time of enforcement are available to satisfy the creditor. Such a pledge is assimilated under French law to a pledge of intangible property (see 'Charge over intangible property and contractual rights' p 92 above). For this reason, a written instrument of pledge is always required and perfection is accomplished by service of such instrument by *huissier* upon the underlying debtor (ie the bank at which the account in question is maintained) or acceptance of the assignment in a notarised deed. However, as in the case of the *gage espèces*, it is considered by certain authors of *doctrine* – but this position is by no means unanimous – that, since the subject of the security is a right to obtain cash, there is no requirement upon enforcement for the pledgee to sell the pledged account or seek judicial attribution the pledgee being entitled to the cash on balance in the account at the time of enforcement.

Charges over aircraft

Although aircraft are considered to constitute personal property (*biens meubles*) for the purposes of the Civil Code, a separate body of laws, rules and regulations related to aircraft (including title to and security over aircraft), airports, air transport and flight personnel are grouped in the French Civil Aviation Code (*Code de l'Aviation Civile*) (the 'CAC'), and the relevant form of security is the aircraft mortgage, modelled in certain respects more closely to the real estate mortgage than to the pledge of personal property.[20]

France maintains a centralised nationwide aircraft register open to the public, under the direction of the French Civil Aviation Authority (*Direction Générale de l'Aviation Civile* or 'DGAC') and located in Paris. Information concerning aircraft registered on the national register is available for a nominal fee upon request in person at the offices of the DGAC and are also displayed on a database which may be consulted via the nationwide 'Minitel' network. Any aircraft duly registered in the French register is considered to have French nationality; any aircraft previously registered outside of France must be deregistered before being admitted to the French register, and any aircraft registered in France loses French nationality if registered abroad.

Mortgages over aircraft will generally not be recognised in France unless the aircraft over which such a mortgage is granted is also registered on the French aircraft register. However, France is a signatory to the Geneva Convention on the International Registration of Rights on Aircraft and will therefore recognise and give effect to mortgages and other security granted over aircraft in other jurisdictions which are also parties to the Geneva Convention.

20 The CAC is divided into three sections, containing, respectively, provisions enacted by law, provisions adopted by Decrees of the *Conseil d'Etat*, and provisions adopted by other decrees or regulations. Articles adopted by law are preceded with the letter 'L', those adopted by the *Conseil d'Etat* are preceded with an 'R,' and those adopted by other decrees are preceded with a 'D'.

In order for an aircraft to be registered in France, it is generally necessary for the owner of the aircraft to possess the nationality of a member state of the European Union (the 'EU') or the European Economic Area (the 'EEA'). In the case of legal entities, the entity must have been constituted in conformity with a member state of the EU or the EEA and have its registered office (*siège social*) or its principal establishment in the territory of France, another EU member state or an EEA member state.

However, the CAC provides specifically that application may be made to the proper authorities for a derogation permitting the registration of aircraft the owners of which do not satisfy the foregoing requirement. The CAC provides no guidance as to the reasons which will justify the granting of such an exoneration, but past experience shows that non-EU owned aircraft leased to a French operator will usually qualify.

Registration in the aircraft register is proof of title. The CAC specifies that aircraft constitute movable property for purposes of the Civil Code; however, transfer of property rights must be effected in writing and is binding upon third parties only if so noted in the aircraft register. Indeed, pursuant to the CAC, the following operations relating to the aircraft *must* be inscribed on the register:

1 original registration;
2 change in ownership;
3 creation of a mortgage;
4 lease;
5 attachment;
6 modification to characteristics of the aircraft;
7 discharge of lease, mortgage or attachment;
8 deregistration.

Mortgages on aircraft must be in writing and, to be binding upon third parties, must be registered in the aircraft register. The CAC provides specifically that mortgages on aircraft may be granted only by agreement between the parties; thus, unlike real estate mortgages (see 'Charges over land: real estate mortgages' p 79 above), aircraft mortgages may not be created by operation of law or upon court order. Only the registered owner of the aircraft may create a mortgage.

So long as they are also owned by the owner of the aircraft, an aircraft mortgage automatically covers the hull, engines, propellers, on-board equipment and any other equipment intended to be used for service of the aircraft, whether installed or temporarily separated from the body of the aircraft. Provision is made for the granting of a single mortgage over all or part of an entire fleet owned by the same owner, so long as the different portions of the fleet are separately stated in the instrument. Spare parts may also be covered by the mortgage if individually itemised; however, such spare parts must be stored in a place where notice of the mortgage (including a statement of the register in which the mortgage is inscribed) is displayed, and an inventory of such spare parts must be attached to the instrument as registered. Any such spare parts which are used on the aircraft must be replaced by other parts, and the creditor must be notified of such use.

The mortgage agreement must mention the elements over which the mortgage is granted, and may be made out 'to order'; in such case, endorsement of the agreement automatically results in transfer of the mortgagee's rights. The CAC provides that, where the deed of sale for an aircraft recites that all or part of the purchase price remains due to the seller, this will (unless the deed specifies otherwise) automatically result in the creation of a mortgage for the amount so due, provided that the seller requests inscription of such mortgage in the register.

Mortgages may be granted over aircraft under construction, but must be declared to the DGAC, such declaration indicating the main characteristics of the aircraft under construction.

In the event of loss of an aircraft, the mortgagee is automatically subrogated to the rights of the insured party up to the amount of the debt mortgaged, unless stipulated otherwise. Prior to effecting any payment, the insurer must request a statement of any mortgages on the aircraft, and any payment made in disregard of the rights of the creditors appearing on such statement will not liberate the insurer from its obligation to pay.

The priority of a mortgage is determined by the date of registration. In the event that two mortgages are registered on the same day but at different times, they are considered as having identical priority. A validly registered mortgage is considered valid for ten years, and may be renewed prior to expiration. The mortgage covers principal and three years' interest in addition to the year of registration.

Registration of a mortgage will be cancelled only upon production of a document setting forth the agreement of the parties to such effect, or a judgment incapable of appeal; unlike the case of real estate mortgages, there appears to be no requirement that the cancellation agreement be notarised. Except in the case of compulsory sale of the aircraft (see below), an aircraft cannot be deregistered from the registry until all mortgages have been discharged; however, where the aircraft is to remain on the French register in the name of the purchaser, title to the aircraft may be transferred subject to any registered mortgage.

Duly registered mortgages have priority over all other liens created by operation of law, except those created for the following reasons:

1 legal costs incurred for the sale of the aircraft and the allocation of the purchase price thereof in the common interest of the creditors;
2 amounts due for rescue or salvage operations; and
3 amounts expended for indispensable conservation measures.

Such liens are privileged in the order set forth above (except that, as among themselves, the second and third privileges are preferred in inverse order of the date of the event giving rise thereto), and expire three months after the act in respect of which they arose occurs, unless they are themselves registered. Any other statutory privileges are ranked after any mortgages which have been duly registered prior to the act in respect of which such privileges occur.

As in the case of a real estate mortgage, aircraft mortgagees enjoy a *droit de suite* preserving the mortgage in the event of sale of the aircraft to a third party. In the case of forced sale of an aircraft, the purchaser may 'purge' the mortgage by notifying the mortgagee of the purchase and offering to pay the mortgagee out of the proceeds of sale. If the pledgee does not accept the offer of 'purge', it has five days (or longer depending on the location of the mortgagee) in which to request that the mortgaged aircraft be sold at auction, by undertaking to offer to submit a bid of at least one-tenth higher than the planned purchase price.

In the event of default, the mortgagee is entitled to apply to the court for an ex parte authorisation to attach the aircraft (*saisie conservatoire*) by showing that such attachment is urgent (which could be justified by showing that the aircraft is about to be flown out of the jurisdiction), that the existence of the debt is well-founded and that the recovery of the debt could otherwise be difficult. However, an amendment to the CAC in 1987 provides that such seizure will not generally be permitted where the aircraft, whether French or foreign-registered, is assigned to State service or to 'public transport' (ie the carriage of passengers or cargo for commercial purposes). Hence, such aircraft may be attached only after a judgment on the merits. However, an exception to the rule provides that such pre-trial attachment is permitted where the amounts owed by the owner of the aircraft arise out of the acquisition of the aircraft or contracts for training or maintenance related to the operation of the aircraft. Loans granted to finance the purchase of the aircraft and secured by a mortgage are likely to qualify under such exception.

Technically, in the event that the mortgage has been executed before a notary (*acte authentique*) or where a judgment has been entered even if not executory, it is not necessary to obtain judicial authorisation to attach the aircraft. In practice, however, such authorisation is advisable. It is not the general practice to execute an aircraft mortgage before a notary.

The CAC provides specifically that where an aircraft is registered in a State which is a party to the Geneva Convention is the subject of an attachment in France, no forced sale may occur if any claims which rank superior to those of the attaching creditor would not be satisfied out of the proceeds of the sale or if the purchaser does not agree to satisfy such creditors, unless the attachment is requested by surface victims of an accident occurring on French soil.

Once the aircraft is attached no further disposition may be made of the aircraft. The mortgagee then has one month in which to commence proceedings on the merits (which, when there is no arguable defence to the claim, can be by way of summary proceedings (*référé*)). In the event that a favourable judgment is obtained, then forced sale (*vente forcée*) of the aircraft may occur, provided that the mortgagee must first serve upon the owner by bailiff (*huissier*) a formal notice to pay (*commandement de payer*). Where the mortgagor is not domiciled in France and has not 'elected domicile' (ie named an agent for service of process) in France, all notices and service of process may be made upon the captain of the aircraft.

Upon attachment, the bailiff (*huissier*) will prepare minutes of attachment (*procès-verbal de saisie*) which must be served upon the owner together with a summons to the owner to appear at the court hearing at which a decision will be made as to whether to proceed to the forced sale of the aircraft. The minutes must also be filed with the DGAC within five days of the attachment. Within eight days of such filing, the DGAC will, upon request by the mortgagee, provide the mortgagee with details of all other registered claims upon the aircraft. Within three days thereafter, the mortgagee must notify the attachment and the date of the court hearing in respect of the forced sale to all such registered creditors, either by bailiff or by registered mail, receipt requested by return. The court will fix the conditions of the sale, including the minimum bid price, and the sale will be announced by means of official publication and posters affixed both at the courthouse and the DGAC, as well as on the aircraft itself.

Upon sale, the proceeds are deposited with the *Caisse des Dépôts et Consignations* (a specialised French bank), and creditors are paid out of the proceeds, in the order of the ranking of their security. In the event that the creditors are unable to agree on an amicable basis as to the distribution of the proceeds, the court will issue a judgment apportioning the proceeds. Such judgment can be appealed within ten days. When the court has issued orders entitling the creditors to seek payment from the *Caisse de Dépôts et Consignations*, any interested party (in practice, the mortgagor) is entitled to request the DGAC to cancel registration of any mortgages which have been satisfied by the sales proceeds. Mortgagors who have not been satisfied out of the proceeds retain their rights against the mortgagee.

Charges over ships

As in the case of aircraft, specific rules relating to registration of both title and security interests, set forth in Law no 67-5 of 3 January 1967 (the 'Ship Law') and Decree no 67-967 of 27 October 1967 (the 'Ship Decree'), apply to the creation of charges over ships, with the relevant security being the ship mortgage (*hypothèque maritime*)[1] . Unlike the case of aircraft, France does not maintain a nationwide ship register, but relies on local registration of interests in ships effected at the home port (*port d'attache*) of the vessel.

Subject to certain exceptions described below, in order for a ship to be registered in France (and therefore to become subject to a French ship mortgage), it is necessary for the ship to obtain French nationality (a process known as *francisation*), which, in turn, requires that the ship be owned in one of the following manners:

1 at least 50% by nationals of a member state of the EU (or, with respect to commercial or pleasure vessels, of the EEA) who, in the event that they reside in France less than six months per year, must elect domicile in France for any administrative or judicial matters relating to the ownership of the ship; or

2 entirely by legal entities having their registered office in France or another member state of the EU (or, with respect to commercial or pleasure vessels, of the EEA), provided in the last two instances that the operation and use of the vessel are controlled from a permanent establishment in France, provided that such principal office may be in another foreign country if:

    (a) such country is a party to an international treaty with France permitting a company organised under French law to exercise its activity in such foreign country and have its principal office there, and;

    (b) the operation and use of the vessel are controlled from a permanent establishment in France, and provided further that in any event, and notwithstanding the location of the principal office the following (or their closest equivalent in the relevant jurisdiction) must be French, EU or EEA member state nationals:

        (i) in the case of corporations (*sociétés anonymes*), the Chairman of the Board, any officers and a majority of directors;

1 The rules described in this section are applicable to seagoing vessels (*navires de mer*). Slightly different rules apply to a mortgage over a vessel used in river navigation (*hypothèque fluviale*). These rules are set forth in the French Code of River Navigation (*Code du domaine public fluvial et de la navigation intérieure*).

(ii) in the case of limited partnerships by shares (*sociétés en commandite par actions*), the majority of the supervisory committee (*conseil de surveillance*) and each 'manager' (*gérant*); and

(iii) in the case of limited partnerships (*sociétés en commandite simple*), private limited companies (*sociétés à responsabilité limitée*), general partnerships (*sociétés en nom collectif*) and non-commercial 'civil companies' (*sociétés civiles*), the owners of a majority of shares and each 'manager' (*gérant*); or

3 be owned entirely by a combination of nationals of a member state of the EU (or, with respect to commercial or pleasure vessels, of the EEA) qualifying under the first category and by legal entities qualifying under the second category; or

4 be the subject of a finance lease with purchase option (*crédit-bail*) pursuant to which, upon exercise of the purchase option, the ship will be owned by any of the three categories.

The Ship Law also provides that application may be made to the authorities for registration of a ship in France in either of the following cases:

1 in those cases where the ship is owned entirely by legal entities or by a combination of natural persons and legal entities, the nationality requirement as to ownership may extend to only one-half of the ship, so long as the management of the ship is assured directly by such persons or by other persons fulfilling the requirements of the first two categories described above; or

2 the ship is bareboat chartered to an owner/operator (*armateur*) fulfilling the requirements of paragraphs (a) or (b) above, responsible for the outfitting, the operation and the nautical management of the ship, and where the law of the foreign flag state permits the abandonment of the foreign flag.

Any ship which has been registered in France must carry on board at all times its French registration instrument (*acte de francisation*).

Registration of French ships is effected by the customs authorities, and all French ships, as well as any vessels under construction the declaration of which is mandatory, must be so registered. The registry is classified by name of vessel, with each vessel being allotted a separate register (*fiche matricule*). The register of the ship sets forth the information necessary to identify the vessel, the name of the owner (or, in the case of multiple ownership, the names of all owners and the numbers of their respective shares), and additional information, including the following:

1 any instrument, deed or act by which property rights in the ship are created, transferred or terminated;

2 any time or bareboat charter of one year or greater and any clauses thereof which give the charterer the status of *armateur*;

3 any foreign contractual liens created prior to *francisation* of the ship which are recognised pursuant to the Ship Law;

4 election, resignation or revocation of any *gérants* of ships owned in syndication;

5 any mortgages granted over the whole or any part of the ship; and

6 any attachment of the ship.

When the ownership of a ship is transferred, the name of the new owner must be registered and a new *acte de francisation* issued. Unless this formality is effected, the transfer is not binding on third parties. Sale of a French-registered vessel to a person or entity not qualifying as an authorised national under the rules described above requires the seller to remit the instrument of *francisation* for cancellation.

The ship registry is open to the public and may be consulted by any interested party. Registration is effected at the home port (*port d'attache*) of the ship; unlike the case of aircraft, there is no national ship registry. In order to provide an alternative to the 'open' registers operated by countries offering flags of convenience, France created in 1987 an 'offshore' registry in the Kerguelen Islands, a French-controlled archipelago located in the French Austral and Antarctic Territories ('TAAF'). Vessels registered in the TAAF registry enjoy reduced minimum French crew percentage requirements.

Any ship registered in France may be the subject of a ship mortgage. As in the case of aircraft, ship mortgages must be in writing and may be granted only by agreement between the parties and not by operation of law or upon court order. Also as in the case of aircraft, a ship mortgage need not be signed before a notary, but a notarised mortgage will qualify as an 'executory title' in the event it subsequently becomes necessary to attach the vessel.

A French ship mortgage may be granted only by the owner of the ship or by its duly authorised agent pursuant to a specific mandate. Where the ship is owned in syndicated share ownership (*copropriété*), each shareholder may grant a mortgage over his individual share, and the syndicate manager (*gérant*) may mortgage the entire vessel if this is approved by a majority of the shareholders representing three-quarters of the value of the ship. Unless otherwise specifically agreed, a French ship mortgage automatically covers the body of the ship and all its accessories, machines and apparatus, but does not extend to cargo on board.

French law permits the registration of a ship mortgage against a vessel under construction, so long as the fact of construction has been declared to the authorities. Such declaration is made to the mortgage registration authorities (*conservateur des hypothèques*) with authority over the administrative area (*circonscription*) in which the ship is being built; in the case of ship mortgages, this activity is carried out by the local customs authorities (*recette des douanes*). Publication of a ship mortgage is effected by entry thereof on a special register maintained by such authorities in the district in which the vessel is being built or, once built, where registered.

In the case of vessels being built outside of France or purchased abroad, the Ship Law provides that mortgages granted by the purchaser prior to the *francisation* of the vessel are valid and enforceable in France on condition that they are validly published in France, ie at the future port of registry. In theory, other contractual liens (*sûretés conventionnelles*) granted in respect of a ship prior to its *francisation* should also be valid and enforceable in France subject to the following conditions:

1 they have been published in conformity with the laws of the foreign flag state (or, in default thereof, the laws of the place in which the vessel was built);
2 they have been notified to the purchaser prior to the transfer of ownership of the vessel; and
3 they have been duly published in France at the time of *francisation*.

However, the text of the Ship Law states that subsequent decrees will determine which foreign contractual liens will be covered by this provision and, to date, no such decrees have actually been promulgated. In any event, however, France is a party to the 1926 Brussels Convention on the Unification of Certain Rules Relating to Maritime Liens and Mortgages (but not to the 1967 Brussels Convention).

The priority of a ship mortgage is determined by the date of registration. Two mortgages registered on the same day but at different times are considered as having identical priority. A validly registered ship mortgage is effective for ten years, and may be renewed prior to expiration; the mortgage covers principal and two years of interest in addition to interest for the year under way at the time of enforcement of the mortgage.

A French ship mortgage may be made 'to order': in such case, endorsement of the agreement automatically results in transfer of the mortgagee's rights. Registration of a mortgage will be cancelled only upon production of a document setting forth the agreement of the parties to such effect, or a judgment incapable of appeal.

The mortgagee enjoys a *droit de suite* and the mortgagee's rights follow the vessel into the hands of any purchaser thereof. In the event of voluntary sale of the ship, mortgagees are entitled to be paid out of the purchase price of the vessel, according to their rank. In the event that only a portion of a vessel has been mortgaged, the mortgagee's rights extend only to the portion of the vessel so mortgaged; however, if more than one-half of the vessel is mortgaged, the mortgagee may cause the entire vessel to be sold and share the proceeds among the other mortgagees. The purchaser can 'purge' the mortgages by notifying all registered mortgagees, within 15 days of the purchase of the vessel, of the fact of purchase, the purchase price and the current registered mortgages, and offering to pay off all such mortgages. Any creditor may, within 10 days thereafter, require the vessel to be put up for sale at public auction, upon offering to bid at least 10% over the original purchase price and providing sufficient security for the payment of such increased price.

In addition to those statutory liens existing pursuant to ordinary legislation, the Ship Law provides a number of specific maritime liens which take priority over any mortgage, notwithstanding the ranking of the mortgage, and which extend to the ship, its freight charges and to certain accessories (ie amounts due to the owner for damage to the ship or loss of freight, for general average and for assistance or salvage operations). Such liens include the following:

1 judicial fees incurred for the sale of the ship and the distribution of the sales price;
2 tonnage taxes, port fees and similar taxes and duties, pilots' expenses, expenses for the conservation of the ship from the time of entry of the ship into its last port;
3 amounts owed to the captain, the crew and other ship personnel;
4 remuneration due for salvage and assistance and contribution of the ship to general average;
5 amounts due resulting from collisions or other navigation accidents, or for damage to ports or other constructions, amounts due for physical injury to passengers and crew or for damage to cargo and baggage; and
6 amounts contracted by the captain outside of the port of registry, by virtue of his legal powers, for the conservation of the ship or the continuation of the voyage, whether or not the captain is also the owner of the ship and whether the amounts are due by the captain, the suppliers, repairers, lenders or other parties.

These liens rank in the order listed for any particular voyage undertaken by the ship, and such liens incurred during any voyage are preferred to those incurred during a previous voyage, unless resulting from a single multi-voyage agreement. The liens survive a transfer of the ship and expire one year from the time they are incurred (except for the liens referred to in the last subparagraph, which expire six months from the time incurred). The liens are automatically discharged in the event of confiscation of the ship for violation of customs rules or police or security regulations, by the judicial sale of the ship, or by voluntary sale, two months after publication of the sale.

'Ordinary' statutory liens (ie liens arising by laws other than the Ship Law) may also be invoked by creditors, but they rank behind mortgages, notwithstanding the ranking of such mortgages.

In the event of default by the mortgagor, the mortgagee is entitled to obtain an arrest of the vessel or an attachment leading to its forced sale, and will have a priority claim to the proceeds of the forced sale over all other creditors except those benefiting from prior-ranking mortgages or the specific maritime liens described above.

Arrest (*saisie conservatoire*) of a vessel may be obtained upon ex parte application to the president of the commercial court, by establishing a debt which 'appears founded in theory'. The granting of an arrest order prohibits the vessel from departing from the port but does not otherwise affect the owner's rights in the vessel, and the court may, upon deposit of security, authorise the departure of the vessel for one or several voyages determined in advance. If the vessel has not returned by the deadline fixed by the court, the security is forfeited to the creditors, unless the vessel has been lost and insurance paid. France is a party to the 1952 International Convention Relating to the Arrest of Seagoing Ships, and arrest in France of non-French vessels is possible.

Attachment (*saisie exécution*) is effected in aid of execution so as to permit the forced sale of the vessel. The creditor must be in possession of an executory title (*titre exécutoire*), which may be either a court judgment or a notarised deed. The attachment procedure may commence only 24 hours after the creditor has served the debtor with a formal request for payment (*commandement de payer*); in practice, however, the port authorities will not permit the vessel to leave the port once the request for payment has been served.

If the payment is not effected within 24 hours, a *huissier* retained by the creditor may then board the vessel and issue formal attachment minutes (*procès-verbal de saisie*), as well as naming a guardian of the vessel (frequently, the port authority). At this point, the vessel may no longer leave the port unless, as in the case of an arrest, the President of the commercial court authorises specific voyages and the debtor provides specific security.

A copy of the attachment minutes, coupled with a summons to appear at the local court, must be served on the debtor or his representative (typically, the captain of the vessel) within three days thereafter (or a longer period if the owner is not in France) and must be filed with the ship and mortgage registry (or, if the vessel has not been *francisé*, with a special register maintained by the customs authorities), within seven days. The authorities then deliver to the creditor a list of all mortgages obtained over the vessel, and the creditor must notify all mortgagees of the existence of the attachment and the imminence of the court hearing.

At the hearing, the court renders a judgment fixing the date and the conditions of the forced sale, including the minimum bid price. The auction takes place at a special audience of the court, preceded by publicity by way of posters on the vessel itself, the courthouse door, the port, the local chamber of commerce, the customs authorities and the local merchant marine office, and by newspaper publication. At the auction, the vessel is adjudicated to the highest bidder; unlike the case for voluntary sale, *surenchère* is not permitted. The proceeds of the auction are paid to the *Caisse des Dépôts et*

Consignations and title to the vessel is passed. The purchase price is divided among the creditors; if an initial attempt to obtain an amicable distribution is not successful, the court will determine allocation of the price upon examination of the various creditor claims. The decision of the court is appealable within 10 days.

FORMALITIES

Board resolutions

The French Company Law Art 98 (recently codifed as Art L. 225-35 of the Commercial Code) provides that, in order for a guarantee (which would include both a *caution* and a first-demand guarantee) issued by a *société anonyme* (corporation)[2] to be valid, the guarantee must first be approved by a resolution of the board of directors (*conseil d'administration*) of the corporation. Decree no 67-236 of 23 March 1967 (the 'French Company Decree') Art 89 provides, as an alternative to requiring a specific board resolution for each guarantee, that the board may adopt a general resolution authorising the chairman of the board (who may subdelegate such power) to issue during one or several guarantees during a period up to one year in an aggregate amount which does not exceed the global limit determined by the board. Such authorisation may also establish an individual limit beyond which no single guarantee may be issued. If a proposed guarantee exceeds either the global or the individual limit, a specific authorisation is required in each case. In practice, the procedure of adopting a 'blanket annual resolution' is typically used only in fairly large-sized companies in France, so that it will usually be necessary, in the context of a cross-border transaction, to seek specific Board authorisation for a guarantee granted by a *société anonyme*.

The French Company Decree Art 89 further provides that if the aggregate amount of guarantees issued during a given period exceeds the global limit determined by the board for such period, then the fact that the limit was exceeded is not opposable to third parties who were not actually so aware, unless the amount of the guarantee in and of itself exceeded either the global limit or the individual limit determined by the board.

The original French-language text of Art 98 requires authorisation for the issuance of '*cautions, avals et garanties*'. Literally, this language includes not only outright guarantees but security (the French word '*garanties*' encompassing not only 'guarantees' in the English sense of the term but also other forms of undertaking which provide further security to a creditor that the debt will be repaid). However, the *Cour de Cassation* has specifically ruled that security provided by a corporation to secure its own debt and not that of a third party does not require authorisation by the Board of Directors. Hence, such authorisation is required only if the corporation provides either an outright guarantee of another person's debt, or a third-party charge over its own assets to secure the debt of another person.

The requirement of board authorisation must in practice be taken very seriously. Under prevailing court decisions, a guarantee executed on behalf of a *société anonyme* without the required prior board approval is null and void (not merely voidable). The courts have steadfastly refused to recognise any theory under which a third party

2 See footnote 20 for a description of the different forms of French companies.

relying in good faith on the representations of the guarantor that proper authorisation has been obtained, or on the apparent authority of the signatory of the guarantee, is entitled to benefit from the guarantee if such authorisation was not actually given. Moreover, the courts have ruled that the Board authorisation must be given prior to execution of the guarantee: failure to authorise the issuance of a guarantee cannot be cured by a subsequent ratification by the board. The fact that the guarantor and the guaranteed party are closely related is irrelevant; thus, the fact that the guaranteed party was the direct subsidiary of the guarantor has been held to be irrelevant where the chairman of the parent company guarantor failed to obtain the authorisation of the board of the parent. Nor is any distinction made between ordinary *cautions* and first-demand guarantees.

An area that is particularly fraught with difficulties is that of letters of intention, which are usually drafted in a manner intended to fall somewhat short of an outright guarantee, yet provide a certain level of comfort to the beneficiary. Typically, in the event of a dispute over the exact scope of a letter of comfort, the provider of the letter is likely to argue that the letter did not constitute a full guarantee. In an ironic twist, however, in several French court decisions the provider of the comfort letter has, in order to escape liability thereunder, argued successfully that the letter did in fact constitute an outright guarantee, but that, since the execution of the letter had not been authorised by the board of directors, it was null and void.

For the foregoing reasons, it is strongly advisable for the beneficiary of a guarantee provided by a French *société anonyme* to insist on actual sight of a certified copy of the board resolution authorising the issuance of the guarantee. If the beneficiary is informed that the guarantee is being given pursuant to a blanket annual resolution of the type described earlier, then, in addition to requiring a certified copy of such resolution, the beneficiary should require a certificate signed by an officer of the guarantor to the effect that the granting of the guarantee will not cause the global and any individual limits set forth in such resolution to be exceeded.

In the event that the guarantee is to be given in favour of an affiliated company, it may also be necessary for further specific authorisation to be obtained from the board of directors under the 'interested director' provisions of the French Company Law (Arts 101ff (recently codifed as Arts L. 225-38 ff of the Commercial Code)). Under these provisions, any contract to which a French company is a party between the company itself and one of its directors or officers, or with any company any of the directors or officers of which are also directors or officers of the company, require board approval prior to signature thereof (with any 'interested director' being required to abstain from the vote), unless certain restrictive conditions are met. In the event where, as occurs frequently, a parent company guarantor shares some directors or officers with a subsidiary the obligations of which are being guaranteed, and if the text of the guarantee is incorporated into the underlying loan agreement or some other document which is to be signed by both the guarantor and the underlying debtor, then such authorisation will usually be necessary[3]. Agreements falling within the scope of the 'interested

3 The French Company Law Art 102 (recently codifed as Art L. 225-39 of the Commercial Code) excepts from the requirement of prior Board authorisation agreements relating to 'ordinary transactions concluded at normal conditions (*opérations courantes et conclues à des conditions normales*'). Certain authors of *doctrine* have taken the position that guarantees concluded by parent companies for the obligations of wholly- or nearly wholly-owned subsidiaries fall by nature within such exception and are therefore not subject to prior authorisation even when the parent and the subsidiary share common directors.

director' provisions which are not submitted to the prior approval of the board may be annulled within three years of signature if they have had damaging consequences for the guarantor, unless they have been approved by the shareholders of the guarantor following a report of the statutory auditors (*commissaires aux comptes*) of the guarantor explaining to the shareholders why the procedure for board approval was not followed.[4]

Beneficiaries of guarantees in jurisdictions in which resolutions of the board of directors of corporations may be adopted by telephone or by unanimous action in writing should be cautioned that neither of such procedures is valid for the holding of a meeting of the board of directors of a French *société anonyme*. The French Company Law requires the physical holding of a meeting of the board and the physical presence of at least one-half of the members of the board at the meeting in order for any action taken at the meeting to be valid. Although proxies can be given by one director to another, such proxies count only for purposes of counting a majority, not for quorum purposes.

A separate question may also be raised in the event that the *société anonyme* has a labour-management committee (*comité d'entreprise*). In such an event, representatives of such committee must be invited to attend all meetings of the corporation's board of directors (although they have only a consultative role). Failure to invite the committee members does not void the action taken at the directors' meeting but it does constitute a penal violation by management, and certain labour-management committees have been known not to take the matter lightly.

It is therefore strongly advisable to plan the holding of a board meeting authorising the issuance of a guarantee by a French *société anonyme* well in advance. In the event that the French guarantor is not organised as a *société anonyme*, then there is no requirement that the guarantee be approved prior to execution unless the articles of association (*statuts*) of the guarantor so requires. Thus, no such approval would ordinarily be required if the guarantor was a limited liability company (*société à responsabilité limitée*, or SARL), a general partnership (*société en nom collectif*), or a limited partnership (*société en commandite simple*). However, in the case of SARL's, a procedure similar to that of the 'interested director' provisions requires that any agreement entered into between the SARL and any of its managers (*gérants*) or shareholders, or with any company in which the *gérant* or shareholder of the SARL is also an officer or director or a partner with unlimited liability, be submitted to the shareholders of the SARL (French Company Law Art 50 (recently codifed as Art L. 223-20 of the Commercial Code)). If the shareholders do not approve the agreement then the agreement will nevertheless be effective, but the *gérant* or shareholder in question will be jointly and severally liable with the SARL for any consequences of the contract which are prejudicial for the SARL.

Execution

As explained earlier, France does not possess a unified regime for the taking of security over assets; each category of assets is subject to a different set of statutory provisions

4 Shareholder approval is often obtained where, due to the requirement that 'interested directors' abstain from voting on the board resolution, a sufficient quorum of 'non-interested directors' does not exist.

which provides the framework pursuant to which charges over such assets are created and perfected. For this reason, there is no single set of rules applicable to formalities of execution of documents relating to security interests; rather, each type of security is subject to separate rules of form. Certain forms of security, such as the pledge of tangible goods with dispossession, do not, theoretically, even require the execution of a written instrument. Others, such as the pledge of shares and other securities, require as a matter of law the execution of certain documents but not necessarily the signature of a formal contract of pledge. Still others, such as the pledge of a going business (*fonds de commerce*) or the aircraft mortgage, require signature of formal documentation which must, in order to create valid security, contain specific language, whilst others, such as the real estate mortgage, require the signature of a highly stylised document before a notary. For this reason, the requirements relating to the execution of documentation for different forms of security are described under 'Types of security' (p 78 above), dealing with the rules concerning each such form of security. In this section, certain basic concepts relating to execution of documents in France will be discussed and their relevance to the creation of security mentioned.

At the outset, a basic distinction should be made. French law and practice distinguishes between the 'civil act' (*acte civil*) and the 'commercial act' (*acte de commerce*). Although the French Commercial Code Arts L. 110-1 and L. 110-2 set forth an illustrative list of 'commercial acts', the list is not exclusive. However, any act which is effected by a *commerçant* (a 'merchant', which by law includes any commercial company of the sort which are most likely to be encountered in the course of transactions requiring cross-border security) in the furtherance of its business activities will be considered to be a 'commercial act'.

The practical significance of this distinction is that certain formal requirements relating to contracts executed in the context of 'civil acts' are inapplicable in the case of 'commercial acts'; in addition, as explained in more detail under 'Remedies and enforcement' (p 117 below), certain remedies of secured parties are facilitated when the security interest is deemed to be 'commercial' rather than civil. Moreover, due to the French system of dual jurisdiction, disputes arising under 'civil' contracts are subject to the jurisdiction of different courts than those in respect of 'commercial' disputes.[5] For purposes of this chapter, it is assumed that the transaction in respect of which cross-border security is sought and the identity of the parties thereto render the security a 'commercial act'.

Commercial contracts do not have to be in writing unless so required by statute (although, of course, it is certainly prudent to execute a written instrument); as described under 'Types of security' (p 78 above), many of the laws relating to different forms of

5 Civil disputes will be heard in the *tribunal d'instance* or the *tribunal de grande instance* (depending on the amount in dispute), staffed by professional judges, whilst commercial disputes will be litigated in the commercial court (*tribunal de commerce*), a court staffed by business persons elected to the position by their peers and frequently assisted by very able law clerks. Appeal from both jurisdictions is to the appeals court (*cour d'appel*) and further appeals (but only as to disputes of law rather than of fact) to the *Cour de Cassation*, the highest French court for civil and commercial matters.

Other consequences which differ depending on whether a contract is deemed to be 'civil' or 'commercial' include validity of arbitration clauses (*clauses compromissoires*), which are valid in commercial but not civil agreements, statutes of limitations (the general statute of limitations regarding commercial agreements is shorter), and rules of evidence.

security do in fact require a written instrument as a condition to validity of the security. In most cases, such instruments may be simple signed agreements (*actes sous seing privé*), which need not be executed before a public official or before any witnesses but which must be signed at the least by the party against whom the contract is sought to be enforced.[6] In the case of bilateral agreements (*contrats synallagmatiques*), the Civil Code requires that, in order for the agreement to be valid, there be signed at least as many originals as there are parties in interest (a single original document being sufficient for several parties all of which share the same interest). Documents evidencing a unilateral obligation to pay a sum of money or to deliver a fungible good must contain the signature of the obligor together with a manuscript statement of the obligor setting forth, both in figures and in words, the sum or the quantity of the obligation. The French courts have held that this latter obligation does not apply where the unilateral contract is commercial in nature, but in practice this procedure is typically followed in the case of guarantees.

The date set forth in an *acte sous seing privé* is binding on the parties to the agreement (although any party may prove the contrary by appropriate evidence), but is not automatically binding as against third parties. In the case of commercial agreements, the actual date (*date certaine*) of the agreement may be proved by any appropriate evidence. Otherwise, a *date certaine* is obtained only by registration of the agreement with the tax authorities (see 'Registration and stamp duty' below) or by executing the agreement as an *acte authentique* (see following paragraph).

In certain cases, the law requires that agreements be executed as 'authentic deeds' (*acte authentique*); in practice, this means that the agreement is signed before a notary and complies with certain requirements as to form. As explained under 'Charges over land: real estate mortgages' (p 79 above), the signature of an *acte authentique* is required in order to create a valid real estate mortgage capable of being filed with the land registration authorities as required for perfection, and in order to remove a pledge of going business or a purchase money security interest from the public register. An *acte authentique* is also considered to constitute an executory deed, enabling attachment of the pledged asset without a court order. More generally, an *acte authentique* provides a *date certaine* and the facts set forth in the document are binding unless fraud is proven. Despite these advantages, however, it is not common for commercial agreements to be executed as an *acte authentique* unless required by law, due to the costs associated therewith.

Registration and stamp duty

As with the case of formalities of execution above, the absence of a unified regime for the taking of security over assets has a consequence that there is no single set of rules applicable to requirements of stamping and registration of documents relating to creation and perfection of security interests.

6 Strictly speaking, the courts have determined that a signature on a document binds the signatory thereof to the entire text of the document, irrespective of the date upon which the signature was executed, even where the signature was executed prior to the full text of the contract being completed (signature *blanc-seing*). In practice, a party may always allege that the final text of such an agreement does not in fact reflect the will of the parties, but in that case the party must supply proof to the contrary.

At the outset, a distinction should be made between stamp duty and registration duty. Strictly speaking, stamp duties (*droits de timbre*) alone are fees which must be paid for the purchase of tax stamps (*timbres fiscaux*) which are required to be affixed to certain documents as a matter of law. Outside of stamps required in the case of certain administrative documents, the French General Tax Code (the 'Tax Code') requires that stamps known as *timbres de dimension* be affixed to any instrument having as its sole or principal purpose an undertaking for the payment or the reimbursement of cash or negotiable securities (but not to such undertakings which are ancillary to other obligations). Failure to pay such stamp duties does not result in the invalidity of the undertaking in question but can result in fines or penalties. At the time of publication of this book, the cost of *timbres de dimension* amounts to FRF 40 per A4 size sheet of paper; however, this tariff is reduced to FRF 20 per page if only one side of the sheet is used and the reverse side is clearly marked to indicate that it is cancelled in accordance with the relevant provisions of the Tax Code. Stamp duties are also payable (in addition to registration duties) whenever an instrument is required to be or is voluntary submitted to registration, as described below.

Registration duties (*droits d'enregistrement*) are amounts required to be paid whenever an instrument is submitted to the formalities of registration. Registration consists in submitting the instrument in question to the local tax authorities, who emboss the instrument to indicate that it has been registered and retain one copy of the document for their files. Any document can be submitted for voluntary registration to the tax authorities; such registration conveys a *date certaine* on the document, ie the date of execution cannot be challenged by third parties except in the case of fraud. Certain documents, however, *must* be submitted to registration. In many cases, such requirements stem from the Tax Code, meaning that failure to obtain registration does not invalidate the instrument but can be subject to fines and penalties. In certain cases, however, such requirements stem from the legislation pursuant to which the document is executed. In such cases, failure to submit the instrument to registration can result in the instrument being invalid or unenforceable. As explained under 'Types of security' (p 78 above), registration is required in the case of the following types of security:

1 charges over going business (see p 87 above);
2 purchase money security interests over material and equipment (see p 90 above);
3 in certain cases, charges over intangible property and contractual rights (see p 92 above); and
4 real estate mortgages (see p 79 above);

The amount of registration duties varies depending on the instrument to be submitted for registration. In many cases, registration is subject only to a fixed duty of FRF 500 per instrument (irrespective of the number of executed copies submitted for registration). In certain cases, such as real estate mortgages, however, registration duties are payable as a percentage of the security taken. In all cases in which an instrument is submitted for voluntary or mandatory registration, stamp duty is also payable.

Foreign parties should take note of the fact that, as a practical matter, the French tax authorities will typically refuse to accept for registration an instrument which is not in the French language, unless accompanied by a translation into French prepared by a translator authorised to do so by the local court (*traducteur assermenté*). The cost of preparing 'sworn translations' can be considerable, and thought should be given, in the case of security which is to be submitted to registration, to preparing the document in the French language in the first place.

As explained under 'Types of security' (p 78 above), certain forms of security require, either in addition to or in lieu of registration, filing with various public authorities. Such filing is also subject to the payment of fees, which vary depending on the kind of security taken.

Governmental consents

The taking or enforcing of security over assets located in France is generally free from any requirement to obtain governmental or administrative consents except where the assets are utilised by an entity which itself requires such an authorisation to use such assets. The effect of French exchange controls on the enforcement of share pledges is described under 'Exchange controls' (p 85 above).

Obligatory use of the French language

Law no 94-655 of 4 August 1994 (the '*Loi Toubon*') strengthened previous legislation intended to protect the use of the French language by requiring its use in certain circumstances, including advertisements, posters, descriptions of goods and services and the warranties relating thereto.

Under Art 5 of the Law, any contract to which a public entity or a private entity which performs a public service is party must be written in the French language, and cannot contain any foreign expression for which there is an officially-approved equivalent expression in French (the government has issued from time to time lists of such officially-approved French equivalents).

There are no criminal penalties for violation of Art 5 of the Law. However, Art 5 provides that a party to a contract which violates the provisions of Art 5 cannot enforce any provision of the contract written in a foreign language which would 'prejudice' the counterparty. The term 'prejudice' is not defined and it is not clear whether this means simply a provision which is detrimental to the other party or a provision which harms the other party only because such party was not able to understand the terms.

Article 5 provides that where at least one of the parties to the contract is foreign, the contract may be written in another language in addition to French, and that the versions in both languages may have equal force. A contract may not be written only in a foreign language, or, if written in French and a foreign language, the foreign-language version may not be the only one having force.

Article 5 also contains an exception: contracts to which public entities who engage in industrial or commercial activities are parties and which are performed entirely outside of France are not subject to the provisions. This is a difficult exception to interpret. 'Public entities engaging in industrial or commercial activities' is easy enough to understand: certain public entities under French law, such as Electricité de France and Gaz de France (the state-owned electricity and natural gas companies), are incorporated specifically to perform such services, and many other entities, such as the French postal services, do so as a matter of practice. However, determining when a contract is to be performed 'entirely' outside France is another story. Obviously, certain commercial contracts will fit easily into the definition, but cross-border security is granted in an international context in which the contract will inevitably have at least some portion performed in France.

In order to resolve certain of these difficulties, Article 5 was modified in 1996 in order to provide that loans benefiting from the exemption from withholding tax provided under the Tax Code Art 131 quater (ie Eurobonds/loans and other debt 'outside' of France) will be considered performed entirely outside France.

As a practical matter, it is usually recommended that any contract purporting to create a security interest under French law be executed in the French language. As in the case of the French tax authorities (see 'Registration and stamp duty' p 110 above), in the case of litigation before the French courts, such courts will require that any agreement submitted to them for interpretation be in the French language or accompanied by a 'sworn translation'.

PRIORITIES

Priority as between competing charges

The issue of priority as between competing charges arises rarely under French law, since, as described above, in most cases each specific category of asset is subject to different security. Where such conflict does arise, priority is determined according to the following rules:

1 where a tangible asset over which security has been taken under specific legislation permitting the granting of security without physical dispossession (eg pledge of going business (see p 87 above) or purchase money security interest over material and equipment (see p 90 above)) is pledged anew by physical dispossession (see 'Charges over goods – pledge of stock-in-trade' p 86 above), the second pledge will have priority unless the pledgee was aware of the existence of the prior pledge;
2 where an asset which forms part of a pledged going business is made subject to a purchase money security interest over material and equipment, the purchase money security interest has priority if notified to the pledgee of the going business within two months of the creation of the security interest;
3 a purchase money security interest over granted over material and equipment which, upon installation, becomes a fixture (*immeuble par destination*) ranks ahead of any real estate mortgage which is extended to such fixture;
4 assets which form part of a group of pledged assets but which are the property of a third party are not subject to the pledge.[7]

7 For example, in one case a ship motor was sold to the ship operator subject to a reservation of title in the event of failure to pay the full price of the motor over time. The court ruled that the reservation of title had priority over a mortgage granted over the ship, including the motor.

Priority as against unsecured creditors (eg judgment debts, garnishee orders etc)

As described under 'Possessory lien' (p 120 below), unsecured creditors are entitled in certain cases to exercise a possessory lien (*droit de retention*) over assets of the debtor or to obtain seizure and forced sale of such assets. The possessory lien is effective as against all other creditors, including those with security over the asset. The right of seizure and forced sale may be exercised notwithstanding the existence of security over the asset, but the secured creditor will be entitled to priority over the proceeds of the sale. The reader is referred to 'Remedies and enforcement' (p 117 below) for a more detailed description of these remedies.

Preferential debt

As in other legal systems, French law provides for a number of categories of preferential debt (*créances priviligées*), some of which have priority over contractually-created security interests. Occasionally, the specific legislation pursuant to which the security interest is created itself provides for certain liens which rank ahead of such security regardless of the date of the lien; this is the case, for example, of certain aircraft and maritime liens, as discussed under 'Charges over aircraft' and 'Charges over ships' (at pp 97 and 101 above).

More generally, various categories of French legislation, including the Civil Code, the Labour Code, the Tax Code and the Bankruptcy Law provide for a number of *privilèges* which rank ahead of contractual security either in the case of specific assets (*privilèges spéciaux*) or on all assets of the same category (*privilèges généraux*). A full description of all of the various categories of preferential debt would be beyond the scope of this work; however, the following kinds of *privilèges* are among the most significant:

1 court costs and expenses (*frais de justice*) disbursed in the interest of all creditors for the conservation or the forced sale of the asset (Civil Code Arts 2101 and 2104);
2 liens of the tax administration for payment of various taxes, duties (including customs duties) and imposts (Tax Code Arts. 1920ff), and privileges of the social security administration for payment of compulsory employers' and employees' contributions to the comprehensive French health, unemployment and retirement insurance system (Social Security Code Arts L. 138 and 139);
3 wages and certain comparable payments such as redundancy payments and payments in lieu of holiday period, including a special lien (*superprivilège*) in the case of the opening of bankruptcy proceedings, ranking ahead of all other preferred debts and all security interests, securing payment of salaries for the last 60 working days (90 days in the case of certain employees) up to a maximum monthly amount fixed by decree (Labour Code Art L. 143-10). Immediately upon the opening of bankruptcy proceedings, the bankruptcy administrator must, on simple request of the *juge-commissaire*, set aside an amount of one month's unpaid salary for employees of the bankrupt debtor, even before a claim in respect thereof is formally established, and the remainder of such payments must be made within ten days of

a formal judgment of the *juge-commissaire* ordering such payments to be made. In practice, these sums are paid by an insurance organisation, the *Association pour la gestion du régime d'assurance des créances des salariés*), which advances the funds necessary upon receipt of the claim;

4 the 'Article 40' lien described under 'Administrators' right to continue agreements' (p 122 below), pursuant to which claims arising against the debtor following the opening of bankruptcy proceedings rank ahead of all debt incurred prior thereto during the 'observation period' and thereafter unless the debtor is placed in judicial liquidation;

5 various 'special' liens relating to amounts due in respect of specific assets, such as the lien of the seller of certain assets for payment of the purchase price, the lien of the lessor of real estate for rental payments, transporters' and commissioners' liens and innkeepers' liens (Civil Code Art 2102);

6 various 'general' liens relating to substinence payments, medical payments, funeral costs and similar expenses (Civil Code, arts. 2101 and 2104).

Outside of the bankruptcy situation, most contractual security ranks behind the lien for court costs and the liens for tax and social security, equally with 'special liens' and ahead of 'general liens'; complex rules govern the priority of the general liens as among themselves. Aircraft and ship mortgages rank behind special aircraft and maritime liens and the lien for court costs, but ahead of tax and social security liens and both special and general liens. The purchase money security interest for material and equipment ranks ahead of all liens other than the lien for court costs. In the event of bankruptcy, however, these rules are modified so that the employees' '*superprivilège*' ranks ahead of all other liens and all security, followed by the 'Article 40 lien'.

Subordination

France possesses a number of pieces of specific legislation relating to subordinated debts.

Law no 78-741 of 13 July 1978 created the participating loan (*prêt participatif*), the reimbursement of which ranks by law behind all secured and unsecured creditors in the event of the judicial liquidation of the borrower. Such loans may (but are not, except when granted by the State, required) to provide that a portion of the interest payable thereon may be calculated as a function of the performance of the borrower (including by participation in the net profits of the borrower). Participating loans are considered for accounting purposes as equity (*fonds propres*) of the borrower. The granting of security for such loans by the borrower is prohibited, but a third party may provide a guarantee or security over its own assets for such loans.

Law no 83-1 of 3 January 1983 created a class of negotiable securities known as *titres participatifs*, issuable only by companies operating in the public sector.[8] Fixed interest must account for at least 60% of the return on investment, with the remainder being calculated as a function of the issuer's revenues or otherwise as a function of the activity of the issuer. *Titres participatifs* rank behind all secured and unsecured

8 Historically, the law creating *titres participatifs* was passed a year after the wave of nationalisations following the 1981 elections, as it became clear that certain recently nationalised entities required further injections of equity.

creditors, including lenders under *prêts participatifs*, in the case of liquidation of the issuer.

Law no 85-1321 of 14 December 1985 added a new article (Art 339-7) to the Company Law, providing that negotiable debt securities, or securities providing rights to subscribe to or acquire other debt securities, may provide that they will not be reimbursed until all other creditors (except holders of *prêts participatifs* or *titres participatifs)* have been paid. This law, which legitimised a practice already prevalent in the securities markets, has given rise to numerous variations of subordinated debt instruments, including perpetual subordinated bonds (*titres subordonnés à durée indéterminée*), reimbursable subordinated bonds (*titres subordonnés*), occasionally issued with warrants to acquire bonds redeemable in shares, and a host of others.

Despite this abundance of specific legislation, the majority view of the learned commentary is that contractual subordination in the absence of a legislative text is also permitted under French law, and in fact such contractual subordination is frequently employed in France, particularly in the case of management buy-outs and buy-ins making use of 'mezzanine debt'. In the absence of definitive *jurisprudence* on the subject, however, it is unclear whether such contractual subordination is effective as against a bankruptcy administrator.

A particular problem arises with respect to the contractual subordination of security interests. As explained in more detail under 'Types of security' (p 78 above), security which is perfected by registration in a public record (eg real estate, aircraft and ship mortgages, pledges of a going business and purchase money security interests over material and equipment) can be created over the same asset several times over, with ranking of successive security generally following chronological order of filing. In certain cases, it is possible for a higher-ranking secured creditor to transfer the benefit of the higher ranking to a lower-ranked secured creditor through an arrangement known as *cession d'antériorité*. Such arrangements must be noted on the public register in order to be effective against third parties.

In the case of other security interests, however, it is not clear whether security interests can be contractually subordinated, or even, for that matter, whether security interests of different ranking may exist over the same asset. This is the case, for example, for pledges over dematerialised shares (see under 'Dematerialisation of securities: creation and perfection of share accounts or fractional ownership interests' p 82 above), in which creation and perfection of the pledge results in the shares being transferred to a special account in which the pledge is recorded. In the view of some practitioners, the creation of second-ranking security over such shares is impossible, since under the literal language of the law this would require transferring the shares to yet another account, thus destroying the first security. Such practitioners generally prefer the signature of a private agreement between the various secured creditors and the debtor (*convention sur le rang*) under which a single pledge is taken in the name of all secured parties securing the aggregate amount of the debt of all such parties, but a contractual order of priority of the payment of the proceeds of such security is agreed. This practice complies with the letter of the law but does not put third parties on notice of the existence of two levels of security. Other practitioners prefer to record both levels of security in the same shareholders' account in the issuer's share register, even though this does not appear to be authorised by the letter of the law, arguing that it is more important that other creditors be put on notice of the existence of the subordination.

REMEDIES AND ENFORCEMENT

The absence of a unified regime for the taking of security in France means that the remedies of secured creditors under French law depend to a considerable degree on the kind of asset over which the security is taken and the form of security obtained. The distinction between the different kinds of security available and the remedies available to creditors in the case of each specific kind of security is described under 'Introduction: lack of a comprehensive security structure and other differences with Anglo-American practice' (p 78 above). This section will describe more generally the nature of remedies available to secured creditors of security, and the limitations and restrictions on such remedies, including those resulting from the opening of French bankruptcy proceedings.[9]

Power of retention

In the case of ordinary charges over tangible assets, where the security is perfected by delivery of the pledged asset to the pledgee (see 'Charges over goods – pledge of stock-in-trade' p 86 above), the creditor is entitled to retain the pledged asset until the secured debt, including principal, interest and expenses, has been repaid in full (Civil Code, Art 2082). This right of retention does not entitle the pledgee to employ the asset for its own use or to sell the asset to a third party, but merely to refuse to surrender the asset to the owner until the debt is repaid. Obviously, similar rights do not exist in the case of pledges which do not require physical dispossession, such as the pledge of going business (p 87 above) or the purchase money security interest over material and equipment (p 90 above). However, the revisions to the law of 1983 relating to the pledge of financial instruments (see 'Charges over share accounts and fractional ownership interests in French companies' (p 82 above) create a right of retention in favour of the pledgee over all financial instruments and cash in the pledged account. Holders of a real estate mortgage (see p 79 above) have a quasi-right of retention, since they are entitled to obtain the expropriation of the debtor from the mortgaged premises (Civil Code Art 2204). Unsecured creditors with physical possession of an asset also enjoy a right of retention (see 'Possessory lien' p 120 below).

Power of sale or attribution of the secured asset

The principal remedy afforded to secured creditors under French law is the right to cause the pledged asset to be sold and to be satisfied out of the proceeds of the sale or, in certain cases, to obtain attribution of the asset. However, except in extremely limited cases, the secured creditor is not entitled to effect such sale or self-attribution on its own: sale must be effected at public auction and, where permissible, self-attribution must be authorised by court order. The security instrument may not entitle

9 The procedures of the appointment of a receiver or an administrative receiver are unknown in France.

the secured creditor to self-appropriate the pledged assets in the event of default by the pledgor. Any provision of a security agreement which permits the secured party to self-attribute the assets (*pacte commissoire*) or to dispose of them by private sale (*clause de voie parée*) is null and void. The public policy reason behind this rule is that the value of the pledged asset may be greater than the amount of the debt secured, and attribution or private disposal of the asset upon default of the pledgor may result in unjust enrichment of the pledgee. This policy is considered to be a cornerstone of French security law, and some courts have even held that where a clause of such nature was central to the pledge agreement, the entire pledge (and not merely the remedies clause) was null and void.

In the case of pledges of assets, whether tangible or intangible, the relevant provisions of the French Civil and Commercial Codes provide that in the event of a default by the pledgor, the pledgee has only two remedies under French law:

1 to petition the court to permit self-appropriation of the assets or the sale of such assets at public auction, but only after the court has actually ruled to such effect, which may require an expert's evaluation of the value of the assets (Civil Code Art 2078); or
2 (in the case of a commercial pledge only) following eight days' notice to the pledgor, to sell the assets at public auction or (in the case of shares) through an authorised stockbroker (Commercial Code Art L. 521-3).

Similar restrictions exist in the case of a pledge of a going business (except that judicial self-attribution is not available), and for a purchase money security interest of material and equipment, and as discussed above, also apply in the case of shares deposited in a pledged account and not traded on a regulated market.

Similar rights and restrictions apply in the case of mortgages. The mortgagee of real estate is entitled to exercise the remedy of 'expropriation', as described in under 'Charges over land: real estate mortgages' p 79 above, to cause the mortgaged real estate to be sold at auction and to be satisfied on a priority basis out of the proceeds of the sale. Clauses permitting the mortgagee to occupy the premises or to sell the real estate outside of the auction procedure are void. Similarly, beneficiaries of aircraft and ship mortgages are entitled to arrest or attach the aircraft or vessel and to cause the forced sale thereof at auction, being satisfied on a priority basis out of the proceeds of the sale.[10]

Lenders to French companies occasionally attempt to evade these rules by requiring the French party to grant an assignment by way of security over the asset rather than a pledge. Where the asset is actually located outside France (which is arguably the case in the event that the asset being assigned consists of intangible rights arising under a contract with parties in other jurisdictions)[11], there is some merit to adopting

10 As explained in under 'Forced sale' (p 121 below), unsecured creditors also have the right to cause the forced sale at auction of assets owned by a defaulting debtor. However, creditors with security over the asset in question enjoy rights of priority (*droit de préférence*) to satisfaction of their debts out of the proceeds of such sale.

11 The Rome Convention on governing law (Art 12) provides that the obligations of assignor and assignee under a voluntary assignment of a right against another person is governed by the law which under the Convention applies to the contract between the assignor and assignee, which in most cases is the law chosen by the parties. However, the law governing the right to which the assignment relates determines its assignability, the relationship between the assignee and the debtor, the conditions under which the assignment can be invoked against the debtor and any question whether the debtor's obligations have been discharged.

this approach, at least where the security assignment is made contractually subject to a law other than that of France and such choice of law is justified by the international element of the transaction.

However, outside of the special case of the assignment of book debt to a credit institution pursuant to the *Loi Dailly* described under 'Security assignment or pledge of book debt' p 93 above, where the notion of security assignments has received specific statutory recognition, the status of security assignments under French law is very unclear. At least one French court has ruled that where a debtor transferred ownership of certain shares to a creditor accompanied by an agreement that the shares would be returned upon repayment of the debt, this was a disguised attempt at operating a *pacte commissoire* and therefore unenforceable. Alternatively, parties attempting to create a security assignment over French assets risk the possibility that a French court will misconstrue their intention and rule that an outright assignment of the asset has occurred.

The problem is compounded by the fact that there is no concept under French law equivalent to that of the trust, so that it is not possible under current law to transfer legal title to assets whilst retaining beneficial ownership. For several years, the French parliament has been considering the possibility of enacting proposed legislation to permit the creation of trust-like arrangements, known as *fiducie*, similar to legislation existing in Luxembourg. However, this legislation has been stalled due to fears that the *fiducie* will be used in order to avoid taxation.[12]

Survival of the security interest in the case of sale of the secured asset: *droit de suite*

In all of the categories described under 'Types of security' (p 78 above) in which security is taken over tangible assets which are not delivered to the secured party, the security interest survives any sale of the asset to a third party, and the secured party continues to have the rights described above with respect to such assets. This right is known as the *droit de suite*. However, in each such case, the transferee can defeat such rights by using a procedure known as 'purging' the security interest, offering to pay the purchase price of the asset directly to the secured party. If the secured party accepts such payment, the security interest is 'purged' (although the creditor retains its ordinary

12 The scope of this chapter is limited to the taking of security in the context of international financing transactions. In the case of commercial transactions, the Bankruptcy Law recognises the enforceability of retention of title clauses where goods are sold on trade credit (Bankruptcy Law Art 121). In such a situation, such goods can be reclaimed in the course of the bankruptcy proceedings so long as they have not been transformed or resold.

Similarly, assets owned by a third party and used by the bankrupt debtor (eg assets leased to the debtor) may be reclaimed in the course of the bankruptcy proceedings, so long as a claim is filed within three months from the opening of the *redressement judiciaire* (Bankruptcy Law, article 115). Thus, assets which have been financed by sale and leaseback transactions may be recovered so long as the relevant filing is made. However, where the business of the bankrupt debtor is sold to a third party in the course of the proceedings (see below), the court may determine that the benefit of certain finance leases (*crédit-bail*) necessary to the preservation of the business are to be transmitted along with the business (although the views of the lessor must in such cases be solicited).

right to sue the debtor for the difference between the proceeds of sale and the amount of the debt). If the secured party refuses to accept payment of the purchase price (in practice, because the amount is insufficient to discharge the debt), it must request that the secured asset be put up for auction, and undertake to submit or cause to be submitted at such auction a bid for 10% higher than the purchase price.

Rights and powers of unsecured creditors

Possessory lien

As in the case of secured creditors (see under 'Power of retention' p 117 above), unsecured creditors enjoy a possessory lien known as the *droit de retention* which permits in certain cases a creditor to retain physically assets owned by a defaulting debtor but which have come into the possession of the creditor until complete payment of the debt in question. Unlike a genuine security interest, the *droit de retention* does not give the creditor the right to be satisfied on a priority basis out of the sale of the proceeds of the asset in question.

The *droit de retention* is specifically recognised by statute in certain circumstances but both the *jurisprudence* and the *doctrine* has extended the benefits of the lien to all creditors, provided that the following conditions are met:

1 the existence of a claim which is certain (ie the existence of which is undisputed), liquid and payable (although the courts have held that the conditions of 'liquidity' and 'payable' can be satisfied as late as the time of any court decision ruling on the amount of the claim);
2 the asset must consist of tangible property capable of being materially possessed, and the creditor must actually have physical possession of the asset; and
3 there must be a nexus (*lien de connexité*) between the asset possessed and the claim. Both the courts and the learned commentary have distinguished between two kinds of nexus:
   (a) a 'physical nexus', ie where the claim of the creditor has arisen directly in connection with the property sought to be retained, either because the property has caused damage to the creditor, or because the creditor has expended sums for the conservation, the improvement or the transformation of the property; and
   (b) a 'legal nexus', ie where the claim of the creditor has arisen in connection with a contract or other legal relationship between the debtor and the creditor.

The *droit de retention* is a powerful tool for an unsecured creditor. Although it does not in and of itself grant the beneficiary thereof the right to cause the asset to be sold and to satisfy its claim out of the proceeds thereof on a preferential basis, the possessory lien remains enforceable even against the purchaser in a sale of the asset (including a judicial sale following attachment) until the debt giving rise to the lien has been paid; hence, the beneficiary of the lien can continue to refuse to return the property until the debt is paid. As a practical matter, this means that secured creditors will usually pay off the debt subject to a *droit de retention* if the value of the property retained is greater than the amount of the claim of the secured creditor.

Arrest

Unsecured creditors are entitled in certain circumstances to arrest (seize) certain assets of a defaulting debtor, even when they are in the hands of a third party. Under Law no 91-650 of 9 July 1991, precautionary arrest (*saisie conservatoire*) of tangible moveable assets or debts (*créances*) or other intangible property may be authorised on an *ex parte* basis by the courts upon petition of the creditor or be effected directly by the creditor possessing an executory title (eg a judgment on the merits). The debtor is entitled to obtain a release (*mainlevée*) of the arrest order if certain conditions are not met or to substitute any other measure which safeguards the interests of the parties. Similar provisions in the relevant legislation permit the arrest of vessels and aircraft. In the case of real estate, an analogous procedure exists permitting a creditor who fears that the debtor will shortly become insolvent to obtain a 'judicial mortgage' (*hypothèque judiciaire*) over real estate owned by the debtor, and similar provisions in the FDC law permit a 'judicial pledge' (*nantissement judiciaire*) of a going business.

Forced sale

Unsecured creditors holding an executory title (eg a judgment debt) are, like secured creditors having obtained the necessary court order, entitled to obtain the forced seizure (*saisie-vente*) and sale (*vente forcée*) of assets belonging to a defaulting debtor. However, creditors holding security over such assets are entitled to priority over the proceeds of such sale. The creditor must then serve a notice to pay (*commandement*) on the debtor; in the event that payment is not forthcoming in eight days then the property is seized, and may be sold at auction. Similar procedures permit seizure of amounts owed to the debtor by a third party in order to obtain forced attribution (*saisie-attribution*).

Procedures which can restrict/prohibit enforcement; the fate of security in bankruptcy proceedings

As is the case in other jurisdictions, the French bankruptcy law (Law no 85-98 of 25 January 1985, hereinafter the 'Bankruptcy Law' (recently codifed as Arts L. 620-1 ff of the Commercial Code)) imposes several restraints on the creation[13] and enforcement of security. The current Bankruptcy Law, which replaced an earlier law of 1967, reflected the concerns of the French parliamentary majority at the time to discourage unemployment resulting from bankruptcy by directing post-bankruptcy efforts at saving the enterprise, occasionally at the expense of creditors. In 1994, substantial revisions were made to the Bankruptcy Law by amending legislation (Law no 94-475 of 10 June 1994), including measures designed to improve the position of creditors, particularly secured creditors. The following discussion describes the effect of a bankruptcy filing on the claims of secured creditors.

13 The effect of the 'hardening rules' contained in the Bankruptcy Law Arts 107 and 108 (recently codifed as Arts L. 621-107 and 621-108 of the Commercial Code) are discussed under 'Security created at point of insolvency' (p 128 below).

Administrator's right to continue agreements

French bankruptcy proceedings are triggered by the inability of a debtor to meet current liabilities with current assets, a situation known as 'cessation of payments' (*cessation des paiements*). Once the debtor is in cessation of payments, it has an obligation to petition the court for the opening of bankruptcy proceedings within 15 days thereafter.[14] Prior to the 1994 amendment of the Bankruptcy Law, the initial petition was required to be for judicial reorganisation (*redressement judiciaire*), proceedings akin to administration in the UK and 'Chapter 11' proceedings in the United States, rather than for judicial liquidation (*liquidation judiciaire*), proceedings akin to 'Chapter 7' proceedings in the US. Except in the case of small bankruptcies, the opening of reorganisation proceedings results in the opening of a period of observation of from six to 20 months during which the enterprise continues to transact business while the court considers whether it is possible to save the enterprise by the conclusion of a payment plan with creditors or to sell all or part of it as a going business and satisfy the creditors out of the proceeds of such sale.

Under the prior law, the court was obliged to order the liquidation of the business only if neither of the foregoing solutions was possible. Under the amended Bankruptcy Law, the initial petition may request and the court is entitled to order the immediate judicial liquidation of the enterprise, with no period of observation, where the enterprise has ceased all activity or if recovery is manifestly impossible. This has important consequences for secured creditors, since, as will be explained in more detail below, the principal benefits of security are suspended during the observation period.

On the opening of *redressement judiciaire* proceedings, the court appoints three persons with different responsibilities: an administrator (*administrateur*) who, depending on the scope of the judgment, either 'supervises', 'assists' or actually 'assures' the management of the debtor company, a creditors' representative (*représentant des créanciers*), who can be assisted by one or several 'comptrollers' (*contrôleurs*) named from among the creditors themselves,[15] and a supervising judge (*juge-commissaire*) who supervises the development of the proceedings.

Although the creditors' representative is typically the closest link to individual creditors, since all claims for unpaid debts are filed with the representative,[16] it is the administrator who frequently makes the decisions which have the most bearing on the creditors' rights. Under the Bankruptcy Law Art 37 (recently codifed as Art L. 621-28 of the Commercial Code), once *redressement judiciaire* proceedings have been opened, the administrator alone, and no other party (ie including any creditor) has the option of

14 The petition for the opening of the proceedings may also be filed by any creditor, by the public prosecutor, or by the court acting *sua sponte*. Employee representatives may also inform the court of any facts which tend to show that an enterprise is in *cessation des paiements*.

15 Prior to the 1994 amendments to the Bankruptcy Law, the maximum number of comptrollers was two. Under the amended legislation, the maximum number is five, and, if more than one is named, at least one is to be chosen from among secured or privileged creditors. Comptrollers are also given increased power to file motions at various stages of the procedure.

16 In addition, under the new legislation any creditor who so requests by registered letter sent to the creditors' representative is entitled to be informed by the representative of essential developments occurring in the course of the proceedings. Creditors benefiting from security which has been published in the public record are entitled to be personally informed of the opening of the bankruptcy proceedings (Bankruptcy Law Art 50(recently codifed as Art L. 621-43 of the Commercial Code)).

requiring further performance of any contract then under way, on condition that the administrator itself furnishes future performance of the bankrupt debtor's obligations. If the administrator determines to 'continue' performance of the contract, then the co-contractant is required to provide further performance of its own obligations, even if the bankrupt debtor had defaulted in its own performance of payment obligations prior to the opening of the bankruptcy proceedings. In such case, the pre-bankruptcy default gives rise solely to a bankruptcy claim made to the creditors' representative.

The administrator has no deadline period in which it must make known to the co-contractant whether or not he intends to continue performance of the contract. However, Art 37 provides that the administrator will be deemed to have waived his right to continuation of the contract if he does not respond to a formal request for a determination (*mise en demeure*) made by the co-contractant within one month of such *mise en demeure* (unless the *juge-commissaire* requires a shorter period or grants an additional period of up to two months). If the administrator does not exercise the option to continue the contract, then failure to perform during the period following the opening of bankruptcy proceedings can give rise to damages, which themselves can be the subject of a creditor's claim[17]. Article 37 further provides that, notwithstanding any contractual clause to the contrary, a contract cannot be terminated solely due to the opening of the bankruptcy proceedings (similarly, the Bankruptcy Law Art 56 provides that the judgment opening the bankruptcy proceedings cannot, in and of itself, render due amounts which were not otherwise due at such date, and provides that any contractual clause to the contrary is deemed to be inexistent).

Under the amendments made to the Bankruptcy Law in 1994, the powers of the administrator in this respect have been somewhat tempered. The power of the administrator to decide in his sole discretion whether a contract will be 'continued' is limited by requiring, in the case that the contract relates to the payment of a sum of money, the administrator to pay such amount in cash or to obtain payment delays from the co-contractant. The administrator must, on the basis of the provisional documents available to him, determine whether the bankrupt debtor actually possesses the funds necessary to make the payments. In the event of contracts calling for payment in instalments, the administrator must terminate (ie refuse to continue) the contract if it appears to him that he will not possess the funds necessary to make payment of the next instalment. If the administrator continues the contract but does not make payment, then the contract is automatically terminated and an application may be made for the termination of the observation period as well.

The practical effect of Art 37 in the context of international lending is that once bankruptcy proceedings are opened with respect to a French debtor, it is nigh impossible to enforce security during the observation period. Provisions in the loan agreement providing that the occurrence of bankruptcy is automatically an event of default will be considered unenforceable. The administrator alone can determine whether to continue the agreement by promising future performance (subject to the limitations

17 Creditors, secured or otherwise, other than salaried employees, must file a creditor's claim within two months of the publication of the opening of bankruptcy proceedings in the French official gazette (this period being increased to four months for creditors outside of France). Creditors with security which has been filed in the public record are personally notified of the requirement to file a claim, and may not be foreclosed for failure to file such claim on a timely basis if they have not been so informed.

described in the previous paragraph resulting from the 1994 amendments); payment defaults of the debtor which have occurred prior to the opening of the bankruptcy proceedings will not permit termination of the loan agreement following the opening of the proceedings, but will give rise only to the right to file a creditor's claim.[18] Hence, if the full amount of the loan facility has not been drawn prior to the opening of the bankruptcy proceedings, the borrower could conceivably have the right to draw the remaining amount following the opening of the proceedings, even if amounts previously drawn have not been repaid when due, such amounts giving rise solely to a creditor's claim.

On the other hand, if the administrator does decide to continue performance of the agreement following the opening of the bankruptcy proceeding, then the lender is entitled to priority of repayment of new sums advanced, pursuant to the Bankruptcy Law Art 40 (recently codifed as Art L. 621-32 of the Commercial Code). Until the 1994 amendments to the Bankruptcy Law, this so-called 'Article 40 priority' ranked ahead of all other creditors, even secured creditors, except for certain liens of employees for salary and the costs of the bankruptcy proceedings. The policy behind this provision was to encourage lenders to make new moneys available to the bankrupt debtor in order to enable it to recover. Under the 1994 amendments, 'Article 40 priority' continues to rank ahead of secured debtors in the event that the bankrupt enterprise agrees on a reorganisation plan with the creditors or if the enterprise is sold in order to satisfy creditors out of the proceeds. However, if the bankrupt debtor is placed in judicial liquidation, then, under the amendments, all pre-bankruptcy security consisting of either mortgages, pledges coupled with a right of retention or purchase money security interests over material and equipment will have priority over post-bankruptcy 'Article 40 debt'. This means that the security described on pp 79, 86, 90, 97 and 101 above will benefit from such priority in the case of *liquidation judiciaire*.[19]

Due to the rather extraordinary power of the administrator under the Bankruptcy Law Art 37, once bankruptcy proceedings are opened, any loan agreement in which a French party may draw on the facilities must be carefully drafted so as to trigger a default situation (and resulting acceleration) upon the occurrence of events which typically occur chronologically prior to the opening of bankruptcy proceedings but which presage an impending bankruptcy filing.

Even so, in France as elsewhere, speed is of the essence. Under the Bankruptcy Law Art 47, the judgment opening the bankruptcy proceedings suspends or prohibits any judicial action on the part of any creditor whose debt originates prior to the judgment and which relates either to the payment of a sum of money or the termination of a contract for default in the payment of a sum of money, as well as any measures of execution (eg arrest or seizure of assets) commenced by creditors with respect to movable or

18 However, the 1994 amendments provide statutory recognition to a case law gloss on the law permitting set-off (*compensation*) of pre-bankruptcy debts against amounts owed to the bankrupt debtor by the creditor where the two debts are 'connected' (Bankruptcy Law Art 33 (recently codifed as Art L. 621-24 of the Commercial Code)).

19 Security assignments of book debt under the *Loi Dailly* (p 93) constitute transfers of title and would survive the opening of bankruptcy proceedings. Pledges of going business (p 87) are not covered by the 1994 amendments and will therefore rank behind 'Article 40' debt. It is not clear at the present time whether pledges of intangible rights (p 92) or charges over cash and bank accounts (pp 96-97) would be covered by the 1994 amendments, although in the view of the author this would be the case, since such security entails constructive dispossession of the pledged asset to the pledgee.

immovable assets.[20] Nevertheless, there is some case authority for the proposition that a pledgee of a tangible asset who actually holds the asset is entitled to exercise the pledgee's remedy of sale of the asset as described under 'Power of sale or attribution of the secured asset' (p 117 above). In addition, the Bankruptcy Law Art 33 permits the debtor, on application to the *juge-commissaire*, to pay debts which arose prior to the opening of the bankruptcy proceedings if such payment is necessary to release a pledge over an asset which is necessary for the continuation of the bankrupt's business.

The fate of guarantees and security in a bankruptcy proceeding

Guarantees

Creditors of bankrupt debtors benefiting from guarantees are generally entitled to enforce such guarantees despite the opening of bankruptcy proceedings against the underlying obligor[1] . However, under the 1994 amendments to the Bankruptcy Law, actions against *cautions*[2] who are physical persons are suspended until the court orders a reorganisation plan or the liquidation of the company, following which the court may grant extensions to pay of up to two years (Bankruptcy Law Art 55 (recently codifed as Art L. 621-48 of the Commercial Code)). The Bankruptcy Law contains specific provisions dealing with situations where the guarantor is also the subject of a bankruptcy proceeding. In that case, the beneficiary may file a creditor's claim in both bankruptcy proceedings for the full amount of the debt (Bankruptcy Law Art 58). Where there are more than two guarantors, neither guarantor may file a claim in the bankruptcy procedure of the other, unless the total of all amounts paid under each procedure exceeds the amount of the debt, in which case the excess amount is paid, in the order of the undertakings to those guarantors who are guaranteed by the others (Bankruptcy Law Art 59 (recently codifed as Art L. 621-52 of the Commercial Code)). In the event that the creditor has received partial payment prior to the opening of the bankruptcy proceedings, it may file a creditor's claim solely for the amount remaining due. Any guarantor who has made such partial payment may file its own creditor's claim against the underlying debtor for the amount of such payment (Bankruptcy Law, Article 60 (recently codifed as Art L. 621-53 of the Commercial Code)). In the event that the

20 The bankruptcy judgment also prohibits the perfection of any security interest the perfection of which requires recording on a public register (such as the pledge of a *fonds de commerce* and the real estate mortgage) (Bankruptcy Law Art 57 (recently codifed as Art L. 621-50 of the Commercial Code)). Suits against the bankrupt debtor which are actually under way are suspended until the creditor has filed a creditor's claim; thereafter, the suit can be continued, but only in order to determine that a debt is due and the amount thereof (Bankruptcy Law Art 48 (recently codifed as Art L. 621-41 of the Commercial Code)). Interest, including default interest, on any loan agreement concluded for a period lesser than one year ceases to run (Bankruptcy Law Art 55 (recently codified as Art L. 621-48 of the Commercial Code)). However, this suspension does not apply to guarantees or co-sureties of the bankrupt debtor.

1 A number of decisions of the *Cour de Cassation* have held, however, that failure of the creditor to file a creditor's claim in respect of the underlying obligation may be invoked by a *caution* as a defence to payment under a *cautionnement*. In addition, it should be recalled that under the Bankruptcy Law Art 56 (recently codifed as Art L. 621-49 of the Commercial Code), the mere opening of bankruptcy proceedings will not render the underlying debt immediately due; hence the opening of such proceedings will not give the creditor an independent right to call on the *cautionnement*.

2 The amendment uses the word '*cautions*'. It is unclear whether the same treatment extends to physical persons who have granted a first demand guarantee.

bankruptcy court adopts a reorganisation plan which provides for delayed payment by the bankrupt debtor, *cautions solidaires* do not benefit from such postponement (Bankruptcy Law Art 64 (recently codifed as Art L. 621-65 of the Commercial Code)). In the event that the court orders judicial liquidation of the bankrupt and the proceeds of such liquidation are insufficient to pay off all creditors, creditors benefiting from a *cautionnement* or a first-demand guarantee are entitled to bring an action against the guarantor for the difference.

Security

During the observation period, security over assets of the bankrupt debtor is essentially frozen. The bankrupt debtor or the *administrateur* may propose to holders of security the substitution of 'equivalent security', and may, if the holders do not consent, apply to the *juge-commissaire* for an order to this effect. In the event that any assets of the debtor which are subject to security are sold during such period, the proceeds thereof are deposited in a special account maintained at the *Caisse des Dépôts et Consignations* (a special state-owned bank). When the observation period is over (ie the debtor presents a plan accepted by the creditors or is declared in judicial liquidation), the secured creditors are paid the amounts in order of priority (subject to payment of certain employee liens) (Bankruptcy Law Art 34 (recently codifed as Art L. 621-25 of the Commercial Code)). Under the 1994 amendments to the Bankruptcy Law, the *juge-commissaire* is even given power to order the provisional payment by the debtor of all or part of debt secured on the assets of the debtor, prior to the end of the observation period, provided that the secured creditor posts a bank guarantee.

At the end of the observation period, the administrator either proposes a plan of recovery or the liquidation (ie 'straight' bankruptcy) of the bankrupt debtor. The recovery plan in turn can consist either of the continuation of the enterprise or the total or partial sale of its business (*cession totale ou partielle de l'entreprise*) to a third party. Even if the enterprise is to be continued, parts of the business can be sold to third parties (*cession partielle de l'entreprise*). The fate of security granted prior to the opening of the bankruptcy proceedings will be considered in each of these scenarios:

Continuation of the enterprise pursuant to a recovery plan

The administrator will have proposed to all creditors either the postponement or the reduction of their debt, or both, which each creditor, whether secured or not, has the liberty to refuse (Bankruptcy Law Art 24 (recently codifed as Art L. 621-60 of the Commercial Code)). However, the court may unilaterally impose on all creditors who have not accepted the administrator's proposition, whether secured or unsecured, a postponement of reimbursement and may propose a reduction in lieu thereof (Bankruptcy Law, articles 74 and 75 (recently codifed as Arts L. 621-76 and 621-77 of the Commercial Code)). Although any security over the debt will survive, the debt itself will thus have been weakened.

The court may order, as part of the continuation plan, either the isolated sale of assets or the sale of a line of business. In either case, if such assets are subject to security, then the proceeds are subject to the same procedure as sales of such assets during the observation period : the proceeds thereof are deposited in a special account maintained at the *Caisse des Dépôts et Consignations* and the secured creditors are paid the amounts in order of priority (subject to payment of certain employee liens). Amounts payable to secured creditors as part of the general continuation plan (as postponed or reduced pursuant to the procedure described in the previous paragraph) are reduced by any amount payable as the proceeds of such sales. The court may order that alternative security be given to the creditor in substitution of the security originally granted on the asset sold (Bankruptcy Law Art 78).

If the bankrupt debtor does not honour the recovery plan, then any creditor may petition the court for the conversion of the *redressement judiciaire* to *liquidation judiciaire*. Prior to the 1994 amendments, such a petition could be filed only by one or several creditors having 15% or more of the outstanding debts of the debtor.

Total sale of the enterprise

If the total business is sold to a third party, then the judgment adopting the plan of sale renders any debts not yet due immediately due (Bankruptcy Law Art 91 (recently codifed as Art L. 621-94 of the Commercial Code)). If the sale includes assets which are subject to security, then the court must allocate a portion of the proceeds of sale to each of such assets for the allocation of the purchase price and the exercise of preferential rights (Bankruptcy Law Art 93 (recently codifed as Art L. 621-96 of the Commercial Code)). Except in cases of fraud or certain criminal proceedings, this is the sole right of the creditors; they do not recover their individual rights against the debtor at the close of the proceedings. However, any security granted by the debtor to secure the financing of the acquisition of assets on which the security is granted survives the sale of the secured asset to the third party, who is thereafter obligated to reimburse the financing according to its terms unless extended payment terms are granted by the court or the parties agree otherwise.[3]

Judicial liquidation

If the administrator is unable to propose either an acceptable recovery plan or a sale of the business or if a recovery plan proves unworkable, (or, if pursuant to the 1994 amendments, it is clear at the time of the opening of the bankruptcy proceedings that the enterprise has ceased all activity or if recovery is manifestly impossible), then the debtor enterprise is placed in judicial liquidation, and the assets are sold and the proceeds used to satisfy creditors. Where the judicial reorganisation proceedings are converted into liquidation proceedings, the creditors' representative is usually named liquidator for such purposes.

Real estate is normally sold at auction, with the reserve price (*mise à prix*) being determined by the *juge-commissaire*. However, the *juge-commissaire* may also decide to sell the real estate privately if circumstances so permit (Bankruptcy Law Art 154 (recently codifed as Art L. 622-16 of the Commercial Code)). The proceeds of the sale are distributed in the same manner as described above. Units of production consisting in whole or in part of movable or immovable property may be sold pursuant to a special procedure of public solicitation of offers, and the proceeds allocated to creditors.[4] All other assets are sold at auction or privately by the *juge-commissaire* (Bankruptcy Law Arts 155 and 156 (recently codifed as Arts L. 622-18 and 622-19 of the Commercial Code)).

3 Prior to the 1994 amendments, this exception applied only to purchase money security interests for the acquisition of materials and equipment. Henceforth the exception applies to any security granted to secure the acquisition of an asset, eg real estate mortgages.

4 In order to cease an obvious abuse of the procedure which occurred frequently, the 1994 amendments provide that in such case neither the bankrupt debtor itself nor any officer or director thereof or any of their close relatives may offer to purchase the assets pursuant to such proceedings.

However, certain special rules apply to assets subject to security. If the liquidator so wishes, he may, by payment of the debt secured thereby, liberate from a pledge any tangible assets which have been made subject to pledge. If the liquidator does not do so, he must, within six months of the judgment declaring the debtor in liquidation, request from the *juge-commissaire* authorisation to sell the asset. The creditor is notified of the impending sale at least two weeks prior to the sale and may petition the court for the judicial attribution of the asset (Bankruptcy Law Art 159 (recently codifed as Art L. 622-21 of the Commercial Code)).

The judgment which opens judicial liquidation proceedings (or converts reorganisation proceedings into liquidation proceedings) renders immediately due all debts which are not yet due (Bankruptcy Law Art 160 (recently codifed as Art L. 622-22 of the Commercial Code)). Creditors with mortgages over real estate or recordable security over personal property (eg pledgees of a *fond de commerce*) may, if such assets have not been sold by the liquidator within three months from the judgment opening the liquidation proceedings, recover their individual rights and may enforce their security in the manner described in under 'Remedies and enforcement' (p 117 above) (minus any payments they may have received in the course of the recovery plan). However, pursuant to the 1994 amendments, the *juge-commissaire* may order the provisional payment of all or part of a debt, and may condition such payment on the submission of a bank guarantee (Bankruptcy Law Art 161-1 (recently codifed as Art L. 622-24 of the Commercial Code)). In the event that debts owing to secured creditors are not fully satisfied out of the proceeds of the sale of the secured assets, such creditors rank equally with unsecured creditors for the remainder of the debts owed to them (Bankruptcy Law Art 164 (recently codifed as Art L. 622-27 of the Commercial Code)).

VITIATING FACTORS

As in the case of other jurisdictions, certain circumstances exist under which security is intrinsically invalid under French law. The following section describes those instances which are most likely to occur in the case of cross-border security.

Security created at point of insolvency

Pursuant to the Bankruptcy Law Art 57 (recently codifed as Art L. 621-50 of the Commercial Code), security cannot be perfected by filing following the opening of bankruptcy proceedings. In addition, the Bankruptcy Law Arts 107 and 108, which are the French equivalent of the 'hardening rules' found in the bankruptcy laws of other countries, provide that certain transactions are either automatically null and void or are voidable at the discretion of the court if such transactions have been entered into by the bankrupt debtor during the so-called 'suspect period' (*période suspecte*). The suspect period begins at the time when the bankrupt debtor is in cessation of payments (*cessation des paiements*), ie is unable to make payments as they become due. Although in theory a debtor which finds itself in a situation of cessation of payments is required to file for bankruptcy at the latest 15 days thereafter (Bankruptcy Law Art 3 (recently codifed as Art L. 621-1 of the Commercial Code)), in practice the court is entitled to fix the date of cessation of payments (and thus the beginning of the suspect period) as early as 18 months prior to the judgment opening the bankruptcy proceedings (Bankruptcy Law Art 9). Thus, in the event that a pledgee files for bankruptcy at any time in the 18-month period following the signature of a security instrument, there is a hypothetical possibility that the security could be set aside if the security falls within one of the transactions described in the Bankruptcy Law Arts 107 or 108 (recently codifed as Arts L. 621-107 and L. 621-108 of the Commercial Code).

Article 107 contains a specific list of transactions which, if accomplished during the suspect period, *must* be set aside (ie the court has no discretion to refuse to do so). Several such transactions can apply to the taking of security. Article 107(1) provides that any instrument by which real or personal property (which would include intangible rights) is conveyed (which has been interpreted by the French courts as including the creation of security thereon) for no consideration (*à titre gratuit*) must be set aside[5]. Article 107(2) provides that any bilateral contract pursuant to which the obligations of the debtor exceed significantly the obligations of the other party must also be set aside. Finally, Article 107(6) provides that any mortgage or pledge granted during the suspect period as security for previously contracted debts (ie not for new money) must be set aside.

Article 108, unlike Art 107, provides that the court may in its discretion (but is not required to) set aside any transaction involving payment for consideration (no specific list is given) after the date of *cessation des paiements* if the parties having dealt with the debtor had knowledge at the time of contracting that the debtor was in fact in cessation of payments. Obviously, the question of whether or not parties granting a loan – particularly a loan coupled with security – to a debtor actually knew that the debtor was in cessation of payments is a delicate question, and the court is entitled, on the basis of the evidence, to find that this was indeed the case; however, the burden of proof lies on the party seeking the setting aside of the transaction.[6]

In addition to the foregoing, lenders should be aware that a French court is entitled to find the supplier of credit liable in damages to other creditors of a debtor (whether or not the debtor is in bankruptcy, although the question arises most frequently in that situation), if at the time of granting the credit the lender knew that the financial situation of the debtor was 'irremediably compromised'. Actual knowledge is required (although such knowledge can be inferred from the facts), and the notion of 'irremediably compromised' is delicate: the courts have held that the fact that the debtor was admitted to bankruptcy at the time of the granting of the credit does not necessarily mean that its situation was irremediably compromised if the lender reasonably believed that the lending of new money could help the debtor to recover. Conversely, the fact of lending even to a start-up entity can result in the liability of the lender if the circumstances make it clear that the lender knew that the borrower's business plan was entirely unrealistic.

One other source of lender liability resides in the action for *comblement de passif*. Under the Bankruptcy Law Art 180 (recently codifed as Art L. 624-3 of the Commercial Code), when the *redressement judiciaire* or *liquidation judiciaire* proceedings of a legal entity make it clear that there is an insufficiency of assets to pay off all liabilities, the court may decide that the debts of the bankrupt debtor will be paid in whole or in part by the *de jure* or *de facto* managers (*dirigeants de droit ou de fait*) of such entity, where the fault of such persons has resulted in the insufficiency of assets. The notion

5 In this particular case, the court is also entitled (but not obliged) to set aside such transactions if they occurred during the six-month period prior to the beginning of the 'suspect period'.

6 Actions under Arts 107 and 108 may be brought by the administrator, the creditors' representative, the liquidator, or the plan commissioner (an officer named by the court to oversee performance of the reorganisation plan).

of *de facto* manager is wide, and encompasses any person or entity which in fact exercises management decisions. In several instances, the French courts have found that the actions of a bank in enforcing covenants contained in a loan agreement was such that the bank was actually acting as *de facto* manager of the debtor, thus justifying the application of Art 180.

'Financial Assistance'

The French Company Law Art 217-9 (recently codifed as Art L. 225-216 of the Commercial Code)provides as follows:

> 'A corporation[7] may not advance funds, grant loans or give security for the subscription for or purchase of its own shares by a third party.
>
> The provisions of this article do not apply either to current operations of credit companies or to transactions undertaken with a view to the acquisition by employees of shares of the corporation or one of its subsidiaries.'

Article 217-9 represents the codification into French law of the provisions of the Second Company Law Directive of 13 December 1976 Art 23. Unfortunately, the text is very sparse and contains none of the language of its English counterpart (Companies Act 1985 Arts 151ff) which both explain in greater detail the scope of the prohibition and provide specific exemptions therefrom and a procedure for 'whitewashing' in certain cases.[8] Hence, a great many questions remain open, few of which appear, to date, to have been the subject of any French court decisions which would provide the answers.

First among these issues is what is meant by the term 'security' in the first paragraph. The French term used in the text of the statute, '*sûreté*', does not correspond to a perfectly defined legal category, and can be construed either narrowly, as the equivalent of the term 'security', or more generally to include any preferential right, including *cautionnements* and first-demand guarantees. Such doctrinal authorities as have considered the issue are inclined to follow the more general interpretation, including *cautionnements* and guarantees. If this interpretation is correct (and, in the absence of any court decisions, it would be prudent to assume that it is), then the granting of even an unsecured guarantee by a French company would be caught in the net of prohibited 'financial assistance.'

A second issue is whether the provisions of Article 217-9 are applicable to security granted for the purchase of shares of a company other than that which actually grants the security. Typically, the question arises where a subsidiary is requested to provide security for the acquisition of the shares of its parent company, a situation which arises

7 The literal wording of the statute here is 'company' (*société*); however, the positioning of the statute in the French Company Law makes it clear that only corporations (*sociétés anonymes*) are intended. Where the company is organised as a *société à responsabilité limitée* (limited liability company) rather than as a *société anonyme*, then it does not fall within the ambit of the provision in the first instance. However, there is no distinction made in the French statute between 'public' and 'private' companies similar to that effected in the English Companies Act 1985.

8 For example, the English Companies Act 1985 provisions prohibit specifically the extension of financial assistance by subsidiaries of the company being acquired, while no direct mention is made of this in the French text (see discussion below). The Companies Act also provides for specific exoneration in the case of 'private companies', subject to certain requirements.

very frequently in practice in the context of management buy-outs/buy-ins of foreign companies which have a French subsidiary.

While there is no case law authority on this point, it appears possible to argue that the strict wording of the statute, which refers to financial assistance granted by a company in view of the acquisition of 'its own shares,' would not apply to such a case. Unfortunately, it is just as possible to argue that, where a subsidiary of the company whose shares are being acquired provides financial assistance for the purchase of such shares, it is also indirectly financing the purchase of its own shares, since such shares are in the portfolio of its parent company, and therefore that such assistance falls within thc ambit of Art 217-9. The text of the French statute is regrettably totally silent on this point (unlike the English Companies Act 1985 Art 151, which deals specifically with the issue) and there does not appear to exist any case law on the subject at this point in time. Some of the doctrinal authorities appear to be in favour of a strict reading of the statute, thus excluding subsidiaries from the scope of the restriction, but even those commentators have cautioned that they are reluctant to exclude the proposition entirely where the subsidiary grants the security acting on the orders of its parent company the shares of which are being acquired.

Article 217-9 does not prohibit the granting by a company of a pledge over the shares of another company which it is in the process of acquiring to secure the purchase price of the shares of the company being acquired, since in such instance it is not the company being acquired which is granting the security. A 1994 decision of the *Cour de Cassation* has also taken the view that the payment of dividends by a company to the holding company which has been constituted in order to purchase its shares does not fall within the prohibition enunciated by Article 217-9.

Commercial benefit

In the case of all French companies, regardless of the form under which they are constituted, the issue of corporate interest (*intérêt social*) will be important. Under prevailing principles of French case law, financial concessions granted by one company in a group of companies to another may constitute an 'abuse of company assets' (*abus de biens sociaux*) of the first company (thereby triggering liability of the corporate officers who authorise such concessions) unless the following conditions are met:

1 the two companies belong to a genuine 'group' of companies (which presupposes the existence of structural bonds between the companies and a genuine common strategy in order to accomplish a common objective, as opposed to a 'conglomerate' situation), and the operation is dictated by an economic, social or financial interest which is common to the members of the group; and
2 the financial concession must not be devoid of consideration or break the equilibrium between the respective undertakings of the companies, and must not exceed the financial capabilities of the company granting the concession.

Various court decisions have held that these rules apply to the granting of inter-company guarantees as well as the granting of outright loans or advances. The application of these general principles to the potential granting of guarantees by a French company is, however, a complex issue which will depend in great part on the actual facts of the transaction.

The first test, that of group interest, appears easy enough to meet in the case of an ordinary loan to a multinational group of companies, in which upstream and cross guarantees are frequently sought by the lending banks. However, there appears to be no case authority as to whether the test is met in the case of an acquisition facility for a management buy-out/buy-in, where the new holding company created for the purposes of the transaction is frequently required by the banks financing the acquisition to obtain guarantees and security from the various companies being acquired. Obviously, a rather facile argument could be made to the effect that the success of the MBO/MBI will result in more dynamic management at the group level and thus to each of the companies in the group, including any French company from which guarantees or security are sought and that this alone should enable the test to be met. Not surprisingly, the doctrinal authority on the subject does not go quite that far. However, certain authors are of the view that if the acquisition facilities are accompanied by other lines of credit (eg working capital facilities) permitting the refinancing of existing debt, or if the credit facilities made available to the parent are to be used in part for on-lending to the other companies, in the group, it can be considered that the ensemble of credit granted constitutes a single whole, guaranteed by the guarantee sought from the French company and therefore that the granting of a guarantee by the French company corresponds to the interest of the group as a whole.

Other authors are less favourable to such an argument, pointing out that in order for the operation to be dictated by an economic, social or financial interest which is common to the members of the group, there must first exist a true group of companies. These authors are of the view that the creation of an ad hoc entity for the sole purpose of obtaining leverage in the acquisition, does not constitute a true 'group of companies,' and that the test is therefore not met.

The second test (consideration, equilibrium and financial capacity), also raises issues the solution of which will depend on the contours of the actual transaction. Unless the benefit of the facilities can somehow be linked to the French company from which a guarantee is sought, it might be difficult to show that the guarantee was not devoid of consideration; as for the first test, this test is commonly met by showing that the proceeds of the loan being guaranteed will be made available in whole or in part to the entity giving the guarantee, either because the guarantor is itself a permitted borrower under the credit facility, or because the proceeds of the loan will be (or at least are capable of being) on-lent in whole or in part to the entity granting the guarantee.

In order to meet the second test, it is also necessary to show that the granting of the guarantees did not break the economic equilibrium between group companies or exceed the financial capacity of the entities granting the financial assistance. Obviously, the courts here are concerned with the possibility that the assets of a financially sound company may be used to shore up the failing financial health of another company. This test is generally dealt with by negotiating a monetary limitation on the amount of the guarantee, either an absolute amount calculated as a function of the value of the French company at the time that the guarantee is executed, or an agreed-upon percentage of the net worth of the French company from time to time.

Error, duress, fraud

Under the Civil Code, all contracts (including those relating to the granting of security) can be declared void (*nul*) or rescinded in the event that the court determines that consent to the contract was flawed by error, duress or fraud (Civil Code Art 1109).

Error may result in the voiding or rescission of a contract only where the error relates to the substance of the thing contracted for. Mere error in the identity of the other contracting party is not a cause for rescission unless such identity is the principal cause of the contract (Civil Code Art 1110). The victim of the error must show that it would not have concluded the contract had it been aware of the error, and that the error was not imputable to itself.

Fraud (*dol*) is a cause of voidness of a contract when the manoeuvres exercised by one of the parties are such that is clear that in the absence thereof the other party would not have entered into the contract (Civil Code Art 1116). The courts have held that the counterparty must have intentionally intended to deceive or mislead the party seeking rescission; mere negligence or involuntary omission will not suffice to prove fraud. However, intentional withholding of information (*réticence*) can constitute fraud. Fraud will not vitiate the contract unless it emanates from the other contracting party and not from a third party. Fraud will not be presumed, and must be proven by the party seeking to rescind the contract. Where the fraud did not incite the party to conclude the agreement, but only to accept less favourable conditions than it would have otherwise obtained, the contract cannot be rescinded, but damages may be claimed.

Duress (*violence*), whether exercised by a contracting party or a third party (Civil Code Art 1111) can result in the voiding of a contract when it is of a nature to cause a reasonable person to fear that his own person or his assets will be exposed to significant and present harm. The court is entitled to take into account the age, the sex and the condition of the person in question (Civil Code Art 1112). Where the contracting party is a legal entity, duress exists where it is exercised on the physical persons representing the entity. Duress exercised on the spouse, descendants or ascendants of the contracting party will also suffice to void the contract (Civil Code Art 1113).

ENFORCEMENT OF FOREIGN GUARANTEES AND SECURITY

Basis of recognition

As explained earlier, the domestic French rules governing both guarantees and security are complex: French law recognises two types of guarantee, the statutory guarantee (*cautionnement*) and the first-demand guarantee, and the rules governing security generally follow the type of asset over which the security is to be taken rather than a unified regime. It follows that the rules governing recognition in France of guarantees and security governed by foreign law and/or executed outside France will be somewhat complex as well.

Statutory guarantees (cautionnement)

As described under 'guarantees' (p 67 above), the determining characteristic of the *cautionnement* under French law is its strong link to the underlying obligation. For this reason, the French courts initially adopted the principle that the proper governing law of a guarantee was the same as that of the underlying obligation, and often refused to enforce a foreign guarantee executed to guarantee the obligation of a party to a contract governed by French law. Gradually, however, the French courts abandoned this theory and now hold that the parties are free to provide that a guarantee executed in the context of an international transaction will be governed by a foreign law, even if the underlying obligation is subject to French law. In the absence of a choice of law in the guarantee, however, the courts are inclined to presume that the parties intended to apply the same law to the guarantee as that which governs the underlying obligation. This presumption is rebuttable, and the courts usually apply the law of the jurisdiction of the bank in the case of a bank guarantee.

Issues of capacity of a party to enter into the guarantee and proper authorisation remain governed by the law of the domicile of the party in question. For example, the French courts have held that the requirement referred to under 'Board resolutions' (p 106 above) that a guarantee entered into by a French corporation be approved by a resolution of the board of directors remains applicable in the case of a guarantee governed by a foreign law.

First-demand guarantees

Unlike the case of the statutory guarantee, the essence of the first-demand guarantee is its independence from the underlying obligation. Hence, the initial preference of the French courts for application of the law of the underlying obligation which existed in the case of the *cautionnement* has never existed with respect to the foreign-law first-demand guarantee, which the French courts generally enforce in international transactions. In the absence of an express choice of law, the French courts are inclined to apply the law of the bank granting the guarantee to the relationship between the underlying obligor and the bank, but the law of the place of the beneficiary to the relationship between the bank and the beneficiary; in practice, of course, it is extremely rare for an international bank guarantee to fail to include a governing law clause.

Security instruments

The French rules relating to recognition of foreign security over assets are particularly complex, and tend to distinguish between the creation of such security and the effects thereof.

With respect to the creation of the security, the French *doctrine* and *jurisprudence* appear to give preference to the law applicable to the source of the security (law governing the contract, the court decision or the provision of law pursuant to which the security is created); the French courts will recognise such security only if the source is valid and binding in the relevant country and gives rise to an effective obligation to create such security. However, the French courts will also require that the security purported to be created actually corresponds to a type of security recognised by the jurisdiction in which the asset over which the security purported to be created is located, the *lex rei sitae*. Thus, for example, it is theoretically possible to create security over an asset located in France pursuant to an agreement governed by the laws of England, provided that the agreement in question is the valid and binding source of such security under English law, *and* that the type of security so created exists under French law. It is for this reason that an English-law agreement purporting to create a floating charge over assets situated in France will not be recognised and enforced by a French court.

With respect to the effects of security, the *lex rei sitae* is given virtually exclusive effect. The law of the location of the asset will therefore govern issues such as the rights of the secured party to preferential payment of the proceeds of sale of the asset, *droits de suite*, and the causes of termination of the security. Delicate issues may arise where the asset is in one jurisdiction at the time of creation but is located in another jurisdiction at the time that the security is sought to be enforced. In such case, the tendency of the French courts is to apply the new *lex rei sitae* to the effects of the security.

The remainder of this subsection will deal with issues relating to specific categories of security.

Real estate mortgages (*hypothèques*)

The Civil Code Art 2128 provides specifically that, in the absence of international treaty, an agreement entered into outside France is invalid to create a mortgage over real estate situate in France. Hence, it is inadvisable to execute a mortgage over French real estate otherwise than in accordance with the procedures described in under 'Charges over land: real estate mortgages' (p 79 above) (execution before a French notary), except in the rare cases where international treaty permits the execution of such mortgages before a French consular officer[9] or before local authorities. Article 2128 has been interpreted restrictively, however, so that neither an agreement pursuant to which a party promises to create a mortgage nor an agreement relating to subrogation to or transfer of a mortgage need be executed before a French notary, although in the latter case other legislation requires that the foreign document be legalised by a French civil servant and registered with a French notary.

Pledge of tangible assets

It is a constant principle of French jurisprudence that a pledge of tangible assets must comply with the *lex rei sitae*. For this reason, the French courts have strictly applied the requirement of physical dispossession (under 'Charges over goods – pledge of stock-in-trade' p 86 above) to any purported pledge of goods located in France, even if the agreement is executed in a country which recognises the creation of such pledges without dispossession. Where French law recognises the creation of pledges without dispossession (eg in the cases described under 'Charges over going business' and 'Purchase money security interest over material and equipment' pp 87 and 90 above), a foreign agreement will be recognised, but only if the procedures required under French law for the creation and perfection of such security are effected. For the same reason, it is strongly recommended to avoid execution of agreements purporting to create a security assignment of tangible assets located in France, as such agreements run a strong risk of being declared invalid in France as a *pacte commissoire*.

Aircraft mortgage

France is a party to the Geneva Convention on the International Recognition of Rights in Aircraft, under which the contracting states agree to recognise mortgages and similar rights in aircraft, provided that such rights have been constituted in accordance with the law of the contracting state in which the aircraft was registered as to nationality at the time of their constitution, and are regularly recorded in a public record of the contracting state in which the aircraft is registered as to nationality.

9 Even in the absence of international treaty, French consular authorities are competent in the case of a mortgage instrument executed solely between French parties.

Where the aircraft is registered in a country which is not a member state of the Convention, the tendency of the courts has also been to apply the law of the state in which the aircraft is registered to mortgages and other security created over the aircraft. Hence, it is possible that the French courts would recognise the validity of a foreign mortgage created over an aircraft registered in the country of such mortgage, even if the aircraft is temporarily in France at the time of the creation of the mortgage.

Ship mortgage

France is a party to the 1926 Brussels Convention on the Unification of Certain Rules Relating to Maritime Liens and Mortgages. A description of the recognition in France of mortgages and other security created over vessels being built outside of France or purchased abroad is provided under 'Charges over ships' (p 101 above).

Competing receiverships

The French courts subscribe to the principle of 'territoriality of bankruptcy proceedings' (*térritorialité de la faillite*), under which different bankruptcy proceedings can be brought in respect of the same bankrupt debtor in as many places as the debtor does business or owns assets, rather than that of 'universality of bankruptcy' (*unité ou universalité de la faillite*), under which proceedings may be brought only before a single court, usually that of the domicile or principal place of business of the bankrupt debtor. Consequently, in several highly-publicised instances, the French courts have granted petitions for the opening of bankruptcy proceedings (or instituted such proceedings *sua sponte*) in respect of foreign companies having branches in France, or even (as in the case of the bankruptcy of BCCI) simply on the grounds that the foreign company had a 'genuine commercial presence' in France. The fact that bankruptcy proceedings have already been brought in respect of the same debtor in another jurisdiction (including that of the principal office of the debtor) is not a bar to the opening of proceedings against the debtor in France unless the judgment opening the foreign proceedings has been the subject of execution (*exequatur*) proceedings in France or there is a treaty to the contrary.[10] Such bankruptcy proceedings will be conducted pursuant to the French Bankruptcy Law.

For this reason, it is possible for creditors, whether French or foreign, to file a creditor's claim in a French bankruptcy opened in respect of a French or foreign debtor, even where another proceeding regarding the same debtor has already been opened outside of France. Secured creditors may therefore find themselves in a position where their rights will be accorded different levels of priority in two different bankruptcy proceedings. The position of the French courts is that, subject to the rules described under 'Security instruments' (p 134 above), the law governing the security instrument will be applied to determine if such security will be validly created and the effects thereof,

10 The Brussels Convention on Jurisdiction and Enforcement of Judgments specifically excludes bankruptcy proceedings from its scope. France is a party to bilateral treaties which include provisions on enforcement of bankruptcy proceedings with Belgium, Italy, Monaco and Austria. A draft European treaty on bankruptcy has been signed by France but has not entered into effect at the date of publication.

but French law will govern the priority to be accorded to such security in a French bankruptcy proceeding, even where both the creditor and the debtor are not French.

The effect which foreign bankruptcy proceedings, whether brought against a French or foreign debtor, will have in France will depend on whether the judgment opening such proceedings has been the subject of an execution order (*exequatur*) in France. In the absence of such an order, the French courts will take judicial notice of the foreign bankruptcy, but will not enforce any order made by the foreign bankruptcy court. Under general principles of French law as enunciated by the *Cour de Cassation*, a judgment of a foreign court will be enforced in France without a re-examination of the merits only (in the absence of treaty) if the following conditions are satisfied :

1 there is a significant connection between the dispute and the court that has rendered the judgment and French courts do not have exclusive jurisdiction over the dispute;
2 fundamental procedural rights were duly fulfilled by the court rendering the judgment;
3 the laws of the jurisdiction which would be applicable under French conflicts of laws principles were applied by the court rendering the judgment; and
4 the judgment is not contrary to French public policy (*ordre public*) as applicable in the context of enforcement of foreign judgments and is not tainted by fraud.

In the event that a foreign bankruptcy judgment receives *exequatur* in France, it is entitled to full *res judicata* effect (*force de la chose jugée*), impeding the opening of similar proceedings in France and subjecting to the law of the forum of the bankruptcy proceedings the question of priority of security.

On a practical level, more than one respected author of *doctrine* has stated that the French courts have generally applied a pragmatic approach to the issue of 'competing' bankruptcies. Where the interests of French creditors requires that a foreign bankruptcy judgment be granted *exequatur*, the French courts will do so. Where such interests will be better protected by the opening of bankruptcy proceedings in France, the courts will order the opening of such proceedings, even if similar proceedings have already been opened outside of France.

4 Germany

Florian Wolff

Rossbach & Fischer, Frankfurt am Main

CATEGORIES OF SECURITY AVAILABLE UNDER GERMAN LAW

As a general rule, under German law all types of tangible or intangible assets can serve as collateral and security interests can be created over them. Unlike certain other jurisdictions, Germany does not recognise a global or floating charge over a group of assets or over all the assets of a company. Security interests can only be created on an asset-to-asset basis, although techniques have developed allowing a general description of the collateral in the security documentation. In practice it is therefore possible to take security on future assets, stock and receivables which change on a daily basis.

By way of overview, security interests can be categorised in three ways: personal security vs real security, security over chattel vs security over real estate and, finally, abstract vs what in German legal parlance is called 'accessory' security.

Personal and real security

While in the case of personal security a person or entity promises to make up the loss suffered by a third party (guarantee or indemnity), real (*dingliche*) security is created over an asset, which is given as collateral to the holder of the security. The holder of a real security interest has a preferential right to realise that asset and apply the proceeds towards the discharge of the secured claim.

Security over chattels and security over real estate

Whereas security over real estate can only be created in the forms described by law, security over movables and rights benefit from the freedom to contract, enabling the conversion of ownership interests into security interests by contractual agreement. The main difference between security over chattels and security over real estate is, however, that security over real estate is created only once it has been registered in the land register, whereas no registry exists for movables or rights. Generally, the registration of a security interest over real estate requires an application signed before, and certified by, a German notary as a prerequisite for the registration. Subject to the agreements on the order of priority to which the holder of the affected rights have to be a party, priority issues in real estate matters are decided by strict reference to the date and time of registration. The realisation of security over real estate is governed by a special statute, the *Zwangsversteigerungsgesetz* (ZVG), which provides a very detailed and separate scheme for the execution of mortgages.

Accessory (*Akzessorische*) security and abstract security

In Germany, most types of security are available in an abstract and in an accessory form. By way of example, the accessory guarantee is the counterpart of the abstract indemnity, and the hypothec (*Hypothek*) is the accessory counterpart of the abstract charge over land (*Grundschuld*). An accessory right is strictly dependent and attached to the secured claim. It only exists to the extent the secured claim exists; it can only be exercised and enforced to the extent the secured claim can be exercised and enforced. All exceptions and defences, which are available against the secured rights, can be exercised also against the holder of the accessory security interest. As a consequence of the accessory nature of a security interest, it can only be held by the secured. Accessory rights are automatically transferred together with the secured claim. Holding a security interest on trust, eg by a syndicate of banks in the case of an accessory security, is only possible if the underlying claim is transferred to the trustee as well.

In contrast, abstract security interests do not legally depend on the existence of a secured right at all. They are created independently, ie abstractly, from the secured right. The discharge of the secured claim does not automatically discharge or even reduce the security interest. The connection between the interest and the claim it secures is made by a separate agreement in which the purpose of the security arrangement is defined as between the giver of the security and its holder and which is therefore referred to as the 'Security Purpose Agreement' (*'Sicherungszweckbestimmung')*.

German statutory law, ie the German Civil Code (*Bürgerliches Gesetzbuch, BGB*), contains express provisions relating mainly to accessory security interests such as the pledge (*Pfandrecht*), the guarantee (*Bürgschaft*) and the hypothec (*Hypothek*). Abstract security interests are often not specifically codified, with the exception of the abstract charge over land, the *Grundschuld*.

Abstract security interests have often developed over the years through case law and legal practice, adapting other forms of interests over assets to be security interests. Thus an assignment for security purposes uses the title to receivables and, by adding a security purpose, tailors the full proprietary right to the receivable to be effectively reduced to a security interest only. All abstract security interests contain a fiduciary element in that the secured creditor has rights and legal positions much more complete and far-reaching than its rights vis-à-vis the giver of the security. The holder of the assignment for security purposes has the power to assign the assigned receivable, regardless of whether the debtor of the secured claim is in default and even if the secured claim has already been discharged. Therefore, abstract security always bears a certain risk of abuse, since the holder can enforce its interests regardless of whether doing so may be a breach of the security purpose arrangement. The fiduciary position allows the private sale of the collateral, even though the secured claim may be void, may not have matured or may have even been paid off or offset. The restrictions on the creditor's rights to exercise abstract security interests are only contractual in nature and thus, under German law, independent (abstract) title to the underlying collateral. They will often not be described in much detail in the security documentation, but may be implied by law.

In practice, abstract security interests are, for a variety of reasons, much more commonly used than accessory security interests. Normally they require fewer formalities and are easier to administer. Most of them do not require notification or publication and can thus be concealed from the general public or trade debtor until they are enforced. They are also more practical, since they can remain in place after the secured claim has been discharged and the secured claim can later be exchanged for another. They can be assigned to a third party. Finally, only abstract security interests permit the administration of the security by a trustee who holds and administers the interests for third parties (eg a syndicate of banks) without being the legal owner of the secured claim. This feature is particularly important when a security trustee must be appointed for the day-to-day administration of a security package designed to secure claims held by various creditors. Then often the security trustee must be able to enforce the security interest and any change in the composition of the group of creditors should not necessitate the creation of a new security interest. For reasons of clarity, simplicity and probably mere tradition, syndicates of banks and their agents often tend to include new banks in existing security arrangements by way of novation and not by way of assignment of one bank's interest to the new bank. As long as this tendency continues, banks will insist on abstract security interests in order not to lose the (accessory) security interest upon novation. From a practical viewpoint, it would be easier to proceed by assignment of the old bank's interest to the new bank and any accessory security would simply follow the secured claim. If the new bank is, however, included by novation, accessory interests necessarily lapse and must be created anew, a process which is cumbersome, and, in case of security which requires notarisation, costly.

PRIVATE INTERNATIONAL LAW

Law applicable to personal security

Personal security is always created by way of contract. Although in practice guarantees, indemnities, letters of support and the like are often simply signed by the obligor and thus appear to be unilateral declarations, they are in fact contracts concluded, as all contracts are, by an offer and a corresponding acceptance. The acceptance by the beneficiary is most frequently not issued explicitly. Under BGB Sec 151 sentence 1 the acceptance need not be received by the offeror (ie the guarantor of the security) if an explicit and express acceptance is not to be expected according to general usage in the relevant trade, or if the offeror has waived its right to an express acceptance. This will generally be the case if the guarantee is worded as an unilateral declaration.

Once qualified as contractual arrangements, the Introductory Code to the German Civil Code (EGBGB) Arts 27ff apply and provide that the parties to a contract are free to choose the law by which they want the agreement to be governed. Thus guarantees, indemnities and other personal security can be subject to virtually any law either explicitly, by specific reference contained in the documentation, or implicitly. In the absence of an express or implicit choice, conflict of law rules in Germany, as in all jurisdictions which have ratified and adopted the EEC Convention on the Law Applicable to Contractual Obligations (the Rome Convention) of 19 June 1980, and in particular its art 4, submit a contract to the laws of the country to which it has the closest connection. This rule is coupled with the, albeit rebuttable, assumption that the contract is most closely connected with the country in which the party who has to effect the 'characteristic performance' has its seat or residence. In the case of a guarantee or an indemnity this is generally the place of residence of the guarantor or the guarantor of the indemnity. These rules offer a considerable amount of freedom and discretion to a judge and it is therefore strongly advisable when drafting any form of personal security documentation to specify which law is to govern the contractual relationship. In view of discrepancies in traditional techniques of contractual interpretation, it should also be clearly stated that the same law is to govern the construction of the instrument.

With respect to the requirements of form, EGBGB Art 11 allows for alternative points of contract. Under this provision a transaction is valid if it is made in the form prescribed by the law governing it or the law of the jurisdiction in which it is made.

Finally, EGBGB Art 4 provides that, if German private international law refers to a foreign jurisdiction to govern a certain set of facts, this reference is not only to the foreign substantive law but also to the foreign conflict of law rules. It is therefore possible that foreign conflicts of law rules refer back to German law (*renvoi*) or transmit forward to the law of a third country. In EGBGB Art 35 , however, both the *renvoi* and the transmission forward are excluded when the applicable law has been contractually specified. Thus, a contractually specified choice of law is to be interpreted to refer to the substantive law of the chosen jurisdiction only.

Law applicable to real security

Altogether different rules apply to real security. Granting such security always entails conferring rights over or interests in the asset serving as collateral. The assignment of receivables for security purposes (*Sicherungsabtretung*) for example, requires the actual transfer of the ownership of that receivable. The same applies to the fiduciary transfer of title in movables for securities purposes (*Sicherungsübereignung*). A hypothec entails the partial transfer of ownership insofar as the owner passes its right to the beneficiary to sell the real estate by the way of a public auction. These aspects of the establishment of security interests, ie the giving up or transfer to the beneficiary of all or parts of the proprietary rights over assets, take such cases out of the scope of application of EGBGB Art. 27. Consequently, under German conflict of law rules, the parties are not free to choose the governing law.

Lex rei sitae

Although not explicitly laid down by statute, it has been consistently held that the creation and transfer of rights over corporeal assets and thus the creation of security over real estate and movables, including negotiable instruments, is governed by the so-called *lex rei sitae*, ie the law applicable at the place at which the collateral is located at the time of creation of the security interest. The same applies to changes to such rights, which must be effected in compliance with the laws of the jurisdiction in which the collateral is located at the time of such change. In particular, the *lex rei sitae* rule determines what forms of security interests are available at all. By mandatory German conflict of law rules, therefore, any form of security over real estate is governed by German law. Thus the only forms of security available over German real estate are the hypothec (*Hypothek*) and the abstract land charge (*Grundschuld*, a variant of which is the *Rentenschuld*). Security interests in chattels located in Germany also have to be created in accordance with, and are governed by, German law, and only those security interests provided for by German law are available to the creditor. A security interest over property owned by a German or a German company but located outside of Germany cannot be created pursuant to German law.

Law governing rights

A similar rule applies to rights. Security interests over receivables and other rights can be created only in accordance with the law governing such rights. Receivables governed by English law are thus not available as collateral for pledges or assignments for security purposes under German law (EGBGB Art 33). Similarly, the shares in a German GmbH, for example, since they are not being considered a security and are not evidenced by an instrument or by any other document, are qualified as 'rights' and can for this reason serve as collateral only if pledged or assigned in accordance with German rules.

Movables in transit

In the case of movables, the *lex rei sitae* rule can create considerable risks. In view of the fact that by far the most important types of security over movables do not require possession in most jurisdictions, the *lex rei sitae* rule described above which, on first glance seems quite straightforward, may turn out to be extremely complicated in cases where the movable is, for whatever reason, shipped or transported outside of the jurisdiction which originally governed the security interest. Once a movable over which a German security interest exists leaves the territory of the Federal Republic of Germany (and the same applies in most jurisdictions), a new *lex rei sitae* automatically applies to the movable and the effects on security interests it may be encumbered with are often quite unclear. The beneficiary of a security interest will therefore have a vital interest in controlling the whereabouts of the encumbered asset. It is, for example, very possible that a German supplier delivers automobile parts to a German automobile factory on a retention of title basis (see 'Retention of title', p 158 below for more details). Before the full payment of the purchase price the manufacturer delivers these as spare parts to an English distributor without transferring title. Under German conflict of law rules, as a consequence of the parts being shipped to England, English law now governs the supplier's retention of title.

It is accepted, at least by German doctrine, that the security interests validly created under one jurisdiction continue under the jurisdiction to which the asset has been shipped, within the legal framework of that new jurisdiction. Such new jurisdiction will generally govern the rights over the movables once they have entered the territory governed by it, to the extent the foreign rights have been perfected before the movables were moved to the new jurisdiction but only to the extent that they comply with the general legal framework of the new jurisdiction. The particulars of such transport into a new jurisdiction and of the resulting transformation of the interest by its new legal environment must be considered very carefully in light of the particular facts and circumstances of each case. In the event that a change of the *lex rei sitae* is already contemplated at the time of the creation of the security interest, it is advisable to carefully scrutinise the possibility of meeting the requirements of all possible jurisdictions.

Generally, transjurisdictional and cross-border security matters involve many, often unresolved, theoretical and practical issues. For example, what if the new *lex rei sitae* requires possession for security interests in movables or only accepts such interests if they are registered? What if the new *lex rei sitae* has no equivalent procedures for the execution of the interest? Security interests over collateral transported into another jurisdiction will only be acceptable if they are 'compatible' with the rules of the receiving country. In effect, this means that the courts of the new country will only recognise the interest if it somehow fits into its own legal system, it can be 'translated' into its legal system and only to the extent that the necessary formalities and other prerequisites for creation or perfection provided for in that new jurisdiction are fulfilled.

In short, one could say that foreign security interests would be enforced by a new jurisdiction only if and to the extent that they are compatible and meet all continuing requirements for the validity under the new *lex rei sitae*. The real consequences can only be ascertained on a case-by-case basis by looking at the relevant jurisdictions and at the security interests involved.

TYPES OF SECURITY, THEIR CREATION AND THEIR ENFORCEMENT

Accessory guarantee (*Bürgschaft*)

Types of accessory guarantees

The guarantee is the most important form of personal security. Although often worded as a unilateral declaration of the guarantor, it is a contract between the guarantor and the creditor by which the guarantor undertakes to be liable for the performance of a certain liability owed by a third party. The third party is referred to as the 'main debtor' (*Hauptschuldner*) and the secured obligation owed by him shall be referred to as 'main debt' or the 'main obligation'. Since the creditor itself does not, in general, undertake any obligation towards the guarantor and thus there are no mutual obligations, the guarantee is a unilateral contract. In practice guarantees are mainly used to secure payment obligations but they can also cover other kinds of liabilities, such as, for example, the obligation to deliver certain goods or to complete a construction project. In the case of a guarantee as security for a non-monetary obligation, it is a question of drafting and of interpreting the text of the guarantee as to whether the guarantor undertook actually to perform the obligation in kind, eg deliver the goods or see to the completion of the project, or whether it is only to cover the financial loss of the beneficiary from and in connection with the non-performance of the main debt.

Without going into particular details the following typical forms of guarantees are used in practice:

1 *Guarantee as principal (Selbstschuldnerische Bürgschaft)*. In such a guarantee the subsidiary nature of the guarantee is removed by the guarantor waiving the defence that its obligation does not fall due before the beneficiary has unsuccessfully tried to levy execution proceedings against the main debtor (BGB Sec 771 in conjunction with BGB Sec 773 para 1 lit 1). Unless otherwise agreed, accessory guarantees given by merchants in the course of their business are always guarantees as principal.

2 *Deficiency guarantee (Ausfallbürgschaft)*. This type of guarantee stands on the opposite end of the spectrum from the guarantee as principal, in that its subsidiary nature is reinforced by the guarantor being liable only for the amount of the shortfall which the beneficiary was unable to recover from the debtor. The beneficiary will have to establish that all possible remedies, including all attempts to realise all other security given for the secured liability, were insufficient to realise enough funds to satisfy the debt or the secured liability. Obviously this type of guarantee is the most subordinated form available and is often used by public bodies, such as municipalities, governments and their agencies.

3 *Partial and maximum amount guarantee (Teil-und Höchstbetragsbürgschaft)*. This guarantee is designed to share the risk of default by limiting the guarantor's exposure either to a certain percentage of the secured liability (partial guarantee) or to an overall maximum of the secured amount.

4 *Joint guarantee (Mitbürgschaft)*. If a second guarantor guarantees all or parts of a liability already guaranteed, both guarantors are automatically jointly and severally liable (BGB Sec 769), thus allowing the paying guarantor to take (partial) recourse against the other.

5 *Re-guarantee (Rückbürgschaft)*. The re-guarantor guarantees for the benefit of the primary guarantor the due performance of the main debtor's obligation to reimburse the guarantor. It offers 'reinsurance' to the primary guarantor and shifts the insolvency risk to the re-guarantor.

6 *Guarantee restricted in time (Zeitbürgschaft)*. The guarantor can either restrict its obligation and exposure to liabilities arising or falling due no later than a certain date or go even further and limit its liability to those defaults which have led to an actual claim against it before that date. The latter form offers comfort to the guarantor that after that date it will not be confronted with any new demands under the guarantee.

7 *Accessory guarantees on first-demand (Bürgschaft auf erstes Anfordern)*. Guarantees are more and more frequently worded as 'payable on first-demand'. This clause is obviously designed to detach the guarantor's obligation to a certain extent from the underlying main debt, so that even if the latter does not exist, the guarantor would have to pay. Upon first glance, therefore, an accessory first-demand guarantee seems like a contradiction in terms. Nonetheless, the German Supreme Court in Civil Matters (BGH) has held that the first-demand clause does not automatically convert a guarantee into an indemnity or an abstract guarantee. The court interpreted the first-demand clause to mean that the guarantor agreed to pay up front immediately whatever amount was demanded and that the exceptions and defences available to him would only be available in judicial

proceedings it may subsequently bring for the repayment of the amount advanced. Using reasoning largely based on the Act on Standard Terms and Conditions (*AGB-Gesetz*), a number of disputed recent court cases have held that guarantees, although drafted as instruments on first demand, are only so payable if given by banks and insurance companies. It is not yet finally settled to what extent these cases would also apply to sophisticated companies and businessmen who are not banks or insurers.

Creation

Although generally the guarantee agreement is concluded between the guarantor and the creditor, it can also be embodied in an agreement between the guarantor and the main debtor made in favour of the creditor as the third party beneficiary without any involvement of the latter as a contractual party (BGB Sec 328). Although strictly accessory to the main obligation, the validity of the guarantee itself does not depend on the validity of such obligation. Under BGB Sec 766 Sentence 1, the declaration of the guarantor by which it offers to enter into the contract of guarantee has to be in writing, unless the guarantor is a merchant for all legal purposes (*Vollkaufmann*) under the Commercial Code ('*Handelsgesetzbuch*' HGB) and such declaration is given by him in the course of the operation of its business (HGB Sec 350). In view of the extremely onerous nature of the guarantee and the fact that the guarantor will be liable for the obligation with all its assets, this form requirement is designed to protect the guarantor from rushing into the guarantee. In the event that a guarantor has entered into the guarantee orally, the invalidity due to the non-compliance with BGB Sec 766 Sentence 1 the form requirement will be retroactively remedied (*Heilung*) pursuant to BGB Sec 766 Sentence 2 if the guarantor subsequently honours its obligations under the guarantee. It is an important nuance that the form requirement does not extend to the entire contract but is limited to the declaration: ie the contractual offer – of the guarantor ('*schriftliche Erteilung der Bürgschaftserklärung*'). Thus acceptance of the offer can be made orally or tacitly, and almost always is. As already stated above, in practice, guarantees are almost always worded as unilateral declarations by the guarantor and the contract is concluded by operation of BGB Sec 151, which provides that no receipt by the guarantor of an express acceptance is necessary to conclude a contract if the offeror has waived such receipt or no express receipt is required under prevailing and generally accepted practice. This is so in the case of guarantees (see also 'Law applicable to personal security', p 141 above).

As is the case with all contractual agreements, a guarantee can be void if it is in violation of *bonus mores* and in particular if it is contrary to public policy or unconscionable (BGB Sec 138). A very important line of recent cases, which was triggered by a decision of the Constitutional Court handed down at the end of 1993, has held this to be the case in circumstances where young and inexperienced family members or relatives, who had no own economic interest or benefit from the transaction they were securing, guaranteed obligations of relatives. In some of these cases creditors were held to have exploited the close family relationships and the social pressure exercised through them or other personal ties of the guarantor with the debtor to bring them to accept obligations, which in view of their financial positions, and their inexperience in commercial matters, they would not be able to live up to. The courts have taken the view that the inequality of the bargaining positions and the exploitation thereof by the creditor in these family scenarios can vitiate the entire guarantee. This area of law is still in a state of flux and great care has to be taken by creditors to avoid going too far when requesting guarantees as security from individuals as guarantors.

As the guarantee is accessory to the main debt, the contents and the status of the main obligation determine the extent to which the guarantor is liable. If this main obligation does not or ceases to exist, the liability under the guarantee is automatically extinguished. If the main obligation is reduced by partial payment or otherwise, the guarantee is automatically reduced accordingly. The accessory nature, which is subject to very limited exceptions in cases of bankruptcy or insolvency of the main debtor, is the main difference between an accessory guarantee on the one hand and an abstract guarantee or indemnity (*Garantie*) on the other hand: under the latter the guarantor undertakes to perform its side of the bargain without any regard to the extent to which the main debtor is bound. The accessory nature is most apparent in the fact that the assignment of the main debt automatically and necessarily also operates the assignment to the assignee of the rights under the guarantee (BGB Sec 401 para 1). This direct effect of the status of the main debt on the guarantee makes it crucial that the document establishing the guarantee defines such main debt in a very detailed manner. This holds particularly true when it comes to securing future obligations and obligations which bear interest, since such interest is only covered by the guarantee if there is a specific agreement to that effect.

Other corollaries of the accessory nature are that the guarantor, if not otherwise provided for in the guarantee – can raise all defences against the beneficiary's claim under the guarantee, which the main debtor would have against a claim under the main debt. He can therefore, in particular, raise the defence that the main debt is already prescribed (statute barred), that it has been deferred, that the main debt or the contract it is based on can be rescinded by the main debtor (*Anfechtung*) or that the creditor could seek satisfaction of its claim against the main debtor by way of set-off against a liability the creditor has against the main debtor. In the absence of an agreement to the contrary and outside the area of commercial transactions of merchants, the guarantor can withhold payment as long as the main debtor has not exhausted all procedural remedies against the main debtor, including having unsuccessfully attempted to execute a judgment against the debtor and its assets (BGB Sec 771). The guarantor, as is the underlying intent of the statutory provisions, should only be liable once the main debtor has been unsuccessfully pursued for payment of the main obligation. This subsidiarity of the guarantor's obligation is in practice, however, excluded by an express provision to that effect in the text of the guarantee.

The subsidiary nature of the guarantee is also evidenced by BGB Sec 776, which provides that the guarantor is released from its obligations under the guarantee if the creditor waives or relinquishes other security interests given as security for the main obligation and the guarantor would have been able to be reimbursed by exercising rights under these other security interests.

Enforcement

The rights under the guarantee are exercised like any right in persona by claiming payment against the guarantor and, if such payment is not forthcoming, by bringing action against him. After a final court order has been obtained, the creditor can then levy forced execution proceedings against the guarantor. To the extent the guarantor owns assets which are not protected against seizure (ie clothing, personal items etc), all such assets are available to the secured creditor for the satisfaction of its claim.

If the guarantor has paid the creditor under the guarantee, the main debt is not extinguished. Rather, the guarantor becomes creditor of this obligation by operation of law by way of an automatic statutory assignment to him (*cessio legis* pursuant to BGB Sec 774 para 1). As a consequence, accessory and ancillary rights are then also vested in the guarantor who is thereby put in a position enabling him to be reimbursed for its payment by availing itself of all rights so conferred upon him by the subrogation. In addition, the guarantor almost always has a legal relationship with the main debtor (such as a banking agreement or a credit facility, which can be drawn down in the form of guarantees). The guarantor's recourse can also be based on this relationship

Abstract guarantee or indemnity (*Garantie*)

Types of guarantees or indemnities

The non-accessory, ie abstract, guarantee is not systematically covered in German statutory law but various, mostly not exhaustive regulations may be found in different legislative acts. An exception is the bill of exchange (*Wechsel*), a very commonly used credit instrument in commercial practice in Germany, which is covered in detail by statutory regulations based on international conventions. Other types of abstract guarantees and indemnities have been developed in detail by legal practice under the principle of freedom of contract and were further shaped by a large number of court cases. Without going into too much detail, typical uses for abstract guarantees in modern financial practice include:

1 the guarantee of the bank issuing eurocheque cards for the cashing of an eurocheque up to DM 400;
2 the guarantee of a manufacturer in favour of the consumer that its product will work for a certain time without defects;
3 bank guarantees (eg standby letters of credit), which are widely used in international trade and trade financing; and
4 bills of exchange (*Wechsel*).

Creation

Like the accessory guarantee, the abstract guarantee is an agreement between two parties, the guarantor and the beneficiary. By this agreement the guarantor undertakes to be responsible for the occurrence or achievement of a certain event or result (hereinafter 'promised event'). In most cases the guarantor will not undertake to be liable for specific performance and will promise only to indemnify and hold harmless the beneficiary against all loss it may incur or suffer as a result of the non-occurrence of the promised event. In these cases the abstract guarantee is simply an indemnity and the amount payable will be calculated in accordance with the rules governing the calculation of damages for breach of contract.

On the other hand, an abstract guarantee could well be worded in a way that the guarantor undertakes not only to indemnify the beneficiary, but also specifically to perform the beneficiary's contractual obligation to bring about the promised event. It is, for example, conceivable that a completion guarantee for a construction project be given by a construction company for the performance of its contractor subsidiary, undertaking to build the project itself if the subsidiary cannot or will not do so or fails to do so within a specific time frame. That having been said, such a structure is rare and for all practical purposes abstract guarantees are almost always indemnities. Specific requirements of creation of an obligation under a bill of exchange have to be observed.

Structurally, the abstract guarantee is very different from an accessory guarantee, although distinguishing the two can become very complex, if the promised event is defined in the abstract guarantee documentation as the 'due and timely performance of an obligation to pay money' owed by a third party. The real difference between the two is that the abstract guarantee and its validity are completely independent of the fate or even the existence of the secured claim. The parent company of the contractor in the above example, which gave an abstract guarantee to the financing bank as a security for the timely completion of the project, will have to pay the indemnity even if the construction contract between the employer and the contractor was invalid, unenforceable or voidable. Deciding which of the two – abstract or accessory guarantees – have been intended in the face of an existing agreement can be a very difficult and complex exercise in contractual interpretation. The distinction can, however, have far-reaching legal effects. The abstract guarantee does not have to be issued in writing, all of the exceptions related to the accessory nature are not available and the guarantor is not automatically subrogated into the rights of the beneficiary against the main debtor, if such rights exist at all.

There is no typical abstract guarantee. The legal rights and obligations arising under them are determined by the wording of the particular guarantee agreement and therefore vary widely. The most important feature of an abstract guarantee is that the guarantor must pay even if the secured obligation does not exist, is reduced or if the main debtor has a right of retention, a right of set-off or another defence against the creditor's claim. If coupled with a first-demand clause, an abstract guarantee brings about an extremely strict and onerous liability. The only available and difficult defence of the issuer of such a guarantee is the '*abus de droit*' (abuse) defence, which was accepted by courts in cases where the demand for payment, was fraudulent on its face. In such cases obvious, and clear (*liquide*), proof must be presented that, although the conditions precedent for a claim under the guarantee were fulfilled, the event guaranteed against had not occurred, ie the main debtor was not liable.

In the absence of an agreement to the contrary, when the guarantor makes a payment it is not paying to discharge the secured debt. Consequently, no automatic subrogation takes place. The guarantor's recourse is simply based on the (contractual) relationship (mandate) which it has with the main debtor and which may contain an agreement that all payments made under the guarantee shall be reimbursed by the debtor.

Enforcement

The abstract guarantee or indemnity is a personal security and as such is enforced by claiming payment against the guarantor. Mostly no further requirements will be necessary nor any defences of the guarantor originating in the contractual relationship between guarantor and main debtor may be brought forward. Thus the enforcement of an abstract guarantee or indemnity is straightforward, making this type of security desirable for creditors, provided the guarantor is solvent.

Pledge (*Pfandrecht*)

German law provides for pledges over both movable physical assets (BGB Sec 1204ff) and over rights (BGB Sec 1273ff). Thus, virtually all kinds of assets including such things as credit balances on bank accounts, receivables, securities etc are available to be pledged if they are transferable and their 'pledgeability' is not excluded by statute (or in the case of rights, by agreement to that effect) and as long as the asset to be pledged does not form part of, or is deemed to be, real property (cf 'Security over real estate', p 161 below).

Pledge over movable physical assets

A pledge confers the right to the pledgee to discharge the secured claim by selling the pledged asset, albeit only by public auction, once the secured claim has become due.

Generally, the pledge is created by agreement between the pledgor and the pledgee that a pledge be established and the transfer to the pledgee of the direct possession of the asset. The rules governing the transfer of the asset to be pledged apply *mutatis mutandis*. There are certain pledges which arise by operation of law (*gesetzliche Pfandrechte*) such as the pledge in favour of the landlord over assets the tenant brought onto the leased premises (BGB Sec 559ff) or the pledge in favour of the contractor (*Werkunternehmer*) over movables of the employer produced or repaired by the contractor (BGB Sec 647). Such statutory pledges arise automatically in the situations described by the relevant provisions and thus require no agreement between pledgor and pledgee. Once so established, however, they are governed by substantially the same rules as a contractual pledge.

The pledge subsists only as long as the pledgee continues to hold possession of the asset. This feature makes the pledge awkward to handle in practice and undesirable for the pledgor. As a rule banks are neither willing nor equipped to hold assets such as trucks, tools or machinery in their possession. In addition, the pledgor will generally want to continue to use such assets, which normally means that it, rather than the pledgee, must have physical control over them. The requirement of continued possession is the main reason why in commercial practice the pledge has largely been replaced by its abstract counterpart, the transfer of title for security purposes (cf 'Transfer of title for security purposes', p 152 below).

Another inconvenience of the pledge is that, in the event of its enforcement, the pledged collateral must only be sold by way of public auction. An agreement that, in the event of the pledgor's failure to satisfy or timely satisfy the pledgee's claim, title to the asset reverts to the pledgee in satisfaction of the secured debt, is void under BGB Sec 1229 if made before the pledge falls due, ie before such failure occurs. The purpose pursued by the legislator when introducing this provision back when the BGB was drafted was to protect the pledgor against losing an asset worth more than the secured debt. It was thought that only a publicly-supervised auctioning procedure would avoid selling below market price and disputes over such price between pledgor and pledgee. Whether this is in fact true can be disputed with good reasons. Mainly in cases where there is no real market for the kind of objects pledged or if they are generally only purchased after a due and careful inspection or with appropriate warranties, this way of exercising the rights under the pledge may considerably impair or diminish the economic value of this form of security. Only if the collateral has a determined market price or is quoted on an exchange can it be sold outside an auction, albeit always by special persons publicly authorised to effect the sale.

As soon as the secured claim becomes due the pledgor will become entitled to enforce the pledge, ie have the pledged assets auctioned or sold, without having to obtain a court order or satisfy other procedural formalities.

Pledge of receivables and other rights

Under German law, rights, and in particular receivables, can also be pledged (BGB Sec 1273). In practice this happens quite frequently in the form of pledges over shares and participation in companies and over credit balances (from time to time) on bank accounts. In fact the general terms and conditions used by German banks routinely provide for such a pledge in favour of the account bank, putting it in quite a comfortable position in case of financial difficulties of their client. However, the assignment of rights for security purposes, which contrary to the pledge does not have to be notified to the debtor of the pledged right, is much more flexible. Therefore, other than in the cases described above the pledge of rights is not very commonly used in German legal practice.

The pledge is created by applying *mutatis mutandis* the rules applicable to the transfer, ie assignment, of the relevant right (BGB Sec 1274). It is therefore essential to ensure that neither the assignability nor the pledgeability of such rights has been excluded or subjected to particular prerequisites, whether by agreement or otherwise. The pledge itself is different from a simple assignment in that it is valid only once notice has been given to the debtor of the assigned right or receivable (BGB Sec 1280). This means that a silent or unrevealed pledge of rights is not possible under German law. Since, however, debtors are not particularly keen on making it publicly known that they have given security over receivables and since unless there is only a limited number of debtors under a particular agreement, the benefits of which are to be made available as collateral (eg a supply agreement) it is quite onerous from an administrative point of view to give notice to every single customer of the pledgor of the fact that it has pledged rights under a supply agreement, the pledge of receivables is not very widely used. In practice, it is mainly used to take security over shares in companies and partnerships. Security over bank accounts and security custody accounts under the General Terms and Conditions of German Banks Sec 14 and under corresponding provisions of standard terms and conditions of savings banks and other financial institutions is, as mentioned above, typically in the form of a pledge. A pledge of shares will often be an appropriate form of security because, in most cases, the person taking security is not interested in assuming the full position and responsibility of a shareholder and the pledgor will generally want to retain the responsibility, the management and the voting rights.

Transfer of title for security purposes (*Sicherungsübereignung*)

Creation

This type of security over physical assets is specifically not provided for in the German Civil Code or elsewhere in statutory law. It was developed by legal practice and is now generally accepted by case law. As described above, the pledge, which is the form of security over movables contemplated by the code, requires continued physical possession of the pledged object by the pledgee. Due to that feature it is impossible for the provider of security to continue to make use of the assets given as security. If, for example, a transportation company wants to finance a truck, pledging the truck as security for a loan is pointless, since only the use of the vehicle generates the revenue flow necessary to service and eventually to retire the loan.

Creditors, in turn, are generally also interested in permitting and ensuring the most productive use of the debtor's assets and not in storing them. Therefore, it is apparent that a form of security is needed that allows the transferor to retain possession of the security. The transfer of title for security purposes (*Sicherungsübereignung*) achieves this and is now the most customary way of providing collateral for financing of movables. Another advantage of the transfer of title for security purposes over the pledge is in the case of the execution of rights granted by the security: the relevant documentation normally provides for realisation by private sale and not by public auction, as is required in the case of pledges.

The transfer of title for security purposes is an abstract security by design and is created by way of an agreement between the transferor, as the owner of the asset, and the transferee (the secured creditor or a trustee for the secured creditor) to the effect that:

1 full title to the asset is transferred to the transferee;
2 the transferor shall keep the possession while holding the property also for the transferee thus leaving the transferee with 'indirect possession' of the security (Sec 929 and 930 BGB).

Regularly, there are a variety of covenants and agreements regarding the purpose of the transfer and the relationship between the transferor and the transferee. As between the secured creditor and third parties, this type of security confers full title with all rights and obligations. As between the transferor and the transferee, the security purpose elements of the agreement limit and restrict the exercise of such rights on the part of the transferor. Contractually these are in addition to, but quite independent from, the transfer itself. The transfer and the other arrangements are, notwithstanding their distinct nature from one another, often contained in one document. The security purpose agreement determines the obligations to be secured by the transfer, under what conditions the assets can be repossessed by the transferee, what grace periods are to be permitted, when and to what extent the transferor/possessor is entitled to sell the assets to third parties and how the proceeds of such sale are to be used etc. Finally, of course, the security purpose agreement will contain the obligation of the transferee to retransfer the property once the secured obligation is repaid.

The transfer of title for security purposes, like all abstract security interests, creates a fiduciary relationship between the transferor and the transferee, in that the latter receives full title and all rights to the assets (albeit generally not economic ownership for tax purposes) but undertakes not to avail itself of these rights, except in accordance with the terms of the security purpose agreement. Thus, as a matter of principle, the transferor can at any time sell the collateral to a third party and confer good title, even if such sale is in breach of the security purpose agreement. The transferee's default under the security purpose agreement gives rise to the transferor's claim for breaching the security purpose agreement.

Legal requirements

In practice the most important and often very difficult legal requirement to meet when creating a transfer of title for security purposes is the definition of exactly what assets are to be transferred. Although this may sound fairly straightforward, a vast number of transfers have been held invalid for not fulfilling this requirement. The collateral is only defined with the necessary degree of certainty (*Bestimmtheit*) if any unrelated third party can certainly and unequivocally identify the transferred assets by consulting the transfer agreement (and the attachments to it, if any) without having to resort to circumstances outside of the agreement or to any judgement of law or facts. Typically one would therefore find either exact lists of assets, often making reference to an inventory number which would preferably be marked on the asset transferred, or clauses to the effect that all assets stored or to be stored in a certain marked area or room are to be transferred. Clauses not sufficiently defining such assets are dangerous, as for example wordings such as 'all assets stored in warehouse A *which are owned by the transferor*' (the unrelated third party would have to research ownership before it could decide if a particular asset was included or not) or 'all widgets located in room 15 *up to an aggregate value of DM X*' (an evaluation would be necessary).

The transfer of title to movable assets such as stock for security purposes is frequently not only used for individual assets but *globally*, ie on a group of assets present and future, such as stock which frequently changes. Typically, in such a global form of a transfer, the transferor is authorised to sell the assets (or use them up in its business) notwithstanding the fact that they are owned by the secured creditor. Such a transfer will often be combined with an assignment, also for security purposes, of all of the receivables of the debtor or all of the receivables resulting from the sale of the assets subject of the title transfer. The assignment of the receivables for security purposes, again, would normally be on terms that the assignor remains authorised to collect them notwithstanding that after such assignment they are 'owned' by the assignee. Thus, economically, this form of security interest provides something like a floating interest in that the identity of the underlying assets is changing during the life of the security interest but, at the time of enforcement or crystallisation, it is fixed and defined.

Typical problems a transfer of title may fall foul of are:

1. The existence of statutory pledges, as described above (typically, landlord's pledge: BGB Sec 559, 581; pledge of commercial warehouser: HGB Sec 421; pledge of commercial carrier: HGB Sec 440, 410; factor's pledge: HGB Sec 397 and contractor's pledge: BGB Sec 647).

2 The collateral transferred includes assets supplied to the transferor under a retention of title arrangement. Under well-established case law, the retention of title arrangement takes priority over the transfer of ownership for security purposes.
3 The asset is an integral part (*wesentlicher Bestandteil*) of another object (BGB Sec 93) and can therefore not be the subject of rights and obligations separate from that object.
4 The asset is considered to be a, or to be part of a, real estate as an accessory (*Zubehör*) and is as such encumbered by an interest in such real estate prior to the transfer of title agreement (BGB Sec 1120).

Enforcement

Since there is no statutory basis for the transfer of title for security, enforcement is governed by the security purpose agreement itself rather than by statute. It would usually stipulate that once the debtor defaults in the payment of the secured claim, the transferee can repossess 'its' assets and sell them by private sale. As long as the debtor does not default and maintains direct possession of the assets, which it is entitled to do under the security purpose agreement, he is protected against the transferee selling the collateral. The security purpose agreement will preclude a purchaser from acquiring good title to the assets (BGB Sec 932 para 2). If the transferor, or whoever has possession at the time the security is sought to be enforced, refuses to surrender the assets, the transferee will first have to obtain a court order for the surrender of the assets (which could turn out to be quite a lengthy process).

Another aspect which may influence the value of the security for the transferee is that it will want to exclude to the maximum extent possible its liability as seller (for implied or express warranties) which, depending on the asset, may reduce the proceeds considerably. Any excess proceeds not required to retire secured obligations will have to be surrendered to the transferor or to its trustee in insolvency, as the case may be.

It has been discussed under 'Pledge over movable physical assets' p 150 above that pursuant to BGB Sec 1229 an agreement providing that, in the event of a payment default by the debtor, the pledgee becomes owner of the pledged collateral in satisfaction of the secured debt is invalid. Sec 1229 BGB is not applied by analogy on transfer of title for security purposes, so that such a provision in the security purposes agreement is valid, if it is not violating good business morals for being too excessive in respect to the secured claim.

Assignment for security purposes of receivables and other rights (*Sicherungsabtretung*)

Creation

The difference between an assignment for security purposes and a transfer of title for security purposes is quite simple. While the collateral in the latter case is a tangible movable, in the former case it is a right, most frequently a receivable or a group of receivables. Consequently assigning such right or rights creates the security interest.

This is done not by transfer of title but by way of an assignment. Except for these differences and the problems which arise as a consequence of the fact that the collateral is not a movable tangible but a receivable or other right (hereinafter collectively referred to as 'receivable' or 'receivables') the rules governing the assignment for security purposes are structurally identical to those governing a transfer of title for security purposes.

The need for the assignment for security purposes originates from the fact that a pledge of receivables is only valid once it has been notified to the debtor of the receivable used as collateral. No business could therefore use the unpaid receivables as collateral for credit which it may need to bridge the time until the receivables have been paid, unless it is prepared to disclose the fact that it was compelled to do so to the clients. In the same way as giving movable collateral to the pledgee is largely unworkable in most situations, the notification of the pledge to the client is impractical or simply resisted by debtors for other, often quite irrational, reasons. Normally businesses do not want to involve their clients in their affairs and shy away from disclosing their liabilities and sources of finance to them. In addition, once notice of a pledge of a receivable is given the debtor of such receivable can no longer settle its debt by simply paying to the pledgor but must pay to the pledgor and the pledgee jointly (BGB Sec 1281). This brings about considerable administrative inconvenience, which businesses want to spare their clients.

The structure of the assignment for security purposes is as follows. The creditor is owed a debt by the debtor for which it wants security (hereinafter the 'secured debt'). For this purpose the debtor assigns a receivable or a group of receivables which it has against a third party debtor (most often purchasers under contracts for the sale and purchase of goods or services). The assignment for security purposes relies on the fact that under German law the assignment of a receivable, to the extent that its assignability is not excluded by agreement between the debtor and the third party debtor (BGB Sec 399), is valid without notice thereof being given to the third party debtor. The third party debtor is, however, protected under BGB Sec 407, which provides that payment to the assignor by the third party debtor has discharging effect towards the assignee if notice of the assignment has not been given to the third party debtor. In the event of such discharging payment the assignee, who chooses not to notify the third party debtor of the assignment, is entitled to claim against the assignor under the principles of unjust enrichment (BGB Sec 816 para 2). In satisfaction of the secured debt, the assignee can claim from the assignor whatever the latter has received from the third party debtor.

As in the case of a transfer of title for security purposes, the assignee becomes the owner of the receivable and can theoretically assign it on to third parties. The security interest is abstract but a security purpose agreement stipulates that the assignee is restricted to enforcing the assigned receivable only in case of default by the debtor/assignor under the secured debt. It is sometimes argued that, even if no express provision to that effect is contained in the relevant security documentation, the assignment for security purposes is always made under the implied suspensive condition (*aufschiebende Bedingung*) that the secured right comes into existence and is valid and under the resolutory condition (*auflösende Bedingung*) of its extinction. To infer this, however, from the simple use of the assignment as a security device would, in our view, stretch the rules of contractual interpretation a little too far and case law does support such an argument. Still, if an assignor wants to obtain as much of the protection offered by the accessory nature of security rights as possible without the inherent disadvantages of a pledge described above, such conditions should be included. This technique saves having explicitly to reassign the receivable once the security purpose has been fulfilled (ie the secured debt has been discharged). It also protects against the secured creditor's further unpermitted assignment of the assigned receivable. This protection is offered by operation of BGB Sec 161 para 1, which provides that if a person has disposed of any object under a resolutory condition (assignment for security purposes in the above example) then any subsequent disposal (assignment) of that same object pending the occurrence of the condition is invalid to the extent it would frustrate or make impossible the effect of the occurrence of the condition (reversion of the assigned receivable to the grantor of the security interest).

The assignment for security purposes is most frequently used in a global form. This means that all or a group of receivables, including future receivables, are assigned for one or more specified security purposes, often a particular bank loan or all obligations vis-à-vis a bank. Such a global assignment is valid as long as the assigned receivables are 'determinable' ie as long as the assignment is defined in general terms so that at the time a receivable comes into existence it can be ascertained on the basis of the assignment agreement and the circumstances surrounding it whether or not it is covered by the assignment. The requirement of ascertainability is much less strict than the corresponding requirement (*Bestimmtheit*) in the case of a transfer of title for security purposes, thus allowing the draftsman of an assignment for security purposes much more leeway. It is satisfied even if the determination requires a considerable amount of work and interpretation.

Similar to the right of the transferor for security purposes to retain possession of the movable, the security purpose agreement of an assignment for security purposes will contain a provision permitting the assignor to continue to receive and claim payment of the assigned receivables in the ordinary course of business. Often this provision is supplemented by an undertaking by the assignor to book the payments received on a special proceeds account and/or account to the assignee for the payments received on a regular basis. It is also possible to provide that the proceeds must be immediately applied to discharge the secured debt.

Legal requirements

One of the main problems a secured creditor will be faced with in connection with the assignment for security purposes is a restriction on the assignability of the receivables, which are intended to serve as collateral. Under BGB Sec 399 the assignability of receivables can be restricted by a simple agreement between the debtor and the creditor of such receivable. Any assignment (for security purposes) of a receivable so restricted would be ineffective at least as long as the third party debtor has not waived the non-assignability. The security assignee will seek protection against this by duly investigating that no such restrictions exist and will further include a warranty as to the free assignability of the receivable and a covenant in the security purpose agreement not to enter into a non-assignability agreement with respect to future receivables assigned. Even if compliance by the assignor with these covenants is supervised, they do not offer full protection to the assignee. Powerful debtors have a tendency automatically to exclude the assignability in their general terms and conditions because they want to avoid the administrative expense and hassle of verifying and dealing with assignment notices and investigating to whom they can pay with discharging effect. Until recently assignees were powerless against such standard clauses.

Often due to the unequal bargaining position of suppliers such restrictions on the assignability in standard terms of trade are frequently coupled with long payment periods (such as 90 days after delivery). The suppliers are faced with the following dilemma: on the one hand, they have to supply their goods and services on a credit basis, because the purchaser is allowed a grace period for payment. On the other hand, they cannot use the receivables to collateralise bank loans or third party credits which they need to continue their production. This credit crunch, which affected mostly medium-sized business with relatively little bargaining power and limited financial resources, was recently tackled by the legislator with the enactment of HGB Sec 354a, which provides that, in certain cases, agreements which restrict the assignability pecuniary obligations are void. It applies to all receivables, which arise under a contract between two merchants (*Kaufmann*). On the other hand, Sentence 2 of the same section provides that the debtor can continue to pay with discharging effect to the assignor. This provision seems to suggest that even if the third party debtor has been notified of the assignment following a default by the assignor under the secured debt, the third party debtor may continue to make payments to its original contractual partner, ie the security assignor with discharging effect. This would, if applied strictly, make such receivables quite unsuitable as collateral, because the assignee could not prevent payment to the debtor. If so applied, HGB Sec 354a would have largely failed its main purpose to make available to these medium-sized businesses all their receivables to back up their urgently needed credit requirements. Due to the wording of HGB Sec 354a it is not likely that it will have much impact on the availability of receivables as collateral.

Under German conflict of law rules the law which governs the receivable also governs its assignability, the relationship between assignee and the debtor, the conditions under which the assignment can be held against the debtor and the discharging effect of payment by the debtor (EGBGB Art 33). An assignment, which follows the German rules, can therefore only ensure the transfer from assignor to assignee if the receivable is also governed by German law or by a law that does not provide for additional requirements for the assignment. As a consequence it is advisable for a secured creditor to ensure that non-German law governs none of the assigned receivables with stricter rules for an assignment than German law. A creditor faced with a debtor who has receivables from transjurisdictional trade must therefore be particularly watchful to ensure, by way of due diligence, current monitoring of the debtor's activities, covenants not to contract under any other law but German law and warranties, that the debtor does not contract under foreign law. Faced with one or a group of foreign receivables, the assignee will have to ensure that whatever conditions such foreign law may require are satisfied by the assignment agreement.

Another classic problem in connection with assignments for security purposes is the conflict between a supplier to the assignor of goods who retains title to the goods and extends the retention of title to all receivables which the purchaser generates by way of a sale of the goods delivered. If that same purchaser had previously assigned all its receivables to a bank as security for a loan then obviously there is a conflict between the purchase money creditor (supplier under the extended retention of title agreement) and the bank. This will be dealt with in more detail under the heading 'Retention of title'(p 160 below).

Enforcement

The enforcement of the assignment for security purposes will generally take place as follows: the authority of the assignor to claim payment of the assigned receivables will be revoked once the assignor is in default under the secured debt. After giving notice to the security assignor the assignee will also disclose the assignment to the third party debtors. Once this has occurred, the payment of the latter to the assignor would cease to have discharging effect and it must forthwith pay only to the assignee.

Creditors of the assignee can seize the assigned receivable by way of forced execution proceedings against the assignee since the assigned receivables form part of its estate. Due to the fiduciary nature of the assignment, however, the courts allow the 'real' owner, ie the assignor, to stop the execution proceedings against the receivables as long as no default under the secured debt has occurred. In the reverse scenario, ie, in the case where other creditors of the assignor seize the assigned receivables, the right to stop the execution proceedings is granted to the security assignee. In this case the other creditors of the assignor are unable to seize the assigned receivables as long as such receivables have not been reassigned or have automatically retransferred (in the case of a resolutory condition) to the assignor. Failing this, other creditors of the security assignor can only seize the security assignor's claim against the security assignee for reassignment of the secured receivable once the security purpose has been fully achieved. In the event of the assignor's insolvency (see 'Security interests in insolvency' p 170 below), the assignment for security purposes, exactly like the transfer of title for security purposes, confers a right to separate satisfaction and not to separation. If in turn the assignee goes bankrupt, the courts permit the assignor to reclaim the receivable (right to separation) provided it discharges the secured liability in full.

Retention of title (*Eigentumsvorbehalt*)

Creation

This accessory form of security is widely used by suppliers and providers of purchase money credit. It is created under one of the clauses, generally contained in the sale and purchase agreement, to the effect that the seller/supplier delivers goods before full and final payment has been made and defers the transfer of ownership until final settlement of the purchase price.

Although not covered in any detail by the Civil Code the retention of title as an instrument to secure a creditor's position is specifically referred to in BGB Sec 455 and is thereby contemplated by it. BGB Sec 455, which is systematically located in the chapter dealing with general provisions on the sale and barter of goods, provides that if the seller of a movable asset has retained title to the asset until payment of the purchase price, then in case of doubt the transfer of the title is deemed to have been made under the suspensive condition of full and final payment of the purchase price. It only creates a simple contractual obligation on the seller to transfer title at some specified date by entering into a transfer agreement in consummation of the sale contract from which it is legally separate. It is then further assumed that the seller shall have a right of recession (*Rücktritt*) of the contract if the purchaser is in default of payment of the purchase price.

Reading this provision carefully immediately reveals that the BGB does in fact not consider retention of title to be a security interest for the payment of the deferred purchase price. Rather it is designed to secure the right of the supplier (seller) against the purchaser to reclaim and repossess the goods supplied in case (a) the purchaser does not pay the purchase price, and (b) as a consequence thereof, the seller withdraws from the contract.

The scenario in which the retention of title is used and the risks which the players encounter and attempt to manage by using the device are as follows. The supplier (seller) sells goods to the purchaser (debtor) who does not want, or is simply unable, to pay immediately. Often the debtor is a dealer in this particular type of goods and wants the purchase price to be credited so that it can resell them to its clients and use the proceeds from that on sale to discharge suppliers' claims against him. Under German law this sales contract does not automatically operate a transfer of the ownership to the property. From a legal point of view the transfer of ownership in the property is thus a completely separate agreement from the contract of sale, the latter giving rise to the obligation to perform the former. The supplier will be reluctant to give to the purchaser more than possession in the goods. If he conveys title immediately, then the purchaser can sell the goods on to the client. Even if the purchaser refuses to pay the purchase price it could still validly transfer ownership of the assets to its clients and even if the seller would and could rescind the contract it would be unable to claim the sold asset back.

The alternative route is that the seller agrees to the transfer of title only once the full purchase price has been paid. This would not satisfy the interests of the purchaser since between the sale and the full payment the purchaser would not be able to sell the goods on to a third party. This dilemma is resolved by a simple transfer of title agreement made immediately, ie at the same time as the purchase agreement providing that the transfer is conditional upon full and final payment. This means that once payment is made the transfer of title to the purchaser operates automatically and the purchaser is protected against dispositions made by the seller between the time of the purchase agreement and the full payment of the purchase price under BGB Sec 161 para 1. The only risk the supplier bears is that, due to the possession of the client, the latter can provide good title to a bona fide purchaser in good faith.

Most frequently a retention of title arrangement is contained in general terms and conditions of the seller. According to general contract principles such agreement must be contained in the purchase agreement and if it is too late the supplier attempts to impose it on the purchaser only once the transfer or delivery must be made. in the absence of such a provision, delivery under a retention clause would constitute a breach of the sale agreement.

Types of retention of title

The retention of title with a 'processing clause' (*Verarbeitungsklausel*) is designed to accommodate the interests and risks of a seller of raw materials. The most prominent legal risk arises from the operation of BGB Sec 950, which provides that the person who creates a new movable from raw material acquires title to the new movable unless the value of the work invested in the processing is materially lower than the value of the raw materials. The operation of BGB Sec 950 is normally circumvented in such a way that the purchaser of the raw materials undertakes to process them for and as an agent for the seller so that the seller becomes the first owner of the new movable under Sec BGB 950. This clause can also operate in case of raw materials of several suppliers. They would then simply become co-owners pro rata to the relative value of the raw material they each supplied.

The most important permutation, however, is the 'extended or prolonged' retention of title arrangement (*Verlängerter Eigentumsvorbehalt*) which is actually a simple sum of (a) a retention of title, (b) the permission to sell the retained goods in the ordinary course of business, topped off with (c) an assignment to the retaining owner of the asset of the future claims which the purchaser will have against his clients. It has been described under 'Assignment for security purposes' p 157 above, that banks often take security over a whole set of globally defined present and future receivables. For example, a bank would grant a working capital facility to a computer dealer against a global assignment of all receivables that dealer may have against his retail clients himself. The dealer himself most certainly purchases computers from the manufacturer under an extended retention of title agreement. This inevitably leads to the claims against the retail clients being assigned twice: once to the bank under the global assignment for security purposes and once to the manufacturer under the extended retention of title (assignment of the receivables created by reselling the retained goods). Generally, if a receivable is assigned twice the first assignment takes priority. Thus if a future receivable was assigned to the bank on 2 January and the retention of title agreement would have been signed on 2 February, the bank would take priority. As early as the 1950s the Supreme Court in Civil Matters has, however, preferred the purchase money creditor (supplier) by invalidating global assignment of receivables under BGB Sec 138 (violation of public policy) if the bank knows that the receivables are generated by reselling assets which the assignor acquired under an extended retention of title arrangement. The argument runs as follows. The bank requesting such a global assignment due to the fact that extended retention of title is so commonly used will generally know that the assignor will not disclose to its suppliers the prior assignment to the bank. If it did so, obviously, it would not be supplied with goods. Thus the bank participates in or induces its debtor to committing future breaches of his supply agreements. This, so the court ruled, vitiates the global assignment leading to the result the court was probably aiming for, ie a general priority of the purchase money creditor retaining title to his goods to the financial creditor. The credit industry has long since adjusted and yielded to the arguments and to the relevant rulings by excising from all global assignment agreements those receivables generated by the sale of assets supplied to the global assignor under extended retention of title arrangements. Thus the relevant receivables are not even affected by the assignment to the bank which will go to the supplier who retained title.

The conflict between a global assignment to a factoring company and the assignment under the extended retention of title agreement is decided by the courts in a differentiated manner: If the factoring company to whom the claims are assigned takes the insolvency risk (*delcredere*) of the clients (in German legal parlance 'real factoring' (*echtes Factoring*)), the global assignment prevails against the assignment under the extended retention of title agreement if agreed earlier. The 'breach of contract theory' described above is not brought forward in this case since, so the argument goes, the supplier is in no worse position than it would be had the client paid the receivable. If the factoring company in the agreement with the purchaser does not take the insolvency risk ('false factoring' (*unechtes Factoring*)) the global assignment to the factoring company is held to be invalid, since in this case the global assignment is nothing different than a security for a loan of the factoring company to the purchaser.

Enforcement

It follows from the above that creditors of the purchaser cannot execute against the asset because it is clearly still owned by the seller. All the purchasers have a vested expectancy right (*Anwartschaft*), which to the extent that payments or partial payments have already been made could be seized as such. The same applies in the event of the purchaser's insolvency. The asset is not part of the estate and therefore the seller can reclaim the goods in kind (right of separation: *Aussonderungsrecht*). Since the sale is a synallagmatic agreement which has not been fully performed by either party, ie an executory contract, (the seller under German law has to confer full and unrestricted title), the trustee in insolvency has the option to rescind the contract. In these cases the seller can avail itself of the above right of separation. Alternatively, the trustee can elect fully to perform its side of the bargain, in which case the seller has to do the same. Then the purchase price has to be paid in full (InsO Sec 209). This is of course often impossible since the purchaser has sold the goods on to a bona fide third party that has acquired full title. In that event, ie in the case that title to the asset cannot be separated, the seller has a right of separation with respect to the surrogate, ie the purchase price paid by the bona fide third party.

Absent insolvency, rights under the retention of title arrangement are executed as follows: the seller can rescind the contract of sale for non-performance if the purchase price has not been paid (BGB Sec 455). Once it has done so the parties have mutual claims of restitution. Each of them has to give back to the other whatever they have received under the rescinded agreement (BGB Sec 346ff). The seller has yielded to the buyer possession of the goods and can reclaim this possession either on the basis of its contractual right under BGB Sec 346 (restitution) or simply under BGB Sec 985 which allows the owner of an object to reclaim possession from whoever possesses its assets without a right to do so. Alternatively the seller can set a default date for payment goods only under a retention of title arrangement himself. Often the authority to resell itself is restricted accordingly. This attempts to prevents the third party acquirer (client of the purchaser) from acquiring title before the seller has been fully paid.

Security over real estate (*Grundpfandrechte*)

Creation and Transfer

The German Civil Code provides for two basic types of security interests over real estate, which again come in a number of variations and which allow the secured creditor to use the proceeds generated and/or the value represented by the real estate to discharge the secured liability. One is the accessory mortgage or hypothec (*Hypothek*). The other is the abstract land charge (*Grundschuld*). A sub-category of the latter is the annuity charge (*Rentenschuld*) under which a sum of money is to be paid 'out of the real estate in scheduled instalments' (BGB Sec 1199).

Other than tradition and historic coincidence, there is no reason or necessity for these different types of security interests. The differences between them largely boil down to legal technicalities. Before the enactment of the German Civil Code each of the various regions of Germany, which themselves often consisted of a number of jurisdictions, had developed their own traditional techniques of securing rights on real estate. The local legal professions and the Code's draftsmen, had become so attached to these techniques and the legal traditions associated with them, that it was eventually decided to retain practically all of them in the uniform Code which was to apply in all of Germany from 1 January 1900. The complexity created by this today is not justified by any inherent economic or legal requirement. One unified and simple form of mortgage over real estate could conceivably fulfil all the intentions pursued by the variations offered by the Civil Code, but a reform on that issue is not high on the agenda of the legislature. In practice, contrary to the expectations of the historic legislators, the abstract land charge (*Grundschuld*) to which the Civil Code dedicates only a few sections has become by far the most popular and widely used instrument for securing debt on real estate. This is due to its flexibility. Furthermore, by clever draftsmanship it can be assimilated to a large extent by a hypothec to offer almost the same degree of protection to the landowner as the accessory hypothec does.

Both the hypothec and the land charge, like any interests on real estate, need to be registered in the local land register to become valid. The priority ranking between interests in real estate, ie among security interests as well as among security interests and other encumbrances (such as rights of way, building restrictions etc), is determined by the chronology of their registration. Such priority can, however, be changed later by an agreement between the owner and all of the beneficiaries of the encumbrances affected by such change. That agreement takes effect against third parties once it has been registered in the land register (BGB Sec 879, 880).

Land charge and hypothec are both coming in two forms: one with a certificate representing the right and one without. The hypothec or land charge with a certificate is more easily transferable because no registration of the transfer in the land register is necessary, saving the parties time and formalities. The transfer of the charge with a certificate and the assignment of the claim secured by a hypothec with a certificate are done 'outside the register' by an agreement between transferor and transferee coupled with the delivery to the transferee of the certificate. Both interests can be created in a global form to encumber several plots of land (*Gesamthypothek, Gesamtgrundschuld*).

Both can be created for the owner himself or can revert to the owner. Although upon first glance this may seem somewhat absurd, the function of a security interest over real estate in favour of the owner of the plot encumbered (*Eigentümergrundschuld* or *Eigentümerhypothek*) becomes apparent in view of the economic importance of the priority ranking. In an enforcement scenario the value of an interest over real estate is determined by its priority ranking, since the holder of the better-ranking right retains such right or has to be fully repaid before anybody holding a junior-ranking right can benefit from his right. While an unlimited number of land charges, one ranking after the other, can theoretically be created over a plot of land, certain banks and financial institutions insist, or have to insist, on a first-ranking security interest or one which, together with any interest senior to theirs, does not exceed a certain percentage of the value of the land (which will be determined by using certain, frequently rather conservative, valuation guidelines). Even if they do not insist on a particular priority ranking, banks determine the terms of the loan they are prepared to extend by taking into account the ranking of the security they are offered for it. In particular, in view of the lower deficiency risk they will grant much more advantageous interest rates on loans backed by a first-ranking security interest. In view of that, the owner will want to make sure it keeps control over which of his creditors enjoys which rank. He may want to block a particular rank to raise additional funds in the future on cheaper terms. This applies in particular if a (cheap) loan secured by a first-ranking hypothec or charge is retired while there are still (more expensive) loans outstanding, which are secured on subsequent security interests. Once the secured debt is discharged, the hypothec, due to its accessory nature, would theoretically automatically cease to exist. If there was no mechanism to block that rank the second-ranking charge would take its place, offering better security to the second-ranking lender than he originally bargained for. This result, which in some legal systems seems to be acceptable, would create a windfall advantage for the beneficiary of a second-ranking security interest who, after all, factored into his pricing (interest rate) the fact that he was unable to achieve the comfort of enjoying first- (or better-) ranking security. To prevent this unjustified improvement, the hypothec is automatically converted into a land charge in favour of the owner and this land charge can and will be (re-)transferred to the owner of the plot. Both thereby cease to be a proper security interest since there is no secured claim. Later they can then be transferred on to a new lender, thus allowing the re-use of the rank they originally occupied. In fact, the security interests in favour of the owner are just a legal device to block a particular priority rank for the amount of the discharged hypothec or land charge. It is like an empty shell which can be re-used and transferred to a new lender who will then enjoy that rank.

The assets covered by the security interests over real estate, ie the extent to which they are available to the beneficiary for his satisfaction, are also identical for both hypothec and land charge. They are defined in BGB Sec 1120–1130. Although some of them are chattels by nature they are treated like real estate for purposes of the enforcement of the security interests on immovables. They are, therefore, covered by the hypothec or land charge and are no longer available as collateral for other security interests created over them. These assets are/may be:

1 Products separated from the encumbered plot of land and components of the real estate (BGB Sec 1120).
2 'Accessories' of the plot of land (*Zubehör*: BGB Sec 1120 in conjunction with BGB Sec 97). This category of assets is of particular importance because it is not always obvious that they be identified with the real estate. Movables, to the extent they are intended to serve the economic purpose of the real estate, are considered to be accessories to such real estate if they have a certain geographic closeness or relationship to it. The following are some examples of movables that have been held by courts to be accessories to the property they serve: the shuttle bus used

by a hotel with respect to the plot of land on which the hotel was built, supplies of coal and heating oil, machinery in a production site, animals on a farm and excavators in a pebble pit.

3 Rights to lease and other regular payments (BGB Sec 1123, 1126) with respect to the encumbered real estate.

4 Insurance payments for insurance taken out for the real estate or objects covered by the interest (BGB Sec 1127, 1128, 1129).

Abstract land charge

By far the most popular and commonly used type of security over real estate is the abstract land charge or *Grundschuld* provided for in BGB Sec 1191ff. The land charge confers a 'real' right to the secured creditor to receive the payment of a certain amount of money to be paid 'out of the real estate' (BGB Sec 1191). This peculiar wording means that the creditor holds the right against the owner from time to time of the encumbered plot to use the real estate by either having it administered by an administrator who would then deliver the proceeds from the use of the land (such as rent etc) to discharge the secured claim or, more commonly, by having the real estate sold by public auction and applying the proceeds from such sale to discharge and retire the secured claim. The land charge cannot provide for a right of the creditor to sell the plot by way of a private sale. Different from the hypothec the abstract land charge is independent from the claim it secures and is therefore again, like the assignment and transfer for security purposes, a fiduciary security interest. The connection between the 'real' right and the secured claim is again made in a security purpose agreement.

The charge as such is created by an agreement between the chargor and the chargee and registration. The motion to register the charge must be signed by the original owner of the real estate original and certified by a notary since it can only then be registered in the land register. The charge as such does not exist before it is registered in the land register. In terms of creation in addition to the above the abstract land charge with certificate requires the creation and delivery of the certificate to the chargee.

The charge will (and that is the real difference to the hypothec) be valid even without a secured claim and can be assigned without that claim. In addition to the creation of the charge itself, chargor and chargee will enter into a separate security purpose agreement, which defines and determines in particular the secured claim. It usually contains certain information, covenants and an undertaking to keep the real estate insured. Often the position of the bank is reinforced by an assignment by the debtor/owner of any claim against better ranking chargees for reassignment of their charges to the owner and the necessary clauses for such an assignment will also be contained in the security purpose agreement. It will further define when the bank is entitled to use its rights under the charge and will give details on the application of payments to the bank (banks will want them to be applied to the secured claim only and not to the claim under the charge so that the charge is not diminished). The treatment of the charge after full and final payment of the secured debt and the right to request reassignment before such full repayment are additional topics usually covered by that security purpose agreement.

The security purpose agreement is of course valid only as between the chargor and the chargee and does not affect the charge itself. If the chargee, however, violates the security purpose agreement, this would trigger contractual remedies such as recourse in damages or, in case of a blatant breach, would allow the chargor to apply for injunctive relief to prevent the chargee from using its rights.

An assignment of the abstract land charge requires a written statement of assignment and the delivery of the mortgage certificate or, if there is no certificate, the registration of the transfer in the land register.

The abstract nature of the land charge becomes apparent upon full repayment of the secured amount. The land charge itself is generally not affected at all by such repayment. It remains registered and retains and blocks the priority ranking it has been registered with. As described above, the 'shell', however, can, and often is, re-used as security for new debt by a simple new security purpose agreement between the parties involved to that effect and assignment to the new creditor of the land charge. The charge is extinguished by cancellation and deregistration (BGB Sec 875ff). This requires the consent of the owner of the real estate (BGB Sec 1183), since it may want the charge to be re-used for its purposes (see above). A land charge is neither extinguished by the creditor's simply waiving his rights under it nor by the owner's paying the outstanding amount to the creditor. In these events the charge remains in place and reverts to the owner.

The land charge allows the use of 'real estate' to satisfy the chargee's claims. The term is used as a legal term of art and includes not only the actual piece or plot of land but also the assets described in more detail 'Security over real estate' p 163 above. This may in practice lead to conflicting security interests. While, for example, a transfer of all machinery for security purposes could by its wording include a forklift situate on the real estate, in fact that forklift is part of the real estate for purposes of the charge which takes priority.

*Accessory mortgage or hypothec (*Hypothek*)*

The hypothec is the form of security over real estate to which the Code dedicates 80 sections and which it regulates in great detail. It is the model security interest over real estate which the legislators used when drafting the Code and all the provisions governing the hypothec apply *mutatis mutandis* to the land charge, unless 'the fact that the land charge does not presuppose a claim' requires otherwise (BGB Sec 1192). Thus the Code itself defines the difference between the land charge and the hypothec: the latter 'presupposes' the secured claim, and is necessary to the hypothec, whereas the land charge is not. The hypothec must therefore be created as security for a particular and defined claim. This claim has to be expressed in a certain sum of money in domestic currency (plus interest and accessory rights), which sum must be registered in the land register. The claim can be conditional or future as long as it is determinable. Since the hypothec cannot be separated from the claim it secures (BGB Sec 1153) the creditor of any future claim must be determined and identified and must be identical with the hypothecary creditor who is registered in the land register.

Otherwise the hypothec is created in the same way as the land charge. Obviously there is no security purpose agreement. In the event that the secured claim does not (yet) exist and the hypothec is (already) registered the registration is incorrect in that legally a concealed land charge was created.

The hypothec as such is not assignable. It does, however, automatically transfer to any assignee of the secured claim. Any assignment of a claim secured by a hypothec is created under and governed by BGB Sec 1154. In case a certificate was issued the assignment of the secured claim requires a written assignment agreement and the delivery of the certificate. The claim secured by a hypothec without a certificate is assigned by an agreement to that effect (which does not require any particular form) and registration (which requires a motion with a signature certified by a notary) (BGB Sec 1154 para 3 in conjunction with BGB Sec 873, 878).

Execution of the rights under security over real estate

The realisation of the rights conferred by the hypothec and the land charge is carried out 'by way of forced execution proceedings' (BGB Sec 1147, 1192 para 2). The Code simply refers to the statutes governing forced execution over immovables and in particular to the Act on Forced Public Sales (*Zwangsversteigerungsgesetz ZVG*)). The two ways of enforcement offered by the *ZVG* are:

1 the sequestration or forced administration of the real estate aimed at making available to the beneficiary current revenue streams generated by the economic use of the real estate (such as lease payments etc); or
2 the outright sale of the real estate effected by way of public sale, which follows strict and complex rules.

The following overview will be restricted to the public sale, which is the more important form of realising rights under charges and hypothecs.

Once the secured claim (in the case of a hypothec) or the real claim (in the case of a land charge) are due, the rights can be exercised against the real estate. If a default notice is necessary to render the secured claim due, this notice has to be addressed to the owner of the real estate as well, since he is equally affected by it.

The next step towards the enforcement of the interest is to obtain an enforceable instrument allowing forced execution proceedings against the encumbered real estate. This is done by bringing action against the owner and obtaining a judgment against him in which it is ordered to 'tolerate forced execution against his property' (*Duldung der Zwangsvollsteckung*). In practice this step is abbreviated by experienced lenders who insist that, at the time the charge or hypothec is created, ie long before any default on the secured claim occurred, their borrowers execute or procure that the owner issues a notarial instrument in which the owner submits to immediate execution against the real estate (Sec 794 para 1 lit 5 Code of Civil Procedure). Such declaration becomes enforceable by issuance of an enforceable copy of the declaration by the acting notary without involvement of a court. It is then equivalent to a judgment of a court for purposes of execution proceedings and economically this procedure really amounts to a waiver of the requirement of an enforceable judgment by the owner. The declaration of submission to immediate execution can be issued in a way that it is binding on a successor in title (Code of Civil Procedure Sec 800).

The creditor makes a motion to the court to order the forced sale of the real estate (ZVG Sec 15). Once the motion is granted the court order to that effect is served upon the creditor and a notice of the proceedings is registered in the relevant land register. The court order leads to the attachment of the real estate and all the assets, which are covered by the security interest (ZVG Sec 20). Then the court schedules a first date for public auction and a notice setting that date has to be served upon the participants of the proceedings no later than six weeks before the scheduled date.

The conditions of the sale prescribed by the ZVG are designed in a way that all rights with a better priority ranking than the one held by the executing creditor will not be affected and to a certain extent the debtor, the owner and beneficiaries of junior security interests are protected against a sale at an unrealistically low price. The so-called *Mindestgebot* or minimum bid absolutely prevents the sale on the first auction date at a price which is lower than half of the fair market value determined by the court. If the highest bid on that first date does not reach seven-tenths of that value the sale has to be cancelled provided a motion to that effect is filed and the person bringing that motion (a junior creditor) can show that his claim is not covered but would have been so covered by a higher bid. Both minimum bid requirements only apply on the first auction date.

On the other hand, rights senior, ie with a better priority ranking, to the ones held by the creditor pursuing the sale will not be discharged by a payment in cash and must not be affected by the forced sale. They are being retained and continue to encumber the real estate then owned by the highest bidder and acquirer. Therefore under ZVG Sec 44 para 1 the lowest bid (*Geringstes Gebot*) must cover (a) senior, ie better ranking, rights (by way of taking them over), and (b) costs of the execution proceedings (to be paid in cash). Anything above the amount of the lowest bid will be available to the creditor pursuing the sale and will also have to be paid in cash by the acquirer. With the acceptance by the court of the highest bid in the public auction the highest bidder becomes the owner of the real estate by operation of law. Only those encumbrances, which ranked before the right of the creditor who pursued the forced execution remain in place and have to be assumed by the bidder. The security interest of the creditor who brought the proceedings against the real estate continues and encumbers the proceeds as surrogate of the real estate. While the highest bidder immediately has to pay up the amount of the bid, which must be discharged in cash, the distribution of the proceeds to the secured creditor by the court is made in a separate distribution hearing.

Security interests over particular types of assets

Security interests in all types of assets follow the principles described above. Security interests in certain 'rights' in principle follow the rules described in respect of receivables, except that the enforcement may be by sale at public auction rather than collection, and carry with them certain peculiarities, which largely depend on the nature of the asset concerned. The following, although certainly not exhaustive, are noteworthy:

1 Rights evidenced by bearer certificates (bearer shares or bearer bonds): For most purposes, including the citation of security interests over them, these will be treated like movable assets, so the rules described above in respect of movables apply. The pledgee of bearer bonds, however, can collect them at maturity.
2 Registered securities: A combination of the rules applying to movable assets and rights apply.

3 Shares in a limited liability company ('GmbH'): Security interests available over 'rights' (pledge, assignment) are available. The GmbH is treated as if it were the 'third party debtor' so that a pledge must be notified to the GmbH in order to become effective (debated). Upon a security transfer of the shares, the transferee becomes subject to rights and obligations of a shareholder under German company law. This may particularly have the effect of tainting debt outstanding to the transferee from the GmbH, which may be subordinated by effect of law as being as a shareholder's loan in lieu of equity (*kapitalersetzendes Gesellschafterdarlehen*). The same could occur if one relies on one, albeit atypical and highly disputed case, where shares in a GmbH are pledged with very far-reaching covenants to put the pledgee in a position which *de facto* corresponds to one of a shareholder.

4 Industrial property rights and other intangibles. Quite specific rules may apply depending on the nature of the individual intangible concerned. By way of example, until 1992, a trademark could be transferred only together with the business or part of the business to which it belonged. Therefore, a security interest in a trademark, whether as a pledge or as a transfer for the security purposes, was not legally possible unless the business was transferred as well. This requirement of transferring the business together with the trademark was abolished in 1992, so that now a security interest in a trademark is legally possible. So far there is, however, not much practical experience in this area.

GENERAL LIMITS TO THE VALIDITY OF SECURITY INTERESTS

There are some general principles under German law which creditors must consider when deciding what kind of security interest they wish to be have created in their favour and to what extent they want to secure their claims. While some of the principles set out below are quite complex and much of the case law governing them is in a state of flux, an attempt will be made here to give a very general overview on some of the pitfalls a creditor may encounter when receiving or requesting security from a German debtor or under German law.

Excessive security interests

Particularly in cases of cross-border acquisition financing in which one of the legal systems involved is accustomed to global charges, attempts are frequently made to create security interests on all assets a certain company or a group of companies own for debt of each individual member of the group. While such strong and far-reaching security can be extended under German law, there are a number of problems connected with such an approach and in particular there are general principles which may have an adverse effect on the secured creditor. There is, in particular, a potential risk of security interests being held invalid if a court considers them to be excessive and to violate the principles of good business morals. These problems frequently arise before the courts, since trustees in insolvency often raise them to enrich the estate to the detriment of secured creditors. Consequently, there is abundant case law, which does not, however, always provide clear guidance to the lawyer and the creditors attempting to stay within the limits of the permissible collateralisation.

Undue restrictions on debtors

A security interest or a package of security interests can also be held invalid if, without constituting excessive security, it restricts the debtor's ability to carry on its business in an unacceptable way.

1 This situation could arise in theory if the security interests relate to all assets of the debtor so that it has no asset base for other necessary credits and is therefore in the grip of one or a group of creditors. However, this feature should not invalidate security interests in a case where the mere existence of the debtor is due to the financing of that creditor or that particular group of creditors, ie in the case of a single purpose company, which takes on debt in connection with that purpose. If the mere existence of the debtor, or the business activity it is engaged in, is possible only because of that financing, then the extension of security interests over all its assets is justified.
2 The security interests could be invalid if they make the carrying on of the business impossible. For instance, if inventories and receivables were transferred to the banks without a right for the borrower to sell the stock and collect the receivables in the ordinary course of business absent an event of default under the loans.
3 Far-reaching security interests in conjunction with very burdensome covenants for the borrower could create a situation where the ability of the borrower properly to conduct its business is unduly impeded, resulting in the invalidity of the security interest. This aspect must be kept in mind when drafting or reviewing covenants not only in security documentation but in loan documentation as well.

Conflicts of interests

Security interests have also been held to be invalid if they are structured in a way which will inevitably conflict with necessary security interests of others. It is customary in Germany for a supplier to sell goods only under a retention of title arrangement with further provisos that the retention of title, within certain limits, carries over into products made from the supplies and, upon a sale of those products, will be replaced by an assignment of the receivables resulting therefrom for security purposes. It is established case law in Germany that these rights of suppliers have priority over the rights of banks and, in order to avoid invalidity of the security interest given, the security documentation of the banks must expressly reserve the positions of the suppliers. This issue has been described in more detail under 'Retention of title' p 160 above.

Securities in groups of companies

Finally, great care has to be taken when a German subsidiary secures obligations of its parent company or any of its group companies (up-stream security). German rules protecting a company's capital may under certain circumstances vitiate or otherwise make a security interest invalid or unenforceable in whole or in part. This applies in particular, but not exclusively, in the event of a German Stock Corporation giving financial assistance in the form of security in connection with the acquisition of its shares (German Stock Corporation Act – AktG Sec 71 and 71a).

Also the reverse case of a security provided by a parent company for a liability of a German affiliate may bear substantial risks, since providing the security may be considered to be contribution in lieu of equity. If the daughter company in a state of crisis pays back the secured claim and thereby relieves the parent company from its obligations under the security and later the daughter company becomes insolvent, the trustee in insolvency may under certain conditions claim the secured amount back from the parent company. The repayment of the secured claim could be considered an undue repayment of equity.

SECURITY INTERESTS IN INSOLVENCY (*INSOLVENZ*)

Overview

As of 1 January, 1999 the new German Insolvency Code ('*Insolvenzordnung*', or 'InsO'), replaced the existing insolvency statutes of the Federal Republic of Germany, namely the Bankruptcy Code ('*Konkursordnung*', 'KO'), the Aggregate Execution Code ('*Gesamtvollstreckungsordnung*', the insolvency law of the territory of the former German Democratic Republic) and the Act on Court Composition ('*Vergleichsordnung*'). For the purpose of this chapter on German securities it will suffice to provide information on the new legal situation under the InsO. It has to be observed, though, that all bankruptcy proceedings which go back on applications on or before 31 December 1998 are subject to the old laws, which may differ in detail substantially from the InsO.

Insolvency proceedings under the *Insolvenzordnung*

The filing of an application to the court (InsO Sec 13 para 1) commences insolvency proceedings. Creditors have a right and the debtor has (under certain circumstances, which are defined in a variety of statutes) a duty to file such an application. In the case of a corporation which is insolvent or over-indebted, each individual member of the management board (*Vorstandsmitglied*) of a stock corporation or each individual general manager (*Geschäftsführer)* of a GmbH has the right and the obligation to file the application (AktG Sec 92 para 2, GmbHG Sec 64 para 1). Failing to do so in time can lead to criminal liability and can also render the persons obliged to file for insolvency personally liable in damages vis-à-vis the creditors.

Once the application is filed, the insolvency court, which supervises the proceedings, will determine if preliminary measures must be taken to secure the assets and prevent manipulation of the estate by the creditors or the debtor (InsO Sec 21). The most common measures are sequestration of the assets owned by the debtor and appointment of a sequester charged with the administration of these assets. If there is a reason for insolvency (over-indebtedness or inability to pay liabilities currently due) and no circumstances exist which would prevent the opening of insolvency proceedings, the court issues a declaration that the proceedings are officially opened (*Eröffnung des Insolvenzverfahrens*). The most common reason for not opening the proceedings is if the assets available to the debtor would not even cover the costs of the proceedings (InsO Sec 26 para1). In that event, however, each creditor is free to provide sufficient funds to cover such costs and the proceedings will then be opened.

Once the proceedings are opened the debtor ceases to be able to dispose of its assets. By operation of law the trustee in insolvency is vested within the rights and obligations of the debtor. Any court proceedings pending in which the insolvent entity is a party are interrupted (Code of Civil Procedure Sec 240). In the court order opening the proceedings, the trustee is appointed (InsO Sec 27, Sec 56 para 1). He must be a natural person and can therefore not be an auditing company. The trustee in insolvency virtually replaces the debtor for all practical purposes. He takes possession of the assets and if sequestration is ordered pursuant to InsO Sec 21 para 1, the sequester will release the sequestrated objects to the trustee. Often, however, the sequester will be appointed as trustee in insolvency so that he will already have and retain possession.

The trustee's task is to liquidate the entity's assets and supervise the distribution of the proceeds to the creditors, who are prevented from bringing enforcement action individually against the insolvent entity during the insolvency proceedings. Other than the former KO, an explicit task of the insolvency proceedings is now to prevent the liquidation of the insolvent entity whenever possible and to continue the business after restructuring (InsO Sec 1). During the proceedings many important decisions are subject to the consent of, or may be taken by, the creditors' meeting (eg the replacement of the trustee).

If the continuation of the business after a restructuring of the entity according to an insolvency plan ('*Insolvenzplan*' InsO Sec 217ff) is not possible the proceeds from the sale and liquidation of the assets owned by the estate shall eventually be distributed by way of a dividend. The trustee in insolvency takes possession of all the assets belonging to the estate. Under German law, possession carries the presumption of ownership (BGB Sec 1006). Thus at the opening of insolvency proceedings, there is a presumption that the assets in the insolvent entity's possession at that time are part of its estate. Third parties who have rights or interests in any of these assets can avail themselves of these rights. Depending on the nature of their interests they may claim either a right of separation (*Aussonderungrecht*) pursuant to InsO Sec 47 or a right of separate satisfaction (*Absonderungsrecht*) pursuant to InsO Sec 49ff.

*Right of separation (*Aussonderung*)*

Obviously, assets which are in possession of the insolvent entity and consequently pass into the possession of the trustee, but which are owned by a third party, will not be available for the trustee to sell and liquidate. Assets such as cars leased by the insolvent entity, assets stored on its premises and supplies delivered to it on the basis of a retention of title arrangement are not owned by the estate. The insolvency does not expropriate them and unless the trustee fully honours the contract on which the right to possess is based, they have to be returned in kind to their lawful owner. The corresponding right to claim against the estate that the asset is surrendered is called *Aussonderungsrecht* (right of separation). It is simply the right of the owner to claim delivery of these assets outside of insolvency pursuant to those laws and arrangements, which governed the relationship before the occurrence of insolvency proceedings.

*Right of separate satisfaction (*Absonderungsrecht*)*

Most security interests and in particular those referred to in InsO Sec 49-51 (hypothec, abstract land charge, contractual and statutory pledge etc) confer to the holder a right to separate satisfaction (*Absonderungsrecht*). In short, this means that the trustee will liquidate the asset and the secured creditor has a preferred or separate right to the proceeds, which it can apply to satisfy its claims against the estate.

The claim for separate satisfaction must be brought against the trustee in insolvency. The relevant asset will be realised and liquidated using the appropriate procedure, ie the procedures, which would apply absent insolvency proceedings. The trustee in insolvency may surrender the asset to the holder of a claim for separate satisfaction against a contribution for the administrative costs of the trustee (see p 174 below). If liquidated by the trustee, the holder of a claim for separate satisfaction has a claim against the estate for the release of the proceeds realised from the sale. It will be paid in full minus a contribution for the administrative costs (see p 174 below) provided the proceeds from his security interests fall short of the amount still outstanding under the secured claim. To the extent that the sale of the collateral does not generate enough proceeds to satisfy the secured claim in full, the secured creditor will obtain the appropriate dividend on the unsatisfied part of the secured claim, as would any other unsecured creditor.

Security interests in the insolvency proceedings

Retention of title

The only security interest, which entitles one to the strong right of separation, is a retention of title arrangement. InsO Sec 47 allows the supplier and owner of the delivered goods to exercise a right to separation, ie to reclaim his property provided the trustee in insolvency does not elect to fulfil his side of the sale and purchase agreement, which he has a right to do until the reporting hearing (*Berichtstermin*), ie up to three months after the opening of the insolvency proceedings (InsO Sec 103 para 2 in conjunction with Sec 107 para 2). In this reporting hearing the creditors decide on the further fate of the estate and on the way the proceedings are to be continued. Until that time, the asset shall be generally available to the estate for further use. This right and the rather long period of uncertainty is in line with the idea of keeping the estate together until it is decided whether or not there is a chance to continue or restructure the business of the insolvent entity.

Transfer of title and assignment for security purposes

From a purely systematic standpoint, it would be logical also to grant the right of separation to the transferee of a transfer of title agreement (*Sicherungsübereignung*) and to the assignee of an assignment for security purposes (*Sicherungsabtretung*). After all, both of them hold full and legal ownership to the asset or claim, respectively. German courts have under the former bankruptcy regime, however, consistently held that the purely legal analysis shall not prevail when it comes to deciding whether a holder of an interest in an asset is granted the right of separation or a simple right to separate satisfaction. They have taken a more functional view and held that the limitations on the transferee's/assignee's rights usually contained in the security purpose agreement are such that economically these arrangements amount to simple 'security interests' and are therefore much more akin to a pledge than to full ownership. Consequently the legislator now in InsO Sec 51 lit 2 set forth that the transferee/assignee for security purposes has to content itself with a simple right to 'separate' satisfaction.

Transfer of title and assignment for security purposes and extended forms of the retention of title arrangements are subject to a moratorium on realisation once insolvency proceedings have been opened. Although this is not spelled out very clearly it is implied when InsO Sec 166 provides under the heading 'Realisation of Movables':

> '(1) The trustee in insolvency is entitled to sell privately a movable which is subject to a right of separate satisfaction provided such movable is in his possession.'

Paragraph 2 then goes on to state that the trustee has a general right to collect or otherwise use and realise claims and InsO Sec 173 finally spells out that the secured creditor who holds a right to separate satisfaction is only entitled to enforce his right if and to the extent the trustee is not itself authorised to do so.

The impact of these restrictions on secured creditors who do not hold possession in the collateral is, of course, quite obvious. The fact that the debtor wanted and did retain possession is proof of the fact that the assets form a direct and integral part of his business and would be most efficiently realised if sold by or together with the business unit they are used for and form part of. The chance that a higher price can be achieved for the business in its entirety demand the sacrifice of the immediate right of the affected secured creditors to seize and sell the asset.

Pledge

The connection between the estate and the collateral is, of course, much less close if it was openly pledged rather then assigned/transferred in a concealed way. Where the insolvent entity did not have a need for direct control and use of the asset given as security, ie where he could part with possession, there is a presumption of fact that the trustee will not need the collateral concerned for the most efficient sale or liquidation of the estate. *E contrario* InsO Sec 166 and 173 confirm that the pledgee can avail itself of his rights over the asset and that his entitlement to have the pledged asset sold remains unaffected by the insolvency proceedings.

Security interests over real estate

According to InsO Sec 49, holders of security interests over immovables, ie of hypothecs and abstract land charges, are not subject to an automatic stay of their right to enforce their interests pursuant to the law on the forced sale and forced administration of real estate (ZVG). If, however, the trustee in insolvency can establish that the interest of the estate in staying realisation proceedings, and in particular an auction of the land, outweighs the interest of the secured creditor in an immediate sale, he can obtain a court order staying further measures of execution (new ZVG Sec 30d).

Contributions of secured creditors towards administrative expenses

Obviously, one of the main tasks of a trustee in insolvency is to determine if and what kind of third party rights and security interests encumber the assets belonging to the estate. Once these interests have been determined the trustee will have to ascertain if they are valid and if so will have to take appropriate steps to honour them. The drafters of the new InsO felt that the costs and expenses for these measures, including the cost of the trustee's time, should not burden the estate to the detriment of the unsecured debtors. The new InsO therefore provides that a lump sum of 4% of the proceeds from the sale of the collateral will be paid to or retained by the estate as a contribution to the costs of determining the security interests and the assets encumbered by them (InsO Sec 170 para 1 in conjunction with Sec 171 para 1). This contribution is levied only on the proceeds generated by the realisation of that collateral which the trustee is charged with disposing of pursuant to InsO Sec 166 (mainly transfer of title and assignment for security purposes and extended retention of title arrangements).

A similar and additional contribution can be deducted by the trustee for the costs of realisation, ie the cost of selling the collateral (Sec 170). The lump sum for this is 5% unless the actual costs and expenses are considerably lower or higher, in which case such lower or higher costs are to be withheld. In addition, VAT triggered by the sale, if any, shall be deducted from the proceeds. From any sale pursuant to the InsO, not organised by the secured creditor, such costs and VAT will normally be deducted up front and will be retained by the estate.

These contributions do not necessarily mean that any secured creditor whose interest is realised by the trustee will automatically recover 9% less than the actual proceeds of its secured claim. If carefully drafted, the security documentation will ensure that the amount of the contributions will be included in the definition and description of the secured claim as costs of the realisation. The only risk a secured creditor then runs is that the sale of its collateral does not yield the amount of the actual claim plus 9% for the trustee. It is conceivable that the courts will not permit such drafting to achieve its purpose since it would effectively once again burden the unsecured creditors with the costs of the trustee. One will have to await the respective court rulings before being able to answer this question conclusively.

Compensation of secured creditors

Through delays and discussion with the trustee in insolvency the new regime may result in additional burdens for the secured creditors. Due to the safeguards for the estate and the unsecured creditors, the secured creditors are liable to receive the proceeds from their security later than under the old KO. To the extent that the security documentation will contain provisions to that effect, interest for late payment of the secured claim can and will in most cases, be covered by the security interest. But even if the security agreements do not contemplate this and the trustee prevents the individual secured creditor from immediate realisation of his interest he will under the new InsO automatically receive default interest payments for late payment by way of compensation. Such interest will, however, only start to accrue after the reporting hearing, which shall not take place later than three months from the opening of the insolvency proceedings, leaving the secured creditor with a potential interest rate loss for at least that period.

5 India

Shardul Thacker

Mulla & Mulla & Craigie Blunt & Caroe

INTRODUCTION

The external commercial borrowings policy of the Government of India permits the parties to a loan transaction to determine the security for the borrowing. *These guidelines, known as the ECB guidelines are reissued every year amending, altering and adding to the old guidelines.* The fundamental statutes relating to the creation of cross-border security and the rights of the security holder are as follows:

1 the Indian Contract Act 1872 (ICA);
2 the Transfer of Property Act 1882 (TPA);
3 the Registration Act 1908 (RA);
4 the Companies Act 1956 (CA);
5 the Foreign Exchange Regulation Act 1973 (FERA); and
6 the Foreign Exchange Management Bill 1998 (FEMA) (when in force).

THE INDIAN CONTRACT ACT (ICA)

The ICA is not an exhaustive enactment of the law of contract to be applied by the courts in India, as it is only an amending and consolidating Act. This is reiterated in its preamble which specifies that the statute is enacted in order to define and amend certain parts of the law relating to contract. The ICA s 1, which enunciates the short title, extent and commencement of the Act, expressly specifies that it does not effect 'any usage or custom of trade, nor any incident of any contract, not inconsistent with the provisions of this Act'. Since the Indian legal system is mainly based upon the common law system, principles of common law will apply in the area of the law of contracts, to the extent that they are not inconsistent with the provisions of the Indian Contract Act or the Constitution of India.

INDEMNITIES AND GUARANTEES

Chapter VIII of the ICA governs the law of indemnity and guarantee.

Contract of indemnity

A contract of indemnity is defined as a 'contract by which one party promises to save the other from loss caused to him by the conduct of the *promisor himself, or by the conduct of* any other person' (*not being the promisee*): ICA s 124.

The definition of a contract of indemnity, contained in the ICA, is a narrow definition as it is concerned only with loss caused to one person (the indemnified) by the conduct of another person. It does not address situations where loss may be caused from events or accidents which do not depend on the conduct of any person, eg a natural hazard. Nor does this Section include contracts of insurance. In India, such cases would more appropriately be covered under the ICA s 31 defining 'Contingent Contracts'. Essentially, a contract of indemnity covers all obligations imposed on one person to make good a loss suffered by another, without any qualification as to the nature of loss giving rise to the performance of the obligation. However, since the law of indemnity as contained in the ICA is not exhaustive, other forms of contracts of indemnity are governed by principles of common law.

The liability of the indemnifier commences as soon as the loss of the indemnified becomes absolute. Hence, it is not necessary for the indemnity holder to first pay off the claim against him, prior to calling upon the indemnifier to make good his loss.

Essential features of a contract of indemnity

To enable the indemnity holder to sue upon a contract of indemnity, it is necessary that the indemnity holder must have suffered a loss before he can claim compensation for the loss. The indemnity holder can, however, call upon the indemnifier to compensate him before the actual discharge of the loss, and thus it is not a condition precedent that the loss must have been made good. But it should also be noted that a contract of indemnity where the object is contrary to the law of the land or against public policy, is either unlawful or void depending upon the legal provision which applies.

Rights of the indemnity holder

In the event that the indemnity holder is sued by a third person with respect to a loss arising to that person on an aspect covered by a contract of indemnity, the indemnity holder may, so long as he acts within the scope of his authority under the contract of indemnity, recover the following payments from the indemnifier (ICA s 125):

1 all damages which he may be compelled to pay in any suit in respect of any matter to which the promise to indemnify applies;

2 all costs which he may be compelled to pay in such suit if, in bringing or defending it, he did not contravene the orders of the promisor, and acted as it would have been prudent for him to act in the absence of any contract of indemnity, or if the promisor authorised him to bring or defend the suit:

3 all sums which he may have paid under the terms of any compromise of any such suit, if the compromise was not contrary to the orders of the promisor, and was one which it would have been prudent for the promisee to make in the absence of

any contract of indemnity, or if the promisor authorised him to compromise the suit.

Besides the above rights, the indemnity holder can also sue for specific performance of the contract of indemnity, if he incurs absolute liability which is covered by the contract of indemnity.

Express or implied indemnity

In a number of cases, the contract of indemnity is to be implied from the circumstances of the case. The ICA s 124 includes an express or implied promise to indemnify. However, the duty to indemnify in certain cases, may also be annexed by operation of law, for example, under the Companies Act 1956, a transferee of shares is bound to indemnify the transferor against future calls on shares.

Contract of guarantee

A contract of guarantee is defined as 'a contract to perform the promise, or discharge the liability, of a third person, in case of his default' (ICA s 126).

The person who gives the guarantee is called the 'surety'; the person whose liability is guaranteed is called the 'principal debtor'; and the person to whom the guarantee is given is called the 'creditor'. It is essential that there be three parties who are privy: namely the principal debtor, the creditor and the surety. It is necessary that their implied assent or express participation be proved by the person who relies on the contract of guarantee.

Essential features of a contract of guarantee

Co-extensive liability

The liability of the surety is co-extensive with that of the principal debtor, unless it is otherwise provided by the contract (ICA s 128). While elaborating on the co-extensive nature of the liability of the surety, the Supreme Court of India observed that the liability of the surety to fulfil his obligation under the guarantee is not automatically suspended when the liability of the principal debtor is suspended under any statutory provision/ liquidation proceedings against the principal debtor, or if the principal debtor is referred to the Board of Industrial and Financial Reconstruction under the Sick Industrial Companies (Special Provisions) Act 1985, since the contract of guarantee is an independent contract between the creditor and the surety (*State Bank of India v Saksaria Sugar Mills Ltd* AIR 1986 SC 868). Similarly, the creditor is not bound to exhaust his remedy against the principal debtor before he may sue the surety under the contract of guarantee.

Consideration

Since an essential element of a valid contract is the existence of consideration, a contract of guarantee has to be on the basis of some consideration flowing towards the surety, in return for which the guarantee is given. On the aspect of consideration, of the ICA s 127 specifies:

> 'Anything done, or any promise made, for the benefit of the principal debtor may be a sufficient consideration to the surety for giving the guarantee.'

Surety for past debt is valid when there is fresh consideration for the promise. The intention to include a past promise must be made clear so as to bind the surety for a past debt. The Act also contemplates past consideration as valid consideration.

Guarantee may be oral or written

The ICA s 126 specifically reinforces the validity of oral guarantees, placing them on a par with written guarantees, by inter alia providing that a 'guarantee may be either oral or written'.

Principal debt

Since the object of guarantee is to secure the payment of debt, the existence of a recoverable debt is necessary. The term 'liability' means liability enforceable by law and there cannot be a contract to guarantee a time-barred debt.

Consent of the surety should not have been obtained by misrepresentation or concealment

Any guarantee which has been obtained by means of misrepresentation by the creditor or with his knowledge and assent, concerning a material part of the transaction, is invalid (s 142). And any guarantee which the creditor has obtained by means of keeping silent as to the material circumstances is invalid (s 143).

For a guarantee to be invalidated in this way two points have to be proved: first that there was misrepresentation as to a material part of the transaction, or silence as to material circumstance; and, second, that the guarantee was in fact obtained by means of such misrepresentation or silence.

Indian courts have, however, distinguished between fiduciary guarantees by persons in favour of banks. But, where the suretyship is with regard to an advance to be made by a bank, the bank need not disclose part indebtedness to the surety.

Legal

A contract of guarantee must also satisfy the element of legality. Illegality of object or consideration vitiates a contract of guarantee. The term 'liability' under s 126 envisages a liability enforceable by law. Therefore a contract to guarantee a time-barred debt is void for illegality.

Kinds of guarantee

1. *Conditional guarantee.* A surety may require a condition precedent to be fulfilled by the creditor, failing which he should not be made liable.
2. *Limited guarantee.* A surety may, while undertaking to guarantee a debt, place a

limit upon his liability, by which he expressly declares that his liability under the guarantee shall not at any time exceed the limit.

3 *Continuing guarantee.* The ICA s 129 defines a continuing guarantee as one which extends to a series of transactions. This kind of guarantee is intended to cover a number of transactions over a period of time. The essence of a continuing guarantee is that it applies not to a specific transaction but to any number of transactions and makes the surety liable for the unpaid amount at the end of the guarantee.

Rights of a surety against the principal debtor, creditor and co-sureties

Principal debtor

Under ICA s 140, a surety on payment of the amount due under the contract of guarantee to the creditor steps into the shoes of the creditor and is invested with all the rights which a creditor had before such payment.

However, if the surety is given for a part of debt and payment is made thereof, which amounts to payment of the whole debt as between him and the creditor, then such payment gives the surety a right over the securities.

In every contract of guarantee there is an implied promise by the principal debtor to indemnify the surety; and the surety is entitled to recover from the principal debtor whatever sum he has rightfully paid under the guarantee, but no sums he has paid wrongfully.

Rights against creditor

The rights of a surety as against the principal debtor is also embodied in s 141, by which he is entitled to the benefit of every security which the creditor has against the principal debtor whether he knows of its existence or not. If the security is lost or parted with or without his consent, he is entitled to a partial discharge of his liability. However, loss arising due to an act of God does not fall within s 141 so as to give the surety a right of discharge.

The right under the section is limited to the securities existing at the time of the formation of the suretyship contract.

Rights against co-sureties

The liability of co-sureties is joint and several. Although the creditor can choose to release one or more of them, such a release will not amount to a discharge of the other co-sureties. A necessary implication of the principle of joint and several liability is that the surety/sureties who is/are released by the creditor will still remain responsible to the other sureties. This principle is enunciated in the ICA s 138 which states as follows:

> 'Where there are co-sureties, a release by the creditor of one of them does not discharge the others; nether does it free the surety so released from his responsibility to the other sureties'.

The liability of each co-surety will be to pay an equal share of the whole debt, or of that part of it which remains unpaid by the principal debtor. The sharing of the liability in the above manner, amongst the co-sureties, is irrespective of whether the co-sureties have given their respective guarantees under the same or different contracts and irrespective of whether the co-sureties issued their respective guarantees with or without the knowledge of each other. the above principle of sharing of liability is a statutory stipulation under the ICA s 146 which reads:

> 'Where two or more persons are co-sureties for the same debt or duty, either jointly or severally, and whether under the same or different contracts, and whether with or without the knowledge of each other, the co-sureties, in the absence of any contract to the contrary, are liable, as between themselves, to pay each equal share of the whole debt, or of that part of it which remains unpaid by the principal debtor.'

There will be no right of contribution between sureties whose obligations are distinct and which do not relate to the same debt, but relate to different portions of a single debt or which relate to different debts between the same principal debtor and creditor.

If two or more co-sureties extend their respective guarantees on the same debt but are bound in different amounts, the sharing of the liability amongst the co-sureties will not be in proportion to their respective obligations, but will instead be equal 'as far as the limits of their respective obligations permit' (ICA s 147).

The above principle is explained by the following illustrations:

1 A, B and C, as sureties for D, enter into three guarantees, each with a different liability, namely, A's liability is Rs 10,000, B's is Rs 20,000, C's is Rs 40,000, guaranteeing D's obligations to E. D defaults to the extent of Rs 30,000. A, B and C are each liable to pay Rs 10,000.
2 A, B and C, as sureties for D, enter into three guarantees, each with a different penalty, namely, A's liability is Rs 10,000, B's is Rs 20,000, C's is Rs 40,000, guaranteeing D's obligations to E. D defaults to the extent of Rs 40,000. A is liable to pay Rs 10,000, and B and C Rs 15,000 each.

Discharge of surety

The surety is discharged from his liability in any of the following situations:

Revocation by the surety

ICA s 130 provides that a continuing guarantee may at any time be revoked by the surety as to future transactions by notice to the creditor.

Under this section only a continuing guarantee can be revoked and only in respect of future transactions. It is worth noticing that revocation becomes effective for the future transactions while the surety remains liable for transactions already entered into.

When the consideration is single and indivisible, for instance where a continued relationship is established on the faith of a certain guarantee, no revocation of the same is possible.

Surety's death

Section 131 reads:

> 'The death of surety operates, in the absence of any contract to the contrary, as a revocation of a continuing guarantee, so far as future transactions.'

If there is any contract to the contrary, the surety's death would not automatically revoke the guarantee.

Variance in the terms of the contract between the principal debtor and the creditor
The ICA s133 stipulates that any 'variance, made without the surety's consent in the terms of contract between the principal debtor and the creditor, discharges the surety as to transactions subsequent to the variance'.

Any form of variance of the contract between the principal debtor and the creditor will not discharge the surety. Only *material* alterations, made without the knowledge of the surety, will result in a discharge of the surety. Material alterations depend upon the circumstances of each case and are those alterations which will materially affect the surety's interest in an adverse manner and which will be prejudicial to the surety. Unsubstantial alterations which are not disadvantageous to either the principal debtor or the surety will not discharge the surety.

The Supreme Court of India reiterated the above principle in a case where the surety pleaded discharge of his liability on the basis of an alteration of a contract between a bank and the debtor for the grant of an overdraft facility by the bank. In this case a blank guarantee form was issued by the bank to the debtor, who completed the form stating that the maximum debt guaranteed was Rs 25,000. The bank was not prepared to give an overdraft facility exceeding Rs 20,000. Hence, the principal debtor altered the guarantee form and reduced the debt guaranteed from Rs 25,000 to Rs 20,000. In a case by the surety for the discharge of liability on the ground of the above alteration in the maximum debt that was guaranteed, the Supreme Court held that the surety would not be discharged since the alteration was neither substantial nor to the detriment of the surety.

Release or discharge of the principal debtor on account of the creditor
The ICA s 134 specifies that:

> 'The surety is discharged by any contract between the creditor and the principal debtor, by which the principal debtor is released, or by any act or omission of the creditor, the legal consequence of which is the discharge of the principal debtor.'

A discharge which the principal debtor may secure by operation of law in bankruptcy or in liquidation proceedings does not result in a discharge of the surety.

A restated issue is whether a surety will be discharged if the creditor does not sue the surety within the limitation period, but instead allows the debt to be time-barred. Although there were divergent views on this question by the lower courts, the Supreme Court has held that a creditor is entitled to recover the debt from the surety even though the suit against the principal debtor is time-barred. This dictum was on the basis that the legal consequence of the termination of the limitation period is not the extinction of the debt. Neither is the liability of the debtor nor the debt extinguished. Instead, the creditor only loses his right of recovery through the courts of law.

The above principle is strengthened by ICA s 137, which reads as follows:

> 'Mere forbearance on the part of the creditor to sue the principal debtor or to enforce any other remedy against him does not, in the absence of any provision in the guarantee to the contrary, discharge the surety.'

Contractual undertaking by the creditor either to give time or not to sue the debtor

The ICA s 135 specifies as follows:

> 'A contract between the creditor and the principal debtor, by which the creditor makes a composition with, or promises to give time to, or not to sue, the principal debtor discharges the surety, unless the surety assents to such contract.'

Although a mere forbearance on the part of the creditor to sue the principal debtor does not discharge the surety, as explained above (ICA s 137), a contractual undertaking by the creditor within the ambit of ICA s 135 will discharge the surety. In relation to the failure on the part of creditor to sue the principal debtor, the distinction between s137 (which does not discharge the surety) and s 135 (which discharges the surety), rests upon the assumption of a contractual obligation on the part of the creditor, restraining him from suing the debtor.

Impairment of the rights of the surety through an act or omission on the part of the creditor

The ICA s 139 specifies that if the creditor performs any act which is inconsistent with the rights of the surety, or omits to perform any act which his duty to the surety requires, and the eventual remedy of the surety himself against the principal debtor is thereby impaired, the surety is discharged.

Subrogation

The principle of subrogation, whereby on discharging the liability of the principal debtor the surety steps into the shoes of the creditor, is enshrined in the ICA s 140 which reads:

> 'Where a guaranteed debt has become due, or default of the principal debtor to perform a guaranteed duty has taken place, the surety, upon payment or performance of all that he is liable for, is invested with all the rights which the creditor had against the principal debtor.'

In a particular instance, the surety sought to invoke the principle of subrogation prior to his payment of the debt to the creditor, by requesting the court to grant a temporary injunction restraining the principal debtor from disposing of his personal properties until the disposal of the suit for recovery of the money filed by the creditor against the principal debtor. The High Court of Calcutta upheld the application of the surety and granted the temporary injunction as requested (*Mahatma Ghosh v United Industrial Bank Ltd* AIR 1987 Cal 280). Although the principle of subrogation as enshrined in ICA s 140 arises only upon payment or performance of all that the surety is liable for, in the above-mentioned case the equitable doctrine of subrogation was applied by the High Court even prior to the discharge of the liability by the surety.

The surety's right of subrogation entitles him to benefit from all the securities held by the creditor against the principal debtor at the time of entry into the contract of guarantee. The ICA s 141 contains this right in the following terms:

'A surety is entitled to the benefit of every security which the creditor has against the principal debtor at the time when the contract of suretyship is entered into, whether the surety knows of the existence of such security or not; and, if the creditor loses, or, without the consent of the surety, parts with such security, the surety is discharged to the extent of the value of the security.'

SECURITY

Security may be created through any of the following methods:

1 mortgage;
2 charge;
3 pledge; and
4 hypothecation.

The Transfer of Property Act 1882 (TPA), which deals only with the transfer of immovable property, distinguishes between a mortgage and a charge over immovable property, whereas the CA regards a mortgage as a form of charge, in the context of the regulatory provisions on the registration of charges.

Immovable property

Immovable property may be made surety either by way of a charge or a mortgage.

Mortgage

A 'mortgage' is defined by the TPA s 58 as:

'A mortgage is the transfer of an interest in specific property for the purpose of securing the payment of money advanced or to be advanced by way of loan, an existing or future debt, or the performance of an engagement which may give rise to a pecuniary liability.'

The transferor is called a mortgagor; the transferee a mortgagee; the principal money and interest of which payment is secured for the time being are called the mortgage-money and the instrument (if any) by which the transfer is effected is called a mortgage deed.

The types of mortgages that are recognised under Indian law are:

1 *Simple mortgage*. Where, without delivering possession of the mortgaged property, the mortgagor binds himself personally to pay the mortgage money, and agrees, expressly or impliedly, that, in the event of his failing to pay according to his contract, the mortgagee shall have a right to cause the mortgaged property to be sold and the proceeds of sale to be applied, so far as may be necessary, in payment of the mortgage money, the transaction is called a simple mortgage and the mortgagee a simple mortgagee (as contained in the TPA s 58(b)).
2 *Mortgage by conditional sale*. Where the mortgagor ostensibly sells the mortgaged property:

(a) on condition that on default of payment of the mortgage money on a certain date the sale shall become absolute; or
(b) on condition that on such payment being made the sale shall become void; or
(c) on condition that on such payment being made the buyer shall transfer the property to the seller, the transaction is called a mortgage by conditional sale and the mortgagee a mortgagee by conditional sale. However, no such transaction will be deemed to be a mortgage, unless the condition is embodied in the document which effects or purports to effect the sale (as contained in the TPA s 58(c)).

3 *Usufructuary mortgage.* Where the mortgagor delivers possession or expressly or by implication binds himself to deliver possession of the mortgaged property to the mortgagee and authorises him to retain such possession until payment of the mortgagee money, and to receive the rents and profits accruing from the property or any part of such rents and profits and to appropriate the same in lieu of interest, or in payment of the mortgage money, or partly in lieu of interest or partly in payment of the mortgage money, the transaction is called an usufructuary mortgage and the mortgagee an usufructuary mortgagee (as contained in the TPA s 58(d)).

4 *English mortgage.* Where the mortgagor binds himself to repay the mortgage-money on a certain date and transfers the mortgaged property absolutely to the mortgagee, but subject to a proviso that he will re-transfer it to the mortgagor upon payment of the mortgage-money as agreed, the transaction is called an English mortgage (as contained in the TPA s 58(c)).

5 *Mortgage by deposit of title deeds.* Where a person in any of the following towns, namely, the towns of Calcutta, Madras and Bombay, and in any other town which the State Government concerned may, by notification in the *Official Gazette*, specify in this behalf, delivers to a creditor or his agent documents of title to immovable property, with intent to create a security thereon, the transaction is called a mortgage by deposit of title deeds (as contained in the TPA s 58(f)).

5 *Anomalous mortgage.* A mortgage which is not a simple mortgage, a mortgage by conditional sale, an usufructuary mortgage, an English mortgage or a mortgagee by dèposit of title deeds within the meaning of the above definitions, is called an anomalous mortgage (as contained in the TPA s 58(g)).

Charge

Section 100 of the TPA defines a 'charge' as follows:

> 'Where immovable property of one person is by act of parties or operation of law made security for the payment of money to another, and the transaction does not amount to a mortgage, the latter person is said to have a charge on the property; and all the provisions hereinbefore contained which apply to a simple mortgage shall, so far as may be, apply to such charge.
>
> Nothing in this section applies to the charge of a trustee on the trust property for expenses properly incurred in the execution of his trust, and, save as otherwise expressly provided by any law for the time being in force, no charge shall be

enforced against any property in the hands of a person to whom such property has been transferred for consideration and without notice of the charge.'

Under the TPA, the fundamental difference between a mortgage and a charge is that, in the case of the former, there is a transfer of interest in the property to the person in favour of whom the security is granted whereas, in the case of the latter, there is no transfer of interest in the property. In a charge, there is only a creation of a right of payment out of the property over which the charge is created. The charge-holder does not enjoy the right of foreclosure, available to the mortgagee under the TPA.

Movable property

Pledge and hypothecation are forms of creation of security over movable property. While a pledge is governed by the ICA, there are no statutory provisions in relation to hypothecation. However, since the ICA is not exhaustive on the law of contracts, hypothecation is recognised in India and is governed by principles of common law.

'Pledge' is defined by the ICA s 172 as the 'bailment of goods as security for payment of a debt or performance of a promise'. The person creating the pledge is called the 'pawnor' and the person in whose favour the pledge is created is called the 'pawnee'.

'Bailment' is defined by the ICA s 148 as 'the delivery of goods by one person to another for some purpose, upon a contract that they shall, when the purpose is accomplished, by return or otherwise be disposed of according to the directions of the person delivering them.'

The essential elements of a pledge are:

1 actual/constructive delivery of the property to the pawnee; and
2 the delivery of the property is to be by way of security for payment of a debt due by the pawnor to the pawnee.

Although the pawnee has the right to the possession of the property, he does not have any interest in the property that is pledged. The rights enjoyed by the pawnee in relation to the property are:

1 the pawnee may retain the goods pledged, not only for payment of the debt or the performance of the promise, but for the interest of the debt and all necessary expenses incurred by him in respect of the possession or for the preservation of the goods pledged (ICA s 173);
2 the pawnee is entitled to receive from the pawnor extraordinary expenses incurred by him for the preservation of the goods pledged (ICA s 175); and
3 if the pawnor makes default in payment of the debt, or performance, at the stipulated time of the promise, in respect of which the goods were pledged, the pawnee may bring a suit against the pawnor upon the debt or promise and retain the goods pledged as a collateral security; or he may sell the thing pledged, on giving the pawnor reasonable notice of the sale.

If the proceeds of such sale are less than the amount due in respect of the debt or promise, the pawnor is still liable to pay the balance. If the proceeds of the sale are greater than the amount so due, the pawnee shall pay over the surplus to the pawnor.

The following items of movable property are usually secured in consideration for a debt:

1 goods;
2 shares;
3 ships; and
4 aircraft

Goods

Goods may either be pledged or hypothecated by way of security. Where the actual or constructive possession of the goods is given to the creditor, it will amount to a pledge. Where possession of the goods is retained by the owner and the right to seek payment against such goods is granted to the creditor, the goods are said to be hypothecated. Although there are no statutory provisions in relation to hypothecation, the same is governed by principles of common law.

Shares

Shares are defined by the CA s 82 as movable property, in the following terms:

> 'The shares or other interest of any member in a company shall be movable property, transferable in the manner provided by the articles of the company.'

Shares may be given as security either by way of pledge or mortgage. Although the TPA does not deal with the mortgage or movable property, the concept of mortgage of shares in specific cases has been recognised by courts. The distinction between pledge and mortgage of shares is usually drawn on the basis of the nature of the transaction and the rights enjoyed by the security-holder. A pledge usually differs from a mortgage to the extent that the pawnee has no right of foreclosure since no interest in the property is transferred to the pawnee, unlike in the landmark judgment in the case of the mortgage of shares where the facts were as follows (*Shahzadi Begum v Giridharlial*).

A, the owner of certain shares, delivered the share certificates by way of security for a loan, to the tender (B). The agreement for the creation of security was called an agreement of pledge and it required B to lodge the shares for transfer in his name. In order to enable the transfer, share transfer certificates were executed by A in favour of B. A was given the right under the agreement to repay the loan including the transfer fee and take delivery of the shares within a period of two years from the day of the loan. A further period of one year thereafter was also given to A to take back the shares from B by paying the loan, the transfer fee and interest at the rate of 9% (referred to as the 'amount'). The agreement expressly conferred a right on B to dispose of the shares, after giving a prior notice to A, in the event of A's default in the repayment of the loan as stipulated above.

The shares were registered in B's name, on their delivery, and the voting rights on the shares were enjoyed by B during the entire term of the loan, ie three years. On the completion of the term of the loan, A failed to repay the amount and redeem the shares despite several notices in this regard by B. The shares were then sold by B for the recovery of the amount from A. Subsequently A's heirs challenged the sale of shares by B and raised the plea that the transaction was one of sale from A to B, with a right of repurchase to A.

The court held that the transaction was one of mortgage of shares and not sale. Nor was the transaction a pledge, since along with possession of the shares the right of enjoyment was also given to B. The court explained that under the ICA the person to whom goods are pledged does not receive any rights of enjoyment of the goods. In the event of a mere deposit of share certificates without any deed of transfer, the transaction would be one of pledge. In the present case a transfer of shares was effected in favour of B who also exercised voting rights over the shares. Thus the court held that the transaction was one of mortgage and explained the legal position on the mortgage of movable property as follows:

> 'although the hypothecation and mortgage of movables are not specifically mentioned in the Contract Act, that Act not being exhaustive law on the subject, and the above said transactions having long been recognised as valid in India, these transactions will have to be given effect to. In the absence of specific rules applicable to any matter, the principle recognised in the various Civil Courts Act is that the courts should decide according to justice, equity and good conscience whatever is considered to be equivalent to the English Law wherever such law is applicable to Indian conditions. It is only under this principle that the hypothecation or mortgage of movable property, although not specifically provided in the Contract Act, are valid and a decree can be passed in enforcement of such transactions.'

Ships

Mortgage of Indian-registered ships is governed by the Merchant Shipping Act 1958 ('MSA'). The MSA defines an Indian ship as a ship registered under the MSA and includes any ship registered at any port in India at the commencement of this Act which is recognised as an Indian ship. The MSA requires every Indian ship ie every ship owned by an Indian citizen or an Indian company, or a co-operative society to be registered with the Registrar of Indian Ships Mercantile Marine Department. A mortgage may be created only over a registered ship or share therein and the instrument creating the mortgage has to be in the prescribed form, ie the statutory mortgage form, and has to be recorded in the Register of Ships and the ship's port of registry. The statutory mortgage is usually accompanied by a deed of covenant which is also filed with the Mercantile Marine Department along with the mortgage.

In accordance with general practice, when a ship is mortgaged as security for cross-border transactions, the earnings, insurance and charters (if any) of the ship are assigned in favour of the lenders as further security, pursuant to obtaining the Reserve Bank of India approval for the same. The Reserve Bank of India approval must also be obtained to convert the insurance policy to dollar denomination prior to assigning the same.

Aircraft

Operation of aircraft in India is governed by the Aircraft Act 1934 and the Indian Aircraft Rules 1937. No aircraft may be operated in India unless it is registered in India, under the said Aircraft Rules. Only aircraft which are wholly owned by Indian companies may be registered in India. An aircraft owned by a company with its registered office outside India may be registered in India, provided the company is carrying on business in India (r 30). However, under r 160 of the Aircraft Rules, the Central Government is authorised to exempt any aircraft or any person operating an aircraft from the application of r 30.

There is no prescribed form for the creation of an aircraft mortgage and the same may be governed either by Indian law or by the law of any other country. There are no special formalities for the creation of an aircraft mortgage, but the usual practice adopted is to record the mortgage in the Register of Aircraft maintained at the office of the Director General of Civil Aviation, who is the aviation in India. The Register of Aircraft is open to public inspection.

FORMALITIES FOR CREATING DEBTS/MORTGAGE AND PLEDGE/ HYPOTHECATION

Documentation

Immovable property

Immovable property may be given as security either by way of a mortgage (TPA s 58) or a charge (TPA s 100).

A mortgage (other than a mortgage by deposit of title deeds) can be effected only by means of a written instrument, signed by the mortgagor and attested by at least two witnesses. This is a statutory requirement under the TPA s 59. Similarly, a charge within the meaning of the TPA s 100 can be created only by means of written instrument, signed by the person creating the charge and attested by at least two witnesses.

The term 'attested' has been defined in the TPA s 3 in relation to an instrument as:

> 'attested by two or more witnesses each of whom has seen the executant sign or affix his mark to the instrument, or has seen some other person sign the instrument in the presence and by the direction of the executant, or has received from the executant a personal acknowledgement of his signature or mark, or of the signature of such other person, and each of whom has signed the instrument in the presence of the executant; by it shall not be necessary that more than one of such witnesses shall have been present at the same time, and no particular form of attestation shall be necessary.'

Movable property

A pledge and/or a hypothecation of movable property may either be created by a written instrument or may be by means of an oral contract.

Corporate authorisations

The CA s 292(e) mandates that the board of directors of a company can exercise their power of making loans only by means of resolutions passed at meetings of the board. The proviso to s 292(1) permits the board to pass a resolution delegating the power to make loans to 'any committee of directors, the managing director, the managing agent, secretaries and treasurers, the manager or any other principal officer of the company or in the case of a branch office of the company, a principal officer of the branch office.' A resolution delegating the powers as above may contain restrictions and conditions prescribed by the board for the exercise of the power delegated. Further, s 292(4) stipulates that every resolution of the board delegating the power to make loans will have to specify the total amount up to which loans may be made by the delegate, the purposes for which the loans may be made and the maximum amount of loans which may be made for each purpose in individual cases.

The power to make loans includes the power to create security in consideration for the loans. However, in the event that the security is a usufructuary mortgage of the whole, or substantially the whole, of the undertaking of the company, or where the company owns more than one undertaking (of the whole or substantially the whole of any such undertaking) then prior consent of the company in general meeting will be required for the creation of such mortgage (CA s 293(1)(a)).

Registration

Registration of immovable property

The Registration Act 1908, s 17 requires registration of all

> 'non-testamentary instruments which purport or operate to create, declare assign, limit or extinguish, whether vested or contingent, of the value of one hundred rupees and upwards, to or in immovable property.'

Hence a mortgage and/or a charge of immovable property will have to be registered under the Registration Act 1908. The implications of registration are set out in the TPA Explanations of s 3 as follows:

1 Any person acquiring immovable property or any share or interest in such property, which acquisition is required by law to be and has been effected by a registered instrument, shall be deemed to have notice of such instrument as from the date of registration thereof.

2 Any person acquiring any immovable property or any share or interest in any such property shall be deemed to have notice of the title, if any, of any person who is for the time being in actual possession thereof.

3 A person shall be deemed to have had notice of any fact if his agent acquires notice thereof whilst acting on his behalf in the course of business to which that fact is material.

The implications of non-registration of an instrument that is compulsorily required to be registered are that a non-registered instrument shall not:

1 affect any immovable property comprised therein; or
2 confer any power to adopt; or
3 be received as evidence of any transaction affecting such property or conferring such power.

Registration under the Companies Act for movable property

Under the ICA s 125 specified charges will be void against liquidators or creditors unless they are registered with the Registrar of Companies within 30 days of the creation of the charge. Once a charge becomes void on account of non-registration, the money secured thereby becomes immediately payable (ICA s 125(3)).

Under the ICA, 'charge' includes a mortgage. The following charges are required to be registered:

1 a charge for the purpose of securing any issue of debentures;
2 a charge on the uncalled share capital of the company;
3 a charge on any immovable property, wherever situate, or any interest therein;
4 a charge on any book debts of the company;
5 a charge, not being a pledge, on any movable property of the company;
6 a floating charge on the undertaking or any property of the company including stock-in-trade;
7 a charge on calls made but not paid;
8 a charge on a ship or any share in a ship; and
9 a charge on goodwill, on a patent or a licence under a patent, on a trade mark, or on a copyright or a licence under a copyright.

Registration of ships with the Mercantile Marine Department (MMD)

The creation of a mortgage on a ship has to be registered with the MMD with whom the ship is registered. Registration of the mortgage is done by filing the Statutory Form 11 with the MMD. The MMD takes on record the details of the mortgage and makes an entry of the same in the Register of Ships maintained by the MMD. The Register is open for public inspection and acts as deemed notice to any party taking inspection of the Register.

Regulatory authorisations

The regulatory provisions governing foreign exchange and securities and import and export of currency and bullion are governed by the Foreign Exchange Regulation Act 1973.

Transfer of any interest in immovable property

The Foreign Exchange Regulation Act 1973 (FERA) s 31 prohibits foreign citizens and foreign companies, except with prior permission of the Reserve Bank of India, from acquiring or holding or transferring or disposing of by way of sale, mortgage, lease, gift, settlement or otherwise, immovables situated in India. The above prohibition does not apply to the acquisition or transfer of any immovable property by way of lease for a period less than five years.

Export and/or transfer of securities

The FERA also places restrictions on the export and transfer of securities, ie shares, debentures etc of Indian companies, without the prior permission of the Reserve Bank of India. In particular, persons are prohibited under FERA s 19 from:

1 taking or sending any security to any place outside India;
2 transferring any security or creating or transferring any interest in a security to or in favour of a person resident outside India;
3 issuing, whether in India or elsewhere, any security which is registered or to be registered in India, to any, person resident outside India; and
4 acquiring, holding or disposing of any foreign security.

In terms of the above, since prior Reserve Bank of India permission is required before creating or transferring any interest in a security to or in favour of a person resident outside India, any cross-border mortgager over Indian shares will require prior Reserve Bank of India permission.

Guarantee issued by an Indian resident in respect of an external borrowing

FERA s 26 prohibits persons resident in India from giving a guarantee, without the general or special permission of the Central Government or the Reserve Bank of India, in respect of any debt or other obligation or liability of the following nature:

1 of a person resident in India and due or owing to person resident outside in India; or
2 of a person resident outside India.

Since 1993 FERA has been reviewed several times as it was felt that substantial changes needed to be incorporated in the light of the process of economic liberalisation relating to foreign investments and foreign trade. It was subsequently felt that it would be better to repeal the existing Foreign Exchange Act and enact new legislation. Keeping this in view the Central Government decided to introduce the Foreign Exchange Management Bill 1998. The provisions of the Bill aim at consolidating and amending the law relating to foreign exchange, with the objective of facilitating external trade and payments and promoting the orderly development and maintenance of foreign exchange markets in India. At the time of writing the FEMA Bill is awaiting enactment by the Indian parliament.

PRIORITY OF THE MORTGAGOR'S/CHARGE-HOLDER'S RIGHTS

Priority as between competing charges

The TPA s 48 embodies the principle of 'prior in point of time is prior in point of law', while stipulating the priority of rights created by transfer. Section 48 enacts that:

> 'where a person purports to create by transfer at different times rights in or over the same immovable property, and such rights cannot all exist or be exercised to their full extent together, each later created right shall, in the absence of a special contract or reservation binding the earlier transferees, be subject to the rights previously created'.

The only exception to the above rule of priority is contained in the TPA s 78, which specifies that:

> 'where, through the fraud, misrepresentation or gross neglect of a prior mortgagee, another person has been induced to advance money on the security of the mortgaged property, the prior mortgagee shall be postponed to the subsequent mortgagee'.

The doctrine of marshalling securities is also incorporated in the TPA, whereby in the event that the owner of two or more properties mortgages them to one person and then mortgages one or more of the properties to another person, the subsequent mortgagee, in the absence of a contract to the contrary, would be entitled to have the prior mortgage debt satisfied out of those properties which have not been mortgaged to him but have been mortgaged to the earlier mortgagee (TPA s 81). However, the subsequent mortgagee may exercise his right of marshalling only to the extent that it does not prejudice the right of the prior mortgagee or of any other person who has, for consideration, acquired an interest of any properties.

Priority of ship mortgages

If there is more than one registered mortgage on an Indian flag vessel then, notwithstanding any express, implied or constructive notice, the mortgagees acquire priority according to the date on which each mortgage is recorded in the register book, ie Register of Ships, and not according to the date of each mortgage itself. This is a statutory rule of priority contained in the Merchant Shipping Act 1958 s 49.

Priorities in payments during winding-up of a company

The ICA s 511 stipulates the fundamental rule on the application of the assets of a company in the satisfaction of its liabilities by specifying that:

> 'Subject to the provisions of this Act as to preferential payments, the assets of a company shall, on its winding up, be applied in satisfaction of its liabilities pari

passu and, subject to such application, shall, unless the articles otherwise provide, be distributed among the members according to their rights and interests in the company.'

In the event that a company's assets are insufficient to fulfil its liabilities, during winding-up the principles of priority of payments will apply in the repayment of the debts of the company. The principle mainly contained in s 529 is that all unsecured creditors will have to prove their debt and all such debts will be paid pari passu.

A secured creditor may either rely only on his security and proceed to realise his debt in the ordinary course of law, ie outside the winding-up proceedings, or he may choose to relinquish his security and prove his debt in the winding-up proceedings. In the event that he chooses to rely on his security and if, after exhausting his security any amount is still due to him, he may prove for the deficiency/balance in the winding-up proceedings.

The security of every secured creditor is deemed to be subject to a pari passu charge in favour of the workmen of the company to the extent of the workmen's portion therein. 'Workmen's portion' in relation to the security of any secured creditor of a company, is defined under the ICA s 529(3)(c), as:

> 'the amount which bears to the value of the security the same proportion as the amount of the workmen's dues bears to the aggregate of:
> (i) the amount of workmen's dues; and
> (ii) the amounts of the debts due to the secured creditors'.

The above principle is illustrated through the following example. The value of the security of a secured creditor of a company is Rs 1,000,000. the total amount of the workmen's dues is Rs 1,000,000. The amount of the debts due from the company to its secured creditors is Rs 3,000,000. The aggregate of the amount of workmen's dues and of the portion of the security is, therefore, one-fourth of the value of the security, that is Rs 25,000.

Section 529A stipulates the 'overriding preferential payments' which are to be paid in priority to all other debts of a company during its winding-up. The two fundamental overriding preferential payments are:

1 workmen's dues; and
2 so much of the debt to a secured creditor as could not be realised by him by virtue of his security being subject to a pari passu charge in favour of the workmen to the extent of the 'workmen's portion' therein.

Thereafter the following debts are to be paid in full, unless the assets are insufficient to meet them, in which case they will abate in equal proportion;

1 debts provable; and
2 the valuation of annuities and contingent liabilities.

Preferential payments

As provided in the ICA s 530:

1 In a winding up, subject to the provisions of s 529A, there shall be paid in priority to all other debts:
   (a) all revenues, taxes, cesses and rates due from the company to the Central or a State Government or to a local authority becoming due and payable;
   (b) all wages or salary of any employee, in respect of services rendered to the company and due;
   (c) all accrued holiday remuneration becoming payable to any employee, or in the case of his death to any named beneficiary;
   (d) all amounts due in respect of contributions payable by the company under the Employees' State Insurance Act 1948 (34 or 1948);
   (e) all amounts due in respect of any compensation or liability for compensation under the said Act in respect of the death or disablement of any employee of the company;
   (f) all sums due to any employee from a provident fund, a pension fund, a gratuity fund or any other fund for the welfare of the employees, maintained by the company; and
   (g) the expenses of any investigation held in pursuance of s 235 or 237, in so far as they are payable by the company.

REMEDIES

Mortgage of immovable property

Right to sue for mortgage money

A mortgagee has a right to sue for mortgage money in the following cases (see TPA s 48):

1 where the mortgagor binds himself to repay the same;
2 where by any cause other than the wrongful act or default of the mortgagor or mortgagee, the mortgaged property is wholly or partially destroyed or the security is rendered insufficient, and the mortgagee has given the mortgagor a reasonable opportunity of providing enough further security to render the whole security sufficient and the mortgagor has failed to do so;
3 where the mortgagee is deprived of the whole or part of his security by or in consequence of the wrongful act or default of the mortgagor; and
4 where the mortgagee being entitled to possession of the mortgaged property, the mortgagor fails to deliver the same to him, or to secure the possession thereof to him without disturbance by the mortgagor or any person claiming under a title superior to that of the mortgagor.

Power of sale of the property

A mortgagee may sell the mortgaged property or any part thereof, in default of payment of the mortgage money, without the intervention of the court, only in the following cases:

1 where a power of sale without the intervention of the court is expressly conferred on the mortgagee by the mortgage deed and the mortgagee is the government; and
2 where a power of sale without the intervention of the court is expressly conferred on the mortgagee by the mortgage deed, and the mortgaged property, or any part thereof, was on the date of the execution of the mortgage deed situated within the towns of Calcutta, Madras, Bombay or any other town specified in this regard by the State government.

A mortgagee may exercise the above power of sale only on the fulfilment of the following conditions:

1 a notice in writing requiring payment of the principal money has been served on the mortgagor and there is a default in the payment of the principal money for three months after such service; or
2 some interest under the mortgage, amounting to at least Rs 500, is in arrears and unpaid for three months after becoming due.

Right to foreclosure or sale

In the absence of a contract to the contrary, the following types of mortgagees have a right to foreclose, ie a right to institute a suit to obtain a degree that the mortgagor shall be absolutely debarred of his right to redeem the mortgaged property:

1 a mortgagee by conditional sale; and
2 a mortgagee under an anomalous mortgage by the terms of which he is entitled to foreclosure.

In the absence of a contract to the contrary, the following types of mortgagees have a right to institute a suit to obtain a decree that the mortgaged property be sold:

1 usufructuary mortgagee; and
2 mortgagee by conditional sale.

The above rights may be exercised by the mortgagee at any time after the mortgage money has become due and before a decree has been made for the redemption of the mortgaged property.

Pledge of movable property

In the event of a default on the part of the pawnor in payment of the debt secured by the pledge of movable property, the pawnee may institute a suit against the pawnor upon the debt and retain the goods pledged as a collateral security; or he may sell the goods pledged after giving the pawnor a reasonable notice of the sale. If the proceeds of such sale fall short of the amount due in respect of the debt, the pawnor is liable to pay the balance. Similarly, if the proceeds of the sale are greater than the amount due to the pawnee, the latter is under a duty to pay the surplus to the pawnor.

Mortgage of ship

MSA s 51 provides that where there is only one registered mortgagee of a ship, he is entitled to recover the amount due under the mortgage, by selling the mortgaged ship without approaching the High Court. However, where there are two or more registered mortgagees of a ship, they are entitled to recover the amount due under the mortgage only by instituting proceedings in the High Court and obtaining a decree/direction from the High Court that the mortgaged ship be sold in execution of the decree.

In the event that the sole mortgagee of a ship intends to recover the amount due under the mortgage by selling the mortgaged ship, he is required to give an advance notice of 15 days, relating to such sale, to the Registrar at the ship's Port of Registry. Such a notice should be accompanied with proof of payment of wages due to seamen and other amounts.

All wages and other amounts due to seamen in connection with their employment on the ship will acquire priority over the claims of the registered mortgagee.

VITIATING FACTORS

Corporate authorisations

The corporate formalities that are necessary preconditions for the taking of a loan or creation of a security by a company have already been discussed. It is necessary to ensure that a company's steps to take a loan or create security are not ultra vires its constitutional documents, ie its memorandum and articles of association. It is also necessary to ensure that the borrower obtains the mandatory corporate authorisations for the taking of the loan and/or creation of the security.

The interpretation of 'ultra vires' under Indian law is identical to the settled decisions under English law and this doctrine is accordingly interpreted by Indian courts.

Contravention of the Companies Acts 293(1)(d)

Under this section the board of directors of a company cannot take a loan or create a debt under a guarantee, where monies to be borrowed or debt to be created, together with the monies already borrowed or debt created by the company, will exceed the aggregate of the paid-up capital and free reserves of the company. Such borrowing or creation of debt can only be done with the consent of the company in its general meeting of shareholders.

Absence of consideration

Like any other contract, a contract of guarantee would be invalidated by the absence/ total failure of the consideration for giving the guarantee, eg where the consideration for an intended guarantee was postponing the sale of the debtor's goods, but the creditor was unable to postpone the sale for want of the consent of other necessary parties, or where the consideration was withdrawal of a criminal prosecution against the debtor, but the court would not sanction the withdrawal, the offence being non-compoundable, the contracts were held to be invalid on account of absence of consideration.

Coercion, undue influence, fraud, misrepresentation and mistake

All contracts, including contracts of guarantees and indemnities are required to be entered into with free consent of the parties.

The CA s 14 stipulates that consent is free when it is not given as a result of:

1. coercion, as defined in s 15;
2. undue influence, as defined in s 16;
3. fraud, as defined in s 17;
4. misrepresentation, as defined in s 18; or
5. mistake, subject to the provision of s 20, 21 and 22.

Coercion

'Coercion' is committing, or threatening to commit, any act forbidden by the Indian Penal Code (XLV of 1890), or the unlawful detaining, or threatening to detain any property, to the prejudice of any person whatever with the intention of causing any person to enter into an agreement. (CA s 15)

Undue influence

A contract is said to be induced by 'undue influence' where the relations subsisting between the parties are such that one of the parties is in a position to dominate the will of the other and uses that position to obtain an unfair advantage over the other.

A person will be deemed to be in a position to dominate the will of another:

1. where he holds a real or apparent authority over the other, or where he stands in a fiduciary relation to the other; or
2. where he makes a contract with a person whose mental capacity is temporarily or permanently affected by reason of age, illness, or mental or bodily distress.

Where a person, who is in a position to dominate the will of another, enters into a contract with him and the transaction appears, on the face of it on the evidence adduced, to be unconscionable, the burden of proving that such contract was not induced by undue influence shall lie upon the person in a position to dominate the will of the other (CA s 16).

Fraud

'Fraud' means and includes any of the following acts committed by, or with the connivance of, a party to a contract, or by his agent, with intent to deceive another party thereto or his agent, or to induce him to enter into the contract:

1 the suggestion, as a fact, of that which is not true, by one who does not believe it to be true;
2 the active concealment of a fact by one having knowledge or belief of the fact;
3 a promise made without any intention of performing it;
4 any other act fitted to deceive; or
5 any such act or omission as the law specially declares to be fraudulent (ICA s 17).

Misrepresentation

'Misrepresentation' means and includes:

1 the positive assertion, in a manner not warranted by the information of the person making it, of that which is not true, though he believed it to be true;
2 any breach of duty which, without an intent to deceive, gains an advantage to the person committing it, or any one claiming under him, by misleading another to his prejudice or to the prejudice of any one claiming under him; or
3 causing, however innocently, a party to an agreement to make a mistake as to the substance of the thing which is the subject of the agreement (ICA s 18).

Mistake of fact

A mutual mistake on a matter of fact essential to the agreement would make an agreement void. There may be some defect that is unknown to both the parties whereby the contract is so fundamentally affected that there is good ground for holding the contract void because of mutual mistake of fact (ICA ss 20, 21 and 22).

The general rule laid down in s 19 above has been applied to the special case of a guarantee, under s 142, as follows:

> 'Any guarantee which has been obtained by means of misrepresentation made by the creditor, or with his knowledge and assent, concerning a material part of the transaction, is invalid.'

Similarly, the ICA s 143 deals with guarantees obtained by concealment:

> 'Any guarantee which the creditor has obtained by means of keeping silence as to material circumstances is invalid.'

Another vitiating factor in a guarantee is when a person gives a guarantee on the basis that another person has to be joined as a co-surety, the guarantee will be invalid if the co-surety does not join. This is dealt with by the ICA s 144, which specifies that where 'a person gives a guarantee upon a contract that a creditor shall not act upon it until another person has joined in it as co-surety, the guarantee is not valid if that person does not join'.

ENFORCEMENT OF FOREIGN JUDGMENT IN INDIA

Under the Civil Procedure Code 1908 ('CPC' s 13), a foreign judgment shall be conclusive as to any matter thereby directed upon except in the following circumstances:

1 where it has not been pronounced by a court of competent jurisdiction;
2 where it has not been given on the merits of the case;
3 where it appears on the facts of the proceedings to be founded on an incorrect view of international law or a refusal to recognise the law of India in cases in which such law is applicable;
4 where the proceedings in which the judgment has been obtained are opposed to natural justice;
5 where it has been obtained by fraud; or
6 where it sustains a claim founded on a breach of any law in force in India.

The CPC s 44A specifies that any decree or judgment under which a sum of money is payable (not being a sum payable in respect of taxes or other charges of a like nature or in respect of a fine or other penalty), of a superior Court of any reciprocating territory, may be filed in a district court and may be executed in India as if it had been passed by the district court. hence, a decree or judgment rendered by a superior court of any reciprocating territory may be filed in a district court in India and may be executed as if the judgment had been passed by the relevant court in India.

CONCLUSION

The new External Commercial Borrowings ('ECB') Policy 1999–2000, recently amended by the government of India, has further liberalised the raising of foreign loans by domestic companies. The annual cap for commercial borrowings has been raised to $10 million. All domestic companies are now permitted to borrow up to $10 million with a simple maturity of three years, for the purposes of meeting rupees expenditure, provided that only one such loan may be outstanding at any point of time. There is also an exemption on the payment of withholding taxes on interest payments and fees payable to foreign lenders of external commercial borrowings.

6 Italy

Roberto Cornetta

Norton Rose, Milan

INTRODUCTION

Security under Italian Law is a specific legal category, encompassing several instruments, aimed at reinforcing the position of the creditor.

The key legislation governing security in the Italian legal system is contained in the Civil Code Art 2740, according to which the assets of the debtor represent the security available to the creditor.

This security is general, in the sense that it aims to cover any debt with any asset of the debtor, which is available to the creditor. The Italian Civil Code Art 2740 is just a general principle which in itself does not give the creditor any specific rights other than to seek restoration before the courts and to seek seizure of the assets of the debtor once in possession of an irrevocable judicial decision. Needless to say, if no specific security is granted, creditors cannot be certain that their credit will be satisfied, in the case of default, through recourse to a given asset of the debtor.

Any asset, in fact, may in the meantime have been sold to a third party, and thus removed from the scope of the guarantee in favour of the creditor, or may have become subject to a judgement in favour of other creditors, who may have acquired rights over it.

The security granted by the debtor or a third party aims to fulfill the principle indicated under Art 2740 of the Italian Civil Code in two different and related ways. It identifies the object of the guarantee (shares, credit, movable goods, real estate, etc.) but also specifies the time at which the guarantee is given. This latter characteristic is crucial in order to resolve conflicts among different creditors, or to determine the validity and the enforceability of the security where bankruptcy and related actions seeking to revoke the security, are brought against the creditors.

A security can be 'real' or 'personal'. Real security is where a creditor takes security over assets whether movable or real estate to secure the payment of the liability of the debtor to the creditor. Personal security is where a person, other than the debtor, agrees to become liable for an obligation of the debtor normally by means of a guarantee. Security can be given under Italian law as a result of an agreement between the parties or can also be granted by law or by order of a court.

Forms of real security are the pledge and the mortgage:

1 the pledge concerns movables, rights of credit (Italian Civil Code Art 2784) or other rights (Italian Civil Code Art 2806); and
2 the mortgage is based on real estate, or registered movables (Italian Civil Code Art 2810).

Pledges and mortgages are therefore real security: the asset remains in the property of the debtor or third party, who has given it by way of pledge or mortgage, and may be freely sold by the owner. But the creditor acquires a dual right over the asset as discussed below.

The right to the amounts secured by the asset even if the asset has been purchased by a third party purchaser

The pledge or mortgage, in other words, follows the asset through any subsequent changes of ownership, until the debt is discharged.

The right of payment on the proceeds of sale on enforcement of the asset with priority over any other creditors of the same debtor

It is the right of pre-emption which pledges and mortgages have in common with other causes of pre-emption, such as liens (Italian Civil Code Art 2741): if the asset given in pledge or in mortgage raises on enforcement, a sum equal to or lower than the sum of the credit guaranteed, the entire sum will go to the pledgee or mortgagee with the total exclusion of other eventual creditors. If, however, a higher sum is received as a result of the sale, what remains after satisfying the pledgee or mortgagee will be distributed between the remaining creditors. If lastly, after satisfying all the creditors, a sum still remains, this goes to the owner of the asset given in pledge or mortgage, be it the debtor or a third party.

The asset which is the object of a pledge or mortgage may perish or deteriorate, in such a way that it is insufficient security for the creditor. The latter may demand that he is given further security or failing this, may ask for the immediate repayment of the debt (Italian Civil Code Art 2743). If the object of the guarantee was insured, the right of pledge or mortgage on the goods which have perished or deteriorated, is converted into a pledge on the credit of the insured party towards the insurer.

The asset given in pledge or subject to the mortgage, may have and normally has, a value exceeding the sum of the debt it guarantees. The creditor may not take advantage of this greater value to the detriment of the debtor or of other creditors, according to the Italian Civil Code Art 2744, which states that an agreement is invalid if the creditor and debtor agree that in the case of failure to pay, the asset given in pledge or mortgage passes into the ownership of the creditor.

On the basis of the Italian Civil Code Art 2911, the creditor with real security may seek repayment out of other assets of the debtor if he does not first look to the assets subject to the pledge or mortgage for satisfaction of the debt.

Another principle typical of a civil law system such as the Italian system is that any security must be clearly ascertainable. A clear description of the asset and the estate given as security must be given. Security may be created over a future asset but the security will formally come into existence as soon as the asset is acquired. Security may also be created over assets or rights belonging to a third party (which the debtor is supposed to acquire). It follows that the security will come into existence only once the debtor has acquired the relevant rights to the assets. Based on the need for clear identification (or potential identification) a general right of security granted to the creditor is not a security enforceable under Italian Law even with the agreement of the debtor over any property or good belonging to the debtor.

Security can also be categorised according to its effects. That is:

a) security which merely gives the creditors rights over assets;
b) security whereby ownership of the assets can be transferred to the creditor as the result of the proper enforcement procedure, such as a mortgage; and
c) security under which the creditor has actual physical possession of the secured assets such as a pledge, for example, or what under Italian law is defined 'privilegi'.

Each of these categories will be examined below. At this stage however it is worth clarifying some terminology. The words ownership and possession are sometimes used in a way so that these words can be interchangeable. However in the context of security interests, the two words have distinct meanings under Italian law: ownership means having title to an asset whereas, possession is the factual situation and means having physical possession of an asset. These will be the meanings attributed to ownership and possession in this chapter.

Under Italian law security granted by a third party or by the debtor may give right to possession but will never give the creditor an automatic right to ownership of goods pledged or mortgaged.

The transfer of ownership will follow upon the enforcement of the creditor's rights, which are set out in the security documentation. To give an example, a mortgage is a right over real estate given by the debtor or a third party to the creditor. The mortgage and its registration procedure under Italian law does not transfer the property to the creditor. Such ownership will be transferred only upon enforcement of the mortgage. The same considerations apply for pledges over assets such as a pledge over shares of a company, or a pledge over cash or movable goods. Under Italian law the person who has been granted the pledge will never automatically become owner of the goods just because the debtor has failed to fulfil its obligations. The creditor will acquire an ownership interest in the asset only upon fulfillment of the judicial procedure, which will allow transfer of property.

REAL SECURITY

Pursuant to the Italian Civil Code art 2784, the debtor or a third party, may secure or guarantee certain obligations, by pledging movables, debts and other rights relating to movables. The pledge therefore represents security established over a certain asset with a conventional nature, regards goods which may even be heterogeneous, and is established in a variety of ways depending on the asset pledged.

In order for the right of pre-emption to be activated, which allows the creditor in possession of the security to have priority over others, the pledge contract must be in a written form and be dated, whether it refers to movables (Italian Civil Code Art 2783, (3)), or whether it regards credits or other rights (Italian Civil Code Art 2800). The written form is not required either for the validity or proof of existence of the contract. But a notarization of the signature is required for certainty of the date on which the endorsement of the security was given.

Pledging movables

Pursuant to the Italian Civil Code art 2784, establishing a pledge of movables requires the delivery to the creditor or to a third party of the asset or the document, or at the very least the pledgor must not be able to use the asset without the co-operation of the creditor (Italian Civil Code Art 2786, (2)).

Art 2786 of the Italian Civil Code specifies the requirements for establishing a pledge of movables. The law requires that exclusive possession is withdrawn from the pledgor and that possession or joint-possession be given to the creditor or to a third party. The pledge of movables contains:

1 a secured obligation, consisting of pre-emption rights and the right to expropriate the asset from a third party purchaser;
2 the right to retain the asset;
3 the right to recover the asset;
4 the right to earnings from the asset;
5 the rights of sequestration of the asset; and
6 the power of sale.

These aspects of a pledge of movables are discussed in more detail below.

In relation to the pledge and its effect on third parties, it should be stated firstly that the pledgee's possession of the asset is necessary to establish the pledge. The pledge is valid as against third parties as long as the asset remains in the pledgees possession. This is stated in Italian Civil Code Art 2787 (2) with reference to the right of pre-emption, but is valid in general also for the purchasing third party. Moreover, it is valid for all the effects of the pledge. Without possession there is no pledge, but only a personal right against the pledgor to obtain or recover possession to establish the pledge. It follows that as long as the debtor has or re-obtains possession of the asset, the other creditors may treat the asset as if it is unencumbered, even if they are aware of a valid deed for the establishment of the pledge; and that a third party purchaser acquires the asset or the right as if it were unencumbered, even if he is aware of the security. Even if third parties know of the existence of a deed for granting the pledge, it is not considered established or valid without possession. It follows that the loss of possession by the pledgee means extinction of the pledge.

The right to retain the asset

The right of retention cannot arise if there is no dispossession of the debtor.

The right to recover the asset

Possessory actions and claims cannot be made by the creditor, unless he or his representative has possession or joint-possession (Italian Civil Code Art 2789).

The right to earnings from the asset

The right to the earnings generated from the asset on the basis of the Italian Civil Code Art 2791 also presupposes that the creditor or his representative is in possession or joint-possession: otherwise this *de facto* power could not be exercised, but would be, if anything, an obligation on the debtor to deliver the income from a given asset to the creditor.

The sequestration of the asset

Sequestration or seizure of the asset obviously cannot arise, if the asset is not in the possession of the creditor or his representative.

The right of sale

When the creditor or his representative does not have possession or joint-possession, it is not possible to proceed with the quicker forms of sale, as provided for in the Italian Civil Code Art 2797, involving the intervention of the bailiff.

The pledge of securities

As we have seen, the pledge is established by way of contract between the owner of the asset and the creditor. The pledging of securities is a specific case of a pledge on movables. The securities subject to the pledge discussed in this section could be: drafts, commodities orders, warehouse warrants, company bonds and bonds of other institutions, company shares, etc. These are instruments that give rise to rights distinct from the security created by actual possession of the asset. These are securities for which the document is the only proof of title to the assets concerened. In other words, in these cases, the subject of the pledge is the particular nature of the right incorporated in the document, whereas documents of title concern the assets themselves.

The pledge of documents of title, as identified, has various peculiarities in terms of how it is established. The method of constituting a pledge is established by the Italian Civil Code Art 1997, on the basis of which: 'the pledge of a right mentioned in a document of title has no effect if it is not activated on the security'. The consequences of this are as follows:

1 *For bearer securities.* The pledge is established by the transfer of possession of the document to the creditor or to a third party or with the application of common

custody, so that 'it is impossible for the establishing party to make use of the security without the co-operation of the creditor' (Italian Civil Code Art 2786). The activation of the right of pre-emption is provided for by the Italian Civil Code Art 2787, which we will examine in detail in the course of this chapter.

2 *For trade financing documents*. The pledge is established with the endorsement 'value guaranteed', 'value in pledge' or similar. The transfer of the security to the creditor will be necessary, because otherwise, the possession of the security by the debtor gives rise to the presumption that the debtor has paid and is once more free to dispose of the security. To establish pre-emption, a written deed is also necessary, according to the Italian Civil Code Art 2787. Since the Italian Civil Code Art 1997 foresees that the pledge should be activated on the security, it is also possible to establish the pledge by transferring the security, without the endorsement of value guaranteed, and with a deed drawn up according to the Italian Civil Code Art 2800; in this case the creditor may not demand the security itself, but only the right to sell it.

The right of sale may also be exercised according to the Italian Civil Code Art 2797, with the intervention of a public official; since guaranteed endorsement does not per se authorise full endorsement allowing a forced sale after a default.

If for security purposes, a full endorsement is performed, a fiduciary endorsement is effected. The pledge relationship will remain only between the parties, but the creditors of the endorser can enforce it, if they so wish.

3 *For registered securities*. The pledge can be established in two ways: either with registration on the security (made by the issuing institution) and on the register of the issuer; or with the transfer of the security endorsed with the clause 'guaranteed' or equivalent to the creditor or third party. It must however be registered in the shareholders' book for it to be effective against the issuing company. In the first case it is not necessary to deliver the security, since publication visible to third parties is provided by registration in the register and on the security.

The content of the pledge of the debt instruments depends on the nature of the right inherent in the security, which may be: (i) a right to money or goods; (ii) shareholders' rights.

In the case of pledging debt instruments, containing a right over money or goods, regardless of the way it is established, the pledge of securities has the same content as the pledge of debts which we will examine below (Arts 2802, 2804, 2807), in addition to pre-emption and the right of retention of the security. The same is also true for that part of the shares relating to the right to dividends and to a share of the net assets in liquidation.

Pledge of shares

In the case of a pledge on shares, the method of establishing the pledge varies depending on whether the company whose shares are pledged is a public limited company ('società per azioni') or a limited company ('società a responsabilità limitata').

In the case of a pledge of shares of a 'società per azioni', the execution of the security and the validity of the pledge as against third parties is subject to certain formalities.

Pursuant to the Royal Decree n° n. 239/42 Arts 3 and 4, the pledge over the shares must be registered with an annotation ('annotazione') in the shareholders' register by one of the directors and on the share certificate. Alternatively, the pledge can be registered by delivering the share certificate to the creditor along with the endorsement of the clause 'in guarantee' ('in garanzia'). In both the cases, such procedures need to be notarised by an Italian notary public. The annotation must indicate the full name and all the data relating to the holder.

Shares can be sold and transferred even though they are pledged. If one of the shareholders intends to sell its shares to a third party or to another shareholder, the shares will remain pledged in favour of the creditor regardless of who acquires them.

In case of default of the debtor, the creditor who has taken security over the shares in the form of a pledge, will not automatically become owner of the shares but will need to obtain title by a court order, if the shares are not intended to be sold through an auction.

If a pledge of shares is given and the company's constitution does not contain any pre-exemption rights in relation to the shares the creditor wishing to enforce the pledge should be aware of the following points:

1) the creditor never automatically acquires title to the shares;
2) the creditor must either agree the criteria for the sale with the other shareholders or the creditor must ask the court to proceed to a public auction;
3) the sale will not take effect however if, 'within ten days from the court order, the Company submits the offer of another purchaser who offers the same price' (Italian Civil Code Article 2480).

Alternatively, the creditor may ask the judge that the shares pledged be transferred to the creditor at a value that has to be ascertained by a court appointed expert.

In the case of a pledge of shares given where the company's constitution contains a pre-emption clause, the same conditions under points 1 and 2 above will apply. As to the condition under point 3 above, the only difference is that instead of waiting for 10 days, the creditor must wait for 30 days before the sale is effective.

As to voting rights, the general principle under Italian Civil code Art 2352 is that in the absence of agreement to the contrary the voting rights belong to the pledgee. This is true both for ordinary and extraordinary shareholders meetings, bearing in mind that one of the general principles of the pledge is that the conduct of the pledgor must not reduce the value of the goods pledged. Based on this assumption some discussion exists as to whether the pledgor could vote in order to agree changes of corporate purpose and to the business of the company or whether the pledgor could be liable, because of its vote, if the value of the shares was adversely affected.

The role of pledgor and of debtor being the same person could sometimes give rise to a conflict of interest. In other cases, especially for long term loans where the right of pledge is given for an extended period, the creditor could be deemed to have exercised control over the company if he were given a pledge over a significant portion of shares. For these reasons and also to meet the requirements of the Central Bank, it is usual (at least for a pledge over shares in banks) that parties agree to the debtor retaining the voting rights until an event of default or acceleration of the loan has occurred.

As to share options, if the share ownership also involves options, these belong to the shareholder; if however, the shareholder has taken no action within three days of the due date for payment of sums necessary for the exercise of the options, the right must be sold on behalf of the shareholder. The sale of the options will be made through a broker or a bank.

If payments for the shares are required, the shareholder must pay the necessary sums at least three days before the due date; otherwise, the pledgee may have the shares should through the broker or bank.

A pledge gives a preferential right to the creditor in comparison with other creditors. It should be noted that unlike a mortgage, different priority rankings do not technically exist under Italian Law for pledges. In fact, the Italian Civil Code Article 2792 also prohibits the creditor with a pledge from pledging the same asset to a new creditor. One solution would be that the second pledge is agreed upon immediately but it comes into existence only after the first one is terminated.

With regard to companies 'a responsabilità limitata' the same rules relating to 'società per azioni' (Italian Civil Code Art 2352) are applicable with some exceptions, which depend on the nature of the quota of an S.r.l.

Quotas are intangible goods. Pledges of quotas cannot be executed through endorsement and there is no certificate issued which refers to them. It follows that the pledge over quotas only has to be registered in the shareholder's books and then registered also on the commercial register.

Pursuant to the Italian Civil Code Article 2479, the document establishing the pledge must be notarised by an Italian public notary and filed by such public notary at the commercial register.

Pledging government securities

In the case of pledging government securities managed centrally by the Bank of Italy, the subject of the pledge is represented by an obligation to act.

In effect, as already mentioned, the phenomenon of the dematerialisation of national debt securities precludes their use in pledges as a tangible asset for two precise reasons:

1 the intangible nature of the security; and
2 the impossibility of singling them out.

This has in part led the Italian courts to abandon considering the pledge of government securities as a pledge of movables and instead to see it as a pledge of credit, held in favour of the creditor by the bank, for the transfer of the securities or their economic equivalent at term.

In this case, the establishment of the pledge on the securities is provided for by the Ministerial Decree of 27 May 1993 Art 4, subsequently modified by the Ministerial Decree of 5 January 1995 Art 1, which states that securities are to be identified exclusively in terms of type and quantity. The bank deals with collection of government securities which should come to term during the pledge relationship and is authorised to use the sums collected for the purchase of other securities of the same type, quantity and duration of those expired and at the rates in force at the moment of renewal and so on at every subsequent expiry of the securities due to their renewal or from renewals performed. The bank is, however, obliged to inform the establishing party about the identifying data of the new securities. The sums collected and the securities purchased are subject to the original pledge. To this end the bank is authorised to carry out the eventual transfers of securities and/or stocks in custody for deposit and/or custody administration concerning securities and/or stocks given in guarantee, as well as to proceed with the registration that may be necessary in the register as per Ministerial Decree of 27 May 1993, modified by Ministerial Decree of 5 January 1995. The pledge remains in force until the definitive extinction of the bonds depending on the guaranteed operations, including eventual interest and costs, although the bank retains the right to exercise the shares owed to it both towards the debtor and other co-obligors. Moreover, the pledge has full effect regardless of any other personal or real guarantee, which was issued or provided by anyone, under any form, in favour of the bank.

Pledge of debt or other rights

In the case of a pledge of a debt or other rights, pre-emption takes place only when the establishment of the pledge has been notified to the debtor or has been accepted by the latter in writing on a known date.

As far as regards its establishment, we should distinguish between: 1. relations with the third party debtor and with the acquirers of the debt itself or rights over it; and 2. relations with other creditors (exercise of the right of pre-emption).

1 The pledge is established with the notification, even verbal, to the third party debtor, or with the acceptance by him, according to the requirements of the Italian Civil Code on the transfer of the debt (Arts 1264-1265). If disputes should arise, it will obviously be necessary to prove the date of the notification or acceptance. It will also be necessary to identify the secured debt; but it will not be necessary for this identification to result from a security in written form, in that if the notification to the third party debtor is in writing, it will also specify the secured debt. It is always advisable to notify the relevant parties by means of registered letter or notarization.
2 In relation to the other creditors, the pledge is established with the notification in writing (the actual date of the pledge should be clear) or with the acceptance of the third party debtor, which is based upon a security in written form essential for the validity of the pledge, whatever the sum of the guaranteed debt may be.

Mention should also be made of the identification of the debt: this will occur with the written notification to the third party debtor; the identification of the debt is also necessary and must be evident from the security and from the notification or acceptance (Art 2787 and 2807). A fixed date however does not seem necessary for the security, since it is evident from the notification to, or acceptance by, the third party debtor.

Pledging fungible assets – the 'irregular pledge'

Lastly, the concept of the 'irregular pledge' should be mentioned or, as it could also be termed, a caution pledge, when the asset given in pledge is a sum of money or other quantity of unidentified fungible assets which the creditor has been given the right to use.

An irregular pledge is provided for under the Italian Civil Code Article 1851, which refers specifically to bank loans, although its general applicability is uncontroversial.

The assets given in pledge become the property of the creditor, who must return them at the moment of discharge of the debt or, in the case of default, must return the part that exceeds the sum of the secured debt, determined in relation to the value of the assets at the time of the expiry of the secured debt.

In the case of a pledge over fungible assets, the law makes a clear exception to the principle whereby a pledge gives the pledgor the right to retain possession and properties without judicial co-operation. In fact, in the case of a pledge over fungible assets such as money, the pledgor retains the property and is bound to give back the same amounts at the termination of the pledge agreement. This arrangement is often used in project financing where excess cash flow can be pledged or given in escrow.

The right of pre-emption

The Italian Civil Code Art 2787 resolves the conflict between the creditors regarding the forms of sale to be used as per the Italian Civil Code Art 2797. The rule in question states that the pledgee has the pre-emptive right for its debt to be discharged using the asset received in pledge.

When the asset is assigned to the creditor in payment (where assignment is possible) together with other creditors, or if the value of the pledge exceeds that of the debt, the remainder must be paid to the next ranking creditors. If there are liens over the pledge, the pledgee must pay these, in order to be able to become the assignee.

Pre-emption, according to the provisions of the Italian Civil Code Art 2788, can be extended to include interest incurred during the course of the year in which the security was given or, on the date of the notification of proceedings. Pre-emption also affects any interest accrued subsequently, within legally established limits, up until the date of sale. It is also extended to include the costs related to establishing the pledge and collection of the debt (legal costs) and to the costs of custody of the pledge, on the basis of the provisions of the Italian Civil Code Art 2790.

The effect of the pledge

As for any other security, the pledge has an ancillary nature with regard to the debt guaranteed, since if the main relationship is invalid, the pledge is also invalid.

The ancillary nature of the pledge is linked, on the subject of the pledge of debt to the regulations of the Italian Civil Code Art 2805, on the basis of which the debtor may raise all the defences that he could bring to bear on his creditor against the pledgee himself, unless he has accepted the establishment of the pledge without reservation.

In the Italian legal system a pledge may also secure a future debt, provided that, at the moment of the establishment of the pledge, the legal relationship from which the debt could arise already exists; it is not sufficient that such a relationship could exist in the future between the parties.

As indicated above, the object of the pledge must be determined and it is not possible that goods given in pledge be given as security for any future debt of the debtor.

The invalidity of a pledge written in general terms can be inferred from Art 2787, (3), which states that the pledge must contain sufficient information not only regarding the asset but also the debt. Therefore the pledge may not be extended to cover credit which may arise from possible future relationships between the parties.

This restriction is confirmed in relation to mortgages (Italian Civil Code Art 2852) registered as security for debt that may eventually arise from a pre-existing relationship.

If the debtor pays the capital and interest (Italian Civil Code Art 2788) of the debt secured by a pledge on movables, the creditor must return the asset to him (Italian Civil Code Art 2794). If, however, he does not pay, the creditor, after having invited him to pay, may have the asset sold by a mediator authorised to do so, or may ask the judge for it to be assigned to him in ownership. In the first case, any excess of the price received from sale compared to the sum of the credit, will go to the debtor (or to the third party providing the pledge) or if there are any, to other creditors; in the second case, it will be necessary to estimate the value of the asset and ascertain that its value does not exceed the sum of the credit (Italian Civil Code Arts 2796, 2798).

In principle, the pledge is indivisible and, in line with the dictates of the Italian Civil Code Art 2799, secures the credit until this has been satisfied in full, even if the debt or asset given in pledge is divisible. However, this principle is not rigid, and it is in fact subject to exceptions, for example in the case of a bank loan (Italian Civil Code Art 1848). There is in fact no doubt, in case law and in doctrine, that the divisibility of the pledge may be allowed on the basis of an agreement between the parties, with the obligation of the pledgee to perform partial returns of the pledge corresponding to the payment by the debtor of parts of the debt.

THE MORTGAGE

Definition, subject

The mortgage is a real right of security which gives the creditor the right to proceed with a sale of the asset and to be paid in priority to other creditors from the sums obtained from the sale (Italian Civil Code Art 2808, comma 1).

If the debtor does not repay the debt, the mortgagee may sell the secured asset, and be repaid from the money obtained in priority to non-guaranteed mortgage creditors or those with a mortgage which ranks lower in priority.

In general, the mortgage may concern assets of the debtor or of a third party. More precisely, according to Italian Civil Code Art 2810, the following may be subject to mortgage:

1 real property and its fixtures and fittings;
2 the use of these goods;
3 building rights;
4 the right of a lessee pursuant to a long-term lease and that of the lessor;
5 the earnings of the State as established by the laws on public debt; and
6 ships, airborne vehicles and motor vehicles according to the legislation which regulates them.

The Italian Civil Code Art 2811 also states that the mortgage extends to include improvements to and constructions on the mortgaged property, apart from the exceptions established by law.

The mortgage is established through registration with the Land Registrar of the place in which the real property is found. Registration is necessary for a mortgage to be valid (Art 2808(2)): ie the mortgage exists only if it appears in the registers and only from the moment of registration.

The mortgage must be registered over assets specifically identified at the moment of registration (Italian Civil Code Art 2809(1)). This is not possible in the case of the registration of future assets, since the mortgage may be validly registered only when the asset already exists (Italian Civil Code Art 2823); or in the case of assets of others, since the mortgage granted by someone who is not the owner of the asset may be considered valid only when the asset is purchased by the grantor himself (Italian Civil Code Art 2822).

It is common in project financing or in any case of construction finance that the bank and the debtor agree to register the mortgage over the construction once it has been completed. In this case the agreement shall only have taken effect in the sense that parties shall need to enter into a new agreement for registering the mortgage once the asset comes into existence.

The mortgage must also be registered for a certain sum of money: this means that the claim that the creditor has on the mortgaged asset is only valid up to the sum for which the mortgage is registered. Moreover, the credit secured by the mortgage need not necessarily be for a sum of money, there is no reason in fact why a mortgage should not be granted to secure the transfer of certain assets or the performance of certain services.

The mortgage fixes on all the mortgaged assets and on every part of them; in the case in which the secured credit, is already partially extinguished or the value of the mortgaged goods has subsequently increased compared to the sum of the credit guaranteed, the mortgage extends to cover all the constituent parts of the asset, unless otherwise stated in the mortgage deed.

The eventual reduction of the mortgage may be obtained only with the consent of the creditor or with a judicial ruling which reduces the sum for which the mortgage was registered or limits the registration to cover only a part of the assets initially mortgaged (Art 2872 ff).

Voluntary, judicial and legal mortgages

In order for the mortgage to be valid a right giving rise to the mortgage and the right to registration, and registration in the public registers are both necessary. The cause which allows the creditor to register the mortgage, may derive from the will of the owner of the asset, from a legal measure, or from a particular situation foreseen by law: respectively voluntary mortgage, judicial mortgage and legal mortgage.

The voluntary mortgage is based on a contract between a debtor and a third party grantor of the mortgage and a creditor or on a unilateral act (excluding the will of the debtor or of the third party grantor of the mortgage). The contract or the unilateral declaration must be made in writing or otherwise may be considered void; it must contain the information necessary to identify the mortgaged property (Italian Civil Code Arts 2821, 2826).

The owner of the asset can grant a voluntary mortgage; if the mortgage is granted on the asset of a third party or by a person who acts as a representative without having the authority, the registration may be considered valid only once the asset has become the property of the person who has granted it, or once the effective owner has approved it (Art 2822). The same principle applies for the mortgage on future assets (Art 2823), on which a mortgage may be validly registered only when the thing has come into being. A mortgage on ships or airplanes in construction may however be validly registered once they have been registered in the register of ships or airplanes in construction.

According to the Italian Civil Code Art 2818 , valid bases for the registration of judicial mortgages on the debtor's assets of the debtor are:

1 any sentence, which orders the payment of a sum of money, the fulfilment of an obligation or the payment of damages (Art 2818(1));
2 any injunction (Italian Code of Civil Procedure Art 655);
3 any judicial ruling allowing this effect (Art 2818(2));
4 arbitrators' awards (Art 2819); and
5 foreign judgments which have been declared effective by the Italian judicial authorities (Art 2820).

The recognition and enforcement of 'foreign judgments' is governed by the Italian Civil Procedure Code Arts 796–99. Foreign judgments have been defined by the Italian courts to include any judicial act having the nature of a judgment in so far as it rules on a given judicial dispute on a definite basis, (any applicable rights of appeal having expired, or having been otherwise extinguished) regardless of the form in which the foreign judicial act has been issued under the law of the jurisdiction where it was rendered. Therefore, the term 'foreign judgment' would include any decree, order, decision or arbitration award that complies with the above mentioned definition. However, judgments containing provisional remedies and/or rulings on procedural matters only cannot be the subject of recognition proceedings.

The Italian Code of Civil Procedure prescribes certain prerequisites for the recognition of foreign judgments in Art 797, and the courts have the power, indeed the mandate, to refuse recognition of a foreign judgment in the event that any of these requirements have not been satisfied. Although some of the provisions contained therein will be the subject of further discussion below, Art 797 provides as follows:

The Court of Appeal shall declare a foreign judgment effective within the Territory of the Republic of Italy, upon determining:

1 that under the principles of jurisdiction in force in the Italian legal system, the court of the state in which the judgment was rendered had jurisdiction over the case;
2 that the summons was served in accordance with the law of where the case was heard and that a reasonable time was given to the defendant to appear in court;

In expressly specified cases, the law grants certain creditors the right to obtain registration of the mortgage on the assets of the debtor, even against the wishes of the debtor. The following have the right to this so-called legal mortgage:

1 the assignor of real property or of a registered movable which has not been paid for by the acquirer. In this case, the mortgage is based on the asset assigned and secures payment of the price (Art 2817(1); Arts ss rd no 436, 1972);
2 each heir on inheritance of real property, as security over the payment of money owed to him (Art 2817 no 2); and
3 the State, on the assets of a person accused or responsible for a crime, as security for payment for fines, legal costs and maintenance of the convicted person in prison (Italian Civil Code Art 2817(3); Italian Penal Code Art 189).

The establishment of the mortgage

The contract or unilateral deed for the voluntary mortgage, the judgment or other judicial measure for the judicial mortgage, and the deed of sale of the asset for the legal mortgage are the prerequisites for registration of the mortgage.

A mortgage is established exclusively by *registration* in the public registers (Art 2808(2)). Registration is a necessary condition for the creation of the right of mortgage; only after satisfying this duty does the creditor have the power to proceed with the sale of the mortgaged asset and receive payment from the sum thus obtained, in that only from that moment is the mortgage considered valid (Arts 2827 ff). A single asset may be subject to various mortgages registered as security for different debts. At the moment of registration, the mortgage is given an order number which depends on the order of registration and which specifies the degree of priority on the mortgaged asset (Italian Civil Code Art 2852 ff). In the case in which the mortgaged asset is subject to sale on enforcement, the sum thus obtained will be used to repay first of all the secured creditor with a first ranking mortgage; the eventual remainder will go to the second ranking mortgagee, and so on (Art 2852 ff).

In the case of a number of mortgagees depending on the same first ranking asset, at varying degrees, the so-called mortgage subrogation for payment may occur: a creditor, with a lower ranking mortgage may repay a creditor with a higher ranking mortgage, replacing him in the order of priority.

The subrogation of a lower ranking creditor is different. A creditor, with a mortgage on one or more items of real property may (if the sums obtained from the sale on enforcement of the assets completely satisfy another creditor of higher degree, whose mortgage extended to cover other assets of the same debtor), replace the repaid creditor in the registered mortgage, and acquire rights of priority over later creditors (Art 2856(1)).

Registration lasts for 20 years, after which the mortgage is extinguished, unless registration is renewed before its expiry on application of the creditor (Art 2847). If renewal is requested after the expiry, it will be equivalent to a new registration or a new right of mortgage which will take effect from the new date (Italian Civil Code Art 2848). This means that the new registration will not affect those who have already registered mortgages, even during the duration of the 20-year period, or those who have acquired rights over the mortgaged asset (Italian Civil Code Art 2847 ff).

The enforcement of the mortgage

In case of a breach of an obligation incurred pursuant to a credit facility agreement, the creditor has the right to proceed with the forced sale of the mortgaged asset. This will occur according to the Italian Code of Civil Procedure Art 555. On the sum obtained from a sale on enforcement, the mortgagee will receive payment with priority over the creditors without mortgages and those who hold mortgages with lower priority. Naturally, the procedure will also be the same if the sale on judgment is instigated by another creditor.

The sale on enforcement of the asset is valid against the third party acquirer, or the person who has acquired the mortgaged asset after registration (see below).

The *third party acquirer* who has satisfied the registered creditors or has released the real property or who has had his asset sold on enforcement, has recourse against the debtor, and may take action against the debtor for compensation (Art 2866).

The *third party grantor of the mortgage* security is in the same position, he is at risk of a sale on enforcement unless he offers to pay the mortgagees. After having paid the registered creditors or after the sale has gone ahead he may take action against the debtor to obtain reimbursement of sums paid or he may take the place of the creditor who has been repaid (Art 2871).

The third party purchaser of the mortgaged asset

Being established through registration, the mortgage will be valid against whoever purchases the real property after registration of the mortgage, or in other words valid against a third party purchaser.

This purchaser is exposed to the eventual sale of the asset is because he has purchased an asset already subject to a mortgage (Art 2858). To avoid sale on enforcement, the third party purchaser may:

1 pay the creditors registered before the registration of his deed of purchase (Arts 2827; 2852) (this will be convenient if the sum secured does not exceed the value of the asset or assets mortgaged);
2 release the assets mortgaged, therefore waiving ownership, with a specific declaration made at the office of the clerk of the relevant court (Art 2861); this will be convenient if the sum secured exceeds the value of the asset(s) mortgaged; or
3 free the real property from the mortgage, through the redemption of the mortgage, offering the mortgagee/s a sum equal to the purchase price of the asset (or equal to the value of the asset, if the asset was transferred for free). If no creditor offers to purchase the asset for a price exceeding at least 10% of that offered by the third party purchaser, the asset is freed from the mortgage following the payment of the sum offered by the third party purchaser (Arts 2889 ff).

The third party purchaser, who has satisfied the registered creditors or has released the asset or whose asset has been sold on enforcement, has the right to obtain payment of damages from the debtor (Italian Civil Code Art 2866(1)). He is also recognised as having the right of participating in the mortgages established in favour of the creditor who has been repaid out of the other assets of the debtor; if these assets have been purchased by third parties, he will be able to take action only against those who have registered their purchase subsequent to the registration of his security (Art 2866(1)).

The third party grantor

The position of the third party grantor of a mortgage is similar in many ways to that of the third party debtor. The third party grantor is at risk from a sale on enforcement and the only way in which he is allowed to avoid it is by paying off the mortgagees. In fact, once the mortgage has been established to secure the debt of someone else, he cannot request that the creditors take action against the debtor first to obtain payment, unless this has been specifically agreed (Art 2868).

Naturally, being a third party outside the relationship of debt, if he pays the creditors, he has the right to be reimbursed by the debtor and may eventually acquire the right of mortgage belonging to the satisfied creditor (Art 2871).

The reduction and extinction of the mortgage

The mortgage covers all the goods that make up the object secured and every constituent part of them, even if the secured amount is partially extinguished or the value of the goods mortgaged has subsequently increased.

On the basis of the Italian Civil Code Art 2872 ff, it is nevertheless possible to proceed with the reduction of the mortgage by reducing the sum for which the mortgage was registered or limiting the registration to cover only a part of the assets. The reduction may take place even if the mortgage is based on a single asset, as long as this has separate parts which can be easily distinguished from each other.

The discharge of the mortgage occurs firstly with the cancellation of registration from the register (Art 2878(1)). The land registrar may not proceed with cancellation on his own initiative, since the interested party must first make a request, which must be accompanied by the express consent of the creditor for its cancellation (Arts 2882, 2883), or a final judgment or any other definitive ruling issued by the competent authorities (Italian Code of Civil Procedure Arts 2884; Art 324), who, having ascertained a valid reason for the discharge of the mortgage, order its cancellation.

The mortgage is also extinguished if registration is not renewed within 20 years of the date when it was established (Art 2878(2)).

If renewal does not take place within the term foreseen by Italian Civil Code Art 2847, the creditor may reserve the right to re-register, provided that the terms of the security allows him to do so, but the ranking of the mortgage will depend on the date of the new registration (Art 2848). Consequently, a negligent creditor, who does not promptly renew registration, will be subordinate to both a creditor who has registered another mortgage (Art 2848 (2)) and to a third party purchaser who has registered his security before renewal of the registration (Art 2644).

The Italian Civil Code Art 2878 lastly provides for discharge of the mortgage in the following cases:

1 the discharge of the secured amount;
2 the destruction of the mortgaged asset;
3 the express waiver of the creditor;
4 the expiry of the term to which the mortgage was limited or the occurrence of the cancelling condition to which the mortgage is subject; or
5 the assignment of the right of expropriation to the purchaser and the cancellation of the mortgage.

The discharge of the mortgage is noted in the margin of the register (Italian Civil Code Art 2882). The reason for discharge of the mortgage takes effect even if cancellation does not occur, which may in fact be performed subsequently. Likewise, cancellation discharges the mortgage even if this has been consented to by the creditor by mistake (there is, however, naturally the possibility of renewing the registration, according to the rules and with the effects already described above).

LIENS

Liens in general

The Italian legal system provides for three distinct forms of security giving pre-emptive rights: the pledge, mortgage and lien. The lien covers a specific asset or category of assets. The legal concept of lien consists of a 'legal' cause of pre-emption, that is granted by law in relation to assets that, on the basis of their nature, are considered to require greater protection than others. The Italian Civil Code governs the subject of liens in book VI, Section II, from Art 2745 to Art 2783 *bis*.

The main feature of the lien is that it is granted by law on the basis of the nature of the debt. This means that the Italian legislator has reserved to himself the exclusive right to evaluate the characteristics and importance of the debt and the advantages in its being subject to lien. Private parties, moreover, may not create liens which are different from those provided for by law.

Nevertheless, under Italian law the establishment of the lien may be subordinated to the agreement of the parties; this is the so-called conventional lien. In a conventional lien the content and scope of the lien are determined by law and the contracting parties are only free to choose the objects which they intend the lien to cover; these objects are however already generally indicated by the law.

Case law has defined the lien as 'ancillary' to the debt itself, granted by law in specific cases and extinguished automatically if the right of the creditor is extinguished. The lien, therefore, does not represent an independent right, but is linked to the debt in question.

It is worth remembering that a lien does not involve any derogation from the fundamental general principle provided for by the Italian legal system (Italian Civil Code Arts 2740-1), whereby the debtor is liable for payment of the debt out of all his present and future assets and the creditors have equal rights to be repaid from the assets of the debtor. The creditor, therefore, may validly enforce his rights by proceeding with execution on any asset of the obligor, even if it is not the asset over which the lien was established.

Liens may be general or special.

General lien

A general lien affects all the movables of the debtor (Italian Civil Code Art 2746). The main characteristic of a general lien lies in the fact that it does not allow the pursuit of goods that the debtor has sold to third parties. The result is that if the debtor disposes of the asset on which the general lien is established, for example by selling it, the creditor cannot exercise his lien and thus have recourse against the third party purchaser who has the right of ownership on the asset the subject of the lien.

The law provides a list of the debts giving rise to a general lien. These are debts regarding 1. payment for employment or professional work, 2. earnings of farmers, craftsmen or productive co-operatives, 3. national insurance contributions, 4. necessary expenses for the debtor (for food, medical care, and others) and 5. direct taxation. Ranking in first priority among the debts giving rise to a general lien are the payments and indemnities owed to employees.

Special lien

A special lien is exercised on certain movables and real property. This type of lien is characterised by the particular connection between the debt and the asset the subject of the lien. Consider the following debts which may be secured by special lien on certain goods:

1 the debt owed by the hotel guests and the lien the hotelier has over the goods brought into the hotel and which continue to be there; and
2 the lien of the car salesman over the car for the price of the car.

Unlike the general lien, a special lien follows the asset even if it has been acquired by a third party. More generally, it can be enforced against third party creditors subsequent to the establishment of the lien. However the third party creditors may avoid the restrictive effects of the lien by purchasing the asset in good faith and keeping possession provided that the lien is not evident from the purchase deed. This measure, which protects the circulation of movables, is provided for by a specific article of the Italian Civil Code (Art 1153).

In some cases the special lien may also be exercised to the detriment of pre-existing rights of third parties. The debts secured by lien which have such features include:

1 debts for the performance and cost of conservation and improvement of movables;
2 the debts owed to the hotelier, already mentioned, have effect even if the goods brought into the hotel by the guest belong to a third party, unless the hotelier was aware of this from the start;
3 the debts owed to the carrier, sender, depositor and sequestrator;
4 the debts owed to the lessor on the assets that serve to supply the leased property.

The fact that the special lien will be valid against third party purchasers means that it is extremely important to determine and identify the lien itself. Moreover, at the moment when the special lien is established, the goods subject to this form of security must be clearly specified. Some special liens on movables exist only as long as the asset is located at a certain place.

The existence of the lien is not dependent upon particular requirements of publication; it should be noted in particular, that the special liens on real property do not require publication in the land registers.

The special lien, is similar to the pledge and mortgage as it is valid against third party purchasers. However, it differs in that the order of priority between the liens does not depend on when they arose, but only on the nature of the different debts giving rise to the lien.

The subjects of liens

The subject of liens are linked to the debt, since the right of pre-emption is ancillary to the debt existing between creditor and debtor. Naturally, the subject of the lien may be a physical person, or a legal person. For liens on debts with certain types of companies, such as companies of persons who are legal persons, partners with unlimited responsibility may be liable for the debt giving rise to the lien. The subjects of the liens may change both in the case of universal succession (eg inheritance) and in the case of particular succession (eg transfer of credit, company transfer, personal subrogation). However, case law does not consider it possible to sell or transfer the lien separately from the credit to which it is linked.

Order of liens

The order of priority between a number of debts subject to lien does not depend on their order of creation, but only on the importance which the law gives them. The Italian Civil Code Article 2777 establishes the following decreasing order of priority:

1 debts for legal costs (preceding any other debt, including mortgages or pledges);
2 debts for payments owed, in any form, to employees (retirement bonus, payment of damages for the failure to pay national insurance contributions or for unfair dismissal);
3 debts owed for the payment of professionals for the last two years of services and for the commissions deriving from a relationship of agency due for the last year of service; and
4 debts owed to a farmer for the sale of products, and to craftsmen, companies and organisations producing work.

Liens on the basis of the Bank Consolidation Act Art 46

An example of a conventional special lien is represented by the lien governed by the Bank Consolidation Act Art 46(1 September 1993 no 385). This lien may be granted only by a company that is beneficiary of a medium- or long-term loan in favour of the lending bank. In this case, the subject of the lien may not be different from those provided by law.

Medium- and long-term loans are those loans which have a duration of over 18 months. The main feature of this lien is that it enables companies to obtain a loan more easily since they may give security over the assets of the company, without preventing these assets from generating income and, therefore, from being used profitably by the company. Consequently, these forms of security are particularly suited to project financing loans.

Article 46 subdivides the assets which may be subject to liens into the following four categories:

1 existing and future plants and works, concessions and assets destined for company work;
2 raw materials, unfinished products during the production process, supplies, finished products, crops, livestock and goods;

3 assets purchased with the loan granted; and
4 income (future income included) deriving from the sale of the assets indicated in the previous points.

This is an express list of the assets over which may liens may be given, although the terminology used to identify the goods is so generic that it includes all the assets connected with the activities of the company.

In practice, in fact, the debtor makes use of a separate deed to establish the lien already anticipated by the loan contract stipulated with the bank. This contract includes a clause which provides for the establishment – to secure punctual fulfilment of the obligations deriving from the loan contract – of a special lien according to Art 46, concerning real property or plants and machinery, present movables and future works, and the concessions and goods connected with the activity for which the loan was requested. Among the goods which may become subject of the lien there may also be future goods (for example the income of the company) or those which, according to the type of activity performed by the company, will be replaced or made into other goods.

For the lien to be considered valid, it must be confirmed by written deed, which must exactly describe the goods and debts subject to the lien, the creditor bank and the subject who granted the lien, the sum and the conditions of the loan and the sum of money for which the lien was established.

The details to be inserted in the deed do not include its duration, since it is presumed that discharge of the debt ends the lien, since the latter is ancillary to the debt.

In order that the lien may be valid against third parties, on the basis of Art 46 (3), the establishment of the lien must be transcribed in a special register kept at the office of the clerk of the court in the town where the registered offices of the debtor company are situated. Notice must also be given by publication in the journal of legal announcements of the corresponding province.

The overall sum for which the lien is established is identified so as to include and secure every payment owed by the debtor, ie mortgaged capital, interest, legal costs, and connected expenses, insurance premiums, reimbursements of taxes and duty, in addition to sums specified in the loan contract for return or early cancellation of the mortgage.

The debtor must also warrant to the creditor that the goods specified and subject to the lien belong to him, are free from any other lien, pledge or action by third parties. This is to avoid the bank which makes the loan finding itself in competition with other creditors thereby weakening the protection derived from the lien.

The lien foreseen by the Consolidated Bank Act Art 46, like the other liens of the industrial credit sector, is subordinated only to the lien for legal expenses and to the liens specified in the Italian Civil Code Art 2751 *bis*.

REMEDIES AND EXECUTION OF JUDGMENTS

Execution of judgments

The creditor who has not obtained payment from the debtor may proceed with execution of judgment on the latter's property, according to the regulations of the Italian Code of Civil Procedure. If the debt is a sum of money, this is taken from the property of the debtor, or obtained from the expropriation and forced sale of some of his goods, and the proceeds are paid to the creditor (Italian Civil Code Art 2910, Italian Code of Civil Procedure, Arts 483 ff).

If the unfulfilled obligation involves the consignment of a movable or the release of real property, the law sets out special procedures to obtain the consignment or forced release of the asset (Italian Civil Code Art 2930). If an obligation to perform an action has not been fulfilled, the holder of the right may demand that the action be performed at the expense of the obligor (Italian Civil Code Art 2931), unless performance of the action is impossible, in which case he may only obtain payment of damages. If an undertaking 'not to do' an action has been breached, the possessor of the right may obtain the rectification, at the expense of the obligor, of what has been done in violation of the undertaking (Italian Civil Code Art 2933). Lastly, if a contracting party does not perform his contractual obligations, the other party (if this is possible and not prohibited by the terms of the security), may obtain a judgment which produces the effects of the contract had it been performed (Italian Civil Code Art 2932).

The most important and common form of execution judgment is that which orders the expropriation and sale of the debtor's goods to satisfy a debt of money. Forced expropriation begins with distraint, which consists of an injunction served by an officer of the court on the debtor preventing him from taking any action aimed at removing goods from the reach of the creditors. If the distraint order relates to real property, it must be registered in the land register. If it relates to debt owed to a third party, the third party must be notified (Italian Code of Civil Procedure Arts 491, 492, 543, 555).

Deeds of sale of goods subject to distraint are ineffective against the creditors who proceed with execution of judgment. Nevertheless, if we are dealing with a movable not registered in the public registers, and despite the distraint, it is sold to a third party who purchases it in good faith, the purchase by the third party is safeguarded, according to the general rule already mentioned (Italian Civil Code Art 1153). If, however, we are dealing with real property, or other goods registered in public registers, or debts, third parties may protect themselves by consulting the public registers or asking the debtor: therefore distraint orders will be valid against third parties.

As regards transfers made before the distraint, these can be brought to bear against the creditors that proceed with execution judgment only if the fact that they were made before the judgment can be demonstrated by law. More precisely, if we are dealing with real property or movables registered in the public registers, the sale needs to have been registered before the distraint. Movables, meanwhile, must already have been assigned to the purchaser, or the date of the sale must be apparent; if it is a debt, the assignment must have been notified to the debtor or accepted by him on a date before the distraint (Italian Civil Code Arts 2914, 2915 and 2916).

Sale on enforcement of security

Sale on enforcement of security transfers the ownership of the asset; however, if the asset did not belong to the person who instigated the sale, ownership is not transferred to the purchaser unless it is a movable and the purchaser took possession in good faith. In this case, the owner of the movable may enforce his rights in relation to the sum obtained from the sale, but only before this sum has been distributed to the creditors (Italian Civil Code Art 2920). Similar rules are valid if the asset is subject to rights of third parties.

The transfers which are not valid against the distrainor cannot be valid against the purchaser either (Italian Civil Code Art 2919).

The third party purchaser pays the price owing to the creditors who participate in the execution of judgment. More precisely, if there is only one creditor, the sum obtained is paid to him up to the amount of his credit, and the eventual remainder goes to the debtor. If there is more than one enforcing creditor, the sum obtained is shared between them according to the principle of equal treatment, except where there are legitimate priority rights (lien, pledge and mortgage).

MEANS OF PRESERVING SECURITY

Introduction

The property of the debtor represents, as it has been said, the subject of a general security in favour of the creditors. The security is called general because it does not attach to a specific good. Instead it is continually changing: it does not follow the goods transferred by the debtor but instead it includes the new goods that are acquired over time by the debtor. Moreover, it operates in favour of the creditors in general, without distinguishing between creditors on the basis of the date each credit was granted. It follows that each creditor is exposed to the credit risk of the debtor. The financial fortunes and problems of the debtor may have indirect repercussions for his creditors. However, this does not justify them interfering with the administration of the property of the debtor, who preserves his independence. Obviously, the conservation and improvement of the economic situation of the debtor is above all in his own interests, in addition to his creditors. Granting a loan to a person (without demanding real or personal security) presupposes faith not only in his present economic situation, but also in his ability to maintain or improve it.

There are, however, particular situations in which the debtor neglects to exercise his rights, putting in danger the general protection offered by his property, or performs fraudulent acts to remove his assets from the reach of the creditors. In such cases, the respect for his independence is no longer justified, and the law allows the creditors to intervene, replacing the debtor in the exercise of the economic rights that he has neglected and appealing against any fraudulent acts.

Subrogation

The creditor, to ensure that his debts are discharged, may exercise the rights and the actions that are due to the third parties from the debtor and which he neglects to exercise (Italian Civil Code Art 2900). A mortgaged debtor may, for example, fail to collect an asset which is his, or to collect a debt, knowing full well that the asset or sum would not remain in his possession, because it would be due to his creditors. In this case, any creditor may substitute himself for the debtor in the exercise of his right.

A fundamental premise of this subrogation is that the inertia of the debtor means that the creditor risks not being paid. This happens mainly when the property of the debtor does not provide sufficient security. It also happens when the action that the debtor neglects to carry out would allow the creditor to obtain a certain asset that is owed to him.

This opportunity is granted to the creditor even if his credit is subject to conditions or specific terms (Italian Civil Code Art 2901, comma 1). This protection of the debt is linked to the general rule that allows the performance of acts to protect the debt: in this case preserving security. It is understandable that action should also be permitted which protects debt subject to a term which has not yet expired. It should be remembered, moreover, that in circumstances that may justify subrogation, the debtor loses the benefit of the term on the basis of the Italian Civil Code Art 1186.

With subrogation it is only possible to exercise rights and actions of an economic nature, and not rights and actions of a strictly personal and family nature, even if they may bring an economic advantage. Furthermore, the rights and actions that, although of an economic nature, involve a moral judgment (eg the revocation of a donation due to ingratitude: Italian Civil Code Art 801) are also excluded.

Since the right exercised with subrogation belongs in any case to the debtor, the money or asset obtained becomes part of the latter's property, where it may be subject to execution by all his creditors, and not only by the creditor that performed the subrogation.

The exercise of subrogation does not attribute any right of priority to the asset obtained. This is not so in the case of direct action. The principal, for example, may substitute himself for the principal representative and act against third parties, exercising the rights derived from the execution of the power of attorney (Italian Civil Code Art 1705). In this case the asset or the sum becomes the property of the principal and is not subject to the demands of other creditors of the principal representative. This explains why it is termed direct action, whereas subrogation is sometimes referred to as indirect action. For other hypotheses of direct action, see the Italian Civil Code Art 1676, 1717.

Ordinary revocation

With revocation, the creditors may have declared the disposal made by the debtor to defraud their rights to be ineffective. We are referring to effective transfers, and not simply artificial ones. One example is the mortgaged debtor who strips himself of his goods, by donating them or disposing of them with the aim of defrauding creditors.

Given certain conditions, which we will now examine, in similar cases each creditor may appeal against the disposal, in order to seek repayment from the transferred asset (Italian Civil Code Art 2901). This action is granted even if the asset is subject to conditions or terms.

A possible subject of revocation is a deed of economic disposition, with which the debtor intentionally harms the rights of the creditor. This occurs when the chances of the creditor obtaining what he is owed by execution of judgment is diminished. This may result from an act that reduces the property of the debtor (donation, abdication, sale at an undervalue), but can also derive from a sale at a fair price, if the asset sold would have been easily accessible to the creditors and which is in this way replaced by money, which can be easily hidden. In each case, the remaining property of the debtor does not offer sufficient security: otherwise there would be no damage to the creditor.

The performance of guarantees may also be prejudicial in the sense illustrated above, because in the case of default of the guaranteed debt, they lead to the same result of a transfer or assumption of debt; therefore these may also be subject to revocation.

The payment of an expired debt, however, is not revocable (Italian Civil Code Art 2901(3)). This act does not reduce the property of the debtor, because it extinguishes a pre-existing debt. It may determine the advantage of one creditor compared to others that present themselves subsequently and find nothing with which to have their credit satisfied. But ordinary revocation does not have the aim of ensuring equal treatment of the creditors (unlike bankruptcy revocation).

The following are the subjective requirements necessary for the granting of revocation. In each case, the debtor must be aware of the detriment he causes to the rights of the creditor or, in the case of an act carried out before the debt was incurred, this act must have been prearranged with the specific aim of fraud.

The problem does not finish here. One also needs to consider the interests of the third party purchaser, who would be harmed if, subsequent to acceptance of the revocation, the asset were subject to execution of judgment by the appealing creditor. Here as elsewhere if we are dealing with a purchase for valuable consideration the act will be revoked only if the third party purchaser is acting in bad faith.

The effect of the revocation is closely related to the interest of the creditor who has exercised it: the asset is not part of the property of the debtor, yet the creditor may take enforcement action in relation to it, because the transfer is not binding on him. It is a case, not of invalidity, but of ineffectiveness. Therefore the parties cannot take advantage of this, if the creditor does not achieve execution of judgment and one or the other wishes to be released from the contract appealed against. Moreover, the effectiveness of the contract between the parties implies that the purchaser will keep what remains after the creditor's debt has been discharged. Lastly, the purchaser may take action against the transferring debtor, precisely because the contract is considered valid. The relative nature of the ineffectiveness is manifested also in favour of the creditor, who may take enforcement action independently of other creditors.

The purchaser, may, in turn have sold the asset to a third party. Again the problem is of the protection for the bona fide purchaser. The solution is the same as that adopted for the cancellation of the contract: rights acquired by third parties in good faith are not prejudiced, although the effects of the registration of the request for revocation remain valid (Italian Civil Code Art 2901 last comma).

Particular rules are valid for bankruptcy revocation (which we will examine later) and also in criminal law. Revocation is not equivalent to a general principle of rights of creditors towards third parties. In fact, it does not force third parties to deal with and constantly worry about pre-existing commitments of the other party, but only to proceed with caution when faced with insolvency, ie a situation which regards the property as a whole. And since insolvency is a public process (through protests, distraints etc), this rule does not excessively compromise the speed and safety of the proceedings.

The right of retention

Sometimes the law allows the creditor, who holds something belonging to the debtor, to retain it until the latter pays his debt. This right of retention is granted only in particular cases, in which there is a connection between the credit and the asset retained. A typical example is given in the Italian Civil Code Art 1152: the possessor in good faith may retain the asset until he has received the indemnity owed to him for repair or improvements made to the asset. See also the Italian Civil Code Arts 748, last comma, 975 (2), 1006, 1011, 1502 (2), 2040.

Usually, the right of retention is accompanied by a special lien, which gives the creditor the right to repayment of his debt from the asset in priority to the other creditors: this applies to debts arising from actions performed and expenses incurred for the preservation and improvement of movables (Italian Civil Code Art 2756), and also for the debts owed to the carrier, principal representative, depositor and sequestrator (Italian Civil Code Art 2761). Since retention represents a form of self-protection, according to the general principle which forbids self-administered justice, it is allowed only in the cases specifically provided for by law.

PERSONAL GUARANTEES

Real security which we have just examined, and which is given over an asset of the debtor or of a third party, is distinguished from personal guarantees. For these, it is a person who uses his property to guarantee the fulfilment of the obligation of another person.

In the Italian legal system, the most important type of personal guarantee is represented by the 'Fideiussione': this is a contract pursuant to which a person (guarantor) guarantees the fulfilment of someone else's obligation, thus incurring personal liability to the creditor (Italian Civil Code Art 1936 (1)). The effect that the guarantee produces is a joint and several responsibility, of the debtor and his guarantor, towards the creditor.

The creditor, on the basis of the regulations of Italian Civil Code Art 1944, (1), demands payment from one or other of the obligors, without the need to first ask the main debtor, unless this is specifically provided for by the contract (benefit of preventive enforcement towards the main debtor: Italian Civil Code Art 1944 (2)). In this way the creditor may rely on the creditworthiness of two, rather than one, persons, having a guarantee for his credit not only in the property of the main debtor, but also in that of the guarantor. It should, however, be stressed that on the basis of the Italian Civil Code Art 1957, the creditor loses his rights over the guarantor, if the main obligation expires and he does not take legal action against the main debtor (or against the guarantor) within six months following expiration.

The debtor is not party to the contract, the guarantee is effective even if the debtor is not aware of its existence (Italian Civil Code Art 1936, (2)). Once the obligation has been fulfilled, the guarantor may take action for recourse against the debtor even if the debtor is unaware of the existence of the guarantee (Italian Civil Code Art 1950 (1)). In fact, the debtor may only be aware of the guarantee when it is enforced by the guarantor. In normal situations, however, the main debtor is well aware of the situation: the guarantee is issued in favour of the creditor, on the basis of a personal relationship between the debtor and the guarantor, on the strength of which the latter is persuaded to give the guarantee.

On the basis of Italian Civil Code Art 1943, the debtor may need to procure a guarantee under the terms of the agreement between the creditor and the debtor from which the main debt arises. The obligation to provide a guarantee is usually conceived as the obligation of a bank to provide a guarantee (the bank guarantee). The issue of the guarantee by a bank presupposes a contract, normally a current account, existing between the debtor, as customer of the bank, and the bank itself. The bank – or other guarantor – may, however, be persuaded to provide a guarantee on the basis of a further guarantee that guarantees its action for recourse, or on the basis of a policy that guarantees its action for recourse, or on the basis of an insurance policy that guarantees against the risk of insolvency of the guaranteed party.

No written document is required for the contract of guarantee, neither for its validity, nor for proof of its existence. In practice it is almost impossible to prove the existence of a guarantee if it is not given in writing.

The guarantor also becomes a debtor, although his obligation is ancillary to the obligation of the debtor:

1 the guarantee is valid only if the obligation of the main debtor is valid, except for the case where it has been granted to guarantee the obligation of a person without legal capacity. In practice, the reason for the contract of guarantee is the guarantee of the debt of a third party; if the debt of the other person does not exist (for example because the contract from which it derives is declared null or is cancelled), the reason for the guarantee ceases to exist;
2 for the same reason, the guarantee cannot exceed the sum owed by the debtor (Italian Civil Code Art 1941), in the case of the guarantee exceeding the sum owed, the guarantee is affected by partial nullity (Italian Civil Code Art 1941). However, it extends to cover the expenses for the notification to the guarantor of the action brought against the main debtor (Italian Civil Code Art 1942). It may be partial or contracted on less onerous conditions (Art 1942, (2)), and may be contracted for a specified period of time, as sometimes happens with guarantees for future debt and always with bank guarantees; and
3 the guarantor may raise the same defences against the creditor as the main debtor, but excluding the defence of incompetence of the main debtor (Italian Civil Code Art 1945). The consideration is still valid even where a payment by the guarantor to which the main debtor is not liable would be made without cause. If the creditor makes demand on the main debtor, and he pays, the main obligation is extinguished and consequently also the guarantee. If, however, the creditor receives payment from the guarantor, the latter has the choice of subrogation in the rights of the creditor towards the main debtor as established by Italian Civil Code Art 1949, or action for recourse against the main debtor for the reimbursement of the sum he has paid (Italian Civil Code Art 1950). He, however, loses the right of action or recourse if, having omitted to inform the main debtor of the payment made, the latter paid the debt (Italian Civil Code Art 1952). The recourse of the guarantor is assisted by the action for release: even before having paid, the guarantor may take action against the main debtor so that he releases him or, failing to do so, gives him suitable guarantees. This occurs in a series of situations, such as the following: if he has been called to court for payment, if the debt has become subject to execution, or if independently of this the main debtor has become insolvent (Italian Civil Code Art 1953). Italian court rulings, however, tend to rule out

application of the norm, if the main debtor is subject to a procedure agreed with creditors before bankruptcy. In this example, the same debtor may not completely repay the creditor, neither may he offer the guarantor greater guarantees than those offered to other creditors, nor in any case obtain the waiver of the creditor to the guarantee. Due to the effect of the reduction of his right towards the main debtor, according to the agreed percentage, such a waiver would deprive him of the only tool which could help him achieve complete repayment. We should also add that the guarantee is extinguished if, due to an act of the creditor, the subrogation of the guarantor in the right of the creditor or in the real guarantees or in the liens which assist him is void (Italian Civil Code Art 1955). A premise of this rule is the obligation of the creditor to preserve the rights of the guarantor towards the main debtor. This principle is violated by the creditor, where for example a bank, that grants credit or extensions to an already insolvent debtor, extends the term of the debt at a moment when the guarantor may no longer usefully take action against him. If the creditor has prejudiced the rights of the guarantor, the latter may oppose, according to Art 1955, the discharge of the guarantee. The guarantee may be jointly offered by more than one person. If not agreed otherwise, the guarantee will be joint and several, ie each guarantor, according to Art 1946, is liable for the whole sum.

Guarantee of a future obligation

The Italian Civil Code Art 1938 provides that a guarantee may also be offered for a future obligation, which does not exist at the moment of the contract of guarantee. This may be an obligation which arises from an already existing relationship between the debtor and the main creditor. In this case the object of the contract of guarantee is not determined, but according to the Italian Civil Code Art 1346, can be determined on the basis of criteria supplied by the contract itself. Thus in the example of a contract of supply, the guarantee may be of all the obligations of the supplier regarding the supplies to be delivered.

Another type of guarantee of future obligations is the guarantee of indemnity, which guarantees the fulfilment of obligations for compensation for damages which may arise from the non-performance or incomplete performance by the main debtor, of contracts concerning the production of goods or services, in particular public works contracts, or forms of abstention such as contracts of non-competition.

Moreover, there is no problem in allowing a guarantee against an illegal act of a third party, which may be committed whilst executing a contractual relationship, such as the illegal acts which an employee could commit whilst performing his working duties.

Guarantee policy

Alongside the bank guarantee we find the guarantee policy, which is a guarantee issued by an insurance company. It differs from the bank guarantee in that the entire sum which links the guarantor to the main debtor is not a bank contract, but an insurance contract. The insurer-guarantor assumes the risk of insolvency of the insured debtor; the debtor-insured party pays premiums to the insurer-guarantor, calculated according to insurance parameters, and based on the risks of the occurrence of an accident, which in this case, is the collection of the debt by the creditor of the insured party. In the relationship between insurer-guarantor and guaranteed creditor, the contract is a guarantee, and the contract is subject to the norms of the Italian Civil Code on guarantees.

The relationship between insured debtor and insurer is an insurance contract, subject to usual conditions: in particular, related to the lapse of the right to the premium that is barred within one year on the basis of the Italian Civil Code Art 2952 (2), and of the regulation contained in the Italian Civil Code Art 1982 on the basis of which the insurance contract may be cancelled if the insurer has been induced to give his consent on the basis of inexact and incomplete statements provided with intent to defraud or of serious fault on the part of the contracting party.

Guarantee omnibus

The concept of *guarantee omnibus* has been developed in Italian banking practice from the guarantee for a future obligation, following the creation of a series of contractual schemes by ABI (the Italian Banking Association).

The typical contract of *guarantee omnibus* is characterised by the fixing of a limit of liability, formulated so that the figure indicated, including both the capital and the interest and the other ancillary costs, constitutes the limit of the guarantee, beyond which the guarantor may not be called on to pay the bank.

In this contract then, the guarantor guarantees the fulfilment of all the obligations depending on banking operations of any kind, already granted or which may subsequently be granted to a certain subject or to whoever may have replaced him. The withdrawal of the guarantor is possible, but the withdrawing guarantor is liable for the obligations of the debtor existing at the moment of the declaration of withdrawal and for every other obligation which may arise or become due subsequently or depending on the relations existing at the aforementioned moment.

The specificity of the *guarantee omnibus* is represented, as emerges from this contractual model by the fact that not only are the guaranteed obligations future obligations with respect to the moment of signing of the guarantee, but so are the economic facts that generate the debt. The guarantee, in fact, in this case, extends also to cover obligations arising from bonds that are granted subsequently. The validity of such a guarantee has long been the subject of discussion and the debate has for some time concentrated on two aspects:

1. the consideration of general evaluations, which can be applied to any *guarantee omnibus*, independently of the subjective intentions of the contracting parties and of the nature of the guaranteed obligations; and
2. the more specific consideration of the *guarantee omnibus* given in favour of banks and to guarantee the fulfilment of obligations arising from bank contracts.

With regards to the possibility of invalidity indicated in point 1 the possibility of determining the object of the obligation on the basis of the Italian Civil Code Art 1346 in the *guarantee omnibus* has been open to question. The answer to this question is affirmative in the sense that the object of the contract of guarantee can be determined with reference to all the obligations that a subject assumes towards another subject.

This argument, however, is not entirely borne out in the case law of the Italian courts: the guarantor on the basis of case law can in no way have a clear idea, at the moment when he gives the guarantee, of the risk he is taking on, since this depends on a series of events which cannot be foreseen at the moment of the agreement, such as for example the increase or decrease in the turnover of the debtor's company. It appears obvious that the unpredictability of the contractual risk is incompatible with the requirement of identification of the guaranteed obligations. To this argument it is, however, legitimate to respond that the ability to terminate the commitment allows the guarantor to contain the risk within the originally foreseen limits.

As far as regards the possibility of invalidity specified in relation to point 2, there is the problem of whether, in the Italian legal system, interests which are subordinate to the *guarantee omnibus* deserve protection.

It appears fundamental at this point, to consider that this guarantee serves a precise economic and social function, which is that of allowing access of the third party to bank credit while protecting savings, of which the bank makes use to issue credit.

The status of the guaranteed creditor has been studied from various perspectives, being a subject regulated by precise and strict legislative control. The function of the *guarantee omnibus* is not, therefore, the same as that of the guarantee for future obligations as per the Italian Civil Code Art 1938.In other words, the *guarantee omnibus* is valid only if offered in favour of banks and as a guarantee of operations arising from banking activity. On the basis of these considerations, it is clear that the guarantee may be requested validly by banks, but not by loan companies, who issue credit with their own capital.

This argument however is not convincing: it is not clear why the assumption of an indeterminable risk, which would prevent the general validity of the *guarantee omnibus*, would cease to prevent the validity of the contract when, since the guaranteed creditor is a bank, there is the need to protect savings. A more correct approach questions rather the *guarantee omnibus* considered *per se*, the single clauses inserted in the contract, and examines these in relation to the various uses of the contract. In the various types of economic relationships, the *guarantee omnibus* is issued:

1 by holding companies in favour of banks who make loans to subsidiary companies; here, the supply of guarantee is set in a context of the specific function of financial assistance that the holding company performs in favour of the controlled companies;
2 by partners in joint-stock companies in favour of the banks who give loans to their subsidiaries; and the supply of guarantee required of them by the bank is usually a consequence of the undercapitalisation of their companies, which do not offer sufficient guarantees for the size of the loan;
3 by company directors (even non-shareholders) in favour of the banks who make loans to the company administrated by them; and
4 by close relations of the customer of the bank.

The validity of individual clauses inserted in bank contracts is affected by this variety of situations: in particular, by the clause whereby the contracting party waives the right to take advantage of the cause for the discharge of the guarantee foreseen by Art 1956. In cases 1–3 the clause may be considered valid because the guarantor is considered aware of the changes of the economic conditions of the guaranteed debtor. He has sufficient information to allow him to withdraw from the contract, with the consequent discharge of his responsibility for obligations arising from operations subsequent to communication of the withdrawal. In case 3, the director who neglects to claim invalidity of the guarantee remains bound by it. The same is valid for case 4: in this case, Art 1956 must be considered compulsory, unless a limit to the risk of the guarantor has been established. Here, the principle of contractual good faith may play a determining role. In case 4 the good faith in the execution of the contract (Art 1375) demands that the bank informs the guarantor of developments, originally unpredictable, regarding the risk represented by the main debtor; in case 3 the bank that finds out about the assignment of the administrator must *bone fide* report to him the existence of the guarantee and ask him what action he intends to take.

The independent contract of guarantee

The ancillary obligation, which in a guarantee binds the obligation of the guarantor to that of the main debtor, is the basis of this contract and cannot be derogated by the will of the parties. It is, however, necessary to distinguish between the general ancillary obligation that characterises the obligation of guarantee as such, and the specific ancillary obligation which belongs to guarantee. Here, the ancillary nature of the obligation of the guarantor with respect to the obligation of the main debtor can be brought to bear against the guaranteed creditor by the guarantor. The guarantor may declare the guarantee void by opposing the other party on the grounds of the invalidity of the main obligation or raising defences that the main debtor could have used against him (Arts 1939, 1945). Moreover, on the basis of Art 1952 it can be argued that, if the guarantor intentionally omits to raise with the creditor the exceptions based on the main relationship, the main debtor may raise them against the guarantor.

In the Italian legislative system, a guarantee is the only typical personal guarantee. On the wider international scene there is, however, alongside the guarantee, another personal guarantee, in which the ancillary nature of the guarantee is established in different terms. This different contract has for some time been used in Germany as and is known as *Garantievertrag*; in Anglo-Saxon countries and, more generally, in international commerce it is the bid bond, a guarantee in respect of a contractual offer, of the performance bond, a guarantee of the correct performance of a contract, and of the repayment bond, a guarantee of the reimbursement of advance payments. In Italy this is referred to as an independent bond contract (or automatic guarantee, first request guarantee, or simple request guarantee); and it is an atypical contract, not governed by the regulations on guarantee, with its own basis, which differs from the guarantee.

The essence of this contract, which is different from a guarantee, is in the fact that the guarantor – usually a bank or an insurance company – waives the right of action in respect of the subordinate guaranteed relationship; since the debtor, if the payment made by the guarantor turns out not to be due (either because the main contract was invalid or ineffective or, more simply, because the main debtor had already paid), will have to take action against the recipient to have the sum not due returned.

The independent contract is, therefore, only relatively independent of the main contract. Precisely because the guarantee is ancillary to the main debt, the payment received by the guaranteed party, if not justified by the main relationship, is subject to reimbursement. In fact, the guaranteed debtor, may act against the recipient for reimbursement claims that should not have been received, if made on the strength of a contract which is ancillary – in so far as it is a contract of guarantee – to the contract which is invalid due to ineffectiveness or discharge of the debt.

However, the guarantor may and, moreover, should, refuse payment in presence of documented proof or, at least, certain and evident bad faith of the creditor, as when the guarantor is able to produce the document from which it can be seen that the guaranteed debt has already been paid or, at least, proof that the main debt is extinguished. The enforcement of the guarantee may, on request of the guarantor, be prohibited by the judge using emergency measures (Italian Code of Civil Procedure Art 700), whereas it is doubtful whether the debtor has the right to ask for the guarantor to be prohibited from paying. The most he may obtain is for the guarantor – if he has paid the creditor in bad faith – to be prohibited from seeking recourse against him.

The interest deserving protection, which justifies the independent contract of guarantee along the lines of Art 1322 (2), has sometimes been studied in terms of its structural difference compared to a guarantee. It has been said that in the former, unlike in the latter, there is not necessarily a link between the main debt and the guaranteed debt, since the automatic guarantee is given to secure non-pecuniary obligations, as in the cases of the bid bond and of the performance bond. However, the *fideiussio indemnitatis*, which has already been mentioned, is also possible outside the independent contract of guarantee, as an obligation ancillary to the main obligation. On the other hand, the waiver clause to the exceptions based on the subordinate relationship is widely practised in guarantees offered in favour of banks, where the guaranteed obligation is a debt; the justification for these clauses is the same as those indicated for the independent contract of guarantee.

The real reason why the automatic guarantee is considered valid is, due to the widespread international use of the concept. It is not possible, without commercially isolating Italy, to consider a contract null which is universally considered valid. The Court considers 'the needs of increasingly extended international commerce and of the relative inter-bank relations which have determined the practice of guarantee contracts partly detached from the main guaranteed transaction'. Other judges also state that 'not recognising the possibility would be the equivalent of preventing a increasingly large series of transactions, whose speed and reliability has been improved by this form of guarantee', and above all the judges recognise 'the legal system, apart from economic needs, also has to recognise the influence of legal concepts already codified abroad' which basically means that the judgment of worthiness as per Art 1322 (2), may be expressed, not only with respect to the Italian legal system, but also with respect to other similar legal systems.

It is understood then, that once it has been introduced into the Italian system due to the needs of international commerce, the first request guarantee has ended up being recognised where, as in the ordinary guarantees demanded by the banks from their clients, the needs of international commerce are not taken into direct consideration. It can be said that the 'adaptability of our legal system', evidenced by case law, has gradually absorbed the operations connected with international commerce and, there is no distinction between international relations and domestic relations and also those inherent in current bank lending.

The power of attorney or letter of credit

The term 'letter of credit' Art 1958 identifies the contract with which a subject, usually a bank (promisor), commits itself towards another subject (promisee) to provide credit to a third party, in his own name and on his own behalf. From the contract obligations arise for both parties: the promisor is obliged to give credit to a third party; the promisee guarantees the obligations of the third party as the 'guarantor of a future debt'. Therefore, the first gives credit to the third party with his own money, but at the risk of the second.

It is not, strictly speaking, a power of attorney, since the promisor acts (as specified in Art 1958 (1)) 'in his own name and on his own behalf'. The idea of the power of attorney is evoked by the fact that the risk of the deal, is borne by the promisee; but the technique of transfer of the risk of the deal is different here from a real power of attorney (Arts 1719–1720). In fact, the promisee always, has an interest in the promisor giving credit to the third party, for himself, as in the case of the holding company that asks the bank to give credit to a subsidiary company, for third parties, such as in the case of the national bank that, on behalf of a customer, gives credit to the overseas supplier of their customer. The regulation of Article 1958 (2) also refers to the power of attorney: the promisor may not, once he has accepted it, renounce the power of attorney, whereas the promisee is free to renounce it at any time, although is obliged to pay damages to the other party. The promisee is thus seen as the stronger party in the deal, stronger than pursuant to a power of attorney *in rem propriam*, that according to Art 1723, (2), can be revoked only if there is just cause.

The contract is initiated by the promisee, according to Art 1958 (1), who thus assumes the role of proposer. Since a guaranteed obligation is borne by the proposer and from the contract, the proposal must have the 'free will' required by Art 1937: general requests or intercessions or solicitations or recommendations aimed at obtaining credit for a third party are not valid letters of credit. The acceptance of the promisor may not be a tacit acceptance, according to Art 1333: this is true of contracts with the obligation to give credit to a third party. Article 1327 is, however, applicable since the acceptance may be valid, if the nature of the dealings allow it, from the date of execution, ie from the issue of credit to the third party, provided that the issue of credit, in terms of amount and methods of issue, conforms to the proposal and provided that it immediately follows the receipt of the proposal, and that the acceptor has, in accordance with Art 1327 (2), promptly informed the proposer of the completed execution.

In accordance with Article 1959 (1) which governs the consequences of the insolvency of the promisee or of the third party, in line with the general principle of Art 1461, the principal promisor may withdraw if the economic situation of the other party or third party becomes, subsequent to signing of the contract, such that payment of the debt becomes extremely unlikely. The insolvency of the third party may, due to the reference in Art 1959 (2) to Art 1956, release the promisee. The two articles, moreover, have different contents: Art 1959, (1) stresses the objective fact of the change in the economic situation of the other party or third party; Art 1956, however, requires that the creditor is aware of the changed economic conditions of the third party.

7 Japan

Masaru Ono and Daniel C Hounslow (senior foreign counsel)

Nishimura & Partners, Tokyo

INTRODUCTION[1]

Japan has a civil law system largely derived from the French and German codes one and a half centuries ago. The types of security (*Tanpo*) which can be created are determined primarily by the Civil Code, though partly also by the Commercial Code, while the Civil Execution Law provides the procedures for the enforcement of such security interests. Other kinds of security interests are, however, recognised by the courts, and parties to a personal security arrangement can, to the extent permitted by law, exclude or vary the application of the relevant legislation as between themselves by agreement. The Codes etc are interpreted in the light of judicial decisions and academic comment, which are given weight according to the level of the court in question and the reputation and experience of the commentator, respectively.

While the nature of and creation of security interests is a fairly settled area of Japanese law, questions of perfection and priorities are, at times, somewhat complex and this chapter necessarily only provides an outline of them.[2]

Security interests in Japan fall into one of two principal categories: personal security (*Jinteki Tanpo*); and real security (*Butteki Tanpo*). The most important form of personal security is the guarantee (*Hosho*) (which may be joint and several or simple),[3] though this paper also considers the indemnity,[4] joint and several obligations (*Rentai Saimu*)[5] and the assumption of obligation (*Saimu Hikiuke*).[6] All of them may rely on substitute performance by a third party of the principal obligation.

1 The author would like to acknowledge the contribution made to the preparation of this paper by Daniel Hounslow (Senior Foreign Counsel of Nishimura & Partners) and thank Kozo Kawai and Toshihiro Maeda (Partners of Nishimura & Partners) for their assistance.

2 In this paper the 'principal obligation' means the secured obligation (the corresponding right being the 'secured right'), the 'principal obligor' means the party owing the principal obligation, the 'beneficiary' means the beneficiary of the security interest and 'in rem guarantor' means any third party providing personal or real security.

3 See 'Guaranties' p 238 below.

4 See 'Indemnities' p 244 below.

5 See 'Joint and several obligations' p 244 below.

6 See 'Assumption of obligation' p 245 below.

Real security is a security interest created by agreement or by operation of law over property or rights belonging to the principal obligor or a third party (ie an in rem guarantor); the principle types of real security are the mortgage (*Teitoken*) (including the bracket type or root mortgage (*Ne-teitoken*)),[7] the pledge (*Shichiken*),[8] transfer as security (*Joto Tanpo*),[9] provisional registration security (*Karitoki Tanpo*),[10] retention rights (*Ryuchiken*)[11] and liens (*Sakidori Tokken*).[12]

As with any other jurisdiction, the party taking security should consider carefully what security to take, having regard to the interests to be protected, the flexibility of the various options available, the rights (or potential rights) of third parties and the ease or otherwise of enforcement. An investigation of the proposed subject matter or grantor of the security is advisable, especially if the security is to be granted over land or buildings which constitute separate real property under Japanese law. Even if a valid and enforceable security interest is granted, enforcement can be both expensive and time-consuming (even if only the enforcement of a foreign judgment[13]), enforcement against land or buildings being particularly burdensome even though recent legislative movement has eased the procedures somewhat. If a beneficiary acquires property as a substitute for performance of a principal obligation, it is generally obliged to realise that property or have it valued and pay over the excess, if any, over the amount of the principal obligation satisfied to the security provider. Naturally, the more security taken, the better from the creditor's point of view and where more than one security interest exists in respect of a principle obligation, the creditor may generally choose to seek performance from any security granted in its discretion. Further, if there is any deficiency after the enforcement of the security interest, the secured creditor can seek to make up that deficiency from the debtor's other assets and a secured creditor can, in any event, seek payment from the debtor other than through the security interest.

PERSONAL SECURITY

Guarantees

Legal nature

A guarantee is an undertaking from a third party to perform the principal obligation in substitution for the principal obligor if the principal obligor fails to perform that obligation.[14] While a guarantor usually assumes a guarantorship at the request of the principal debtor, a guarantee agreement itself is an agreement between the guarantor and the creditor, the principal debtor not being a party. A guarantee is a collateral

7 See 'Mortgage' and 'Bracket type' or 'root' mortgage p 248 and p 251 below.

8 See 'Pledge and transfer as security' (shares of stock), p 253, 'Pledge of rights' p 254 and 'Pledge' (movable property) p 254 below.

9 'Transfer as security' (real property), p 252, 'Pledge and Transfer as security' (shares of stock), p 253 'Transfer as security' (rights) p 256 and 'Transfer as security' (movable property) p 258 below.

10 See 'Provisional registration security' (real property) p 252 below.

11 See 'Retention rights' p 260 below.

12 See 'Liens' p 261 below.

13 See 'Enforcement of foreign judgment' p 273 below.

14 Civil Code Art 446.

obligation and generally supplemental to the principal obligation. In their ordinary business, Japanese banks issue guarantees at the request of their customers, as debtors to third parties, particularly in respect of bonds and debentures issued by the customers. Standby letters of credit are not used by Japanese banks in their domestic banking business.

Collateral nature

It is a general principle of Japanese law that a simple guarantee obligation can only exist on the precondition that the relevant principal obligation validly exists (*Fujusei*) Accordingly:

1 if the principal obligation is void, nullified or ceases to exist, the guarantee obligation also ceases to exist;
2 the scope of the guarantee obligation cannot exceed that of the principal obligation;
3 if the principal obligation is reduced, the guarantee obligation is also reduced;
4 the guarantor can invoke any defences available to the principal obligor in respect of the principal obligation; and
5 if the creditor assigns the secured right, the assignee also automatically takes the benefit of the guarantee, without further action (*Zuihansei*).

Supplementary nature

A guarantor under a 'simple' guarantee (as against a 'joint and several' guarantee) is only liable to the extent that the principal obligation has not been performed and, accordingly, can require that:

1 the creditor first demands performance from the principal obligor; and
2 the creditor first attempts execution against the assets of the principal obligor.

A guarantor under a simple guarantee can thus turn the creditor away twice, though, since a guarantor under a joint and several guarantee, the form of guarantee most common in Japan,[15] does not have these defences, they are seldom available in practice and can, in any event, be excluded by agreement between the creditor and guarantor.

Types of guarantee

There are two types of guarantee under Japanese law; the simple guarantee (*Tanjun Hosho*); and the joint and several guarantee (*Rentai Hosho*). If several parties assume a guarantee obligation for a single principal obligation, it is called a co-guarantee (*Kyodo Hosho*) (see 'co-guarantors' p 242 below). A joint and several guarantee is an agreement under which the guarantor assures the performance of the principal obligation by assuming performance of that obligation jointly and severally *with* the principal obligor (and any other joint and several guarantor), though it does not become a principal obligor and the principal obligation, as such, still only exists as between creditor and principal obligor; a simple guarantee is the basic form of guarantee and if there is no express wording to the effect that the guarantee is given 'jointly and severally' (or *Rentai Hosho*) in the agreement, the guarantee is considered to be a simple guarantee under the Civil

15 See 'Types of guarantee' p 239 below.

Code. Banking practice invariably requires that a joint and several guaranty be obtained. If a guarantee itself is a commercial transaction, or if the principal obligation arises out of a commercial transaction, the Commercial Code[16] deems it to be a joint and several guaranty.

The most distinctive characteristic of a joint and several guarantee is that it is *not* of a supplementary nature, the joint and several guarantor being a joint and several primary obligor with the principal obligor.[17] Therefore, if the principal obligor defaults in performance of the principal obligation, the creditor can immediately demand performance from the joint and several guarantor without demand against the principal obligor or attempted execution against its assets,[18] though the requirement that the principal obligation (ie the obligation of the principal obligor) exist still applies.

Unless otherwise limited under the terms of its guarantee, a guarantor will be liable for principal, interest, liquidated damages, damages and any other associated liabilities,[19] though its liability will not exceed that of the principal obligor. A guarantor is entitled to set off against its guarantee liabilities any rights it or the principal obligor may have against the creditor.

Rights of reimbursement; subrogation

Reimbursement from the principal obligor

While a guarantor discharges the principal obligation by the performance of its guarantee obligation, that performance is, in substance, the performance of the principal debtor's obligation, and constitutes the basis of a guarantor's right of reimbursement from the principal obligor. However, the substance of that right depends on the legal relationship between the principal obligor and the guarantor. Where a guarantee is made at the request of the principal obligor, the guarantor's right of reimbursement is analogous to the right to reimbursement of expenses incurred in the contractual management of another's affairs and the Civil Code provides that a guarantor is entitled to be reimbursed for payments made under the guarantee, interest on those payments and related necessary expenses.[20] On the other hand, if a guarantee is provided, but not at the request of the principal obligor (which is unusual), the nature of the guarantor's right of reimbursement depends on whether the guarantee is made against the wishes of the principal obligor or not; if it is, the right is analogous to the right of restitution from unjust enrichment and, if not, the right is analogous to that for reimbursement of expenses incurred for voluntary acts undertaken for the benefit of another. In the former case, the scope of the indemnification is limited to the extent that

16 Commercial Code Art 511.

17 See 'Joint and several obligation' p 244 below regarding joint and several obligations.

18 The creditor is not even required to notify the joint and several guarantor of the principal obligor's default (or of any other matters vis-à-vis the principal obligor which may affect the joint and several guarantor) unless the guarantee agreement provides so.

19 Civil Code Art 447.

20 The guarantor is entitled to be reimbursed (a) its expenses incurred and damages suffered, and (b) any amount expended in performance of the principal obligation (including the value of rights lost, eg the waiver by the guarantor of a right of set-off against the creditor, or of property rendered as substitute performance) and interest on that amount at the rate of 5% per year specified by statute (Civil Code Art 459; the Commercial Code specifies a rate of 6% per year as statutory interest for delayed payment).

the principal obligor benefited from the discharge of the principal obligation at the time the claim for reimbursement was made;[1] in the latter case, the principal obligor is liable to indemnify the guarantor to the extent that the principal obligor benefited from the discharge creditor at the time of the discharge.

In addition, the Civil Code allows a guarantor which provided a guarantee at the request of the principal obligor a right of advance payment of reimbursement in limited cases (for example, if the principal obligor becomes subject to bankruptcy proceedings and the creditor does not participate in those proceedings or if the principal obligation is due[2]).

In principle, a principal obligor has the same defences against the creditor in respect of the principal obligation as it has against the guarantor in respect of the guarantor's right of reimbursement, though it does not have any defences if the guarantor gave it prior notice that it would perform its guarantee obligation, except for defences which were notified to the guarantor by the principal obligor and which the guarantor did not invoke against the creditor.[3]

Reimbursement from other guarantors

A co-guarantor which has satisfied more than its due proportion of the principal obligation is entitled to reimbursement from the other co-guarantor(s); if there is more than one other co-guarantor, their liability to reimburse the performing co-guarantor(s) is determined by reference to their proportionate liability in respect of the principal obligation.[4]

Subrogation

Regardless of whether or not a guarantee is given at the request of the principal obligor, a guarantor has a legitimate interest in the performance of the principal obligation. By performing the obligations of the principal obligor, the guarantor is automatically subrogated as creditor,[5] and the rights of the creditor against the principal obligor are, accordingly, transferred to the guarantor.[6] In order to secure the guarantor's right of subrogation, the creditor is obliged to deliver to the guarantor the document(s) establishing the principal obligation and the security together with evidence of

1 That is, the scope for reimbursement would be affected by events affecting the principal obligor (eg a right of set-off against the creditor) occurring between the date of performance of the guarantee obligation and the date of the claim for reimbursement and which would have resulted in the reduction or discharge of the principal obligation as against the principal obligor.

2 Civil Code Art 460.

3 Thus, a guarantor should notify the principal obligor of its intention to perform the principal obligation under its guarantee; the principal obligor should similarly notify the guarantor offences against the creditor.

4 The defences available to a co-guarantor against claims for reimbursement from another co-guarantor are broadly the same as those available to the primary obligor in respect of a claim for reimbursement from a guarantor (as are the exceptions to those defences); a co-guarantor would be well advised to notify the other co-guarantors of its intention to perform, and of performance of, its guarantee obligations.

5 This subrogation is effected by operation of law and regardless of whether or not the guarantee was requested by the principal obligor. The guarantor, in effect, takes a transfer of the creditor's rights in respect of the principal obligation. A guarantor does not have any rights to subrogation before performance of the guarantee obligation (in whole or in part).

6 Civil Code Arts 501–504.

performance by the guarantor; the creditor is also required to transfer registration of related registered security (eg a mortgage) and possession of the subject matter of related possessory security (eg a pledge) to the guarantor.[7] Should the creditor subsequently receive the benefit of performance under any other security interest in respect of the principal obligation performed by the guarantor, it would be obliged to account to the guarantor accordingly.

Co-guarantors

A co-guarantee (ie the guaranteeing of an obligation by more than one guarantor, either as a simple or a joint and several guarantee) can be established by agreement or as a matter of fact. It can be founded on an agreement between two or more guarantors to guarantee a principal obligation, or a subsequent additional guarantor guaranteeing an already guarantied principal obligation (and even if the co-guarantors do not know of each other's existence). As against the creditor, co-guarantors are, in principal, liable for a proportion of the guarantied principal obligation equal to the amount of that obligation divided equally between all the co-guarantors; this principle does not apply, however, where the co-guarantors are joint and several guarantors As between themselves, co-guarantors' shares of the principal obligation are determined by agreement between them. In the absence of such an agreement, shares are divided equally between the co-guarantors, though if a co-guarantor has benefited from the principal obligation that fact will be material in determining its share.

If co-guarantors exist, a creditor has the benefit of a number of different guarantee obligations in respect of the same principal obligation. For example, some guarantors may have given joint and several guarantees and some simple guarantees; the creditor will need to determine the potential liability of each guarantor and the likelihood of successfully enforcing the guarantee obligations of each of them before deciding from which guarantor(s) to seek substitute performance.[8]

Defences

Events affecting the principal obligor

In principle, an event affecting the principal debtor affects the guarantor in the same manner, although the extent of a guarantor's obligations is primarily governed by its

7 If the creditor has the benefit of security which would have been transferred to the guarantor on subrogation and the value of that security is diminished through the negligent or intentional acts of the creditor (eg failure to register a security interest or loss of possession of the subject property), the guarantor's obligations are reduced to the extent it is thereby not able to obtain indemnification pursuant to its right of subrogation (Civil Code Art 504).

8 Eg a principal obligation is guaranteed by A and B jointly and severally and by C and D as simple co-guarantors, shares being divided equally between the four of them. The guarantors' liabilities to the creditor are:

A whole amount;
B whole amount;
C 25%;
D 25%.

(The principal obligor is also, of course, liable for the whole amount.)

contractual relationship with the creditor: for example, an agreement between the principal obligor and the creditor to increase the amount of the principal obligation would not affect a guarantor, unless the guarantor otherwise agreed; a guarantor can also take the benefit of any variation of the principal obligation which is to its advantage.[9]

Collateral extinction

As has been mentioned, extinction of the principal obligation as against the principal obligor also operates to extinguish the guarantee (whether simple or joint and several). Similarly, if the principal obligation is reduced or waived, the guarantee obligation is varied accordingly.[10]

Extension of the limitation period

Under Japanese law, a contractual right not exercised within a certain limitation period (*Jiko*; the length of the limitation period depending on the nature of the right and of the contracting parties) may be extinguished. If the obligor acknowledges the right during its limitation period, the period will be extended, recommencing from that acknowledgment. If the right has not been exercised by the end of the relevant period, the obligor may thereafter either acknowledge the right (in which event the limitation period is reinstated and runs again in full from that acknowledgment) or deny the right, in which event the right is extinguished.

The extension of the limitation period by the principal obligor in respect of the secured right also operates against the guarantor in respect of the guarantee obligation. However, reinstatement of a lapsed limitation period in respect of the principal obligation does not reinstate the guarantee obligation without the agreement of the guarantor.

Concomitant nature

As mentioned above,[11] if a creditor effectively assigns the guaranteed right, the assignee takes the benefit of and can enforce the guarantee against the guarantor without any obligation to notify the guarantor of the assignment.

If the principal obligor consents without objection (the legal effect of which is the loss of any defences which otherwise existed prior to that assignment) to the assignment by the creditor of the guaranteed right, the guarantor does not lose the defences available to it prior to that assignment, while the principal obligor may no longer invoke those defences.

Events affecting guarantors

Generally, the extension or reinstatement of the limitation period in respect of a joint and several guarantee due to demand under the guarantee by the creditor also operates against the principal obligor by similarly extending or reinstating the period in respect of the principal obligation. A guarantor who has independent rights against the creditor can offset its guarantee obligation against those rights.

9 On the other hand, to avoid any defences being available to the guarantor, any adverse variation of the underlying contract establishing the principal obligation should be approved by the guarantor.

10 A joint and several guarantor will not be liable under its guarantee if the principal obligation ceases to exist.

11 See 'Collateral nature' p 239 above.

Indemnities

An indemnity is an agreement under which the indemnifier agrees to indemnify the beneficiary for losses suffered by the beneficiary. The most notable difference between an indemnity and a guarantee is that there is no requirement for a principal obligation under an indemnity. Even where an indemnity does relate to an act or default in the nature of a principal obligation, the indemnity and that act or default are not collateral (as described under 'Collateral nature' p 239 above). Also, unlike a guarantee, an indemnity is not automatically transferred to the assignee where the principal obligation is assigned by the creditor. However, an indemnity is sometimes utilised in lieu of a guarantee and in some cases it is not clear whether an agreement is a guarantee or an indemnity.

Indemnities are a type of contract not contemplated by the drafters of the Civil Code. Accordingly, it is not necessarily appropriate to apply the Civil Code provisions applicable to a guarantee to an indemnity by analogy.

Joint and several obligations

Nature

A joint and several obligation is an obligation for which there is more than one obligor and under which each of the multiple obligors is jointly and severally responsible for the performance of the entire obligation and, if one obligor fully performs the obligation, all obligors are discharged. While joint and several obligations are similar to joint and several guarantees, there are certain differences. Joint and several guarantees have a collateral relationship with the principal obligation in that if the principal obligation is extinguished, the guarantee obligation is also extinguished. However, since the obligations of each joint and several obligor in respect of a joint and several obligation are several and separate from each other and there is no collateral relationship between them, nullification or cancellation of the obligation as against any one of the joint and several obligors will not affect the validity of the obligations of the others.

Formation

Whether a contract with more than one obligor establishes joint and several obligations or several obligations depends on the interpretation of the intentions of the parties and the description of the obligations, though to create a joint and several obligation there must be an agreement (express or implied) to be liable jointly and severally. Joint and several obligations can arise by agreement, as a result of the contract being a commercial act on the part of any obligor (where the obligors have the same obligations under a single contract) or by operation of law.[12]

12 For example:
1 obligations of members of a partnership company (*Gomei-kaisha*);
2 obligations to pay national taxes on co-owned property; and
3 obligations owed by successive carriers of goods for damage caused.

Most of the principles referred to above in respect of joint and several guarantees also apply in respect of joint and several obligations (other than those which relate solely to the principal obligation and the principal obligor).

As between themselves, each joint and several obligor's share of the obligation is determined primarily by agreement between them. If there is no such agreement, the shares will be apportioned having regard to the benefit each joint and several obligor has received from the underlying contract.[13] If shares cannot be established on either of these two bases, they will be divided equally. As with co-guarantors, the question of each joint and several obligor's share is relevant in respect of matters such as reimbursement, subrogation and release.

Release

If one joint and several obligor is released from its obligations, this is effective as against the other obligors in that the amount of the joint and several obligation is reduced by an amount equal to the released obligor's share,[14] even if the obligee is unaware of the obligor's respective shares. The obligee can also relieve a joint and several obligor of its obligations in part by releasing it from the 'joint and several' nature of its obligation.[15] Once so relieved, the former joint and several obligor is only thereafter liable to the creditor for his own share of the obligations though, unlike a release from obligations, relief from joint and several liability does not impact on the other joint and several obligors' liabilities (they remain liable for the whole amount of the obligations) or their reimbursement rights against the relieved obligor.[16] In any event, a creditor should exercise great care when varying the obligations of less than all joint and several obligors.

Assumption of obligation

An assumption of obligation is simply the assumption by one person of the obligations of another, either in substitution for or jointly with that other. There are two types of assumption of obligation: the 'discharging assumption of obligation' (*Mensekiteki Saimuhikiuke*) and the 'aggregative assumption of obligation' (*Heizonteki Saimuhikiuke*). Under the former there is a change of principal obligor and it is therefore not appropriate for use as a security interest. Under an aggregative assumption, the

13 Unlike co-guarantors, this will usually be the applicable test as joint and several obligors are, in effect, principal obligors.

14 The remaining joint and several obligors' reimbursement rights against the released obligor are, however, also extinguished.

15 A novation as between obligee and one joint and several obligor or rescission as against one joint and several obligor extinguishes the obligations as against all joint and several obligors. However, if the underlying contract is void (or is voided) as against one joint and several obligor, while that obligor is not liable, this does not, in principle, affect the obligations of the other joint and several obligors.

16 The principles stated under 'Reimbursement from other guarantors' p 241 above, in respect of reimbursement as between guarantors, in general, apply in respect of reimbursement as between joint and several obligors.

original principal obligor remains liable and the party assuming the obligation becomes a joint and several obligor, the obligation then being treated as a joint and several obligation and would not be affected if an obligor ceased to exist. The creditor's consent is required for a discharging assumption of obligation, but not, in principle, for an aggregative assumption of obligation.

SECURITY OVER PROPERTY AND RIGHTS

Floating security

A floating security interest (ie a security interest over a fluctuating group of assets or rights) can be created over the entire assets from time to time of a joint-stock company (*Kabushiki Kaisha*) as collective collateral.[17] This is called an 'enterprise security' (*Kigyo Tanpo*) and is prescribed by the Enterprise Security Law. Obligations so secured are limited to those arising under bonds or debentures issued by the joint stock company granting the security. The effect of enterprise security is weak in that a creditor so secured only has preference over general unsecured creditors in the enforcement of the security or bankruptcy of the debtor company. It is also, in principle, possible to create transfer as security over a varying group of assets, though the matter is open to debate.

'Bracket type' or 'root' security

'Bracket type' or 'root' security (*Ne Tanpo*) is security in respect of a principal obligation or obligations, the amount of which varies from time to time. Security interests are generally created in respect of a specific right to a certain amount existing at the time of the creation of the security interest (or, exceptionally, created within a short period thereafter); if the amount of the secured right is later reduced by partial performance etc or extinguished, the amount secured is correspondingly reduced or extinguished. Even if the principal obligor incurs new obligations to the creditor (or increases its existing obligations) in respect of the same matter, the amount secured by the original security interest is neither increased nor is that security interest reinstated and a new security interest would need to be created to secure the new obligations. This new security interest would only rank in priority from its date of perfection, not the date of perfection of the original security interest. This is sometimes both impracticable and undesirable and the concept of 'Bracket type' or 'root' security' is intended to overcome this; the amount secured by a bracket type or root security interest is unaffected by any increase or decrease (even to zero) of the amount of the secured right. However, the only bracket type or root security recognised by statute is the root mortgage (*Ne-*

17 In addition, there are several kinds of quasi floating security interests provided for in specific statutes and which relate to particular industries (eg railways) or assets; for example, a factory hypothecation (*Kojo Teito*) covers a factory (consisting of immovable (land and buildings), their fixtures and movables used in them) by regarding the factory etc as a single immovable. It should be noted that these specific security interests are only available within strict limits; for example, equipment in a business not a factory could not be made subject to such security.

teitoken),[18] though other types of security interests, such as the guarantee and the transfer as security, are also created in bracket type or root form and, as such, have been recognised in practice and by case law; there is, however, a divergence of views as to which provisions of the Civil Code applicable to the root mortgage should be analogously applied to these other forms of bracket type or root security.

Security over real property

Investigations and title

It should be noted that, although a building always attaches to land and cannot legally exist without title to or a right to use the land on which it stands, as has been mentioned, a building and the lot on which it stands are separate and independent real properties under the Civil Code and, accordingly, can be the subject of separate security interests.

As with probably every other jurisdiction, a party seeking to take security over real property in Japan should conduct searches and investigations to ensure that the subject property conforms to the description etc given by the security provider, is of sufficient value and is not unexpectedly encumbered. These investigations should comprise a physical examination of the property itself and a legal investigation of the security provider's title and the interests of any third party in the property. While an investigation of the physical state of the property can be conducted by the beneficiary or a competent surveyor or land agent, given the complex nature of the Japanese real property registration system, investigations into the security provider's title and third party rights over the property require detailed knowledge of that system and should be conducted by appropriately qualified persons.

As has been mentioned, land and buildings constitute separate immovables and, as such, each has its own immovable register dealing with matters such as title, etc. Each register comprises three parts: the heading (which describes the property); section 1 (which gives details of ownership rights); and section 2 (which gives particulars of other rights, eg mortgages and registered leases over the property). While each of these sections should be checked to ensure that it accords with the details of the property etc given by the security provider, entries in the registers are not conclusive and reported to only have the effect of public notification of the matters stated. For example, if a registered owner of property does not have any beneficial interest in the property, but nevertheless creates a mortgage over the property, the beneficiary of the mortgage will not be entitled to the benefit of that mortgage as against the beneficial owner of the property (unless the beneficiary is protected by its registration of the mortgage in terms of earlier perfection). A prospective mortgage beneficiary would be well advised therefore to conduct its own investigation into the security provider's title to the property, for example through establishing the bona fides of the recent chain of transfer of ownership. An investigation at the property should not only have regard to its physical condition but also make inquiries of any tenants to establish the nature of their tenancy rights and check the physical details of the property against those registered. Any building on land to be used as security should be checked against the details of the building as registered. In deciding whether to take real property as security,

18 Civil Code Art 398–2.

in addition to the investigations of title and factual investigations referred to, the beneficiary should have the property professionally appraised. It should then consider whether that value is sufficient security, having regard to any impediments on, and costs likely to be incurred in, the realisation of the property and also taking into account matters reducing the value of the property, such as prior ranking security interests.[19]

Mortgage

Legal nature

A mortgage (*Teitoken*) is a security interest prescribed by the Civil Code[20] created over real property and created by the debtor or a third party (ie an in rem guarantor). The mortgaged property is still owned, used and economically exploited by the mortgagor and does not change possession. A mortgage may be created also as bracket type or root security (ie a root mortgage).[1]

A mortgage has the following legal characteristics, which are common to all types of security interests in Japan over real property.

Collateral nature

Generally a mortgage cannot exist without a secured right and a mortgage (though, subject to its terms, not a root mortgage) is extinguished on the extinction of that secured right.

Concomitance

If the secured right is effectively transferred by way of assignment etc,[2] the mortgage is also transferred as between transferor and transferee, unless they otherwise agree. If the secured right is attached, the effect of that attachment also operates on the mortgage. However, transfer of the mortgage must be registered to be effective against third parties.

19 Land may also be subject to one or more of a number of statutes regulating its use or disposal (eg agricultural land)

20 Civil Code Art 369.
A mortgage can also be created over a variety of immovable property (eg trees), registered aircraft and registered ships and rights (eg mining and fishing rights), though it is most commonly used as security over real property and over businesses, including factories and equipment. Fixtures are usually included in the mortgaged property, though non-essential items, decorations and the mortgagor's personal property are not.

1 The mortgage is itself a valuable right which may be dealt with independently of the principal obligation. For example, it can be used by the creditor as security for its own obligations (a 'remortgage; *Tenteito*'), though this is usually effected with the consent of the mortgagor; the procedures, etc relating to remortgage are somewhat complex and its use as security other than in a purely domestic context is probably unlikely.

2 Assignment of the secured right would require perfection in a similar manner to that for perfection of a pledge of rights (see 'Pledge of rights' p 254 below and 'Notice or consent' p 265 below).

Indivisibility

If a part of the secured right is extinguished by partial performance etc, the scope of the mortgage is not diminished, the mortgage continuing to attach to the entire mortgaged property.

Substitution of property

If the mortgaged property is lost, damaged, sold or leased, the mortgage operates on the compensatory damages, insurance money,[3] etc accruing in respect of that loss or damage or the proceeds of sale or the rent payable under the lease.

Formation

The mortgage agreement should set out certain material matters (for example, the sum secured, interest rate, default rate[4] and time for performance). The agreement often restricts the mortgagor's powers to dispose of or grant rights over the mortgaged property and requires it to be kept in good repair. In addition, having regard to the difficulties which can be encountered in the enforcement of a mortgage and the disposal of the mortgaged property, the agreement sometimes provides the beneficiary with a right to dispose of the property or acquire the property (as substitute performance) or a right to require the mortgagor to dispose of the property, thereby avoiding the need to enforce the mortgage through public auction etc, though the validity of such a provision is questionable and in practice the foreclosure of the mortgage is usually effected pursuant to the provisions of the Civil Execution Law.

Relation to usufructuary rights

One distinctive characteristic of a mortgage is that the possession of the mortgaged property is not transferred from the mortgagor to the beneficiary, the possession and benefit of exploiting the mortgaged property remaining with the mortgagor (subject, of course, to the terms of the mortgage agreement). Accordingly, if property is mortgaged, usufructuary rights over it are not affected and it is also, in principle, permissible to create new usufructuary rights over property after its mortgage. However, if the mortgage is enforced (ie through the public enforcement sale of the mortgaged property), it is a general rule that the mortgaged property is conveyed to the purchaser in its original

3 The position with regard to a mortgage beneficiary's rights to insurance proceeds is subject to debate, especially where there are competing claims to such moneys. If the beneficiary becomes aware of an insurance claim and the possibility of insurance proceeds becoming available, it should take steps to secure its rights over those proceeds, eg by obtaining a pledge of the insurance proceeds in its favour.

4 Civil Code Art 374 provides that a mortgage secures the principal sum, the last two years' interest and damages arising from the default, though the parties may agree otherwise (subject, in certain instances (for example, if more than two years' interest is secured) to registration requirements).

condition at the time of mortgage and all rights of use over the property created after its mortgage are generally extinguished.

However, there are two significant exceptions to this principle of extinguishment, being the creation of a statutory surface right and the protection of a short-term lease.

Statutory surface right

As has been mentioned,[5] a building and the land on which it stands constitute separate real properties and consequently an owner of both can mortgage them separately or one and not the other. On enforcement of the mortgage(s) ownership of the land and the building may therefore become vested in different persons. In these circumstances, the owner of the building is granted a right to use the lot on which the building stands by operation of law (a 'statutory surface right' (*Hotei Chijyoken*)),[6] the rent for that use being determined by the court, if not agreed. In order to avoid such a restriction on the benefit of the mortgage, the mortgagor will, in practice, be required to create a joint mortgage over both the land and the building, which will then be sold jointly on enforcement.

Short-term lease

If a mortgage is enforced during the term of a lease granted after the mortgage, the lease agreement ought to be automatically extinguished. This consequence renders the lessee's position too uncertain. To balance the rights of the beneficiary of the mortgage and those of the lessee, the 'principle of short term lease' (*Tanki Chintaishaku*) provides that a registered lease with a short term (five years or less for land and three years or less for buildings) is protected even if entered into after the registration of a mortgage of the relevant land or building.[7] In practice, this right is often abused to block enforcement of a mortgage and, to avoid this, the creditor sometimes requires the mortgagor to undertake not to grant a lease to any third party and to grant to the creditor a right to lease the property, that right being provisionally registered and subsequently perfected on default. A lease granted to a third party in breach of such an undertaking ranks behind the creditor's registered lease.

Variation of mortgage rights

If a bank etc seeks to take security over real property (or any other property), it would naturally prefer its security to rank in priority to pre-existing security granted over the

5 See 'Security over real property' p 249 above.

6 Civil Code Art 388. The following conditions must be satisfied to establish a statutory surface right:
1 the building must have existed at the time of the mortgage;
2 the land and the building must be owned by the same person, ie the mortgagor;
3 the mortgage must have been created over the land, the building or both; and
4 ownership of the land and of the building must have become vested in different persons on enforcement of the mortgage(s).

7 Civil Code Art 395.

same property. In the case of prior ranking mortgage, this can be achieved by a transfer, waiver or alteration of the priority rights attaching to any existing mortgage or the transfer or waiver of the earlier mortgage itself. The rank of a mortgage may be transferred between mortgage beneficiaries by agreement between them; consent of the mortgagor is not necessary, but notice to or consent of the principal obligor is required in order to perfect the transfer as against the mortgagor and principal obligor.[8] The transfer only affects the beneficiaries concerned.

A mortgage beneficiary may waive the priority of rank of its mortgage in favour of another mortgage beneficiary of the same principal obligor; as against each other, the two beneficiaries then have equal rank. A mortgage beneficiary may also waive its mortgage in favour of an unsecured creditor of the principal obligor, the mortgage beneficiary and the unsecured creditor. These procedures are not often used due to their complexity.

An alternative, more comprehensive system is the alteration of rank of priority. This provides for an effective alteration of rank of priority of a mortgage by agreement between all affected mortgage beneficiaries. The transfer also requires the consent of all interested parties and registration to be effective.

'Bracket type' or 'root' mortgage

Most of the principles applicable to a mortgage also apply to a 'bracket type' or 'root' mortgage (*Ne Teito*) though statute requires that the agreement for a root mortgage should provide for a number of additional matters, ie the maximum amount secured, the nature of the principal obligations secured[9] and the identity of the obligor or obligors. Certain of these matters require registration to be valid against third parties, as described below. The agreement may also provide for a date (being less than five years hence) on which the amount of the principal obligation will be fixed. The terms of a root mortgage can, in general, be changed by agreement between the mortgagor and the beneficiary, though a change in the maximum amount will require the consent of the beneficiaries of lower ranking mortgages.

The amount secured by a root mortgage may be determined as agreed between the mortgagor and the beneficiary, as provided by the Civil Code[10] or on the demand of the mortgagor (not less than three years after the creation of the root mortgage and provided a fixed determination date has not been agreed). Once the amount secured is determined,

8 Civil Code Art 376.

9 There must be principal obligations:
1. Arising out of specific successive business agreements with the principal obligor (eg ongoing contracts to supply goods);
2. relating to certain specific agreements with the principal obligor (eg loan and guarantee transactions);
3. arising from certain causes (eg certain claims for damages); or :
4. being rights to claim under promissory notes or bills of exchange. (Civil Code Art 398-2).

10 Civil Code Art 398–20. The principal amount secured by a root mortgage is determined, *inter alia*, on the termination of the related transactions (etc), the attachment of the property, petition for public auction of the property on bankruptcy of the mortgagor or beneficiary.

the root mortgage becomes an ordinary mortgage securing a specific principal obligation.[11]

Provisional registration security

Under the provisional registration security (*Karitoki Tanpo*) system, a creditor secures its rights by entering into an arrangement with the principal obligor or a third party (ie an in rem guarantor) for substitute performance (*Daibutsu Bensai*) of the principal obligation through the transfer of ownership of real property owned by the principal debtor or that third party to the creditor. This is achieved by effecting provisional registration of that transfer of ownership against default in the principal obligation, the property then being transferred to the creditor in satisfaction of the principal obligation. If provisional registration has been made and the creditor triggers the registration (by declaration of an intention to do so, the fulfilling of a contractual condition or as otherwise agreed), the transfer of ownership of the property can be perfected and priority is retroactively effective as of the date of the provisional registration. In some cases this resulted in the creditor acquiring property of greater value than the principal obligation, the creditor not being obliged to repay the excess to the security provider; because of this, the scheme was held to be void under, *inter alia*, the public policy provisions of the Civil Code Article 90.[12] The courts then attempted to prevent creditors with the benefit of provisional registration security from abusing their preferential rights by requiring them to liquidate the property and to repay to the principal obligor or in rem guarantor the excess of the value of the property over the amount of the principal obligation; this requirement is now provided by statute.[13] Provisional registration is of benefit as security to the creditor given the cost, delay and complexity of enforcement of a mortgage and may be of financial value to the creditor as it enables it to acquire an asset which may appreciate in value, rather than the cash proceeds of disposal of the property, although, in practice, the provisional registration security system is seldom used.

Transfer as security

Questions similar to those relating to abuse of creditors' preferential rights under the provisional registration security system have been raised in respect of the transfer for security purpose (*Joto Tanpo*) system. A duty to liquidate the property in satisfaction of the secured right is imposed by case law on a transferee as on the holder of provisional registration security.

11 The beneficiary still has the benefit of the maximum amount in securing related claims for interest and damages, though if the determined amount is less than the maximum amount, the hypothecator may apply for a reduction in the maximum amount.

12 Civil Code Art 90: 'A juristic act which has for its object such matters as are contrary to public policy or good morals is null and void.'

13 Provisional Registration Security Act Art 3.

Pledge

Real property may also be pledged, the pledge becoming effective on the pledgee taking possession of the property. To be effective against third parties a real property pledge would have to be registered, the procedures being much the same as those for registration of a hypothecation. Pledges of real property are not common.

Security over shares of stock

Pledge and transfer as security

Security over shares of stock of joint-stock companies is primarily categorised into either a pledge or a transfer as security, each of which is further categorised into the simple form and the registered form.[14]

A simple pledge becomes binding and perfected (except as against the company issuing the pledged shares) on agreement between the pledgor and pledgee for the pledge and the delivery to the pledgee of the relevant share certificates;[15] uninterrupted possession by the pledgee of those certificates is required for the pledge to be set up against third parties. In the case of a registered form pledge, in addition to the requirements for a simple pledge, the name and address of the pledgee must be entered (as pledgee) in the shareholder list of the issuing company and endorsed on the relevant share certificates. A registered form pledge is more advantageous to a pledgee than a simple pledge in that it can be set up against the company issuing the pledged shares and the registered pledgee is entitled to receive dividends and distributions of assets in priority to other creditors of the pledgor,[16] though both a registered pledgee and a simple pledgee can enforce the pledge as against third parties other than the issuing company.

A simple transfer as security of shares becomes binding and perfected (except as against the company issuing the pledged shares) on agreement between the transferor and transferee and the delivery to the transferee of the relevant share certificates. For a registered form transfer as security (which can be set up against the company issuing the transferred shares), in addition to the agreement and delivery referred to, the transfer of the relevant shares is then registered in the shareholder list of the issuing company. Because the substance of security is not noted in the shareholder list, it is not apparent from the shareholder list that it is other than an absolute transfer of ownership of the shares.

14 A transfer as security is often used as security in respect of security over shares etc or movables.

15 The principles stated in respect of shares of stock apply generally (though there are, of course, differences) in respect of security over negotiable instruments, eg debentures, notes and certain bonds. A creditor taking security over shares should check that the shares are unencumbered and that their transfer is not subject to restrictions under the issuer's articles of incorporation, legislation or otherwise. If the creditor is to become the holder of the subject shares (eg under a transfer as security), it should also ensure that it would not thereby become subject to onerous restrictions or regulatory requirements.

16 It is assumed that registered stock certificates have been issued, as is the case for most listed companies in Japan; if not, different arrangements will be required, which are not discussed in this paper.

While a registered form pledge or registered form transfer as security is evidenced through registration, in the case of the simple form of each, the only visible act is the delivery of share certificates to the creditor and there is no significant difference between the simple form pledge or simple form transfer as security in the manner of creation or effect. In practice, parties appear to create and enforce such simple form security interests in shares without being aware of whether it is a pledge or a transfer as security. Sometimes this ambiguity is intended, the security granted being referred to as a 'security interest' over the subject shares, leaving the security holder, in effect, able to determine the nature of the security according to its needs, including whether or not the security granted is in the registered form.

The major difference between a registered form pledge and registered form transfer as security is that a pledgor and pledgee are registered as the holder and the pledgee of the shares respectively, voting rights being exercised by the pledgor and, in the case of rights issues, subscription rights accrue to the pledgor while the transferee is registered as the holder of the shares and, accordingly, is treated by the issuing company as the holder of the shares being able to exercise voting rights and acquiring subscription rights in rights issues.

Shares held in a depository agency

Where shares of listed stock are deposited with a depository agency, a security interest in this type of shares is usually created by the debtor agreeing to 'offer the shares as security', the creditor opening a pledge account or an ordinary account to which the shares in question are being transferred by book-entry from the account of the debtor to that of the creditor.

Rights as security

Pledge of rights

The Civil Code[17] provides that 'a property right may be the object of a pledge' and it is not doubted that any property right can be pledged and that although the pledge was originally devised as a security interest for tangible property, the subject matter of a pledge is not limited to tangible property, but extends to contractual or any other kind of legal rights.

Creation

A right pledge (*Kenri Shichi*) can be created by agreement between the creditor and the debtor or a third party, ie an in rem guarantor (being a pledgor other than the principal obligor), as the obligee of that right and the delivery of the instrument (if any) evidencing the pledged right to the creditor. If such an instrument exists but is not delivered, the pledge does not become binding,[18] though the pledgee of a right is not otherwise subject to the general requirement of a pledge that the pledgee retain possession of the pledged

17 Civil Code Art 362.
18 Civil Code Art 363.

property. However, in the case of a right arising from a specified obligation (*Shimei Saiken*), such as a right to claim a purchase price, sometimes no evidentiary instrument exists, in which case the agreement between the principal obligor (or in rem guarantor) and the creditor is the only basis on which to establish a binding pledge. Furthermore, a document evidencing such a right of a specified obligee (eg a certificate of borrowing) merely evidences the existence of the right and, in the absence of such a document, the enforcement of the right would still be possible if its existence is otherwise proved. The retention of the subject matter pledged is thus not as effectively secured by the delivery of tangible evidence of the right in the case of a right pledge as in the transfer of possession of the subject property in the case of a pledge of tangible property.

Effectiveness against the obligor of the pledged right

In order to establish a pledge of a right of a specified obligee as against the obligor of that pledged right (the 'right obligor'), notice to or consent of the right obligor is required,[19] as follows:

1. The notice is required to be given by the pledgor to the right obligor; notice given by the pledgee is not effective. If only a notice is given, the defences available to the right obligor prior to receipt of the notice (eg extinction of the obligation, a right of set-off, etc) are still available to it as against the pledgee.
2. Consent can be given by the right obligor to the pledgor or the pledgee. There are two kinds of consent: consent with the reservation of objection, and consent without the reservation of objection; simple consent is understood to be the former. In the case of consent with the reservation of objection, the right obligor can (as for a notice) set up against the pledgee such defences as it could assert against the pledgor as at the date of the consent, but cannot do so in the case of consent without the reservation of objection.

Effectiveness against other third parties

In order to establish a pledge of a right against third parties other than the right obligor, notice to or consent of the third party by an instrument with an authenticated date (*Kakutei Hizuke*) is required.[20] Third parties here are limited to those having a legitimate interest in denying the creation of the pledge, such as an assignee of the pledged right, other pledgees of the same right, an administrator in bankruptcy or corporate reorganisation of the pledgor etc. The authenticated date is necessary in relation to these third parties to avoid fraudulent practices such as the backdating of a notice of or a consent to a pledge.[1]

19 Civil Code Art 364.

20 Civil Code Art 467. An authenticated date is usually established by the relevant instrument being date stamped by a notary public or by posting it by certified registered mail with return receipt, the date of delivery being certified and being the authenticate date. (Civil Code Art 468(1), though this may not be the date of priority (see 'Priority as between security holders' p 266 below).

1 In October of 1998, a new law providing for special measures for perfecting the assignment and a pledge of accounts receivable (the 'Special Perfection Law') became effective. This new law allows the assignment and pledge of accounts receivable by a corporate entity to be perfected by way of registration thereof at the Tokyo Judicial Affairs Bureau, a sub-agency of the Ministry of Legal Affairs with respect to the third parties other than the account debtor. At the time of

Transfer as security of rights

A security interest in a right can be created by transfer as security. It is created by agreement without a requirement for delivery of the evidentiary document. A transfer as security of a right is perfected by notice to or consent of the right obligor in a similar manner to that for a pledge of rights.

Money-on-deposit as security

A right to withdraw money on deposit with a bank etc (a 'deposit withdrawal right') is a useful form of collateral for security, if the deposit agreement does not prohibit it or it is otherwise permitted by the bank, as discussed below, as the liquidity of the third-party debtor (ie the bank etc) is not usually doubted.

Deposits with the bank[2]

A pledge of a deposit withdrawal right against the depositor bank, also being the creditor, ie pledgee, in this situation, becomes binding on agreement between the pledgee and the pledgor and can be set up against any third party by affixing an authenticated date to a notice to or consent of the bank, as outlined above. If an instrument exists evidencing the deposit withdrawal right, such as a certificate of deposit, its delivery to the pledgee is also required for the pledgee to set up the pledge against the bank or any third parties.

Deposits with a third party as bank

For a deposit withdrawal right against a bank other than the creditor bank to be pledged, it is, in practice, necessary to obtain the consent of the bank holding the deposit, with an authenticated fixed date. This consent is required for the perfection of the pledge

---

registration no notice of assignment or pledge needs to be given to the account debtor. Under the Special Perfection Law s 2, para 1, if an assignment or pledge of accounts receivable is registered in the registration files, kept on magnetic disks maintained at the Tokyo Judicial Affairs Bureau, such assignment or pledge is perfected vis-à-vis such third parties, ie the registration itself does not make such assignment or pledge valid vis-à-vis the account debtor. Application for the registration of an assignment or pledge must be filed jointly by the assignor or pledgor and the assignee or pledgee. While the Civil Code perfection procedures always require the account debtor to be informed of the assignment or pledge, the Special Perfection Law allows the assignment or pledge to be perfected with respect to such third parties without knowledge of the account debtor. Thus, the mere registration is insufficient to make the assignment or pledge valid vis-à-vis the account debtor. Under the Special Perfection Law s 2, para 2, the assignment or pledgee shall be valid vis-à-vis the account debtor if (i) either the assignor or pledgor or the assignee or pledge gives a notice of the assignment or pledge by delivering to the account debtor a Certificate of Registered Matters, issued by a registrar, which sets out the matters stated in the registration files, or (ii) the account debtor gives consent to the assignment or pledge. The assignee or pledgee shall, however, be subject to any defence and counterclaim that the account debtor may have had against the assignor or pledgor prior to receipt of such notice or consent.

2 A pledge over deposits with a bank as creditor is not necessarily utilised because the bank (the creditor and pledgee) can easily recover its exposure by setting-off its claim against its obligation to repay the deposits (see 'Set-off' p 261 below).

and also operates as a release from any negative pledge in favour of the bank. A bank deposit agreement invariably contains a negative pledge prohibiting the depositor from assigning or pledging its deposit withdrawal right. The bank's consent is necessary to avoid the assertion of such a negative pledge and, in the absence of the bank's consent, the perfection requirements are not only not met, but the pledge itself is void. In addition, consent without reservation also functions to block the exercise by the bank of set-off rights against the relevant deposit.

Security interests in a group of rights

It is generally understood that an agreement to create a security interest over a group of rights (ie floating security) is valid; such security would usually take the form of a pledge or transfer as security. The Supreme Court has allowed the transfer as security of a group of future rights (that is, rights that have not yet been created) because of the existence of the basis for their creation and if the agreement specifies the period during which the rights are to be created. Based on this and other cases, the use of a group of present and future rights as collateral is possible if the rights are sufficiently identified. Factors such as:

1 the obligee;
2 the obligor;
3 the basis of the creation of the rights;
4 the period during which the rights will be created (if not existing); and
5 the amount of the rights

must be specified to identify the rights.

As mentioned above, a notice to or consent of the right obligor is necessary in order for the security interest to be valid as against the right obligor. However, it is normally difficult to give notice of a transfer as security at the time of execution of the transfer as security agreement between the transferor and transferee, because, in practice, that notice is likely to be regarded as an indication of the transferor being in financial difficulties. Therefore, in practice,[3] the transferor is sometimes required to deposit with the transferee a written notice signed and sealed by the transferor with blank spaces to be filled in with the contents of the transferred claim(s), date of transfer, date of notice, identification of the right obligor(s) and so forth, and that the transferee dispatch that notice with the blank spaces appropriately filled in (by the transferee) at the time of the occurrence of an event of default; this procedure has been held to be valid by lower courts but is still subject to doubts as the notice of transfer should be given by the transferor, not the transferee. Another problem with this procedure is that a notice of transfer made after a general suspension of payments or filing of a petition for bankruptcy may be avoided and considered ineffective and, as a result, the transferee would not be able to enjoy the benefit of the security interest in bankruptcy proceedings.

3 Regarding recent legislation, see n 1, p 255 above. Because of the recent legislation, practice is now shifting to use of the registration file as means of perfection.

Movable property as security

Pledge

A pledge is a creditor's right to obtain and retain the possession of property of a debtor or a third party as security for the principal obligation and to receive substitute performance of that obligation out of the foreclosure of that property in preference to other creditors;[4] a movable property pledge is a pledge the subject matter of which is movable property. A fundamental difference between a pledge and a mortgage is that the pledge is a possessory security interest while the mortgage is a non-possessory security interest. The possessory nature of a pledge operates practically as public notice of the pledge and economically as indirect coercion on the pledgor to perform the principal obligation to recover the use of the pledged property. A bracket type or root pledge can also be created.

A movable property pledge is created by a pledge agreement between the pledgor (which can be the principal obligor or a third party (ie an in rem guarantor)) and the pledgee, but the agreement for a movable property pledge is a real contract and does not become binding merely on agreement between the parties, the delivery of the pledged property also being required, the pledge becoming effective on delivery.[5] Any movable property can be the subject matter of a pledge, except movable property the use and economic exploitation of which the owner should not be deprived of for public policy reasons, eg registered vessels and registered aircraft.

Transfer as security

Although a pledge is a significant and effective form of security, its possessory nature renders it inappropriate in many situations, particularly, for example, where the prospective pledgee does not wish to or cannot take delivery of the subject property or the prospective pledgor needs to retain possession of and/or the ability to deal in the property; the transfer as security system was developed to address these situations.[6] A transfer as security is a transfer of ownership rights as security (with an obligation to retransfer those rights on satisfaction of the principal obligation), the transferor retaining physical possession and use of the subject property. The transferor retains possession as agent of the transferee, by a constructive change of possession of the relevant property (ie the transferor retains the property but declares it to be held for the transferee)[7] in order to establish the date of delivery.

The transfer as security agreement should provide for: (1) the transfer of ownership rights (and the obligation to retransfer on satisfaction); (2) declaration of change of possession; (3) use of the subject property by the transferor (this can be effected as a lease (ie with compensation) or a loan for use (ie without compensation), though in

4 Civil Code Art 342.
5 Civil Code Art 344.
6 The transfer as security system predates the Civil Code and although it is not provided for in the Civil Code is valid and enforceable. A transfer as security can also be effected as a bracket type or root transfer as security (*Ne Joto Tanpo*).
7 Civil Code Art 183.

banking transactions, a loan for use is used); (4) the obligations of the transferor with regard to the possession, use and maintenance of the property; (5) the transferor's obligations to notify third parties that the property is subject to transfer as security; and (6) insurance of the property.

A transfer as security can be used as security over individual items of movable property or over a group of movables, which may or may not fluctuate. As with security over a group of rights, the primary consideration in taking a transfer as security over a group of movables (ie floating security) is certainty as to what the security is being taken over. Where the movables are relatively stable (eg plant and machinery) or where they comprise a clearly identified group which may subsequently be reduced (eg identified stock which the transferor may dispose of in the course of its business) the accurate identification of the subject property should not be difficult. Taking such security over a fluctuating group of movables (ie a group, which may increase and decrease) does, however, present greater difficulties and care needs to be taken in the preparation of the applicable transfer as security agreement to ensure certainty of its subject matter.

Reservation of ownership

Reservation of ownership is a covenant by which a seller of property retains its ownership after its delivery to the purchaser until the purchase price is paid in full. Theoretically, all types of property can be the subject matter of a reservation of ownership, though, in practice, it is mostly used for movable property. Reservation of ownership can be conceptually explained as, ownership of the purchased property having been transferred from seller to purchaser in the same manner as an ordinary sale, the purchaser immediately returns ownership to the seller by a transfer as security. This being so, the academic theories and case law principles developed for transfer as security are analogously applied in the analysis of reservation of ownership.

Vessels

A vessel with a total tonnage of less than 20 tonnes is classified under Japanese law as movable property and security interests in the form of a pledge, lien or reservation of ownership right can be created over it, though mortgage is not permissible. The requirements for the creation and binding effect of these security interests over such a vessel are the same as those for other movable property. Accordingly, in order to pledge such a vessel as collateral, the pledgee must take and keep possession of it, which imposes an excessive burden on the pledgee and would deprive the pledgor of the use and economic benefit of the pledged vessel. For these reasons, a transfer as security, rather than a pledge, is generally used where such a vessel is used as collateral. Reservation of ownership is also used as security over such vessels.

Although any Japanese registered vessel with a total tonnage of 20 tonnes or more is classified as movable property under the Commercial Code, such a vessel is probably of significant value and its ownership is publicly notified through registration in the shipping register (that registration being a requirement for a disposition of ownership to be valid against third parties). Accordingly, mortgage of such a registered vessel is permitted,[8] and a general lien, a special movable lien and a vessel lien can also be created over it.[9] Since a registered vessel can be mortgaged, it cannot be pledged,[10] though non-statutory security interests, such as a transfer as security or reservation of ownership, are permissible.

Aircraft

The aircraft mortgage system is prescribed by the Aircraft Mortgage Law and is the commonly used security interest over aircraft. However, a mortgage pursuant to that law is limited to airplanes and rotorcraft (as defined in the Aircraft Mortgage Law Art 2) that are registered pursuant to the provisions of the Aviation Law Chapter 2. Accordingly, other types of aircraft, such as gliders and airships, even though registered, are treated as movable property for the purpose of security interests, as are foreign aircraft, including airplanes and rotorcraft as so defined. Aircrafts under construction are treated as movable property as they cannot be registered.

Statutory rights

The Civil Code and the Commercial Code provide for two categories of statutory rights, being retention rights (*Ryuchiken*)[11] and liens (or preferential rights) (*Sakidori Tokken*).[12] These rights are governed by the codes (and associated legislation) and cannot be varied by agreement between the parties.

Retention rights

If a principal obligation has arisen in respect of property of the principal obligor and the creditor has possession of that property, the creditor may retain that property until the principal obligation is satisfied; the creditor may also retain anything produced by the property and apply it to satisfaction of the principal obligation, regardless of the rights of other creditors. The creditor may not, however, use, lease (or dispose of) the retained property (unless necessary to preserve it) and is required to look after it. A retention right is extinguished if the principal obligor provides adequate security for the principal obligation or the creditor loses possession of the subject property.

8 Commercial Code Art 848. A registered automobile can also be the subject of a mortgage.
9 Commercial Code Art 842.
10 Commercial Code Art 850.
11 Civil Code Arts 295–302; Commercial Code Art 521 etc.
12 Civil Code Arts 303–341.

Liens

A creditor having a lien may generally obtain satisfaction of its principal obligation from the property[13] of the principal obligor subject to the lien in priority to other creditors.

Types of liens

There are three principle types of lien under the Civil and Commercial Codes, being general liens, movable property liens and real property liens (the latter two being called specific liens).

1 General liens relate to obligations arising from one of four sources; expenses relating to the preservation etc of the principal obligor's property incurred for the common benefit of all obligees, payment of wages of employees, funeral expenses and the supply of daily necessities; a general lien applies to all of the assets of the principal obligor.
2 Liens over movable property accrue to a creditor where the principal obligation relates to one of a number of situations listed in the Civil Code.[14]
3 Where a principal obligation arises from the preservation or sale of, or work on, real property, the creditor has a lien over that property.

The Civil Code[15] provides for the ranking of liens (general against general, general against specific and specific against specific). A general lien must first be enforced against movable property, then, to the extent not satisfied, against immovable property not subject to other security, then against other immovable property.

Set-off

Although, strictly speaking, set-off (*Sosai*) is not a security interest, it often functions as such, especially in the banking field. A business entity wanting to obtain credit from a bank in Japan is required to execute a bank transaction agreement (*Ginko-torihiki Yakujo Sho*), a standard form of which (with minor modifications) is used by nearly all Japanese banks. This agreement contains a provision whereby obligations owed by the debtor to the bank will immediately become due and payable on the occurrence of an acceleration event, including insolvency of the debtor or an order or notice of

13 With respect to the property of the principal obligor, the lien right will apply to movable property the creditor is entitled to receive as a result of the sale or lease of, or damage to, the property, though the creditor must attach such movable property before their delivery to the principal obligor.

14 Civil Code Art 311:
  1 lease of an immovable;
  2 lodging at an inn;
  3 carriage of passengers or goods;
  4 negligence of public officers in the performance of their duties;
  5 preservation of movable property;
  6 sale of movable property;
  7 supply of seeds, seedlings or fertiliser; and
  8 agricultural or industrial labour.

15 Civil Code Arts 329–332.

provisional attachment, preservative attachment or attachment in respect of deposits and/or any other credits with the bank.

As mentioned, a bank does not usually require a pledge or transfer as security of deposits with the bank to have an authenticated date affixed. However, according to case law settled by the Supreme Court, the bank may set off its claim for repayment of a loan against a deposit of a debtor with the bank and this right of set-off has a function similar to a perfected security interest over the deposit. The court held that a bank could set off its claim against a deposit of a debtor even when the deposit was attached by a third party, including the government in respect of a tax liability, so long as the loan etc was made prior to the attachment.

AUTHORISATION AND PERFECTION

Capacity

Corporate capacity

The primary business objects of a Japanese company are set out in its articles of incorporation. In addition, the company may enter into transactions which are 'necessary or advisable' in relation to its primary objects; this phrase is interpreted broadly and it would be unusual for a company to be found to lack capacity on the basis that a transaction not falling within its primary objects was not 'necessary or advisable'.

Certain corporations, eg banks and insurance companies, are, in addition, subject to licensing requirements to carry on their business and may only carry on the licensed business or business incidental to it. What is 'incidental' will depend, to some degree, on the nature of the primary business, and whether business is 'incidental' to the licensed business would be strictly looked at depending on the licensed business.

Board of directors

The governing organs of a Japanese company comprise a board of directors and one or more representative directors. A board of directors has the power to make decisions with respect to the general conduct of the business operations of the company (Commercial Code Art 260(2)), while a representative director has the power to represent the company and to effect its business. The conduct of business and the decision-making process are thus separated, each being vested in a separate body, though a representative director may decide and execute matters not falling within Art 260(2),[16] unless resolved otherwise by the board of directors.

It is generally understood that the granting of security falls within the scope of 'disposition of assets' and that the giving of a guarantee is 'borrowing'; therefore,

16 Commercial Code Art 260:

(2) The board of directors cannot grant authority to a representative director to decide any of the following matters or other material matters regarding the operation of the business of the company:

(i) disposition or acquisition of important assets;

(ii) borrowing of a large amount;'

depending on the degree of materiality for the relevant company, both come within the ambit of Art 260(2). Accordingly, the creation of security over a significant asset, or the incurring of a substantial guarantee obligation, requires a resolution of the board of directors. The necessity for such a resolution is determined on a case-by-case basis and it is therefore generally advisable for a creditor to obtain a resolution of the board of directors of the company granting the relevant security or guarantee. Even if a representative director enters into such a transaction without a board resolution, the default is merely in the company's internal decision-making procedure and the action of the representative director is considered to be valid unless the beneficiary actually knew or could have reasonably known of the lack of a board resolution; what a beneficiary could reasonably have known of would be determined on a case-by-case basis having regard to the nature and value of transaction, the relationship between the parties and other relevant factors.

Evidence

A cautious beneficiary would require the following documentary evidence to establish the capacity of, and due execution by, the security provider, though what would be required in any particular instance would depend very much on the parties' relationship.

1 a certified copy of the security provider's commercial register (*Shogyo Tokibo Tohon*) (to ascertain the valid existence of the security provider and the relevant person having been appointed a representative director);
2 the articles of incorporation (*Teikan*) of the security provider (to ascertain that entering into the transaction is not outside the scope of the security provider's corporate capacity);
3 corporate authorisation of the transaction through either of:
   (a) the relevant board resolution (this may be either specific for the particular transaction or generic as to transactions of a similar type); or
   (b) the rules established by the board of directors showing that the particular transaction is not of a type which must be approved at a board meeting; and
4 Authorisation/identification of signatory:
   (a) if a representative director or a person specifically authorised in the document in item (3)(a) above is the signatory, a specimen signature or certificate of seal impression (*Inkan Shomei Sho*), as appropriate; or
   (b) if another person is the signatory:
      (i) power of attorney in favour of the signatory executed by any of the persons referred to in (4)(a) above; and
      (ii) a specimen signature or certificate of seal impression of both of the signatory and the person executing the power of attorney.

Execution

Real contracts and consensual contracts

The Japanese Civil Code recognises two types of contracts, being classified by their requirements for binding effect: a consensual contract becomes binding on agreement (in writing or not) between the contracting parties; while a real contract requires both agreement between the parties and delivery of the subject matter of the contract.

A pledge of movable property is a real contract, the same as the right pledge (even though the concept of the delivery of a right does not exist under the Civil Code). Transfer as security, for example, is a consensual contract and becomes binding between the contracting parties merely on their agreement.

Manner of execution

A contract made on behalf of a company, regardless of whether or not a resolution of the board of directors is required as noted above, becomes binding on the company on being signed by its representative director (or his attorney-in-fact under a power of attorney granted by him). Execution of a contract or a power of attorney by a representative director can be effected by his signature or, the directors title and name having been stamped on the document, the affixing of his registered seal (*Jitsuin*) either personally or by a third party authorised by the representative director. Execution by seal is common in practice and, in such a case, the representative director should at the same time provide an official certificate authenticating his registered seal. It should, however, be noted that the sealing of a document is not irrebuttable evidence of the formation of a contract; it is advisable to establish the executing party's true intent.

Requirements for perfection

Registration of the security

While security interests are generally effective as between the parties to them, in order to be effective against third parties, security interests in real property as well as in movable property requiring the registration of a transfer of ownership, such as certain vessels, aircraft and automobiles, require appropriate registration thereof in the register recording ownership of the relevant property for perfection.

Application for registration of a mortgage of real property is made jointly by the mortgagor and the mortgagee; the application procedure must be carefully complied with and it is usual to engage a judicial scrivener (*Shiho Shoshi*) to complete the application. A registration tax is payable.

Registration against the security provider

Unlike some jurisdictions and except for certain situations[17], Japan does not have a system whereby security interests created by a company are registered against the company in a public register. Security interests created by a company over any of its assets are only registrable if ownership of the asset is registrable and then only against the asset.

17 See enterprise security as referred to on 'Floating Security' p 246 above and in particular, see note 64 above.

Possession

The perfection of a movable property pledge, a pledge or a transfer as security of share certificates requires the pledgee or transferee to obtain and retain possession of the collateral movable property or share certificates. Delivery is not limited to actual delivery and can be effected by constructive delivery (ie a pledgor delivers pledged property which is already in the possession of the pledgee to the pledgee by a declaration of intent) or by transfer of possession by direction (ie a pledgor directs a third party holding the pledged property to hold it for the pledgee); however, a constructive change of possession (ie a pledgor in possession of the pledged property declaring it is holding that property for the pledgee) is not effective.[18] A transferee of movable property in a transfer as security does not take possession of the subject property and perfection is achieved relatively easily. It should be noted that if the subject movable property is held by the creditor or a third party and is disposed of to a bona fide third party, that third party may be protected and would acquire good title to the property.[19]

Notice or consent

In order that a security interest in the form of a right pledge or transfer as security of a right can be established against the obligor of that right, notice to or consent of that obligor is necessary and, in order to establish such a pledge or transfer as security against third parties other than the obligor, that notice or consent must have an authenticated date.[20]

As a transferor of property which is the subject of a transfer as security will retain possession of the property and as there is no system for registration of transfer as security of movables (other than movables in respect of which the transfer of ownership requires registration), there is obviously a real risk that the transferor may deal with the subject property to the detriment of the transferee. To counter this, steps should be taken to give public notice of the existence of the transfer as security over the property; this could include attaching a label or notice to the property or at the premises in which it is located. These steps would probably prevent a third party from claiming it had effected a bone fide acquisition of the property (and thereby acquired title).

Regulations under the foreign exchange law

Prior to 1 April 1998 the Foreign Exchange and Foreign Trade Control Law (the 'Foreign Exchange Law') strictly regulated 'capital transactions (*Shihon Torihiki*)' such as, for the purpose of this chapter, guarantee agreements or agreements for the creation of a security interest made between a resident and a non-resident (in both cases, including companies), a non-resident's acquisition of real property in Japan and a non-resident's acquisition of shares of stock of a Japanese corporation. However, as a part of the

18 Civil Code Art 345.
19 Civil Code Art 192.
20 See 'Rights as security' p 254 above for a more detailed description of these notice and consent requirements and, in particular, see n 1 p 255 above.

Japanese 'Big Bang', the restrictions under the Foreign Exchange Law such as prior filing or the need to obtain permission were substantially deregulated and cross-border capital transactions liberalised, and now. except for certain extraordinary situations where economic sanctions or other emergency restrictions are necessary, no prior filing or permission is now required under the Foreign Exchange Law in respect of interest arising on the creation or perfection of security interests.

Stamp duty

Certain instruments are liable to stamp duty under the Stamp Duty Law. The mortgage and the pledge are not instruments liable to stamp duty (but, of course, subject to registration fees payable by stamp duty). However, security arrangements inevitably accompany the execution of a loan agreement and other credit arrangements. Under the Stamp Duty Law, a loan agreement is subject to stamp duty (levied on each copy last executed in Japan) and the rate of duty follows the same scale as that for the transfer of real property, whether absolute or as security. The rate of duty varies according to the contract amount specified in the relevant instrument, the maximum duty being ¥600,000 where the contract amount exceeds ¥5 billion. Failure to stamp a stampable document does not render it unenforceable.

PRIORITY OF SECURITY INTERESTS

Priority as between security holders

Security holders with security rights over the same subject matter in principle rank in order of the date of perfection of their security interests,[1] though it should be noted that the Supreme Court has held in respect of right pledges that where the pledge was the subject of a notice with an authenticated date, the reference date for priority is the date of delivery of the notice and, in the case of a consent with an authenticated date, the authenticated date was the relevant date of priority. It has been held in exceptional cases that, with respect to security interests requiring registration for perfection, a security holder acting in bad faith cannot assert its priority against a third party with an imperfect security interest.

Priority over general unsecured creditors

A security holder with a perfected security interest has priority over general unsecured creditors. An 'execution title' (*Saimumeigi*) is required for the compulsory execution of an unsecured right. An execution title is an instrument in the prescribed form certifying the existence and substance of a right enforceable through the compulsory execution procedure; the types of execution title are specified in the Civil Execution Law. A simple example is an irrevocable final judgment. For example, if a general creditor with an irrevocable final judgment in his favour commences compulsory execution proceedings

1 As between security interests requiring possession of the subject property, the security holder with possession has priority.

against the judgment debtor and attaches its property, this attachment operates as a prohibition on the debtor's disposition of the attached property: ie a judgment lien is created for the benefit of the judgment creditor. If a third party has a security interest in the attached property, a conflict occurs between the security holder and the attachment creditor and priority between the security and the attachment is determined by reference to the timing of their perfection.

Preferred rights

Tax claims

Tax claims usually have priority over unsecured rights. Generally, taxes can be collected from the taxpayer's entire assets in preference to other public charges and private creditors' rights. Priority between a tax claim and a security interest is determined on the basis of the statutory due date of that tax; a secured interest created and perfected prior to that due date has priority over the tax claim.

Liens

A lien holder is entitled to apply for a compulsory enforcement sale of the property the subject of the lien and to receive from the proceeds of sale substitute performance of the obligation secured by the lien.

A general lien is, in principle, subordinated to perfected security. In the case of a movable property lien, a lien creditor usually cannot enforce his lien if he does not possess the property the subject of the lien and priority between such a lien and any other consensual security interest is thus primarily determined by possession. Real property liens (other than those arising from the sale of the property) must be registered and, if duly registered, have priority over other security interests with earlier registration, though these liens are not commonly used.

Subordination of rights

The principle of equality of creditors requires that rights cannot be generally subordinated except to a security interest or a preferential right provided by statute law. However, it is possible to subordinate a right to any other specific right(s) by agreement between the beneficiaries of those rights. By use of a contract for the benefit of a third party, it is also possible to create a subordinate right in favour of a third party so long as that third party declares his intent to enjoy that right.

ENFORCEMENT OF SECURITY

Methods of enforcement

The Civil Execution Law prescribes the procedures for enforcing security interests other than those 'enforced' in accordance with their terms (eg perfection of provisional registration of ownership). Satisfaction of a creditor's right in security can be achieved either (a) by the creditor acquiring ownership of the relevant collateral (eg under provisional registration security or a transfer as security), or (b) by selling the collateral and applying the proceeds of sale to the satisfaction of the principal obligation. Enforcement of security interests under the Civil Execution Law usually follows the latter route. When an in rem guarantor has granted security over its property or rights, the creditor does not have a right to claim against the in rem guarantor personally, only against the subject property or rights. However, if the principal obligor defaults, the in rem guarantor can personally perform the principal obligation to avoid enforcement against the property the subject of the security.

Personal security

Personal security, such as a guarantee, relies on substitute performance by a third party of the secured principal obligation and is therefore enforced simply as a matter of contract as between the security provider and the beneficiary.

Security over real property

Mortgage

A mortgage beneficiary may not enforce the mortgage without first giving notice to the mortgagor and any person having rights in respect of the mortgaged property. If a third party has acquired the subject property, the mortgage beneficiary can demand that the purchase price be paid to it (*Daika Bensai*), in which case the mortgage is extinguished as against that third party. Similarly, such a third party may, subject to certain procedures,[2] within one month of receipt of the beneficiary's notice of intention to enforce, discharge the principal obligation, and therefore the mortgage (*Tekijyo*).

In making an application for enforcement, the beneficiary must deposit funds with the court on account of the cost of service of documents, appraisal of the property, auction and taxes.

If the application is in order, the court will order the auction of the property and its attachment. The order for the auction will be served on the mortgagor; the attachment is effective on the earlier of registration of the application for enforcement or service of the order for auction on the mortgagor. The court will then have a number of inquiries conducted into the property in respect of its condition and occupants and third party rights over it. It will then have the property appraised, set a minimum price for the auction and, having set a time, date and location for the auction, give public notice of the auction (including the minimum price). The successful bidder is required to pay a deposit.

If the minimum price is not likely to exceed the aggregate of the costs of enforcement and the value of claims over the subject property having priority over that of the creditor seeking enforcement, the court may require that creditor to provide security for the costs and prior claims and offer to purchase the property himself if no one else bids; if the creditor fails to provide that security etc the court may terminate the enforcement proceedings.

2 Civil Code Arts 378 and 382–384.

The proceeds of sale will first be used to settle liabilities having priority (eg tax which was due before registration of the mortgage, liens, etc), the balance being distributed between mortgage beneficiaries according to the rank of their mortgages.

Provisional registration security

Provisional registration security is enforced by the security holder acquiring ownership of the collateral property through perfection of the provisional registration. Given the potential value of the property to the grantor, the grantor is provided with a brief period of grace before provisional registration may be perfected. The creditor is required to notify the grantor (and third party holders of certain security interests in the property) of the estimated value of the subject property on realisation and may only perfect its registration within the two months after the grantor receives that notice. The grantor is not subject to the perfection of the transfer of the property unless it has received the excess of the realisation value of the property over the amount of the principal obligation. The grantor also has the opportunity to discharge the principal obligation before perfection of the transfer and even after perfection may reacquire the property from the creditor on payment of all outstanding related obligations before the earlier of its receipt of the excess payment and five years from the end of the two-month period referred to (provided the property has not been acquired by a third party).

Transfer as security

The enforcement of transfer as security is effected by the security holder acquiring absolute ownership of the collateral property, the obligation to retransfer the property being extinguished through the principal debtor's failure to satisfy the secured obligation. The transferee may either sell the property as and when it sees fit or retain the property and have its value appraised. As with provisional registration security, if the appraised value exceeds the amount of the principal obligation, the transferee will be required to pay the excess to the transferor and a transferor which has retained possession of the subject property will not have to surrender it to the transferee until so paid. The transferor would be able to reacquire the property from the transferee at any time prior to its receipt of the excess payment on payment of all outstanding related obligations, provided the property has not been acquired by a third party.

Security over movable property

A pledge of movable property is generally enforced against the property by attachment and subsequent public auction sale under the Civil Execution Law.

Attachment against movable property, being the subject of a pledge, is effected by an execution officer (an officer of the court) obtaining possession of the attached property, that possession being effected when the execution officer designates the property as being subject to attachment by attaching a notice to the property. Movable property in the possession of a third party cannot usually be attached unless the third party voluntarily submits to the subject property for attachment. Priority between the attachment creditor and any secured creditor having a security interest in the attached movable property is therefore determined by possession of the property.

However, where an obligation secured by a pledge relates to a commercial transaction (as defined by the Commercial Code), the pledge is classified as a commercial pledge and the Commercial Code has separate provisions for enforcement of such pledges.[3] Unlike an ordinary pledge under the Civil Code, forfeiture of the pledged property is permitted for a commercial pledge. If the pledgor defaults, the pledgee under a commercial pledge can thus acquire ownership of the pledged property, though he must pay the pledgor the balance of the value of the pledged property over the amount of the secured obligation.

A transfer as security of movable property is effected in much the same manner as a transfer as security of real property.

Security over share certificates

A pledge and a transfer as security of share certificates are enforced in a similar manner to that for movable property. In practice, it is thought better voluntarily to sell the collateral shares and apply the proceeds in satisfaction of the principal obligation and the pledgee or transferee should be entitled to dispose of them as they see fit under the agreement creating the security interest. It is advisable to provide in the agreement creating a transfer as security of shares that the transferor does not object to the timing and price of the disposal of the shares by the transferee and the use of the proceeds towards satisfaction of the principal obligation.

Security over monetary rights

It is understood that, under the Civil Code, a pledgee is entitled to obtain direct payment of a pledged monetary right to the extent the secured obligation is not paid and to apply that payment to the satisfaction of the principal obligation.[4] In the case of a commercial pledge, a forfeiture agreement is permitted to the effect that a pledgee will acquire a pledged right on a due date. In such a case, the pledgor is obligated to refund to the pledgee the amount by which the value of the pledged right exceeds the amount of the secured obligation.

Compulsory execution against monetary rights (eg a claim against a deposit) is applied for in the form of an application for a court order of attachment. If the application is in order, the court issues an attachment order and has it served on the right obligor. Priority between the attachment creditor and any secured creditor having a security interest over the attached monetary right is determined by the timing of the right obligor's receipt of service of the attachment order and the perfection of the security.

Security over registered vessels and registered aircraft

The enforcement of a mortgage over a registered vessel or registered aircraft is, in principle, the same as that for a real property mortgage under the Civil Execution Law. Priority between the attachment and any other security interest is determined by the timing of the registration of the attachment and that of the relevant security interest.

3 Commercial Code Art 515.
4 Civil Code Art 367.

Limitations on enforcement of security interests in insolvency proceedings

Insolvency proceedings in Japan comprise bankruptcy (*Hasan*), corporate reorganisation (*Kaisha Kosei*), composition with creditors (*Wagi*),[5] special liquidation and corporate arrangement. Bankruptcy and corporate reorganisation, as summarised below, are the most commonly used of these procedures.

Bankruptcy

Security interests in the assets of the bankrupt, whether statutory or non-statutory, can be established against the bankruptcy trustee and can be enforced in preference to the rights of bankruptcy creditors under the Bankruptcy Law.[6] Such a security interest is called a 'right with exclusive preference' (*Betsujo-ken*).

Corporate reorganisation

Unlike the Bankruptcy Law, the Corporate Reorganisation Law prohibits all holders of security interests in the assets of the corporation being reorganised from enforcing their interests outside the relevant corporate reorganisation proceedings while also empowering them to participate in those proceedings.[7] Security interest holders participating in reorganisation proceedings are afforded certain preferential treatment; a reorganisation plan giving the reorganised corporation grace in the performance of its obligations requires the approval of at least three-quarters of the security interest holders by value and the approval of at least four-fifths of them by value for a reorganisation plan otherwise affecting the rights of security interest holders.[8]

INEFFECTIVE SECURITY

Consideration

The concept of 'consideration' for a contract does not exist in Japanese law and a security interest or guarantee unilaterally offered by a third party, and even against the principal debtor's wishes, without consideration (including legal fictions such as 'deeds') is valid.

5 In lieu of composition of creditors, the Civil Rehabilitation Law is currently being considered by the Diet.
6 Bankruptcy Law Art 92.
7 Corporate Reorganisation Law Art 67.
8 Corporate Reorganisation Law Art 205.

Unlawfulness

In Japan a contract which violates a law is not, in theory and principle, considered to be void and non-existent unless it is against public policy and good morals, as provided in the Civil Code Art 90; though in many situations a violation of law would be considered as against public policy and the contract invalid.

Rescission, avoidance and nullification

Rights to rescind

A right to rescind a fraudulent transaction (*Sagaikoi Torikeshi-ken*) is a right to rescind a transaction made by a debtor with intent to harm its creditors.[9] For a transaction to be fraudulent in this sense it needs to be shown that the debtor is rendered insolvent by the transaction in question and that the debtor was aware that the transaction would harm its creditors. If an insolvent debtor offers a security for existing obligations to only some of its general unsecured creditors, that offer may be held to be a fraudulent transaction. However, it is generally understood that creation of a security interest for a new borrowing would not constitute a fraudulent transaction.

Naturally, a contract may be rescinded if made by fraud or under duress[10] or if recognised as a contract made by a party without mental capacity.[11]

Rights of avoidance

Certain transactions made by a bankrupt when it was on the verge of insolvency and which meet specified statutory criteria may be avoided by a bankruptcy trustee.[12] Avoidance is only executed by a bankruptcy trustee or a reorganisation trustee within the framework of bankruptcy or reorganisation proceedings. The relevant provisions of the Bankruptcy Law relating to avoidance are briefly summarised below; the corresponding provisions of the Corporate Reorganisation Law are similar.[13]

Avoidance for wilful preference

A transaction made by a bankrupt in the knowledge that that transaction would harm its creditors is subject to avoidance if the beneficiary of that transaction also had that knowledge. Also, transactions such as the granting of security or the repayment of a debt made after the bankrupt's suspension of payments or an application for its bankruptcy which will harm the bankruptcy creditors are subject to avoidance if the beneficiary of the transaction knew of the bankrupt's suspension of payments or the application for its bankruptcy.

9 Civil Code Art 424.
10 Civil Code Art 96.
11 Civil Code Arts 4, 9 and 12.
12 Bankruptcy Law Art 72.
13 Corporate Reorganisation Law Art 178.

Avoidance in insolvency

Security granted, eg after a debtor's suspension of payments or an application for its bankruptcy or security granted within 30 days prior to either such fact, is subject to avoidance, without fraudulent intent of the bankrupt unless the bankrupt is obligated to offer a security interest prior thereto. In order to avoid the security, the trustee is required to prove that the beneficiary knew of the suspension of payments or application for bankruptcy of the bankrupt when granted the right.

Avoidance of gratuitous transactions

A gratuitous transaction made within the six months prior to, or at any time after, the debtor's suspension of payments or an application for the bankruptcy of the debtor is subject to avoidance, without any mental element of the bankrupt or the beneficiary being required. For example, a bankrupt's guarantee of a third party's obligation without compensation, such as a guarantee fee, is considered to be a gratuitous transaction.

Avoidance of perfection

An act perfecting the transfer of a right (eg registration or delivery) is also subject to avoidance if that act was made more than 15 days from the relevant original transaction and if the beneficiary knew at the time of the act of the debtor's suspension of payments or an application for the bankruptcy of the debtor. In substance, acts perfecting the transfer made within 15 days after original transaction will not be avoided.

Nullification

A contract is nullified (ie deemed void and non-existent from the beginning) under the Civil Code if it is:

1 against public policy;
2 made without the true consensus of the parties;[14] or
3 made by mistake.[15]

ENFORCEMENT OF FOREIGN JUDGMENTS

A lender etc may, of course, decide to effect personal security given by a Japanese citizen or corporation under the laws of another jurisdiction, even if the guarantor does not have a presence or assets against which the security can be enforced in that jurisdiction. The judgment creditor may therefore seek to obtain judgment from the courts of the governing jurisdiction and then seek to have that judgment enforced in Japan.

While there is a view in Japan that its system for the recognition and enforcement of foreign judgments should be reformed in the light of the globalisation of international trade and that it should be more certain and open in its application, these views have not as yet borne fruit and the procedure is still time-consuming, costly and uncertain

14 Civil Code Art 93.
15 Civil Code Arts 94 and 95.

in its outcome. Japan is not party to any treaty regarding the recognition or enforcement of foreign judgments (other than in respect of specific claims, eg oil pollution) and questions of recognition and enforcement are therefore governed by Japanese domestic law.[16]

Requirements

In order to execute a foreign judgment in Japan, it is necessary for the judgment creditor to obtain an execution judgment rendered by the competent Japanese court based on the foreign judgment. The Japanese court's recognition of the foreign judgment is a prerequisite for the granting of an execution judgment. The Japanese courts would recognise as a valid judgment any final judgment obtained in a foreign court against a Japanese guarantor in an action, and would give effect thereto, provided that:

1 the jurisdiction of that foreign court is not denied under Japanese law;
2 the guarantor has received service of process otherwise than by public notice or has appeared before that foreign court;
3 the judgment is not repugnant to public policy as applied in Japan; and
4 there is reciprocity as to the recognition by the foreign court of a final judgment obtained in a Japanese court.

Jurisdiction

Recognition of the foreign court's jurisdiction over the original action is determined by the Japanese court through the application of the relevant Japanese law; the fact that the foreign court determined it had jurisdiction under its own law on the subject is not effective before the Japanese court.[17] The relevant Japanese laws are not provided by statute but based on practice, each case being determined on its facts. It can, however, be said that an agreement as to jurisdiction between the parties and a judgment rendered in accordance with that agreement will be upheld and that a defendant's appearance before the foreign court will provide a basis for recognising the jurisdiction of that court.[18]

16 Japan is a signatory to the 1927 Geneva Convention and 1958 New York Convention on enforcement etc of foreign arbitral awards, as well as a number of bilateral treaties on the subject and arbitral awards falling within the ambit of those conventions or any such treaty will be dealt with accordingly. If a convention or treaty does not apply, the award will be dealt with as a local (ie Japanese) arbitral award would be, the procedure being broadly the same as that for the enforcement of a foreign judgment.

17 The question of the jurisdiction of the foreign court is of particular relevance with regard to courts of jurisdictions (in particular certain states of the US) which take jurisdiction on what is sometimes referred to as a 'minimum contact' basis, and which other jurisdictions may regard as an exercise in extraterritoriality.

18 In either case, unless the agreement ousts the exclusive jurisdiction of Japan or a third country.

Service of process

This principle is intended to ensure that the Japanese defendant was given a proper opportunity to defend itself and, in effect, requires that the defendant actually receive notice of the proceedings, or should have done so. The major issue with regard to the service of process, and one which is often overlooked by parties taking action against Japanese citizens or corporations in Japan before foreign courts, is the question of service of process by post or personally (eg by courier) on the defendant in Japan. Although the Hague Service Convention provides for service of process by post to persons abroad, Japan docs not accept this procedure and a foreign judgment based on service of process by post etc to a Japanese defendant in Japan will, in general, not be recognised. Service of process in Japan is effected by the court and foreign process must be served in the same manner. This will require the foreign court to issue the process, for the process to be forwarded (with a Japanese translation) through diplomatic channels to the Japanese government and thence down through the courts to the court having jurisdiction over the defendant, which will effect service – a lengthy and tiresome process.

Even if process is not served as described above, the defendant's response to the merits of the issue, or its appearance before the foreign court without any reservation of its rights to oppose the jurisdiction of that court is sufficient to recognise the jurisdiction of the foreign court.

Public policy

Although the Japanese courts are, in principle, prohibited from reviewing the merits of a foreign judgment in an enforcement action,[19] a foreign judgment will not be enforced in Japan if it is contrary to Japanese public policy in respect of either its substance or process and, in determining this issue, the Japanese court will look not only at the actual decision of the foreign court but also at the reasons for it. While one would not expect a Japanese (or any other court) to enforce a foreign judgment requiring an act illegal under its local laws, the public policy principle has been more widely applied, for example, to deny enforcement of a judgment of a California state court which imposed punitive damages.[20]

Process of a foreign judgment may be repugnant to Japanese policy where, for example, it was obtained by fraud or if there was obvious bias against the defendant.

Reciprocity

This simply means that a judgment of a Japanese court would be recognised in the jurisdiction of the court whose judgment is the subject of the enforcement proceedings in Japan;[1] appropriate evidence must be produced to the Japanese court.

19 Civil Execution Act Art 24.

20 The court regarded the punitive damages as being in the manner of a sanction for anti-social behaviour – a concept not recognised in Japan, and therefore not enforceable (though the remainder of the judgment was upheld).

1 Eg New York, California and Hawaii have been held to satisfy this requirement, while Belgium has not and Hong Kong has not in one case but has in another.

Finality

For a foreign judgment to be enforceable in Japan, it must be 'final and binding' ie there is no readily available means of appealing against the judgment; orders for temporary relief and preliminary awards are therefore not enforceable.

Procedure

Even though a foreign judgment which satisfies all of the required criteria can be recognised automatically, the judgment creditor must still seek an execution judgment from a Japanese court before being able to enforce the judgment in Japan. The judgment creditor will therefore have to commence an action for an enforcement judgment before the appropriate Japanese court and incur the attendant costs and suffer the consequential delays. On commencing the action, the judgment creditor will be required to pay a petition fee (usually referred to as 'stamp duty'). The fee is calculated on a scale by reference to the amount of the claim and can be substantial.[2]

The Japanese court will then review the foreign judgment in the light of the principles stated above and render an order. The proceedings are, in essence, like any other civil action and the defendant is party. The progress of the proceedings depends to no small extent on the attitude of the defendant: if the defendant disputes the foreign judgment as, for example, arising from bias, the proceedings could take a considerable length of time.

If the judgment creditor is successful in obtaining an enforcement order, the court will usually order the costs of the proceedings, including the stamp duty and other costs (but excluding legal fees) to be paid by the defendant. Legal fees are not automatically recoverable by the successful party to an enforcement action, a separate action for recovery (itself incurring further costs) being required; it is unusual to commence such an action and the judgment creditor should be prepared to regard its legal fees as sunk costs.

Once an execution judgment is obtained and becomes final, judgment will be enforced by an officer of the court.

Practicalities

Having regard to the principles and procedures referred to above (and their attendant costs and delays) a creditor seeking to enforce a guarantee (etc) in Japan against a Japanese security provider resident in Japan would be well advised to bring its initial action in Japan (albeit under another law) rather than obtain a foreign judgment (with its costs etc) and then seek to enforce that judgment in Japan; better still, it should ensure that the Japanese party has assets etc against which the foreign judgment can be enforced in the jurisdiction of that judgment.

2 As at 30 November 1999, the fee for a ¥100 million claim is ¥417,600; for a ¥1 billion claim the fee is ¥3,117,600; other fees and expenses would also be payable.

8 The Netherlands

Roel Botter and Bas Boris Visser

Trenité Van Doorne

GUARANTEES AND INDEMNITIES

Surety

In The Netherlands the concept of suretyship (*borgtocht)* is specifically provided for by law. A suretyship is an agreement under which a party (the surety) undertakes vis-à-vis another party (the creditor) to perform the obligations of a third party (the principal debtor) against the creditor. In principle, a suretyship is not limited to monetary obligations, but may also be issued in relation to other obligations of the principal debtor. Unless otherwise agreed, the suretyship is in such case assumed to be issued as security for claims for damages of the creditor in case of the non-performance by the principal debtor. The main characteristic of a suretyship is that it is dependent on the existence of the obligations of the principal debtor. Should the obligations of the principal debtor be void, the liability of the surety would cease to exist. In addition, any defences available to the principal debtor may be invoked by the surety unless otherwise agreed. In cases where the principal debtor would be entitled to suspend the performance of its obligations, the surety would equally be entitled to suspend its obligations under the suretyship. Unless otherwise agreed, a surety would only be under the obligation to pay under a suretyship upon the principal debtor being in default. Under Netherlands law the default of the principal debtor only occurs upon a notice of default having been issued and the principal debtor being given a reasonable term to comply with its obligations. In practice, beneficiaries of suretyships would consider any such restrictions to be too burdensome and would normally require that no defences of the principal debtor would be available to the surety and that the surety may not suspend its obligations under the suretyship. Also, it is common practice to agree that upon the mere non-performance of the principal debtor, the surety will be under the obligation to pay under the suretyship, without any notice of default being required. It would, however, not be possible to agree that the suretyship is independent from the obligations of the principal debtor and that the obligations of the surety under the suretyship will not be affected by the avoidance of the obligations of the principal debtor. A suretyship may be issued with respect to future obligations of the principal debtor, but only to the extent that any such future obligations are identifiable at the time of the issue of the suretyship.

There are specific provisions under Netherlands law for the protection of private persons issuing suretyships.[1] A suretyship issued by a private person should comply with certain additional requirements as to the form in which it is drawn up. In such a suretyship the maximum amount of the liability is to be set out and any such suretyship is to be made up in writing. A suretyship issued by a private person in relation to future obligations of a principal debtor may be terminated at any time with respect to obligations arising after the date of the termination. Should a suretyship issued by a private person have a fixed term it may, however, only be terminated after the expiry of five years from the date of the issue of the suretyship. Again, any termination would only have effect with respect to obligations of the principal debtor arising after the date of the termination. With respect to suretyships issued by private persons it cannot be agreed that the surety is not entitled to the defences of the principal debtor or that it is not entitled to suspend its obligations. Also, it would not be possible to agree that the surety would have to comply with its obligations to pay under the suretyship prior to a default of the principal debtor having occurred. Finally, a suretyship issued by a private person may not be made subject to more onerous conditions than are imposed upon the principal debtor. In principle, any instruments similar to suretyships and issued by private persons are subject to the same restrictions.

Guarantees

Unlike suretyships there is no legal basis for guarantees. Generally, it is held that the main distinction between guarantees and suretyships is that the obligations of a guarantor are independent from the obligations of the principal debtor, while under a suretyship this is not the case.[2] To avoid any obstacles or delays in the payment under a suretyship, a guarantee would normally be preferable to beneficiaries. In order to qualify as a guarantee, it should be made clear that the obligations of the guarantor are independent from the obligations of the principal debtor. Typically, guarantees would contain wording to the effect that the guarantor will pay the obligations of the principal debtor as if it were its own debt and that any avoidance will not affect the obligations of the guarantor. As a result, beneficiaries of guarantees would have the option to demand payment either from the principal debtor or from the guarantor. Should this be undesirable and the guarantor wishes the guarantee only to be called upon a default of the principal debtor, the guarantee would in principle qualify as a suretyship and the relevant provisions of Netherlands law would apply. In The Netherlands it is not customary to provide for an indemnity in addition to a guarantee. It is generally considered sufficient if a guarantor assumes the obligation to pay certain obligations and that the obligations are independent from the obligations of the guarantor. As in relation to suretyships, guarantees can also in principle be issued for obligations that are not monetary obligations. In the building industry performance guarantees and completion guarantees are issued on a regular basis.

In The Netherlands it is common practice for banks to issue bank guarantees as security for certain of the obligations of their clients vis-à-vis third parties. Typically,

1 Any such provisions are set out in Sections 857 through 864 of Book 7 of the Netherlands Civil Code Book 7 ss 857–864.

2 See Bertrams *Bank Guarantees in International Trade* (2nd edn, 1996) pp 3ff.

bank guarantees are independent guarantees and may be called upon first demand. Bank guarantees are considered to be comparable to letters of credit. A bank which issues a bank guarantee would be under the obligation to pay immediately upon a demand being made and no defences will be available. Only when a demand is fraudulently made may the bank refuse to pay. It has been held by the Supreme Court of The Netherlands that banks issuing bank guarantees should take into account principles of reasonableness and equity.[3] Any such principles are to be taken into account both as against the bank's clients and the beneficiaries of the bank guarantees. On the basis of the duty of care to be observed as against clients, banks may in theory be prevented from making payments under bank guarantees if they have knowledge that the secured obligations are not due. Should a bank nevertheless make payments, its ability to recover the monies paid under a bank guarantee from the client may be limited. The principles of reasonableness and equity to be taken into account against beneficiaries would result in an obligation for the bank to advise a beneficiary in case a demand under a bank guarantee has not been made in the prescribed form.

Joint and several liability

In cases where obligations are due by two or more debtors each of them is liable for equal shares, upon otherwise agreed or otherwise provided for by law. In this respect it would normally be agreed that each of the debtors is jointly and severally liable for the total indebtedness. Under Netherlands law there are specific provisions relating to joint and several liability (*hoofdelijk schuldenaarschap*). Where debtors are jointly and severally liable, the creditor may demand performance of the obligations from each of the debtors for the total amount. In principle, no defences would be available to any of the debtors other than any defences which the debtors as such may have as against the creditor. The creditor will not have to concern itself with the relationship between the debtors. Where one debtor pays all the obligations, the other debtors are automatically discharged from their obligations. So as to create security for the obligations of a debtor, third parties are sometimes included as joint and several co-debtors without part of the financing being disbursed to such parties. It is assumed that in this way better security becomes available to the beneficiaries than under a suretyship or guarantee, since performance of the obligations may be demanded from the co-debtors without the (principal) debtor being in default. It is, however, disputed whether a third party can be a joint and several debtor if it is not a borrower. Should this be the case, the co-debtor would be considered as a surety or a guarantor with the associated uncertainty for the beneficiaries. In addition, in case of joint and several liability the avoidance of the obligations would in principle extend to the obligations of the co-debtors. Accordingly, an independent guarantee may be preferable from the viewpoint of beneficiaries.

Recourse and subrogation

Where a surety pays under a suretyship it can take recourse against the principal debtor and the principal debtor is under an obligation to indemnify the surety by operation of

3 See Hoge Raad 9 June 1995/NJ 1995, 639.

law. In principle, this would extend to any interest and costs which would have been paid by the surety to the creditor under the suretyship. Should the surety have paid the creditor without advising the principal debtor and the principal debtor has subsequently paid, the principal debtor may discharge its obligations against the surety by way of the assignment to the surety of its claim for repayment on the creditor. Any defences available to the principal debtor against the creditor may also be invoked against the surety. The same principle would apply where the creditor demands payment from a joint and several debtor and the debtor has paid obligations exceeding its share. In addition, it is provided for by law that a joint and several debtor which pays obligations in excess of its share, will to the extent of the excess, be subrogated in the rights of the creditor against the co-debtors and should a co-debtor become insolvent, its liability will be shared pro-rata by the other co-debtors. As a result of the payment by a guarantor under a guarantee, the guarantor will in principle not have any recourse as against the principal debtor or be subrogated in the rights of the creditor. Basically, where payment is made under a guarantee, the guarantor would pay its own obligations rather than the obligations of the principal debtor. Indeed, under a typical guarantee the obligations of the guarantor are independent from the obligations of the principal debtor. In order to avoid this undesirable effect, it is normally agreed that a guarantor has recourse and is subrogated in the rights of the creditor against the principal debtor. For subrogation Netherlands law requires that at the time of payment by the guarantor, the creditor had knowledge of the existence of the agreement by way of which the guarantor and the principal debtor agreed that the guarantor would be subrogated in the rights of the creditor. In addition, Netherlands law provides that anyone whose assets are sold in order to pay the obligations of the principal debtor or would pay any such obligation in order to avoid setting its assets at risk, is subrogated in the rights of the creditor against the principal debtor. In The Netherlands it is customary that any recourse rights and rights of subrogation are subordinated to the remaining obligations of the principal debtor against the creditor until such moment that any such obligations are discharged in full. Sometimes the subordination is enhanced by way of the creation of a right of pledge by the surety/guarantor in favour of the creditor over its recourse rights and rights of subrogation against the principal debtor.

TYPES OF SECURITY

Mortgage/pledge

Under Netherlands law a clear distinction is to be made between personal rights and rights in rem. Rights in rem relate to property (immovables, movables, tangibles and intangibles) and may be exercised against third parties. The most comprehensive right in rem is the right of ownership. Security interests are limited rights in rem (*beperkte rechten*).[4] In The Netherlands there are two types of security interests: right of mortgage (*hypotheekrecht*) and right of pledge (*pandrecht*). A security interest over immovable property, ships and aircraft is created by way of a right of mortgage. Immovable property, ships and aircraft qualify as registered property in respect of which there are public

4 Other limited rights in rem are, inter alia, leasehold (*erfpacht*), building rights (*opstal*) and usufruct (*vruchtgebruik*).

registers of ownership and security interests. Security over movable property, rights and claims, shares, intellectual property rights and any other property is created by way of a right of pledge. Under Netherlands law assets subject to a security interest are to be identified and specific security is to be taken over the various types of assets. It is not possible to create a security interest over all of an NVs or a BVs undertaking and assets without identifying the same. An NV (*naamloze vennootschap*) is a company limited by shares, a BV (*besloten vennootschap met beperkte aansprakelijkheid*) is a private company with limited liability (see 'Formalities' p 286). A right of mortgage and a right of pledge are dependent rights (*afhankelijke rechten*) in that they are dependent on the existence of the secured obligations. Should the secured obligations have been fully discharged, the right of mortgage/right of pledge will in principle terminate by operation of law. Netherlands law provides for certain mandatory rules with respect to rights of mortgage and rights of pledge. It is specifically set out that a right of mortgage and a right of pledge can be created over any and all property which is capable of being transferred/assigned and extends to any and all accessory and additional rights (*nevenrechten*) attaching to the property. Rights of mortgage/rights of pledge are indivisible also in the case where there are two or more creditors or obligors of the secured obligations. A right of mortgage and a right of pledge may be created for existing obligations and future obligations, provided any such obligations are sufficiently identifiable. By operation of law a right of mortgage/right of pledge entails a right of pledge over claims for compensation which substitute the secured property (eg insurance claims). Any such right of pledge has a preference over any other right of pledge over such claims. Any provision allowing the mortgagee/pledgee to appropriate the secured property is null and void. The transfer or assignment of property with the purpose of creating security is not valid. Indeed, under Netherlands law a security interest is to be created by way of either a right of mortgage or a right of pledge.

A security interest should in principle be created in favour of the creditor of the secured obligations. Accordingly, it is questionable whether a security interest created in favour of a security agent/security trustee on behalf of beneficiaries is enforceable. Although there is no clear case law in this respect, normally the security agent/security trustee is made a creditor of the secured obligations and a direct relationship between the obligor and the security agent/security trustee is created. This can be done by way of a parallel debt structure under which the obligor undertakes to pay to the security agent/security trustee any and all of the obligations which may from time to time be due to the creditors or to make the security agent/security trustee a joint creditor of the secured obligations. In either case the right of mortgage/right of pledge would secure the obligations due to the security agent/security trustee (as a creditor of the secured obligations), rather than the obligations due to the creditors. Now that Netherlands law explicitly provides for the concept of joint creditorship and as such there is a legal basis to make the security agent/security trustee joint creditor, this structure may be preferable. It is sometimes argued that the parallel debt structure is artificial and may be challenged on this basis. As an alternative, occasionally a structure is set up under which the security agent/security trustee issues a suretyship in favour of the creditors and the right of mortgage/right of pledge is created as security for the right of recourse of the security agent/security trustee as against the obligor resulting from the enforcement of the suretyship by the creditors. This structure is, however, rather complicated and there may be doubt whether a security interest created on this basis would be enforceable under all circumstances, since the secured obligations only arise upon the suretyship being enforced (which may very well be subsequent to the insolvency of the obligor). On the basis of the Convention on the Law applicable to Trusts and their Recognition of 1 July 1985 (the 'Trust Convention') as implemented in The Netherlands by the Act on Conflict of Laws of Trusts (*Wet conflictenrecht trusts*), there is a strong argument that the creation of a security interest in favour of a security trustee should be recognised in The Netherlands.[5] Sometimes it is, however, argued that the Trust Convention only relates to the recognition of foreign trusts as such and not the way in which a security interest may be created under Netherlands law.

Immovable property

In The Netherlands a distinction is normally made between two types of mortgage: the bank mortgage (*bankhypotheek*) and the fixed mortgage (*vaste hypotheek*). A bank mortgage secures all present and future obligations of an obligor against the creditor. Basically, a bank mortgage is created as security for all of the obligations (all monies) arising from or in connection with the relationship between the obligor and the creditor. In principle, a bank mortgage only terminates upon there being no outstandings and no new outstandings are anticipated (in effect the termination of the relationship between the obligor and the creditor). A fixed mortgage only secures certain obligations of an obligor against the creditor and terminates upon such obligations having been fully discharged. A right of mortgage is created by way of the execution of a notarial deed before a civil law notary in The Netherlands and the registration of the deed of mortgage in the public registers. In the deed of mortgage the secured obligations are to be set out or, alternatively, it should be referred to on the basis of which facts the secured obligations may be determined (ie the relationship in case of a bank mortgage). In addition, the amount of the secured obligations is to be mentioned and in case such amount is not yet determined a maximum amount is to be referred to. Unless otherwise provided in the deed of mortgage, the right of mortgage secures three years of statutory interest. Normally, however, under a right of mortgage a 30% mark-up over the principal amount is included in the secured obligations so as to cover interest and costs. In a deed of mortgage a lease stipulation (*huurbeding*) is often included which prohibits the mortgagor from leasing the mortgaged property to third parties. Should no such lease stipulation be agreed upon, the right of mortgage can only be enforced subject to the existing lease which would not terminate as a result of the sale of the mortgaged property. In case of the termination of a right of mortgage, the mortgagee is under the obligation to submit a confirmation to that effect to the mortgagor which confirmation may be registered in the public registers. The procedures for the creation of rights of mortgage over ships and aircraft are similar to the procedures for the creation of a right of mortgage over immovable property. Given the specific nature of ships and aircraft, there are certain additional requirements.

Movable property

A right of pledge over movable property may be a possessory right of pledge (*vuistpand*) or a non-possessory right of pledge (*stil pand*). Under a possessory right of pledge

5 The Trust Convention came into effect in The Netherlands on 1 February 1996.

the pledgee (or a third party on behalf of the pledgee) would take possession of the pledged property, whilst under a non-possessory right of pledge the pledged property will remain with the pledgor. In The Netherlands it is customary for banks to take a non-possessory right of pledge over the inventory and trading stock of customers. Under such arrangement the customers may continue their operations and would normally be allowed to dispose of the pledged property in the ordinary course of business. A right of pledge over movable property is created by way of a pledge agreement between the pledgor and pledgee. In respect of a non-possessory right of pledge there is the additional requirement that the pledge agreement is registered with the tax authorities in order to fix the date thereof and the right of pledge will only be effective upon the registration having been made. Alternatively, it would be possible to have the non-possessory right of pledge created by way of a notarial deed passed before a civil law notary in The Netherlands. A right of pledge may be created over existing assets and any future assets which may from time to time be owned by the pledgor. However, the right of pledge will not extend to any assets acquired by the pledgor subsequent to its insolvency and any such assets will fall in the bankrupt estate of the pledgor. There is no requirement whatsoever to list the assets in the pledge agreement and in principle a general reference to the movable property will suffice. It is not necessary that the pledgor submits pledge lists to the pledgee as and when assets are acquired by the pledgor. In case of a non-possessory right of pledge it would, however, be advisable for secured parties to require that the pledgor submits an overview of the pledged property on a regular basis, so as to determine the value of the security from time to time. Netherlands law provides that in case of a default or an expected default under the secured obligations, the pledgee may take possession of the pledged property and convert the non-possessory right of pledge into a possessory right of pledge. In practice, secured parties would wish to have the flexibility to take possession at any time without any evidence having to be submitted of the default or expected default and normally this provision is contracted out. In principle, subject to certain exceptions, a non-possessory right of pledge is as strong as a possessory right of pledge and the conversion (ie taking possession of the pledged property) may also be effected subsequent to the insolvency of the pledgor, although in such a case the pledgee may have to share in the bankruptcy costs. In The Netherlands there is no public register of security (other than in respect of immovable property, ships and aircraft). Accordingly, it would not be possible for secured parties to verify whether there would be any prior security interests and normally an undertaking to that effect by the pledgor is relied upon.

Rights and claims

A security interest over claims is created by way of a disclosed right of pledge or an undisclosed right of pledge. Under a disclosed right of pledge notice of the right of pledge is given to the debtors of the claims, whilst under an undisclosed right of pledge no notice will be given. A disclosed right of pledge is created by way of a pledge agreement between the pledgor and the pledgee and the notification of the right of pledge to the debtors of the claims by either the pledgor or the pledgee. Under an undisclosed right of pledge the pledge agreement would have to be registered with the tax authorities to fix the date thereof or, alternatively, an undisclosed right of pledge may be created by way of a notarial deed passed before a civil law notary in The Netherlands. In case of registration the right of pledge will only be effective upon the registration having been made. Under a disclosed right of pledge the pledgor would no longer have the authority to collect the claims and give discharge in respect thereof and any such authority would be vested in the pledgee. Indeed, under a disclosed right of pledge the debtors of the claims may only validly discharge their obligations against the pledgor by payment to the pledgee. Under an undisclosed right of pledge the authority to collect the claims and give discharge in respect thereof will remain with the pledgor and banks in The Netherlands would normally take an undisclosed right of pledge over trade receivables of customers. In case of a default or expected default under the secured obligations, the pledgee would have the authority to notify the debtors of the claims of the right of pledge. Again, this is normally contracted out in that notice may be given at such time as the pledgee shall deem appropriate. Upon notice having been given and the undisclosed right of pledge having been converted into a disclosed right of pledge, the pledgee may collect the claims and should it do so the right of pledge will attach to the proceeds by operation of law until enforcement. A right of pledge over claims may be created over existing claims and future claims. In respect of future claims under an undisclosed right of pledge there is the additional requirement that any such future claims are based on an existing relationship between the pledgor and the debtor of the claims (such as eg under a lease agreement or a licence agreement). A right of pledge over future receivables which are not based on an existing relationship (such as eg trade receivables) is created by way of pledge lists (in effect supplemental pledge agreements) from time to time. By way of the pledge lists the pledgor would give security over the claims which have come into existence since the entering into the pledge agreement. Normally, in a pledge agreement the obligation is imposed upon the pledgor to submit pledge lists on a monthly or a quarterly basis. In the absence of any such pledge lists no right of pledge will be created in respect of future receivables and the right of pledge would only be effective upon the registration of the pledge lists with the tax authorities. A right of pledge (whether disclosed or undisclosed) will not have any effect in respect of claims arising or – in the case of continuing certain obligations – becoming due and payable subsequent to the insolvency of the pledgor. Notice of the right of pledge may also be given to the debtors of the claims subsequent to the insolvency of the pledgor and in such case the pledgee may have to share in the bankruptcy costs. The same principle would apply to the taking of security over bank accounts. In this respect it should be noted that the claims of the pledgor as against its bank from time to time are considered not to be based on an existing relationship and, accordingly, it would be necessary to create a disclosed right of pledge (or to make the bank a party of the pledge agreement) or, alternatively, to prepare pledge lists from time to time. A right of pledge over copyrights is created by way of a pledge agreement in which the copyrights are identified and there is no distinction between an undisclosed right of pledge and a disclosed right of pledge. Although there is no legal requirement to do so, normally pledge agreements in respect of copyrights are registered with the tax authorities in order to fix the date thereof.

Shares

Under Netherlands law security over bearer shares is created in accordance with the rules relating to the creation of a right of pledge over movable property. This principle applies to bearer shares held or deposited in The Netherlands irrespective of whether the shares relate to Netherlands companies or foreign companies and irrespective of whether the bearer shares would be held through security depositaries such as Euroclear. A right of pledge over bearer shares may be a possessory right of pledge or a non-possessory right of pledge. As regards Netherlands securities which are included in the giro-system under the Act on the Securities Giro System (*Wet giraal effectenverkeer*) there are specific requirements. A right of pledge over any such securities is created by way of a book entry in the name of the pledgee in the administration of the custodian. Where the security interest is created in favour of the custodian, the right of pledge is created by way of a pledge agreement between the pledgor and the pledgee. A right of pledge over registered shares in an NV or a BV is created by way of a notarial deed passed before a civil law notary in The Netherlands and the acknowledgment of the right of pledge by the NV or the BV. In the absence of any such acknowledgment the right of pledge will be without effect and normally the NV or the BV would be a party to the deed of pledge for the purpose of the acknowledgment. In the articles of association of an NV or a BV the possibility of creating a right of pledge may be excluded and in such case it would not be possible to take any security interest. A right of pledge over shares extends to the dividends and, accordingly, the pledgee would in principle be entitled to collect any dividends. It is, however, common practice to authorise the pledgor to collect the dividends until the occurrence of a default under the secured obligations. Under a right of pledge over registered shares there is the option to transfer the voting rights attaching to the shares to the pledgee, unless this would not be allowed under the articles of association of the NV or the BV. If a pledgee could exercise the voting rights it would have effective control over the NV or the BV. Accordingly, a pledgor would normally require to retention of the voting rights until the occurrence of a default and in such case the voting rights would be transferred to the pledgee under the condition precedent of the occurrence of a default. Although it is generally felt that any such conditional transfer of voting rights is enforceable, there may be doubt in this respect now that Netherlands law provides that a pledgee is entitled to exercise the voting rights if so provided at the time of the creation of the right of pledge (and not at a later stage). As an alternative it would be possible to transfer the voting rights to the pledgee at the moment of the creation of the right of pledge and to authorise the pledgor to exercise the same on the basis of a contractual arrangement. Where the pledgee would be entitled to exercise the voting rights the fiscal unity (*fiscale eenheid*) between the pledgor and the NV or the BV (if both the pledgor and the NV or the BV are Netherlands companies) might be affected. As a result, the pledgor and the NV or the BV would be prevented from being treated on a consolidated basis for Netherlands corporate income tax purposes. A pledgor who is not entitled to exercise the voting rights and a pledgee who is entitled to exercise the voting rights, have the rights conferred by Netherlands law upon holders of depositary receipts for shares issued with the cooperation of the NV or the BV Any such rights would include the right to receive notice of a general meeting of shareholders and the right to attend the same. A pledgee who is not entitled to exercise voting rights would have such rights as provided for in the articles of association of the NV or the BV unless otherwise provided in the deed of pledge. In respect of the priority of a right of pledge over registered shares, secured parties would normally rely on an undertaking of the pledgor and the shareholders register of the NV or the BV. In this respect it should, however, be borne in mind that the shareholders' register is an administrative record only and does not provide any conclusive evidence as to the ownership of the shares or the existence of any prior security interests.

FORMALITIES

Board resolutions/internal authorisations

Netherlands private international law provides for the so-called 'incorporation theory' (*incorporatiestelsel*) as opposed to the theory of the '*siège réel*' (*stelsel van de werkelijke zetel*). This means that the incorporation, existence, structure, internal organisation and dissolution of a legal entity is governed by the law of the jurisdiction under which such legal entity is incorporated. Under the theory of the *siège réel* this would be the law of the jurisdiction where the legal entity is situated, irrespective of the jurisdiction of its incorporation. The incorporation theory is assumed to be conducive to international trade, where it recognises foreign legal entities. This principle is confirmed by recently-introduced legislation: the Act on Conflict of Laws of Legal Entities (*Wet conflictenrecht corporaties*). In addition, the Act on Conflict of Rules of Legal Entities provides that if the statutory seat of a foreign legal entity is moved to another foreign jurisdiction, this does not affect the recognition of the legal entity. In such case the incorporation, existence, structure, internal organisation and dissolution would be governed by the law of the jurisdiction to which the statutory seat of the legal entity is moved, unless in such jurisdiction it would be provided that such aspects are governed by the law of the jurisdiction of the incorporation of the legal entity (ie the incorporation theory). So as to avoid the misuse of foreign legal entities, further legislation has been introduced: the Act on Formal Foreign Companies (*Wet op de formeel buitenlandse vennootschappen*).[6] Under the Act on Formal Foreign Companies, foreign legal entities which conduct their business exclusively or almost exclusively from The Netherlands and do not have any material connection with the jurisdiction of their incorporation, will have to comply with certain provisions of Netherlands company law. This mainly sees to the registration at the Commercial Register (*Handelsregister*), minimum capitalisation, personal liability of directors and reporting requirements. On the basis of the incorporation theory the question whether board resolutions will have to be passed, in which form and whether internal authorisations are required, is governed by the law of the jurisdiction under which a legal entity is incorporated. Where all corporate action necessary under the laws of the jurisdiction under which a legal entity is incorporated is complied with, this will be recognised in The Netherlands. This would only be different if the statutory seat of a foreign legal entity moved to another foreign jurisdiction and such jurisdiction did not recognise the incorporation theory. Anyhow, Netherlands law is only relevant with respect to the corporate action required to be taken by legal entities incorporated under Netherlands law. This would also be the case for foreign legal entities which would be subject to the Act on Formal Foreign Companies. Netherlands law does not override the provisions of foreign law as to the required corporate action.

The most important legal entities in The Netherlands are the company limited by shares (*naamloze vennootschap* or NV) and the private company with limited liability (*besloten vennootschap met beperkte aansprakelijkheid* or BV).[7] The main distinction

6 Both the Act on Formal Foreign Companies and the Act on Conflict of Rules of Foreign Entities came into effect on 1 January 1998.

7 Other legal entities are the association (*vereniging*), although certain associations do not have legal personality and the foundation (*stichting*). Generally, neither associations nor foundations conduct a business.

between an NV and a BV is that shares in a BV cannot be freely transferred to third parties. The articles of association of a BV must contain restrictions on the transfer of shares. The articles of association of an NV normally do not contain restrictions on the transfer of shares. Shares in a BV are always registered shares, whilst shares in an NV may be registered shares or bearer shares. The minimum issued and paid-up share capital at incorporation is NLG 100,000 for an NV and NLG 40,000 for a BV. NVs and BVs are managed by a management board (*bestuur*), consisting of one or more managing directors (*bestuurders*). It is possible to create a two-tier system and to provide for a supervisory board (*raad van commissarissen*), consisting of one or more supervisory directors (*commissarissen*). The duty of the supervisory board is to supervise and assist the management board. For certain large companies – so-called 'structure companies' (*structuurvennootschappen*) – it is mandatory to have a supervisory board.[8] Although it is not customary in The Netherlands to provide for underlying board resolutions for each transaction to be entered into by an NV or a BV, it must be assumed that these are required. Such board resolutions may be passed in a meeting or, alternatively, by way of unanimous consent (unless the articles of association prevent the same). The procedures for board meetings are generally set out in the articles of association. Should board resolutions be passed by unanimous consent, the resolutions must be executed by all the managing directors. In principle, no internal authorisations are required for the entering into of transactions, although the articles of association may provide that certain resolutions of the management board require the prior approval of the general meeting of shareholders or the supervisory board. Generally, such resolutions are specified in the articles of association, but the articles of association may also provide that such resolutions will be specified by the general meeting of shareholders or the supervisory board and submitted to the management board at a later date. Finally, the articles of association may provide that certain resolutions of the management board must be adopted with a certain majority of votes or unanimity. For structure companies, certain resolutions of the management board require the prior approval of the supervisory board by operation of law. Whether an NV or a BV is a structure company may be verified with the Commercial Register. The absence of the prior approval of the general meeting of shareholders or the supervisory board (as the case may be) or the absence of a required majority in the management board, would in principle not affect the validity of transactions entered into by an NV or a BV. Should the other party to the transaction have knowledge that not all internal authorisations have been complied with and that any such authorisation would not have been given had it been asked for, there is an argument that such party may not benefit from the non-compliance. This would also seem to apply to the absence of underlying board resolutions. In addition, non-compliance with required internal authorisations or the absence of underlying board resolutions may trigger personal liability of the managing directors.

In principle, there are no specific requirements for an NV or a BV to issue guarantees or to provide security. However, it is held that where all the assets of an NV or a BV are encumbered, the prior approval of the general meeting of shareholders is required,

8 An NV or a BV is a structure company if the following criteria are met during a consecutive period of three years:
(i) the issued share capital increased with the reserves is in excess of NLG 25,000,000;
(ii) a works council (*ondernemingsraad*) has been established; and
(iii) generally, more than 100 employees are employed in The Netherlands.

because the transaction may lead to the dissolution of the NV or the BV. Where security is to be provided for 'important' indebtedness of another enterprise, under the Works Council Act (*Wet op de ondernemingsraden*) it would be necessary to obtain the prior advice from the works council.[9] Any such advice should be sought at such time that it may have an influence on the decision whether or not to provide the security. Where the works council provides negative advice the NV or the BV must postpone any resolution for a one month-period during which the works council may institute proceedings with the Enterprises Division (*Ondernemingskamer*) of the Court of Appeal in Amsterdam. In the proceedings the basis for the appeal of the works council is limited to the ground that the NV or the BV could not reasonably have decided to provide the security. The Enterprises Division may order the NV or the BV to revoke a resolution and to undo any consequences and may also order the NV or the BV not to implement the resolution. In principle, any such measures of the Enterprises Division would not affect any existing rights of third parties.

Execution

Netherlands law provides that transactions may be entered into on behalf of an NV or a BV by its management board and any one of the managing directors, unless it is provided in the articles of association that the authority to bind the NV or the BV only vests in two or more managing directors acting jointly. Also, in the articles of association certain managing directors may be excluded from the authority to bind an NV or a BV.[10] Whether a managing director has the power to enter into transactions on behalf of an NV or a BV may be verified with the Commercial Register, where specimen signatures of the managing directors are deposited. Each managing director and – if the 'two or more signatories' clause applies – two or more managing directors acting jointly, may execute an agreement on behalf of an NV or a BV, provided that they are not excluded from the authority to bind the NV or the BV. The authority of the managing directors to bind an NV or a BV may be limited in case of conflicts of interest between the managing director personally and the NV or the BV. Any conflict of interest between a managing director entering into a transaction on behalf of an NV or a BV and the NV or the BV would in principle result in a lack of authority of the managing director to bind the NV or the BV and would as such have external effect. There is, however, an additional requirement that the other party to the transaction at the time of entering into the transaction knew or should have known that there was a conflict of interest.[11] In The Netherlands there is no specific form in which an NV or a BV is to execute agreements. An NV or a BV does not have a corporate seal and no witnesses are required. Normally, it is simply stated by whom an agreement is executed and in which capacity. In respect of security to be created by way of a notarial deed, any such notarial deed should be

9 Under the Works Council Act an NV or a BV (basically the enterprises conducted by the NV or the BV) is under an obligation to create a works council if they generally employ more than 35 employees in The Netherlands.

10 On the basis of the First EC-Directive on Company Law (Directive 68/151), no further restrictions are permitted.

11 See Hoge Raad 22 March 1996, RvdW 1996, 76 C and Hoge Raad 11 September 1998, RvdW 1998, 150 C.

passed before a civil law notary (*notaris*) in The Netherlands. In principle, the parties to the notarial deed would have to appear before the civil law notary. It is, however, customary that the parties give a power of attorney to personnel in the office of the civil law notary to appear on their behalf. The Netherlands is a party to the Convention on the Law Applicable to Agency of 14 March 1978 (the 'Agency Convention').[12] The Agency Convention applies to relationships of an international character entered into on behalf an NV or a BV by an attorney. On the basis of the Agency Convention the relevant requirements of the laws of the jurisdiction where the attorney has its office or entered into the agreement would have to be complied with, irrespective of the proper law of the power of attorney.

Registration/stamp duties

The creation of security over immovable property and over ships and aircraft registered in The Netherlands is effected by the registration of the deed of mortgage in the public registers. This will be dealt with by the civil law notary before whom a deed of mortgage is executed immediately subsequent to the execution thereof. Also, any deed of pledge providing for an undisclosed right of pledge over movable property or claims (and any subsequent pledge lists providing for an undisclosed right of pledge over claims) are to be registered with the tax authorities, unless the deed of pledge (and the pledge lists) are made by way of a notarial deed. The registration is only intended to fix the date of the creation of the right of pledge. In The Netherlands there is no public register of security, other than in respect of immovable property, ships and aircraft. No other filings, registrations or recordings are required in order to ensure the validity, enforceability of admissibility in evidence of guarantees or security or to create, perfect or preserve security or priority of security. In addition, no stamp duties exist in The Netherlands, although court fees are payable in case of the enforcement by way of proceedings in the courts.[13]

Consents

No consents are required for an NV or a BV to enter into guarantees or to provide security. Also, there are no exchange control restrictions in The Netherlands. However, pursuant to the External Financial Relations Act 1994 (*Wet financiële betrekkingen buitenland 1994*) and the Reporting Instructions on Foreign Payments (*Rapportagevoorschriften buitenlands betalingsverkeer*), an NV or a BV which is regularly involved in financial transactions with non-residents is under the obligation to register with the Netherlands Central Bank (*De Nederlandsche Bank NV)* and any foreign bank accounts opened and maintained and any in and outgoing payments in excess of NLG 25,000 should be reported for the purpose of determining the composition of the balance of payments of The Netherlands for financial statistical purposes. In addition, on the basis of the External Financial Relations Act 1994 the Ministry of Finance may from time to time restrict

12 The Agency Convention came into effect in The Netherlands on 1 October 1992.

13 The court fees range from NLG 400 to NLG 9,350 depending on the amount of the claim and the competent court.

payments to and from third countries. In principle, such restrictions may only be imposed in relation to sanctions based on EC legislation with respect to such third countries. The violation of the restrictions imposed on the basis of the External Financial Relations Act 1994 is an economic offence.

PRIORITIES

Priority of security

The priority of a right of mortgage is based on the time of the registration of the deed of mortgage in the public registers. So as to ensure the ranking of a right of mortgage, the civil law notary will verify the public registers so as to see whether there are any prior mortgages or any intermediate attachments. It is possible to agree with prior mortgagees that a different priority will apply. Any such priority should be included in the deed of mortgage and the agreement from prior ranking mortgagees should also appear. The priority of rights of pledge is in principle based on the date of the execution of the deed of pledge. In the case of a non-possessory right of pledge over movable property and an undisclosed right of pledge over claims, the date of the registration of the deeds of pledge with the tax authorities is decisive. No other priority is relevant. As regards non-possessory rights of pledge over movable property there is one important exception to the priority rules. A subsequent possessory right of pledge over movable property will have priority over a prior non-possessory right of pledge, provided that the subsequent pledgee acts in good faith (ie did not or should not have knowledge of the prior non-possessory right of pledge). This would not apply to an undisclosed right of pledge over claims, although the debtor may validly discharge its obligations to a subsequent pledgee under a disclosed right of pledge. Any such subsequent pledgee would, however, be under the obligation to pay any monies collected to the prior pledgee under the undisclosed right of pledge.

Attachments/garnishments

Creditors wishing to take recourse against assets of an obligor will in principle have to make an attachment on the assets. Under Netherlands law there are two attachment procedures: attachment prior to judgment and attachment subsequent to judgment. The procedures for an attachment prior to judgment are rather straightforward. The only requirement is that an application be made to the president of the competent district court to allow the attachment. Generally, any such attachment will be allowed provided the party wishing to make the attachment can briefly substantiate its claim. In principle, an attachment may be made with respect to all of the assets of an obligor. In addition, it would be possible to levy a garnishment on any and all monies due from a third party to the obligor. This would effectively freeze the payments between the third party and the obligor. Since the procedure for making attachments prior to judgment is fairly easy, this is often used as a manner to impose pressure upon an obligor. The only option for an obligor who wishes to be released from an attachment is to enter into summary proceedings before the president of the competent district court. Generally, the president will not order the release of the attachment, unless it is crystal clear that the party which made the attachment does not have any claim whatsoever. In case of an attachment prior to judgment the party making the attachment is under the obligation to institute proceedings on the merits of the matter within such time period as set by the president (normally two weeks). Any such proceedings may take several years and only upon a final judgment having been obtained would it be possible to enforce the attachment. Pending the proceedings the debtor is prevented from disposing of the assets subject to an attachment. Enforcement of an attachment in principle takes place by way of a sale through a public auction. Mortgagees and pledgees do not have any right to prevent the enforcement of an attachment, but they have the right to take over the sale. As a result of the bankruptcy of an NV or a BV any attachments made prior to the date of the bankruptcy will be released and will effectively be replaced by a general attachment on behalf of all of the creditors.

Preferential rights

Under Netherlands law creditors may seek recourse against all of the assets of an obligor. Basically, all the creditors rank *pari passu*, unless they have a certain preference (*voorrang*). Any such preference is based on a right of mortgage, right of pledge or preferential rights (*voorrechten*). A right of mortgage and a right of pledge have priority over preferential rights, unless otherwise provided for by law. Preferential rights cannot be agreed upon by contract and are always based on a specific provision of Netherlands law. Certain preferential rights relate to specific assets of an obligor only, whilst other preferential rights relate to all of the assets. On the basis of preferential rights creditors only have preference on the enforcement proceeds and not on the underlying assets. The most important preferential rights with respect to all the assets are the claims of the tax authorities and the national insurance authority (*bedrijfsvereniging*) with respect to certain unpaid taxes and social security premiums. In addition, under Netherlands law creditors who are given the authority to retain assets until their claims have been paid, have a preference with respect to such assets. Although this would not create any preference, under Netherlands law creditors have extensive opportunities to set off their obligations with any claims on the obligor. In addition to the preferential rights on the assets of an obligor, the tax authorities have limited preferential rights with respect to assets which are located on the premises of an obligor but are owned by third parties, eg under lease arrangements or in respect of which third parties have a security interest. Any such preferential rights would be limited to assets used for the operation of the business, such as machinery, equipment, furniture, etc. but not trading stock.[14] The preferential rights of the tax authorities would in principle prevail over the ownership rights and security interests of secured parties. If third parties have 'real ownership rights' with respect to the assets, their rights would, however, be respected. Generally, ownership rights under an operational lease arrangement would qualify as 'real ownership rights', whilst ownership rights under a finance lease arrangement would not. In the latter case it is assumed that the lessor only has a financial interest and should be treated on equal footing as other creditors of the obligor.

14 New legislation is proposed so as to extend the preferential rights of the tax authorities to other assets. As yet it is not clear when such new legislation will come into effect.

Subordination

Under Netherlands law subordination will have to be agreed upon by way of an agreement between the creditor and the obligor. Subordination can be agreed upon with respect to all or certain of the creditors of the obligor. In principle, any such arrangement would be enforceable also in the bankruptcy of an NV or a BV. Should the arrangement be included in eg an intercreditor agreement to which the obligor is not a party, it is questionable whether a receiver in the bankruptcy of an NV or a BV would be bound by the terms of the subordination. Where the subordination is agreed upon with respect to specific creditors only, different layers of debt arise and it is possible that a subordinated creditor will receive payment prior to the creditors in relation to which the subordination is agreed upon having been paid in full. In case of subordination the claims of the creditors remain in existence, but simply have a lower ranking. As an alternative, it may be agreed that creditors will not seek recourse against all or certain of the assets of an obligor. As such, Netherlands law provides for a legal basis for limited recourse and non-recourse arrangements.

REMEDIES AND ENFORCEMENT

Power of sale/enforcement

In case of a default under the secured obligations a mortgagee may sell the immovable property subject to a right of mortgage by way of a public auction before a civil law notary in The Netherlands. In this respect the formalities provided for in the Civil Procedures Act (*Wetboek van burgerlijke rechtsvordering*) are to be complied with. These formalities relate to notification of the mortgagor and minimum notice periods and also provide for detailed instructions in relation to the sale. Also, subsequent-ranking mortgagees have the power to sell the mortgaged property. In case of the sale by a subsequent-ranking mortgagee, (part of) the purchase price will have to be forwarded to the prior-ranking mortgagee. A prior-ranking mortgagee also has the opportunity to take over the sale, but cannot prevent or postpone the sale. As an alternative, both the mortgagee and the mortgagor may request the president of the competent district court to allow a private sale. Any such request should ultimately be made one week before the proposed sale and a complete draft of the purchase agreement should be submitted to the president. Generally, a private sale will be allowed in case a higher purchase price can be realised than may be expected in case of a sale through a public auction. The enforcement of a right of mortgage by way of a sale through a public auction or a private sale is mandatory. Other ways of enforcement are null and void and, in particular, a mortgagee may not appropriate any mortgaged property. The procedures for the enforcement of rights of mortgage on ships and aircraft are similar to the procedure for the enforcement of a right of mortgage on immovable property. In respect of the enforcement of a right of pledge on movable property there are fewer formalities than in relation to the enforcement of a right of mortgage on immovable property. Again, a pledgee would only be entitled to enforce the right of pledge in case of a default under the secured obligations. There is a specific provision in Netherlands law which enables the pledgor and the pledgee to agree that enforcement would only be possible upon having obtained a court judgment confirming the existence of the default. This would result in substantial delays in the enforcement process and normally secured parties would not agree to any such provision. Again, the enforcement of a right of pledge should in principle be effected by way of a sale through a public auction. There are no specific provisions governing the way in which the sale is to be effected, other than that it is to take place in accordance with local customs and local conditions. In case the pledged property consists of goods which are traded on exchanges or other markets the sale may be effected through such exchanges. A pledgee would not be entitled to appropriate the pledged property, but may purchase the pledged property in the public auction. Also in relation to a right of pledge each of the pledgee and the pledgor may request the president of the competent district court to allow a private sale. Unlike in relation to a right of mortgage the authority to make an application to the president may be excluded in the pledge agreement and this is normally done in relation to the pledgor so as to prevent the pledgor interfering with the enforcement process. In addition, the pledgee may make an application for an order that the pledged property be transferred to the pledgee for such amount as to be determined by the president. The pledgor and the pledgee may agree to a private sale amongst themselves, though this may only be agreed upon once a default has occurred. Also subsequent-ranking pledgees have the power of sale. Higher ranking rights of pledge would, however, remain in existence and, accordingly, the movable property can only be sold subject to any such higher ranking right of pledge. There are no provisions which allow a pledgee with a higher priority to take over the sale, but in practice it is not very likely that the sale of pledged property subject to a right of pledge would be successful. There are various notice requirements, but generally these may be validly waived by the pledgor in the pledge agreement. Upon a sale having been effected, the pledgee may set off the proceeds with the secured obligations and is under the obligation to remit any excess to the pledgor.

There are no specific provisions for the enforcement of a right of pledge on claims. In principle, the procedures with respect to the enforcement of a right of pledge on movable property would *mutatis mutandis* apply. This would mean that a right of pledge over claims would in principle have to be enforced by way of a sale through public auction. Where a pledgee of claims would, however, have the right to collect any claims subject to a right of pledge upon notice having been given to the debtors, the pledgee may simply collect the claims, and in case of monetary claims set-off any monies so collected against the secured obligations. The enforcement of a right of pledge on registered shares in a BV is rather complex. In principle, the rules relating to the enforcement of a right of pledge on movable property apply, but in addition any transfer restrictions included in the articles of association of the BV would have to be observed. Where the right of pledge has not been created with respect to the total issued share capital of the BV, this may result in the requirement to have the transfer of the shares to a specific purchaser approved by the general meeting of shareholders or to have the shares offered to the other shareholders first by way of a sale through a public auction. This is highly impractical and for this reason it would be advisable for secured parties only to take a right of pledge over the total issued share capital. In addition, a right of pledge over other assets, such as copyrights, will have to be enforced in accordance with the rules relating to the enforcement of a right of pledge over movable property.

Accordingly, it would in principle be necessary to enforce such right of pledge by way of a sale through a public auction.

Rights of creditors

In principle, creditors do not have any right whatsoever to prevent the enforcement of a right of mortgage or a right of pledge. Mortgagees and pledgees can simply enforce their rights and would as such not be bound by any restrictions. The enforcement would, however, be subject to the general principles of reasonableness and equity under Netherlands law. Such principles would have to be observed as against other creditors, but also as against the mortgagor/pledgor. To prevent or postpone enforcement a mortgagor/pledgor may try and obtain an injunction to that effect. Although it would be difficult to give any guidelines in this respect, it should be assumed that enforcement may only be prevented or postponed where such enforcement would clearly be in violation of the principles of reasonableness and equity. This may be the case in the situation where the mortgagee/pledgee would from one day to the other demand payment of the secured obligations and would subsequently wish to enforce the right of mortgage/right of pledge. Additionally, where there is considerable doubt whether or not the secured obligations are due and payable, the mortgagor/pledgor may try and obtain an injunction to prevent enforcement. In cases where third-party security has been provided and assets of the principal debtor are subject to a security interest, the third party may require that the security over the assets of the principal debtor be enforced first. In theory, third-party creditors could also try and obtain an injunction so as to prevent the enforcement of a right of mortgage/right of pledge on the basis of the principles of reasonableness and equity, but in practice there would only be a limited chance of success. Conversely, third-party creditors may force a mortgagee/pledgee to enforce the rights of mortgage/rights of pledge should they not do so within a reasonable time period. In cases of the bankruptcy of an NV or a BV the receiver may set a reasonable term to mortgagees/pledgees to enforce the rights of mortgage/rights of pledge. If the mortgagees/pledgees will not comply with such term, the receiver may require delivery of the mortgaged/pledged property and sell the same himself. In such a case the mortgagees/pledgees would be entitled to the proceeds, but would have to share in the costs of the bankruptcy.

Insolvency procedures

In The Netherlands, there are two insolvency procedures: bankruptcy (*faillissement*) and suspension of payments (*surséance van betaling*). A bankruptcy may be applied for by an NV or a BV or their respective creditors, if the NV or the BV has got into a situation in which it has ceased to pay its debts. An NV or a BV is considered to have ceased to pay its debts if it leaves at least two creditors unpaid. In a bankruptcy a receiver (*curator*) will be appointed to liquidate the assets of the NV or the BV and to distribute the proceeds thereof among the creditors, with due observance of their respective rights. A suspension of payments may be applied for by an NV or a BV if it anticipates that it can no longer pay its debts and effectively works as a freeze of payments. An administrator (*bewindvoerder*) will be appointed to manage the NV or the BV in suspension of payments jointly with the management board, with a view to the continuation of the activities of the NV or the BV. Normally, a provisional suspension of payments is granted for a period of two to three months, which will be followed by a definitive suspension of payments for a period of 18 months. In this period a 'composition' (*akkoord*) may be offered to the creditors which, under certain circumstances, will be binding on all creditors. It is not possible to provide for a binding composition other than in a suspension of payments or a bankruptcy. In most cases a suspension of payments will be followed by a bankruptcy prior to the expiry of the term for which the (provisional) suspension of payments was granted. An application for a suspension of payments by an NV or a BV is often used as defence to an application for the bankruptcy of the NV or the BV by the creditors. A bankruptcy and a suspension of payments should be applied for at the district court in the jurisdiction where the NV or the BV has its statutory seat. In The Netherlands no extra-judicial insolvency proceedings exist and the concept of administrative receivership is unknown. Creditors who apply for the bankruptcy of an NV or a BV in principle do not have any influence over the appointment of a receiver (in most cases, receivers and administrators are solicitors (*advocaten*)). In a bankruptcy a receiver is supervised by a court magistrate (*rechter-commissaris*); in a suspension of payments the court magistrate has an advisory role only.

A bankruptcy and a suspension of payments do not have effect against mortgagees and pledgees. Mortgagees and pledgees may in principle enforce their rights of mortgage and rights of pledge as if there were no bankruptcy or suspension of payments. They are entitled to sell the mortgaged property and the pledged property and set-off the proceeds against the secured obligations. Under the Bankruptcy Code there is a cooling-off period (*afkoelingsperiode*) with respect to bankruptcies and suspensions of payments. A cooling-off period is ordered by the court magistrate on the application of any interested party. The period for which a cooling-off period may be ordered is one month, with a possible extension of one further month. During this period creditors, including mortgagees and pledgees, may not take any action against an NV or a BV. As a result, during the cooling-off period, mortgagees and pledgees (and all other creditors) are prevented from enforcing their respective rights. Before any distribution may be made to the creditors, the fees of the receiver and any other costs expended for the benefit of an NV or a BV during the bankruptcy (*boedelkosten*) should be paid. In principle, mortgagees and pledgees would not have to share in the costs. As a result of the termination of the bankruptcy of an NV or a BV, the NV or the BV is dissolved and ceases to exist. Accordingly, any unpaid claims can no longer be recovered.

VITIATING FACTORS

Nullity

Netherlands law makes a distinction between transactions which are null and void *ab initio* (*nietig*) and transactions which are capable of being avoided (*vernietigbaar*). Transactions are null and void if the content or intended effect is in conflict with good morals or public policy. Further, transactions which are in conflict with mandatory provisions of Netherlands law are void, provided that where the mandatory provisions are designed to protect one of the parties to a transaction, the transaction may only be avoided by such party. Also, transactions which are not entered into in the prescribed form are null and void, unless it is otherwise provided for by law. Where the basis for a transaction being null and void only applies to part of the transaction, the remaining part of the transaction remains valid, unless it forms an indissoluble part with the part which is null and void. In addition, Netherlands law provides that if the intended effect of a void transaction is similar to another transaction which may be deemed to have been entered into (should such transaction not be void) the void transaction will be deemed to have the effect of the other transaction. This would only be different if this would be unreasonable vis-à-vis third parties. Transactions may be avoided if specifically provided for by law, inter alia, in case the entering into the transaction transgresses the objects of an NV or a BV, the transaction is a preferential transaction or the transaction is entered into on the basis of threat, fraud, abuse of circumstances or mistake. The avoidance of a transaction may be claimed by mere extra-judicial statement or by the entering into legal proceedings. Should a transaction be successfully avoided, this will have retroactive effect.

Capacity

The capacity of an NV and a BV is limited by their objects. Object has a dual meaning: not only does it mean the object of the NV or the BV described in its objects clause as embodied in its articles of association, but also the corporate object of making profits (the corporate benefit). If as a result of a transaction entered into by an NV or a BV the object of the NV or the BV is transgressed (ie the transaction is *ultra vires*), the NV or the BV (which would include a receiver in its bankruptcy but not any creditors) may contest the validity of the transaction, but only if the other party to the transaction was aware or should have been aware that the object of the NV or the BV was transgressed.[15] In principle, the other party is not required to investigate independently the object of an NV or a BV. In order to determine whether the object of an NV or a BV is transgressed, the objects clause as embodied in the articles of association of the NV or the BV is relevant but not decisive. All relevant facts and circumstances should be taken into account.[16] If an NV or a BV provides security for its own indebtedness, it is not very likely that the courts of The Netherlands would hold that as a result the object of the NV or the BV was transgressed. This would also be the case even if the providing of security is not explicitly referred to in the objects clause as embodied in the articles of association. This may be different when the NV or the BV issues guarantees or provides security for third party indebtedness. There is an argument that if the issue of guarantees and the providing of security for third party indebtedness is not explicitly referred to in the objects clause as contained in the articles of association, the issue of guarantees and the providing of security may transgress the object of an NV or a BV.

15 The subject matter is laid down in of the Civil Code Book 2 Section 7, which reads as follows: 'A legal act performed by a legal person may be avoided if, as a result, its object was transgressed and the other party was aware thereof or, without personal investigation, should have been so aware; only the legal person can claim avoidance on this ground.'

16 See, inter alia, Hoge Raad 7 February 1992 NJ 1992, 438.

However, if an NV or a BV has a clear interest in and benefits from the issue of guarantees or the providing of security for third party indebtedness, the same should be deemed to pertain to the object of the NV or the BV (ie it is included in the corporate object). In particular, this will be the case if a guarantee is issued or security is provided for the indebtedness of a parent company/group financing company which makes cash facilities available to an NV or a BV. On this basis it is also argued that upstream guarantees/ security are more vulnerable than downstream guarantees/security. In the latter case, the parent company is likely to benefit from the issue of the guarantees and the providing of security. On the other hand, if the issue of guarantees or the providing of security for third party indebtedness is provided for in the objects clause as embodied in the articles of association, this does not necessarily mean that the entering into such guarantees and the providing of such security may not be successfully contested. In particular, if the issue of guarantees or the providing of security for third party indebtedness leads to the insolvency of the NV or the BV (as a result of a demand being made under the guarantees or the enforcement of the security), the issue of such guarantees and the providing of such security is clearly outside the object of the NV or the BV. For this reason it is often provided that an NV or a BV when issuing guarantees or providing security for third party indebtedness, will not be liable in excess of its net assets (at the time of a demand being made or enforcement). If the validity of a transaction is successfully contested, the transaction will be avoided and the obligations of an NV or a BV under the avoided transaction will cease to exist. As a result, the secured party may have an (unsecured) claim for damages. Also, the entering into transactions which transgress the object of an NV or a BV may result in personal liability of the managing directors and the supervisory directors (if any).

Preferential transactions

If a transaction entered into by an NV or a BV is prejudicial to the interests of the creditors of such NV or BV, the transaction may, under certain circumstances, be contested (*actio pauliana*). The rights of creditors of an NV or a BV will be prejudiced if preferential treatment is given to the other party to the transaction. Under Netherlands law transactions may be contested on the basis of the *actio pauliana* in the bankruptcy of an NV or a BV and otherwise.[17] Other than in a bankruptcy of an NV or a BV each creditor whose interests are prejudiced may contest the preferential transaction, but only if the transaction was entered into by the NV or the BV without having any legal obligation to do so and the NV or the BV and the other party to the transaction were aware or should have been aware that the transaction was prejudicial to the interests of the creditors. It is not always clear under which circumstances there is or is not a legal obligation to enter into a transaction. However, a clear example of where there is no legal obligation is the providing of new or additional security for existing indebtedness, while in the underlying documentation there is no obligation to provide such security.[18] In practice it may be difficult for creditors to prove that the other party

17 The *actio pauliana* in a bankruptcy (*faillissementspauliana*) is provided for in the Bankruptcy Code; the *actio pauliana* other than in a bankruptcy in the Civil Code Book 6.

18 See, inter alia, Hoge Raad 10 December 1976/NJ 1977, 617 and Hoge Raad 22 May 1992/NJ 1992,526.

to the transaction was aware or should have been aware that the interests of the creditors were prejudiced. Therefore, by operation of law it is provided that with respect to certain specified transactions (such as the providing of security for indebtedness that is not due) the awareness is deemed to exist with the NV or the BV and the other party, if the transaction was entered into within a (suspect) one-year period prior to the date it is contested. The NV or the BV and the other party should prove that they were not or ought not to have been aware that the transaction was prejudicial to the interests of the creditors. If a transaction is successfully contested it will be avoided, but only as against the creditor contesting the transaction and to the extent required to eliminate the prejudicing effect with respect to such creditor. Any transaction being avoided will not have effect as against third parties acting in good faith.

In a bankruptcy of an NV or a BV preferential transactions may be contested by the receiver in the bankruptcy on behalf of all the creditors of the NV or the BV. The conditions under which the transaction may be contested are similar to the conditions other than in a bankruptcy. Again, a transaction may only be contested if it was entered into without having any legal obligation to do so and the NV or the BV and the other party to the transaction were aware or should have been aware that the transaction was prejudicial to the interests of the creditors. In a bankruptcy the awareness of the NV or the BV and the other party that the transaction was prejudicial to the interests of the creditors, is deemed to exist if the transaction was entered into within a (suspect) one-year period prior to the date of the bankruptcy (again with respect to certain specified transactions only). In case a preferential transaction is successfully contested by the receiver in the bankruptcy of an NV or a BV, the transaction will be avoided without limitation. In addition, in the bankruptcy of an NV or a BV, transactions which are entered into with the legal obligation to do so may also be contested, if the other party at the time the transaction was entered into knew that an application had been made for the bankruptcy of the NV or the BV, or where the transaction is the result of discussions among the NV or the BV and the other party with the purpose to prejudice the other creditors.

Financial assistance

An NV or a BV may not provide financial assistance by issuing a guarantee or providing security for the purpose of the subscription or acquisition by third parties of shares in the share capital of the NV or the BV. A BV may extend loans to third parties for the purpose of the subscription or acquisition of shares in its capital, but only to the extent it has sufficient distributable reserves and if so permitted under its articles of association. Unlike a BV, an NV may not provide financial assistance in the form of extending loans to third parties.[19] Any guarantee issued or security provided in violation of the prohibition to provide financial assistance is null and void. In such case the secured party may have an (unsecured) claim for damages. The prohibition to provide financial assistance extends to subsidiaries of an NV or a BV. It is disputed whether this only applies to subsidiaries incorporated under Netherlands law or also to foreign

19 The prohibition on providing financial assistance is based on the Second EC-Directive on Company Law (Directive 77/91). This Directive only applies to NVs. The application for BVs is more or less voluntarily and, as a result, not as strict as for NVs.

incorporated subsidiaries. The prevailing view is that foreign incorporated subsidiaries are indeed subject to the prohibition to provide financial assistance. As a result, such foreign incorporated subsidiaries would be prevented from providing financial assistance for the purpose of the subscription or acquisition by third parties of shares in the capital of the NV or the BV, even if this would be allowed under the jurisdiction of their incorporation or the jurisdiction in which they are situated.[20] Conversely, it is sometimes argued that NV's and BV's may not provide financial assistance for the purpose of the subscription or acquisition of shares in their foreign incorporated parent company, even if this is allowed under the laws of the jurisdiction under which the parent company is incorporated or situated. This is, however, not the prevailing view.

Threat/fraud/abuse of circumstances/mistake

A transaction which is entered into on the basis of threat (*bedreiging*), fraud (*bedrog*), abuse of circumstances (*misbruik van omstandigheden*) or mistake (*dwaling*) may be avoided. Threat is considered to exist if a person is induced to enter into a transaction under the unlawful threat of personal loss or loss to any property. The threat should be such that a reasonable person would be influenced by it. Fraud is considered to exist if a person is induced to enter into a transaction as a result of the provision of inaccurate information or the concealing of information which should have been disclosed, or as a result of any other artifices. Untrue representations in general terms would as such not constitute fraud. Abuse of circumstances is considered to exist if a person enters into a transaction as a result of special circumstances, such as state of necessity, dependency, wantonness, abnormal mental condition or inexperience and the other party knew or should have known that the transaction was entered into on that basis and that the party to which the special circumstances relate should have been prevented from entering into the transaction. Mistake is considered to exist if (i) the mistake is the result of information volunteered by the other party to the transaction, (ii) the other party should have disclosed the mistake and (iii) both parties to the transaction were under influence of the mistake and the transaction would not have been entered into if there would have been a correct assessment of the subject matter. Avoidance cannot be based on a mistake as to circumstances arising exclusively in the future or if the mistake must be deemed to remain for the account of the party acting under influence of the mistake.

ENFORCEMENT OF FOREIGN GUARANTEES AND SECURITY

Basis of recognition

The Netherlands are a party to the Convention on the Law applicable to Contractual Obligations of 19 June 1980 (the 'Rome Convention').[1] Basically, the Rome Convention

20 On basis of the Second EC-Directive all member states of the European Union have similar prohibitions to provide financial assistance. In other jurisdictions it may be allowed to provide financial assistance.

1 The Rome Convention came into effect in The Netherlands on 1 September 1991.

lays down the existing unwritten principles of Netherlands private international law. The Rome Convention applies irrespective of whether or not the other party to the transaction has its corporate seat or its place of business in a country which is a party to the Rome Convention. On the basis of the Rome Convention the courts of The Netherlands will recognise the choice of a foreign law as the proper law of an agreement, provided such choice of law is made in accordance with the Rome Convention. The Rome Convention provides that, in order to be valid, a choice of law should be expressly made or demonstrated with reasonable certainty by the terms of the agreement or the circumstances of the subject matter. There is no requirement that the law chosen by the parties be connected with the transaction. However, a choice of law will not prejudice the application of the rules of the law of a country which may not be derogated from by contract, if all elements of the transaction are connected with such country only. In the absence of a choice of law the courts of The Netherlands will determine the proper law of an agreement in accordance with the rules of the Rome Convention, which provide that an agreement, in the absence of a choice of law, will be governed by the law of the country with which the transaction is most closely connected. The transaction is deemed to be most closely connected with the country in which the party which is to effect the performance which is characteristic of the agreement has its principal place of business. In applying the Rome Convention the courts of The Netherlands may give effect to the mandatory rules of any country (including The Netherlands) with which the situation has a close connection, if and insofar as under the law of that country those rules must be applied whatever the proper law of an agreement. In considering whether to give effect to the mandatory rules of another country, the nature and purpose of the mandatory rules and the consequences of their application or non-application will be taken into account. Moreover, the law chosen by the parties (or applied on the basis of the Rome Convention) will not be recognised by the courts of The Netherlands to the extent that any of the terms and conditions of the agreement, or any of the provisions of such law, are manifestly incompatible with the public policy of The Netherlands.

The Rome Convention in principle only applies to agreements made by an NV or a BV and the contractual relations resulting therefrom. The Rome Convention does not apply to security and the effect as against third parties (including creditors and the receiver in a bankruptcy or the administrator in a suspension of payments of an NV or a BV). The question as to how valid security over assets is to be created should under Netherlands private international law be determined in accordance with the *lex rei sitae*, ie the law of the country where the assets are situated at the time of the creation of the security. This means that security over immovable property and movable property situated in The Netherlands is to be created in accordance with Netherlands law.[2] Similarly, security over Netherlands registered ships and aircraft should be created in accordance with Netherlands law. As the *situs* of claims (other than claims to bearer or order) cannot be easily determined, there used to be much confusion in accordance with which law security over such claims should be created so as to have effect as against third parties. It was sometimes argued that security over claims would have to be created in accordance with the law governing such claims (*vorderingsstatuut*). Conversely, it was sometimes argued that security over claims would have to be created

2 The General Provisions Act (*Wet algemene bepalingen*) s7 provides that immovable property is governed by the law of the country where such immovable property is situated. This *lex rei sitae*-rule has been construed as to extend to movable property.

in accordance with the law of the relevant security agreement (*cessiestatuut*) so that the parties would effectively be free to choose the law which would govern the security. To avoid uncertainty as to whether valid security over registered claims is created, it was considered that such security should be created in accordance with all the laws with which the security and/or the claims have a connection, ie (i) the law governing the claims, (ii) the law of the country where the party giving security has its corporate seat or principal place of business, (iii) the law of the country where the secured party has its corporate seat or principal place of business, (iv) the law of the country where the debtor of the claims has its corporate seat or its principal place of business and (v) the law governing the security agreement. Obviously, this was very impractical and in a landmark judgment the Supreme Court of The Netherlands made an end to the debate.[3] Surprisingly, the Supreme Court recognised a German law security assignment by a Netherlands assignor to a German assignee over claims governed by Netherlands law. On this basis it is held that in international situations (ie the assignor and assignee being situated in different jurisdictions) security may be created in accordance with the proper law of the security agreement so as to have effect as against third parties. Any such effect is, however, subject to the Rome Convention Section 12, Sub-Section 2, in that whether the claims are assignable should be ascertained in accordance with the law governing the claims. In addition, the law governing the claims is relevant with respect to the relationship between the assignor and the assignee, any defences which are available to the debtor and whether the debtor validly discharged its obligations. In The Netherlands doubt has been expressed whether the above principle would equally apply to security interests other than security assignments (eg a charge or a pledge) where the decision of the Supreme Court of The Netherlands is very much based on the Rome Convention which only refers to assignments (and not to other security interests). It is, however, the prevailing view that other security interests may also be governed by the proper law of the security agreement. It is doubted whether in purely Netherlands situations it would be possible to make use of this solution by simply creating the security in favour of a secured party situated outside The Netherlands. Generally, it is felt that this is not possible and that in such case the security will have to be created in accordance with Netherlands law. Under Netherlands private international law security over claims to bearer or order should be created in accordance with laws of the country in which the bearer or order documents are situated.

Foreign security interests

Under Netherlands private international law security over immovable property and movable property situated outside The Netherlands should be created in accordance with the laws of the country in which the assets are situated. In case of proceedings in the courts of The Netherlands with respect to the creation, enforcement or priority of security which is governed by foreign law (eg because the assets after the date of the giving of security have been moved from a foreign country to The Netherlands), such security would be upheld as valid, binding and enforceable provided that the security (i) is valid, binding and enforceable under the foreign law, (ii) fits into the system of the creation, enforcement and priority of security under Netherlands law and (iii) does not

3 See Hoge Raad 16 May 1997/NJ 1998, 585.

conflict with Netherlands public policy. If foreign security is upheld as valid, binding and enforceable it would have the same priority as comparable Netherlands security. Although there is no certainty in this respect the same recognition principles would seem to apply with respect to the recognition of foreign security interests over claims on the basis of foreign law security agreements. The enforcement of foreign security in The Netherlands should take place in accordance with Netherlands law. Foreign security in foreign registered aircraft is subject to the provisions of the Convention on the International Recognition of Rights in Aircraft of 19 June 1948 (the 'Geneva Convention').

Enforcement of foreign judgments

Unless a treaty provides otherwise, a foreign judgment against an NV or a BV will not be automatically enforceable in The Netherlands and, in the absence of applicable treaty provisions, it will be necessary to bring the matter and re-litigate the same before the courts of The Netherlands which may give such effect to a foreign judgment as they deem appropriate. However, a final foreign judgment for the payment of money which is not rendered by default and is not subject to appeal or any other means of contestation and is enforceable in the country in which it is rendered, would generally be upheld and be regarded by the courts of The Netherlands as conclusive evidence when asked to render a judgment in accordance with such final foreign judgment. The courts of The Netherlands will not re-examine or re-litigate the merits of the foreign judgment, provided judgment has been rendered by a foreign court of competent jurisdiction, in accordance with rules of proper procedure and has not been rendered in proceedings of a penal or fiscal nature and its content and possible enforcement are not contrary to Netherlands public policy. Final judgments for the payment of money rendered by a court of a country which is a party to the Convention on Jurisdiction and Enforcement of Judgments in Civil and Commercial Matters of 27 September 1986 (as amended) (the 'Brussels Convention') or the Convention on Jurisdiction and Enforcement of Judgments in Civil and Commercial Matters of 16 September 1998 (the 'Lugano Convention') will be recognised by the courts of The Netherlands, subject to the relevant rules and regulations promulgated pursuant to the Brussels Convention and the Lugano Convention.[4] The Netherlands are a party to the Convention on Enforcement and Recognition of Arbitral Awards of 10 June 1958 (the 'New York Convention'). Final arbitral awards against an NV or a BV for the payment of money issued by an arbitration panel situated in a country which is a party to the New York Convention will be recognised by the courts of The Netherlands, subject to the provisions and the relevant rules and regulations promulgated pursuant to the New York Convention. The enforcement of foreign judgments and foreign arbitral awards in The Netherlands is subject to the Netherlands rules of civil procedure as applied by the courts of The Netherlands.

4 The Brussels Convention came into effect in The Netherlands in 1973; the Lugano Convention in 1992.

Foreign insolvency procedures

In the absence of applicable treaty provisions, foreign insolvency procedures would in principle not be recognised in The Netherlands. Except for a treaty with Belgium, The Netherlands are not a party to any treaty with respect to the recognition of foreign insolvency procedures. Conversely, the scope of Netherlands bankruptcy law is not limited to The Netherlands. However, it is doubtful whether foreign courts would apply the principles of Netherlands bankruptcy law with respect to assets which are situated within their jurisdiction.

9 Spain

Francisco G Prol

Prol & Asociados

INTRODUCTION

In Spain the legal regime regulating guarantees has evolved fundamentally as a consequence of the changes undergone by the commercial and financial world, where guarantees play an important role.

Thus, the early guarantees regulated under the Civil Code, the Commercial Code and the Mortgage Act now co-exist with new guarantees (some of them are not expressly mentioned in the legislation). They form a whole that endows trading with greater security, allowing borrowers to obtain funds under more beneficial conditions.

In Spain guarantees are issued for the following purposes:

1 to secure the fulfilment of an obligation;
2 to secure a creditor or group of creditors in the event of the debtor's insolvency; and
3 to secure preferential collection of some debts in certain insolvency situations.

Guarantees are not the only measures to be taken to force a debtor to comply with his obligations in such a manner that any default could have very serious consequences.

In particular, we should refer to the penalty clause under which, if the debtor does not comply with his principal obligation, he will have to pay a fine or fixed amount under a penalty clause. Though there are some Spanish authors who regard such a clause as a kind of guarantee, it seems more reasonable to side with those who view it as a sanction or punishment.

Concept

The guarantee consists of two basic elements: the 'debt' (either the payment of an amount of money or the obligation to perform an action); and the liability or obligation to bear the consequences of the main obligor's default.

Given that the 'debt' is established in each individual case, we are left with the concept of liability, which we consider here.

In this respect, Spanish law embraces the principle of debtor's total estate responsibility (*responsabilidad patrimonial universal*). Thus, the Spanish Civil Code s 1911 provides that:

> 'The creditor has recourse to all the debtors assets both present and future for the discharge of the debtors liabilities.'

As stated above, the debtor is bound to comply with his obligations irrespective of whether a guarantee has been agreed or not. What is the point, then, of entering into a guarantee agreement, commonly signed in commercial agreements if, pursuant to the principle mentioned above, the creditor has recourse to all the debtor's assets anyway? The answer to this question lies in the purposes of a guarantee which are as follows:

1. it gives the creditor priority ahead of any other creditor who has not agreed a guarantee;
2. it may be enforceable in relation to specific assets of the debtor;
3. it does not apply to all creditors but only to the one in whose favour it has been issued; and
4. sometimes, it does not become extinguished even when the ownership of the assets attached to it passes from the debtor to a third party.

In addition, the issuance of a guarantee securing a third party's obligations makes the debtor-creditor relationship linked to a third party who will not be bound (at least in such debtor-creditor relationship) by the principle of the total estate liability mentioned above.

Under Spanish law, therefore, a guarantee may be defined, albeit broadly, as

> 'any means to secure the fulfilment of an obligation or the enjoyment of a right' [1]

This definition also illustrates one of the main features of guarantees, which is their collateral nature. Indeed, guarantees are constituted to secure the fulfilment of an underlying obligation and are therefore collateral agreements and ancillary to a principal agreement. A guarantee does not create additional rights (other than those under the principal agreement) for the beneficiary, but merely gives him greater certainty that the obligation guaranteed will be properly performed, increases his priority over other creditors and reinforces his right to fulfilment of the obligation guaranteed.

Elements of a guarantee agreement

The elements forming guarantee agreements may be categorised as personal, real and formal.

Personal elements

The parties here are the guarantor (the person who issues the guarantee), the beneficiary (the person in whose favour the guarantee is issued) and the debtor (the person who is bound to perform certain actions).

1 Mr Guilarte Zapatero (comments on the Civil Code).

Those with the legal capacity required to execute agreements will be able to fulfill any of the roles mentioned above. However, there are certain details that need to be discussed with respect to the special regime of guarantees.

1 In the case of mortgages the representative of a mortgagor needs to be authorised not only to issue a guarantee over certain assets but also to dispose of the mortgaged asset.
2 When a guarantee is to secure a third party's obligation, representatives of companies issuing such a guarantee are usually required to be expressly authorised by the general meeting of shareholders for such companies to be bound.[2]

Real elements

These elements are based on the guarantor's undertaking.

For the differences between personal guarantees and guarantees in rem we refer to 'Types of guarantees' below.

In any case, it suffices to say that the guarantor is bound (under the terms of the guarantee agreement) to comply with the debtors obligations if such debtor fails to do so.

Any obligations, either of a pecuniary or performing nature, other than strictly personal obligations (which can only be fulfilled by a specific obligor, such as a painting painted by a certain artist) may be guaranteed.

Formal elements

Under the Spanish Civil Code the general principle is that there are no special requirements in terms of the form of agreement. However, in the guarantees field there are many exceptions to this freedom of form principle.

Thus, for instance, the Civil Code s 1827 clearly provides that the guarantee or *fianza* cannot be implicitly inferred but must be explicitly stated. It therefore must be in writing. The fact that this guarantee has to be expressly issued should not prevent agreement from being proved through means other than a public deed, such as electronic means.

Likewise, real estate mortgages, naval mortgages, chattel mortgages and, in general, all those guarantees required to be registered with a public registry, will need not only to be in writing but to be constituted in a public instrument formalised before a public notary.[3]

Types of guarantees

Spanish authors divide guarantees into two main groups: in rem (real guarantees) and personal guarantees.

1 An in rem guarantee attaches to a specific asset of the debtor in order to secure the obligor's fulfilment of a certain obligation (giving the beneficiary privileged treatment of his debt in priority to the other creditors when it comes to enforcing

2 It is worth mentioning that Spanish legislation allows the issuance of guarantees securing not only the guarantor's debts but those of a third party.

3 Sometimes before an official stock exchange broker.

the guarantee). The mortgage in its several forms – real estate, naval, chattel, etc – can be referred to as an example of this kind of guarantees.

2 Unlike those in rem guarantees, personal guarantees do not link an asset to the compliance of an obligation, yet the beneficiary of such a guarantee may always seek to have the guarantee enforced against the guarantor's property though holding no privilege over any particular asset. The *fianza* and the first call guarantee are examples of this type of guarantee.

International private law rules and special regional systems

The principle of free will present in the Spanish legal system also applies to guarantees. Hence, Spanish legislation[4] allows the parties to a guarantee agreement to choose the law governing this special contractual relationship.

Whereas this principle seems to be applicable to personal guarantees with no special legal issues arising, its application to in rem guarantees may clash with that provided in section 10, 1° of the Civil Code which states that the law governing in rem rights over movables and immovables is the law in force in the place where such assets are located ('lex rei sitae'). Thus, where there is a conflict because, for instance, the parties have chosen a governing law different from that of the place of location, the prevailing law must be thoroughly determined since, for instance, the validity of mortgages in Spain must be registered with the Land Registry and this essential requirement may not be necessary under other jurisdictions.

As for jurisdiction, Spanish law[5] allows the parties to bound by a specific jurisdiction which must be expressly stated. However, section 63, 3° of the Rules of Civil Law Procedure establishes that the court competent to rule on guarantee conflicts will be that which is also dealing with the underlying claim. Furthermore, section 1.828 of the Civil Code provides that the guarantor will be bound by the court with jurisdiction over the place where the obligation has to be fulfilled. If on top of the above we mention that section 22, 1° of the Law of the Judiciary (*Ley Orgánica del Poder Judicial*) provides that Spanish Judges and Courts have jurisdiction in respect of matters relating to real rights over immovables located in Spain (which may affect mortgages) we may notice the complexity of trying to give a general rule. Therefore, the advice would be to submit to the jurisdiction of Spanish Courts if there is the slightest possibility that a guarantee has to be enforced in Spain and, in all cases where there are real guarantees charging assets located in Spain.

One should not overlook the fact that in Spain there are several systems regulating private legal relationships. Hence some regions, such as Catalonia, the Balearic Islands, Aragon, the Basque Country, Calicia and Navarra have their own provisions governing marriage settlements and inheritance.

Some of them also have special provisions relating to guarantees. There are particularities that are worth mentioning because of their likely relevance in commercial relationships; thus, for instance the Compilation of Navarra (embodying the provisions of its own Private Law) includes a special provision of the *fianza* that covers a matter

4 Section 10, 5° of the Civil Code and section 3 of Rome Convention, dated 19 June 1980.
5 Section 56 of the Rules of Civil Law Procedure.

such as the 'promise of *fianza*' (unknown in the Spanish Common Law) and the prohibition that guarantors act as lawyers in actions involving *fianza* issued by them.

Likewise, the Act on Possessive Guarantees over Movables of Catalonia[6] providing for the pledge on rights establishes, for instance, that if the pledge charges an amount of money or instruments representing money the creditor may take possession of them without having an auction, provided the amount claimed is liquid and due and the debtor is duly informed.

The guarantee and insolvency law

When we referred to the formal aspects of guarantees above we mentioned that some of them are required to be constituted by public instrument to the purpose of being registered with the relevant registry. Now we are to refer to a series of cases where it is advisable to fulfill these formalities even though the guarantees do not usually need to be issued by way of public deed.

Such is the case where the debtor of a secured obligation becomes bankrupt. For this situation Spanish law provides for a list of priorities pursuant to which the outstanding debts will be repaid and, it also provides for the possibility of withdrawing certain privileged debts from the bankrupt estate. Amongst these debts qualified for such detachment are the rights of in rem guarantees which confer on their holders the possibility of joint enforcement, and such qualified creditors are entitled to obtain the payment of their debts with the proceeds resulting from such enforcement.

Therefore, this right enabling a creditor to enforce a guarantee against the assets charged with it comes together with other advantages that Spanish law gives to agreements formalised in public instruments, including (i) the certainty on the date of payment, and (ii) the possibility of using bankruptcy proceedings, which are quicker and are more likely to result in seizure of the debtor's property.

Under a situation of '*suspension de pagos*' (similar to receivership) the holders of in rem guarantees that have been formalised in a public instrument enjoy the privilege of not being bound by any creditors' composition that might be agreed between the debtor and his creditors.[7]

Foreign investments

In recent years Spanish legislation on exchange control has undergone significant changes, moving towards almost complete liberalisation.

A good example of this liberalising tendency is that a foreigner nowadays has the legal capacity to be the beneficiary of a guarantee (personal or in rem) securing the fulfilment of obligations. Some years ago, this capacity was conditional on the prior authorisation by the exchange control authorities if the enforcement of the guarantee involved the outflow of funds from Spain.

This has been completely liberalised and guarantees can be issued in favour of non residents without having to obtain any authorisation, the only requirement is the

6 22/1991 Act dated 29 November, of the Government of Catalonia.
7 Section 22 of the Act on 'receivership' and sections 1922 and 1923 of the Civil Code.

notification to the Spanish Central Bank of the outflow of funds (which will be done by the entity in charge of transferring the funds).

Now that we have outlined the general aspects of guarantee agreements, we will address in detail the different kinds of guarantees existing within the Spanish Legal System.

PERSONAL GUARANTEES

As mentioned above, personal guarantees are those that do not link specific assets to the fulfilment of the underlying obligation, since the creditor will have recourse to all the debtors assets. The beneficiary will not be vested with rights over a particular asset.

Set out below are the most frequent types of personal guarantees that can be found in Spain.

Fianza (bond)

A '*fianza*' is a guarantee under which the *fiador* (guarantor) undertakes to fulfil the payment obligation of a third party (principal debtor) if the latter defaults on his obligation. Under the '*fianza*', the guarantor undertakes an obligation distinct from that of the principal debtor, yet it is collateral and ancillary in respect of principal underlying obligation.

These collateral and ancillary elements have been recognised by the doctrine of the Spanish Supreme Court.[8] Thus, the ancillary character means that the *fianza* enjoys the same fate as the underlying obligation and *fianza* cannot be created or subsist without a valid underlying obligation.

Its auxiliary nature is also mirrored in the fact that the *fianza* can not contain terms more burdensome than those in the principal agreement.

If the parties expressly decided to deprive the *fianza* of its accessory character, then we would be faced with another type of guarantee. The 'on demand' guarantee.

The collateral nature is another of its essential features, the guarantor will only be bound to comply with his obligation if the principal debtor defaults on his obligation. Nevertheless, it is worth noting that in the case of a joint and several *fianza*, the creditor of the principal obligation could seek payment directly from the guarantor, leaving the principal debtor aside, in which case the collateral nature of this guarantee would cease to exist.

Another important item to be highlighted is the fact that the *fianza* must be expressly granted (it cannot be presumed or implicit).

This guarantee can be (i) granted without consideration, (ii) granted for a fixed period, (iii) granted in favour not only of the principal debtor but also of another surety and, even, (iv) securing future obligations (which have to be identifiable and not requiring a new declaration of the guarantor and the creditor). As for a *fianza* securing future obligations, it will not be enforceable until the debt is ascertainable.

If on debtor's default the guarantor has to pay the principal obligation, he will become subrogated to the creditor's interests. Conversely, if for reasons caused by

8 Decisions of the Supreme Court of 17 February 1962; 2 June 1976; 2 October 1990 and 15 April 1991.

the creditor such subrogation is prevented, the guarantor will be released from his obligation.

It is important to note that the ancillary nature of this guarantee, collateral to a principal obligation, means that the guarantor will be answerable for the payment of the debt only after the creditor's unsuccessful attempt to settle his credit against the debtor's property, provided that the guarantor had raised this at the moment he was called on for payment. This right will not arise if (a) the guarantor has expressly waived such right; (b) the guarantor is jointly and severally liable alongside the debtor; (c) the debtor is insolvent or bankrupt; or (d) the debtor cannot be sued within the Spanish Kingdom. The guarantor is entitled to raise any objections with the creditor relating to the principal debtor and inherent in the debt, but only those which are exclusive to the debtor. Furthermore, if the guarantor made the payment without advising the debtor, the latter will be entitled to raise any objections with the guarantor which he could have raised with the creditor at the time of payment.

Once the payment obligation has been fulfilled by the guarantor, and on notification of such payment, the debtor must repay the guarantor the amount of the debt so paid, including all the legal interests, expenses and damages the guarantor may have incurred.

Under certain circumstances, Spanish law allows the guarantor – even if he has not made payment – to take legal action against the principal debtor, for example in those cases where the guarantor is faced with legal action relating to the payment obligation or when the debtor is declared bankrupt or there is an ongoing insolvency process.

The *fianza* becomes extinguished at the same time as the debtor's obligation and for the same reasons as other obligations (like offsetting, abatement, etc). It also extinguishes if the creditor allows the debtor an extension of the maturity date without the consent of the guarantor.

Aval

Over the years this term has been wrongly used to refer to suretyship in general, despite the fact that under Spanish law[9] *Aval* should refer only to those *fianzas* issued on negotiable instruments, such as bills of exchange, cheques and promissory notes.

Consequently, we should point out that the *Aval* secures, the partial or total payment of a negotiable instrument. It can be issued by any person already signatory of such instruments or by a third party with no interests in it.

The *Aval* may be issued for a specific period, even after the maturity date of the relevant instrument when its payment has been rejected, provided that at the time of issuance the debtor had not yet been released from his obligation (as it would be the case if, for instance, the holder of a bill of exchange had not called for payment at the proper time).

This guarantee must be written on the relevant instrument or on its supplement – otherwise it will lack effectiveness – and must be expressed by the word '*aval*' or any other equivalent and signed by the guarantor ('*avalista*'). In this respect, any signature stamped on the reverse of the instrument will make the signatory bound and liable for the *Aval*, provided that such signature is not the drawer's or drawee's.

9 19/1985 Act of 16 July on Bill of Exchange and Cheque (*Ley Cambiaria y del Cheque*).

Where a guarantee does not expressly mention the person whose obligation is being secured (the creditor), depending on the kind of instrument involved such person will be assumed to be (i) the drawee of a bill of exchange who, in signing the instrument, has undertaken the payment of the bill on its maturity date; (ii) the drawer of a bill of exchange, in the absence of a drawee; (ii) the signatory of a promissory note; and (iv) the drawer of a cheque.

The guarantor is jointly and severally liable along with the other obligor and to the same extent as the debtor, and is not entitled to raise objections to payment which relate exclusively to the debtor's rights. The *Aval* will be effective even if the secured obligation were declared null and void for any cause other than the infringement of an essential procedural requirement.

In fulfilling the payment obligation, the guarantor acquires those rights attached to the negotiable instrument, which he may enforce against the principal debtor and those who are answerable to the latter. Thus, the guarantor may take action either on an individual or collective basis, without being compelled to follow the order in which the obligors have bound themselves. Furthermore, the action against one of the obligors does not prevent the guarantor from subsequently suing the others, regardless of whether they had become liable at a later date.

Comfort letters

Firstly, it may be useful to point out the essential requirements that must be met for the existence of a comfort letter, which are the following:

1 a statement acknowledging the financial obligation, and
2 details of the holding of a stake in the beneficiary company without the parent company undertaking payment obligations.

Comfort letters may take different forms, amongst which are the following:

1 A statement of participation, where the signatory states his participation in the capital of the company that is applying for a bank loan.
2 A statement of continuing participation, where the parent company undertakes to continue with the participation.
3 A statement of a general policy, containing a declaration of business policy followed by the parent company and its subsidiaries, without any commitment whatsoever.
4 A statement on the situation of the subsidiary with respect to the performance of its obligations and reimbursement of the loan granted, expressing the opinion that the subsidiary is in a position to fulfil its commitments or, even, undertaking to safeguard the subsidiary's preservation of its capability to meet its obligations.
5 A statement of solvency, where the parent company undertakes to help the subsidiary to stay in a solvent situation that enables such subsidiary to fulfil its obligations.
6 A statement of preserving the capital and/or ownership, where the parent company undertakes to maintain a certain level of capital and/or ownership.
7 A statement of fulfilment, where the parent company expressly undertakes that the debt will be reimbursed. This is not easily differentiated from the common forms of guarantee.

Comfort Letters are not regulated under Spanish law and there is almost no case law on this subject, apart from the Supreme Court decision of 16 December 1985 which makes distinctions between declaratory letters and letters containing undertakings and admits the legal effectiveness of comfort letters when they contain undertakings, conferring on them a mere moral obligation when they do not contain undertakings but mere declarations of facts or opinions.

This decision refers to the essential problem that comfort letters represent for the Spanish law, which is the determination of their judicial or extrajudicial nature or, in other words, to resolve whether such comfort letters create an authentic legal bond between the recipient and thc signatory company or if such letters do merely give rise to a moral bond.

Under Spanish law there are no general rules to solve this question, a separate study of each particular case is necessary.

Consequently, where a comfort letter is to be used in an operation subject to Spanish law, it is advisable that such letter be drafted in such a way that clearly involves the assumption of a legal commitment, given that if it only declares a series of facts or intentions, such as the ownership of a subsidiary, its legal effectiveness may be contested.

Finally, it is worth noting that the fact of concluding that a comfort letter does not contain legal obligations does not make the comfort letter irrelevant in legal terms. Under Spanish law such comfort letters may be legally relevant either on the basis of a natural obligation or from the scope of the extracontractual liability or from the principles of good faith and ultra vires.

On demand guarantees

The guarantee on first demand is defined as a guarantee 'where the payment is conditional only upon the mere demand of payment made by the beneficiary (creditor) in writing'. This kind of guarantee intends to confer full autonomy from the principal obligation so as to be enforced and paid without the beneficiary being required to prove the secured debtor's default.

This guarantee is not regulated under Spanish law. Both the Civil Code (ss 1882 to 1856) and the Commercial Code (ss 439 to 442) refer to the *fianza* and provide for a contract where the ancillary character is one of the essential features.

In studying this matter, the Spanish doctrine evaluates the advantages of this kind of guarantee compared to the *fianza*. Thus, for instance (i) on demand guarantees may exist without a valid obligation (contrary to that provided by section 1824 of the Civil Code); (ii) the grantor may bind himself beyond the limits set for both the amount and the terms of the principal obligation (contrary to section 1826 of the Civil Code); (iii) the guarantor may not raise those objections which relate to the principal debtor and are intrinsic to the debtor personally; etc.

The doctrine deems that this is an unusual agreement whose legitimacy comes from the principle of contractual freedom – provided such contracts are not contrary to those provided for in Section 1255 of the Civil Code – and its execution implies the existence of an underlying agreement whose fulfilment is secured. The bargaining power of the parties concerned and the intention of the parties are the most important factors in establishing the scope of this kind of agreement. In this respect, if the free will of the parties clearly shows their intention to agree an autonomous guarantee agreement, all those requirements in the Civil Code in relation to the *fianza* providing for the ancillary nature of the guarantors obligations with respect to the underlying obligation must be excluded.

Existing case law is not clear and conclusive on this matter. However, despite the fact that most recent decisions of the Supreme Court agree with the possibility that this on demand guarantee may exist, they have not conclusively ruled on their validity. From certain decisions (21 April and 14 November 1989) one may assume that the Supreme Court is not absolutely opposed to recognising guarantees apart from the *fianza*, yet the special feature to which both decisions refer (an insurance relationship) gives rise to problems when it comes to making analogies with common commercial relationships.

The decision of 27 October 1992 helped to clarify the issue but not in a conclusive manner. The Supreme Court admits here that based on the free will of the parties (s 1255 of the Civil Code) there may be certain types of guarantees distinct from the *fianza*, given that the latter does not satisfy all the needs of commercial transactions. On the other hand, the Court recognises that it cannot allow further defences to payment of the guarantee other than those arising from the guarantee agreement itself or permit a reversal of the burden of proof which now lies on the guarantor, who must contest the payment of the guarantee by giving enough evidence that the payment demand is inappropriate or fraudulent.

Summarising, we may say that the Supreme Court is moving towards recognising this kind of guarantee, though the existing case law is not enough to clearly and conclusively assert that it recognises these guarantees without reservation.

Procedural aspects

In Spain there are two kinds of proceedings for debt collection, declaratory proceedings and enforcement proceedings. The declaratory proceeding is the common one whereas the enforcement proceeding is more unusual since the obligation claimed must be evidenced in any of the following instruments: (i) a public deed formalised before a Notary Public, (2) commercial agreements signed by the parties and by registered stockbrokers or (iii) bills of exchange, cheques or promissory notes.

Unlike the declaratory proceedings, the enforcement proceedings take less time to be completed and limit the objections that the debtor may raise. From a practical point of view the enforcement proceedings allow seizure of the debtor's property at the time he is notified of the claim, whereas through the declaratory proceedings, normally, the seizure takes place upon judgment.

Personal guarantees may be enforced through one proceeding or the other, depending on whether or not the guarantee instrument gives rise to a right to enforcement proceedings.

As for procedural essentials we may note the following:

- both the Civil Code and the Law of Procedure establish that the jurisdiction for actions relating to personal guarantee obligations corresponds to the Court competent to deal with the underlying obligation:
- in declaratory proceedings: the claim may be addressed to both the principal obligor and the guarantor;

- in enforcement proceedings: if the instrument containing the obligation is a policy or a public deed delivered by credit entities, the guarantor must be notified in advance of the amount claimed;
- in enforcement proceedings: if the relevant instrument is either a bill of exchange, a cheque or a promissory note and the action is brought against the drawee and his guarantor a protest declaration is not required; when the action is against the endorser, the drawee and his guarantors the declaration that the bill has not been paid (recorded on or attached to the instrument itself) will be an essential requirement, except if in the document itself it has been agreed otherwise; finally, the guarantor's responsibility is joint and several with the guaranteed.

'IN REM' GUARANTEES

As has been previously mentioned, the 'in rem' guarantees are those which attach a specific asset to the fulfilment of a particular obligation.

There are two types of 'in rem' guarantees:

1 Those where the attached asset is a movable (the different kinds of pledges).
2 Those where the attached asset is an immovable asset (usually real estate).

Guarantees on movables

Let us broadly describe the general characteristics of the pledge (*prenda*) and then set out the most well known types of pledge in more detail.

The *Prenda* (pledge) is a real guarantee aimed at securing the fulfilment of a principal obligation – once again we note its ancillary nature – of the person whose property is being pledged. The assets charged by the *prenda* must be tradable movables and possession must be freely held. Besides, it should be noted that the *pignorante* (pledgor) does not need to be the debtor of the principal obligation.

Other essential characteristics of the *prenda* are, on the one hand, the transfer of the possession of the movable property pledged – which is transferred to the creditor or to a third party designated by mutual consent – and on the other hand, its individuality – ie the partial fulfilment of an obligation will not result in the release of the pledged assets, except if the pledge is given over several assets where each of them is securing only an specific part of the credit.

The object of this guarantee is that, in case the debtor defaults on his obligation, the *acreedor pignoraticio* (pledgee) may seek the sale of the pledged assets in a public auction and, thus, recover the value of his credit. The beneficiary of the pledge does not become the owner of the pledged asset in case of non-fulfilment, the only right he holds as beneficiary is to seek the sale of the pledged assets and discharge his credit with the proceeds of the sale. Hence, another essential feature of this guarantee is that concerned with tradable assets that will be subject to a sale following the maturity of the principal obligation.

In order to be effective vis-à-vis third parties, a pledge must be formalised in a public deed. Besides, this formalisation gives the beneficiary the right to bring separate enforcement proceedings if the debtor becomes bankrupt.

Pledge on merchandise

In this part we will address the granting of pledges over merchandise where possession is not held by the owner since they are in the course of carriage or deposited either at *Almacenes Generales de Depósitos* (special public warehouses meeting a series of legal requirements and duly authorised) or other entities related to them. To be more precise, we will refer to the pledge constituted over documents representing such merchandise (documents of title ('titulos de tradición')).

These title docuements confer on their legitimate holder the right to have the documented merchandise delivered and to dispose of such merchandise by negotiating the title. The charge over the title document entails the direct charge on the merchandise. Therefore, the pledge right lies in the merchandise itself but it is issued over the title representing it.

The most common documents representing merchandise are deposit receipts and Bills of Lading.

Deposit receipts; warrants

The legally incorporated and authorised warehouses will issue receipts for the merchandise stored. These receipts are transferable either by endorsement or by way of other instrument which may be drawn in favour of a named party or to bearer. Such receipts are required to specify the kind of merchandise with details of the number or amount of merchandise that they represent.

The creation of the pledge requires that documents of title be delivered to the creditor. In this respect, if such documents of titles are in bearer form it will suffice to hand them over to the creditor at the moment of constituting the pledge, recording their numbers in the agreement entered into for this purpose; if the documents of title are to order instruments, the guarantee will be charged by the endorsement of such documents of title; and if the documents of title are in favour of a named party the creation of the pledge must be notified to the issuer so as to enable the new creditor (pledgee) to enforce such pledge.

If the debtor defaults, the creditor (pledgee) may instruct the warehouse to sell sufficient quantity of the merchandise to meet the payment of the debt, as he is in a preferential position as against other debts, except for those debts derived from the transport, storage and maintenance of the merchandise deposited.

The Royal Decree of 22 September 1917 introduces a method that substantially simplifies the creation of the pledge. The title or receipt issued by these warehouses is made up of three parts, namely, a master copy or matrix which will always be held by the warehouse, a deposit receipt that constitutes a legitimate transfer of title to the property of the deposited merchandise and a guarantee receipt or warrant the transfer of which gives rise to a pledge on the deposited goods in favour of the holder of the document.

In short, the endorsement or transfer of the deposit receipt transfers the ownership of the merchandise whereas the endorsement or transfer of the warrant pledges such merchandise in favour of the person specified in the endorsement.

Once the pledge has been created and both parts of the title or receipt are detached, neither of them permits the total disposal of the deposited merchandise. Indeed, the holder of a deposit receipt alone cannot demand the return of the merchandise from the depository (the warehouse) if he has not satisfied the credit secured, payment of which is evidenced only if he also holds the warrant. In turn the holder of a warrant, as pledgee, cannot demand the return of the merchandise from the depository either, he can only seek in due course a forced sale of them for the payment of the debt.

The creation of a pledge by endorsement of a warrant needs to meet a series of requirements as provided by Spanish law. Thus, the endorsement must contain (i) the principal amount of the credit, (ii) the interest agreed, (iii) the maturity date which cannot be later than that set for the termination of the deposit and (iv) the place agreed for payment. The endorsement must be signed by the debtor and the creditor.

Pledges are recorded on deposit receipts, which have to meet the same requirements as above. Both the deposit receipt and the warrant must include mention that the pledge has been registered on the books of the depository entity and on the master copy.

On maturity of the obligation secured the holder of the warrant will be entitled to demand from the depository entity the sale of the goods recorded in the warrant, for the discharge of the debt owed after discount of the storage and maintenance charges and of those arising from the sale. The remainder, if any, will be in the depository's custody at the disposal of the holder of the deposit receipt.

Bill of lading

Since this kind of instrument can be drawn either to bearer, to order or a named party, in issuing a pledge it will be necessary to deliver the documents of title to the creditor and also (i) an endorsement with guaranteeing purposes if the documents of title are 'to order' or (ii) a detailed specification of such documents of title in the pledge agreement if they are drawn to bearer or (iii) a detailed description of the documents of title in the pledge agreement and notification of such pledge to the issuer of the documents of title when they are in favour of a named party.

Banks are the creditors that most usually accept pledges on these documents to secure the documentary credits they make available. In practice, these documents are not really pledged but rather delivered to the relevant bank which keeps them until the debt secured has been fully paid up. Should the debtor default on reimbursement, the bank will exercise its right of disposal that characterises this kind of documents, recovering the amount of its debt with the price obtained from the sale of the merchandise involved.

Pledge on securities

Shares of non-listed companies

Since shares are movable and tradable assets, they are capable of being pledged. Notwithstanding this, we should point out that section 62 of the Companies Act forbids the transfer of shares before their registration with the Commercial Registry or before the relevant resolution of capital increase has been registered. Consistently, doctrine and case law regard shares as being outside commerce and, consequently, incapable of being pledged, so long as the deed creating them is not registered with the Commercial Registry.

Likewise, it is worth noticing that a company can only accept a pledge on its own shares or on those issued by its parent company,[10] within the same limits and requirements as those applying to the purchase of its own shares. That is, (1) that the General Meeting of Shareholders has passed resolution authorising it to do so, (2) that the aggregate of the face value of the shares pledged added to the value of those already pledged does not account for more than 10% of the entire share capital, (3) that a captive reserve may be created without the pledge resulting either in a reduction of the share capital or in a reduction in the captive statutory reserve and (4) that such shares be fully paid up.

Now we should differentiate those shares represented by physical instruments from those represented by book entries.

Shares represented by printed and delivered certificates

A pledge on bearer shares must meet the requirements above mentioned, whereas a pledge on registered shares can be charged by way of endorsement – expressly noting the words 'share given in guarantee' or any other similar expression – being such pledge recorded in the book of registered shares of the company.

As regards this pledge by endorsement, the same procedure will apply – by analogy – as that provided for by the law for transfers of shares by endorsement,[11] ie (i) the endorser must place his signature on the instrument or on its supplement, (ii) an endorsement crossed out will be regarded as void, (iii) it will not be valid to use a multiple instrument representing several shares to endorse in guarantee only a part of such shares – partial endorsement is null and void – and (iv) the endorsement should be placed on the instrument itself rather than on provisional vouchers.

Shares represented by instruments which have neither been printed nor delivered

Given that the shares do not exist physically, the pledge would be constituted on rights. This is not provided for by Spanish law but is accepted in practice.

As regards registered shares, the transfer of their possession (which is an essential requirement of the pledge as already indicated) will be inferred from the notification of such pledge to the issuer of the affected shares. Upon notification the company concerned will record such transfer in its book of registered shares.

Unlike the case above, companies do not keep registers for bearer shares, so any changes or charges relating to these shares cannot be recorded. Some authors deem that companies should hold a register where any notification relating to transfers or creation of real rights over bearer shares may be recorded.

10 Parent Company is that which may stand in any of the following positions:
- a hold the majority of voting shares,
- b hold the power to appoint or remove the majority of the Board of Directors,
- c control the majority of the voting rights pursuant to an agreement with the other shareholders,
- d the majority of the members of the Board who are serving office at the time of submitting the annual accounts report and during the two previous financial years has been exclusively appointed with the voting rights of such company.

11 Section 56 of the Companies Act, which refers to ss 15, 16, 19 and 20 of the Bills of Exchange and Cheques Act already mentioned in the chapter on the 'aval'.

Shares represented by book entries

The regime of the shares represented by book entries is governed by the regulations on the Securities Market and the organisation of companies.[12] Such legislation – section 5 onwards of the Securities Market Act – establishes that the ownership of shares is evidenced by its prior registration in the Book-Entries Registry – since there are no physical instruments representing the shares. The entities in charge of keeping the accounting books of entries will issue and deliver certificates justifying an entry, such certificates are neither transferable nor negotiable. The creation of a pledge over shares represented by book entries is recorded in the relevant account, as a registration equivalent to a change of the possession that, as we have already seen, is an essential feature in the creation of a pledge. It is worth remarking that a pledge is enforceable against any third parties from the moment of its registration.

Shares quoted on the Stock Exchange

Shares quoted on the Stock Exchange may be represented by instruments or by book-entries. However, given the dynamics of the exchange negotiations and the mandatory requirement under the Companies Act, the shares quoted on the Stock Exchange are mainly represented by book entries. Such shares will be registered with the relevant accounting registries.

It should be borne in mind that these registries of shares will be kept following the principles of priority and successive registration.

The principle of priority means that no subsequent registration relating to a particular security and referring to a predated event can be made as long as it opposes or is incompatible with other security created previously. The principle of succession implies that any registration relating to a transfer of securities requires that such securities have been previously registered in favour of the transferor.

The pledge will be constituted by the registered holder of the securities and formalised in a public deed. The entities in charge of the registry will be duly informed about such pledge so as to record it in the relevant account, which is the moment marking the effectiveness of the pledge against any third party.

In order to effect a proper control of the affected securities, they will be itemised separately from the accounts recording their 'history', so as to have them individualised, identified and immobilised. If the pledge only affects one part of the securities with the same reference, the entity participating in the Securities Clearing and Settlement system will ask the Agency to keep the accounting registry of securities separate and to replace the relevant recording reference.

Those securities affected cannot be traded in the Stock Exchange, yet they may be transferred subject to the encumbrance until its cancellation.

Certificates may be issued, if needed, so as to prove the creation of a pledge over book-entry securities. Any registration subsequent to the issue of such certificates will require the return of the certificate so as to make the pertinent accounting entry.

Participation in the share capital of limited liability companies

The commercial law does not provide for a general regime for pledges on share capital, however the regulator of limited liability companies envisages the possibility of such an encumbrance, providing for certain aspects of it of private limited companies.

12 Section 51 of the Companies Act.

Firstly it is worth noting that a participation in the share capital of a private limited company does not have the same characteristics as a share in a public limited company and can be represented neither by physical instruments nor by book-entries. Therefore, any pledge constituted will actually be charging the rights inherent to the status of member of the company.

The pledge has to be formalised in a public instrument – executed before a Notary Public or an official stock exchange broker – and notified to the company concerned for registration with the register of members. The notice should also be served by a Notary or official broker who would note the pledge either on the memorandum of association of the company concerned or on the deed relating to the capital increase, if appropriate.

As for Public Companies, there is disagreement on whether a pledge can be given on the share capital of a company where the memorandum of association – or the deed on capital increase, if relevant – has not yet been registered with the Commercial Registry. Most authors deem that, in such circumstances, participation should not be so encumbered.

These private limited liability companies cannot accept a pledge or any other form of guarantee that charges its own participation or shares or participation issued by a company from the same group, unlike public companies which are allowed to do so within the limits and requirements already mentioned.

Pledges on bills of exchange

The first fact to take into account with respect to this pledge is that it is often used and, therefore, it is required to meet all the conditions of the general regime (ss 1863 and following of the Civil Code, and 320 and following of the Commerce Code).

Section 22 of the Bills of Exchange and Cheques act confers two basic characteristics on this pledge, that is:

1 those individuals bound by a bill of exchange cannot raise objections against the payee of a pledged bill based on their personal relationships with the person who gave the bill in guarantee, except if the payee had knowingly acted to the detriment of a third party; and
2 the pledge creditor (pledgee) or endorsee of the bill, has more rights than a common pledgee as he is authorised to directly enforce the charge through the collection of the bill.

Pledges on bank deposits

This guarantee is mainly issued to secure those obligations undertaken by a depositor in respect of his depository credit entity or any other credit entity. This pledge is often used because of the advantageous terms of prompt liquidity it offers to the banks.

There is neither specific legislation nor established practice on this issue. However, the current trend recognises this kind of pledge and regards the pledgee as holder of the same rights as those the law gives to the pledge on movables.[13]

13 Decisions of the Supreme Court dated 19 April 1997 and 7 October 1997.

The object charged with the pledge is not the deposited money itself – which is property of the bank that undertakes to restore it to its client – but the right of credit held by depositors to have their deposits and relevant interests restored to them.

Consequently, the pledge may be given over any type of bank balance representing the credit right of restoration held by depositors in respect of their deposits. Thus, both long-term deposits and short-term deposits may be the subject of a pledge.

However, since the ultimate target of the creditor is the effective locking up of the amount pledged, pledges of on demand deposits, especially those on current account balances, are almost non-existent in practice.

Short-term deposits

Current accounts. Though in theory there are no problems giving a pledge on current account balances, in practice it is hardly feasible mainly because of the mobility that characterises these accounts that make balances subject to fluctuations (cash services, withdrawals through electronic terminals, etc).

Savings accounts. In banking practice, the pledge on the balances of these accounts is commonplace. In spite of being on demand deposit, the depository bank does not really render a cash service but it merely receives funds to be deposited and meets the payments ordered by the depositor.

In this kind of account the client has access to his funds through presentation of a savings book. Therefore, in the case of a pledge agreement the savings book will record the funds agreed as locked up, thus securing the effective immobility of a minimum balance to be pledged.

Long-term deposits

The balances of these deposits are more easily pledged because of their stability; they may only be available within a certain term previously agreed by the depositor and the depository bank. It might be said that the holder of a long term pledged deposit has a double block on his account, ie firstly that deriving from the deposit agreement itself and secondly that inherent to the pledge agreement which makes the deposit unavailable until the fulfilment of the obligation secured.

The formal requirements for the issuance of this pledge are the same as those mentioned for the pledge over credit rights, that is, its formalisation by an official stock broker and its notification to the depository bank, when the bank is not the beneficiary.

Another feature to bear in mind is its enforcement. In this respect, the pledge on balances has the advantage of the liquidity of money that allows different procedures from that of selling pledged assets in public auctions.

If the beneficiary is the depository bank the execution of the pledge will be carried out by offsetting the debt with the pledged credit, such offset may be direct for on demand deposits, or at maturity date for long term deposits.

When the depository bank is not the beneficiary and such bank has been duly notified of the pledge, the mere demand for payment received by such depository bank will be enough for the enforcement of the pledge. Notwithstanding this, the guarantee may lose its effectiveness if before notification of the pledge the pledgor had incurred debts with the depository bank and such bank has offset those debts.[14]

14 Decision of the Supreme Court of 19 September 1987.

In view of the foregoing it is advisable that the beneficiary and the depository bank be the same, except if the depository bank gives its express consent to the pledge.

Finally, the most recent case law regards this guarantee as a proper pledge, conferring on the pledgee the right to have his debt detached from the bankrupt estate of the debtor and the right to not participate in any creditors' arrangement in the event of depositor's bankruptcy.[15]

Pledge on life insurances

Over recent years some banking entities operating in Spain are resorting to taking pledges over life insurance policies underwritten by clients, linking them to the reimbursement of a debt and as a guarantee collateral to others already issued by the client.

This pledge has been fully recognised by Spanish law and is embodied in section 99 of the 50/1980 Act on Insurance Agreements (AIA) of 8 October 1980.

In analysing this pledge the first question that arises refers to the subject-matter of the pledge, thus questioning if such subject is the insurance policy itself or, rather, the rights arising from such policy.

The most accepted doctrine deems that as per section 9 of the Act on Insurance Agreements (AIA) the insurance policy is not a negotiable instrument, that is, an instrument conveying a right (such as the bill of exchange) and so, therefore, the pledge does not attach to the policy itself – the physical instrument of the life insurance – but, instead, to the rights arising from such policy.

On the premise that the pledge arises over the rights, section 99 of the AIA requires the notification to the insurer of the pledge, so as to ensure the pledge creditor – usually a banker – of the effectiveness of his right, given that upon notification the insurer will not be discharged even when paying the beneficiary.

In order to pledge the policy, the policy-holder is required by section 99 not to have irrevocably appointed a beneficiary. This is consistent with the same provision establishing that the pledge on a life policy implies the revocation of the beneficiary.

The beneficiary's tacit renunciation resulting from pledging the policy does not mean that the pledge creditor (pledgee) will automatically become the new beneficiary, yet if the debtor does not fulfil the obligations secured, the pledgee is entitled to have the amounts of his credit reimbursed against the principal of the policy.

Furthermore, this section 99 establishes that a pledge may be constituted 'at any time', which means that once the insurance policy has been underwritten the policy-holder is fully entitled to pledge the policy at any time, giving the insurer official notification in writing of such pledge.

As to its validity, a pledge does not need to be executed by way of public deed, however as for its enforceability against third parties the Civil Code requires that the date of delivery be evidenced in a public instrument. Besides, this formalisation is advisable for the pledgee given that in this way, and pursuant to the Civil Code, his credit will be preferential to any other credit owed by the debtor (pledgor).

As for the effects of the pledge, the holder of a pledged policy does not lose the rights that the AIA vests in him, yet the exercise of such rights will correspond to the

15 Decisions of the Supreme Court dated 19 April 1997 and 7 October 1997.

pledgee. In any case, the policy-holder continues to be bound to pay the relevant premiums.

With regard to the beneficiary, the pledge on the policy implies the revocation of his designation and the loss of his rights over the amounts secured, which he will keep only with respect to any eventual remainder once the principal debt so secured has been settled.

As for the insurer the pledge implies that, once he has been notified of its existence, he will not be discharged by the mere payment to the beneficiary.

Finally, the effects on the pledgee depend on the moment at which the beneficiary dies. Thus, if on the death of the beneficiary the obligation secured is not due, the pledge on the policy will become an irregular pledge on the amount of the compensation. Conversely, if at such moment the obligation secured was already due but not satisfied, the pledgee will reserve his right to add to the payment of the obligation those moneys the insurer has to pay, being the remainder, if any, for the holder's heir.

Pledge on credit rights

Unlike other legal systems such as the German system, Spanish legislation does not expressly provide for the possibility of creating this kind of pledge. In this sense, the definition contained in section 1864 of the Spanish Civil Code which states that 'all those movables that are in the market may be subject to pledge so long as they are capable of ownership' has opened a doctrinal debate on whether credit, particularly credit rights, can be pledged.

Most recent case law[16] and some authors admit the creation of this kind of guarantee.

Leaving aside the pledge on balances of banking deposits, which is analysed above, any credit right can be charged with a pledge, provided such right is transferable.

The latest Supreme Court decision of 19 April 1997 admits, subject to some adjustments, the application to the pledge on credit rights of those provisions regulating the creation of a pledge on goods. Thus, for instance, such guarantees are required to be executed in a public deed so as to be enforceable against third parties. Likewise, since a pledge on goods requires the pledgor's dispossession, in the case of pledge over credit rights such requirement is replaced by the notification of the pledge to the debtor. In addition, the credit pledged must be identified in a clear and detailed manner.

The pledgee is entitled to receive interest arising from the pledged credit and to withhold it so as to, if necessary, offset the payment of the debt against the eventual default of the pledgor. Likewise, the pledgee is entitled to collect and withhold the principal of the pledged credit if it matures before the debt secured with it; otherwise, if the secured debt matures before the pledged credit but a payment default has occurred, the process to be followed will be the enforcement of the pledge (sale in a public auction).

Finally, as we indicated above, there is a doctrinal debate on whether pledges on credit rights are proper pledges, so therefore, there is no doctrinal consensus on whether the pledgee of the guarantee in hand is vested with the same rights as those the law confers to pledged credit. However, the most recent decisions of the Supreme Court of

16 Decisions of the Supreme Court dated 19 September 1987, 31 May 1993, 19 April 1997 and 7 October 1997.

1997, as seen above, recognise the creation of this pledge and give it protection in the case of the debtor's bankruptcy.

Maritime rights

Like many other rules forming the Spanish law, maritime rights originated in Roman Law. Thus, to boost the maritime traffic which was of the utmost importance for the Roman people, their law-makers established a preferential treatment for those creditors who had contributed to the success of maritime enterprise by granting loans either for the construction or purchase of vessels or for the provisions or repairs required by the vessels in the course of their voyages. This is the historical origin of these rights whose principal features remain alive even today in modern law.

In this view, maritime rights may be defined as a prerogative the law gives to certain debts – those called maritime privileged debts – pursuant to which the creditor is vested with an enforcing, tracing and preferential right in the case of judicial sale of the vessel the origin of the credit to which settlement was attached in guarantee.

In order to have a better understanding of these privileges, we will analyse them separately.

1 *The right of enforcement.* This right reflects the privileged maritime creditors' entitlement to seek the seizure and subsequent judicial sale of the relevant vessel, so as to have the debt settled with the proceeds of sale. This right is effective at any port where the vessel might be located and irrespective of who the shipowner might be. Therefore, the right of enforcement means that the vessel is directly affected by the settlement of the debt even if its owner is not the debtor. Thus, where a vessel is operated by a person other than its proprietor because of an assignment of its use (such as a lease or a charterparty) the vessel will be answerable for the debt even if the obligation had not been undertaken by the proprietor, but by the charterer.
2 *Rights against third parties.* This right enables a privileged maritime creditor to follow the vessel beyond the boundaries of the debtor's property, that is, even if the vessel attached to the payment of the debt has been assigned to a third party the creditor may demand payment from the ultimate successive owner. Consequently, these privileged credits are enforceable against the vessel despite the fact that the ownership has been transferred to a third party not concerned with the outstanding debt.
3 *Preferential right.* Along with the rights mentioned above, this right enables a creditor to have the debt paid with the price obtained on judicial sale of the vessel, having a preferential position before the other creditors.

Once the rights conferred by the privileged maritime debts have been defined, it is worth itemising the debts benefitting from such rights.

Spanish legislation in this respect is quite piecemeal, lacking a systematic framework. The privileged maritime debts are embodied in the Spanish Commercial Code of 1885, but are also regulated by the Act on Ship Mortgage of 1893 and by the International Conventions signed and ratified by Spain, mainly The Brussels Convention of 1926 which prevails over the domestic law.

In a strict sense and leaving aside the expenses arising from the legal proceedings for the sale of the vessel (legal costs, custody or maintenance charges, etc) which are preferential but do not, however, bear the nature of authentic privileged maritime debts, we may distinguish the following qualifying debts:

1 Duties relating to the use of port facilities and the like.
2 Wages of the captain and crew.
3 Debts incurred for the services provided in aid of a ship in danger.
4 Debts owed to the owners whose cargo has been destroyed during the salvage of a ship in danger.
5 Compensation for death or injuries suffered by passengers or crew, or compensation covering losses or damages to cargo.
6 Debts incurred by the captain in the course of the voyage for meeting the necessities of the vessel (such as shipchandler's provisions, fuel, and the like).
7 Debts arising from the construction of the vessel (such as materials or labour).
8 Debts arising from the sale of the vessel (such as any outstanding amount owed to the last seller).
9 Premiums of insurances on the deck, engines, etc.
10 Amounts owed to the Public Treasury.

Pledges without transfer of possession

Pursuant to section 53 of the Chattel Mortgage Act, the legal owners of farms, forestry or cattle may create a pledge without dispossession charged on the following assets:
- The fruits and expected crops in the agriculture year in which the agreement is signed.
- Segregated fruits, specifying the place where they must be deposited if they are not already stored.
- Animals, their offspring and the products obtained from them.
- the machinery and tools relating to these activities.

This kind of pledge can also be given over

- Machinery and any other movables capable of identification that meet the requirements to be charged by way of mortgage on industrial machinery.
- Merchandise and raw materials stored.
- Artistic objects or collections.

Enforcement of a guarantee on movables

In another section we have analysed each of the guarantees on movables and the rights assisting the pledgee that has secured his debt with this kind of guarantee. On top of these rights, there is another advantage which consists of special call proceedings aimed at satisfying a credit against the assets attached to a guarantee.

Thus, on default the pledgee may seek collection of his debt through any of the following procedures:

- The common judicial proceedings on the basis of the amount of the outstanding debt.
- Enforcement proceedings, which under Spanish law are applicable to those cases

where the debt concerned is embodied in certain instruments, such as a public deed, a policy formalised before an official stock broker, etc.

- Special extrajudicial proceedings established by the law for on demand guarantees on movables, and
- in the case of a pledge without transfer of possession, the pledgee may resort to the special judicial proceeding established by the law governing these pledges.

As to the extrajudicial proceedings there is a wide range of them whose application mainly depends on the nature of the assets attached to the guarantee or on the nature of the creditor concerned. Below we will outline the most relevant proceedings.

Enforcement of a common pledge

The Civil Code, section 1872, provides for an extrajudicial call proceeding that takes place before a notary public and is aimed at the sale of the pledged assets at public auction. This proceeding comes from the premise that the assets attached to the pledge are held by the creditor who seeks enforcement (or held by a third party willing to leave such assets to the creditor's disposal).

On failing to have the assets sold at first auction, a second auction may be held under the same conditions as the first. If in such second auction the assets are not sold either, the creditor is entitled to purchase them giving a discharging receipt in consideration acknowledging the full payment of his debt.

The creditor may initiate this proceeding from the maturity date, that is, when the obligation becomes due and payable, a prior demand for payment to the debtor is not required.

Enforcement of a pledge on negotiable instruments

There is a special call proceeding for a pledge on negotiable instruments, which is regulated by sections 320 to 324 of the Spanish Commercial Code. Such sections have undergone quite substantial amendments after the Law 24/1988 of 24 July governing the Securities Market came into force.

The pledgee may initiate this special proceeding within three working days of maturity of the obligation secured, provided the pledge has been formalised in a policy executed before an official stock broker or in a public deed. The policy, or if appropriate the deed, must contain the particulars that allow identification of the negotiable instruments given in guarantee.

Without the need for demanding payment from the debtor, the creditor may resort to the governing bodies of the official secondary market concerned, seeking the sale of the pledged securities. For this purpose, the creditor has to submit the policy or deed together with the securities or the certificates – issued by the entity in charge of the relevant accounting registry and proving the registration of the guarantee – if the securities involved are represented by book-entries.

Upon completion of the relevant scrutiny by the governing body, the securities will be sold through a member of the relevant secondary market.

Enforcement of a pledge on warrants

Pursuant to section 97 of the Commercial Code there is another special proceeding for calls on those pledges charging the receipts (warrants) issued by the *Almacenes*

Generales de Depósitos (special public warehouses meeting a series of legal requirements and duly authorised).

The holder of a right of credit secured with a pledge on warrants may seek the sale from the public warehouse of the deposited merchandise, provided the credit has become due and the debtor has defaulted.

The sale will take place at the warehouse premises at public auction before a Notary public or a chartered commercial broker. The sale will include all that merchandise needed to fully discharge the debt owed to the creditor.

Extra-judicial proceedings for the enforcement of a pledge without transfer of possession

This proceeding is regulated by the Act on Mortgage on Moveables and Pledge without dispossession, of 16 December 1954, section 94. It consists of the sale of the pledged assets at public auction which is held before the Notary public of the town or city where the assets are placed.

On maturity of the obligation secured by the pledge, the Notary public will demand payment from the debtor, specifying the total amount claimed and the reason for maturity of the obligation.

Within the three days following maturity, the debtor must meet the payment or transfer the possession of the pledged assets to the creditor. If on the expiry of this period, the debtor has neither paid nor delivered the assets, this proceeding cannot go any further, so the holder of the secured credit will have to resort to the relevant judicial proceeding. But if the debtor delivers the assets to the creditor, such assets will be subsequently sold in the way explained when referring to the common pledge.

Judicial enforcement proceedings on a pledge without transfer of possession

Along with the extrajudicial proceeding detailed above, the Act and Mortgages on Movables on Pledge without dispossession also establishes a judicial proceeding for the enforcement of this kind of pledge. It is a proceeding aimed at satisfying a debt as against the pledged assets. This proceeding is very similar to those that are to be analysed later when dealing with enforcement, therefore here we will only focus on the particular differing features.

The jurisdiction corresponds to the court of first instance of the place where the assets are located and documented. The creditor is allowed to bring this kind of proceeding based on the public deed establishing the pledge or the pledge agreement executed before an official stock broker.

A depository must be nominated by the creditor in the writ of demand, so on the debtor's default in payment after being summoned by the judge, the depository will receive the pledged assets. If the assets involved can neither be seized nor deposited, this proceeding will not go any further yet the creditor's interests will be preserved.

This procedure permits two auctions and only the first auction is started at a reserve price. Taking part does not require any deposit on the part of bidders. Once both auctions have been held without a successful sale, the creditor may have the assets awarded giving in exchange a letter acknowledging the full settlement of the debt and assuming the legal costs involved.

Guarantee on immovables

Guarantee on real estate

Through this in rem right of guarantee, real estates are directly and promptly linked to the payment of a monetary obligation. This guarantee permits the owner to keep the possession of the estate so charged and, on the mortgage debt defaulting at maturity, it enables the holder of the guarantee (mortgagee) to seek the sale of the mortgaged estate as to satisfy the debt from the proceeds of the sale.

Amongst the characteristics of the mortgage on real estates, we may highlight the following basic features:

- It is an ancillary or guaranteeing in rem right, since it directly and immediately attaches the property charged to the fulfilment of the obligation secured, irrespective of who holds the ownership of such property.
- It is a right of realisation of value, given that it is not aimed at obtaining the property itself but the moneys resulting from the sale of such property which will serve to settle the debt to the creditor's credit.
- It is the guarantee of a monetary obligation. Although mortgages of this kind may secure any sort of obligation, this particular mortgage bears the characteristic of realisation of the property value and, therefore, it needs either to have the amount of the secured obligation fixed or the maximum amount for which the property is secured must be specified. Consequently, when the obligation secured is not monetary, such obligation has to be translated into an amount of money, payment of which is the only and direct object secured by the mortgage.
- It has the benefit of being effective against third parties ('erga omnes'), and the creditor is entitled to follow the mortgaged property and enforce his right against anyone holding the possession of it.
- It limits the right of unencumbered disposal by the owner of the mortgaged property. This means that, even though the sale of such property is not prohibited, any new owner buys the property subject to the mortgage and the possibility of sale of the property if the underlying obligation is not discharged.
- It has to be issued in a public deed and it will become effective after its registration in the Land Registry.
- It takes preference over other debts, and in the event of bankruptcy or temporary receivership the mortgaged property will not be included in the bankrupt estate until the debt secured has been settled.

This kind of guarantee is very often used in the banking sector, mainly in loan operations for the purchase of houses. It directly lies on real estate and does not modify the personal and unlimited liability of a debtor, unless otherwise agreed. Apart from the principal secured, the law provides that a mortgage will secure the interest relating to the previous two years and that the interest already due attributable to in the current year, that is, three years interest that may be extended to five years.[17]

Furthermore, the mortgage can be extended to certain assets that form part of the mortgaged property, such as those which spring up in the land as an act of nature, improvements and indemnities, those personal chattels firmly fixed in place which

17 Section 114 and 115 of the Mortgage Act.

cannot be removed without causing damage, and any extension made and registered with the Land Registry after the mortgage.[18]

Likewise, the mortgage can be extended by express consent to the personal chattels placed permanently in the land, to the income and to the due and outstanding rents.[19]

Any changes in the ownership of the creditor or other modifications to the mortgage of agreement or its cancellation must be recorded in a public deed and registered with the Registry.

It is worth noting that since the mortgage is subject to a particular legal regime, which is different from that of the obligation secured, it is quite common that certain agreements relating to the operation subject to the guarantee, which may be valid and legitimate between the parties, will not be registrable with the Registry. This prohibition against registration deprives the mortgagee of evidence he could otherwise resort to in case of a breach of such agreements so as to recover his debt with the sale of the mortgaged property.

In some cases it is the law itself which does not allow registration of certain agreements prohibiting the raising of subsequent mortgages, those prohibiting the sale of the mortgaged land or those allowing the mortgagor to keep the property (*pactum comisorium*). There are other cases in respect of which the regulations are silent, but for which non-registration has been determined by case-law. Thus, for instance a clause referring to the acceleration of a debt in the event that the debtor's solvency is diminishing is a non-registrable agreement.

In practical terms it is advisable that before accepting this kind of mortgage, the interested party check the real value of the land or estate to be mortgaged and inquire at the Registry if there is another mortgage on the same property which may make the guarantee ineffective.

Notwithstanding the characteristics outlined above, which are common to these guarantees, there are also small differences arising from the kind of debt these guarantees secure. These are as follows:

Mortgage on commercial premises

Despite the fact that the law of 1954 only refers to the Mortgage on Commercial Premises, the scope of this mortgage does also include intangible assets of the company.

This kind of mortgage can be constituted either by the proprietor of the premises or by the *tenant* provided he holds the right to transfer it.

Scope

- The mortgage on commercial premises inevitably includes the rent of the premises and its fixtures, so far as they belong to the holder of the premises.
- Except as otherwise agreed, this mortgage will also include intellectual property and industrial properties, machinery, furniture, tools and other working and manufacturing devices.
- Merchandise and raw materials may also be included by agreement.

18 Sections 109, 110 and 111 of the Mortgage Act and s 215-1 of the Mortgage Rule.
19 Section 111 of the Mortgage Act.

Formal requirements

Besides the execution by way of public deed and the registration under the requirements mentioned above, the law provides that:

1 The public deed must include the rent and the other terms of the leasing agreement.
2 The lessor or owner of the premises containing the business must be informed of the creation of the mortgage.

Mortgage securing a current account

Such a mortgage is issued to secure the future debit balance that may arise on a current account.

Its creation needs to be recorded by way of public deed and registered with the relevant Land Registry. The public deed must detail (i) the maximum amount for which the mortgaged estate is liable, (ii) the duration of the current account and if such term is extendible, in which case the possible extension must be specified, (iii) the instalments for the liquidation of the account and (iv) the way to verify the existence and amount of the balance due.

Mortgage securing a bill of exchange

The bill of exchange mortgage is issued to secure the payment of one or several bills of exchange, irrespective of who the holder is. Since bills of exchange are transferable by endorsement, what the mortgage is securing is the bill itself, irrespective of who its holder may be at its maturity date, so as to avoid obstructing the free circulation of those bills.

It must be issued by way of public deed and registered with the Land Registry at the place where the estate to be mortgaged is located; the deed must specify in full the details of the bills of exchange secured. Besides, such bills must contain a notarial note stating the issuance of the mortgage (details of the deed and of its registration), including the fact that the mortgage is not only in favour of the holder of the bill at any particular time, but also in favour of future holders.

One special feature that makes these mortgages different from others is the transfer by endorsement, which allows the passing of the title without the need to either inform the debtor about such transfer or register such transfer with the Registry.

The holder of the bills who has collected them has to deliver the deed recording its cancellation, presenting such bills to the Notary Public who will note on them the cancellation of the mortgage. As in preceding cases, this deed must be registered with the Registry.

Ship mortgage

Introduction

The Spanish Commercial Code does not contain specific provisions on the constitution of *in rem* rights on ships. Notwithstanding this fact, it should be noted that Section 1 of the Ship Mortgage Act (SMA)[20] establishes that 'merchant ships may be subject to Mortgages in accordance with the provisions of this Law. For these purposes only, such ships shall be considered immovable goods and for this purpose section 585 of the Commercial Code shall be deemed amended'.

Subject matter of the guarantee

Section 1 of the SMA establishes that only ships can be the subject matter of this guarantee. Notwithstanding this, we may point out the following:

1 The mortgage can also charge a ship under construction.
2 The mortgage on a ship does also charge the furniture, fixtures and freights of the ship, except if otherwise agreed.

Mortgage on a ship under construction

Section 16 of the SMA sets out that in order to raise a mortgage on a ship under construction it is necessary that one third of the estimate for the total value of the hull be invested in such construction.

Prior to the delivery of the mortgage the ship to be built must be registered with the Provincial Registry of Ships under Construction.

As to this registration, the shipowner has to lodge with the Registry an application and a certificate issued by the shipbuilder containing the following data:

1 The phase of the ship construction.
2 The length and other measures of the ship.
3 The quality of vessel, if it is a steamer or a sailing boat.
4 The shipyard.
5 The materials to be used.
6 The cost of the hull.
7 The design plan of the vessel.

When the construction is formalised in an agreement, such agreement will have to be registered. Where there is a mortgage, this registration will be temporary until completion of the ship and its registration with the Registry of the Marine Authorities. At this stage, the temporary registration is transferred to the Book of Ships of the relevant Commercial Registry, becoming then a final registration.

Such transference and subsequent conversion into final registration will be effected by application of the concerned party, to which application he will attach *the certificate of registration* and *the public deed of delivery of the vessel* granted by the shipbuilder in favour of the shipowner.

Objective extension of the mortgage

Except if otherwise agreed, alongside the ship there are other items which are also mortgaged and answerable for the commitments attached to the mortgage. Such items are the following:

1 The tackle, stocks, supplies and engines – if the ship is a steamer – that are held by the owner or owners of the mortgaged ship.

20 Of 21 August 1893.

2 The freights due and unpaid, relating to a voyage still in progress or to the last one effected at the time the mortgage credit became effective.
3 Those indemnities relating to the ship as a consequence of collisions or any other accidents or those others relating to the insurance in case of shipwreck.

Should there be several vessels mortgaged to secure one debt, the share borne by each of them must be determined.

As to the obligation secured, a ship mortgage raised in favour of a loan with interest cannot secure other amounts except for the principal and the interest accrued over the last two years together with that already due for the current year.

Requirements for its formation

Personal requirements

A ship mortgage can only be given by those who hold freehold property or, else, by those who are legally authorised to do so.

In this respect, those legally qualified to raise such a mortgage may do it by themselves or by a representative duly appointed and empowered to undertake this kind of obligation, vested of such powers before a Notary Public or an official stock broker.

If the property of the ship is held jointly, the authorisation for raising the mortgage and the formation of such mortgage will require the prior consent of the majority of the owners.

The mortgage on a ship under construction will be issued by the shipowner or by the shipbuilder if he is entitled to do so under the construction agreement.

Objective requirements

The amount of the debt secured must be specified and the mortgage may also secure a fixed amount relating to costs and to two years accrued interest and interest for the current year.

Formal requirements

The agreement conveying the ship mortgage can only be delivered by way of the following instruments:

1 *A Public Deed* before a Notary Public.
2 *A Policy* before an official stock broker.
3 *A Private Instrument* executed by the parties concerned or by their representatives, and such parties or, at least, the mortgagee will submit it to the officer in charge of verifying the registration, giving him sufficient evidence of their identities.

Exceptionally, section 163 of the Rule of the 1959 Commercial Registry establishes that a ship mortgage securing current accounts or bearer documents of title needs to be executed by way of a Public Deed.

A ship mortgage will not be effective unless it is registered with the Commercial Registry of the province recording the registration of the ship subject to the mortgage. In absence of such prior registration, the mortgage will be filed with the Registry of the place where the vessel was built.

As regards the mortgage agreements delivered abroad, such delivery may be effected before the Spanish Consul at the port where it takes place and be registered with the

Registry of the consulate. Then, the Consul will transfer an authenticated copy of the agreement to the Commercial Registry of the place where the ship is registered.

Furthermore, section 160 of the Rule above allows the registration of a mortgage executed before relevant authorities of foreign countries in accordance with the laws of such countries, provided that such agreements are effective in Spain pursuant to International Treaties and the provisions in force.

Effects of the ship mortgage

Preferential right

The ship mortgage gives the creditor priority for the collection of his debt before other debts, except for:

1 Those taxes or contributions due to the State, Province or Council, which relate to the last voyage of the ship or to the year before.
2 Pilotage, weight and other harbour duties, as well as the wages owed to the captain and the crew accrued over the last voyage.
3 The total of the insurance premiums of the vessel relating to the last two years or, in the case of a mutual benefit society, the amount related to the last two dividends allotted.
4 The reimbursement of the cargo sold by the captain to repair the ship, and the compensation to the consignor for the goods which have either not been delivered or which have suffered damage.

There are other items which take priority over the ship mortgage, so far as they meet the legal requirements. Such items are:

a The amount taken by the captain as a bottomry loan during his last voyage.
b The amount corresponding to a general average incurred by the captain in the last voyage.
c The debts relating to repairs or restorations incurred by the captain in the last voyage.
d The rights or credits under litigation that were noted by way of caution in the Commercial Registry before the registration of the mortgage.

Right to follow the asset

The ship mortgage directly and promptly attaches to the assets charged for fulfilment of those obligations for which the mortgage was raised, regardless of the owner of the assets:

1 on the lapse of the term established for the repayment of the principal or of the interest.
2 when the debtor is adjudged bankrupt or in receivership.
3 when any of the mortgaged ships is lost – except if otherwise agreed – or navigation impaired.
4 when the ship is sold to a foreigner.
5 when the conditions agreed as to the termination of the agreement together with those that make the principal and interest callable are met.

Upon the secured credit becoming due and payable, for its enforcement a prior summons for payment needs to be served either by a notary public or by a broker.

In the event that the debtor fails to pay off his credit within three days following demand, the creditor will be entitled to seek payment through the courts, by the seizure of the mortgaged ship and its subsequent sale in accordance with that provided for in sections 43 onwards of the Act on ship mortgage.

Negative prescription and cancellation

Pursuant to that provided for by the law, the right to enforce a ship mortgage *lapses after 10 years* following the date on which it was enforceable.

As regards cancellation, the registration of ship mortgages can only be cancelled by a court order, by a final judgment or by consent of the mortgagee or his successors. Such consent must be stated in any of the following documents: a public deed, a notary's certificate, a policy before a commercial or a ship broker or by the personal attendance of the creditor or his representative before the Commercial Registry.

Chattel mortgage

Introduction

These guarantees came into being to fulfill two requirements, namely to:

1 formulate a guarantee with the force of the mortgage which could be given on movables.

2 create a type of real guarantee on movables that would not compel the owner of the asset given in guarantee to give up possession.

Both conditions are basically regulated by the law of 16 December 1954 and the Regulation of 17 May 1955.

In order to examine these topics, such topic is to addressed under the following headings:

A Definition
B Common Provisions
  B1 Creation
  B2 Scope and Contents
  B3 Discharge
C Mortgage on Movables.
D Pledge without transfer of Possession.
E Mortgage on Commercial Premises.
F Pledge on Bill of Exchange.

Definition

The rights conveyed in these guarantees can be defined as 'in rem' which fall on certain movables previously established by law. These rights arise from registration and allow their holders to continue enjoying the possession of them even after being given in guarantee.

The main difference between such rights is the kind of movables which may be charged. In general terms, the mortgage on movables falls on assets capable of being identified whereas the assets subject to a pledge without dispossession are rarely definable.

Common provisions

Creation

The *assets* capable of being charged with these guarantees must be:

1 Movables
2 Transferable
3 Property other than the guarantee holder's property.

The debts that may be guaranteed are:

1 Any kind of obligations, whether subject to a condition precedent or subsequent.
2 Monetary debts the amount of which is expressed in domestic currency.
3 Those capable of being secured in current accounts or represented by bearer instruments or transferable by endorsement.

As regards formal requirements:

1 Mortgages on movables and pledge without transfer of possession must be formalised in a public deed.
2 This kind of pledge may also be raised in a policy issued before an official stock broker.
3 The deed or policy must however be registered with the special Registry as provided by the law of 1954. Under the law, the lack of registration will deprive the pledgee or mortgagee of the rights vested in them by the law. Therefore registration is essential.

Scope and contents

As regards the obligation secured, these guarantees of an obligation that give rise to interest will secure, apart from the principal, the interest of the last two years and the part due in the current year.

With regard to the contents, we should highlight the following:

1 The debtor cannot sell the charged assets without the consent of the creditor.
2 The creditor may sell or transfer the credit secured by a mortgage on movables or by a pledge without dispossession, following formalities similar to those required for the creation of the encumbrance and for notifying the debtor – notarial notification – of such sale or transfer.
3 When it comes to collecting his debt, the creditor secured will enjoy the preference and priority the Civil Code establishes for the pledge, maintaining however the priority of wage and tax debts.[1] Besides, there are special rules for the pledge without dispossession – as we will detail later – and for the Movable Mortgage on Aircrafts (where credits for salvage and maintenance expenses are preferential).

1 Section 10 of the law of 1954.

Discharge
In general, since these guarantees are ancillary to a principal right, the discharge of the latter entails the cancellation of the former because there cannot be a mortgage or a pledge without an obligation to be secured.

The law of 1954 sets out that the action to enforce the rights under a mortgage or a pledge lapses after three years from the time at which the secured obligation becomes due.

Mortgage on movables
Pursuant to that provided for in section 12 of the law of 1954 only the following assets may be mortgaged:

1 Commercial premises.
2 Motor cars and other motor vehicles.
3 Aircrafts.
4 Industrial machinery.
5 Intellectual and industrial property.

Apart from the general formalities required by the law, the public deed of a mortgage on movables must contain (i) identification of the debtor, the creditor and, if appropriate, the person who gives the assets in guarantee; (ii) a description of the mortgaged assets; (iii) the proof of title to the assets and a declaration by the mortgagor that such assets are not already encumbered; and (iv) relevant address for serving notices and summons to the debtor and, if relevant, to the third party mortgaging the assets.

Anticresis *(Antichresis)*

The *anticresis* is regulated under sections 1881 to 1886 of the Spanish Civil Code.

Rather than a guarantee securing a payment failure, the *Anticresis* is a contract under which a creditor secures payment of his credit by applying the income of a real estate of a debtor. Thus, such income will serve firstly to cover the interest of the debt and then to settle the principal, the debtor is deprived from enjoying the real estate until the full settlement of the debt or the return of the property by the creditor.

This guarantee may be issued by the debtor himself – or by a third party separate from the debt – to secure any kind of obligation. It has the same indivisible nature as the mortgage and the pledge and it may be extended to new debts – due and payable before extinction of the former debt – even if it had not initially provided for such an extension.

In the event of default, the creditor does not obtain the ownership of the property – any agreement to the contrary will be null and void – but may take legal action seeking payment of the debt or the sale of the estate.

Unless otherwise agreed, the creditor will pay and deduct from the income from the property those taxes and charges attached to the estate and needed to meet the expenses relating to its maintenance and repairs until the moment possession of the estate is reinstated to the debtor.

Sections 1152 to 1155 of the Civil Code provides for a penalty clause under which the parties to these agreements will assess their respective liabilities in the event of breach, the amount so agreed will replace the compensation and interest that might have applied. In case of a partial breach the court may give a new formula for such amount.

Enforcement of 'in rem' guarantees

Enforcement of a mortgage on real estate

The extrajudicial enforcement proceeding was held unconstitutional by a decision of the Supreme Court dated 4 May 1998 and therefore it was prohibited.

After such prohibition, where a mortgaged credit has become due and the debtor does not proceed with payment, the creditor may seek payment either by way of the ordinary procedures or by a special proceeding regulated in the Mortgage Act in its section 131. Such proceeding is named 'Mortgage Summary Judicial Proceeding' (*Procediminto Judicial Sumario Hipotecario*) and its formal requirements are the following:

1 Jurisdiction. Irrespective of the amount of the secured credit involved, enforcement falls into the jurisdiction of the Courts of First Instance (*Tribunales de Primera Instanci*) of the place where the mortgaged real estate is located. If such estate extends to more than one district the creditor will be entitled to choose to lodge his claim with any of the jurisdictions involved.
2 Legislation. The proceeding is initiated by the creditor (mortgagee) and directed against either the debtor (mortgagor) or any third party who has possession of the mortgaged real estate.
3 Procedure. This kind of proceeding requires the participation of a lawyer and a '*Procurador*'. The latter is a special lawyer who represents the plaintiff before the courts, his presence is mandatory under Spanish law.
4 The title on which proceedings are initiated has to be the original deed raising the mortgage, which must be formalised before a Notary Public and registered with the Land Registry (if the title does not appear as registered, a Registral Certificate proving the registration and actual existence of the mortgage must be annexed to the original mortgage deed). The deed has to include two items, namely, the value established by the parties to the mortgage of the estate or land, which will serve as the reserve price for a public auction, and the address of the debtor (mortgagor) where he may be served notices and summons.

Broadly speaking, the proceeding starts with a writ of demand lodged with the competent court, to which the claimant must annex the mortgage deed and the demand for payment he should have sent with 10 days prior notice to the debtor or, if appropriate, to that third party in possession of the estate or land. If such demand for payment had not been made, it would be done in the course of the proceeding. The court will serve notice of the proceedings to those who have any interests in the estate so as to enable them to either take part in the auction or repay the outstanding debt.

The public auction will be preceded by a public announcement. Those wishing to take part are required to deposit with the court an amount, representing at least 20% of the reserve price. Only the mortgagee is exempt from making such deposit. The bids may be put either in 'viva voce' or in writing with the bidding specifications.

The property is awarded to the highest bidder exceeding the reserve price. If in this first auction, no bid reaches the reserve price, the mortgagee may ask either to have the estate awarded to him at the reserve price in payment of his debt or to hold a second auction where the reserve price will be the 75% of that of the first auction. If on this occasion there is not an admissible bid, the creditor may have the estate awarded to him at the new reserve price. Otherwise, a third auction will be held without a reserve price, but if the bids do not reach the reserve price of the second auction, either the mortgagee or the mortgagor or a third party appointed by them may improve on low bids before the estate is awarded to the highest bidder. If at this third auction the estate is not awarded because of the lack of bidders, the mortgagee may request that successive auctions be held.

The successful bidder (whether at the first, second or third auction) has to deposit with the court the remaining balance, that is, the difference between the price at which the estate has been awarded and the amount previously deposited. If such bidder were the mortgagee himself he would only deposit the difference between the highest bid and the mortgage debt and interest.

Once the price has been deposited by the awarded bidder, the mortgagee's credit is promptly repaid and if there is any remainder, this will serve to pay off the subsequent creditors. The award of the property entails the cancellation of the mortgage and of any other encumbrances subsequent to that of the mortgagee, but it does not mean the cancellation of previous encumbrances to which the awarded bidder will become subrogated.

Enforcement of a chattel mortgage

In view of the decision of the Supreme Court, dated 4 May 1998, which deemed the extrajudicial enforcement proceedings for mortgages on real estates to be unconstitutional, there are reasonable doubts about the continuance of such enforcement for mortgages on movables. Although it has not been expressly held unconstitutional, reasons of legal logic drive us to consider it as prohibited for being unconstitutional in the same way.

Leaving aside, then, this extrajudicial procedure before a Notary Public, Spanish legislation also contains a special procedure for the enforcement of mortgages on movables. Thus, the creditor of debt which has become due and is secured with a mortgage on movables may resort to the proceeding under the Act on Movable and Chattel Mortgage of 16 December 1954, which is called 'Mortgage Summary Legal proceeding', which also applies to mortgages on real estate.

The procedure is very similar to that contained in section 131 of the Mortgage Act. However, there are slight differences resulting from the different nature of the assets mortgaged.

As regards jurisdiction, and given the movable character of the assets mortgaged, it does not depend on the place where the assets are located but on the place where the mortgage is registered.

The document allowing the creditor access to such proceeding is the original deed granting the mortgage that must be registered and must include a breakdown of the price given to each of the personal chattels by the concerned parties, together with the debtor's address for serving notices.

Like the mortgage on real estate, holders of subsequent interests in the assets will be notified of the enforcement, enabling them to either participate in the auctions or be subrogated to the creditor's prior payment rights, interest and costs of proceedings.

In the special procedure for the enforcement of movable mortgages the law only provides for two auctions, the first one subject to a reserve price and the second free from such requirement. Upon award of the assets and payment to the creditor the mortgage on movables and any subsequent encumbrance are cancelled.

Enforcement of a ship mortgage

The Act on Ship Mortgage, of 21 August 1893, includes a special procedure for the enforcement of a ship mortgage. Like the mortgage on movables and real estates, this is a real enforcement proceeding which is aimed at satisfying a creditor's debt by direct sale of the mortgaged ship. Pursuant to section 39 of this Act, a creditor is entitled to enforce a ship mortgage on any of the following grounds:

1. Maturity of the term fixed for the repayment of the principal.
2. Maturity of the term fixed for the payment of interest.
3. The debtor is adjudged bankrupt.
4. Damage to the mortgaged ship make it impracticable for sailing.
5. Sale of the ship to a foreign national.
6. Fulfilment of either the conditions agreed as to the termination of the loan agreement or those clauses providing for the enforcement of the credit or its interest, and
7. Loss of the mortgaged ship, except if otherwise agreed.

In the absence of express submission of the parties to a specific court, the plaintiff may at his own discretion choose the court: (1) with jurisdiction in the place where the mortgage agreement was entered into; (2) with jurisdiction in the port where the mortgaged ship is located; (3) with jurisdiction in the place where the debtor is resident; or (4) with jurisdiction in the place where the mortgage agreement was registered.

The document serving as the basis for claiming the right to enforcement, must be annexed to the claim, and varies depending on the causes giving rise to such enforcement. Thus, when enforcement is due to either maturity as seen above, ie maturity for the repayment of the principal or interest, the document concerned is the deed containing the loan agreement, registered with the Registry, to which the request for payment to the debtor must be attached. If the cause for enforcement is the debtor's bankruptcy, the relevant document is the court's decree adjudging the debtor bankrupt. Finally, if the reason is the sale of the ship to a foreigner or its total loss, the title backing the request for enforcement is the public deed formalising the purchasing agreement or the certificate of total loss.

Whereas the procedure prior to the enforcement sale of the mortgaged ship does also vary depending on the reason for claiming the enforcement, the subsequent stages, that is, the auction, the award and payment of the credit to the creditor, are common to all the cases and are developed in a similar way as those already mentioned for the enforcement of a mortgage on real estate.

Enforcement of a mortgage securing the balance of a current account

If on expiry of the term agreed by the parties or, where appropriate, the expiry of the extension agreed, the mortgage creditor (mortgagee) has not been repaid he may seek the enforcement of the mortgage by resorting to the summary proceeding. As for common mortgages, this proceeding is regulated in the Mortgage Act, s 131 onwards, though with some particular features resulting from the fact that the amount owed is not determined.

Thus, the instrument serving as a basis for the initiation of the proceeding, ie the public deed conveying the mortgage registered, must be accompanied by the document certifying the liquidated amount of the debt.

The Mortgage Act provides for two kind of documents confirming the balance which are regulated differently:

1 A book kept by the creditor. It implies that the parties interested (creditor and debtor) have been keeping two books where, over their contractual relationship, each of them has been recording the entries of the current account concerned, with their agreement and signature. The Notary Public attesting the deed embodying the formation of the mortgage will stamp, seal and sign all the pages of these books, of which the first page will state the total of pages included.

   It is worth noting that nowadays this system of books has become obsolete.

2 A creditor's banking certificate. This document confirming the balance is legally used for current accounts opened in banks, saving banks and credit entities duly authorised. This system requires the notarial or judicial service to the debtor of the bank statements issued by the credit entity. On receipt the debtor may challenge such statement within eight days on grounds of error or misrepresentation in the entries.

If the debtor alleges error, the court will summon the parties to a hearing, then in view of such hearing and the documents submitted, the court will rule accordingly.

If the grounds for the challenge is misrepresentation, criminal proceedings will be initiated and the judicial summary proceeding will be discontinued until completion of the criminal proceeding.

Enforcement of the bill of exchange mortgage

If upon maturity of a bill of exchange, whose payment has been secured with a mortgage, payment is not made, the creditor may seek enforcement of his right against the mortgaged estate for repayment of his debt by the sale of the estate. As mortgage creditor he may resort not only to the common proceedings but to the mortgage summary proceeding.

The procedure is the same as that already studied when dealing with the enforcement of mortgages on immovables in general, though there are certain particularities that should be noted.

As to the legitimacy required for the initiation of this proceeding, and given the nature of the bill of exchange, the mortgage action will be legally exercised by the ultimate payee of the bill on its maturity, regardless of whether he is the initial payee – at the time of raising the mortgage – or a subsequent one – as a result of the bill.

The exchange mortgage creditor must annex to the lawsuit the defaulted bill or bills of exchange together with the deed of the mortgage registered with the Registry. If the creditor does not have the deed because he is not the initial payee, instead he will annex a certificate issued by the Registry attesting the registration and the existence of the mortgage (stating the amounts relating to the relevant bills of exchange that must coincide with those submitted by the creditor).

If it is a partial enforcement (involving only some of the defaulted bills) it must be accurately determined which are the bills giving rise to enforcement and which remain live, since the mortgage will continue securing the remaining titles that bear the same rights as those affected by the partial enforcement. Thus, the purchaser of the estate at auction assumes the burden of the mortgage securing the remaining bills. The proceeds of such auction will not be used for the payment or cancellation of such mortgage.

OTHER FORMS OF GUARANTEES

Seguro de caución

The '*seguro de caución*' originates with the underwriting of an insurance policy that aimed to replace the guarantee which certain individuals must issue – either under a contract or pursuant to law – to secure the fulfilment of the obligations under a contract. The *seguro de caución* ultimately intends to secure collection by the creditor.

The *seguro de caución* is regulated in section 68 of the 50/1980 Act on Insurance Agreements, of 8 October, which provides as follows:

> 'Under the *seguro de caution* the insurer undertakes that in the event that the policy-holder fails to comply with his legal or contractual obligations such insurer shall compensate the beneficiary of the policy as to reimburse him for the losses or damages suffered to his property, within the limits of the law or under the relevant contract. The policy-holder shall reimburse the insurer for any such payments made'.

Therefore, the *seguro de caución* is an insurance for damages, since its aim is to compensate for damage caused to property. It is an insurance policy in favour of a third party given that in entering into the insurance agreement the policy-holder (the debtor in the underlying relationship) is not securing his own interests but the interests of the creditor.

The practice and case law have been debated as to whether the *seguro de caución* bears the character similar to a *fianza*, a guarantee or is like insurance.

Certain arguments based on the theory of contractual consideration, champions its character as a *fianza* or as a guarantee, maintaining that the insurer becomes a guarantor who binds himself personally to the insured – who is the creditor in the underlying relationship – so as to secure the fulfilment of the obligation of which the policy-holder is debtor.

However, other arguments stress the fact that policies of *caución* are a common product of insurance companies, since section 5, paragraph 10(b) of the 30/1995 Act on the Ruling and Supervision of Private Insurances prohibits and declares null and void the 'issuance of guarantees different from those used in the insurance business'. Consequently, the fact that the *seguro de caución* is part of the insurance business – as it is governed by the legislation on insurances and is agreed with an insurance company – implies that it has insurance characteristics.

Types of seguro de caución

Apart from the common type of *seguro de caución* securing the payment of commercial operations, basically the following types may be noted:

1 Bond insurance securing the amounts advanced for housing. This insurance is regulated by the Act 57/1968, of 27 July, which compels property developers to secure the reimbursement of the amounts advanced for housing, through a bank guarantee or an insurance policy if for any reason the construction is not successfully started or completed within the proper time.
2 *Seguro de caución* in favour of the Public Administration. This insurance is regulated by the Act 13/1995, of 18 May, on Agreements of the Public Administration, which provides for this insurance as security of the bid bonds for the award of public works contracts or the carrying out of public works or provision of supplies, covering the risk of an eventual compensation to the insured – the Public Administration – arising from the bid or the performance of the works.

   Other types are the *seguro de caución* securing customs liabilities or that securing legal or regulatory duties towards the Administration which a great deal of professionals underwrite, such as insurance brokers, real estate agents, gas licensees, societies or agencies of securities, etc.
3 S*eguro de caución* originated in a contract. These insurances are very often used, for instance, in the field of works contracts so as to secure the satisfactory completion of certain work.

Retention of title

According to the case law of the Supreme Court[2] a covenant on retention of title is a guarantee securing the collection of a deferred payment mainly used in the sale of movables.

In this sense, where sales of movables involve deferred payment they usually include a covenant under which the concerned parties agree that though the asset sold is delivered to the purchasor, there will not be a passing of title until the purchasor has paid off the price.

Conversely, as for sale of realty this covenant is less frequent since there are more satisfactory guarantees securing payment, for example the real estate mortgage.

The covenant on retention of title is not expressly regulated by the Spanish Civil Code. However, the jurisprudence of the Supreme Court[3] recognises this covenant under the aegis of the general principle of free will stated in section 1255, since it is a covenant which is not contrary to the law, the moral or the public order.

The Supreme Court case law[4] defines the covenant on retention of title as a condition of the purchaser's acquisition of the ownership.

Consequently, during the term affected by the condition, that is, until the full payment of the deferred price, the purchaser will only hold the possession and enjoy the use of the asset bought but he will not be entitled to freely dispose of it.

In this view, if the purchaser transfers the asset to a third party, whether voluntarily or not, before the deferred price has been paid off, the vendor may take legal action to recover the asset, that is, action for the recovery of possession or the vendor may bring a third party ownership claim if the asset has been seized.

2 Amongst many we may highlight its decision dated 22 March 1993.
3 Those decisions of 10 June 1958 and 10 January 1989.
4 The Supreme Court decisions dated 19 May 1989 and 12 March 1993.

Summarising the foregoing, the covenant on retention of title provides the vendor with the security that he may claim the return of the asset as its legitimate owner if the payment of the deferred price is not made.

Furthermore, as stated in the decision of the Supreme Court of 19 May 1989, despite the retention of title the vendor lacks the entitlement to freely dispose of the asset so long as the purchaser complies with his obligation of deferred payment. Under such circumstances, the vendor cannot transfer the relevant asset to a third party, and the purchaser is entitled to bring all legal actions required for the preservation of his right.

Notwithstanding the above, there is an exception that must be noted which applies to the sale of real estate in which respect section 34 of the Mortgage Act[5] provides for the protection of registrar notarisation. Thus, when the purchaser of a real estate is a third party who purchases it in good faith and for valuable consideration from a person recorded in the Land Registry as entitled to transfer the title, such purchaser will be held to be the owner of the estate.

Act of 1998 on the sale of movables

The general regime governing the covenant on retention of title must be adjusted in view of the new Act on Credit Sale of Movables of 1998[6] (hereinafter referred as 'the ACSM') which has replaced the former Act of 1965.[7]

In this sense, section 15 of the ACSM provides that '... those retentions of title included in agreements governed by this Act will only be enforceable against third parties if they are registered with the Registry of Credit Sales of Movables'.

Therefore, pursuant to the section above the covenant on retention of title needs to be registered with the Registry of Credit Sales of Movables in order to be enforceable against any third party.

This registration must be made in the standard form authorised by the General Direction of Registries and Notaries, pursuant to that provided for in section 10 of the Order of 15 November 1982 approving the Ordinance for the Registry of Credit Sales of Movables (which has been kept in force by the derogatory provision of the ACSM) which states that '... in order to register those agreements to which section 2 refers, ie agreements of credit sales of movables, there the official form must be used authorised by the General Direction of Registries and Notaries'.

The ACSM sets out a special procedure of enforcement in the event of breach of the obligation to pay the instalments derived from an agreement of this kind, which procedure allows the creditor or vendor to act directly and exclusively in relation to those assets so purchased.

In short, we may point out that currently the enforceability and effectiveness of the covenant of retention of title against third parties are contingent upon its registration with the Registry of Credit Sales of Movables.

Consequently, in practical terms the security that the covenant of retention of title provides to the purchaser and the vendor with respect to the fulfilment of their reciprocal obligations is closely linked to registration of the covenant with the Registry, otherwise the covenant will not be enforceable against third parties.

5 Decree of 8 February 1946 passing the Mortgage Act.
6 Act 28/1998 on Credit Sales of Movables of 13 July.
7 Act 50/1965 of 17 July on Credit Sale of Movables.

To conclude, for these covenants to be subject to registration with the Registry, the agreements of credit sale containing them must comply with the provisions of the ACSM and meet the conditions required by it.

Leasing

From a doctrinal view point this is the involvement of a credit entity which – having legal capacity to do so – acts on behalf of a client and – pursuant to his instructions – purchases from a vendor a specific asset possession of which is vested in the client who will enjoy it in return for a payment made at regular intervals and during a determinate and irrevocable term. On the expiry of such term the client may opt either to return the good or to extend its enjoyment in exchange for a lesser consideration or to purchase the ownership at a residual value previously fixed.[8]

In legal terms the 7th additional provision of the Act 26/1988 expressly regulates leasing and states the following: 'Finance leases are those contracts whose subject-matter is the assignment of the use of movables and immovables as purchased for such purposes in compliance with the specifications of the user-to-be in exchange for a consideration consisting of those periodic instalments to which the 2nd paragraph of this provision refers. The goods that are the subject-matter of such assignment shall only become attached to the user's industry, ie agriculture, fisheries, manufacturing, commerce, crafts or services. The leasing needs to include a purchasing option in favour of the user which may be exercised on the termination of the lease agreement.'

As for its legal treatment it is inferred that this is a commercial financing contract, given that there must be the involvement of a credit entity – the leasing entity – that is providing its client with the funds to purchase a certain asset.

Leases are also shaped as standard contracts, since they are defined and even regulated by the law which requires the compliance of certain requirements and allows the parties little discretion as to their regulation.

The lease is a contract for valuable consideration given that it involves the payment of a rent and it can be defined as 'in rem' since it entails the transfer of an asset, either movable or immovable.

Finally the lease must be in writing.

As for the jurisprudence, it is a complex and unusual contract that is governed by its own specific terms. The goods the subject of the contract are investment goods acquired by a leasing company selection by the end user, to whom the use of such goods is transferred with the option to purchase them.[9]

On the other hand, in comparing this contract with other contracts we find similarities with, for instance, the sale with guarantee, the sale with retention of title or the credit sale with retention of title. Thus, the lease has elements in common with these other contracts but at the same time it contains other elements that until the Act 26/88 made this contract regarded as an unusual contract governed by the parties' freedom to bargain.

8 Mr Sixto Sánchez.

9 This is inferred from decisions of the Supreme Court, such as those dated 30 April 1991, 22 May 1992, 31 January 1994 and 7 February 1995 amongst others.

As for the commercial practice, operative leasing or renting and finance leasing are treated in a separate manner, the former being a short or medium-term lease which usually involves the lessor's technical assistance and deals with bilateral operations between a user and the vendor of the good, without the involvement of a credit entity.

The rents paid in finance leasing are calculated so as to amortise the whole or an important part of the price of the asset with the possibility of eventually purchasing the asset. This contract must be trilateral.

Regarding the guarantees, as already mentioned a leasing entity acquires a movable or immovable asset – the property is kept by such entity – following a user's specific instructions. In the same way, we have also referred to the fact that this is a commercial contract of funding in which the lessor's interest does not lie in keeping the asset but in obtaining the rents arising from it, and so serving such asset really as a guarantee of the payment of the rent agreed.

These contracts usually include certain clauses – whose validity is not questioned – that reinforce the guarantees embodied in them. Thus, for instance, (i) the financial entity is released from curing any hidden defect of the leased asset; (ii) the user as purchasor of such asset is subrogated to the rights and obligations of the credit entity with respect to the supplier or vendor; (iii) any insurance covering the asset will be on the user's account for the duration of the lease; and also (iv) there may be a termination clause for the user defaulting on his payment obligations.

In holding the ownership of the leased goods, the credit entity is legally provided with those protections inherent in ownership, which may be reinforced against third parties when the operation is registered with the Land Registry or that of Credit Sales.

Regarding formal requirements, this kind of contract has to be executed in writing in accordance with most recent practice.

As for the enforceability against the user, leasing contracts involving real estate and registered with the Property Registry must also be formalised in a public deed; whereas those involving movables will have to be executed in a public deed or in the standard authorised form and be registered with the Registry of credit sales of movables.

El mandato de crédito (The credit mandate)

The '*mandato de crédito*' may be defined as a contract by which a person (mandator) instructs another (mandatory) to grant credit in favour of a third party – on behalf and on account of the former – credit understood in the wide sense, encompassing items such as the delivery of a certain amount of money, the issuance of a *fianza*, the extension of an existing debt, etc.

Even though this financial figure is not regulated under Spanish law, jurisprudence has recognised it pursuant to the principle of contractual freedom allowing individuals or entities to enter into contracts.[10]

Basically, it may be said that this is an unusual contract which has particular characteristics and is linked to a funding operation. Although it is quite similar to both the *fianza* and the ordinary mandate, authors do not consider it to be a proper *fianza* or an ordinary mandate but rather an obligation or promise of payment with its own

10 Decision of the Supreme Court dated 22 December 1941 and Commentaries by Mr Antonio Polo. Private Law Magazine.

identity, where the mandator's obligation with respect to the mandatory is for payment of compensation.

The *mandato de crédito* does not have to be delivered in a specific form – it can even be express or tacit – yet for evidentary purposes it should be in writing, setting out in a clear way the obligations relating to the mandatary.

The mandator is entitled to revoke the mandate at his own discretion and at any time, provided the mandatory has not complied yet with the obligation to grant the credit.

In accepting the mandate, the mandatory binds himself to comply with the agreed terms within the limits set by the mandator, except if the mandate may be complied in a manner which is more beneficial to the mandator without having to advance any amount for the execution of the mandate.

Should the final beneficiary of the credit – the debtor – eventually fail to pay, the mandator will be bound to reimburse the mandatory for the amount of the credit, together with the interests attached to it – as compensation – and those damages that may result from the performance of the contract, provided that such damages had been caused by reason other than the mandatorys own negligence.

Stand-by letters of credit (SBLC)

All those arrangements consisting of a payment made against the delivery of a document operate as guarantees. Thus, a creditor is reasonably certain that he will receive payment of the debt he holds from either a documentary credit or a stand-by letter of credit.

In both types of SBLC, that is the direct SBLC (in which a bank undertakes to meet payment in the event of debtor's default) and the indirect SBLC (where the debtor approaches a domestic bank to procure that a bank from the creditor's country grants a direct SBLC to the latter), the securing component seems to be evident; the bank (either if it is the debtor's bank or its correspondent in the creditor's country) will meet the payment due in the event of debtor's default.

As compared with traditional guarantees, the SBLC have a material advantage, as the payment can be conditional upon delivery of certain documents – even if they are only evidence of non-fulfilment – which prevent abuses that might derive from an abstract guarantee where a creditor could effect a fraudulent enforcement.

Spanish authors have been discussing in great detail the legal nature of the SBLC and its differences compared to similar guarantees, such as the documentary remittance, the documentary discount or the abstract guarantee. In this respect, the abstract guarantee is similar to the SBLC since in both cases the bank undertakes to meet the payment if the debtor fails to do so, though in the former – the abstract guarantee – there is no need to submit documentation other than the demand for payment.

Given that the regime of the SBLC is regulated by Standard Rules and Practices relating to the Documentary Credits (see section 1 of the said Standard Rules and Practices), attention should be paid to the likely application of such rules under Spanish law. Thus, the Supreme Court (for instance in its decision of 9 October 1997) does not recognise the argument that regards such rules as a part of the Spanish legal system as a ground for an appeal to the Supreme Court for infringement of the statutory law system, in the event of a likely breach of the Rules and Practices.

The foregoing does not mean that submission to the Rules and Practices will not be valid in Spain. On the contrary, the Supreme Court regards them as valid and binding on the parties as it has given them the character of contractual clauses that the parties may adopt under the contractual freedom existing in the Spanish legal system (decision of the Supreme Court dated 30 March 1976) or considers them as common law (its decision of 27 October 1984), as a valid custom having the force of law.

TAXATION OF GUARANTEES

Broadly speaking guarantees, both personal and real, may involve services that are either subject to Value Added Tax (VAT)[11] when such services are rendered by entrepreneurs or professionals in the performance of their activity in exchange for a valuable consideration, or subject to Transfer Tax and Stamp Duty (*Impuesto sobre Transmisiones Patrimoniales y Actos Jurídicos Documentados*) (TTSD)[12] when they are rendered by individuals.

It should be borne in mind that those guarantees that, in principle, would have been subject to the TTSD as Real Property Transfers will not be subject to such tax when they are ancillary to financial operations subject to VAT.

In this respect, section 20.1.18.f) of the VAT Act regards as financial operations subject to VAT the issue of *fianzas, avales* and any other in rem or personal guarantee collateral to financial operations subject to VAT. According to the doctrine, this collateral nature seems to be applicable not only to 'stricto sensu' financial operations but also to any operation subject to VAT but not to the TTSD that has a guarantee attached.

In view of the foregoing, the general principle here is that operations secured with guarantees are subject to VAT but exempt from it pursuant to section 20.1.18 of the VAT Act that provides for exemption for *fianzas, avales* and any other in rem or personal guarantees.

In addition to the above, since in rem guarantees are subject to registration – for example the mortgage – they are liable to stamp duty at a rate of 0.5% but exempt from VAT. Conversely, *fianzas* are not so liable, nor charged with such tax.

A guarantee might (unusually) not be subject to VAT but it will certainly be charged with Transfer Tax at a rate of 1%, payable by the creditor whose credit is secured.

The tax base for mortgages, pledges and 'antichresis' is the final amount owed (principal plus interest and costs) secured by the guarantee; in the absence of such specific amount the principal plus three-year interest will be taken as such tax base.

On the other hand, guarantees are usually issued to secure a loan/credit. In this respect, as already mentioned for guarantees in general, loans may be subject either to VAT if comprising services rendered by entrepreneurs or professionals in the performance of their activity in exchange for a valuable consideration, or to TTSD.

The doctrine and jurisprudence, in general, limits the levy of VAT to those loans granted by entrepreneurs or professionals during the exercise of their activity, while individuals lending money with interest are not considered to be liable to VAT. Under this criterion a person liable to VAT is strictly speaking, subject to such tax when he

11 Act 37/1992 of 28 December.

12 Legislative Royal Decree 1/1993 of 24 September.

grants loans in the operation of his business activity and those loans granted by private individuals are subject to Transfer Tax even when granted for valuable consideration.

Within the VAT scope the taxation of complementary guarantees, as already mentioned, is governed by the ancillary principle, in such a manner that the guarantees attached to a loan subject to VAT cannot be liable to Transfer Tax even when such guarantees have been issued subsequent to the underlying credit agreement. This is so because section 20.1.18 of the VAT Act confers guarantees with the same nature as that of the financial operations giving rise to them. Consequently, both the guarantee and the loan subject to VAT are financial operations exempt from VAT under the VAT Act.

Furthermore, section 25 of such TTSD adds one more requirement as to the taxation of the loan and complementary guarantees, ie these guarantees must be executed simultaneously to the underlying debt or, if executed afterwards, the loan agreement must provide for them.

10 Sweden

Bengt Kärde

Hammarskiöld & Co

GENERAL

Swedish law is essentially a continental legal system with statutes as the main source of law. Precedence is viewed as a complement to statute, and the status of legal writing is the subject matter of considerable debate.

Sweden has a strong tradition of public and administrative openness, and virtually all administrative documents related to the drafting of a Government Bill are public. Due to their accessibility, traditionally the preparatory works have been the main source of guidance when interpreting a statute. Because of their importance, the preparatory works are usually drafted in a rather extensive manner and resemble in many aspects traditional continental commentaries. Of particular importance are the statements of the responsible minister of the state in the Government Bill. Swedish laws are therefore often not as exhaustive as continental or Anglo-Saxon laws, rather, both the government, the parliament and lawyers in Sweden rely to a comparatively large extent on the preparatory works.

Further, statutes are interpreted in the light of the decisions of the courts. In this respect, the decisions of the Supreme Court, though not formally binding, are viewed as semi-binding, usually due to their authority. Semi-binding means that the burden of argument and distinction is on the party wishing to deviate from a judgment of the Supreme Court. In the absence of any decisions of the Supreme Court that could be of guidance, the decisions of the Courts of Appeal may also be taken into consideration. The decisions of the district courts are hardly ever invoked, but if and when invoked, they are usually regarded more as a point of argument than as authoritative sources of law. As concerns court practice in general, a judgment is not viewed as authoritative solely due to its nature of being a judgment. Rather, the stringency and weight of argument in the reasoning in the judgment is fundamental in assessing its value as precedence.

Even though Sweden has a continental legal system with statutes as the main source of law, Sweden lacks a major codification of civil law and the Swedish system has sometimes been described as a 'patchwork system'. Some areas of major importance, eg the field of contracts, sale of goods and procedure, are thoroughly regulated by statute, but these statutes are not usually considered to cover areas beyond the field of their direct applicability. Therefore, in many fields, analogies have to be drawn and uncodified principles of law need to be applied.

GUARANTEES AND LIABILITIES

Nature of guarantees and indemnities

In Sweden there is only one legal concept relating to guarantees. The legislation is embodied in the Commercial Code Chapter 10, sections 8-12 and originates from the year 1734. Generally, guarantees and indemnities are interpreted and construed to fit into the provisions of these old statutory provisions which in Swedish is referred to as 'borgen'. The word 'borgen' is often translated as 'guarantee' or 'surety' and, for the sake of clarify, in the following the word 'guarantee' will be used when discussing this legal concept. However, quite often, as in relation to, eg on-demand guarantees, it is not possible to subsume an actual contract made having the effect of an on-demand guarantee under the legislation relating to guarantees. As will be described further below, in such situations general principles of contract law will apply.

Under Swedish statutory law guarantees exist in two different forms, both entailing their own distinctive effects. A guarantee can either be (i) subsidiary, ie a contingent liability where the guarantor undertakes to pay whatever the debtor has been proven to be unable to pay, or (ii) direct, entailing that the creditor may seek whomever he chooses, the guarantor or the debtor, for payment of the debt.

A subsidiary guarantee is of rather doubtful value to a creditor. In order to be able to turn to the guarantor for payment, the creditor will have to establish that the debtor is unable to meet its obligations. This may require instituting enforcement or bankruptcy proceedings against the debtor, and only if such proceedings fail, ie where the creditor does not receive full payment for his claim, the creditor may successfully seek payment for the debt from the guarantor. Consequently, in order to receive payment from a guarantor who has undertaken a subsidiary guarantee, the creditor may need to institute legal proceedings against both the debtor and the guarantor, as well as enforcement proceedings against the debtor in order to prove the debtor's inability to meet his payment obligations.

It should be borne in mind that subsidiary guarantees are regarded as the main rule under Swedish law. Guarantees with direct liability will only be recognised if expressly agreed.

To assume a guarantee with direct liability, the guarantor must assume the debt as 'a debt of his own' (*såsom för egen skuld*). By assuming the debt as a debt of his own, the guarantor assumes direct liability for the debtor's original debt, ie the creditor may claim payment from either the debtor or the guarantor. As between the debtor and the guarantor, the liability will be joint and several. The liability of the guarantor may be limited to a specified amount or to a specified debt. The guarantee may also be general in that it may cover all the debtor's present and future debts to the creditor (*generell borden*). Consequently, the importance of clearly specifying the debt or amount that is covered by the guarantee and the fact that the guarantor assumes the debt, as a debt of his own, cannot be emphasised enough.

Under Swedish law, guarantees relate to liabilities that are closely connected to the main debt of the debtor and situations where the guarantor may raise the same objections against the creditor as could the debtor. This means that if the debtor makes partial payments, the liability of the guarantor will be reduced correspondingly, and if the debtor discharges his debt by taking up a new loan, the new loan will not necessarily (without the guarantor's approval) be covered by the guarantee.

The major parts of guarantees and indemnity undertakings are construed to fit the above-mentioned rules. However, if an undertaking cannot be construed to fit the provisions regulating guarantees, the undertaking will be assessed in the light of general principles of contract law. Such is the case with, eg on-demand guarantees, ie contractual obligations to pay a debt that are conditional upon the occurrence of some specified events, usually only a written request to the guarantor to honour its guarantee. This latter position of Swedish law makes it extremely difficult to predict the legal position of the parties involved, and parties should therefore ensure that their intentions are clearly defined and covered in the undertaking.

Indemnities relating to guarantee undertakings are rather unusual in the Swedish legal environment. They appear in mutual contracts, and are rarely encountered as independent undertakings. To the extent they do exist as independent undertakings, they are usually tightly interwoven with existing mutual contracts. Swedish courts will normally uphold such undertakings according to their wording. It should be noted that the actual wording of an indemnity undertaking could be of particular importance; as indemnities are interpreted as contracts. There may be a difference between 'reimburse', 'indemnify' and 'hold harmless': 'reimburse' most probably relates to the reimbursement of costs, 'indemnify' most probably relates to the actual amount of claims presented by third parties, and 'hold harmless' most probably relates to the reimbursement of all losses, whether direct or indirect, related to a certain event. It is, in short, advisable to draft guarantee undertakings in the form of a guarantee 'as for own debt' or 'on demand', and not to make use extensively of indemnity undertakings. If indemnity undertakings in certain relations must be used, care and scrutiny should be taken on their drafting.

JOINT AND SEVERAL OBLIGATIONS

The basic principle under Swedish law is that obligations undertaken by more than one person are joint and several unless otherwise agreed. In relation to guarantee undertakings made by more than one guarantor, this principle is embodied in the Commercial Code Chapter 10 Section 11. The same principle is also codified in s 2 of the Swedish Promissory Notes Act (Swedish Code of Statutes 1936:81)[1] which, according to the preparatory works, is intended to be applied, by way of analogy, in a field considerably wider than that which follows from its wording. Thus, the said principle applies to all obligations, regardless of whether they are embodied in an instrument of debt or not.

Joint and several liability means, as it is expressed in both the Commercial Code and the Promissory Notes Act, that '[...] one shall be liable for all, and all shall be liable for one [...]'. Thus, the creditor is entitled to approach each and every one of the debtors

1 The Swedish Promissory Notes Act has been translated into English; Legal Language Service, Swedish Commercial Legislation, Nordstedts Juridik, Stockholm.

and require payment in full from that debtor. The debtor being approached cannot defend himself by referring to the other debtors. This rule is expressed in the phrase 'one shall be liable for all'.

The phrase 'all shall be liable for one' refers to the contribution as between the debtors and will be dealt with under 'Contribution' below.

Subrogation

By fulfilling the debtor's obligations, the guarantor is entitled to subrogation of the creditor's original rights against the debtor. However, there is no statute directly addressing the question of subrogation and Swedish case law does not provide any definite answers as to what extent such right will be recognised. The position is therefore not entirely clear. However, there are instances of guarantors having succeeded into the position of the original debtor without any explicit provision to such effect in contract or otherwise. However, legal support for subrogation is found in other acts, such as the Swedish Rights of Priority Act (*förmånsrättslagen*) s 3. According to this provision, the guarantor will be entitled to the same priority as the original creditor in the debtor's bankruptcy estate. Further the guarantor will be entitled to subrogation of the creditor's right to a collateral that the debtor has pledged as security for the main debt.

Due to the present uncertainty in this area, it is advisable to address the question of subrogation by way of contract. Since most Swedish civil law in the field of commerce and finance is non-mandatory, the provisions of a contract between the parties will normally be upheld by the courts.

Thus, guarantee undertakings or indemnities should include a provision giving the guarantor an unambiguous right of subrogation into the position of the original creditor. If the undertaking has to be honoured, it is further advisable to seek to obtain a letter of subrogation. Otherwise, if the debtor refuses to recognised the guarantor's rights, the guarantor may need to prove that subrogation has taken place, and that the guarantor is entitled to present the relevant claim.

Contribution

The issue of contribution arises only after a guarantor has paid at least some part of the original debt of the main debtor. Thus, contribution is of less importance for the creditor than for the guarantor(s) and the main debtor. Contribution may be divided into two separate issues; contribution between the main debtor and the guarantor(s), and contribution between several guarantors of which one has discharged the main debt to the creditor.

As to a guarantor's right of contribution from the main debtor, this right may be argued to be one of the features of, or derived from, the debtor's right of subrogation. Even though this right is definitely regarded as a well-established principle, it is debated among legal scholars how to explain and justify it. Being an established principle, in order to be entitled to contribution from the main debtor, the guarantor must have discharged the main debt to the creditor or at lease a part of it (where interest is included). The debt may be discharged by payment in case or by way of set-off or in some other way acceptable to the creditor. The debtor is most certainly entitled to contribution even if he, as guarantor, were able to avoid his obligation due to defences, such as, eg time-bar. However, at least as a main rule, a condition for contribution is that the main debtor was under the obligation to fulfil or redeem the obligation.

As mentioned above, the basic principle in Swedish law is that guarantee undertakings made by more than one guarantor are joint and several, unless sole liability has been expressly agreed upon, and contribution among several guarantors is only feasible if the undertaking is joint and several.

The right to contribution among several guarantors depends on various factors, such as if the guarantor's undertakings are on same level, if they have made the undertaking at the same time and in the same document and, or course, on any specific contractual agreement made between them. However, as a main rule and provided the guarantee undertaking is joint and several, a guarantor who has discharged at least some part of the main debt of the debtor will be entitled to contribution from the other guarantors provided he has paid more than he was obliged to. Unless otherwise agreed, the liability of each of the guarantors will follow from an analogy of the Swedish Promissory Notes Act s 2 para 2, which reads as follows:

> 'Where one of the makers pays the debt, he shall be entitled to recover from his co-debtors, each co-debtor's share of the debt. If it is clearly apparent that one of the co-debtors has become insolvent, or if his whereabouts are unknown, each of the others shall be liable for a proportionate part of the deficit. The above-mentioned shall also apply where the debtor who paid the debt seeks recovery against a co-debtor of the latter's share, or has sent notice of the claim, by appropriate means, and payment has not been made within fourteen days thereafter.'

Thus, the principle of contribution under Swedish law is such that the liability of several guarantors as against the creditor is joint and several whereas liability as between the guarantors themselves is not.

In general, the liability of the debtors as between themselves follows the number of debtors, ie is proportionate to the number of debtors. This liability as against each other, however, may be deviated from by agreement. In any case, the fellow debtors are proportionally liable for each other as against the debtor having paid the debt. This may be illustrated by an example:

> Creditor C has a claim against the debtors D^1, D^2, D^3, D^4 and D^5, whose liability is joint and several. There is no agreement between the debtors to the effect of deviating from the general proportionate liability as between them. C claims full payment from D^1, who – in accordance with the joint and several liability – discharges the debt in full. When D^1 seeks recourse against his co-debtors, it appears that D^2 is insolvent and cannot meet his debt. His part of the debt (20%) shall then proportionally be borne by the remaining debtors; as there are four of them – D^1 is a remaining debtor as well as D^3, D^4 and D^5 – each of them shall bear

> 25% of what D^2 would have had to pay. In effect, D^1, D^3, D^4 and D^5 shall each bear 25% of the original debt. This rule, however, does not affect C, as he was entitled to receive payment in full for the entire claim from each and every of the debtors.

In principle, the liability between the debtors is not joint and several, meaning that the debtor who has discharged the original claim must seek recourse against each and every one of the remaining debtors. It should, however, be possible to agree on joint and several liability as between the debtors as well. Such an agreement is easily explained by way of example:

> D^1, D^2, D^3 and D^4 are jointly and severally liable as against C for a common debt. D are jointly and severally liable as against C for a common debt. D^1 discharges the debt. If the debtors have agreed on joint and several liability as between themselves, D^1 should be able to require payment of the entire debt not attributable to him from any of D^2, D^3 and D^4. Suppose D^2 pays this remaining debt after D^1 and D^2 having discharged their part. If D^2 chooses to take recourse against D^3, D^3 would then be able to claim half of what he had to pay from D^4.

It is difficult to say whether such agreements are common in Sweden. However, the obvious advantage of such an agreement is that each of the debtors only needs to take action once (assuming none of them is unable to meet his debt), instead of one of them having to take action against each and every of the others, especially as it is in the creditor's hand to decide which one of the debtors will be in the position to take action against the others. The decision, however, as whether or not to deviate from the general principle of proportionate liability, and as whether or not to agree on joint and several liability as between the debtors is, in effect, a commercial one.

Defences

In general, the liability of a guarantor follows the liability of the main debtor, meaning that all objections the debtor can raise, or could have raised, are available to the guarantor as well, eg that the goods sold have not been delivered, that the goods delivered were defective, that the main contract is invalid and that the debt has been settled. Due to the various objections it is possible to raise based on the contractual relationship between the main debtor and the creditor, the opportunity of entering into separate on-demand guarantees is frequently taken. Such undertakings entitle the creditor to claim payment under the guarantee subject to the occurrence of some explicitly specified circumstances or events.

Following general contract law, of course, the guarantor may also raise objections of various kinds related to his own undertaking. However, in this context it should be noted that Swedish courts tend to enforce guarantee undertakings rather strictly and in particular undertakings with direct liability as for 'own debt'. It is rather difficult for a guarantor to retreat from a guarantee undertaking without being able to refer to objections the debtor could have raised.

TYPES OF SECURITY

General

Under Swedish law, a pledge is created by an agreement between a creditor/pledgee and a pledgor and, as will be described further below, together with certain other acts for perfection of the pledge. A pledge confers a right to hold the pledged object for purposes of security only, ie no right of use, and to sell it for the purpose of realising the security if the credit secured is not repaid in time.

Under Swedish property law, the moment of perfection of a charge or pledge (*sakrättsligt moment*) varies with the object concerned. In relation to land, ships and aircraft, the perfection is subject to mandatory registration in an official register. In relation to chattels, ie movable objects, the transfer of possession whereby the delivery of the object becomes decisive is of overall importance (*traditionsprincipen*). Finally, in relation to choses in action, ie 'rights' to objects not possessed, including intangible assets, assignable contracts and promissory notes (negotiable instruments are excluded since in many respects they are comparable with chattels), the moment of perfection will be notification to the debtor/obligor.

Other types of security are 'security sales', ie formal sales used only for the purpose of creating a security interest. Security sales are not governed by any special provisions, but follow the general rules in the Sales of Goods Act. A right of retention (possessory lien) is a right to retain someone else's property in order to enforce payment of a debt. In general, a right of retention is not combined with a right to sell the retained property.

The principle of delivery of possession fulfils two specific requirements: the transaction is made public and the debtor is actually sacrificing his own control over the object. In relation to land and other assets that require registration, the registration procedure replaces delivery of possession but fulfils the same purposes.

In this context it should be noted that, under Swedish law, regardless of its form, a pledge or charge will only be held valid provided there is a claim or an obligation corresponding to it. Thus, it should be borne in mind that it is equally important to secure evidence regarding the claim supported by the security, as it is to secure the security itself.

Chattels

As mentioned above, a pledge over chattels or movable assets is perfected through deliver of possession, whereby the handing over of the object is of overall importance (*traditionsprincipen*). The delivery of possession is the essential event giving protection against competing buyers or pledgees and against other creditors in bankruptcy proceedings. There are no specific requirements as to the form of a contract or pledge.

Thus, a pledge over chattels will not be recognised without delivery of possession and there is no freedom of contract concerning this requirement. Further, the actual control of the object may not be returned to the pledgor during the term of the pledge, but must remain with the pledgee or an independent third party, or the pledge will be invalid. The requirement to release control refers to both actual control, ie the pledgor must actually hand over the object to the pledgee, and to legal control, ie the pledgor must not be entitled to reclaim actual control after once having released it. This point is illustrated by the Supreme Court decision NJA 1986 p 409:

> A son had pledged his hunting rifles to his mother. The rifles were locked away, but the son could gain access to them through either the father or the mother, both of whom were holding keys to the closet in which the rifles were locked. In fact, the son was always able to gain access to the weapons when hunting season had arrived. The Supreme Court found that such alteration of physical possession as is required by Swedish law had not taken place and refused to accept that the rifles had been validly pledged. This decision also shows the influence of the Principle of Sacrifice mentioned above under C1.

In some situations possession can be replaced by certain other events. Where the chattel is in the hands of an independent third party, notice of the transaction to that third party is sufficient pursuant to the Act on Pledges over Chattels in a Third Party's Possession (Swedish Code of Statutes 1936:88).

Chattels can also be sold by means of a 'registered chattel sale' (lösöreköp), where registration at the local district court and certain publicity measures protect the buyer against the property being distrained in the seller's hand and in the event of the seller's bankruptcy. The provisions concerning registered chattel sale are found in the Act on Registered Chattel Sales and will be discussed further under 'Registered Chattel Sales' p 402 below.

Choses in action

A pledge over choses in action, such as intangible assets, assignable contracts and promissory notes (other than negotiable instruments) is legally perfected by notifying the debtor/obligor. Notification will also be used for perfection of a secondary pledge over assets already pledged.

This rule is laid down in the Swedish Promissory Notes Act s 31, para 1 first sentence (which according to its wording refers to transfers, but according to s 10 of the same Act shall be equally applied in relation to pledges), which read as follows:

> 'Where a person transfers a non-negotiable promissory note, the transfer shall not be valid as against his creditors, unless notice of the transfers is given to the debtor by either the transferor or the transferee.'

Thus, both the pledgor and the pledgee may notify the debtor of the pledge. The aim of the notification is to prevent the debtor from making a valid payment to the pledgor. It is important to ensure that the debtor is aware of the legal meaning of a notification, since there have been cases in which the courts have disregarded a notification due to its unclear wording.

The primary effect of a notification is that the debtor is no longer entitled to pay the debt to the original creditor. This applies not only to a creditor receiving money on his own behalf, but also to situations where the pledgor/original creditor and the pledgee have agreed that the pledgor/original creditor shall receive the money due in the capacity of agent for the pledgee.[2] This requirement of the pledgor relinquishing control should be made clear, particularly when dealing with consumers (eg when receivables have been pledged). There must not be any uncertainty on the debtor's side as to whether he is entitled to pay the original debtor or not. If there is uncertainty, the situation may arise in which the debtor cannot validly pay the original debtor, and yet the pledgee does not have an enforceable security. The exact extent of the duty to make the effects of the pledge clear to the debtor is, of course, dependent on the circumstances in the individual case, and the requirements for clarity are probably less strict against banks than against consumers.

Charges over land

All land in Sweden, including any buildings on the land, are divided into units that are registered with the local land registration authority. The land registration authority is a division of the local district court for the area in which the land is situated. The authority also keeps a register over title, mortgages and other charges over land, such as leases.

Mortgages (*inteckning*) over land represent an abstract credit potential of a specified amount and a firm order of priority in the event of an executive sale of the unit. The legislation relating to land is found in the Real Property Code of 1971, as amended, and, as concerns mortgages, Chapter 6 in particular.

A mortgage on a unit of land is entered in the register upon application of the registered owner of the unit. It is evidenced by a mortgage deed (*pantbrev*) issued by the registration authority. The deed will be delivered to the registered owner and the owner will thereby have a document which evidences security over the property (*ägarhypotek*). Thereafter, the owner can use the mortgage deed in accordance with the rules relating to ordinary chattels, ie by delivery of possession of the mortgage deed to the creditor and there is no other formal requirement of the agreement to pledge. The holder of the deed is protected by the possession of the deed but may improve his position for purposes of notification etc by having his possession registered. In the event of the sale of the unit of land, the holder of a mortgage deed, including the registered owner, will be paid in relation to the rank of their mortgages. In this context it should be noted that a mortgage deed is a negotiable instrument and must therefore be kept safe. Loss of a deed requires application to the district court for a time-consuming cancellation procedure in accordance with the rules of the Cancellation Act (Swedish Code of Statutes 1927:85 as amended).

There is no lower or upper limit to the amount in which a mortgage may be issued. Consequently, a mortgage deed may very well be issued for a total amount exceeding the value of the land. In order to assert the number of deeds issued and other encumbrances on the land, it is necessary to obtain a certificate of encumbrance from the land register authority containing all necessary information.

Finally, it may be noted that in 1994, Sweden introduced the option to register a mortgage deed electronically. Although the system is only available to major, financial

2 Torgny Hâstad, Satkätt avseende lös egendom, 6th revised edition, Nordstedts Juridik, Stockholm 1997.

institutions, it has rapidly spread, and in 1997, approximately six million of the eight million mortgage deeds in circulation in Sweden have been replaced by a registration in the register for electronic deeds.

The system is intended to substitute the requirement for possession, and thus it cannot serve as a register over existing and valid charges over land.[3] It is the registered holder of an electronic deed who is entitled to make changes in the register. The owner of the land will only be informed of the changes, but is not entitled to make alterations by himself. The electronic deed can only be registered in the name of a licensed user who, in order to receive the license, must fulfil a number of specified conditions. This means that, in reality, an electronic deed never will be registered in the name of the owner of the land.

Charges over ships

The system for pledging ships resembles the system for pledging land in all material aspects and the rules are found in the Swedish Maritime Code Chapter 3.[4]

Both ships and ships under construction can be pledged. The owner applies to the ship register to be granted a mortgage and to obtain a mortgage deed. The deed may be pledged as security to a creditor. As described above under 'Charges over Land', there is a requirement as to the existence of a claim secured by the pledge and the owner will be entitled to proceeds from a sale on enforcement if the owner holds a deed by himself and if the claim related to a certain deed is less than the nominal amount of the deed. Further, in order to verify the total amount for which the ship or the ship under construction is pledged as well as the ranking of a certain deed, it is necessary to obtain a certificate of encumbrance. As concerns the latter, it should be noted that maritime liens do not appear in the register.

If the construction of a ship is pledged, the pledge will remain in the ship when it is transferred from the register of ship constructions to the register of ships.

Charges over aircraft

The process of pledging aircraft still represents the old Swedish system. It is about to be reformed in order to resemble the system for pledging land and ships, but for the time being, the old system is still in force.

The central registry for charges over aircraft is located at the City Court of Stockholm. In order to pledge an aircraft, the pledgee must be able to prove the claim, which shall be secured by the pledge. On the document evidencing the claim, the registered owner of the aircraft shall note his consent to the aircraft being pledged, this consent being

3 As already stated, the possession of a deed of pledge is useless, if the claim it is intended to secure cannot be established. Thus, the fact that a certain financial institute is registered as the holder of a deed of pledge does not necessarily mean that it has a valid claim to which the deed refers. Cf Ulf Jensen, Panträtt i fast egendom, 5th edition, Iustus förlag, Uppsala 1997.

4 The Swedish Maritime Code has been translated into English by the Institute for Maritime and Other Transport Law at Stockholm's University; Axel Ax:son Johnson institut för sjörätt och annan transporträtt, The Swedish Maritime Code, Juristförlaget, Stockholm 1995, supplemented 1997.

certified by the signature of two witnesses. It should be noted that partial ownership, cannot be pledged: the aircraft must be pledged in its entirety. The document evidencing the claim and the consent of the owner to the pledge shall then be filed with the Stockholm District Court, where the competent judge makes a notation in the register showing the fact that the aircraft is pledged and the order of the pledge in relation to other pledges. The charge over the aircraft arises when the notation in the register of charges has been entered.

It should be noted that the system regarding the owner's right to proceeds of sale on enforcement if and when he holds a certificate evidencing the registration, or if and when the claim secured by the pledge is less than the amount of the charge, applies to aircraft as well as to land and ships. It is possible to obtain a notation of registration on a separate document, thus enabling the owner to track back the actual certificate when the claim secured by the pledge is paid, and to reuse the certificate for new pledges. The new pledge will then have the same priority as the old one, as the system of priority is related to the order the certificates were made out (cf 'Priorities' p 405 below).

Pledges over aircraft may also encompass stocks of spares. Spares are defined as parts belonging to an aircraft and intended to replace parts of the aircraft that have been removed. The stock of spares to be pledged needs to be reasonably identified in the document evidencing the claim and showing the consent to the pledge of the registered owner of the aircraft. It shall, further, be certified by a 'trustworthy person' that the person stated to be the owner of the spares, in fact, is the owner.

It is possible to obtain a certificate of encumbrance for aircraft. Such certificates show the number and the order of charges over the aircraft granted by the registry. The certificate is issued by the registry at the Stockholm District Court.

Charges over shares

In Sweden publicly traded securities, including shares, have been completely dematerialised. Thus, a Swedish stock market company may in its articles of association include a provision to the effect that any person who, on a specific recorded date, is registered in the share register shall be deemed to be authorised to receive dividends, exercise the voting rights etc. Companies whose articles of association contain such a provision (record data provision) are referred to as 'VPC companies' (*avstämningsbolag*). According to the Swedish Act on Share Account-keeping of Financial Instruments (Swedish Code of Statutes 1998:1479), physical certificates may not be issued by VPC companies. In relation to VPC companies, the Swedish Central Securities Depository (*Värdepapperscentralen VPC Aktiebolag*) (the 'VPC') or another licensed central securities depository will, among other things, maintain the share register, deal with matters regarding registration of share holders and pledgees, provide print-outs of the share register etc.

Each holder of shares kept and administered by a central securities depository shall have at least one share account opened by an account operating institute, on which the shares held are registered. Pledges of shares held will also be registered on the account together with information about the pledgee.

Thus, when shares are pledged, in order to perfect the pledge, it must be notified by the registered shareholder to the relevant account operating institute administering the account. The person notifying the institute will have to prove its competence to make such notification and its right to have certain registrations on the accounts altered. The pledge will be effective when registered and the shareholder may thereafter not exercise control over the shares without the pledgee's consent.

Registered chattel sales

Due to the fact that both transfer of title and pledges over chattels are perfected through delivery of possession, sale and lease back transactions would, in principle, be invalid under Swedish law. However, as already mentioned under 'Chattels', above, legal title to chattels may be transferred without the need for delivery of possession under certain circumstance by means of a 'registered chattel sale' (*lösöreköp*). The provisions concerning registered chattel sale are found in the Act on Registered Chattel Sales[5] (Swedish Code of Statutes 1845:50 p 1).

In general, registered chattel sale may be used for all chattels and movable objects with the exception of some specified property. Thus, the Act is not applicable to ships, to marked timber and to buildings on someone else's land, although these objects, in general, are categorised as movable objects. There has been some debate as to whether the Act is applicable to, eg aircraft, and it should therefore always be ascertained whether the Act is applicable to the relevant object.

The procedure is rather complicated and is therefore usually not used for objects of comparatively small value. The purchase must be evidenced in writing, the object(s) purchased being evidenced in the document. This document must then be certified by two witnesses and the sale be published in a local newspaper at the place where the seller is domiciled. In the advertisement, the name and profession of both seller and buyer, the day the purchase was made and the purchase sum shall be stated. Within eight days from publishing the advertisement, the sale and purchase document together with a certificate evidencing the publishing of the advertisement shall be filed with the bailiff (*kronofogdemyndigheten*) at the place where the object of the purchase is located. The executive authority will thereafter register the purchase.

It should be noted that the Swedish courts are rather strict on the point of time limits when assessing purchases according to the Act. It should therefore be ensured that the eight-day time limit is not exceeded.

When the purchase has been registered, the buyer enjoys title to the object bought, and is free to lease it back. However, should the seller officially be declared bankrupt, or the relevant property be seized by the bailiff within 30 days from the time the documents were filed with the bailiff, the buyer's title will be disregarded. Thus, there is a certain delay in receiving full title to the object.

Floating charges

The legal concept of floating charges, as such, does not exist in Swedish law. However, there is a similar concept in both its effects and its technical construction to a floating

5 Lag (1845:50 s 1) om handel med lösören, som köparen låter i säljarens vård kvarbliva.

charge called 'industrial hypothec' (företagshypotek) and the legislation is embodied in the Floating Charges Act (Swedish Code of Statutes 1984:649)[6].

The procedure to obtain a floating charge resembles the procedure to pledge land in that the enterprise (a businessman or the board of directors, as the case may be) applies for the issue of a deed representing the floating charge. The application is submitted to a special registry, the Registry of Floating Charges, which is located at the Malmoe District Court. The deed will be issued with a specified nominal amount, and the floating charge will be perfected by the delivery of the deed to the creditor.

As when pledging land, deeds regarding floating charges can be issued in an unlimited number and the priority as between the deeds will be dependent on the respective date of application: an earlier application having higher priority than a later one. The Registry of Floating Charges issues certificates of encumbrance.

A floating charge entitles the use of both industrial as well as other enterprises as security. It encompasses all property relating to the enterprise, such as actual stock for production, chattels, etc but with the exception of short-term assets such as cash, bank account balances, shares and other securities, objects that may be pledged by way of registered mortgages and property that cannot be seized in enforcement proceedings.

Finally, it should be noted that floating charges enjoy a rather low priority under the Rights of Priority Act and creditors may therefore attempt to obtain other security besides a floating charge and to grant loans and credits secured by a floating charge on a rather restrictive basis.

FORMALITIES

Board resolutions

In Swedish companies limited by shares, there are, in general, three bodies with authority to act for and on behalf of the company; the general meeting of shareholders, the board of directors and the managing director.

According to the Swedish Companies Act (Swedish Code of Statutes 1975:1385) the organisation of a company and the management of its affairs is the task of the board of directors. Consequently, the board of directors will always be entitled to provide security in any form on behalf of the company.

The managing director is charged with the day-to-day management of the company in accordance with guidelines and instructions provided by the board of directors. However, the managing director may also, without authorisation from the Board, take measures which, in consideration of the scope and nature of the company's operations, are of an unusual nature or of great significance, if a decision by the board cannot be obtained without significant harm to the operations of the company.

It is often rather difficult to decide which matters are of a day-to-day character and the borderline will be different depending on the kind of business the company in question is engaged in and on the size of the company. However, providing security is in general not a matter of day-to-day business under Swedish law. Although in many

6 The Floating Charges Act has been translated into English; Legal Language Service, Swedish Commercial Legislation, Nordstedts Juridik, Stockholm.

cases the managing director will be the one conducting negotiations on the company's behalf, the provision of security will require authorisation in some form from the board of directors. Depending on the kind of business operation the company is engaged in and the size of the company, authorisation from the board of directors may be given in written instructions or powers of attorney. However, all forms of authorisation must be derived from a decision of the board.

Without authorisation of the board of directors, the managing director will be acting outside the scope of his legal competence, and the company may not be legally bound by the acts and statements of the managing director.

The same applies, mutatis mutandis, where the security is altered and replaced in any way. It is therefore advisable that, as concerns security and, in general, all major contracts outside the daily business of the company in question, that the other party ascertain to what extent the managing director is empowered by the board of directors.

Consequently, a certified excerpt from the minutes of the meetings with the board of directors, authorising the managing director to take certain steps on behalf of the company should be required.

Execution

There are no company seals or the like in Sweden.

As to execution of documents, according to the Companies Act, the board of directors has the right to represent the company against third parties and to sign for and on behalf of the company. The board of directors may also authorise any other person to represent and sign for the company and it is very common that such authorisation is given to two or more persons jointly. The managing director is always authorised to represent and sign for the company in day-to-day matters (see further under 'Board Resolutions', above).

The persons entitled to represent and sign for the company are listed in the certificate of incorporation, which may be obtained from the Swedish Patent and Registration Office. However, it should be noted that there could be a delay in the registration proceedings for various reasons. If somebody who is not covered by the certificate of incorporation offers to sign on behalf of the company, a certified copy of the document evidencing such person's authority should be required. If a person who is covered by the certificate of incorporation as authorised to sign for the company is in fact no longer empowered with such authorisation, the legally binding character of the agreement signed by such a non-competent person will be dependent on the good faith of the other party. However, the fact that a certain person is stated as being entitled to sign for the company in the certificate of incorporation will normally be sufficient for proving good faith.

Registration

As described under 'Types of Security' p 397, above, the change of title and the providing of security will not be legally perfected upon the mere agreement between the parties. An element of perfection, such as delivery of possession or registration, depending on the kind of asset concerned, needs to be fulfilled. Apart from those types of securities where registration constitutes the moment of perfection, there are no requirements of registration with the exception of mortgages over aircraft (see further under 'Charges over aircraft' p 400, above).

Consents

The change of title to, or the pledging of, property may only be effected by the legal owner of the property in question. (In the case of a pledged asset the pledgee can, however, re-pledge the asset). In relation to property encumbered with any rights of use or other liens for the benefit of a third party, the consent of the third party may be required depending on the structure of the encumbrance in question. Further, property that is pledged or otherwise used as security may not be sold or transferred without the consent of the pledgee or holder of the security.

Stamp duty

Stamp duties are levied in accordance with the Stamp Duty Act (Swedish Code of Statutes 1984:404) in connection with the issuing of mortgage deeds over land, ships, aircraft and floating charges. The amount of the duty varies in relation to the kind of property concerned and the registered nominal amount of the mortgage, but a minimum amount of SEK 50 will always be charged. Thus, stamp duty will be levied (i) on mortgages over land, with SEK 20 for every complete amount of SEK 1,000, (ii) on mortgages over aircraft and floating charges, with SEK 10 for every complete amount of SEK 1,000, and (iii) on mortgages over ships with SEK 4 for every complete amount of SEK 1,000. (The figures apply as of May 1999.)

Upon substitution of a mortgage by way of simultaneous applications for cancellation and registration of a new mortgage, stamp duty will not be levied due to an exemption in the Stamp Duty Act.

PRIORITIES

General

The question of priority between debts in general, and between charges, is regulated in the Swedish Rights of Priority Act[7] (Swedish Code of Statutes 1970:979). The Act is divided into several parts: (1) Introductory provisions, (2) Specific rights of priority, (3) General rights of priority, (4) The relationship between specific and general rights of priority and (5) Claims without any right of priority.

7 The Right of Priority Act has been translated into English; Legal Language Service, Swedish Commercial Legislation, Nordstedts Juridik, Stockholm.

The Act is applicable in the event of bankruptcy, insolvent liquidation or enforcement of a debt obligation.[8] The Act divides priority claims into general claims, which enjoy general priority and specific claims, which enjoy priority only in specified property. Claims that enjoy general priority are primarily employees' claims for salary and public taxes and charges.

The specific rights of priority in defined property are listed in ss 4-7 of the Act, where the ranking of the various specific rights of priority, according to s 9, para 1, will be the order of appearance of the various rights of priority in the Act. According to the Rights of Priority Act, the order of priority between the various types of security described under 'Guarantees and liabilities' p 392 above, is the following: (i) charges over chattel, including dematerialised shares, (ii) mortgages granted over ships and aircraft, (iii) floating charges, and (iv) mortgages granted in real property or land. In addition to these types of security, the Rights to Priority Act enumerates a variety of other securities, though these are without any commercial importance in the present context, such as maritime liens and policy holders' rights in the event of an insurance company's bankruptcy.

In general, the various securities mentioned in the Rights to Priority Act will not be in conflict with each other, ie a charge over a ship will hardly compete with a charge over land. In the event different types of security have been granted in the same object, the principle laid down in s 9, para 1, will apply. Thus, the earlier a certain type of pledge or mortgage is mentioned in these sections, the higher the ranking of the priority of that particular security. Thus, for example, a maritime lien (s 4, item 1) has higher priority than a mortgage over the same ship (s 4, item 3). This principle, as stated above, applies throughout all the relevant sections of the Act.

The Swedish system of priority rights are rather straightforward and, in general, competition between charges hardly ever arise.

Priority as between competing charges

According to s 1 of the Rights of Priority Act, 'provisions which prescribe that creditors shall have equal rights to payment mean that each creditor shall be entitled to payment in proportion to his claim'. Thus, in general, several instances of the same type of security enjoy equal priority. Thus, maritime liens enjoy the same priority as between themselves. Having regard only to the provisions of the Rights of Priority Act, also charges over land, ships, aircraft etc enjoy equal priority as between themselves.

However, the provisions of the Rights of Priority Act are supplemented by the provisions of various other statutes, such as, eg provisions in the Real Property Code in relation to mortgages of land. Thus, mortgage deeds over land enjoy priority as between themselves according to the day of the application for the respective mortgage.

8 The Swedish text refers to 'konkurs' and 'utmätning'. The concept of konkurs, unlike English law, describes both the bankrupscy of an individual and the insolvent liquidation of a company. I shall, for the sake of readability, hereinafter only refer to bankruptcy, which term in the context of the present article thus covers both the concept of bankruptcy and the concept of insolvent liquidation as these concepts are understood in English law.

Under 'Types of security' p 397 above, it has been stated that pledges registered the same day enjoy equal right to priority. The effects of provisions giving equal priority rights are provided by the Rights of Priority Act s 1, para 1. If thus, for example, charges over land enjoy the same right to priority, the holders of these charges shall be paid according to their respective claims. This shall be illustrated by the following example:

> C^1 and C^2 enjoy the same right of priority for their charges over a certain estate. C^1's claim amounts to SEK 100,000, and C^2's claim amounts to SEK 50,000; both claims are in their entirety secured by C^1's and C^2's respective charges. Upon sale of the estate, SEK 75,000 are received. As the relationship between C^1's and C^2's claim is 2:1, the moneys received will be divided into three parts, whereof C^1 shall receive two, and C^2 shall receive one, ie C^1 shall received SEK 50,000 and C^2 shall receive SEK 25,000.

Priority as against unsecured creditors

As for guarantees, the problem of priority as against unsecured creditors does not arise, guarantees in themselves being of the nature of an unsecured claim. Only the situation for mortgages and pledges will be discussed below.

The issue of priority against unsecured creditors is regulated in the Rights of Priority Act s 15. The relevant sentence in this section states that '[s]pecific priority rights take priority over general priority rights'. In the event of a debtor's bankruptcy, a mortgage granted in the debtor's real property does not compete with unsecured claims. The real property will be the sold , whereupon the creditors secured by mortgages will distribute the receivables of the sale between themselves. Only if and when the amount of the receivables exceeds the collective amount of claims related to the real property, will the remainder of the receivables become part of the general estate of bankruptcy.

To the extent the claim related to the security does not exceed the value of the security upon sale, secured claims do not compete with unsecured claims. To the extent, however, the claims secured by the securities exceed the value of the securities, the remainder of the claims, pursuant to the Rights to Priority Act s 18, will be treated as unsecured claims. This means that the balances will receive a certain proportion of their value, depending on the assets remaining in the estate after all claims with a right to priority have been satisfied (cf as stated under 'Preferential debts' below). It is therefore important to ensure that the amount of the claim corresponds to the value of the security even in the event of a sale on enforcement of the property serving as security.

Preferential debts

As described under 'General' p 391 above, claims which, due to the security provided, enjoy specific priority rights enjoy priority only in relation to the specific property in question, ie in relation to the pledged property. Special priority applies in all kinds of enforcement procedures, while general priority only applies in bankruptcy. With regard to proceeds received on realisation of specific security, claims with specific priority in that particular asset are preferred to those claims having only general priority, with the exception of costs for the execution procedure.

Sales on enforcement of security of an object to which claims with specific rights of priority are attached are viewed as proceedings outside the actual proceedings in the bankruptcy. However, before any receivables from the sale on enforcement are distributed, the costs of such a sale will be paid. It can generally be said that the costs of the proceedings in both bankruptcy and enforcement proceedings unconnected with bankruptcy will always be met before any amounts are distributed among the creditors.

As this general principle also applies in ordinary bankruptcy proceedings, claims pursuant to guarantees will suffer a number of other debts being preferential to them in the case of the guarantor's bankruptcy. The debts of the bankrupt estate as such ie costs for the bankruptcy or execution proceedings, will be paid first, and thereafter claims that enjoy general priority such as public tax claims, certain claims on salary and certain pension claims will be paid. Finally, the unsecured claims will be paid from the remaining proceeds of the bankruptcy estate, in strict proportion, eg 10% of each claim. Usually, however, unsecured claims will not receive payment at all, as the value of the estate usually will not be sufficient to make payments for such claims.

Subordination

Under Swedish law, subordination will be reached through an agreement to that effect entered into between the debtors. This form of agreement is primarily used in situations where a pledge has already been granted and another pledge is to be granted in the same property, ie in the surplus value.

In general, subordination agreements are three party agreements between the first and the second pledgees and the pledgor and where the right of priority between the pledgees is altered to the benefit of the second pledgee. A subordination agreement can be entered into in various ways; the pledgees enter into an agreement independent from the respective pledge agreements with the pledgor, or the second pledgee enters into an agreement with the pledgor but with the consent of the first pledgee. Obviously, the first pledgee's consent will always be necessary.

A subordination agreement is regarded as an agreement giving rise to a claim, but no title, between the first and the second pledgee, ie the second pledgee acquires a legal claim against the first pledgee for a part of the proceeds corresponding to the amount agreed upon in the subordination agreement. The second pledgee does not, however, acquire direct title to a part of the proceeds from the sale on enforcement of the object pledged.

In this context it should be noted that the courts are rather strict in interpreting the wording of subordination agreements and the use of 'subordination', as such, is not necessarily enough, as is evident from the Supreme Court's decision in NJA 1997 p 382:

> S and W had granted a loan to I. S held a pledge of first priority in the shares of I as security for the loan, W held a pledge of second priority in the same shares. Between S and W, there was an agreement regulating the event that I would not be able to meet its obligations as to instalments. In this agreement, it was provided that W should be entitled to first priority of instalments up to a certain amount of

the proceeds from I's sale of its subsidiaries. The transaction for which the loan was granted was never closed and I was eventually declared bankrupt. After the shares in I had been sold in its entirety for the benefit of S, W raised a claim against S for such part of the purchase sum that was related to the value represented by the subsidiaries covered in the agreement between S and W.

The courts (all three instances, two out of five judges in the Supreme Court dissenting) found that, as the relevant clause in the agreement between S and W related to instalments, W was not entitled to the proceeds relating to the relevant subsidiaries. The argument supporting this decision was that instalments were of no substance in the event of bankruptcy, and that the agreement, although the word 'subordination' (efterställning) was explicitly mentioned, did not give rise to a legally founded claim by W as against S.

The decision has been much criticised. However, in the light of it, it should be made absolutely clear in a subordination agreement that the subordination is intended to apply also in the event of the debtor's bankruptcy.

REMEDIES AND ENFORCEMENT

Powers of sale

If a debtor is unable to fulfil its payment obligations when due, the creditor is entitled to seek payment from the security provided. As described under 'Nature of guarantees and indemnities' p 392 above, a creditor with a guarantee with direct liability will be entitled to claim against the guarantee immediately on the due date, while a creditor with a subsidiary guarantor first has to establish, by way of initiating enforcement or bankruptcy proceedings against the debtor, that the debtor is unable to meet its obligations. In relation to on-demand guarantees, issues relating to enforcement of the guarantee will, of course, be dependent on the wording of the guarantee in question.

As to enforcement of pledges, there is only an old statutory provision in the Swedish Commercial Code Chapter 10 s 2 (from the year 1734). The provision prescribes a very time-consuming procedure with public offering of the pledged property at 'the court' etc. It has even been argued among Swedish scholars whether or not the old provision is obsolete. However, this statutory provision is always, and must always be, contracted out of. Such an agreement may be entered into either in connection with the pledge agreement or when the question of realisation of the pledge arises. At the same time, the parties should agree upon the procedure to be used for the sale of the property. In this context it should be noted that, according to the Swedish Contracts Act (Swedish Code of Statutes 1915:218) s 37, a condition whereby a pledge or other security interest shall be forfeited in the event of non-fulfilment of the undertaking in respect of which it was given, shall be null and void (*lex commissoria*).

As to the enforcement of mortgages over land, ships and aircraft, such mortgages may only be enforced through enforcement proceedings held by the bailiff (*kronofogdemyndigheten*). This is also the case in situations where a creditor and a pledgee have not come to an agreement upon the procedure for the sale of the pledged property.

The request to the bailiff for enforcement must be based on a distraint title (‘*exekutionstitel*’), which means a document in which the payment obligation has been legally determined. The Swedish Enforcement Code (Swedish Code of Statutes 1981:775) mentions eight groups of accepted distraint titles, of which, in the present context, performance judgments (*fullgörelsedom*), decisions from a bailiff in summary debt recovery proceedings and arbitral awards are of importance. Settlements between the parties out of court may also be considered valid distraint titles provided the settlement has been confirmed by a court.

As concerns mortgages over real estate, ships, ship buildings and aircraft, a distraint title in the form of an ‘order to pay’ (*betalningsföreläggande*) is fairly easily obtainable from the bailiff through summary proceedings (the Act on Summary Civil Procedure (Swedish Code of Statutes 1990:746)) and such an application may be combined with a requirement that the payment shall be made out of the mortgaged property. In such case, the decision from the bailiff will at the same time be a distraint title and a declaration of execution of the property in question.

Upon an application for an ‘order to pay’, the bailiff may not make a substantive examination of the claim. If the debtor does not object to the demand within a specified period of time, the Enforcement Authority must issue an order in accordance with the application. On the other hand, even a flat denial from the debtor will cause the bailiff to inform the creditor of the denial. If the creditor maintains his claim he can request that the case be transferred to the district court. Otherwise, the bailiff will dismiss the case. Thus, if a creditor knows beforehand that the debtor will deny a payment obligation, an application for summary proceedings will only result in the loss of time. In such situations, the creditor should instead file a complaint directly with the district court.

When the debtor has a distraint title, the debtor may request enforcement with the bailiff. After identifying seizable property, the bailiff will issue a declaration of execution, mark the property or carry it away and thereafter provide for the sale of the property in question by way of a compulsory auction (*offentlig auktion*). Finally, the bailiff will distribute the proceeds from the auction.

The bailiff will consider the priority as between various rights. The auction will be announced in the local newspaper, the advertisement stating a certain period of time within which creditors secured by a mortgage need to notify the bailiff of their claim. Thereafter, the date of the auction itself will be announced separately. After the auction has been held, the bailiff will distribute the proceeds in accordance with the order of priority attached to the various claims.

Coercive measures

In general, no coercive measures may be taken until a court has rendered a judgment or until some form of distraint title has been received. However, in many situations it would be risky to wait for the court's judgment. In such cases there are exemptions from the general rule and temporary enforcement may take place at various stages of the procedure. Under Swedish law it is not possible to appoint a receiver for these kinds of situations.

A court may order 'attachment of property' (*kvarstad*) or other security measures to be taken both before and during a trial. Attachment of property is granted as means of securing, eg a claim for payment or for a better right to property in the possession of the defendant/debtor, and the property is attached which means that the defendant may not dispose of it. The legislation relating to attachment is found in the Swedish Code of Judicial Procedure[9] (Swedish Code of Statutes 1942:740) Chapter 15.

For other types of claims there are enforcement rules where the security measures are adapted to the kind of claim concerned, such as a ban on the defendant to undertake certain activities, to undertake a specific act or to protect the interests of the plaintiff in some other way. The security measure will be in the form of a prohibition under penalty by way of fine.

To succeed with an application for attachment or another security measure, there are three prerequisites that must be fulfilled. The plaintiff must show that he is likely to succeed with his claim. The plaintiff must also show that the defendant can reasonably be suspected of removing or hiding the property or in any other manner taking actions that would make the enforcement of a judgment difficult. Finally, the plaintiff must provide valid security for any damages that the defendant may suffer.

(The court may under certain circumstance allow an exemption from the requirement to provide security).

As regards the decision by the court, an order concerning attachment of property aims at securing property of a certain value, which may later be seized. The enforcement will be carried out by the bailiff and the enforcement procedure is, due to its nature, the same as for ordinary execution proceedings, but includes only the first steps, ie the decision on attachment and a declaration on attachment.

Appointment of administrative receiver and court supervision

When a debtor finds himself in immediate difficulties in meeting his payment obligations, he may apply to the district court for the reorganisation of his company pursuant to the Company Reorganisation Act (Swedish Code of Statutes 1996:764). Such an application may also be filed by a creditor. An application filed by a creditor, however, may only be granted if the debtor has consented.

In addition to the requirement of the debtor's consent, there are two further requirements to be met to obtain an order in respect of a company reorganisation. First, the debtor must be deemed to be unable to pay his debts as they fall due, or such inability will exist within a short period of time. Second, an order in respect of company reorganisation may not be issued in the absence of reasonable cause to assume that the purpose of the reorganisation can be achieved.

Reorganisation is handled by an administrator appointed by the court. The administrator shall be an experienced and suitable person. The objective of his appointment is to investigate whether the business, which the debtor is operating, is capable of continuing, in whole or in part, and if so, the manner in which the business can continue. He shall also investigate whether it is possible for the debtor to reach a financial agreement with the creditor (composition).

9 The Swedish Code of Judicial Procedure has been translated into English; Justitiedepartementet, The Swedish code of judicial procedure, Ds 1998:65, Fritzes Offetnliga Publikationer, Stockholm 1998.

In general, the administrator will carry on his duties in close co-operation with both the debtor and the debtor's creditors, and the administrator must act in order to ensure that the interests of the creditors are not neglected. The administrator's work aims to remove the cause for the debtor's financial difficulties, either by way of agreements or reorganisations.

Upon the request of the debtor in proceedings for company reorganisation, the court may also order the commencement of proceedings for judicial composition (offentligt ackord). The proceedings follow a rather strict schedule and are handled by the court.

Upon request of the debtor, the court may call the creditors to a public meeting in order to negotiate the composition. Only creditors whose claims have arisen prior to the application for company reorganisation, and whose claims are subject to any rights of priority are entitled to participate in the meeting. The proposal as for judicial composition shall normally not provide for a reduction of claims below 25% of their original amount, unless all creditors whose claims are affected by the proposed composition consent, or there are special reasons for a lower percentage. If the proposal envisages a percentage of at least 25 but not 50%, the proposal is deemed to have been accepted if at least 75% of the creditors participating in the vote and representing at least 75% of the total debt consent to the proposal. If the proposed percentage is 50% or higher, the proposal is deemed to have been accepted if at least 60% of the creditors participating in the vote and representing at least 60% of the total debt second the proposal. If the proposal has been accepted by a sufficient number of creditors, and if there are no other particular reasons not to confirm it, the court shall confirm the decision of the creditors. By this confirmation, all creditors are bound by the proposal, and have to accept the reduction of their claims to the amount stated in the confirmation.

For creditors having security for their claims, this means that in the event the security is not sufficient to cover their respective claims, the remaining amount of the claim will be reduced to the percentage stated in the confirmation.

A company reorganisation expires upon order by the court. Such an order will be rendered either upon the fulfilment of certain conditions, eg the objectives of the reorganisation have been fulfilled, or after a period of three months from issuing the order for company reorganisation. The court may, however, order the reorganisation to continue for another period of three months where special cause exists.

Finally it should be noted that, during the course of a company reorganisation, no enforcement proceedings or other enforcement measures may take place in respect of the debtor. However, enforcement of claims for which the creditor possesses a charge over chattels (*handpanträtt*) or possessory lien (*retentionsrätt*), or for claims regarding alimony or maintenance may be enforced. Nor may orders be entered regarding attachment or other debt enforcement measures. Further, company reorganisation is not applicable in relation to banking companies, credit market companies, benevolent societies, insurance companies, securities companies, clearing companies or the Swedish Central Securities Depository.

Rights and powers of unsecured creditors

As mentioned under 'Powers of sale' p 409 above, in order to enforce a claim against a debtor, the creditor, first of all, needs a distraint title, ie a document in which the obligation to pay is legally determined. For unsecured creditors, amongst them those wishing to enforce a guarantee against a guarantor unable to meet his obligations, the only way to enforce their claims is to obtain a judgment from a court or an 'order to pay' from the bailiff.

After receiving a distraint title, the creditor must apply for the assistance of the bailiff in order to enforce the judgment or decision in accordance with the procedure described under 'Powers of sale' p 409 above. Thus, the bailiff will make a search for property that can be seized in satisfaction of the debt. Such assets will thereafter be sold and the proceeds will be distributed among the creditor(s). In this context it should be noted that, if the debtor is an individual, certain property is exempted from enforcement. The debtor will able to retain what is required for his and his family's immediate support. Such property consists generally of personal property, such as clothes, furniture and objects that are used solely for the family's personal use. Additionally, the tools necessary for the debtor's work are exempted from execution.

Procedures which can restrict/prohibit enforcement

There are two procedures that may restrict or prohibit enforcement, namely the initiation of bankruptcy proceedings and the issuing of an order for company reorganisation.

During bankruptcy proceedings, enforcement procedures are, in general, prohibited. However, a creditor in the possession of a pledge or mortgage with priority for his claim is entitled to apply for and receive a declaration of enforcement in relation to that claim. The reason for this exemption is that the proceeds from the sale of the property in question already, due to the priority rights, are destined for that creditor.

During the course of a company reorganisation, however, only creditors secured by a charge over chattels are allowed to enforce their claim. Claims secured by any other form of security, including guarantees and indemnities, are thus prevented from being enforced during a company reorganisation.

VITIATING FACTORS

Security intrinsically invalid

In Sweden the basic rules on the formation and validity of agreements and other undertakings in the economic sphere (*förmögenhetsrätt*) are found in the Contracts Act (Swedish Code of Statutes 1915:218). The Contracts Act deals with parties supposed to have full legal capacity to enter into contracts and applies in the absence of a clear contractual structure.

Under the Code Relating to Parents, Guardians and Children (Swedish Code of Statutes 1949:381), individuals below the age of 18 are minors and, as such, have, in general, no power to enter in to contracts or undertake legal obligations. Thus, agreements made by a minor are void, and on demand of the minor or his guardian or, in fact, the minor's counterparty, both the minor and the counterparty must return whatever they have received under the agreement. If such return is impossible due to consumption, loss or damage, the equivalent value must, in principle, be repaid. However, unless the minor has positively mislead the other party, the minor will be under no obligation to repay consumed values in situations where the consumption did not serve his maintenance or otherwise involve a profit for the minor. Thus, sellers of ordinary useful objects for minors, such as, eg schoolbooks, will normally get payment.

Under the Act on Contracts made under the Influence of Mental Derangement (Swedish Code of Statutes 1924:323), mentally incapacitated individuals, like minors, are relieved from bearing the full effect of their undertakings. Contracts entered into with such persons are normally void. In addition to the duty to compensate for enrichment obtained, mentally-incapacitated persons must also compensate a good faith counterparty to the extent a court may find it just and fair.

As described under 'Board resolutions' and 'Execution' p 403 above, a company limited by shares is represented by the board of directors and, under certain circumstances, the managing director. However, signatory power may also be granted to other individuals. Who they are will be evident from the certificate of incorporation.

If the board of directors or an authorised signatory of a company has performed legal acts on behalf of the company and thereby acted in contravention of the provisions in the Companies Act regarding authorisation for the various corporate bodies (*behörighet*), such acts will be unenforceable against the company (Companies Act Chapter 8). That is also the case if a managing director has exceeded his authority under the Companies Act, provided, however, that the company demonstrates that the other party realised or should have realised that the authority had been exceeded. Further, according to the second paragraph of this provision, legal acts will not be enforceable against the company if the board of directors, the managing director or any authorised signatory has exceeded their respective authority (*befogenhet*), if the company demonstrates that the other party realised or should have realised that such authority was exceeded. However, if the board of directors or the managing director has acted in contravention of the objects of the company or other provisions set forth in the articles of association or established by another organ of the company, the above-mentioned principle does not apply and, thus, performed legal acts will be enforceable against the company irrespective of good or bad faith of the other party.

In relation to the providing of security, in this context the rule of '*lex commissoria*', mentioned under 'Powers of sale' p 409 above, should also be mentioned. According to the Swedish Contracts Act (Swedish Code of Statutes 1915:218) s 37, a condition whereby a pledge or other security interest shall be forfeited in the event of non-fulfilment of the undertaking in respect of which it was given, shall be null and void. Thus, the pledge or security as such is valid but any penalty or forfeiture clause will be liable to being modified by at the discretion of a court.

The Swedish Contracts Act Chapter 3, containing among other provisions the above-mentioned s 37, is wholly devoted to the issue of invalidity of contracts. The remaining provision concerning invalidity will be dealt with under 'Undue influence, duress and fraud' p 420 below.

There are three kinds of security that cannot be pledged or mortgaged by the pledgee: land, patents and trademarks. If somebody other than the owner of the respective kind of title pledges or mortgages such object or title, such security is intrinsically invalid and will not be recognised by the courts.

As for land, it is stated in the Real Property Code Chapter 6 s 2 that mortgages over land may be granted by the owner of the land. This means that only the owner can legally grant mortgages over land. Thus, it is not possible for the holder of a charge over land validly to grant a mortgage in the land mortgaged to him. This should not be confused with the owner being able to grant two mortgages in the same deed of pledge; the latter is perfectly possible and, in fact, happens rather frequently, in the manner, and with the consequences, described above under 'Chattels' p 397 above. However, the holder of the mortgage is not entitled to use this mortgage to furnish security to a third party.

As for patents and trademarks, the judicial-technical solution resembles that for land: it is stated in the respective law that only the owner of such right, or the applicant for such right, may seek registration of a pledge of such intellectual property rights. Being the owner who has the exclusive right to apply for the registration of a pledge, it is impossible for the pledgee to use the patent or trademark to give security for the benefit of third parties.

Strictly speaking, the term invalidity only applies for the mortgage of a mortgage over land; as for patents and trademarks, one should speak of impossibility, rather than of invalidity. An application for the registration of a mortgage in a patent or trademark will, rather simply, not be granted, and by the application not being granted, a mortgage will never arise. As regards land, however, it should, at least in as far as physical deeds of pledge are concerned, be possible to hand over the deed to a third party, thereby at least giving the appearance of being entitled to mortgage a mortgage in land. The invalidity of such mortgage will then have to be assessed ex post, with the courts as a last resort, should disputes arise.

As concerns land, therefore, a party requiring security should always ascertain whether the holder of the deed of pledge is, in fact, the owner of the estate to which the deed refers. This is easily done by checking the title issue with the registration authority: as already stated, Swedish registration systems are quite developed, and thus, unpleasant surprise can easily be avoided. As concerns the pledge of patents and trademarks, the consideration for the security should not be released before it is certain that the pledger is accepted by the registration authority as competent to apply for the registration of a pledge of such intellectual property rights.

Illegality

As stated under 'Powers of sale' above, the Swedish Companies Act Chapter 3 is devoted to the issue of invalidity of contracts. As will be evident from the section headed 'Undue influence, duress and fraud' p 420 below, the Contracts Act is, however, very limited in its scope and does not mention every kind of invalidity or illegality that may affect a contract. Swedish law copes with this problem in various ways. Some special matters are dealt with on the basis of unwritten general principles, more or less firmly established by case law, while other instances of invalidity are dealt with by way of analogies from statutes relating to special contracts.

Under a general but unwritten principle, a contract may be deemed null and void due to the fact that its content contravenes the law or good custom or practices. That is the case with, eg an agreement where one of the parties undertakes to act or do something that would imply a criminal offence of some other act that would definitely be contrary to accepted moral behaviour or custom (*pactum turpe*). Other examples of illegal agreements are agreements relating to gambling.

These kinds of illegal agreements, however, are not treated as if they did not exist. Instead, they will be impossible to enforce by any legal means and the fact that they are null and void will be observed ex officio by the courts.

Although freedom of contract is a fundamental principle in Sweden, as in many other countries, there are exemptions in many areas such as in relation to consumers and in relation to employees. Such exemptions from the basic principle are laid down in mandatory legislation that makes the divergent provision in a contract void. In such situations, in general, the legislation will provide solutions. Thus, the contract will continue to be effective but with other legal effects.

Security created at the point of insolvency

Rules relating to security created at the point of insolvency are laid down in the Swedish Bankruptcy and Insolvent Liquidation Act (the 'Bankruptcy Act') (Swedish Code of Statutes 1987:672) Chapter 4. The Chapter contains rules as to the relevant point of time when the debtor is regarded as having been in an economic state in which the creation of security is viewed as unconscionable, as well as rules relating to the effects of security created at the point of insolvency.

The point of time relevant for the assessment of whether a security has been created at the point of insolvency is the so called 'day of grace' (*fristdag*). According to the Bankruptcy Act Chapter 4 s 2, the day of grace is the day on which the petition to declare the debtor bankrupt was filed with the district court. However, if such a petition has been filed when attempts were made to reorganise the company in accordance with the Company Reorganisation Act[10], the day of grace shall be the day on which the application for reorganising the company was filed with the court.

The day of grace is important for the assessment of whether the bankrupt estate could recover any assets following transactions made by the debtor. In relation to creation of security, there are primarily two situations in which recovery may be made.

First of all, the creation of a security interest must be assessed in the light of the general rule on recovery in the Bankruptcy Act Chapter 4 s 5. According to s 5, a legal act whereby a particular creditor has been favoured in an unfair manner in preference to others, or the property of the debtor has been concealed from the creditors, or the debts of the debtors have been increased, is annulled if the debtor was or by the procedure, solely or in combination with other factors, became insolvent, provided that the other party knew or ought to have known of the insolvency and the circumstances making the legal act improper. From the second paragraph of the provision it is also evident that a close relative to the debtor will always be considered to have knowledge of insolvency and the circumstances making the legal act improper, unless the opposite is proved. Further, if the legal act in question took place more than five years prior to the day of grace, it is only annulled in relation to close relatives.

10 The Company Reorganisation Act has been translated into English; Legal Language Service, Swedish Commercial Legislatino, Nordstedts Juridik, Stockholm.

The effects of applying s 5 are potentially enormous and therefore the requirements as to its application are rather strict. Thus, there are a number of requirements to be fulfilled. First of all there must have been a transaction. However, the word transaction covers the entire variety of legal transactions provided in Swedish law and will nearly always be fulfilled. Secondly, the transaction must have been unfair. This requirement, on the other hand, is not easy to define, and the wording of s 5, in fact, gives some examples, such as that a certain creditor has been provided with a benefit he was not entitled to, or that the debts of the debtor were augmented. Which transaction is, or is not, unfair, will, to a large extent, be decided in the individual case: it is impossible to give a general rule of any significant application. Thirdly, the debtor must, at the time of the transaction, have been insolvent, or by the transaction, alone or in connection with other transaction, have become insolvent. This requirement obviously covers a large variety of transactions, namely all transactions in which the debtor appears to have been the losing party, as the mere fact that the debtor, when the question of recovery arises, is bankrupt is to show that a number of transactions have led to the bankruptcy. This potentially wide field of application for s 5 is, however, decisively narrowed by the requirement that the other party knew, of the debtor's insolvency and of the circumstances that made the transaction unfair. As for the latter requirement, it is not necessary that either the other party or the debtor himself classify the transaction as unfair, it suffices that the other party knew of the circumstances which made the transaction unfair. The location 'knew or ought to have known' introduces a certain amount of blameworthiness of the other party, which requirement serves to further narrow the field in which s 5 can be applied.

In addition to Chapter 4, s 5, the creation of security may be recovered in accordance with the provision of the Bankruptcy Act, Chapter 4 s 12. These two sections of the Bankruptcy Act are not subsidiary one to the other, but, rather complementary. Thus, a transaction which, in principle, may be assessed in accordance with s 12 may just as well be assessed pursuant to s 5.

According to the Bankruptcy Act Chapter 4 s 12, a security that the debtor has transferred up to three months prior to the day of grace is annulled unless the security was provided at the same time the debt was created or was transferred without delay after the creation of the debt. In this context other measures by the debtor or the creditor intended to secure the rights of the creditor, such as registration or notification, is equated with a transfer (of possession). Further, it is explicitly stated that, in situations where the creation of a security interest requires registration, the delay referred to in this section shall be considered to exist if the application for registration of the security was made later than on the first registration day occurring two weeks after the creation of the debt.

The effect of recovery is, in general, rather straightforward. The object recovered shall be transferred back to the estate, and the estate shall give back what has been paid for the object. As concerns security, however, the effect is that the security shall be released to the estate without any corresponding or additional obligation arising for the bankruptcy estate. Unless other security has been provided, the creditor will only have an unsecured claim in the debtor's bankrupt estate. This is due to the fact that the security recovered was provided either under such circumstances that made the transaction unfair, or was required at such late stage that the creditor has tried to gain an undue advantage as compared to other creditors. Such procedure is not deemed to be worth protecting, and the adverse consequences this may entail for honourable creditors are therefore accepted.

A recovery action may be instituted at the district court within one year from the decision to declare the debtor bankrupt, or within six months from the time the grounds for recovery became known to the estate.

For practical purposes, it is important to require security when the debt arises. From a Swedish perspective, it is, due to the rules on recovery, not advisable to react only when the debtor's financial problems have become clear. To require security at an early stage is thus not proof of lack of trust, it is important for effectively securing the creditor's position. When security is required, it should also be ensured that the debtor, without delay, fulfils his obligation to hand over the security. The content of the latter requirement is dependent on the kind of security required. A pledge in the form of a movable object should be handed over to the creditor immediately; a mortgage should be registered the next possible day. If this requirement is not met, the courts may refuse to accept the security as effectively provided, and the creditor might find himself in an unsecured position at a time when the forthcoming or existent insolvency has already become apparent.

Commercial benefit

Under 'Board Resolutions; and 'Execution' p 403 above, the necessity of board resolutions when dealing with companies limited by shares and the provisions concerning signatory power and the respective corporate bodies' authority have been described. Further, under 'Security intrinsically invalid'above, the provisions concerning situations where the various corporate bodies have exceeded their respective authority have been explained in some detail. However, these provisions refer to some extent to the provisions in the Companies Act regarding authorisation for the various corporate bodies, ie the provisions which provides the limits for a company's activities.

The basic purpose of a company limited by shares is to make profits for the shareholders. According to the Companies Act Chapter 12 s 1, disbursement to the shareholders of the company's funds may only take place pursuant to the provisions of the Act regarding distribution of profits, disbursements in respect of reduction of the share capital, statutory reserves, or share premium reserves, and in respect of distributions in connection with the solvent liquidation of the company. Further the articles of association shall contain provisions governing utilisation of profits and retained assets upon solvent liquidation of the company, if the objects of the company's operations, in whole or in part, are other than to provide profits to the shareholders. As a consequence, a company limited by shares has no interests of its own which are independent of the interest of the shareholders.

Furthermore, the possibility for corporate bodies to act on the company's behalf is strictly limited by the so-called 'general clauses' in Chapter 8, s 34 (applicable in relation to the board of directors and other representatives) and Chapter 9, s 37 (applicable to the general meeting of shareholders).

According to the general clause in Chapter 8, s 34, the board of directors or other representative of the company may not perform legal acts or other measures which are intended to provide undue advantage to a shareholder or other person to the disadvantage of the company or another shareholder. Companies Act Chapter 9 s 37 contains a similar provision relating to resolutions adopted by the general meeting of shareholders). Further, a representative of the company shall not comply with a resolution adopted by a general meeting of shareholders or other corporate bodies if such resolution is void as a consequence of the fact that it contravenes the Companies Act, applicable legislation governing annual reports, or the articles of association.

If the board of directors or another representative of the company performs a legal act in contravention of the above-mentioned general clause, the provision of Chapter 8, s 35, the second paragraph, mentioned above under 'Security intrinsically invalid' p 413 above, will apply. This means that the legal act will not be enforceable against the company if the company demonstrates that the other party realised or should have realised that such authority was exceeded.

In this context it should be noted that the authority to provide security (guarantees or pledges), where the entering into such agreements do not explicitly contravene the objects of the company or other provisions of the articles of association, in general is to be determined in accordance with Chapter 8, s 35, second paragraph. Thus, the security may not be enforceable against the company if the representatives have exceeded their authority and if the company demonstrates that the other party realised or should have realised that such authority was exceeded.

In this context the limitations of granting loans and providing security to certain individuals and entities should be briefly discussed.

According to the Swedish Companies Act Chapter 12 s 7, a company may not grant cash loans or provide security, including guarantees, to shareholders of the company, or to a member of the board of directors or the managing director in the company or in another company within the same group[11]. Exemptions are made for situations where the ultimate debtor is a company within the same group as the lender/guarantor and situations where the debtor conducts business operations and the loan or security is justified by sound business reasons and is intended to be used exclusively in the debtor's business. Further, this provision also includes a rule stating that a company may not grant a loan or provide security for the purpose of financing the acquisition of its shares or shares in another company within the same group.

However, a violation or breach of the Swedish Companies Act Chapter 12 s 7 does not, in general, entail the invalidity of the loan granted or security provided. Although violations of prohibitions may entail invalidity of contracts, according to general principles of Swedish contract law, the question of invalidity is dependent on the reasons upon which the legal prohibition rests. The prohibition against granting loans and providing security by companies to certain parties rests upon the interest of the creditors as a group and of the shareholders, and is not deemed to be of such nature as to entail the invalidity of the contract. However, in relation to the representatives of the company granting the loan, there is a penal provision contained in the Swedish Companies Act Chapter 19 s 1. The violation is a criminal offence and a person who intentionally or due to gross negligence violates the Companies Act Chapter 12 s 7 shall be fined or sentenced to imprisonment for a maximum one year.

11 The group of persons is further extended to defined close relatives as well as to legal entities over which any of the already mentioned persons or entities have a controlling influence.

Finally, the Companies Act Chapter 12 s 2 concerning distribution of profits may be applicable in cases of granting loans or providing security. According to established case law, the issuance of a guarantee, the granting of a loan or another similar financial transaction can be regarded as a form of distribution of profits to shareholders. If a transaction has been entered into with a third party, a sister company or a subsidiary, the provisions have been held to apply by analogy. If the amount which has been distributed exceeds what is available (considering statutory reserves etc), the transaction is null and void and the recipient has to repay the funds, unless he has acted in good faith as to the lawfulness of the transaction. To the extent that the recipient is not able to make reimbursement, any person who took part in the transaction may be liable to repayment.

Undue influence, duress, fraud

As already mentioned under 'Security intrinsically invalid' p 413 above, the Swedish Companies Act Chapter 3 is wholly devoted to issues relating to invalidity of contracts. Normally invalidity is considered to be a lack of something existing when the contract was entered into. However, in some situations later occurrences will make a contract wholly or partially void, eg where it is considered unconscionable to insist on a contract in view of circumstances that have occurred after it was made (see further below Contracts Act s 36.)

The provisions of the Contract Act aim primarily at invalidity affecting the whole contract. Invalidity may also affect only a particular clause of a contract. In some situations invalidity could have affected the whole of the contract but only if contested before performance of the contract had begun. In such situations it may not be justifiable to terminate the complete contractual relationship, but the contract will be maintained in a modified form.

Further, invalidity under the Contracts Act may be divided into situations of absolute invalidity, which will be effective in relation to any contracting party or beneficiary, and situations of relative invalidity, which invalidity will be effective only against a party in bad faith.

Before describing the various causes for invalidity in detail, it should be noted that Swedish law adheres to the Roman concept of legal acts. Thus, a contract is considered to be entered into step by step by the performance of various legal acts, eg offer and acceptance. Each and every one of these acts may be invalid due to causes such as duress etc. It is therefore, from a theoretical point of view, quite incorrect to state that the contract as such is invalid due to eg duress. Rather, one or several of the legal acts leading to the emergence of a binding contract may be invalid and thereby render the contract void. In the following reference will therefore be made to legal acts rather than to the contract as such, thereby following the terminology of the Swedish Contracts Act[12].

The Contracts Act contains provisions on duress (ss 28 and 29), fraud (s 30) and usury or undue influence (s 31).

12 The Swedish Contracts Act has been translated into English; Legal Language Service, Swedish Commercial Legislation, Nordstedts Juridik, Stockholm.

Duress is defined in s 28 as 'violence to the person or threats of imminent danger to the person'. Such violence, or threat of violence, is, if exercised by the person in respect of whom a certain legal act is extracted, an absolute cause of invalidity. However, if the violence, or threat of violence, is exercised by some other party than the one in respect of whom the legal act is performed, and the latter has acted in good faith, the party being subject to the duress must inform the other party without unreasonable delay if he wishes to plead the duress. Should he fail to do so, the legal act and the contract will be deemed to be binding.

Section 29 refers to duress of a less serious kind, ie 'a legal act which a person has been coerced into performing other than as a consequence of duress as stated in s 28'. Examples of such coercion are, eg the threat to cause scandal to the person performing the legal act, or even an illegal condition in the decision of an authority[13]. A legal act performed under coercion will not be valid if the party in respect of whom the legal act was performed exercised coercion, or if he knew or should have known, that the act was performed as a result of coercion exercised by someone else.

The consequences of fraud are regulated in the Contracts Act s 30. The effects of fraud follow the above-mentioned effects of duress and coercion. If the person in respect of whom the legal act is performed knew, or should have known, that the legal act was induced by fraudulent deception, the legal act, and thereby the contract, shall not be binding upon the person being fraudulently deceived.

Usury is defined as the exploitation of the 'distressed circumstances, lack of mental capacity, irresponsibility, or dependence on another' (Contracts Act s 31). If such circumstances are exploited in order to attain benefits which are manifestly disproportionate to the consideration paid or promised, the legal act will not be binding upon the exploited. As in relation to the above-mentioned causes for invalidity, if the fraudulent practice was performed by a third party, the legal act will be deemed void only if the person in respect of whom the legal act was performed knew or should have been aware of the circumstances.

It should be noted that these causes are frequently pleaded in court, but hardly ever applied. Swedish courts are rather reluctant to declare legal acts, or contracts, invalid. The requirement that the person in respect of whom the disputed legal act was performed must have been in bad faith further ensures that it is very difficult to apply these provisions, even in situations where a court might be inclined to do so. In general, good faith is rather strictly protected under Swedish law and it is very difficult to secure one's position against a party acting in good faith.

The policy of protecting a party acting in good faith is also the reason for the provision contained in the Contracts Act s 32, which deals with typographical errors and other mistakes that have a meaning other than was intended. The provision states that, if the promisee realised or ought to have realised the mistake, the promisor is not bound by it. Even more important is the conclusion to be drawn *e contrario*, that is, that when the promisee neither realised nor ought to have realised the mistake, the promisor is bound by the contents of his promise.

The provisions of ss 28-32 are supplemented by a more general provision in s 33. According to this provision, a legal act which would otherwise be deemed valid may

13 Rolf Dotevall, Johnny Herre, Eric M Runesson, Avtals- och köprätt, Nordstedts Juridik, Stockholm 1997, p 42.

not be relied upon where the circumstances in which it arose were such that, having knowledge of such circumstances, it would be inequitable to enforce the legal act, and the person against whom the legal act was performed must be presumed to have had such knowledge. The actual meaning of the provision is extremely unclear but it is usually used to cover certain situations where the requirements of the other provision of Chapter 3 are not fulfilled, as well as in situations of error in underlying assumptions (bristande *förutsättningar*).

The Contracts Act s 34 provides that written promissory notes, contracts or other instruments made for the sake of appearance (shame documents) only are void as between the parties but acquire effect not only in relation to a good faith promisee, but also in relation to a good faith assignee.

Section 35 refers to bearer instruments (negotiable instruments). If signed by the debtor, such instruments shall, notwithstanding that it has been removed from the possession of the debtor against his will, be valid in the hands of a good faith assignee.

A general invalidity and adjustment or modification provision is found in the Contracts Act s 36. This provision is commonly pleaded as a last resort by a debtor who wants to get out of a contractual relationship that is found to be more burdensome than expected. It allows the modification or setting aside of a contractual term which is unreasonable, having regard to the contents of the agreement, the circumstances prevailing at the time the agreement was entered into, subsequent circumstances and circumstances in general. Further, where a term is of such importance for the agreement that it would be unreasonable to demand the continued enforceability of the remainder of the agreement with its terms unchanged, the agreement may also be modified in other respects or even set aside in its entirety.

The prohibition against forfeiture clauses found in the Contracts Act s 37 has already been commented upon under 'Security intrinsically invalid' p 413 above.

ENFORCEMENT OF FOREIGN GUARANTEES AND SECURITY

Basis of recognition

Swedish choice of law rules and the foreign law that they identify, are generally applied ex officio by the Swedish courts, ie even without being pleaded by the parties. Further, Swedish courts strive to interpret and apply applicable foreign law in the same manner as would the courts in that particular legal system. Thus, an agreement between the parties as to the contents of applicable foreign law will not bind the court. When a Swedish court is to apply foreign law it may request a party, primarily the one relying on that foreign law, to present proof of its content, but the court may also try to obtain such information based on its own efforts. Both the court as well as the parties may request assistance from the Foreign Ministry in this respect.

On 1 July 1998, the Rome Convention on the Law Applicable to Contractual Obligations, opened for signature in Rome on 19 June 1980, came into force as applicable law in Sweden (the Swedish Code of Statutes 1998:167). Based on the Rome convention, Swedish courts will, as general rule, enforce a choice of law agreement entered into between the parties. In the absence of a choice of law agreement, in accordance with Article 4 of the Convention, the contract will be governed by the law of the country with which it is most closely connected. In this respect, however, with some exceptions, the contract shall be presumed to be most closely connected with the country where the party who is to effect the performance which is characteristic of the contract has, at the time of conclusion of the contract, his habitual residence or, in case of an enterprise, its central administration.

The law of the contract (*lex contractus*) will be applied to determine the material validity of the contract, ie as to questions of offer and acceptance, as well as to defences to liability such as duress, fraud and mistake. It also determines the scope of the parties' rights to freedom of contract. The law of the contract will also be used for the purpose of filling any contractual gaps and applied to damages for breach, limitations on actions assignments etc.

As described under 'Guarantees and liabilities' p 392 above, these are, from a Swedish perspective, viewed as contractual obligations. In relation to these types of securities, as well as in relation to other contractual obligations, the parties' choice of law will be respected and upheld by Swedish courts. In the absence of such choice, the *lex contractus* will be applied.

As a general rule, rights in real and personal property (typically title and security), are determined in accordance with the principle of *lex rei sitae*, ie the law of the jurisdiction where the property in question was situated at the time of the event (sale, pledge, etc). (In relation to real property, this principle is laid down in the above-mentioned Rome Convention as a situation to which the *lex contractus* does not apply (Article 9, paragraph 6).) Thus, with regard to security interests in personal property acquired in other countries, the question of the interest validity will be determined by the foreign *lex rei sitae* at the time the interest arose. However, the question of whether that interest has terminated once the property has been moved to Sweden, will be determined by Swedish law. Thus, following the Swedish requirement for delivery of possession, personal property pledged abroad will lose its effects in relation to third parties if the object is moved to Sweden and returned to the debtor.

As concerns mortgages in ships and aircraft, Sweden adheres to all important international conventions. Thus, ships and aircraft are deemed to be situated in their respective country of registration and, consequentially, the law of the country of registration will be decisive upon questions concerning the validity of the pledge etc.

Public policy

Under the doctrine of public policy, or ordre public, which is an acknowledged part of Swedish international private law, Swedish courts and other authorities will refuse to apply provisions of foreign law, if such application would lead to a result that is clearly inconsistent with the fundamental principles of the Swedish legal system.

Public policy is, in Sweden, applied ex officio, ie without the need to be pleaded by any of the parties in the proceedings. Further, the lack of express authorisation under any international private law to apply order public will not prevent its application. On the other hand, an express rule to that effect, will not result in its application on a routine basis.

Swedish courts are and have always been very reluctant to apply the doctrine of public policy, and the principles under Swedish law to be considered fundamental and therefore worthy of protection are not easily identified. Though, foreign law provisions that discriminate against racial, ethnic or religious minorities are some examples of the types of provisions that a Swedish court could refuse to apply based on public policy. However, it is difficult to imagine under what circumstances a discussion regarding Swedish public policy may arise in relation to different types of security. In the event that certain foreign jurisdictions deprive the pledgee, or the mortgagee, of all rights, and provide for extensive rights of the pledgor, or the mortgagor, this may, in exceptional circumstances, provoke the application of Swedish public policy. It should also be noted that this is rather unlikely to happen.

Jurisdiction

Swedish jurisdictional rules applicable in cases of contract are mainly based on case law and by analogy on the rules of the Swedish Code of Judicial Procedure (Swedish Code of Statutes 1942:740, as amended) Chapter 10.

As in most countries, a fundamental basis is jurisdiction over persons domiciled in Sweden and enterprises where their board has its registered office (according to its articles of association) in Sweden. Further, when a claim concerns a debt obligation and the defendant has assets in Sweden, the court may hear the claim even if there is no connection between the claim and the Swedish assets. When the dispute relates to personal property situated in Sweden, a party may be sued in Sweden if the dispute concerns rights in or to the property. If a claim is secured through a pledge of property situated in Sweden, the claim may also be deemed situated in Sweden. Under Swedish law a person may also be sued on a contract or debt in Sweden even if not domiciled in Sweden if he has entered into the contract or incurred the debt in Sweden. Finally, Swedish jurisdiction will also apply in connection with real property situated in Sweden when the dispute concern questions of, eg title or other rights to the property.

In most situations where Swedish law permits the parties to reach a binding settlement, an agreement between the parties to have their existing or future disputes adjudicated in Sweden (or in another country) will be accepted by the Swedish courts. The agreement must, however, be made in writing.

Sweden is a party to both the Brussels and the Lugano Conventions on the Jurisdiction and Enforcement of Judgments in Civil and Commercial Matters. In general, the Lugano Convention will apply when the defendant is domiciled in a state that is not a member of the EU and otherwise the Brussels Convention. Furthermore, in this context it should be noted that the Swedish Supreme Court has declared that the principles laid down in the Lugano Convention are to be recognised as applicable principles under Swedish international private law. Consequently, these principles may also be applied outside the immediate field of application of the Lugano Convention, ie also in relation to states that are not parties to the Convention.

Although the Lugano Convention coincides with Swedish international private law in most respects, it does to some extent narrow the scope of those rules. Thus, the Swedish rule that permits debt recovery suits in Sweden based solely on the fact that the defendant has assets in Sweden is expressly prohibited by the Convention.

In general, Swedish courts will hear a case if the defendant appears in the proceedings without raising any objection to jurisdiction. However, neither a silent appearance nor an agreement between the parties is necessarily sufficient to establish jurisdiction if the case lacks every connection to Sweden. At least some connection to Sweden or at least the international character of the dispute will be required.

Competing receiverships

In this summary of Swedish law, the issue of competing receiverships will be limited to, primarily, the Swedish position in relation to declarations of bankruptcy.

In relation to applications for bankruptcy, Swedish courts will have adjudicatory power, if the debtor is an individual, the debtor is domiciled in Sweden, or, if the debtor is a legal entity, if the entity has a registered office in Sweden. A debtor without known domicile may also be declared bankrupt in Sweden provided, however, that the debtor has assets in Sweden or the application is based upon a debt incurred in Sweden. In general, a Swedish bankruptcy is considered to encompass all the debtor's assets (and liabilities), ie both assets in and outside of Sweden. Whether or not the Swedish bankruptcy will be recognised abroad will, of course, be dependent on each foreign countries' international procedural law.

In a Swedish bankruptcy foreign creditors, or creditors domiciled abroad, will be in the same position and have the same rights as Swedish creditors. In reality, however, a foreign creditor may be in a slightly worse position due to the fact that they may not be reached through the ordinary publicity efforts made and, therefore, may not announce his claim in due time.

A foreign bankrupt estate, ie a bankruptcy declared in a country other than Sweden, which has capacity to stand trial and to enter into contracts under the laws in the country issuing the receiving order, will be recognised in Sweden. Further, it is probably undisputed that a foreign receiver will be in the position to dispose of the debtor's assets which, at the time of the issuing of the receiving order, were located in that country. On the other hand, it is also quite clear that a foreign bankruptcy does not have any effect on the debtor's right to dispose of his assets located in Sweden and, further, does not prevent Swedish bankruptcy proceedings or enforcement proceedings in relation to the assets.

In short, and mooted by a well-recognised Swedish legal scholar, foreign declarations of bankruptcy 'do not have any legal effect in this country'[14].

14 Karl Olivecrona, Konkursrätt efter föreläsningar av prof Karl Olivecrona, 9th edition, Lund 1963, p 57, as cited in Michael Bogdan, Sverigs och EU's internationella insolvensrätt, 1st edition, Stockholm 1997.

11 England

Charles Proctor

Norton Rose, London

GUARANTEES AND INDEMNITIES

This section deals with contracts of guarantee and indemnity, which are frequently an important part of an overall covenant 'package' given to secure obligations of the borrower in a typical banking or loan transaction. On occasion, the guarantee may be the sole source of credit which underpins a loan facility, eg where the facility is made available to a subsidiary or to a special purpose vehicle in reliance upon a parent company guarantee.

The following issues will be covered in this section:

1 characteristics of guarantees and indemnities;
2 formalities;
3 liabilities and defences;
4 rights of subrogation;
5 financial limits; and
6 multiple guarantors.

Charactersitics of guarantees and indemnities

The term 'guarantee' is a general term used to describe the contractual relationship between the first person (guarantor) who promises to answer for a liability of a second person (debtor) to a third person (creditor). In the event of a default by the primary debtor, the guarantor is answerable for his obligations.

Since every guarantee is a form of contract, it must be construed in accordance with its terms and taking account of the circumstances of the individual case. But in essence, the guarantor promises to be answerable for the guaranteed debts of the principal debtor, should the latter default in respect of his obligations.

It should be appreciated that a guarantee does not create any immediate rights over the guarantor's assets; it merely creates an additional avenue of personal recourse. This is in contrast to any security (in a strict, proprietary sense) which the debtor himself may have given to the creditor. If, for example, the primary contract is secured by a mortgage on the debtor's property, then (following a default) the creditor has a right to enforce his security and to retain the proceeds of sale in priority to any other claimants against the principal debtor. By contrast, the creditor's only claim against the guarantor is a contractual claim for payment or damages. The creditor has no direct or priority claim against the assets of the guarantor unless the guarantor (in support of his purely contractual obligations) has separately executed a mortgage or charge over some or all of his assets.

Guarantees are a form of 'unilateral' contract, in the sense that they are usually executed and delivered solely by the guarantor; it is not necessary for the creditor or the debtor to sign these documents. Usually, the guarantee becomes binding upon the guarantor when (acting in reliance upon that document) the creditor makes an advance or activates an overdraft facility in favour of the primary debtor. However, guarantees may be given under other circumstances, eg to induce the creditor to extend the maturity date, or to persuade him not to call a default in respect of an existing facility which has already been fully drawn. In such cases, no new money is made available to the debtor, but the guarantee is nonetheless a binding obligation.

As noted earlier, all guarantees are individual contracts and must be construed accordingly. Inevitably, however, most guarantees will share certain common characteristics. In particular:

1 guarantees are often described as 'collateral' or 'secondary' contracts. A guarantor will not be liable to the creditor unless the debtor is in default under the primary contract;
2 it follows that the creditor must first prove that the debtor is actually in default under the primary contract before any claim can be made against the guarantor (although the guarantee may stipulate the evidence or mode of proof which is to be sufficient for these purposes);
3 the rule stated above applies even where (as is often the case) the moneys guaranteed are expressed to be payable 'on demand'; and
4 a guarantee will generally be unenforceable if the primary contract is for any reason void, illegal or otherwise unenforceable. Again, this should follow from the 'secondary' character of the guarantor's obligations. In practice, however, standard forms of guarantee will endeavour to preserve the guarantor's obligations, even where the primary obligations cannot be enforced.

Guarantees must be carefully distinguished from contracts of indemnity. In contrast to a guarantee, an indemnity is a primary obligation of the indemnifier; the indemnifier undertakes to keep the lender harmless against any loss which might be suffered as a result of making the loan. The distinction between these two types of contract is important in three respects, namely:

1 since the indemnifier is a primary (as opposed to a secondary) obligor, his liability is not dependent upon the default of the principal debtor, nor can the indemnifier avail himself of the defences which may be invoked by a guarantor by virtue of his 'secondary' status (see 'Guarantor's defences' below);
2 the contract of indemnity remains valid and binding even though (for some reason) the underlying transaction is void or otherwise not binding on the borrower. Again, this consequence flows from the 'primary' nature of the indemnifier's obligations; and

3 a contract of guarantee may only be enforced if reduced to writing, whereas an indemnity may be enforced even if given orally (see 'Formalities' below).

Although they differ in some detailed respects, it should be appreciated that both guarantees and indemnities are intended to form legally binding commitments in favour of the lender. This will depend upon the proper interpretation of the words used in the document concerned, which should be both clear and unconditional. Occasionally, lenders may accept less specific undertakings from an intended 'guarantor', eg a promise by a parent company to retain ownership of the borrower and confirmation that it is the present policy of the parent to maintain the solvency of its subsidiaries. Statements of this kind (often referred to as 'comfort letters') merely reflect the current policies or intentions of the parent company and do not represent firm or binding obligations. A lender would not generally have a legal claim against the parent if the subsidiary later becomes insolvent.

Formalities

In order to avoid the possibility of abuse, English law prohibits an action to enforce a guarantee unless it has been reduced to writing and executed by the guarantor[1]. It follows that an oral guarantee is of no value. It might be thought that this will rarely be a problem in commercial transactions, but this rule has nevertheless been at issue in a number of recent cases. This is, in part, because the requirement for writing applies to contracts of guarantee but *not* to contracts of indemnity. Parties seeking to rely on verbal assurances have thus sought to classify the spoken words as an indemnity, rather than a guarantee. In practice, standard forms of guarantee in use by banks tend to combine both a guarantee (in the strict sense) and an indemnity by:

1 rendering the guarantor liable or answerable for the borrower's debt (the 'guarantee' aspect); and
2 providing that the guarantor is liable as a principal obligor, and not merely as surety (the 'indemnity' aspect).

Liabilities and defences

The nature and extent of the liability of the guarantor (or indemnifier) depends largely upon the terms of the contract itself. Some care is required in drafting guarantees especially where there is some unusual feature (eg because the guarantor is only assuming responsibility for a specific part or portion of the underlying debt). Great care must be taken to ensure the clarity of the guarantee wording; any ambiguity will be resolved by adopting the interpretation which is most favourable to the position of the guarantor.

Whilst the use of clear and adequate language is important when the guarantee is initially prepared and executed, this is not sufficient to ensure that the guarantor will always be bound into his obligations. For this purpose, care must be taken in the administration of the underlying facility and the guarantee itself; the 'secondary' nature

1 Statute of Frauds 1677 s 4.

of the guarantee means that the guarantor may be discharged if the lender agrees to vary the primary obligation itself. In particular, care must be taken in the following cases:

1 where the primary debtor requests additional time for payment. The debtor may seek a deferral of the repayment date for a number of reasons. He may be in genuine financial difficulty or the deferral may be more convenient than negotiating a new or substitute facility. But the motivation for the time extension does not matter; if the creditor grants time without the guarantor's consent, then the guarantee is discharged. At first sight, this rule appears curious, an extension to the underlying repayment date may defer a call on the guarantee, and thus operate to the guarantor's advantage. But the rule is justifiable upon further examination. The guarantor has only agreed to assume the debtor's risk for the original period of the transaction (and not for an extended period). Furthermore, if the financial condition of the borrower deteriorates during the extended facility period, then the effective value of the guarantor's right of subrogation (see 'Rights of subrogation' below) may be adversely affected;
2 where the terms of the primary contract are varied. The guarantor has undertaken a secondary liability only in respect of the original contract between the primary parties. If that contract is varied, then this operates to discharge the guarantee unless (i) the variation is obviously minor or (ii) the variation clearly operates to the advantage of the guarantor (eg a reduction in the underlying interest rate);
3 where the primary debtor is released. We have previously noted that the obligations of the guarantor effectively 'mirror' those of the primary debtor. Thus, if the debtor is released (eg through agreement or by repayment) then the obligations of the guarantor must necessarily come to an end;
4 where other guarantors are released from liability by the creditor. A guarantor has a right of contribution against other persons who stand as surety for the same guaranteed debt (see 'Multiple guarantors' below). The release of co-guarantors clearly acts to the detriment of those guarantors who would otherwise remain liable, for they are deprived of their contribution rights. A guarantor is automatically discharged under such circumstances, at least if the existence of a 'group' of guarantors formed part of the original understanding between the parties;
5 where security given by the principal debtor is discharged. If the creditor releases a charge over property or assets of the principal debtor, then the guarantor is again discharged. Such action clearly prejudices the guarantor, because he is deprived of his right of subrogation in respect of that security (see 'Rights of subrogation' below);
6 where the creditor has been responsible for a misrepresentation. As noted earlier, a guarantee is a form of contract and is thus subject to the general law of contract. If the creditor has misrepresented the terms of the underlying contract or some other material point, then the guarantor may be able to rescind the contract of guarantee and thus avoid liability upon it;
7 where the creditor acts in bad faith towards the guarantor. The precise scope of this rule is unclear, but the primary creditor appears to owe a limited duty of good faith to a guarantor; and
8 undue influence, duress and fraud. A guarantee may be vitiated if it has been obtained through the use of undue influence, or as a result of duress or fraud. However, considerations of this type (along with other potentially vitiating factors)

apply to any form of security and they are thus considered in under 'Vitiating factors' p 459 below.

It should be appreciated that the considerations noted in paragraphs 1–6 above (which may perhaps be regarded as traps for the unwary creditor) can be excluded by the express provisions of the guarantee, thus ensuring that the liability of the guarantor continues under such circumstances. This factor explains some of the lengthy and detailed provisions found in English law guarantees and which (at first sight) appear somewhat obscure. The consequences of bad faith or fraud (paragraphs 7 and 8 above) cannot be excluded by the terms of any contract.

It should also be noted that the defences listed above are in many cases only available to the guarantor by virtue of the 'secondary' nature of his obligations. Consequently, these defences will generally not be available where the document concerned amounts to an indemnity (that is, a primary obligation of the party giving it).

Finally, it should be appreciated that the creditor may have immediate recourse to the guarantor as soon as the primary debt has become due and payable in accordance with its terms. The creditor is under no general obligation to pursue the primary debtor as a condition to his recourse to the guarantor (unless such a duty has been expressly written into the guarantee itself).

Rights of subrogation

Assuming that there is no defence to a call under the guarantee, the guarantor must of course meet any demand for payment which is validly made by the creditor.

It then becomes necessary to consider a variety of matters, as follows:

1. first of all, the guarantor acquires an immediate right of reimbursement against the principal debtor because (in substance) the guarantor has paid the moneys owing on behalf of that debtor. It should be appreciated that this right of reimbursement ('subrogation right') is an equitable right which arises in consequence of the debtor's original request for the issue of the guarantee. There may be difficulty in claiming a right of subrogation where the guarantee was given in the absence of such a request, but in commercial terms such cases are naturally rare. Where a guarantee is given by a bank or financial institution for the account of one of its customers, it will not normally rely merely upon the *equitable* right of subrogation. Instead, it will have required the customer to undertake a *contractual* obligation of reimbursement by executing a standard form of counter indemnity;
2. in essence, the right of subrogation entitles the guarantor to 'stand in the shoes' of the primary creditor and to enforce any claims and remedies to which the creditor would otherwise have been entitled. Apart from the personal right of recourse noted in 1 above, it follows that the guarantor will be entitled to the benefit of (and to enforce) any security which the creditor had taken from the primary debtor;
3. accordingly, a creditor who has been fully paid by a guarantor must take care in dealing with the security after the closure of the loan account. It must bear in mind the subrogation rights acquired by the guarantor, and must ensure that any title or security documents held by it are sent to the guarantor (ie and not mistakenly returned to the primary debtor); and

4 if there are multiple guarantors, then a guarantor who has discharged the debt may be entitled to a contribution from his co-guarantors. This point is further explored under 'Multiple guarantors', below.

Financial limits

Where a guarantee is given by a parent company to facilitate borrowings by a subsidiary, the guarantee will frequently cover all moneys from time to time owing by the subsidiary to the creditor concerned. This does not involve an undue exposure for the parent guarantor because it controls the affairs of the subsidiary and can thereby regulate the level of borrowings from the creditor in question.

In the absence of such a relationship between the guarantor and the primary debtor, however, the guarantor must ensure that his liability is satisfactorily limited; he does not wish to write a 'blank cheque'. This is especially the case where the guarantee is given by a bank: for credit and regulatory purposes, the bank must be able to quantify the maximum level of its exposure at any given time.

There are some fairly difficult rules which surround the drafting of financial limitations of this type. Suffice it to say that (from the creditor's point of view) the guarantee should cover all moneys owing by the debtor, up to a set monetary limit. This will ensure that the guarantor cannot acquire any subrogation rights until the underlying debt has been paid in full. If the guarantee merely applies to a set *percentage* or proportion of the debt, then the guarantor may be entitled to exercise his subrogation rights in competition with the primary creditor. This rule may seem both anomalous and artificial, but it must be carefully borne in mind in negotiating and drafting financial limits in guarantees.

Multiple guarantors

A variety of issues may arise where the same debt or loan has been guaranteed by a number of guarantors, eg where borrowings by one member of a corporate group are guaranteed by several other members. These issues may be summarised as follows:

1 first of all, it is common to state that the liability of the co-guarantors is 'joint and several'. Although perhaps no longer strictly necessary, this language is intended to confirm that a judgment obtained against one guarantor will not operate to prevent subsequent proceedings against the remaining parties;
2 secondly, if one of the guarantors pays the debt in full, he is entitled to a pro-rata contribution from the other guarantors; and
3 thirdly, as noted earlier, the release of one co-guarantor may have the effect of releasing the other guarantors. Standard forms of bank guarantee will contain language designed to avoid this rule.

TYPES OF SECURITY

Lenders will often require security to be provided over some or all of their borrower's assets in return for the provision of the loan; alternatively, a guarantor may be asked to provide security for the contingent obligations under its guarantee. Security can take the form of fixed or floating charges, depending on the nature of the asset and the level of security required by the lender. Standard form debentures in use by banks usually incorporate both forms of charge. In very general terms, fixed charges are given over assets which are ascertainable and identifiable at any given time such as land, shares, ships and aircraft. Floating charges attach to both present and future assets which are intended to be bought and sold in the ordinary course of business (eg stock-in-trade). For convenience, it is proposed at the outset to examine various forms of fixed charge over specific assets. Thereafter, the nature and effect of a floating charge will be considered. The following topics will therefore be covered:

1 charges over land;
2 charges over shares;
3 charges over cash;
4 charges over contracts;
5 charges over goods;
6 charges over ships and aircraft;
7 floating charges;
8 legal charges; and
9 equitable charges.

It should be noted that (if created by a company) registration requirements may apply to the forms of security about to be discussed, but these aspects are considered in under 'Formalities', below.

Charges over land

Security over real property may be taken either by means of a legal mortgage or by way of an equitable charge.

Legal mortgage

A legal mortgage (which must comply with all formalities applicable to this type of security) will usually be the preferred form of security over a legal interest in land, largely because this form of security is more readily enforceable following a default. The charge must be executed as a deed, whether it relates to a freehold[2] or leasehold[3] interest and this requirement applies equally in the context of a registered title[4]. A legal mortgage affecting a registered title must be registered in order to preserve its priority[5]. Pending registration, the charge only takes effect as an equitable mortgage and is vulnerable in the event that subsequent charges are registered against the title.

2 Law of Property Act 1925 s 85.
3 Law of Property Act 1925 s 86.
4 Land Registration Act 1925 s 25.
5 Land Registration Act 1925 s 26 (as amended).

Equitable mortgage

In essence, an *equitable* charge is a form of security where the chargor has agreed to create the mortgage concerned but not all of the relevant formalities for a legal mortgage have been met, eg because the document creating the security has merely been signed by the chargor (and not executed as a deed). The document recording the security arrangements must be comprehensive, recording all of the agreed terms and it must be signed by both the chargor and the chargee.[6] Where possible, the chargee should take physical possession of the title documents; registration requirements may again apply. The priority of consecutive security interests over land is generally governed by the respective dates of registration of the charges concerned: see under 'Priorities' p 449, below.

It should be remembered that a charge created by a company must be lodged at Companies House[7] in addition to the further registration requirements outlined above.

Finally, a certain amount of 'due diligence' will generally be required on the part of the prospective chargee. In particular:

1 he will need to investigate title to the property, in order to ensure that his security will enjoy its anticipated priority and that the property is not subject to the unusual covenants or restrictions which might affect its value; and
2 he will wish to make local enquiries to ascertain proposals which might have an impact on the value or marketability of the property, eg planning approvals or other local proposals.

Charges over shares

At the outset, it should be noted that a charge over shares is, in many respects, an unsatisfactory form of security. If the issuing company is wound up, then all of the obligations of that company must be met before any moneys become available to the shareholder and, hence, to the chargee. In the case of insolvency, the chargee would recover nothing through this form of security. On the other hand, there may be two advantages, namely:

1 if the charged shares are listed on a stock exchange, there should be a readily available market for their disposal in an enforcement situation; and
2 if the charged shares represent a majority stake in a private company, then this may afford to the lender a degree of control and facilitate disposal, should that prove necessary.

A charge over shares in a company may be taken in different forms, depending upon the precise level of security required by the lender. In the present context, it is proposed to consider:

1 the procedures involved in taking legal charges over shares;
2 the corresponding procedures in the context of equitable charges; and
3 certain disclosure issues applicable to shares in public companies.

6 Law of Property (Miscellaneous Provisions) Act 1989 s 2.
7 Companies Act 1985 s 395.

The relative advantages and disadvantages of each form of security will be noted in each case.

Legal charges

A legal charge involves (i) the execution of a document creating the charge and (ii) the formal transfer of title to the shares to the chargee or to a nominee acting on its behalf. The transfer of title involves the issue of a new share certificate in the name of the chargee or nominee. Alternatively, if the shares are held through the 'paperless' system for listed securities operated by CREST, the relevant shares will have to be credited to the CREST account of a member representing the chargee or nominee concerned.

Where the shares consist of an interest in a private company, a resolution of the board of directors will usually be required before the necessary transfer of shares can be registered in favour of the chargee/nominee.

A 'full' legal charge carries the following advantages:

1 since the chargee/nominee is the registered owner of the shares, his title to the charged property is easily demonstrated, thus facilitating enforcement;
2 as the registered owner, the lender will be entitled to receive payment of all dividends and notice of shareholders' meetings (although the lender would usually agree to pass on any dividends to the chargor, unless and until a default occurs); and
3 if the charge covers more than 50%. of the share capital of the company concerned, then (upon enforcement of the security) a purchaser of the shares will have considerable freedom of action, eg he could effectively appoint and remove members of the board of directors. This will clearly enhance the value of the shares. It should, however, be noted that the chargee should not generally be entitled to vote before enforcement becomes necessary, otherwise, the company concerned could be treated as a subsidiary of the lender itself[8].

There remain, however, certain difficulties with a legal charge over shares. For example:

1 as noted above, the registration of a transfer may (in the case of a private company) require the approval of the board of directors in accordance with the company's articles of association. This may not be forthcoming unless the intending chargor controls the company and can thus effectively compel the directors to provide the requisite approval;
2 from the point of view of the chargor, the need for registration of the transfer results in the disclosure to the company of his borrowing arrangements. The chargor may prefer to maintain the confidentiality of such arrangements and (for that reason) may resist any request for a full, legal charge; and
3 a legal charge is inappropriate in the context of *partly paid* shares, because (as registered owner of the shares) the chargee would become personally liable for any calls made with respect to those shares.

8 Companies Act 1985 s 736 A (7).

Equitable charges

An equitable charge involves (i) the execution of a document creating the charge and (ii) the delivery to the lender of the relevant share certificate and a form of transfer executed in blank. When a default occurs, the lender may complete the transfer form (either in favour of itself or a purchaser) and application can be made for the registration of the transfer. In the case of a listed or public company, this arrangement is frequently satisfactory because the issuing company will generally be obliged to register the transfer. But an equitable charge is of limited value where the issuing entity is a private company because:

1 (as noted above), the articles of association of a private company usually allow to the directors a discretion to refuse registration of a transfer; and
2 there is no guarantee that the directors will co-operate in approving a transfer once the bank finds it necessary to enforce its security. Unless and until the lender can become the registered owner of the shares, it cannot exercise voting rights or claim payment of dividends.

It may be possible to mitigate these problems, eg (i) by seeking an undertaking from the directors to register the transfer upon presentation or (ii) by amending the articles of association so as to deprive the directors of their discretion in the context of the enforcement of a security interest. For a variety of reasons, however, these approaches are not entirely satisfactory; in addition, they frequently involve extensive negotiation with the issuing company and its directors.

For the reasons noted earlier, a charge over *partly paid* shares should only be effected by means of an equitable charge.

Disclosure requirements

A certain amount of care is necessary where a lender or creditor takes security over shares in a *public* company because:

1 formal notice must be given to the company by a person who acquires an interest in three per cent. (or more) of the nominal share capital of the company;[9] and
2 failure to comply with this obligation constitutes a criminal offence.[10]

However, a lender which is a bank will usually be exempt from the notification requirement, provided that the security is taken in support of a transaction in the ordinary course of the lender's banking business.[11]

If, upon the enforcement of its security, a lender or creditor is to dispose of any listed shares which have been charged to it, then care must be taken to ensure that individuals within the organisation do not thereby commit an offence under the 'insider trading' régime.[12]

9 Companies Act 1985 s 198.
10 Companies Act 1985 s 210.
11 Companies Act 1985 s 209.
12 Criminal Justice Act 1993 s 52.

This might occasionally pose difficulty where the lender is also banker to the issuing company, and may thus hold non-public information about that company's affairs.

Charges over cash

It is perhaps something of a misnomer to speak of a charge over 'cash', for security is never taken over physical notes and coins. Rather, a charge will be taken over a bank's contractual obligation to repay moneys to the chargor, as represented by a credit balance on a bank account. The method of taking security depends upon the identity of the deposit-holding bank.

If the funds are lodged with the chargee bank, then in substance the bank is taking a charge over its own indebtedness or liability to the customer. For some years, there was doubt about the validity of such an arrangement, largely because a charge should be taken over an asset (rather than a liability). Nevertheless, the position has recently been clarified and there is now no doubt that a charge structure of this type is operative under English law. A short form of charge over deposit is sufficient to create this type of security. In the event that the intended security is void for any reason, the bank (acting in reliance on statutory rights of set-off available in the liquidation of a company) may still be able to retain the funds in satisfaction of the chargor's obligations, if the latter should become insolvent.[13]

The position becomes more complex where the deposit is placed with a bank other than the intended beneficiary of the security, and the involvement of a third party bank inevitably involves a greater degree of formality. As before, the security may be created by a short form of charge or assignment. In addition, however:

1 the chargor must instruct the deposit-holding bank to operate the account solely on the instructions of the lender or chargee; and
2 the deposit-holding bank should be asked to acknowledge that (i) it has received notice of the charge, (ii) it will not itself exercise any rights of set-off which it may have or may acquire with respect to the charged account (eg in respect of an overdraft facility on a separate account), and (iii) it has not received notice of any prior security interest over the same account (questions of priority are considered in under 'Priorities' p 449, below).

Charges over contracts

A lender may wish to take security over the benefit of a contract to which his customer is a party. For example, a long term supply contract or lease may provide a relatively secure source of cash which may (if necessary) be applied in reduction of the customer's indebtedness.

Once again, a relatively short form of assignment will suffice to create the security as between the chargor and the lender, but a number of steps are necessary to ensure that the arrangements are binding as against the other party to the assigned contract and the creditors of the chargor. In particular:

13 Rule 4.90, Insolvency Rules 1986.

1 the contract which is to form the subject matter of the assignment must be examined. If the contract contains a prohibition against assignment, then the consent of the other contracting party should be sought in order to regularise the security arrangements; and
2 the other contracting party should be asked to acknowledge that he is aware of the assignment, and that he has not received notice of any prior charge affecting the contract concerned.

Charges over goods

A security interest in physical goods may be taken in one of the following ways:

1 by way of legal charge. This involves the transfer of legal title (although not necessarily physical possession) to *identified* or *ascertained* goods to the lender, subject to a provision for re-transfer following the discharge of the secured debt. There is little merit in taking a legal charge over goods, because (notwithstanding that a full legal charge has been created) a purchaser from the chargor will still obtain good title if he acts in good faith and without notice of the creditor's security interest;[14]
2 by way of equitable charge. The chargor would execute a document evidencing the charge but the relevant goods will remain in the possession of the chargor itself. Neither possession of the goods nor a document of title is delivered to the lender (security in this form is frequently referred to as an 'hypothecation'). But once again, equitable charges may be overridden in favour of a purchaser who acquires the charged assets in good faith. The security over goods, machinery and other assets commonly charged to lenders under standard form debentures will take effect as an equitable charge; and
3 by way of pledge. The creation of a pledge involves the delivery of the physical goods (or their documents of title) to the lender or his nominee, with the intention of creating a security interest. In favour of the lender, a pledge implies a power of sale of the pledged goods following default (although prior notice should generally be given to the pledgor).

Charges over ships and aircraft

Ships

A mortgage over a British registered vessel must be in a prescribed form in order to be registered at the Registry of Ships under the applicable legislation.[15]

The prescribed form of mortgage is very brief and merely creates a charge over the ship itself. The formal mortgage is therefore usually supplemented by a deed of covenant. The latter document will create separate assignments over insurances and payments due under any charter with respect to the vessel. In order to perfect such

14 Factors Act 1889 ss 8 and 9, and Sale of Goods Act 1979 s 25.
15 Merchant Shipping Act 1995.

assignments and in order to preserve their priority, notice should be given to the counterparties to each contract or policy in question.

Aircraft

The Civil Aviation Act 1982 provides for the maintenance of a register of aircraft mortgages under a régime which is essentially similar to the corresponding framework for ship mortgages.[16] Regulations made under previous legislation[17] remain in force. The salient provisions of those regulations may be summarised as follows:

1 an aircraft registered in the UK (together with any store of spare parts) may be mortgaged by way of security for a loan or other indebtedness;[18]
2 a mortgage may be entered into the Register of Mortgages maintained by the Civil Aviation Authority;[19] and
3 the fact that a mortgage is registered against an aircraft does not prevent or affect the exercise of any possessory lien (eg in respect of the cost of work done) or right of detention affecting the aircraft.[20]

Floating charges

A floating charge has been described as 'ambulatory' and 'shifting' in nature, in the sense that:

1 the charge affects all of the general class of assets of the company as specified in the charge (both present and future); but
2 the chargor company retains authority to deal with and to dispose of assets in the ordinary course of business, unless and until that authority is suspended in accordance with the terms of the floating charge itself. To describe the nature of the charge in a different way, a floating charge creates an equitable charge over a class of a company's assets, both present and future, which crystallises on the occurrence of certain events and becomes a fixed charge over the specific assets within the class at the time of crystallisation. The advantage of a floating charge is that it enables the company to deal with its stock within the ordinary course of business. Thus the chargor can sell assets falling within the ambit of the floating charge without having to seek the prior consent of the lender. Equally, when the chargor purchases new assets within the class specified in the charge, they will automatically fall within the scope of the security, without the need for any further document to be executed for that purpose. A fixed charge over stock would not enjoy this flexibility and would (in commercial terms) be wholly impractical.

16 Civil Aviation Act 1982 s 86.
17 Civil Aviation Act 1968, s 16.
18 Mortgaging of Aircraft Order 1972 reg 3.
19 Mortgaging of Aircraft Order 1972 reg 4.
20 Mortgaging of Aircraft Order 1972 reg 14(5).

Crystallisation

Once a floating charge crystallises, it becomes a fixed charge over all the assets previously covered by the floating charge. From the moment of crystallisation the company is no longer free to deal with those assets in the normal course of its business. After the charge has crystallised it still continues to apply to assets acquired subsequent to its crystallisation; it has ceased to 'hover' over the assets and has become fixed, but continues to be attached to assets owned both at the time of crystallisation and in the future.

For these reasons, it is important to know what type of event may trigger the crystallisation of a charge. In essence, a floating charge may crystallise:

1 where the chargor ceases to carry on its business, eg because a resolution has been passed or a court order has been made for the winding up of the company;
2 where the chargee takes positive steps for the enforcement of his security, eg by appointing a receiver; or
3 some other event occurs which is stated to cause crystallisation in accordance with the express terms of the charge itself. For example, the chargee may be entitled to give notice crystallising the charge if the chargor defaults on the underlying loan or breaches some provision of the debenture.

Convenience and purpose of floating charges

A floating charge is thus a convenient method of taking security over a company's assets and undertaking, because:

1 the lender obtains a general charge over the entire business with a relative minimum of formality, but enjoys effective enforcement mechanisms should that ever become necessary (see 'Remedies and enforcement', below); and
2 the company remains free to conduct its business in the normal course.

So far as the lender or chargee is concerned, the main disadvantage of a floating charge is that certain preferential creditors will enjoy priority over his security interest (see the discussion under 'Priorities' p 449 below).

FORMALITIES

This section considers the formalities which must usually be observed in completing a security package. In this context, it must be recognised that an intrinsically valid and binding security document is not, of itself, sufficient. The document must be approved and executed in a manner which 'attaches' the obligations to the intended chargor and to its property and assets. This process involves the observance of certain corporate and other formalities on the part of the company concerned. Furthermore, the price of priority over unsecured creditors is often a degree of publicity, and registration requirements may therefore apply.

Accordingly, this section considers the following matters:

1 capacity matters;
2 statutory protection;
3 formalities of execution;
4 registration of charges;
5 official consents; and
6 stamp duty.

Capacity matters

Under this heading, we will consider the need to check both the corporate existence and the contractual capacity of the intending chargor. Although the emphasis will be on borrowers which are limited companies, other forms of entity will also be considered.

Due incorporation

It hardly needs to be stated that an entity can only incur obligations if it has an independent existence as a corporate person. But this existence obviously needs to be checked. In the case of a company established in England and Wales, a certificate issued by the Registrar of Companies is conclusive evidence as to the existence and due incorporation of the company concerned. A lender should accordingly insist upon a copy of this document, and should also independently verify the existence of the entity by means of a search at Companies House.

Capacity and authority

Subject to the points noted under 'Statutory protection' (below), a valid security document will bind the intended chargor company if:

1 the company has the corporate *power* or *capacity* to assume the obligations created by the security document; and
2 the necessary corporate steps have been taken to *authorise* the exercise of that power (ie the execution of the security document) on behalf of the company.

The incorporation documents of a company established in England and Wales comprise:

1 the memorandum of association, which will set out the objects of the company[1] and will thus address questions of corporate *capacity*; and
2 the articles of association, which will deal with questions of corporate *authority*.

So a two stage approach is required. First of all, the memorandum must be examined to ascertain the company's capacity to undertake the transaction in question. Most standard forms of memorandum will incorporate power to borrow, to give guarantees and to create security for obligations. But the precise terms of the memorandum must be examined to ensure that they encompass the transaction in hand. In some cases, the

1 Companies Act 1985 s 2(1)(c).

memorandum may simply state that the object of the company is to carry on business as a 'general commercial company'. Such an entity has the corporate power (i) to carry on any trade or business and (ii) to do all things incidental to any such trade or business carried on by it[2]. The latter provision clearly allows such a company to borrow and to give security in order to finance any business which it has chosen to conduct.

The articles will govern the internal steps necessary to *exercise* the powers conferred by the memorandum. For example, it will establish the number of directors required to form a quorum and will set out the voting procedures at board meetings. Usually, the directors will have an unfettered right to exercise the company's powers to borrow and to give guarantees, but the specific provisions must be examined. In particular, the articles will occasionally limit the borrowing powers of the directors to an amount equal to (say) a set multiple of adjusted capital and reserves. If such a provision is found, then further investigation is necessary; the approval of shareholders may be required if it is proposed to exceed the pre-set borrowing limit.

If the incorporation documents are found to be inadequate for any of the purposes described above, then it may be necessary to pass special resolutions to introduce appropriate amendments.[3] This is a straightforward matter for private or closely held companies, but may pose practical difficulties for public or listed entities.

Finally, the prospective lender will wish to examine a copy of the resolution of the directors sanctioning the transaction in hand. There is no prescribed format for such resolutions, but it should in some way be made clear that (i) the meeting concerned was quorate, (ii) the directors understood the nature and scope of the proposed transaction and (iii) authority has been given for the due execution of all necessary documents. For the reasons given in under 'vitiating factors' (p 459 below) it is occasionally desirable to include a discussion of the corporate rationale for the transaction and of the benefits which the company expects to derive from it. Special care must be taken where an individual director has a *personal* interest in the subject matter of the meeting, partly because his vote cannot necessarily be taken into account and partly because a failure to disclose such an interest may constitute an offence.[4] Where all of the directors have a personal interest in the subject matter, then the relevant transaction should be sanctioned at the shareholder level.

A lender is entitled to rely upon the minutes of the board meeting as adequate evidence of the proceedings, provided that it has been signed by the chairman of the meeting concerned, or by the chairman of the ensuing meeting.[5]

As noted earlier, it is advisable for the lender to obtain search details from the file of the company as maintained by the Registrar of Companies. The search offers a check/confirmation of a number of matters, including:

1 the due incorporation of the company and its correct corporate name;
2 the identity of the directors;
3 details of any existing security registered against the assets of the company; and
4 details of any receiver appointed by an existing debenture holder.

2 Companies Act 1985 s 3A.
3 Companies Act 1985 ss 4 and 9.
4 Companies Act 1985 s 317.
5 Companies Act 1985 s 382(2).

Other types of borrower

It is appropriate briefly to outline some of the issues associated with particular types of borrower, as follows:

1 local authorities are created by statute and thus have only those powers which are conferred upon them by legislation. In this context, a local authority has power to borrow for the purpose of carrying out and discharging any of its functions,[6] and for the purpose of bridging anticipated revenues (eg in respect of council taxes or payments for services).[7] Borrowings in a currency other than sterling or from a bank outside the United Kingdom are only permitted with the consent of the Treasury.[8] In general terms, it may be advisable for a lender to ensure that a transaction with a local authority falls within its statutory powers. However (in the context of a loan transaction only) a person dealing with a local authority is relieved of any duty to enquire into the propriety of the arrangements so far as the local authority is concerned;[9]

2 partnerships established in England and Wales have no separate, corporate personality. Each partner is the agent of the firm and all of his other partners, and all partners are bound by any act carried out by one partner in the ordinary course of the firm's business.[10] However, this provision does not entitle an individual partner to raise loans or to give guarantees on behalf of the firm. Consequently, a prospective lender should ensure that the partners with whom it deals have actual authority to bind the firm to the transaction at hand. In the event of insolvency of the firm, the partners must individually contribute in order to make good the deficiency;[11]

3 the power of trustees to raise money by way of borrowings is regulated by the terms of the document creating the trust in question. A prospective lender should accordingly examine that document, although (i) certain powers to borrow are extended to trustees by the law[12] and (ii) a lender advancing money by way of a mortgage on trust property is not obliged to enquire into the application of the proceeds of the loan.[13]

Statutory protection

Some of the precautionary steps noted above can occasionally be burdensome, and may create traps for the unwary. This general comment applies not merely to transactions involving a financing or security, but to any arrangement involving obligations incurred by a company. In many cases, it is unrealistic to expect the outside party to make detailed checks of the type just described. This state of affairs has been recognised, and steps

6 Local Government Act 1972 s 111.
7 Local Government Act 1972 Sch 13, para 10.
8 Local Government Act 1972 Sch 13, para 3.
9 Local Government Act 1972 Sch 13, para 20.
10 Partnership Act 1890 s 5.
11 Partnership Act 1890 s 44.
12 Trustee Act 1925 s 16.
13 Trustee Act 1925 s 17.

have been taken in an effort to alleviate the burdens placed on an outside party dealing with a company.

To this end, the Companies Act 1985 contains provisions to the following effect:

1 the validity of a transaction entered into by a company cannot be challenged on the grounds that the company lacked the capacity to enter into that transaction;[14]
2 a party dealing with a company in good faith may assume that the power of the directors to bind that company is not limited by the company's constitution;[15] and
3 a party dealing with a company is not bound to investigate the terms of its constitution;[16]
4 where the prospective borrower is incorporated or is otherwise established outside England and Wales, then its corporate or other capacity to enter into the transaction will be governed by the law of the country concerned (see 'Enforcement of foreign guarantees and security' p 465). Under those circumstances, enquiries should be made in that country in order to ensure that the transaction is within the borrower's powers and will thus be binding on the entity concerned. It will frequently be advisable to obtain a formal legal opinion from lawyers qualified in that jurisdiction.

At first glance, it might be thought that this provision would dispose of many of the issues noted above. In some respects, this is true; it appears, for example, that a prospective lender can simply disregard any limitations on the corporate capacity of the borrower, as set out in its memorandum of association. Unfortunately, however, these rules do not entirely obviate the need for enquiry by the intending lender. For example:

1 as noted earlier, it is still necessary to check the very existence of the corporate borrower, and a search at Companies House therefore remains a desirable precaution; and
2 in addition, the statutory protection extends only to persons dealing with 'the directors' of a company. Again, it is advisable to verify the identity of the directors and a search at Companies House is a necessary part of that process. Furthermore, the protection only applies to a person dealing with the *board of directors*, and will not necessarily be available in the context of separate dealing with *individual directors*. Consequently, it remains advisable to obtain a copy of a board minute recording the approval of the transaction by the board as a whole.

Given that a degree of inquiry remains necessary, many banks (although not all of them) continue their former practice and require sight of the incorporation documents and board authorities. It is, perhaps, also unappealing to a bank to rely on statutory provisions which enable it to 'close its eyes' to documents which can readily be examined and checked, without undue strain upon the time and resources of the bank or its employees. Nevertheless, the statutory protection may remain valuable where (for some reason) it is later discovered that the customary corporate verification procedures were not followed. But in general terms, it should be remembered that these

14 Companies Act 1985 s 35.
15 Companies Act 1985 s 35 A.
16 Companies Act 1985 s 35 B.

protections are only available when dealing with a *company*, and will not extend to other types of borrowing entity.

Additional protections may be available in specific cases. For example, where a document creates security over property in England and Wales, the chargee may assume that the document is binding on the company if (i) it has been executed as a deed and (ii) it has been signed by a director and secretary of the company concerned[17].

Formalities of execution

Loan agreements and many other contractual documents are not subjected to any special formalities of execution. They may be executed by a single director or by any other person, so long as this is done in conformity with the relevant board resolution (above).

However, certain categories of documents are required to be executed as a deed, eg a document which is intended to create a legal mortgage over land. A document intended to take effect as a deed only becomes a 'live' document if (i) it has been executed in accordance with the rules about to be described and (ii) it has been delivered to the lender with the intent that the company should be immediately and unconditionally bound by it. In the case of a deed executed by a company in favour of a purchaser or mortgagee, execution and delivery of a deed are deemed to occur simultaneously:[18]

If a document is required to be executed as a deed then:

1 it may be executed by the company under its common seal (if it has such a seal) in the manner prescribed by the articles of association;[19]
2 alternatively, a document executed by the director and a secretary (or by two directors) will take effect as a deed provided that it is clear from the document that it was intended to be a deed;[20]
3 where the document is executed outside this country, then the company may (by deed) appoint an attorney to execute on its behalf, or it may have a separate official seal for use abroad;[1] and
4 a foreign company may execute deeds and other documents in the manner allowed under the laws of its country of incorporation.[2]

Registration of charges

A lender who holds a valid security interest over the assets of a company enjoys a priority right of payment out of those assets in the event of the chargor's liquidation, and also enjoys powers of sale in order to enforce his security. Since these privileges may adversely affect the right of unsecured creditors, certain types of security must be registered at Companies House, thus enabling persons dealing with the company to

17 Law of Property Act 1925 s 74.
18 Companies Act 1985 s 36A(6).
19 Companies Act 1985 s 36A(2).
20 Companies Act 1985 s 36A(5).
1 Companies Act 1985 s 39.
2 Companies Act 1985 s 36(A)(2) and Foreign Companies (Execution of Documents) Regulations 1994.

verify the existence of any prior, secured claims. Furthermore, additional registration requirements may apply for the protection of third parties dealing with a particular class of asset, eg land, ships and aircraft. Other steps, while not legally required to preserve the intrinsic validity of the security – may nevertheless be desirable for a variety of reasons.

These general propositions are readily understood, but it is necessary to examine five specific areas to elaborate on these broad statements:

1 what types of security require registration?
2 what are the consequences of non-registration?
3 how do the registration requirements apply to foreign companies?
4 attention will be drawn to certain registration requirements outside those prescribed by the Companies Act 1985; and
5 mention will be made of a few miscellaneous formalities which may be appropriate in specific contexts.

Registrable Security

The Companies Act 1985 sets out a list of registrable types of security, and includes the following:[3]

1 a charge to secure an issue of debentures (or debt instruments);
2 a charge on uncalled capital;
3 a charge over chattels which remain in the physical possession of the company;
4 a charge on land (including land situate abroad);
5 a charge on the benefit of book debts owing to the company;
6 a floating charge;
7 a charge on calls made by the company on its nil-paid or partly paid shares;
8 a charge on a ship or aircraft; and
9 a charge on goodwill or intellectual property (such as a patent or a trade mark).

A charge which falls outside these prescribed categories does *not* require registration, and is thus binding without that formality. For example, a charge over shares to secure a bank loan does not fall within the list. A person dealing with a holding company could therefore be unaware that it has mortgaged its shares in all of its subsidiaries, and that another lender would effectively have first call over the assets of the group. A charge of this type would not be revealed by a search at Companies House.

Similarly, a charge over a bank deposit is thought to fall outside the scope of the registration requirements. However, there is some doubt about this point and it therefore remains customary to deliver such security documents for registration. Indeed, this 'safety first' approach is customary for any security which falls on the margins of the registration requirements or in any case of doubt, because compliance with the registration procedures is neither expensive nor burdensome.

3 Companies Act 1985.

Non-registration

The Companies Act requires that a registrable charge must be delivered to Companies House within 21 days, along with a prescribed form giving brief details of the security thereby created. The obligation to register the security is placed on the company,[4] although in practice the lender (or other holder of the security) will undertake this task, in view of its obvious interest in ensuring the continuing validity of its security arrangements. In the latter event, the cost of the registration process can be recovered from the chargor company.[5]

If the 21 day time limit is missed, then it should be remembered that (i) a few extra days may be allowed if the charge document has been executed abroad and relates to property outside the UK[6] and (ii) the court may extend the time for registration in many cases[7] (although it will not usually do so if, by the time of the application, the company is in serious financial difficulty).

If a charge is not registered, then it will be void against the liquidator, administrator or any creditor of the company.[8] In other words, the lender (or chargee) is treated as an ordinary, unsecured creditor. It should, however, be appreciated that the charge remains valid as against the *company itself*. The chargee may therefore exercise his powers of sale (and any other powers) unless and until a liquidator, administrator or creditor intervenes. Furthermore, if a charge becomes void upon the expiry of the 21-day period, then the liabilities intended to be secured by the charge become immediately due and payable, regardless of the intended term or period of the underlying facilities.[9]

Foreign companies

A company incorporated abroad must comply with the various security registration provisions just described if (i) the charge relates to property situate in England and Wales and (ii) the chargor has an established place of business in England and Wales.[10]

Whether or not a company has an established place of business in this country is a factual question and a lender may not necessarily be certain of its answer.

A foreign company which has established a place of business here should have registered its existence with Companies House,[11] but it may have failed to do so. As a matter of precaution, any qualifying charge executed by a foreign company and involving property in this country should be delivered for registration. This ensures that the lender has complied with the registration provisions of the Companies Act, and the security will thus remain valid even if it later transpires that the chargor had an (unregistered) place of business in England and Wales.

4 Companies Act 1985 s 399(1).
5 Companies Act 1985 s 399(2).
6 Companies Act 1985 s 398(2)
7 Companies Act 1985 s 404.
8 Companies Act 1985 s 395(1).
9 Companies Act 1985 s 395(2).
10 Companies Act 1985 s 409.
11 Companies Act 1985 Chapter XXIII.

Other registration requirements

Whilst the focus thus far has been on the requirements of the Companies Act 1985, it should not be forgotten that specialised registration requirements may apply in relation to particular types of security. For example:

1 a charge over registered land will require registration at the Land Registry;[12]
2 certain charges over unregistered land will require registration as land charges;[13] and
3 charges over ships[14] and aircraft[15] may require separate registration under legislation applicable to those types of assets.

It should be appreciated that the various registration requirements are cumulative. Thus, the same charge may require registration both at Companies House and at one of the other registries mentioned above.

Other formalities

We have now completed our brief review of the various statutory formalities involved in taking security. But a number of other, *non-statutory* steps may be desirable to preserve the benefit of the security. Usually, this involves the giving of notice to other parties who have dealings with the borrower in relation to the subject matter of the security. By way of examples:

1 where the security includes a charge over cash flows (or potential cash flows) payable by a third party, notice of the security should be given to that party. This will ensure that the lender retains a first priority security interest in that cashflow, and that the third party can only obtain a good discharge of his debt by payment to the lender. Thus, notice should be given to (and acknowledged by) a tenant whose rental stream has been assigned to the lender, or to an insurer of land and buildings which fall within the scope of the security package;
2 where the security includes a leasehold interest, then notice to the landlord will be required (in some cases, his consent may be needed before the charge is executed); and
3 where other lenders have made secured facilities available to the same borrower, they should be notified of the new loan. It will often be desirable for the lenders to settle the security position among themselves by executing a Deed of Priorities of the kind discussed under 'Priorities' p 449 below.

Official consents

As a general rule, it is unnecessary to obtain the approval of governmental authorities as a pre-condition to the creation of security over assets in the UK.

12 Land Registration Act 1985 s 26.
13 Land Charges Act 1972.
14 Merchant Shipping Act 1995.
15 Mortgaging of Aircraft Order 1972.

It should be remembered that borrowings and the creation of security by overseas subsidiaries of UK parent companies may *occasionally* require the consent of the Treasury under tax rules designed to regulate the migration of companies.[16] However, no such consent is required:

1 where the transaction involves a movement of capital as between Member States of the EU;[17] or
2 where the foreign subsidiary gives security to its bankers for facilities made available in the ordinary course of business.[18]

Stamp duty

Liability to stamp duty is imposed on certain categories of documents, whether executed within or outside the UK. Penalties are imposed if the duty is not paid within the set time limits. Apart from the financial issues, failure to pay the necessary duty has other consequences for a person seeking to rely on a document. In particular:[19]

1 the document may not be admitted in any court proceedings for the enforcement of any contractual obligation or any security; and
2 an unstamped document cannot be accepted for registration by governmental or other authorities, eg the Land Registry.

It is true to say that most documents which create a *security interest* are now outside the scope of the charge to stamp duty. But lenders must remember that stamp duty may be chargeable on the *transfer* of the asset which they intend to finance. Thus, a *mortgage* over land is exempt from duty; but a *transfer* of land is liable to duty calculated as a percentage of the purchase price. A bank which intends to finance the purchase of a property must therefore ensure that the necessary stamp duty has been provided for; clearly, the lender's security cannot be registered if the chargor cannot produce the necessary (duly stamped) evidence of his title to the property in question.

PRIORITIES

A company may borrow money from a variety of different sources. Each lender may take separate charges over the assets of the company. The company may also owe money to creditors who have taken no formal security but who may have some other claim to preferential treatment, employees, the Inland Revenue or judgment creditors who have taken steps to enforce their judgment debts.

In such cases, all creditors will wish to know who is entitled to first call on the charged assets, and the order of priority between the remaining creditors. Accordingly, this section will consider the following matters:

16 Income and Corporation Taxes Act 1988 s 765(1).
17 Income and Corporation Taxes Act 1988 s 765A.
18 Income and Corporation Taxes Act 1988 s 765(2).
19 Stamp Act 1891 s 14(4).

1 the link between registration of security and its priority;
2 the general rules as to the priority of fixed charges;
3 the priority of floating charges;
4 the position of preferential creditors; and
5 priority agreements.

It must be said that priorities among different chargees can be an extremely difficult and confusing area of English law. An attempt will therefore be made to explain this area in rather broad terms, but the limitations of this approach should be appreciated.

REGISTRATION AND PRIORITIES

It has been noted under 'Formalities' (above) that many forms of security require registration (eg at Companies House and/or the Land Registry) in order to preserve the validity of those charges against creditors of the chargor or other third parties.

It should, however, be appreciated that the *registration* of a security interest does not necessarily affect its *priority*. This point can perhaps best be illustrated by reference to the provisions for the registration of charges created by companies,[20] under which a charge will become void as against a liquidator, administrator or creditor unless it is duly delivered to Companies House for registration within 21 days of the creation of the security. Whilst this provision may in some cases *vitiate* the charge, it does not seek to regulate priorities as between two competing charges which are duly registered within the requisite time limit.

Thus if:

1 a borrower company executes a charge on 1 January, with registration at Companies House occurring on 20 January; and
2 the same borrower executes a further charge over the same asset in favour of a different lender on 3 January, with registration occurring on 5 January,

then (as will be explained below) the 1 January charge will take priority since it was the first to be executed. This remains the case even though (i) the 3 January charge was the first to make an appearance on the chargor's records at Companies House and (ii) when taking his security, the second lender would have found no trace of the first priority charge when searching the borrower's register at Companies House.

This example serves to illustrate that the priority of charges is *not* generally determined by their respective dates of registration, although a number of exceptional cases are noted below. It perhaps also demonstrates that (in the example given above) the second chargee is vulnerable to fraudulent conduct on the part of the borrower.

GENERAL PRIORITY RULES

The starting point is that competing security interests rank in accordance with the time of their creation; earlier security interests take priority over later ones.

20 Companies Act 1985 s 395.

The general rule is therefore one of considerable simplicity. But perhaps inevitably, there is a large number of exceptions which tend to obscure the general principle. The following are the most important exceptions (although it should be appreciated that the list is non-exhaustive):

1 special rules apply to security over land in England and Wales. Where title to the property is registered at the Land Registry then successive mortgages over that property will generally rank according to the respective dates of their *registration*.[1] In the case of unregistered land, a first mortgagee takes priority by taking physical possession of the title deeds. Subsequent chargees take priority by reference to the dates on which their respective security interests were registered as land charges;[2]

2 where the benefit of a debt or other obligation has been the subject of successive assignments, their priority will be governed by the dates upon which notice of each assignment was given to the debtor or obligor concerned. Apart from other considerations, this rule is both just and convenient for the debtor. He needs to know to whom payment should be made, and yet he cannot be concerned with the terms of the assignments themselves – he will not generally be a party to those documents;

3 a charge created by a company and which requires registration under the Companies Act will become void against other creditors, an administrator or liquidator if the necessary papers are not delivered to the Registrar of Companies within 21 days of the creation of the charge.[3] An unregistered charge will thus lose its priority as against any *subsequent* charge over the same asset which is duly registered;

4 a lender who takes a *legal* mortgage or charge over property without notice of a prior *equitable* charge will obtain priority over the security interest of the equitable chargee. For these purposes, the legal mortgagee is deemed to have notice of the prior equitable security if (i) in the case of land, that security has been registered as a land charge[4] or (ii) in most cases, the security has been registered against a corporate chargor at the Companies Registry;[5]

5 generally speaking, a first mortgagee can continue to add further advances to the scope of its own security unless and until he is notified that a subsequent security interest has been created. Thereafter, such further advances will be postponed to the second security interest, unless the additional advances are made by the first mortgagee pursuant to an obligation to that effect in the mortgage documents;[6] and

6 a separate registration and priority regime applies to ships[7] and to aircraft.[8] Broadly speaking, (i) all registered mortgages have priority over any unregistered charges and (ii) registered charges rank according to their respective dates of registration.

1 Land Registration Act 1925 s29.
2 Land Charges Act 1972.
3 Companies Act 1985 s 395.
4 Law of Property Act 1925 s 198.
5 Companies Act 1985 s 395.
6 Law of Property Act 1925 s 94.
7 Merchant Shipping Act 1995 Sch 1.
8 Mortgaging of Aircraft Order 1972 reg 14.

PRIORITY OF FLOATING CHARGES

The nature of a floating charge has been considered in 'types of Security' p 432 above. The security 'floats' over the class of assets thereby charged, but does not attach to any specific asset until crystallisation occurs. In view of this peculiar feature of a floating charge, it is necessary to give separate consideration to their priority position as against other charges. For present purposes, it will be assumed that both the floating charge and other security have been duly registered where required. Given that a floating charge does not initially 'fasten' onto the secured assets, the floating charge will rank *after* a fixed charge over the same asset, regardless of the date on which the fixed charge was created. This general rule may not, however, apply where (i) the floating charge prohibits the creation of future security over the chargor's assets and (ii) the taker of a subsequent fixed charge was aware of the restriction concerned.

Where a company has created successive *floating* charges over the same class of assets, then these will generally rank according to their respective dates of creation.

PREFERENTIAL CREDITORS

As a general rule, unsecured creditors will (of course) rank behind secured creditors in relation to those assets which form the subject matter of the charge. Whilst this rule is of general application in the context of a *fixed* charge, the security created by a *floating* charge is in some respects vulnerable to the claims of certain categories of unsecured creditors. In particular:

1 the landlord of the company's premises who distrains for overdue rent will enjoy priority in relation to the assets which are taken for that purpose;
2 a creditor who has obtained judgment and who has completed execution over the assets of the company will enjoy priority over an *uncrystallised* floating charge; and
3 certain creditors enjoy priority over a floating charge even though those creditors have not themselves taken any form of security. Preferential debts in this category include (i) social security and pension contributions, (ii) remuneration owing to employees and (iii) certain moneys owing to the Inland Revenue, Customs and Excise and other government departments[9]. Preferential debts rank for payment equally among all of such debts.[10]

PRIORITY AGREEMENTS

As has been seen, the priority of competing security arrangements is governed by a number of detailed rules. However, it is common practice for successive lenders to enter into express agreements which will govern the priority of the respective security documents in the event that enforcement becomes necessary. There are various reasons why the execution of a priorities agreement may be preferable to reliance upon the bare legal rules. In particular:

1 there may be a desire to alter the priority rules which would otherwise apply. For example, it may be commercially agreed that a first and second charge are to enjoy

9 Insolvency Act 1986 ss 40 and 386 and Sch 1.
10 Insolvency Act 1986 s 375.

an equal (or *pari passu*) ranking, so that the risk of loss on the transaction is shared proportionately between the two lenders; and

2 the lending parties can also cater for matters which would not be covered by the ordinary priorities rules. For example (i) the agreement may set out a requirement for consultation/co-operation as between the lenders in relation to any proposed enforcement action and (ii) the agreement may closely define the secured sums which are to form the subject matter of the priority agreement, and the date on which such amounts are to be finally calculated in the event of the borrower's insolvency.

Priority agreements are frequently used in the context of 'structured' transactions where different layers of debt are to have differing interests in the security, differing levels of risk and (consequently) different interest margins.

ENVIRONMENTAL CONSIDERATIONS

Recent environmental protection legislation provides a revised system for the identification and remediation of contaminated land. This legislation will have a significant impact upon a chargee of such land in two respects:

(a) it will become possible for the chargee/lender itself to be held responsible for the contamination of the land, if he is found to have knowledge of the contamination and either (i) has the ability to rectify the situation by virtue of a right contained in the mortgage deed to enter onto the land or (ii) has a right to direct how the land is used;

(b) the priority of the charge may be postponed to any remedial expenditure incurred by the relevant authority.

It is therefore important for the chargee to consider:

- obtaining a comprehensive environmental audit on the land prior to taking charge;
- including a contractual provision within the mortgage deed for the chargee to be informed immediately of any investigations being carried out by the authorities and of any remediation or charging notice which is served;
- taking out insurance to cover the potential costs of remedial work;
- imposing stricter warranties to ensure compliance with environmental laws and requiring appropriate indemnities as conditions of granting the finance.

REMEDIES AND ENFORCEMENT

The principal purposes of any security package are essentially twofold namely (i) to obtain a priority over unsecured creditors in relation to the charged assets and (ii) to enable the lender to control and enforce the sale of those assets following a default. The procedures and remedies available to the lender are therefore a key feature of any security package.

Accordingly, this section will consider the following matters:

1 the range of available remedies;
2 powers of sale;
3 the appointment of an administrative receiver;
4 the role of an administrator;
5 the position of unsecured creditors; and
6 winding up proceedings.

Available remedies

Clearly, the types of remedy available to a lender will vary and will depend in large measure upon the type of asset which forms the subject matter of the security. In essence, however, a security document will create four main remedies which will be available to the chargee following a default:

1 a power *to sell* the asset concerned;
2 a power *to appoint a receiver* in respect of the charged asset;
3 a right *to take possession* of the charged assets; and
4 a right *to foreclose* the security.

In practice, the last two remedies are rarely adopted. A mortgagee who takes possession of the property is bound to take reasonable care of it and to manage it prudently (thus incurring both the inconvenience and the expense which those activities will entail). In addition, the mortgagee may be liable for any losses which the mortgagor suffers in consequence of any breach of these duties. The procedures involved in foreclosure of security are equally complex; in addition, the charged property is transferred to the lender absolutely and the underlying debt is extinguished. These features are unattractive to a lender, who may not be in the business of property ownership and who may hope to make further recoveries out of the general assets of the chargor.

It is therefore proposed to consider only the first two remedies, namely the power of sale and the appointment of a receiver.

Power of sale

Where a charge over property is given by deed, then the mortgagee has the right to sell the charged property. That right arises as soon as the secured monies have become payable.[11] However, the power of sale only becomes exercisable once notice of demand has been served on the borrower. Other formalities apply but these can be varied or excluded by the terms of the mortgage document.[12]

Security documents which are not executed as deeds may create equitable charges over the property concerned, but a court order may be required in order to procure their enforcement.

Appointment of administrative receiver

Before moving on to consider the substance of this topic, it should be borne in mind that there are two types of receiver:

1 a receiver appointed by a mortgagee, whose role is to receive and manage the income derived from the mortgaged property.[13] A receiver of this kind can only be appointed once the mortgagee's power of sale has become exercisable.[14] The receiver will have limited statutory powers to recover the income in respect of which

11 Law of Property Act 1925 s 101(1)(i).
12 Law of Property Act 1925 s 103.
13 Law of Property Act 1925 s 101(1)(iii).
14 Law of Property Act 1925 s 109(1).

he has been appointed, but these powers may be extended by the mortgage document;[15] and

2 an *administrative* receiver is a person appointed as such in respect of the whole or substantially the whole of the company's property. He is appointed by creditors entitled to the benefit of a floating charge over the entirety of the company's undertaking.[16]

As will be noted later (see 'Administrators' below), the ability to appoint an administrative receiver may be advantageous to the secured lender, in that he may thereby prevent the appointment of an administrator. An administrative receiver has extensive powers to manage the business,[17] and these can be further extended by the terms of the document creating the floating charge. The administrative receiver (with the consent of the court) also has power to dispose of assets charged to *other* creditors, if that step is likely to facilitate a more advantageous realisation of the company's assets.[18]

For present purposes, it is proposed to focus upon the position of the administrative receiver, which is more frequently encountered in practice.

Some care must be taken in ensuring that the administrative receiver is properly appointed at the outset. In particular:

1 the appointee must be a licensed insolvency practitioner;[19]

2 the right to appoint an administrative receiver must have become exercisable in accordance with the terms of the security document. For example, if the chargor has defaulted in respect of the underlying facility, a formal demand for repayment must be made *before* the administrative receiver can be appointed;

3 the valid appointment of an administrative receiver pre-supposes that the security document itself is valid. If the security is void for any reason, then the appointee will incur personal liability for trespassing upon the company's property. The bank or lender may be called upon to indemnify the receiver against such liability, either by virtue of their contractual arrangements or through a court order to that effect.[20]

Notice of the appointment of the receiver must be lodged at Companies House within seven days,[1] and the appointment must also be advertised in the press.[2] All correspondence emanating from the company must state that a receiver has been appointed.[3]

In general terms, the company remains liable on all contracts entered into by it prior to the receivership. The receiver is personally liable on contracts entered into or adopted by him in performing his functions, although the receiver is allowed to disclaim this liability by means of an express term in the contract to that effect.[4] However, the lender or debenture holder is not liable for the acts or omissions of the receiver, because the receiver performs his functions as agent for the company itself.[5]

15 Law of Property Act 1925 s 109(3).
16 Insolvency Act 1986 s 29(2).
17 Insolvency Act 1986 s 42 and Sch 1.
18 Insolvency Act 1986 s 43.
19 Insolvency Act 1986 s 388.
20 Insolvency Act 1986 s 34.
1 Companies Act 1985 s 405.
2 Insolvency Act 1986 s 46.
3 Insolvency Act 1986 s 39.
4 Insolvency Act 1986 s 44.
5 Insolvency Act 1986 s 44(1)(a).

An administrative receiver is allowed extensive powers to dispose of the assets of the company and to run its business. As noted above, these powers are conferred by law[6] and may be further extended by the terms of the debenture itself. However, a third party dealing with the administrative receiver in good faith is entitled to assume (without making enquiries) that the transaction is within the powers of the administrative receiver.[7]

It should be appreciated that the administrator owes his duties primarily to the lender or creditor who appointed him, and not to the company itself or to its general body of creditors (although the administrative receiver must exercise his powers in good faith and take reasonable care to obtain a proper price upon a disposal of the company's assets). Subject only to the payment of certain preferential debts (see 'Priorities' p 449 above) the administrative receiver is to apply the assets coming into his hands in or towards the discharge of the moneys owing to his appointor.[8]

Role of an administrator

It will be apparent that the exercise of a power of sale or the appointment of a receiver are designed primarily to protect the interests of the secured lender. The interests of the company, its shareholders and its other creditors are very much a secondary consideration. This state of affairs may have been highly satisfactory for the secured lender but was felt to be unsatisfactory in a broader sense. Precipitate action by a secured lender could bring down the company, destroying both the business itself and the jobs which depended on it; restraint might allow the company to recover or at least allow for a more profitable disposal of its assets.

In an effort to remedy this situation, a new system, designed to afford a 'breathing space' to companies in difficulty, was introduced in 1986.[9] Under that scheme:

1 at the request of the company, its directors or its creditors, the court may make an administration order if the company is or is likely to become insolvent; and
2 an order may only be made if (amongst other things) it may secure (i) the survival of the company or its business or (ii) a more advantageous realisation of its assets than would be achieved by winding up the company.[10]

The court has a general discretion to make or to refuse the requested order. However, it may not make an administration order if an administrative receiver has been appointed, unless the court is satisfied that (i) the relevant security is void or voidable or (ii) the security holder has consented to the administration order.[11]

After a petition has been presented to the court requesting an administration order, and for so long as such an order (if made) remains in effect, the creditors of the company are subjected to a number of restrictions on their freedom of action. These restrictions are designed to allow the company time to achieve the objectives of the order, eg the survival of the business or a more advantageous disposal of its assets. These restrictions include the following.[12]

6 Insolvency Act 1986 Sch 1.
7 Insolvency Act 1986 s 42(1).
8 Insolvency Act 1986 s 40.
9 Insolvency Act 1986 ss 8–27.
10 Insolvency Act 1986 s 8.
11 Insolvency Act 1986 s 9.
12 Insolvency Act 1986 ss 10–11.

1 no creditor may successfully petition for the winding up of the company, nor may the shareholders pass a resolution to that effect;
2 no security or rights of repossession can be enforced against the assets or property of the company unless the prior approval of the court has been obtained for that purpose;
3 no distress or execution may be levied against the company or its assets, unless the court has specifically approved that course of action; and
4 (after an administration order has been made) no administrative receiver may be appointed.

In the context of security interests, these restrictions are supplemented by the power of the administrator (with the consent of the court) to dispose of assets which have been charged to a lender or creditor on such terms as the administrator may deem appropriate. In such a case, the secured lender will be entitled to the net proceeds of the disposal, but any balance of his claim is unsecured.[13] It follows that the chargee of a particular asset may initially be prevented from exercising his power of sale, and subsequently find that he is not able to control the timing or terms of a disposal approved by the administrator (although the secured creditor would be able to make representations to the court when its approval of the disposal is requested).

These provisions are, of course, advantageous to the company as a whole but may be felt to be inimical to the interests of the secured lender. In particular, the lender loses the right to enforce his security at the time deemed by him to be most advantageous and may be compelled to accept a sale on terms decided by the administrator. For these reasons, lenders will now (in addition to their security over *specific* assets) frequently seek a general floating charge over the assets of the borrower company. The floating charge may not be directly required to support the credit, but it will allow the lender to appoint an administrative receiver of the company *before* a petition for an administration order is presented. Under these circumstances, the various restrictions against action by the creditors (described above) will not apply,[14] and the lender accordingly retains control over his 'core' security and the timing of its sale. In many cases, however, the borrower may be reluctant to grant a general charge in addition to the specific security which forms the commercial basis of the transaction.

Once appointed, an administrator must assume possession or control of the company's assets. He also has power to manage the business and affairs of the company.[15] The precise manner in which these powers are to be exercised will depend upon the original purpose of the administration order (eg to ensure the survival of the company or to realise its assets on the best available terms). Immediately following his appointment, the administrator is required to investigate the affairs of the Company and may require the co-operation of directors and employees for that purpose.[16] Thereafter, the administrator must formulate proposals designed to achieve the stated purposes of the administration order itself[17] and must submit these to the creditors of the company for their approval.[18] Under certain limited circumstances, creditors may

13 Insolvency Act 1986 s 15.
14 Insolvency Act 1986 s 10(3).
15 Insolvency Act 1986 s 17.
16 Insolvency Act 1986 s 22.
17 Insolvency Act 1986 s 23.
18 Insolvency Act 1986 s 24.

apply to the court for directions to regulate the future conduct of the administration or to control the conduct of the administrator.[19]

Unsecured creditors

A lender or other creditor who holds no security for his debt is (for obvious reasons) at a disadvantage if the debtor runs into financial difficulty.

As noted earlier, a secured creditor can frequently take action to enforce payment without the assistance of the court. He may appoint a receiver/administrative receiver or exercise his power of sale. By contrast, the unsecured lender/creditor must generally have resort to legal proceedings in order to obtain payment.

As a first step, the lender must obtain a judgment from the court determining the amount due. This can be achieved relatively quickly if the company does not choose to dispute the obligation, but can become time-consuming if the company has an arguable defence.

Once judgment has been obtained, the creditor has at its disposal a range of options to enforce payment, including the following:

1 a court order directing the seizure and sale of the company's assets in satisfaction of its obligations; and
2 the creditor may seek a garnishee order. This order directs specified persons owing money to the company to pay the judgment creditor instead. This remedy can be valuable where the debtor has credit balances with the bank which maintains its current or other accounts, or where moneys are known to be due to the company under contracts with third parties.

Winding up proceedings

A creditor who remains unpaid may consider petitioning the court for an order to wind up the company. This procedure is available to a judgment creditor but may also be used by an ordinary creditor where his debt cannot be disputed.

Very briefly, a company can be wound up by the court if it is unable to pay its debts.[20] The inability of the company to meet its obligations can be demonstrated to the court by accounting or other evidence demonstrating that the liabilities of the company exceed its assets or that it is otherwise unable to meet its obligations as they arise.[1] In practical terms, however, it is usually more convenient for a creditor to rely on either of the following provisions:

1 a company is deemed unable to pay its debts if a creditor for more than £750 has served a statutory demand on the company and the debt remains unpaid after three weeks.[2] However, it should be appreciated that this procedure cannot be used where the company's liability for the relevant debt is the subject of a genuine dispute; or
2 a company is deemed unable to pay its debts if an attempt to levy execution against

19 Insolvency Act 1986 s 27.
20 Insolvency Act 1986 s 122(1)(f).
1 Insolvency Act 1986 ss 123(1)(e) and (2).
2 Insolvency Act 1986 s 123(1)(a).

the company's assets in respect of a judgment debt has been unsuccessful.[3] In this case, the relevant debt must be the subject of a court judgement. But this procedure may be helpful where the relevant debt is less than £750 and the 'statutory demand' approach described in 1 above cannot be used for that reason.

It may be possible to take winding up proceedings against a *foreign* company, if the company has assets in this country or some other benefit would flow from the winding up.[4]

One of the purposes of a winding up of a company is to ensure that its creditors are treated on a *pari passu* (or equal) basis. In order to support that objective and in order to prevent the dissipation or preferential application of some of the company's assets, the Insolvency Act contains various provisions to preserve the assets of the company once a winding up petition has been presented. For example:

1 any disposition of the company's property after the date of the petition will be void, unless the court orders otherwise;[5] and
2 execution or other enforcement proceedings become void following the presentation of the petition.[6]

The compulsory winding up of the company is conducted by the liquidator, who will be appointed by the court. His functions are to realise the assets of the company and to distribute the proceeds to the creditors rateably.[7] He may apply to the court for decisions or directions on various matters affecting the rights and liabilities of parties involved in the winding up.[8]

It will be appreciated that an unsecured creditor does not obtain any priority through the presentation of a winding-up petition.

VITIATING FACTORS

This section considers a number of factors which may result in the avoidance or failure of the security arrangements put in place to support a loan or other obligation. Clearly, it is important for a lender (and its advisers) to police and monitor these aspects as far as possible; otherwise, the lender may unexpectedly find that its security becomes subject to challenge at the point of insolvency.

Accordingly, the present section will examine some of the factors which may serve to vitiate a contract or security arrangement governed by English law. Although the list of matters to be examined is not exhaustive, it will outline the main areas of relevance in the context of loans or facilities made available to commercial borrowers. The following areas will be considered:

1 misrepresentation;
2 duress and undue influence;
3 'financial assistance';
4 transaction with directors;

3 Insolvency Act 1986 s 123(1)(b).
4 Insolvency Act 1986 ss 220–229.
5 Insolvency Act 1986 s 127.
6 Insolvency Act 1986 s 128.
7 Insolvency Act 1986 s 143.
8 Insolvency Act 1986 ss 147–160.

5 'commercial benefit'; and
6 security created at the point of insolvency.

Misrepresentation

A representation is a factual statement upon which the representee relies and which induces him to enter into a contract. If the representation proves to be false or inaccurate in a material respect, then the representee may be entitled to claim damages from the other party and/or to rescind (revoke) the contract. In a financial or security context, this point is perhaps of the greatest importance in the context of a guarantee or third party security, although it could potentially arise in other fields.

A lending bank is not *generally* under a positive obligation to explain to the guarantor the nature of the relevant loan transaction or the extent of any other security which the lender may hold. If, however, the bank volunteers information and in consequence materially misdescribes to a guarantor the nature of the underlying transaction (eg as to its commercial purpose, duration or as to the nature of the risks involved) then the guarantor may subsequently be entitled to rescind his guarantee and thereby avoid any liability under it. Where the transaction between the bank and its borrower contains particularly unusual features which might affect the guarantor's decision to provide the guarantee in the first instance, then the bank may be under a positive duty to explain the position to the guarantor. The failure to provide such an explanation may again allow the guarantor to avoid his contractual obligations. But it should be emphasised that this special duty of disclosure only applies in very exceptional circumstances and where the transaction includes unusual features which could be prejudicial to the interests of the guarantor.

The same general rules will apply where a third party is merely asked to supply security for the borrower's obligations (but is not assuming personal responsibility for their payment).

Duress and undue influence

The consequences of duress can be briefly stated. A guarantee or any other contract can be set aside if it was executed as a result of a threat of physical violence, or an undue threat to take improper steps which will seriously damage the economic or commercial interests of the contracting party in question. In essence, a contract must be the voluntary act of consenting parties; if one party has been subjected to threat or coercion, then this negatives the free consent which is a necessary ingredient of the contractual relationship. If a lender or creditor accepted a guarantee in the knowledge that it had been obtained as a result of duress, then it would clearly be unable to enforce that document.

Where a guarantee or security has been executed as a result of the exercise of 'undue influence' on the signatory, the guarantee/security may be voidable – at least as against some of the parties involved in the transaction. As its name suggests, 'undue influence' is something less than 'duress'. It is therefore unnecessary to demonstrate outright coercion or threats. But again, the underlying rationale is the same; the guarantor (or other contracting party) was not acting of his own free will when executing the document in question, and is therefore entitled to avoid the transaction.

The law in this area has become complex as a result of a number of recent cases in this field but, in essence, a party seeking to avoid a transaction on 'undue influence' grounds must show that:

1. that party was induced to enter into the transaction by a person who was in a position to influence the contracting party as a result of a special relationship between them (eg solicitor/client, parent/child); and
2. the influence so exercised was undue (excessive) and persuaded the relevant party to enter into the contract.

Once it has been shown that a transaction was entered into as a consequence of the exercise of undue influence, then the party thereby disadvantaged may avoid the transaction as against:

1. the party who exercised the influence; and
2. any other party who knew or ought to have known that such influence had been exercised.

In practical terms, the relationship between the lending bank (on the one hand) and the customer/provider of security (on the other hand) will not normally give rise to questions of undue influence: it is simply an arm's length commercial relationship. However, the bank may be aware of circumstances which fix it with notice of undue influence exercised by *another* party to the overall transaction. This may happen where:

1. there is a special relationship between the borrower and the guarantor of the facility (eg the former is the husband and the latter is the wife, or they are cohabitees); and
2. the guarantor derived no obvious advantage from the transaction.

Cases have arisen recently where the bank has effectively lost the benefit of security over a residential property because (i) the transaction involved a business loan or overdraft for the husband's business, (ii) the facility was secured by a mortgage executed by husband *and* wife over their matrimonial home and (iii) the wife derived no obvious, personal benefit from the facility concerned.

In order to safeguard its guarantee/security under these circumstances, the lending bank should take certain precautions. In particular, the bank should interview the wife (or other, potentially-influenced party) and satisfy itself that she understands the transaction and the consequences of providing security. The bank should also recommend that she takes independent legal advice; in practice, the bank often requires written confirmation from the solicitor who has provided that advice.

'Financial assistance'

Company law has long prohibited a company from purchasing its own shares or financing their acquisition by a third party. The rule is intended to preserve the capital base of the company, for the protection of its creditors. If a company could use its own assets to finance the purchase of its own liabilities (i.e. its shares) then the resources available for creditors would be improperly reduced. The underlying rationale of these rules has been questioned and various proposals for reform have periodically been made. However, the present commentary will focus on the existing rules.[9]

In essence, a company cannot make a gift or loan or enter into any guarantee, indemnity or similar arrangement if its purpose is to assist in the acquisition of either (i) shares in the company itself of (ii) shares in its holding company.[10] The prohibition applies both before and after the relevant shares have been acquired; the financial assistance is unlawful if it was given either to facilitate the acquisition or to reduce liabilities incurred in connection with it. If any form of financial assistance is given in contravention of those provisions then:

1 the company and the relevant officers are liable to criminal prosecution;[11] and
2 the guarantee, security or other assistance will be rendered unenforceable (at least if the lender knew or should have been aware of the circumstances giving rise to the infringement of the financial assistance rules).

The financial assistance regime does not apply to subsidiaries which are incorporated outside Great Britain and (in addition) there are a number of exceptions to the general restrictions just described. The following are most likely to be relevant in the context of a loan or similar transaction:

1 a loan made by a money lending company in the ordinary course of its business does not infringe the financial assistance rules.[12] Thus, it is lawful for a bank to make available an overdraft facility, even though the customer happens to utilise those funds to buy shares in the bank itself, and the customer's repayment obligations thus remain enforceable despite the financial assistance rules. However, it should be carefully noted that the transaction must be in the *ordinary course* of the bank's business. It would therefore remain unlawful for the bank to arrange a loan for the *specific purpose* of enabling the customer to purchase shares in the bank itself;
2 a company is permitted to give financial assistance in connection with employee share schemes and similar arrangements;[13] and
3 a company may provide security or other assistance in connection with the acquisition of its shares provided that (i) the net assets of the company are not reduced as a result of the assistance, (ii) the directors swear a declaration that the company will remain solvent after the assistance has been given, (iii) the arrangements are approved by shareholders (where required) and (iv) certain time limits are observed.[14]

There are various other exceptions which are not generally applicable to loan transactions but which may be available in marginal cases.

It follows from these provisions that any transaction involving (or following upon) an acquisition of shares will require careful scrutiny. There is a danger that any guarantee,

9 Companies Act 1985 ss 151–158.
10 Companies Act 1985 s 151.
11 Companies Act 1985 s 151(3).
12 Companies Act 1985 s 153(4)(a).
13 Companies Act 1985 s 153(4)(b)–(c).
14 Companies Act 1985 ss 155–158.

security or other arrangement given by the company (or any of its subsidiaries) in connection with that acquisition may prove to be unlawful, and thus unenforceable.

Transactions with directors

The Companies Act 1985 includes a number of provisions enforcing a requirement of 'fair dealing' as between the directors and the company itself.[15] Broadly, these provisions are intended to prevent a director from using his position to obtain an improper benefit for himself, at the expense of the company and its shareholders.

Amongst other things (and subject to certain minimal limits) a transaction is prohibited[16] if:

1 it is made between a director (or a person connected with him) and his company or its holding company; and
2 it involves a sale or acquisition of assets as between the director (or connected person) and the company concerned.

A transaction falling within these categories is nevertheless validated if it has been approved at a shareholders' meeting of the company entering into the transaction concerned.

At first glance, it might be thought that these matters are of purely internal concern to a company and its directors, and are of no relevance to an external bank or financier. However, this is not so, because:

1 a transaction which infringes the provisions described above is voidable at the instance of the company;[17] and
2 the rights of a bank which financed the acquisition can be prejudiced as a result, if it knew of the factual background resulting in the contravention. Under such circumstances, the company could (for example) reclaim any property transferred to the director in question, and a bank which provided finance to the acquiring director would thus lose the benefit of any security taken over the asset concerned. The position of a lender is, however, protected if it acted in good faith and was unaware of the breach of the statutory provision.[18]

Commercial benefit

The directors of a company are under a general, fiduciary obligation to act in the best interests of the company itself, and to use the company's assets solely in a manner which furthers the objectives of the company. If the directors enter into a transaction which contravenes these general obligations, then they may incur personal liability to the company for any resultant losses. But (more importantly in the present context) the company may rescind the transaction if the other contracting party knew or should

15 Companies Act 1985 ss 311–347.
16 Companies Act 1985 s 320.
17 Companies Act 1985 s 322(1).
18 Companies Act 1985 s 322(2)(b).

have known that the directors were acting in breach of duty in authorising the transaction.

So far as a lender is concerned, difficulties of this type are most likely to arise where one company guarantees the obligations of another company in the same group, or guarantees the obligations of an associated company. Even though the giving of a guarantee is within the powers of the company and the directors have the authority to enter into the transaction, it may still be set aside by the company or its liquidator if (i) the directors have committed a breach of their fiduciary duty by entering into a transaction which is not in the interests of the company and (ii) the other party to the transaction was aware (or ought to have been aware) of that state of affairs.

The directors must act in what they consider to be the best interests of their particular company and cannot take into account the interests of other companies which are members of the same group. Frequently the interests of the company will coincide with those of the group as a whole, but this is not always the case. For example, a parent may normally guarantee the borrowings of a subsidiary, because it has an obvious commercial interest in the success of its subsidiaries. Equally, it may be appropriate for a subsidiary to guarantee the borrowings of the parent, where the parent intends in turn to make funding available to each other member of the group. But it may be more difficult for the directors of a subsidiary to guarantee loans extended to its parent to acquire a new business or property which will not bring any benefit to the subsidiary concerned. The difficulty for the lender taking a corporate guarantee is that it is almost automatically 'on notice' that the directors may be acting in breach of their duties, because (by definition) a guarantee is given for the benefit of a third party, and thus not necessarily for the benefit of the company itself.

In practical terms this problem may be addressed in two ways:

1 first of all, the directors of the company concerned should be asked to explain why they believe the execution of the guarantee to be in the interests of their company, and to record those reasons in the board minutes approving the transaction; and
2 in cases of doubt, the shareholders of the guarantor company should be asked to approve the transaction and to waive any breach of duty by the directors. Such a waiver will be effective and will prevent a later challenge to the guarantee on the grounds now discussed, provided that the execution of the guarantee does not render the company insolvent. Where there are minority shareholders, their approval should be specifically sought, especially where the guarantee is to be given for the benefit of a party connected with the majority shareholders.

Security created at point of insolvency

Where a company is at or near the point of insolvency, the directors may be tempted to make payments or give security to particular creditors whom they would wish to prefer over the general body of creditors. This may happen where (for example) the directors have separate shareholding or other interests in the creditor concerned. Transactions of this type may effectively subvert the general requirement that unsecured creditors should be treated equally in the event of insolvency. The Insolvency Act seeks to avoid these consequences by allowing the court to adjust or overturn transactions which were intended to give a special benefit to a particular creditor or other party.

The main provisions which may be relevant in this context are as follows:

1 a transaction may be set aside[19] if (i) it was entered into at an undervalue as far as the company was concerned and (ii) it was entered into during the six-month period prior to the insolvency (although this period is extended to two years where the transaction involves a party connected with the company). This provision is very unlikely to be applied where a bank has lent money on the security of the company's assets, even though the value of those assets may significantly exceed the value of the loan. This is because, following a realisation of the security, the bank would be obliged to return any surplus proceeds to the company;

2 a transaction may be set aside[20] if it is intended to give a preference to one of its existing creditors: that is, the company makes a payment or gives security with the intention of placing that creditor in a better position in the event of the company's insolvency. Once again, it is unlikely that security given for a new loan could be set aside on this basis, largely because the bank only becomes a 'creditor' of the company after the security has been given. However, if new security is given to an *existing* lender, then this may amount to a preference and could be set aside on this basis. Once again, these rules apply only to transactions entered into during the six-month period prior to insolvency (or two years, in the case of connected party transactions);

3 thirdly, a *floating* charge over a company's undertaking or property created during the 12-month period prior to the insolvency (or two years, in the case of a connected party transaction) will remain effective for 'new' money advanced in return for the execution of the charge, but may be invalid to the extent to which it secures pre-existing indebtedness.[1] However, a floating charge cannot be avoided under this provision if the company was solvent at the time the charge was given and was not rendered insolvent as a result of its execution;[2] and

4 a transaction entered into by a company for the purpose of defrauding or defeating its creditors may be set aside by the court.[3] It is perhaps unlikely that the execution of security documentation in favour of a bank could be set aside under this provision, unless the bank knew (or should have realised) that the chargor was seeking to avoid its creditors.

ENFORCEMENT OF FOREIGN GUARANTEES AND SECURITY

This section explores the rules which an English court will apply when determining (i) which system of law will govern a guarantee or security which involves a foreign element and (ii) whether security created over foreign assets is capable of recognition and enforcement in this country. With this general objective in mind, this section will consider:

1 foreign guarantees;
2 foreign security;

19 Insolvency Act 1986 s 238.
20 Insolvency Act 1986 s 239.
1 Insolvency Act 1986 s 245.
2 Insolvency Act 1986 s 245(4).
3 Insolvency Act 1986 s 423.

3 public policy and mandatory rules;
4 certain jurisdictional issues; and
5 the implications of a cross-border insolvency.

Foreign guarantees

A guarantee is regarded as 'foreign' for present purposes if it possesses one or both of the following characteristics:

1 it is governed by a system of law other than English law; and/or
2 the guarantor is a corporate or other entity incorporated or established outside England and Wales.

Guarantee governed by foreign law

In proceedings before the English courts, the governing law of a guarantee and indeed any contractual arrangement which involves a choice between the laws of different countries, is determined by application of the rules set down in the Rome Convention on the Law Applicable to Contractual Obligations. This Convention has the force of law in the UK[4] and is intended to be applied uniformly throughout the Member States of the EU.[5]

It should be noted, however, that the system of law determined pursuant to the provisions of the Rome Convention need not necessarily be that of a Member State.[6] It follows that an English court, as the domestic court of an EU Member State, is bound to apply the Rome Convention to any dispute with which it is presented.

The Rome Convention contains no special provisions dealing with guarantees; they are merely treated as a species of contract. Accordingly, the governing law of a guarantee must be ascertained through the application of the ordinary provisions of the Convention. In this context, the following points should be noted:

1 The Rome Convention lays particular emphasis on the notion of freedom of contract. Accordingly, a guarantee or any other form of contract will be governed by the system of law chosen by the parties. The choice must either be (i) express or (ii) demonstrated with reasonable certainty by the terms of the guarantee or the surrounding circumstances.[7] With the latter test, for example, it appears that a term within the guarantee providing for any disputes to be resolved through arbitration in London would be sufficient to demonstrate with reasonable certainty that the parties intended a choice of English law to govern the substantive obligations arising under the guarantee. Most standard forms of guarantee in use by banks will include an express choice of law for these purposes.
2 Alternatively, if it is not possible to determine the governing law on the basis of a specific, contractual choice of law, then the guarantee is considered to be governed

4 Contracts (Applicable Law) Act 1990 s 2.
5 Rome Convention Art 18.
6 Rome Convention Art 2.
7 Rome Convention Art 3(1).

by the law of the country with which it is most closely connected.[8] In most cases, a contractual arrangement will be *presumed* to be most 'closely connected' with the country where the party who is to effect 'characteristic performance' has his or its habitual residence, central administration or principal place of business at the time of the conclusion of the contract.[9] However, it should be borne in mind that this is only a presumption, and that it can be displaced in appropriate circumstances.[10] Thus, if a parent company executes a guarantee in respect of a loan made to one of its subsidiaries, it may often be inferred that the guarantee is to be governed by the same system of law as that which applies to the underlying loan agreement.

3 The reasoning outlined in 2 will not generally apply where a guarantee is given by a bank in the course of its business and for the account of a customer. In such a situation, the bank usually issues the guarantee for a fee as part of its normal business. The guarantee will generally be payable on demand and the bank will not usually have been involved in the negotiation of the underlying documentation or commercial transaction. In such a case (and in the absence of an express choice of governing law), it will be necessary to apply the 'closest connection' test described in 2 above. This will usually lead to the conclusion that the guarantee is governed by the law of the country in which the issuing bank branch is located.

Once the governing law of a guarantee has been ascertained, it will then be applied to determine a number of contractual issues, including the following:

1 the material validity of the guarantee: in other words, whether the guarantee constitutes a legally binding arrangement in the first place;
2 the formal validity of the guarantee, ie whether the guarantee satisfies the requisite formalities by which the existence of the guarantee would be recognised and enforced under the governing law. For example, whether the guarantee needs to be in writing or executed in a particular way (eg before independent witnesses or under seal);
3 the interpretation of the guarantee, including its legal significance and effect: for example, whether the guarantee constitutes security for the whole of the underlying debt or only a part of it;
4 the performance of the guarantee: for example, whether the payment by the primary debtor is considered to discharge the obligation, whether payment in full is considered to be made when a deduction or withholding on account of taxes has been made, and whether the payment complies with the terms of the guarantee;
5 the consequences of a breach of the guarantee: for example, whether the defaulting guarantor can be required to pay overdue interest or other damages; and
6 the discharge of the guarantee: for example, whether the release of the primary debtor would also serve to discharge the guarantor from its obligations.

If a guarantee is found to be governed by a foreign system of law, then experts from the relevant jurisdiction will be called to give evidence as to the effect of the guarantee under that law. The English courts will generally enforce a guarantee which is considered

8 Rome Convention Art 4(1).
9 Rome Convention Art 4(2).
10 Rome Convention Art 4(5).

to be valid and binding under its governing law, unless enforcement would offend English public policy in some way (see 'Public policy and mandatory rules' below).

Foreign guarantor

If a guarantor is a foreign entity (for example a company incorporated abroad or a foreign government) then the law of that country will govern a number of considerations including:

1. the corporate capacity of the guarantor to give guarantees and similar assurances; and
2. the authority or power of particular individuals to act on behalf of that entity: for example, whether such individuals have been validly appointed as officers of the company, whether they are as a group empowered to act as the decision-making body of the company and whether they are entitled to approve the entry into and execution of the guarantee.

If a foreign guarantor has acted outside the ambit of its powers or if its officers were not authorised to act or exceeded the scope of their authority, then the guarantee may be void. The specific consequences will generally be governed by the law of the place of incorporation or establishment of the guarantor.

Where a guarantee is 'foreign' in either of the respects just described, it will be necessary to obtain local advice from lawyers in the jurisdiction concerned. The nature and content of that advice will however vary according to the nature of the foreign element involved in the particular case since (as has been shown) the impact and relevance of foreign law in each case is very different.

Foreign security

A security structure may be 'foreign' in the sense that the asset or right over which the security is taken is located outside England and Wales.

The English courts will recognise and enforce security granted over a particular asset if such security is valid under the laws of the country where the asset is located. However, this formulation begs the question – where is a particular asset deemed to be located for these purposes? The following tests are applied in this context:

1. land and buildings are (naturally enough) deemed to be situate in the country in which they are located. Consequently, a charge over such assets will (so far as the English courts are concerned) be regarded as valid if the security document complies with the relevant local requirements. In practice, however, questions of this type rarely fall for adjudication by the English courts: in such cases, effective enforcement action can only be taken locally;
2. shares issued by a company will generally be deemed to be situate in the place in which the share register is kept. This frequently coincides with the place of incorporation. A charge over such shares must therefore meet the requirements laid down by the law of that place; and

3 a charge over a debt (eg a credit balance on a bank account) will be recognised as a valid security interest if it is so recognised by the law of the foreign State in which the debtor resides or the account is held.

An English court will generally not be called upon directly to order the enforcement of security over foreign property, both for practical reasons and on the basis that it would be outside its jurisdiction. However, English courts may on occasion be required to decide upon the essential validity of foreign security, eg where shares issued by a foreign company are held by a nominee in England and it is necessary to decide whether the beneficial owner or an alleged charge has the better title.

Public policy and mandatory rules

There will be a limited number of cases in which an English court will decline recognition of a foreign guarantee or security interest even though it is undeniably valid and enforceable under the system of law by which it is governed. Such a decision will be made very rarely and the court's refusal must generally be based on one of two possible grounds, namely (i) that recognition of the foreign guarantee or security document would violate English public policy[11] or (ii) rules forming a part of the governing law would come into conflict with the mandatory rules of English law.[12] These two points are considered in more detail below.

Public policy

The English courts will refuse to enforce a guarantee governed by a foreign law if such enforcement would clearly be contrary to English public policy. However, the power to disregard a foreign guarantee on these grounds should be exercised very sparingly. In particular:

1 the English court must restrict itself to deciding whether the particular rule of foreign law in question as applied to the relevant document being considered would be contrary to English public policy in the circumstances of the particular case. It is not entitled to pass judgment on whether a particular rule of foreign law is repugnant to English public policy in a more general sense; and
2 the English court should only refuse to apply a particular rule of foreign law if its effect would be 'manifestly' incompatible with English public policy. Thus, public policy should only be invoked in cases where application of the rule of foreign law would be repugnant to fundamental English law principles of morality or justice. A provision forming part of a foreign system of law cannot be struck down or ignored merely on the grounds that it differs from a corresponding rule of English law.

By way of illustrations, the English courts have in the past refused to enforce contractual arrangements (i) whose performance was illegal in England and which

11 Rome Convention Art 16.
12 Rome Convention Art 7.

involved corrupt activities or (ii) which were valid under the applicable law but which were illegal in the intended place of performance. Any guarantee or security provided in respect of such an obligation would similarly be unenforceable here.

Mandatory rules

In certain circumstances, particular rules of English law will be applied to a guarantee or security structure in spite of the fact that the documentation is expressed to be subject to a foreign governing law. This is based on the principle that parties to an arrangement cannot use their choice of law to circumnavigate mandatory domestic rules of the forum which would otherwise be applicable to their relationship.[13]

There are several statutes which apply to contracts entered into in the course of business conducted in the UK regardless of the purported governing law of the contract, and which may constitute 'mandatory rules' for these purposes.

For example, English domestic law forbids the enforcement of foreign exchange contracts which breach the exchange control regime of any state which is a member of the International Monetary Fund. Thus, a guarantee of such a contract will also be unenforceable in this jurisdiction, regardless of the governing law of the underlying contract. Similarly, foreign contracts guarantees or security arrangements involving a fraud on the UK revenue authorities would not be enforced by the English courts.

Jurisdiction

The foregoing discussion has *assumed* that the English courts will have jurisdiction to determine issues arising under a particular guarantee or security document, notwithstanding its foreign element.

The rules by which an English court will decide whether it has jurisdiction over a particular defendant or a particular matter are determined by the application of two, quite separate regimes. The first regime is encapsulated in the Brussels and Lugano Conventions of which the UK is a party by virtue of its membership of the European Union and the European Free Trade Association respectively. The second regime is based on a mixture of common law rules on conflict of laws and a number of reciprocal arrangements with other states.

The Brussels and Lugano Conventions on Jurisdiction and the Enforcement of Judgements in Civil and Commercial Matters are essentially the same in ambit and substance. The Member States of the EU are party to the Brussels Convention. They are also party to the Lugano Convention together with the Member States of the European Free Trade Association (namely Iceland, Liechtenstein, Switzerland and Norway). The provisions of the two Conventions are to be applied in legal proceedings in the UK.[14]

The Brussels and Lugano Conventions are limited in their ambit to civil and commercial matters. However this limitation will not generally be of importance in the

13 Rome Convention Arts 3(3) and 7(2).

14 Civil Jurisdiction and Judgments Act 1982 (as amended).

present context; a claim against a guarantor or a party to a security arrangement will almost always be a 'civil or commercial matter' for these purposes.

The jurisdiction of the English courts in dealing with such proceedings is not in any way dependent upon or affected by the governing law of the guarantee. Where the Brussels or Lugano Convention applies, the English courts will be the courts of competent jurisdiction over any claims against the following types of guarantor:

1 an individual domiciled in England, unless the guarantor has agreed to submit to the exclusive jurisdiction of the courts of another Contracting State or proceedings have already been instituted in such a State;
2 guarantors who have agreed as a term of the guarantee that the English courts are to have jurisdiction to determine disputes arising out of the guarantee;
3 a guarantor whose obligations were due to be performed in England, eg because the guarantee provided for payment to be made by way of credit transfer to a bank account in this jurisdiction;
4 a foreign guarantor which acted through a branch or agency in England in issuing the guarantee;
5 where one guarantor is domiciled in England, the English courts have jurisdiction over co-guarantors domiciled in other Convention states;
6 a guarantor who has given a mortgage over land in England by way of security for his guarantee obligations; and
7 a guarantor who has entered an appearance at proceedings instituted in England (apart from the situation where the appearance was entered exclusively for the purpose of contesting jurisdiction or if the courts of another Contracting State have exclusive jurisdiction).

Where the Brussels and Lugano Conventions are inapplicable, the English courts will have jurisdiction over a claim against a guarantor in a variety of cases, including the following:

1 where the guarantor is present in England and is served with the proceedings here;
2 where the guarantor has expressly submitted to the jurisdiction of the English courts (eg by way of an express term in the guarantee);
3 in certain cases, where the guarantor is outside England but the court gives permission for the service of process outside the jurisdiction;
4 where the defaulting borrower has been served with English proceedings and the guarantor is a necessary or proper party to those proceedings; or
4 where the contract of guarantee was made in England or is governed by English law.

Finally, it should be appreciated that certain types of entity may enjoy immunity from the jurisdiction of the English courts. In particular, a foreign State and its government are, as a general rule, immune from proceedings before the English courts.[15] However, this general rule is subject to a number of important exceptions which will normally assist the lender in the content of a financial transaction. In particular:

1 a State is not to enjoy immunity in the context of a commercial transaction, such as a sale/purchase of goods or a loan or similar arrangement;[16] and

15 State Immunity Act 1978 s 1.
16 State Immunity Act 1978 s 3.

2 a State is not immune if it has submitted to the jurisdiction of the English courts.[17] For this reason, loan agreements involving foreign States or government departments will usually include a specific submission to jurisdiction.

The property of a State is also immune from proceedings to execute a judgment unless (i) the State has expressly agreed to such proceedings (and a clause may be included in the facility agreement for that purpose)[18] or (ii) the property is held for commercial purposes.[19] It follows that proceedings for the execution of a judgment cannot be issued against the premises of a diplomatic mission, or against bank accounts maintained for the upkeep of that mission.

Cross-border insolvency

A number of private international law issues arise where a foreign company holds assets in England but is the subject of winding-up proceedings or has gone into liquidation in its home State. What is the position of a creditor who is the beneficiary of a guarantee from such a foreign company or who holds security over assets in England which has been granted by a foreign company? Can he proceed against the foreign company in England in order to obtain a judgment against it? Or can he proceed to enforce the security? Different rules will apply in each of these situations.

Guarantees

Assuming that they otherwise have jurisdiction, the English courts would generally recognise and enforce a guarantee issued by a foreign company even if the guarantor was in the course of being wound up under the laws of its home jurisdiction. This will be so even if the home State liquidation would otherwise operate to discharge the guarantee because:

1 if the guarantee is governed by English law then the relevant rule of foreign law could not operate to discharge it; and
2 if the guarantee is governed by the laws of the guarantor's home State, then any rule which discharges the guarantee as a consequence of liquidation is likely to be regarded as a procedural matter. The English courts will not give effect to foreign procedural rules and (assuming the document to be otherwise valid under its governing law) the English courts will proceed to enforce the guarantee in any event.

The result will be that the creditor can, notwithstanding the liquidation proceedings in the home state, seek to obtain judgment against the guarantor and seek to enforce that judgment against any assets which the guarantor may have within the jurisdiction. If, however, the guarantor has been formally dissolved under the laws of its home state,

17 State Immunity Act 1978 s 2.
18 State Immunity Act 1978 s 13(3).
19 State Immunity Act 1978 s 13(4).

then legal proceedings in England become more problematic. The English courts must generally recognise that the guarantor has ceased to exist as a corporate entity, and that it is thus incapable of being a defendant in any proceedings.

Security

A charge granted by a foreign company over property situated in this country (for example, a mortgage over land in England or an assignment of a deposit with a London bank) will be enforced by the English courts even though the chargor is in liquidation under the laws of its home State. The proceeds of such security will be available to meet the claims of the secured creditor and any remaining balance must be paid to the foreign company or its liquidator.

Liquidations

A liquidator (or similar official) appointed under the laws of the guarantor's home state will be recognised by the English courts and will thus be entitled to assume control of corporate assets in England for the purpose of conducting the winding up.

In addition, a creditor of an insolvent foreign company may petition for the compulsory winding-up of that company in England,[20] but such an order will only be made if it can be shown that one or more creditors would benefit from the making of the order. A foreign company may be wound up in England even though its corporate existence has previously been dissolved under the laws of its home state[1] and the applicable procedural rules are similar to those which would be applied in winding up a company incorporated in Great Britain.[2]

20 Insolvency Act 1986 ss 220–229.
1 Insolvency Act 1986 s 225.
2 Insolvency Act 1986 s 229.

12 United States of America

Warren F. Cooke

Milbank, Tweed, Hadley & McCloy LLP

INTRODUCTION

In the US, the rules for the creation, perfection and priority of security interests are, in large part, provided by the laws of each of the 50 states.

Security interests in personal property and in fixtures (tangible property that is so related to particular real property that an interest arises in it under real estate law) are covered by Article 9 of the Uniform Commercial Code or 'UCC' (art 9) as enacted in each state. Article 9 has been under review and a major revision ('revised art 9') has been readied for enactment by the states with a target enactment date of 1 July 2001. Revised art 9 broadens the scope of the article in a number of ways, and modernises and streamlines its provisions.

Security interests in real property (including land and buildings) are governed by the real estate laws of the states, and are excluded from the coverage of art 9. While most states have comprehensive statutory schemes governing real estate liens, there is no 'uniform' law for such liens.

Guarantees and subordination agreements (which are not considered to be collateral security in US parlance although they are intended in a general sense to provide 'security' to a creditor) are contractual relationships which are largely governed by the common law (the accumulation of judicial decisions).

The US has a federal legal system, and therefore there is an interplay between state law and Federal law. For example, the creation, perfection and enforcement of security interests are limited in important respects by principles of the United States Bankruptcy Code, the Federal statute governing bankruptcy and reorganisation proceedings in the US.

This chapter provides an overview of the landscape to be traversed by a creditor who desires to obtain collateral security in the US. The principal focus is on commercial financing (the art 9 provisions relating to certain specialised areas such as security interests in consumer goods, motor vehicles and farm products will not be reviewed in detail). Discussion herein refers primarily to the law of the State of New York, a jurisdiction under whose laws a great many commercial transactions are documented; it is vital to check for variations in state law. Nothing in this chapter should be viewed as a substitute for consulting legal counsel as to specific transactions or circumstances.

SECURITY INTERESTS IN PERSONAL PROPERTY AND FIXTURES

The UCC is a model code, developed by the American Law Institute and the National Conference of Commissioners on Uniform State Laws in the 1960s with a view to simplifying, clarifying and modernising the law governing commercial transactions, and promoting uniformity among the laws of the 50 states of the US on those commercial topics covered. The topics covered by the UCC today are sales of goods, leases, commercial paper (negotiable instruments), bank deposits and collections, funds transfers, letters of credit, bulk transfers, documents of title such as warehouse receipts and bills of lading, investment securities and, in art 9, secured transactions.

Although the UCC calls itself 'uniform', and has been enacted by all 50 states, there are some variations from state to state, so that in fact it is not entirely uniform, and revised art 9 may also be enacted with variations.

Although the UCC is a 'code', it accepts the principle of freedom of contract, so that the effects of its provisions may be varied by private agreement, but certain obligations of good faith, diligence, reasonableness and care imposed by UCC provisions may not be disclaimed by agreement.

Introduction to the Uniform Commercial Code art 9

The 12 headings that follow summarise the basic concepts of art 9.

The scope of Art 9

Article 9 applies to any transaction, regardless of its form, that 'is intended to create a security interest in personal property or fixtures' (revised art 9 changes the wording slightly to refer to any transaction that 'creates a security interest in personal property or fixtures by contract'), subject to certain exclusions as described below under the heading 'Exclusions'.

A 'security interest' is an interest in personal property or fixtures which secures payment or performance of an obligation. Property subject to a security interest is called 'collateral', the party that owes payment or other performance of the obligation secured by the collateral is referred to as a 'debtor' (and if the collateral that secures such obligation is owned by another person, such other person is also a 'debtor'), and the party in whose favour there is a security interest is called the 'secured party'.

The form of a transaction does not determine whether the transaction falls within art 9, and the location of title to (ownership of) the property as between the debtor and the secured party is immaterial for this particular purpose. For example, a transaction may be styled as a 'conditional sale', and documented to provide that the seller retains or reserves title to the property until the payment of the purchase price; nevertheless, for purposes of art 9, the transaction results in an art 9 security interest in favour of the seller (who is the 'secured party'), even though the seller may be recognised for other purposes as continuing to own the property. Similarly, transactions taking the form of chattel mortgages, equipment trusts, field warehousing arrangements, leases intended as security interests, and similar arrangements, though making no reference to any 'security interest' or to art 9, create art 9 security interests in the relevant property. If a transaction falls within the scope of art 9, the secured party must comply with the article, or risk finding that other interests in the property take priority.

Although the location of title as between the secured party and the debtor does not determine whether art 9 applies, the debtor must have 'rights in the collateral' (revised art 9 adds, 'or the power to transfer rights in the collateral to a secured party') in order for the security interest to be valid. Article 9 leaves it to the courts to determine at what point the debtor has such rights.

Although it may be counter-intuitive for someone unaccustomed to art 9, a *sale* of 'accounts' or 'chattel paper' also falls within the scope of art 9. An 'account', under current art 9, is a right (such as the typical account receivable) to payment for goods sold or leased or for services rendered, that is not evidenced by an instrument (such as a promissory note) or by chattel paper. The term 'chattel paper' refers to a writing or writings evidencing both a monetary obligation and a security interest in, or a lease of, specific goods (for example, a conditional sales contract, representing both a payment obligation for and security interest in the sold goods, is chattel paper). A buyer of assets such as accounts receivable or conditional sales contracts is thus treated as having a security interest in them and in particular must take the appropriate steps to 'perfect' its interest as described below under the heading 'Perfection'. Revised art 9 extends this concept in two ways:

1 First, under revised art 9, the definition of 'account' is substantially broadened, to include any 'right to payment of a monetary obligation, whether or not earned by performance, (i) for property that has been or is to be sold, leased, licensed, assigned, or otherwise disposed of, (ii) for services rendered or to be rendered, (iii) for a policy of insurance issued or to be issued, (iv) for a secondary obligation incurred or to be incurred, (v) for energy provided or to be provided, (vi) for the use or hire of a vessel under a charter or other contract, (vii) arising out of the use of a credit or charge card or information contained on or for use with the card …', and even as winnings in a state-sponsored lottery.
2 Second, revised art 9 applies the article to sales of 'payment intangibles' and of 'promissory notes', in addition to accounts and chattel paper. Payment intangibles represent a new category under revised art 9, and are a subset of 'general intangibles', which is an important art 9 catch-all category covering such intangible personal property as does not fall in one of the other art 9 categories (for example, indemnification rights, intellectual property and any number of other miscellaneous claims); payment intangibles are those general intangibles that are for money due or to become due (an example of a payment intangible is a loan participation). The term 'promissory note' is defined in revised art 9 to mean an instrument that evidences a promise to pay a monetary obligation (not an order to pay, nor a bank acknowledgment of a deposit).

In a sale of accounts or chattel paper or, under revised art 9, payment intangibles or promissory notes, the sold property constitutes the 'collateral', the seller is the 'debtor' and the buyer is the 'secured party'.

Revised art 9 further extends the reach of the article to cover consignments, 'agricultural liens' (a new, specialised category consisting of statutorily created interests in farm products in connection with farming operations) and security interests arising under a few other specific UCC provisions.

Creation of a security interest

The security agreement

The creation of a security interest is generally accomplished by having the debtor sign an agreement granting the security interest, referred to as a 'security agreement'. The security interest is said to 'attach' to the relevant property when the security agreement is signed (revised art 9 uses the term 'authenticated' to allow for electronic signing) and 'value' is given (subject to the debtor's acquiring rights with respect to the collateral). The issuance of a binding loan commitment or of a letter of credit constitutes the giving of value for this purpose, even if no funds are advanced.

No special formalities need be observed in connection with the signing of a security agreement (as opposed to 'perfection' of a security interest, discussed below) and no incantation of special language is needed in the security agreement, but it is important that the security agreement contain operative language granting the security interest; a mere statement of intent or an agreement to create a security interest in the future (as distinct from the present grant of a security interest in future property), or a promise not to create a security interest in favour of another creditor (known as a 'negative pledge'), will ordinarily not be sufficient to create a security interest.

There is no particular reason why a security interest in virtually all of the personal property of a debtor cannot be covered in a single security agreement. In practice it is nevertheless common to cover certain kinds of collateral in separate security agreements. For example, shares of corporate stock and other securities are often covered by a separate security agreement (usually called a 'pledge agreement') containing a number of provisions directed to such property, such as appropriate references to the Federal and state securities laws; intellectual property may be covered in one or more separate security agreements, in part in order to simplify the making of any Federal filings that may be required; security interests in aircraft and vessels are generally covered by specialised forms of security agreement; and it is common in some financings to provide for separate assignments of insurance, with a view to simplifying the process of dealing with the relevant insurance company or complying with policy provisions.

The secured party may be the representative of a group of creditors, such as an agent for a bank syndicate or an indenture trustee for bondholders.

The security agreement must contain a description of the collateral that reasonably identifies the collateral, and must, of course, name the secured party and describe the obligations being secured. It is inadvisable for the security agreement to describe the collateral too generically; for example, a security agreement covering 'all the debtor's assets' does not satisfy the requirement for reasonable identification of the collateral. It is permissible to use UCC categories in the description, such as 'all accounts of the debtor, whether now existing or hereafter arising'. Revised art 9 draws a distinction in this regard between the security agreement and the 'financing statement' (which is the public filing that perfects a security interest in many types of collateral, as described below): under revised art 9 the financing statement may include a super-generic description, but the security agreement must still describe the collateral by specific listing, or by category or type, or by quantity or computational or allocational formula or procedure, or by another method if the identity of the collateral is thereby objectively determinable; under revised art 9 expressions such as 'all the debtor's assets' or 'all the debtor's personal property' will still be insufficient for purposes of the security agreement.

By the same token, a secured party can trap itself by defining the collateral too specifically. For example, a security agreement describing property as being located at a specific location might be construed as ceasing to cover the property when it is moved to another location.

Future advances

Under art 9 a security interest may secure future advances or other future value, whether or not the advances or other value are given pursuant to commitment, and a perfected security interest generally has the same priority with respect to future advances as with respect to the first advance. There is an express limitation under art 9 on future advances' priority: a lien acquired by a 'lien creditor' (defined as a creditor who has acquired a lien on the property by attachment or levy or the like, a trustee in bankruptcy from the date of filing of a bankruptcy petition, a receiver in equity from the time of appointment and an assignee for the benefit of creditors, an insolvency concept, from the assignment date) will rank ahead with respect to advances made more than 45 days after the lien creditor acquires the lien, unless such advances are made without knowledge of the lien or are made pursuant to a commitment entered into without knowledge of the lien.

After-acquired property

Under art 9 a security interest may cover after-acquired property. The granting clause of a security agreement may reach, for example, all present and future accounts and inventory of a debtor, and there will be no need to require the furnishing of periodic lists of accounts and inventory, or the making of supplemental assignments or confirmatory agreements, as new accounts are created or new inventory is acquired. A security interest in property arising by virtue of an after-acquired property clause has equal status with a security interest in property in which the debtor had rights when value was first given. The effectiveness of an after-acquired property clause may, however, like other aspects of art 9, be limited by provisions of the Bankruptcy Code.

'Floating' liens

Article 9 validates the 'floating' lien, rejecting US case law which had required a secured party to police a shifting body of collateral, such as inventory, in order to maintain a valid security interest. Specifically, art 9 provides that a security interest is not invalid or fraudulent against other creditors simply because the debtor is at liberty to use, commingle or dispose of or otherwise deal with the collateral without accounting for proceeds or replacing collateral. This does not alter the principle that where 'perfection', discussed below, is based upon the secured party's having possession of the collateral, loss of possession will cause the creditor to lose its perfected interest.

Supporting obligations

Revised art 9 states explicitly that attachment of a security interest in collateral is also attachment of a security interest in a 'supporting obligation' for the collateral. The term 'supporting obligation' is a new term in revised art 9 meaning a letter-of-credit right or secondary obligation (for example, a guarantee) that supports the payment or performance of an account, general intangible, chattel paper, document (meaning a document of title such as a warehouse receipt), instrument (such as a promissory note) or investment property (such as a security). Although revised art 9 makes this explicit, the result under current art 9 is probably the same.

Assignability of intangibles

Current art 9 assures the transferability of accounts and certain general intangibles by rendering ineffective a term in the contract giving rise to them that prohibits their assignment, in the case of accounts, or the creation of a security interest, in the case of general intangibles for money due or to become due (or that purports to require the consent of the obligor for such assignment or security interest). This facilitates taking such assets as collateral as well as the transfer of accounts in connection with securitisations.

Revised art 9 expands the benefit of this commercially useful rule not only by broadening the definition of 'account' as noted above, but also by rendering ineffective such limitations with respect to assignments or transfers of and security interests in chattel paper, payment intangibles and promissory notes, security interests in rights under lease agreements, 'health-care insurance receivables' (a new revised art 9 category meaning an interest in or claim under a policy of insurance which is a right to payment of a monetary obligation for health-care goods or services provided) and general intangibles, and assignments or security interests in 'letter-of-credit rights' (another new term in revised art 9, meaning a right to payment and performance under a letter of credit, but not including the beneficiary's right to draw).

Some specialised kinds of property, for example, a federal licence, may be incapable of being made subject to a security interest for reasons unrelated to art 9.

Perfection

The creation of a security interest is not enough to protect the secured party: an additional step is needed to 'perfect' the security interest if it is to be protected against the interests of other creditors and transferees. The basic idea of perfection of a security interest involves the taking of certain steps designed to put third parties on notice of its existence. The potential challengers to a security interest include a bankruptcy representative: under the Bankruptcy Code, a trustee in bankruptcy for a bankrupt debtor, or a 'debtor in possession', being the bankrupt party operating under court supervision and with the powers of a trustee in bankruptcy, acquires upon the filing of the bankruptcy petition the rights of a hypothetical lien creditor, and thus may invalidate the interest of a secured party whose security interest has not been perfected when the filing of the petition occurs.

The perfection of a security interest in property requires the making of a public filing with respect to the property, or (for some kinds of collateral) taking possession of the property by the secured party, or (for some other kinds of collateral) obtaining 'control' over the property, or (for particular kinds of collateral) notation on a certificate of title, Federal filings or other actions.

Perfection by filing

A security interest in most property, including accounts, chattel paper, goods (a broad term for many kinds of tangible personal property, that is in turn subdivided into the categories of 'inventory', 'equipment', 'farm products' and 'consumer goods'), negotiable documents (meaning negotiable documents of title such as negotiable bills of lading and negotiable warehouse receipts) and investment property (including securities and security entitlements, discussed below), may be perfected by filing.

Perfection of a security interest by filing is easy and involves delivery to a designated public official in the relevant state or states of a simple document (called a 'financing statement') on Form UCC-1, and payment of a filing fee. Revised art 9 recognises the possibility of communicating a record by means other than a writing or other tangible media, so as to encourage filing by means of electronic, voice, optical and other technologies. No description of the secured obligations is required.

A financing statement does not create a security interest, and is not a substitute for a security agreement; reflecting art 9's concept of 'notice filing', it simply provides notice of the existence of a security interest for the benefit of prospective creditors of the debtor and others who may need to know of its existence.

Under current art 9, it is often necessary to file financing statements in more than one state based upon the different categories of collateral involved; for example, in the case of collateral consisting of inventory or equipment it is necessary to file in each state where the collateral is located, while the correct filing location as to accounts, general intangibles and some other collateral is the location of the debtor (usually, in the case of a business entity, where it has its chief executive office). Revised art 9 dramatically simplifies this situation in a variety of ways. Among other things, in the case of a debtor that is a 'registered organisation' (a new revised art 9 term that includes an entity whose state of organisation must maintain a public record of its organisation, such as a corporation, limited liability company or limited partnership), it will generally be sufficient to file in the jurisdiction of organisation of the debtor, even though the collateral is located elsewhere. Revised art 9 also addresses the issue of filing against a non-US debtor: in general, non-US law would govern perfection, but if a debtor is located in a jurisdiction that does not provide for filing or recording of non-possessory security interests, revised art 9 provides that such debtor is deemed located in the District of Colombia for these purposes.

Within a state it is sufficient in most cases to make a single filing at a central location designated by the laws of the state, except for crops or some other collateral that is closely related to real estate, which may involve a local filing. In some states, including New York, a local (county) filing is required in addition to a central filing if the debtor has a place of business only in one county within the state; however, revised art 9 eliminates this dual filing. The question of where to file within a particular state with respect to particular collateral requires that the collateral be placed (or forced) into a recognised art 9 category. This sometimes results in entertaining court decisions: for example, according to various court decisions, farm-raised catfish are livestock (not 'crops') for filing purposes; longhorn cattle used for recreational cattle drives are 'equipment' (not 'farm products' or 'inventory', although rodeo cattle may be 'inventory'); and rosebushes are 'fixtures' if rooted in the ground for the purpose of producing cut flowers (not 'crops' or 'equipment' or 'inventory' or 'consumer goods'), although planted Christmas trees are probably 'crops'. However, since the consequences of failing to file in the correct places are serious and since filing is generally an inexpensive process, a secured party should make multiple filings, based on all plausible classifications of the collateral, whenever there is any doubt as to where to file.

Under current art 9, a financing statement must be signed by the debtor, specify the name and mailing address of the debtor as well as the name of the secured party and an address of the secured party from which information concerning the security interest may be obtained, and, as noted above, describe the collateral. Revised art 9 changes the requirements for a financing statement, primarily to simplify filings and to facilitate electronic filing. Under revised art 9, neither the signature nor the mailing address of the debtor is required, and the information address of the secured party is not legally required (although a filing officer will nevertheless reject a financing statement if it does not include the secured party's or debtor's address). In place of the requirement for the debtor's signature, revised art 9 prescribes who is authorised to make a filing and provides for a penalty and possible liability for damages in case of unauthorised filings.

Article 9 demonstrates a practical bent by providing that a financing statement substantially complying with the requirements of art 9 will be effective even though it contains minor errors which are not seriously misleading. Despite this provision, and even though the requirements for a financing statement are simple, there are many reported judicial decisions in which security interests have been held to be unperfected because of inaccuracy in a financing statement. A common mistake, which courts generally view unsympathetically, and which is even less excusable under the express terms of revised art 9, is to specify the trade name of a debtor, rather than its precise legal name, or otherwise to misstate the debtor's name.

Financing statements are indexed by the name of the debtor. Prior to the closing of the transaction, the secured party will wish to obtain and review the results of a UCC search, in order to determine whether earlier filings cover the proposed collateral. The search may be effected, for a fee, through one of several companies that specialise in providing such services. The search will disclose existing UCC filings against the name of the debtor in the locations identified to the searching company. A listing of any filed tax liens may also be obtained.

The secured party will have a perfected security interest in collateral covered by a financing statement only to the extent that both the security agreement and the financing statement cover the collateral. To state this important practical point from a different perspective, a financing statement cannot enlarge upon the collateral covered by a security agreement, but it can, by omission, narrow the scope of perfection of a security interest. As noted above, revised art 9 allows for a super-generic collateral description in a financing statement, though not in a security agreement. In practice, the description of collateral in the financing statement usually tracks the description in the security agreement.

A financing statement may be filed before the security interest is created, and perfection dates from the time of filing (although attachment may occur later). If perfection (by filing or otherwise) occurs more than ten days after the security interest is created, the security interest may be vulnerable in subsequent bankruptcy proceedings of the debtor to being set aside as a preference (perfection of a security interest is a transfer for bankruptcy purposes, and a transfer for or on account of an antecedent debt, made under certain circumstances during a relatively brief period prior to bankruptcy, may be voidable under the Bankruptcy Code). In commercial lending it is normal to arrange for the filing of the financing statement or financing statements at the time of, or prior to, the first extension of credit.

A financing statement remains valid for five years (slightly longer in a few states) after the filing. Perfection may be continued by filing a 'continuation statement' within six months prior to the end of the five-year period; in the absence of such a filing, the original filing lapses. A continuation statement must be signed by the secured party, identify the original financing statement by number and meet certain other requirements. There are also provisions for the filing of amendments to financing statements (for example, to add collateral).

In the case of a change of the debtor's name, identity or corporate structure that causes a filed financing statement to become seriously misleading, the existing filing will not be effective in perfecting a security interest in collateral acquired by the debtor more than four months after the change, unless a new appropriate financing statement is filed within that period.

In the case of fixtures, a 'fixture filing' is required in the office where a mortgage on the relevant real estate would be recorded or registered. Such a filing must comply with certain real estate-related formalities.

A perfected security interest may be assigned, and no new filing is required under art 9 to continue the perfected status of the security interest against creditors of and transferees from the debtor.

There are Federal filing or recording requirements in the case of certain kinds of property. For example:

1 Aircraft: until a security interest in an aircraft, aircraft engine or propeller is recorded with the Federal Aviation Administration in Oklahoma City, it is not perfected against third parties. The Federal statutes governing the registration of aircraft in the US place significant restrictions on the ability of non-US citizens to register such aircraft. It is therefore common for financing transactions involving US aircraft and lenders that are not US citizens to be structured to include US trustees to represent one or more of the parties.
2 US vessels: mortgages on certain types of US flag vessels must be recorded with the US Coast Guard at the vessel's home port (among other requirements).
3 US railroad rolling stock: perfection of a security interest in such property requires a filing with the Federal Surface Transportation Board.
4 US claims: in the case of an assignment of certain claims against the US Government,

the assignment must comply with the provisions of the Assignment of Claims Act of 1940, a Federal statute.

5 Intellectual property: although Federal law provides a system for the recording of assignments of patents in the US Patent and Trademark Office in Washington, DC, cases have held that security interests in patents need not be perfected by such recording, but are perfected by filing a financing statement under the UCC. It may be advisable to take both steps, so as to avoid any question in the matter. The Federal Copyright Act probably creates the exclusive means of perfecting a security interest in a copyright and in accounts receivable arising therefrom, pre-empting state law; this means that a security interest in a copyright should be recorded in the US Copyright Office in Washington, DC, although it may be prudent to perfect both by making such a recording and by filing a financing statement under the UCC (intellectual property falls within the category of general intangibles). Trademarks can arise under Federal law, state law or common law, and Federal as well as state recording or filing is generally advisable.

Perfection by possession

An alternative means of perfection in some cases is for the creditor to take possession of the collateral. A possessory security interest is often referred to as a 'pledge'. For some kinds of collateral, including goods, negotiable documents, and chattel paper, perfection may be accomplished either by filing or by possession. For a few kinds of collateral, filing is not available as a means of perfection, and the secured party must take possession to perfect; in particular, in the case of money or, under current art 9, an 'instrument' (defined to mean a negotiable instrument or writing evidencing a right to the payment of money that is not itself a security agreement or lease but is of a type which 'in ordinary course of business' is transferred by delivery with any necessary indorsement or assignment, and excluding securities or other investment property), other than an instrument constituting part of chattel paper, the secured party must take possession of the collateral in order to perfect; however, revised art 9 provides for filing against instruments, and provides that as between a secured party who filed and a secured party who took possession, the latter prevails. Under current art 9, in order to perfect a security interest in a letter of credit or advice of credit, the letter or advice must be delivered to the secured party; revised art 9 provides for perfection of a security interest in a 'letter-of-credit right' exclusively through 'control', involving the consent of the issuer to assignment of proceeds.

Perfection may be accomplished by 'possession' even if the collateral is held by a third-party bailee (for example, a warehouse). If the collateral consists of goods covered by a negotiable document of title, a security interest in the goods is perfected by perfecting a security interest in the document. If the goods are held by a bailee who has issued a non-negotiable document covering them, a security interest in them may be perfected by issuance of a document in the name of the secured party, or by notification to the bailee of the secured party's interest, or by filing a financing statement covering the goods. If the goods are held by a bailee who has not issued a document, perfection under current art 9 is by filing or notification, while under revised art 9 an authenticated acknowledgment by the bailee would be necessary rather than mere notification.

Perfection by 'control'

As a result of recent amendments to UCC art 8 ('Investment securities') and art 9, a security interest in 'investment property' may be perfected either by the secured party's acquiring 'control' of the property or, except in a few specialised instances where perfection occurs automatically upon attachment, by filing. Investment property means a security (not defined in art 9), a 'security entitlement', a 'securities account', a 'commodity contract' or a 'commodity account'.

Revised art 8 took effect in New York in 1998. The revisions to art 8 were designed to reflect the realities of today's securities transactions, including in particular what has evolved as the 'indirect holding system', whereby the purchaser of a security through a 'securities intermediary' obtains a bundle of rights and property interests, referred to in art 8 as a 'security entitlement', rather than the actual security. The typical investor in stock through a stock broker thus has a security entitlement with respect to the securities in the relevant securities account.

A 'securities intermediary' is defined in art 8 as a person such as a bank or a broker that 'in the ordinary course of its business maintains securities accounts for others and is acting in that capacity', and also includes a clearing corporation, such as Depositary Trust Corporation, that provides clearance or settlement services with respect to securities and other financial assets. The term 'securities account' is defined in art 8 as an account to which a financial asset is or may be credited in accordance with an agreement under which the person maintaining the account undertakes to treat the person for whom the account is maintained as entitled to exercise the rights that comprise the financial asset. A 'financial asset' includes a security, or a security-like obligation or interest 'which is, or is of a type, dealt in or traded on financial markets, or which is recognised in any area in which it is issued or dealt in as a medium for investment', and any other property held by a securities intermediary for another person in a securities account if the securities intermediary has expressly agreed with the other person that the property is to be treated as a financial asset under art 8. The term 'commodity contract' includes traded commodity futures contracts, options on commodity futures contracts, commodity options and the like, and a 'commodity account' is an account maintained by a commodity intermediary in which a commodity contract is carried for a commodity customer.

Article 9 provides that perfection of a security interest in investment property by 'control' can be accomplished in several ways. In the case of a 'certificated security' (such as the good old-fashioned stock certificate), a security interest may still be perfected by delivery of the certificate to the secured party (and if the security is in registered, rather than bearer, form, the certificate must be indorsed to the secured party or in blank by an effective indorsement, or registered in the name of the secured party). In the case of a security entitlement, control is achieved where the secured party 'becomes the entitlement holder'; in addition, art 8 introduces the concept of perfection by way of an agreement (often referred to by practitioners as a 'control agreement') by the securities intermediary to comply with directions from the secured party without further consent by the debtor (but the secured party's right to give such directions need not be exclusive of the debtor's right to do so as long as the secured party's directions would take preference). In the case of an uncertificated security, control may be achieved by delivery (defined in art 8 as occurring when the issuer registers the secured party as the registered owner, or the registered owner acknowledges that it holds for the secured party) or through an agreement by the issuer of the security to comply with instructions from the secured party without further consent by the owner. As noted above, perfection of a security interest in investment property may also be accomplished by filing; as between a security interest perfected by control and one perfected by filing, the former has priority.

Revised art 9 takes the art 8 concept of control by agreement and applies it, with adjustments to suit the particular kind of collateral, to additional categories of property, namely deposit accounts with banks (a category of collateral expressly excluded as original collateral from the scope of current art 9 but included under revised art 9, as discussed below), 'electronic chattel paper' (a category newly created by revised art 9, meaning chattel paper evidenced by a record or records consisting of information stored in an electronic medium), commodity contracts and letter-of-credit rights. In the case of a deposit account, for example, under revised art 9, a secured party has control if the debtor, the secured party and the bank have agreed that the bank will comply with instructions originated by the secured party directing disposition of funds in the account without further consent by the debtor/depositor (in addition, if the secured party is the depositary bank, or if the secured party becomes the bank's customer on the account, it automatically has control).

Other

For a few kinds of collateral, there are specialised requirements for perfection. For example, in the case of a motor vehicle, a yacht or certain other items the ownership of which is evidenced by the issuance of a certificate of title under state law, a security interest may be required to be noted on the certificate in order to be perfected (there are intricate rules relating to property covered by certificates of title).

To the extent that a Federal statute provides a filing or recording system, as is the case for certain aircraft and vessels, the Federal provisions govern. In certain limited cases, involving instruments, certificated securities and negotiable documents, upon the giving of new value under a written security agreement a security interest is automatically perfected for a limited period (21 days under the current New York UCC) without either filing or possession. In addition, a security interest in certain kinds of collateral such as instruments, certificated securities and negotiable documents remains perfected for a limited time after the collateral is released to the debtor for certain specified purposes (these provisions, for example, enable a letter of credit bank to release documents to the buyer/account party for dealing with the underlying goods).

In a few instances, perfection occurs automatically upon attachment of the security interest. Under revised art 9, this is true in the case of a sale of a payment intangible and a sale of a promissory note, as well as a security interest created by the assignment of a health-care-insurance receivable to the provider of the health-care goods or services (transactions brought within the scope of the article by revised art 9). Perfection is automatic for certain other transactions as well, including a security interest in investment property created by a broker or securities intermediary, and a security interest in a commodity contract or a commodity account created by a commodity intermediary.

Priority

Naturally, a perfected security interest ranks ahead of an unperfected one. The relative priorities as between two or more perfected security interests in the same collateral are generally determined by their respective dates of perfection; priority dates from the time a filing is first made or, if perfection is accomplished earlier in a different way, from the time such perfection is accomplished. The relative priorities as between two or more unperfected security interests are determined by the dates on which they attach. When perfection may occur by either filing or control, the latter prevails.

There are some exceptions to this 'first in time' priority rule. A particularly important exception is for a 'purchase money security interest', meaning a security interest securing either the purchase price of collateral or credit to enable the debtor to acquire the collateral, if such credit is so used. A purchase money security interest in collateral that is not 'inventory' (defined as goods held for sale or lease, or furnished under contracts of service, or raw materials, work in process or materials used or consumed in a business) has priority over a conflicting (prior) security interest in the same collateral or its proceeds if the purchase money security interest is perfected at the time the debtor receives possession of the collateral or within a grace period (20 days in New York) thereafter. The rules governing priority of a purchase money security interest in inventory are more stringent, requiring that the purchase money security interest be perfected at the time the debtor receives possession of the inventory and that the holder of the purchase money security interest give notice, in accordance with certain rules, to the holder of the conflicting security interest. Revised art 9 elaborates on these rules.

There are special provisions dealing with security interests in fixtures and their priority vis-à-vis real estate mortgages, security interests in accessions (goods that are installed in or affixed to other goods), and security interests in goods that are commingled with other goods or processed. Under revised art 9, since deposit accounts with banks are covered as original collateral, there are rules with regards to the relative rights of the depositary bank and the secured party, as noted under 'Exclusions' p 493 below.

Priorities may be altered by agreement among the secured parties.

A security interest duly perfected under state law before the filing of a Federal tax lien against the debtor will normally take priority over the tax lien, although in some instances the tax lien will prevail as to after-acquired property. Certain possessory liens arising by statute (such as warehouseman's liens and mechanics' liens) may have priority over a conflicting security interest in the relevant goods. There are a number of other special priority rules.

Disposition of collateral; proceeds

Under art 9, a security interest generally continues in collateral notwithstanding the debtor's disposition of the collateral, unless the disposition was authorised by the secured party by a provision in the security agreement or otherwise — revised art 9 sharpens this rule by providing for such continuation unless the secured party 'authorised the disposition free of the security interest' — and a secured party should be careful: many court decisions have found that a secured party, by its statements or by a course of dealing, in effect released its security interest upon disposition by the debtor.

Although in general a security interest continues in collateral after its disposition, there are exceptions. For example, there are several exceptions designed to protect the ordinary flow of commerce, such as for a holder in due course of a negotiable instrument, a holder by due negotiation of a negotiable document of title and a protected purchaser of a security (these being technical terms defined in other parts of the UCC). A 'buyer in ordinary course of business' (other than a buyer of farm products from a person engaged in farming operations) takes the purchased property free of a security interest created by the seller even if the security interest is perfected and even if the buyer is aware of the security interest, but the expression 'buyer in ordinary course of business' is somewhat less than meets the eye: it is limited to a person who, in good faith and without knowledge that the sale is in violation of the rights of a third party, buys in ordinary course from a person in the business of selling goods of that kind. UCC changes accompanying revised art 9 clarify that a person buys in the ordinary course if the sale comports with the usual or customary practices in the kind of business in which the seller is engaged or with the seller's own usual or customary practices.

A security interest also continues in identifiable proceeds of collateral. The concept of 'proceeds' is a broad one which is further broadened by revised art 9. In addition to the more obvious kinds of proceeds, the term includes accounts receivable arising upon the sale of inventory collateral, insurance payable by reason of loss or damage to collateral (except to the extent that it is payable to a person other than a party to the security agreement), payments or distributions made with respect to securities or other investment property collateral, and 'second-generation' proceeds (property received upon the disposition of other collateral proceeds).

Article 9 contains elaborate rules that both protect and limit the secured party's right to proceeds. The attachment of a security interest in collateral automatically carries with it the rights to proceeds provided by art 9 (unless otherwise agreed). A security interest in proceeds is a perfected security interest if the security interest in the original collateral was perfected, but, except in certain cases as to identifiable cash proceeds, becomes unperfected after a lapse of time unless certain other requirements are met.

Special provisions relating to accounts, etc.

The inclusion of sales of accounts and chattel paper and, under revised art 9, sales of payment intangibles and promissory notes within the scope of art 9 requires a number of special provisions relating to such transactions:

Exemptions from filing

Although the sale of an account is subject to art 9, it is not necessary to file a financing statement in connection with an assignment of accounts that does not alone, or in conjunction with other assignments to the same assignee, transfer a 'significant part' of the outstanding accounts of the assignor. Under revised art 9, this exemption also applies to assignments of payment intangibles. Since the phrase 'significant part' leaves scope for disagreement, a purchaser of accounts or an assignee of payment intangibles will generally err on the side of filing. Also, under revised art 9, as noted above, perfection of the security interest resulting from the sale of a payment intangible or a promissory note occurs automatically when it attaches (no filing is necessary), and the same is true of a security interest created by assignment of a health-care-insurance receivable to the hospital or other provider of the health-care goods or services.

Transfers of accounts outside art 9

Article 9 does not apply at all to a sale of accounts or chattel paper or, under revised art 9, payment intangibles or promissory notes, as part of a sale of the business out of which they arose. It also does not apply to an assignment of accounts or chattel paper or, under revised art 9, payment intangibles or promissory notes, which is for the purpose of collection only; to an assignment of a right to payment under a contract where the assignee is also obligated to perform under the contract; nor to a transfer of a single account or, under revised art 9, payment intangible or promissory note, to an assignee in whole or partial satisfaction of a pre-existing indebtedness.

Sale treatment

Even though art 9 covers sales of accounts and the like, the article acknowledges that there are important differences between outright sales of accounts and mere security interests in them. For example, art 9 confirms that if a transaction with respect to accounts or chattel paper or, under revised art 9, payment intangibles or promissory notes is a sale, then even though art 9 is applicable, the debtor is not entitled to any surplus nor liable for any deficiency; and the rights of a person who is a transferee of such assets, and who is not a secured party, takes priority over the holder of an unperfected security interest to the extent that the person gives value without knowledge of the security interest and before it is perfected.

Defences against third parties

Article 9 provides that an agreement by a buyer or lessee not to assert against an assignee any claim or defence which the buyer or lessee may have against the seller or lessor is enforceable by the assignee who takes the assignment for value, in good faith and without notice of a claim or defence (other than those few defences that may be asserted against a holder in due course of a negotiable instrument) and, under revised art 9, without notice of a claim of a property or possessory right to the property assigned.

Revised art 9 discards the language that limits this rule to buyers and lessees, and makes it applicable to all 'account debtors' (persons obligated on accounts, chattel paper or general intangibles), and employs a somewhat narrower definition of the expression 'for value'.

In the absence of such an agreement by a buyer or lessee, the rights of an assignee are subject to all the terms of the agreement between the account debtor and the assignor and any defence or claim arising from that agreement. Such rights are also subject to any other defence or claim of the account debtor against the assignor which accrues before the obligor receives notification of the assignment (revised art 9 says that such notification must be authenticated by the assignor or assignee) and the account debtor is authorised to pay the assignor until it receives notification that the amount due or to become due has been assigned and that payment is to be made to the assignee; because of this, assignees of accounts, chattel paper and general intangibles often require notification to the account parties in addition to perfecting by the filing of a financing statement.

Leases

A lease may be a security agreement under art 9. Article 9 governs leases of goods that are intended to create security interests, while UCC art 2A governs other leases of goods (sometimes referred to as 'true leases'). The UCC as amended to include art 2A is sometimes referred to as the 'post-1987 version', and the prior version is called the 'pre-1987 version'.

The problem of distinguishing between true leases and security leases has long been a prolific source of litigation. The issue has major practical consequences: if a lease creates a security interest, the lessee will be deemed to be a debtor, the leased goods will be collateral, the lessor will be the secured party and must duly perfect the security interest, and failure to perfect may result in subordination of the lessor's interest in the leased property.

Under the pre-1987 version, which may still apply to long-term leases entered into pursuant to that version, the fact that the lessee has a purchase option does not bring a lease within art 9, but if the option can be exercised for no additional consideration or for a nominal consideration, the lease is deemed to be 'intended as security' and is covered by art 9. The pre-1987 version generally leaves it to the courts to decide whether a lease is a secured transaction based on the facts of each case.

Under the post-1987 version, art 1 of the UCC (which contains definitions of general UCC applicability) and art 9 provide clearer guidelines as to which leases are covered by art 9. A court will still have to make this determination on the basis of the facts of each case; however, a lease will be deemed to create an art 9 security interest if the consideration the lessee is to pay the lessor is for the term of the lease and not subject to termination by the lessee, and either: (1) the original lease term is equal to or greater than the remaining economic life of the goods (determined with reference to the facts and circumstances at the time the transaction is entered into); or (2) the lessee is bound to renew the lease for the remaining economic life of the goods or is bound to become the owner of the goods; or (3) the lessee has an option to renew the lease for the remaining economic life of the goods for no additional consideration or for nominal consideration; or (4) the lessee has the option to become the owner of the goods for no additional consideration or for nominal consideration.

The post-1987 version indicates, helpfully, that certain factors do not by themselves bring a lease within art 9, including the fact that the present value of the consideration the lessee is obligated to pay to the lessor is substantially equal to or greater than the fair market value of the goods at the time the lease is entered into (a 'full payout lease'); the fact that the lessee assumes the risk of loss of goods or agrees to pay taxes, insurance and various costs and fees relating to the property (a 'net lease'); or the fact that the lessee has an option to renew the lease or to purchase the goods.

Since a lessor seeking true lease treatment will nevertheless not wish to take the risk that a court will find that the transaction results merely in an unperfected security interest, art 9 allows for the filing of a precautionary financing statement, using the terms 'lessor' and 'lessee' instead of 'secured party' and 'debtor', and provides that the filing of such a financing statement shall not of itself be a factor in determining whether or not the lease creates a security interest.

Conflicts of laws

The parties to a security agreement may generally agree that the agreement is governed by the laws of a state bearing a reasonable relation to the transaction.

However, a set of 'conflicts of laws' provisions in art 9 determines which state's law (referred to for convenience in this summary as the 'relevant law') governs perfection, and the effect of perfection or non-perfection, in transactions involving multiple states. Among other things, these are the rules that determine in what state or states a filing must be made.

Current art 9

Under current art 9, the rules are as follows:

1 In the case of documents, instruments and ordinary goods (not including goods covered by a certificate of title as referred to in item 3 below, nor mobile goods of a type normally used in more than one jurisdiction, nor minerals and the like, including oil and gas, as referred to in item 4 below), and in the case of a possessory security interest in chattel paper, the relevant law is that of the jurisdiction where the collateral is when the last event occurs on which is based the assertion that the security interest is perfected or unperfected.

   This is the rule that governs, for example, security interests in most inventory and equipment. It means in practice that if the debtor's inventory of ordinary goods, or its equipment, is located in several different states, filing will be required in each such state. The rule also means that in the case of a security interest in documents and instruments or other collateral perfected by possession, the relevant law is the law of the place where those items are delivered to and held by the secured party or its agent.

   There are special rules to deal with collateral that moves from one state to another.

2 In the case of accounts (other than accounts resulting from the sale of minerals or the like at the wellhead or minehead), general intangibles (not including uncertificated securities) and mobile goods of a type normally used in more than one jurisdiction that are equipment or are inventory leased or held for lease (for

example, motor vehicles, trailers, rolling stock, airplanes, shipping containers, road building and construction machinery and commercial harvesting machinery) but that are not covered by a certificate of title, and also in the case of a non-possessory security interest in chattel paper, the relevant law is the law of the jurisdiction in which the debtor is 'located'.

This is the rule that will generally govern, for example, security interests in accounts receivable and general intangibles.

For this purpose, a debtor is deemed to be 'located' at its place of business if it has one, at its chief executive office if it has more than one place of business and otherwise at its residence. Under current art 9, the debtor's jurisdiction of organisation has nothing to do with the issue of its 'location'.

If the debtor's location changes to a new state, a security interest perfected under the law of the first location remains perfected for four months after the change (or until perfection would have ceased under such law, if earlier), and unless perfected in the new jurisdiction before the end of such period it becomes unperfected thereafter and is deemed to have been unperfected as against a person who became a purchaser after the change.

Another rule applies if the debtor is located in a jurisdiction which is not a part of the US and does not provide for filing or recording of non-possessory security interests: in that case, the relevant law is the law of the jurisdiction in which the debtor has its major US executive office; or in the alternative, if the debtor is located in a jurisdiction which is not part of the US or Canada and the collateral consists of accounts or general intangibles for money due or to become due, art 9 provides that the security interest may be perfected by notification to the account debtor. (The secured party will also, however, wish to investigate and comply with the requirements of the debtor's jurisdiction.)

3 In the case of goods covered by a certificate of title issued under a statute of a jurisdiction whose law requires that a security interest be indicated on the certificate as a condition of perfection, the relevant law is initially the law of the jurisdiction issuing the certificate. This rule applies to many motor vehicles and to some aircraft and vessels. However, perfection continues only for four months after the property is removed from the certificate jurisdiction and thereafter until it is registered in another jurisdiction; after that, it is no longer considered to be covered by the certificate of title. Revised art 9 includes several refinements in this area.

4 In the case of a security interest in minerals or the like (including oil and gas) before extraction that attaches thereto as extracted, and in accounts arising from the sale of the minerals at the wellhead or minehead, the relevant law is the law of the jurisdiction where the wellhead or minehead is located.

5 There are several rules for investment property, as follows:

(a) in the case of a security certificate, the relevant law is the law of the state where the certificate is located at the time;

(b) in the case of an uncertificated security, the relevant law is the law of the issuer's jurisdiction (being the jurisdiction where the issuer is organised or, if permitted by such law, the law of another jurisdiction specified by the issuer); and

(c) in the case of a security entitlement or securities account, the law of the securities intermediary's jurisdiction (this can be designated by agreement between the securities intermediary and the entitlement holder), with corresponding rules for a commodity contract or commodity account.

In the case of perfection by filing, however, the relevant law is that of the jurisdiction where the debtor is located.

Revised art 9

Revised art 9 takes a different approach to conflicts of law rules, as follows:

1 The general rule is that *perfection* is governed by the law of the jurisdiction where the debtor, not the collateral, is located, except that perfection of a *possessory* security interest in collateral, of a security interest perfected by a fixture filing, of a security interest in timber to be cut and of a security interest in 'as-extracted collateral' (minerals) is governed by the location of the collateral (or of the wellhead or minehead in the case of as-extracted collateral). As noted above, a 'registered organisation' will be deemed located in the State of its organisation and many non-US debtors may be deemed located for this purpose in the District of Columbia. These rules mean that most filings in commercial financings under revised art 9 will be made in the debtor's jurisdiction of organisation. In the case of a debtor that is not a registered organisation (for example, a private partnership) the debtor will be deemed located at its chief executive office or, if it has only one place of business, at its place of business.
2 The *effect* of perfection or nonperfection, and priority, of a security interest (referred to in this summary as 'effects') are governed by the law of the jurisdiction where the debtor is located, except that the effects of a possessory security interest, the effects of a non-possessory security interest in negotiable documents, goods, instruments, money and tangible chattel paper, and the effects of a security interest in as-extracted collateral are governed by the law of the location of the collateral (or of the wellhead or minehead in the case of as-extracted collateral).
3 In the case of deposit accounts, perfection and its effects are governed by the law of the bank's jurisdiction (which can be determined by agreement between the bank and the debtor).
4 In the case of investment property, the rules under revised art 9 are substantially the same as under current art 9.
5 In the case of letter-of-credit rights, perfection and its effects are governed by the law of the issuer's jurisdiction or that of the nominated person (such as a confirming bank), determined under UCC art 5.

Exclusions

Security interests in some kinds of property are governed by principles found outside the UCC. The significant exclusions from art 9 are as follows.

Real estate interests

Article 9 does not apply to the creation or transfer of an interest in or lien on real property, including a lease of real property or rents therefrom; state real estate law governs these matters (except to the extent art 9 applies to security interests in fixtures).

Article 9 does apply, though, to a security interest in a promissory note or the like that is itself secured by a mortgage on real estate; this means that a security interest in such an instrument must be perfected under art 9 (it will not be enough to record an assignment of the mortgage).

Federal statutes

To the extent that a US Federal statute governs the rights of parties to and third parties affected by transactions in particular types of property, a security interest in such property is subject to that statute, rather than to art 9.

The pertinent Federal scheme may not be all-encompassing, with the result that various aspects of art 9 will still govern. For example, although perfection of a security interest in US registered aircraft is governed by successor provisions to the Federal Aviation Act of 1958 and related regulations, a security interest in certain equipment on the aircraft will still be governed by art 9.

Rights of set-off

Article 9 does not apply to any right of set-off (revised art 9 adds to this exclusion a right of recoupment) and no filing is needed to 'perfect' such rights.

A right of set-off may arise by common law or by contract or by statute, and can be a powerful right. In New York, a bank has a statutory right under the New York Debtor and Creditor Law s 151 to set off and apply general deposit liabilities owing to its borrower against the borrower's obligations to the bank, even if the latter obligations are unmatured, and such right of set-off is exercisable even after receipt by the bank of notice of attachment or garnishment of the deposit.

The exercise of a right of set-off is, however, limited by the provisions of the Bankruptcy Code.

Deposit accounts

Current art 9 does not apply to a security interest in a 'deposit account' (meaning an account maintained with a bank or similar organisation, other than an account evidenced by a certificate of deposit) as original collateral, although there are art 9 provisions relating to proceeds of other collateral deposited into such an account. Except in a few states, the pledge of a deposit account is therefore governed by common law principles and no filing is needed (or effective) to perfect it. The common law governing the pledge of a deposit account has not been entirely clear. In general, the secured party must obtain exclusive dominion and control over the account in order to have a protected interest.

If a pledged deposit account is evidenced by a certificate of deposit, which is an instrument, art 9 does apply.

Revised art 9 changes the scope of the article by including deposit accounts with banks as original collateral, and provides that a secured party perfects a security interest in a deposit account by taking 'control' over the deposit account. Control would exist where the secured party itself is the depositary bank, or where the secured party becomes the customer of the depositary with respect to the deposit; in addition, control can be obtained by having the depositary bank enter into a control agreement, as noted above under 'Perfection by control'. Revised art 9 adds provisions relating to conflict between a security interest in a deposit account and the depositary bank's right of set-off or recoupment, the effect of which provisions is to preserve such rights of the bank, except that if the secured party has perfected its security interest by becoming the bank's customer on the account, the exercise by the bank of a set-off against the account will be ineffective.

Insurance

Article 9 does not apply to a transfer of an interest or claim in or under any policy of insurance, except with respect to insurance payments as proceeds of other collateral. Assignments of insurance are therefore governed by common law and by provisions of the relevant insurance policies. Revised art 9 narrows this exclusion by carving out of the exclusion an assignment by or to a health-care provider of a health-care-insurance receivable and any subsequent assignment of the right to payment.

New York excludes a contract for an annuity from the scope of art 9. In states that do not exclude annuities, courts have had to wrestle with the question of how to characterise them, as instruments or general intangibles, for perfection purposes.

Tort claims

Article 9 excludes from its coverage an assignment of a claim arising in tort (such as a claim for damages as a result of negligence). Revised art 9 narrows this exclusion so as to provide that art 9 does cover an assignment of a 'commercial tort claim', a new category meaning a claim arising in tort where the claimant is an organisation, or where the claimant is an individual but the claim arose in the course of his or her business or profession. A security interest in a commercial tort claim will not attach under an after-acquired property clause.

Other exclusions

Also excluded from art 9 are landlord's liens, liens given by statute or other rule of law for services or materials (although certain possessory statutory liens are given priority over a perfected security interest), transfers of claims for wages, salary or other compensation of an employee, transfers of rights represented by judgments and certain security interests created by governmental entities.

Remedies

Article 9 contains a variety of provisions relating to the enforcement of the rights of a secured party.

The secured party has a number of remedies, which may generally be exercised when permitted by the security agreement and in any event after default. The remedies are cumulative. Among other things, the secured party may reduce the secured claim to judgment, foreclose or otherwise enforce the security interest by an available judicial procedure, notify account debtors to pay directly to the secured party, and take possession of the collateral without judicial process if this can be done without breach of the peace. If the security agreement so provides, the secured party may require the debtor to assemble the collateral and make it available to the secured party at a place designated by the secured party which is reasonably convenient to both parties. The secured party after default may sell, lease or otherwise dispose of any or all of the collateral in its then condition or following any commercially reasonable preparation or processing. Disposition of collateral may be by public or private proceedings and may be made by way of one or more contracts, subject to certain notification requirements. Such disposition transfers to a purchaser for value the debtor's rights therein and discharges the security interest on the collateral disposed of (and subordinate liens).

An overriding principle is that every aspect of the secured party's disposition of collateral (including the method, manner, time, place and other terms) must be 'commercially reasonable'. This requirement of art 9 cannot validly be waived by the debtor. A considerable body of case law has developed as to what procedures or actions are or are not commercially reasonable in the context of liquidating collateral.

If a secured party with a security interest in fixtures has priority over the owners and encumbrancers of the real estate, the secured party may, on default, remove the collateral from the real estate, but must reimburse the owners or encumbrancers (other than the debtor) for the cost of repair of any physical injury (though not for any resulting diminution of value of the real estate).

The secured party must account to the debtor for any surplus after payment of the secured obligations and, unless otherwise agreed, the debtor is liable for any deficiency. Article 9 provides the debtor with a right to redeem collateral before its disposition.

There is a special procedure (so-called 'strict foreclosure') whereby the secured party in possession of collateral may, after default, retain it in satisfaction of the secured obligation.

Revised art 9 elaborates on secured parties' remedies in various ways.

Lender liability

Article 9 states expressly that a secured party does not subject itself to contract or tort liability for a debtor's acts or omissions merely by having a security interest or authorising the debtor to use or dispose of the collateral. This principle is plainly a comfort to a secured party whose collateral is personal property of a kind that is capable of causing harm (for example, industrial equipment).

It cannot be said, however, that holding a security interest is necessarily irrelevant to lender liability. For example, some case law has imposed lender liability where a creditor has exercised an undue degree of control over the debtor and thereby caused or contributed to the debtor's misfortune; the circumstance that a secured party, through its security agreement, had control over the cash flow and operating accounts of a debtor can be relevant (particularly in the minds of jurors) to the question of the exercise of undue control. Nevertheless, lender liability risk normally arises from the manner in which the creditor deals with the collateral and with the debtor and not from the mere existence of a security interest.

Article 9 imposes certain obligations on a secured party, in addition to the requirement of commercial reasonableness noted above. These include an obligation to use reasonable care in the custody and preservation of collateral in its possession and in the case of an instrument or chattel paper, an obligation to take necessary steps to preserve rights against prior parties unless otherwise agreed (it is common practice for a security agreement to disclaim this obligation).

Additional lender liability issues arise if the collateral consists of securities. It is probably advisable to provide (through security agreement provisions) that voting rights in respect of pledged stock are available to the secured party only after default by the debtor and then only if the creditor makes a determination that it wishes to exercise such rights. In addition, any disposition by the creditor of pledged securities must comply with the provisions of Federal and state securities laws relating to the sale of securities generally.

Addendum

Since revised art 9 changes the requirements as to location of filing, extends the scope of art 9 to reach certain new categories of collateral, and make various other kinds of changes that affect perfection and priority, revised art 9 contains a series of transitional rules. Among the more important are the rules that if the relative priorities of parties with conflicting claims to collateral were fixed before the effective date of revised art 9, current art 9 will still determine the priorities, a security interest that is perfected under current art 9 other than by filing but that would not be perfected under the new rules is a perfected security for one year after the effective date of revised art 9, and a security interest that is perfected under both revised and current art 9 remains perfected without further action. There are various other transitional rules that will need to be consulted by practitioners.

SECURITY INTERESTS IN REAL PROPERTY

The law governing security interests in real property is state law. There is no 'uniform' law concerning mortgages and real estate law remains encrusted with all manner of tenements, hereditaments, easements appurtenant and other evidence of arcane learning.

This section summarises, in the 12 headings that follow, the general considerations facing a party that is lending against US commercial real property (special legal rules relating to residential mortgages are not covered). Real property is inherently local and the legal position must be analysed on a state-by-state basis.

The mortgage

States which follow a traditional mortgage theory consider mortgages to be liens upon real property, which are released when the obligations secured by the mortgage are satisfied. Other states follow a title theory, under which actual title or security title is conveyed by the debtor to a lender or to a trustee for the benefit of a lender by a deed, usually a deed of trust or deed to secure debt, and such title is reconveyed to the debtor when the obligations are satisfied. Under either theory, the debtor has a right of 'equitable redemption' whereby the real property is to be released from the lien of the mortgage or reconveyed upon payment of the secured obligations.

In many states the proper document to create a security interest in real property is called a 'mortgage'; other states, including California, utilise a 'deed of trust' in which the debtor conveys real property to a third party in trust for the benefit of the creditor, or, as in Georgia, a 'deed to secure debt'. Although they are different in form and in legal theory, there is little difference between them in practice, particularly where a mortgage includes a power of sale, and each is referred to herein as a 'mortgage'.

In theory, any interest in real property which is transferable can be mortgaged. In practice, most mortgages cover the interest of the owner of the property (a 'fee mortgage') or the interest of a tenant under a lease (a 'leasehold mortgage'). Incidental interests, such as easements benefiting fee or leasehold properties, are usually mortgaged along with the fee or leasehold interest.

The mortgage document must contain a granting clause in which the property to be mortgaged is described and must identify the party giving the collateral (the mortgagor or trustor), the secured party (the mortgagee or beneficiary), the trustee (in the case of a deed of trust), and the obligations being secured. Unlike the approach taken in many art 9 security agreements, the description of mortgaged real property is highly specific and technical.

Future advances

Many states permit a mortgage to secure indebtedness not yet in existence, such as future advances to be made under a construction loan agreement. When advances are made by a lender after the recording of a mortgage, a question arises as to the priority of the mortgage regarding such subsequent advances. Most states, including New York, provide by statute that future advances may be secured to the same extent and with the same priority (with limited exceptions) as if such advances had been made at the time the mortgage was recorded, subject to the satisfaction of certain requirements (for example, that all advances have been made within a certain time period). In some states, including New York, a revolving credit facility (in which the borrower is entitled to borrow, repay and reborrow) cannot conveniently be secured by real property, because mortgage recording taxes must be paid with respect to each drawdown (which can be costly).

Recording

In the context of real property, 'perfection' involves recording the mortgage. The states and localities in the US employ various systems for recording mortgages and customs and practices vary widely. In practice, lenders generally rely on title insurance companies to search the real estate records and to record mortgages. In issuing a policy of title insurance, these companies insure, among other things, the enforceability of a mortgage and its priority, once recorded, vis-à-vis other interests in the mortgaged property.

Recording fees are typically minimal, but many states impose mortgage recording taxes (sometimes called documentary stamp taxes or intangibles taxes) on the indebtedness secured by the mortgage. These taxes may be significant in amount and the tax rates may vary even within different parts of the same state. In some states, it is possible, in connection with a refinancing of mortgage debt, to have the existing mortgage assigned to the new lender (and simultaneously amended or restated, as necessary) so as to avoid or minimise recording taxes. Mortgage recording taxes and fees are typically paid by the debtor, although local practice or statute may dictate otherwise in a few jurisdictions.

Conditions to real estate lending

A party lending against real estate is likely to require, in addition to the legal opinions, corporate documentation and other items customarily obtained as conditions precedent to any financing commitment, a number of items specifically related to the real property collateral. For example:

1 The lender will require the execution and delivery of the mortgage in recordable form, and will require the payment of all mortgage recording fees and taxes (typically to the title company which will be handling the recording of the mortgage). If the mortgage is being assigned by an existing lender to the new lender, an appropriate instrument of assignment (and contemporaneous amendment or restatement) will be part of the documentation.

2 The lender may require the furnishing of a current survey of the property, certified to the lender, prepared by a surveyor licensed in the relevant state and satisfactory to the lender, setting forth a precise description of the perimeter of the property and the locations of all easements, improvements, parking areas, building setback lines, utilities, means of ingress and egress, adjacent streets and so on.

3 The lender will require title insurance issued by a licensed title company satisfactory to the lender (or, in the case of larger loans, issued by co-insurers, or with satisfactory reinsurance agreements in place), insuring the priority of the lender's interest, subject to such exceptions as the lender may approve. In a transaction where real property is the sole security for the loan, the amount of the title insurance policy obtained is usually equal to the loan amount. Where real property makes up only a portion of the collateral package, the lender will often require title insurance in an amount equal to the appraised value of the real property (often with a cushion to account for appreciation in its value). The debtor is generally required to pay the cost of the lender's policy of title insurance.

The most commonly issued form of title insurance policy is the American Land Title Association (ALTA) policy. The mortgagee's policy will insure the mortgagee that title to the mortgaged property is as represented, that the title is free of liens, judgments, encumbrances or other title interests except as shown in the policy, that there is legal access to the property and that the title is marketable. It also insures the mortgagee against invalidity or unenforceability of the mortgage lien, the existence of any lien or encumbrance having priority over the mortgage lien except as specifically disclosed and lack of priority of the mortgage lien over any statutory mechanic's lien for services, labour or material arising from certain improvements or work related to the real property. If the mortgage was already in existence and is being assigned to the lender, the mortgagee's policy insures the mortgagee against the invalidity or unenforceability of the assignment, or failure to vest the mortgage in the named insured assignee free and clear of all liens except as disclosed in the policy.

The ALTA mortgagee policy contains a number of important requirements, exceptions and exclusions from coverage with which the lender should be familiar, including exclusions relating to certain bankruptcy matters, except as may be modified through the issuance of specific endorsements to the policy.

4 The documentation should require the maintenance of insurance in connection with the collateral and the lender will wish to receive, as a condition to lending, evidence that the insurance is in place. This may include casualty insurance, liability insurance, workers' compensation insurance, business interruption insurance and possibly more specialised insurance such as flood insurance and earthquake insurance.

5 For many improved properties, the lender will require an engineering report with respect to the structure, building systems and general condition of the structures and improvements. If the report recommends remedial work, the lender may require that the mortgagor establish reserves, in the form of cash collateral or otherwise, against the cost of the work.

6 In the case of a newly completed building, the lender may require an architect's certificate to the effect, among other things, that the building has been substantially completed in a first-class workmanlike manner in accordance with approved plans and specifications and in accordance with all applicable laws and regulations (including the Americans With Disabilities Act discussed below). In many areas, including New York City, the various departments of municipal government maintain detailed records of violations of rules and regulations applicable to real property, covering matters from fire safety to defective sidewalks, and a prudent lender will require that such records be searched and all existing violations corrected.

7 A certificate of occupancy is almost always required where available, together with appropriate evidence (which may take the form of architects' certifications, opinions of counsel, confirmatory letters from local authorities, 'zoning endorsements' to the mortgagee's title insurance policy, and the like) that the building complies with all local land use and subdivision requirements, including restrictions on height, bulk and density requirements with respect to building set-backs and adequate parking facilities. In jurisdictions where certificates of occupancy are not issued or where the completion and occupancy of the structure pre-dated certificate of occupancy requirements, lenders must rely upon one or more of the above-described alternatives.

8 In recognition of environmental concerns discussed below, the lender against commercial real estate will require an environmental survey and assessment with respect to the property, prepared by a firm of qualified engineers familiar with the identification of toxic and hazardous substances, based on on-site inspections by such firm and including an historical review of the uses of the property and of the business conducted there. The results of the survey should be provided in a written

report which identifies any conditions or circumstances suggesting the possibility of liability under environmental laws, including site contamination or significant failures to comply with regulatory requirements. If such conditions are identified, the report should estimate the costs of addressing them or recommend further investigation necessary to estimate such costs.

9 For many kinds of real property, such as office buildings or shopping centres, the existence of long-term leases of space may be critical to the lender's credit analysis. In such cases, the lender will wish to evaluate the credit of each major tenant and will wish to assure that the terms of all major leases are satisfactory.

10 Generally, lenders will require a debtor to assign to the lender all its rights in any leases of the real property as well as any rents flowing therefrom. The mortgage may include an assignment of all leases and rents, or such assignment may be separately documented and separately recorded. Notice of the assignment may be served on each tenant. The lender will wish to receive assurance that each major lease is in full force and effect and that no tenant under a major lease has any set-offs, counterclaims or defences to the lease. This is typically done by requiring the delivery of 'estoppel certificates' from the tenants under such leases. The mortgage should prohibit material amendments of major leases. The lender may require that existing tenants enter into subordination and non-disturbance agreements, in order to confirm the subordination of the lease to the lien of the mortgage and to reach agreement as to the rights and obligations of the parties following the foreclosure of the mortgaged property. The mortgage may also provide for the lender to enter into such agreements with respect to future leases, to assure tenants that such leases will not be cut off in the event of a foreclosure. The lender may also wish to review and approve other material contracts relating to the property, such as any major supply contract relating to the property, or the management contract in the case of a hotel. Where the other party to such a contract is an affiliated entity, the lender may require that the affiliate's claims for payment under the contract be subordinated to the loan.

Appraisals

The Financial Institutions Reform, Recovery and Enforcement Act of 1989 ('FIRREA'), imposed on US financial institutions in connection with 'Federally related' transactions a requirement to obtain, as a condition to lending, an appraisal of the real estate by a state-licensed appraiser meeting certain requirements. FIRREA excepts loans in connection with which the real estate collateral is obtained in an excess of caution (for example, where the credit analysis is based on the borrower's cash flow, not on the value of the real property, and the availability or unavailability of real property as collateral would not alter the pricing of the loan).

Mortgage covenants

Mortgages commonly contain a variety of other provisions relating to the real property, including: a warranty by the mortgagor of title to the property; requirements for the maintenance of insurance, payment of insurance premiums and the handling of insurance proceeds; covenants to pay taxes relating to the property; provisions as to the consequences of condemnation of the property and the disposition of proceeds of any condemnation award; covenants to maintain the mortgaged property in good condition and to comply with applicable laws and regulations; restrictions on transfer of the mortgaged property (which may include exceptions for permitted leases of the property); restrictions on transfers of interests of the debtor; restrictions on junior liens; in the case of a condominium development or other developments where portions of the property are expected to be sold, provisions for release of such portions from the lien of the mortgage upon payment to the lender, in reduction of the loan, of a prescribed release price; provisions for maintenance of an escrow fund for payment of taxes and insurance premiums relating to the property (the fund to be pledged as additional collateral); covenants to comply with environmental laws and regulations; covenants to furnish updated appraisals and environmental surveys on a periodic basis; environmental indemnities and general indemnities relating to the mortgage and the mortgaged property; further assurances as to maintenance of the recording of the mortgage and the taking of other steps to assure protection of the lender's interest, at the mortgagor's expense; provisions as to what constitutes a default under the mortgage; and various provisions relating to the mortgagee's remedies.

Remedies

The fundamental rights of the holder of a mortgage, in the event of a significant default such as failure to make a payment of principal or interest when due on the secured debt, are the right to foreclose and become the successor owner of the mortgaged property and to exercise a power of sale to force a sale of the mortgaged property.

Foreclosure and power of sale rights and procedures are governed by state law and the states differ widely on rights of mortgagors and mortgagees in such proceedings, on the rights of lenders to collect 'deficiencies' (where the value of the foreclosed property is less than the debt), on the rights of lenders to maintain lawsuits to collect on a note or guaranty separately from the relevant action and on the rights of borrowers to 'redeem' their property. All states provide for foreclosure proceedings to take place in court under judicial supervision, although some states additionally allow for foreclosures to occur outside of court under a 'power of sale'.

Junior liens

In most jurisdictions, the completion of foreclosure proceedings eliminates liens and other encumbrances junior to the mortgage. However, some states have statutes, commonly referred to as 'lien laws', enacted to protect the liens of those who provided materials and labour, and the ability of a mortgagee to wipe out such junior lienors may depend on compliance, usually at the time the mortgage is granted, with such statutes.

California's one form of action rule

California and certain other states have a 'single action' or 'one form of action' rule relating to collection of indebtedness secured by real property and enforcement of real property collateral, designed to deter a multiplicity of actions and to encourage a creditor to view the collateral as the primary source of payment for the obligations. In cases involving a jurisdiction that has a single-action rule, a creditor with a real property mortgage should proceed with extreme caution in exercising any remedy whatsoever, so that remedies ancillary to foreclosure (including enforcement of guaranties) are not lost.

Environmental law

A lender taking a mortgage on real property located in the US must consider risks arising under US environmental laws. Such laws impose stringent requirements relating to the emission or discharge of pollutants, management of wastes and cleanup of spills of petroleum and other hazardous materials. These laws and associated regulations impose costly requirements upon borrowers and can, under certain conditions, affect lenders directly. When a lender forecloses upon a business or property, for example, it may become subject to the environmental obligations of its borrower. When a lender exercises undue control over a borrower's property, operations or finances, it can become the legal 'operator' of the borrower's facilities, a classification that can result in direct lender liability for environmental cleanup costs.

Lender due diligence should generally cover three distinct areas of risk in order to avoid loan defaults resulting from, and direct liability under, environmental laws and regulations. First, a lender should take some care to verify that the borrower's facilities were constructed and are operating in compliance with applicable laws and regulations. The existence of non-compliance is often difficult to detect, but can result in compliance costs that adversely affect the borrower's credit profile. Second, a lender should be concerned about changing environmental regulations. US environmental law changes regularly, often imposing new and significant costs upon owners or operators of specific types of facilities. For the most part, such costs and their effects upon a borrower's business may be identified and anticipated. Third, US law imposes liability for current and past releases of hazardous substances. It has become customary to review the properties owned and operated by a borrower (and, sometimes even those formerly owned or operated) in order to determine whether the borrower has significant contingent liabilities relating to such cleanup costs.

When a borrower shows signs of failing or a loan goes into default, the prudent lender will implement an environmental risk management programme. This programme should include an assessment of the environmental risks and liabilities associated with the borrower's properties, including particularly those properties that are mortgaged. If the environmental risks associated with such properties are potentially significant, the lender should establish careful controls over its workout activities and maintain detailed records with respect to those activities. The lender should also avoid any action that could constitute 'control' of the operation of facilities presenting such risks. Prior to foreclosure, the lender should conduct a full-scale environmental review, to assess compliance liabilities, risks relating to changing environmental laws and site cleanup risks. Failure to follow these precautions can result in the lender's becoming responsible for compliance or cleanup costs originally belonging to the borrower.

Among the important statutes covering environmental matters is the Federal Comprehensive Environmental Response, Compensation, and Liability Act of 1980 ('CERCLA'). CERCLA imposes liability on an owner or operator of a facility for the 'remediation' or cleanup of contaminated soil and ground water associated with the facility's operations, including off-site waste disposal. Such liability is imposed without regard to fault, so that a new owner or operator (including a foreclosing lender) may be liable for cleaning up pre-existing site contamination.

CERCLA authorises the imposition of a lien on real property to secure the recovery of costs from the owner in cases where Federal authorities have incurred costs to remedy site contamination. Such a lien will not ordinarily take priority over security interests that have been duly perfected under state law prior to the recording of the liens. Such liens are also only rarely imposed, as the Federal government is usually able to obtain the cooperation of responsible parties using other enforcement techniques. A site's value is considerable diminished, however, by formal designation as a 'Superfund' site under CERCLA or by the known presence of contamination that could trigger cleanup liability thereunder.

Many states have environmental laws that parallel the Federal laws and provide independent legal obligations enforceable by state authorities. Such state laws may be more comprehensive than Federal law and may impose restrictions that do not exist under Federal law. For example, the State of New Jersey requires sellers to clean up pre-existing site contamination before property is transferred to a new owner or operator, and several states require sellers to notify buyers of existing contamination conditions.

Credit documentation generally includes indemnities by the debtor against environmental risks.

Americans with Disabilities Act 1990

Under the Americans with Disabilities Act (ADA) Title III, enacted in 1990, certain 'places of public accommodation' and 'commercial facilities' must be made readily accessible to persons who have disabilities.

The statute distinguishes between existing structures, which are required to be made accessible to the extent readily achievable, and new construction, which must be made accessible unless doing so would be structurally impractical. Alterations to existing buildings must be made accessible to the maximum extent feasible.

Given the subjectivity of the statutory requirements and the potentially high costs of ADA compliance, many mortgage lenders have revised their standard forms of loan documentation to include borrower covenants with respect to ADA compliance and, in many cases, to include an indemnity in favour of the lender covering any costs associated with failure to meet the statutory standards. Lenders must also consider state statutes dealing with accommodations for disabled persons, as these are often more stringent than the Federal statute.

Federal taxation

A foreign lender taking a mortgage on US real property generally has no greater exposure to US Federal income taxation than would be the case if it were an unsecured lender, but the Foreign Investment in Real Property Tax Act of 1980 ('FIRPTA') can create additional exposure if the creditor takes a participating interest in or forecloses on the real property.

FIRPTA requires a non-resident alien individual or a foreign corporation to pay US Federal income tax at the normal graduated rates on gain from the disposition of a US real property interest whether or not the foreign person has any other connection with the US Land, buildings and other real property improvements, fixtures and certain personal property associated with the use of real estate are interests in real property for this purpose. Stock in a US corporation that has at least half its assets invested in US real property is also treated as an interest in real property. FIRPTA applies even to lenders that are entitled to the benefit of US tax rules and effectively exempt foreign persons from US taxes on capital gains.

An interest in real property held solely as a creditor is not a US real property interest for FIRPTA purposes. The right to foreclose on the property created by a typical mortgage is therefore not a real property interest for such purposes. A lender that takes a participating interest in the borrower's real estate, however, will be deemed to have an interest in real property other than solely as a creditor (even before foreclosure). A right to share in the appreciation of, or the gross proceeds or net profits from, real property is a real property interest even if the loan is not secured by a mortgage. In addition, a lender that forecloses on mortgaged property and thereby becomes the owner of US real estate will be deemed to have acquired a US real property interest, and the operation of the foreclosed property may cause the lender to become engaged in a taxable business within the US.

To facilitate collection of the FIRPTA tax, the Internal Revenue Code imposes a withholding tax on the buyer of a US real property interest owned by a foreign person at a rate equal to a percentage of the gross amount realised by the foreign person. The rate may be reduced under certain circumstances.

BANKRUPTCY CONSIDERATIONS

It is not sensible, or even possible, to divorce secured transactions law from bankruptcy law. In the US, the creation, perfection and enforcement of any security interest are limited in certain important respects by the US Bankruptcy Code. The Bankruptcy Code is a Federal statute that generally applies to bankruptcy proceedings in connection with US debtors and to certain 'ancillary' proceedings in the US relating to non-US debtors.

The following 12 headings summarise briefly certain concepts and provisions of the Bankruptcy Code that are particularly significant from the standpoint of a secured creditor.

The Bankruptcy Code

For secured creditors, the most significant parts of the Bankruptcy Code are Chapter 7 and Chapter 11. In a Chapter 7 case the debtor is liquidated by an independent trustee, who must collect and reduce to money the debtor's property and distribute it to the debtor's creditors. The consummation of a Chapter 7 case terminates the existence of the debtor. Chapter 11 of the Bankruptcy Code envisages the rehabilitation, or 'reorganisation', of the debtor, rather than its liquidation. The objective of reorganisation informs a number of policies of the Code since, in order to achieve reorganisation, the debtor must continue to operate under the eye of the bankruptcy court, with protection from creditors.

Upon the filing of a bankruptcy petition, the debtor becomes a 'debtor in possession', operating under the control of the bankruptcy court and the regime of the Bankruptcy Code, while an acceptable reorganisation plan is formulated. Under some circumstances, a trustee in bankruptcy may be appointed to administer the debtor's affairs. The powers and responsibilities of the debtor in possession are substantially the same as those of the trustee.

As part of the Chapter 11 case, one or more creditors' committees and equity security holders' committees may be formed to represent various types of creditors and equity security holders. Such committees typically play a major role in the reorganisation.

The goal of a Chapter 11 case is to obtain a court order confirming a reorganisation plan, which is in effect a court-approved contract that restructures the debtor's assets and liabilities. A reorganisation plan can rewrite a debtor's contracts with secured creditors and others. Among other things, it can provide for the sale of property, either subject to or free of any lien; satisfaction or modification of any lien; cancellation or modification of any mortgage, deed of trust, or indenture; cure or waiver of any default; and extension of the maturity date, or change in the interest rate or other terms, of outstanding notes, bonds, and other securities.

A reorganisation plan may be confirmed only after creditors and equity security holders have received court-approved information on the plan and have been permitted to vote to accept or reject the plan. A class of creditors is treated as having accepted a plan if, considering only the creditors in that class that have voted on the plan, creditors that hold at least two-thirds in amount and more than one-half in number of the claims in that class vote to accept the plan. The Bankruptcy Code provides special procedures, commonly referred to 'cramdown' confirmation, for confirming a reorganisation plan even though one or more classes of creditors have voted to reject the plan.

Automatic stay

Upon the filing of a bankruptcy petition, an automatic stay takes effect by operation of law. The automatic stay is an automatic injunction that forbids creditors and others to take actions against the debtor or property of the bankruptcy 'estate'. Property of the estate is broadly defined to include all legal or equitable interests of the debtor in property as of the commencement of the bankruptcy case. Property of the estate is not limited to property in the US, but applies to all the debtor's property wherever located and by whomever held. The automatic stay prevents a creditor from obtaining or perfecting a security interest in the debtor's property, or from enforcing a security interest, including seizing of the debtor's property or commencing litigation. The giving of notice to accelerate the maturity of the debt may also be blocked by the automatic stay. If the creditor wishes to take any such action, it must apply to the bankruptcy court for relief from the automatic stay.

Preferences

In order to achieve a degree of fairness in treatment of creditors, who may become aggressive in the days leading up to the bankruptcy filing, the Bankruptcy Code provides an ability to invalidate transfers of the debtor's property which were made within a period of time before the filing. A payment by the debtor of indebtedness, the grant of a security interest, or the perfection of a security interest previously granted, are transfers of the debtor's property. A transfer of the debtor's property to or for the benefit of a creditor for or on account of an antecedent (existing) debt, made within 90 days before the debtor's filing of a bankruptcy petition, may be deemed preferential (and is referred to as a 'preference') and may be set aside by the trustee in bankruptcy or the debtor in possession under certain circumstances. The 90-day preference period is extended to one year if the transfer is to or for the benefit of an 'insider' (but a commercial lender making a loan on arm's-length terms is not ordinarily an insider).

Fraudulent conveyances

A transfer of property of a debtor, including the creation or perfection of a security interest, or the incurrence of an obligation by a debtor, may be deemed to be a fraudulent conveyance, voidable under either Federal or state law under certain circumstances, if:

1 the debtor granted the security interest with actual intent to hinder, delay, or defraud its creditors; or
2 the debtor
   (a) did not receive reasonably equivalent value in exchange for granting the security interest; and
   (b) at the time, or as a result, of the grant of the security interest, the debtor was or became insolvent, undercapitalised, or unable to pay its debts as they become due.

A security interest granted by a debtor to secure its own borrowing for its own corporate purposes should not raise fraudulent conveyance issues: such a transfer is presumably made for reasonably equivalent value. Fraudulent conveyance issues arise, however, when an entity grants a security interest in its property to secure the debt of its corporate parent, or of a sister corporation, since in such cases it may not be easy to demonstrate that the grantor has received reasonably equivalent value. This is an important legal issue in leveraged buyouts and similar transactions, in which the assets and cash flow of a target company are used to support debt taken on by the acquiror. (Other laws, too, must be considered in this context, such as corporate laws restricting the payment of dividends and other corporate distributions, waste of corporate assets, and the like.)

Limitation on after-acquired property

The Bankruptcy Code cuts off a security interest in after-acquired property by providing that property acquired by the debtor or the bankrupt estate after the commencement of the bankruptcy case ('post-petition') is not subject to any lien resulting from any security agreement entered into by the debtor before the commencement of the case ('pre-petition').

The important exception to this provision is for a pre-petition security interest that extends to property of the debtor acquired pre-petition 'and to proceeds, products, offspring, rents, or profits of such property': to the extent provided by the security agreement and by applicable non-bankruptcy law, the security interest is allowed to reach such proceeds, products, offspring, rents and profits even though acquired post-petition. There is an exception to the exception 'to any extent that the court, after notice and a hearing and based on the equities of the case, orders otherwise'; according to the legislative history, this addresses the situation involving, for example, raw materials (covered by the pre-petition security interest) that are converted into inventory post-petition, at some expense to the estate, or inventory (covered by the pre-petition security interest) that is converted into accounts post-petition, at some expense to the estate, thus depleting the fund available to unsecured creditors; it is intended to be limited to the benefit accruing to the secured creditor.

Rejection of executory contracts

The bankrupt debtor may assume or reject an executory contract or unexpired lease. Among other consequences, if a lease is rejected, the leased property must be surrendered to the lessor, and a lease is assumed, the debtor must cure defaults under it. These provisions can affect a lender whose collateral consists in whole or in part of contracts or leases, as well as a creditor extending credit by way of a lease financing.

Use of collateral; adequate protection of secured creditor

A debtor in reorganisation is generally authorised to use, sell or lease its property, including property that is subject to a security interest. Upon request by the secured party, however, the court may prohibit or condition such use, sale or lease of collateral to the extent necessary to provide the secured party with 'adequate protection' of its interest in the collateral. For example, if the collateral is declining through use or through the passage of time, the court may require the debtor to make periodic cash payments to the secured creditor to offset such decline in value, grant the secured party an additional or replacement lien to offset such decline in value, or grant such other relief as would result in the realisation by the secured party of the 'indubitable equivalent' of its interest in the collateral.

The debtor's failure to provide adequate protection would constitute grounds for the secured party to seek relief from the automatic stay to realise the collateral.

Equitable subordination

Under some circumstances, a bankruptcy court may exercise its equitable powers, after notice and a hearing, to subordinate a creditor's claim and security interest. This is referred to as 'equitable subordination'. Equitable subordination can result in the invalidation or subordination of a security interest or a requirement that the creditor return the proceeds of collateral to the debtor.

The criteria for imposing equitable subordination are not set forth in the Bankruptcy Code. As a result, the courts have fashioned the law of equitable subordination and the outcome in a given case will depend on all the facts.

The cases do make clear that the basis for such action is generally the occurrence of inequitable or unconscionable conduct by the creditor, or the creditor's being in a special position vis-à-vis the debtor that justifies subordination. Equitable subordination is not imposed lightly, although the threshold is lower for insiders than for others.

One possible basis for the imposition of equitable subordination is the creditor's improper exercise of control over the debtor's operations, resulting in damage to other creditors. The incidents of a normal debtor-creditor relationship, including the careful monitoring of the affairs of a debtor and the proper exercise of contractual rights, should not ordinarily give rise to a risk of equitable subordination. However, a creditor's risk increases if it controls the debtor's stock and participates in the appointment of the debtor's directors or officers or in the formulating of the debtor's policies, or instructs the debtor which of the debtor's creditors are or are not to be paid.

Substantive consolidation

The general equitable powers granted to bankruptcy courts include the power to order 'substantive consolidation' of entities. Under substantive consolidation, the assets and liabilities of an entity affiliated with or related to a debtor are combined into the debtor's estate and the two entities are treated as one consolidated entity in the debtor's bankruptcy case; the inter-company claims of the entities are eliminated, their assets are combined into a common pool and claims of outside creditors against any of the entities are treated as claims against that common pool. Whether a court will order substantive consolidation depends on, among other things, whether (1) creditors dealt with the entities as separate entities or as a single, integrated unit, (2) the entities' assets, liabilities, and affairs are separate and distinguishable, or hopelessly commingled and entangled, and (3) the demonstrated benefits of consolidation outweigh the prejudice or harm that consolidation would cause creditors.

Although substantive consolidation can significantly affect unsecured creditors' recoveries in a bankruptcy case, it should have less effect on secured creditors, whose liens generally remain enforceable against collateral in the consolidated estate. Substantive consolidation cannot, however, expand the collateral that is subject to a secured creditor's lien.

In some financings, the debtor is established in accordance with criteria that are intended to make it 'bankruptcy remote' so as to minimise the likelihood of a bankruptcy filing and/or substantive consolidation. Where the debt is rated, the bankruptcy remoteness standards of the rating agencies must be met.

'DIP' financing

In order to enable a debtor's reorganisation to proceed, a bankruptcy court may authorise 'debtor in possession' (or 'DIP') financing. In this connection, the court may order that lenders who provide new money to the debtor shall have a first priority lien on collateral, which lien may rank ahead of existing perfected security interests (provided that the holders of such security interests receive adequate protection as described above).

Special provisions relating to aircraft etc

The Bankruptcy Code provides, in s 1110, a limited exception to the automatic stay for certain financiers of aircraft, aircraft engines, propellers, appliances or spare parts. The exception is available only to a lessor or the holder of a security interest, where the lessee or debtor holds a US operating permit for aircraft capable of carrying ten or more individuals or 6,000 pounds or more of cargo. In the case of aircraft 'placed in service' prior to 22 October 1994, a secured party must have a 'purchase-money equipment security interest' to have the benefits of s 1110. For aircraft placed in service after 22 October 1994, any security interest (whether or not a 'purchase-money equipment security interest') in an aircraft of an air carrier holding such an operating permit will have the benefits of s 1110. The lessee or debtor can prevent repossession by the lessor or secured party only by curing its defaults under the agreement within 60 days of the imposition of the automatic stay and agreeing within that time to perform all its obligations under the lease or credit documentation according to its pre-bankruptcy terms. Similar protection is afforded under the Bankruptcy Code with respect to shipping vessels and railroad rolling stock.

Special provisions relating to 'repos'

The Bankruptcy Code provides special protections to parties to so-called 'derivatives contracts' with counterparties that become bankruptcy debtors. These special protections extend to commodity contracts, forward contracts, securities contracts (that is, contracts for the purchase, sale or loan of securities), repurchase agreements, and swap agreements. The Bankruptcy Code generally entitles such parties to terminate these contracts upon the counterparty's insolvency or bankruptcy filing, excepts from the automatic stay the exercise of such parties' set-off and liquidation rights under the contracts, and protects pre-petition payments and other transfers made to, and pre-petition set-offs effected by, such parties from being 'avoided,' or unwound, in the counterparty's bankruptcy case.

GUARANTEES AND SUBORDINATION AGREEMENTS

Guarantees do not constitute collateral security; a guarantee is a contract involving a promise by which one party, the guarantor, agrees to answer for the obligation of another. A guarantee generally creates a secondary liability, rather than a primary liability, although many US guarantees also contain a provision to the effect that the guarantor's liability is primary.

Similarly, a subordination agreement does not create a security interest. In a subordination agreement, a creditor (the 'subordinated' or 'junior' creditor) agrees that its right to payment is in whole or in part postponed until the payment in full of other debt, which is 'senior'. The junior creditor may also agree to subordinate any security interest it holds to that held by a senior creditor.

The validity of a guarantee under US law is governed largely by common law contract principles and not by any comprehensive code. The same is true of subordination agreements.

In most commercial transactions, a guarantee will be stated to be a guarantee of 'payment' and not of 'collection'; this means that the creditor may, upon default, proceed directly against the guarantor without first being required to take steps to collect from the principal debtor. It may also be stated to be 'continuing', meaning that the creditor may continue to rely upon it in extending credit until it is expressly terminated. A guarantee may consist of a separate instrument which refers to another contract or transaction, or it may be incorporated as part of another document.

At common law, a guarantor is a 'favourite of the law': a modification in the terms of the underlying obligation, an indulgence granted to the principal debtor, a release of collateral or of another guarantor and many other occurrences may discharge the liability of the guarantor unless the guarantor consents thereto. For this reason, it is customary for guarantees to include extensive waivers of all common law defences. Such waivers are generally given effect, although in some narrow circumstances, such as total failure of consideration, this may not be so.

A guarantee must, like any contract, be supported by consideration. The consideration should be expressed, and may consist of some detriment to the creditor (the consideration supporting the contract of the principal debtor is generally sufficient to support the guarantee where both are entered into simultaneously). In order to eliminate questions at common law as to whether past consideration can validly support a guarantee, a New York statute expressly validates a guarantee supported by past consideration, provided that the consideration is expressed in the guarantee and is proven to have been given or performed, and would have been valid consideration but for the time when it was given or performed.

A payment by the principal obligor on a guaranteed obligation may, under some circumstances, be recovered as a preference in connection with bankruptcy proceedings of the principal obligor. Because of this risk, a guarantee should provide that it revives or is reinstated if a payment by the debtor is recovered as preferential.

Because of the possibility of bankruptcy of the principal debtor, resulting in the automatic stay of action against the debtor, including, perhaps, action to accelerate the maturity of the debt, some guarantees include a provision to the effect that the guarantor agrees that, as between the guarantor and the creditor, obligations of the debtor may be declared to be and shall be deemed to be forthwith due and payable for purposes of the guarantee, notwithstanding any stay, injunction or other prohibition preventing such declaration (or such obligations from becoming forthwith due and payable) as against the debtor.

Upstream guarantees (in which a company guarantees the debt of its parent) and cross-stream guaranties (in which a company guarantees the obligation of its sister company) raise fraudulent conveyance issues under bankruptcy law. Such guarantees may have specialised provisions relating to the solvency of the guarantor after giving effect to the guaranty.

There is a wide range of possible subordination arrangements. Subordination may be complete, no payments being permitted on the subordinated debt until payment in full of the senior debt, or it may be 'inchoate', payments being permitted on the subordinated debt until the occurrence of a specified event that triggers the subordination provisions. Most subordination arrangements in commercial financings are inchoate, except in special instances, such as where the subordinated creditor is an affiliate of the debtor.

After the occurrence of an event triggering subordination, until payment in full of the senior debt (the senior creditor will wish to specify that such payment must have been 'in cash or cash equivalents'), payments that would otherwise be made in respect of the subordinated debt should be made directly to the senior creditor and payments that are nevertheless received by the subordinated creditor are required to be turned over to the senior creditor (and, until turned over, are usually stated to be held in trust for the senior creditor). The result is that the senior creditor should receive 'double dividends' in the event of the debtor's bankruptcy: the payments accruing to the senior creditor directly and those accruing to the junior creditor but turned over to the senior creditor.

The definition of the triggering events in connection with an inchoate subordination is of central importance, as is the description of the consequences of the occurrence of any such event. Market practice now dictates certain of the concepts and provisions commonly included in the subordination provisions of publicly issued subordinated debt instruments and debt instruments privately placed with institutional investors. Under such instruments, certain events, particularly bankruptcy of the debtor and failure to make payments when due on the senior debt, typically result in a total blockage of payments on the subordinated debt while the event continues. Other events, such as breach of a senior debt financial covenant, generally give the senior creditor or its representative the right to institute a blockage period, limited in time, often to 179 days or a similar period designed to 'catch' two quarterly interest payments and subject to various other restrictions.

Some subordination provisions include a so-called 'X' clause. This clause is an exception to a clause that otherwise requires a subordinated creditor to turn over to the senior creditor any securities received by the subordinated creditor in connection with the reorganisation of the debtor; it allows the subordinated creditor to retain such securities provided that they are subordinate to the senior debt at least to the same extent as the subordinated debt.

It is important to define the term 'senior debt', or the equivalent, so as to identify the parties that are entitled to the benefit of the subordination provisions. Such definition should include interest that would have accrued but for the filing of a bankruptcy petition in respect of the debtor (such a filing causes interest to cease accruing on the debtor's indebtedness). The senior creditor may wish to have the definition include refinancings of the original senior debt.

It is well established under US law that subordination agreements are valid and will be enforced, both as a matter of contract law and as a matter of bankruptcy law and policy. Since in many instances the senior creditor is not a party to the instrument in which the subordination is created, the third party beneficiary concept is utilised to enforce subordination.

CONCLUSION

If the landscape to be traversed by a creditor seeking collateral security in the US appears to be filled with bogs, thickets and bluffs, this is at least in part because of the diversity of the kinds of property that may be encumbered. The UCC is a modern body of law, practical though intricate, and US real estate law remains subject to many local peculiarities. The interplay between state and Federal law and the existence of separate bodies of law in each of the 50 states lend a peculiarly US complexity to certain aspects of the law. In general, however, with the help of the UCC and a vast body of court decisions on commercial matters, and with appropriate guidance from legal counsel in the pertinent jurisdictions, the landscape can be safely and profitably negotiated.

Index